Detailed Contents

Write Time, Write Place

PARAGRAPHS AND ESSAYS

Mimi Markus

Broward College

Longman

Boston   Columbus   Indianapolis   New York   San Francisco   Upper Saddle River
Amsterdam   Cape Town   Dubai   London   Madrid   Milan   Munich · Paris   Montreal   Toronto
Delhi   Mexico City   São Paulo   Sydney   Hong Kong   Seoul   Singapore   Taipei   Tokyo

Senior Acquisitions Editor: Matthew Wright
Senior Development Editor: Marion Castellucci
Senior Supplements Editor: Donna Campion
Senior Media Producer: Stefanie Liebman
Marketing Manager: Thomas DeMarco
Production Manager: Eric Jorgensen
Editorial Assistant: Samantha Neary
Project Coordination, Text Design, and Electronic Page Makeup: Electronic Publishing
Services Inc., NYC
Cover Design Manager: John Callahan
Cover Designer: Maria Ilardi
Cover Illustration/Photo: Andy Sotiriou/Getty Images, Nikada/iStockphoto
Photo Researcher: Poyee Oster
Senior Manufacturing Buyer: Roy L. Pickering, Jr.
Printer and Binder: Courier Corporation/Kendallville
Cover Printer: Lehigh Phoenix Color, Hagerstown

For permission to use copyrighted material, grateful acknowledgment is made to the copyright holders on pp. 593–597, which are hereby made part of this copyright page.

Copyright © 2011 by Pearson Education, Inc.

1 2 3 4 5 6 7 8 9 10—CRK—13 12 11 10

Longman
is an imprint of

www.pearsonhighered.com

ISBN-13: 978-0-205-64662-3
ISBN-10: 0-205-64662-X
AIE ISBN-13: 978-0-205-64664-7
AIE ISBN-10: 0-205-64664-6

PART 3   Learning Other College Writing Assignments   291

PART 4   Building Powerful Sentences   **335**

Preface for Students

The two most important requirements for major success are first, being in the right place at the right time, and second, doing something a out it.

—Ray Kroc, founder of McDonald's

"Being in the right place at the right time" means to be in a position or place where something good may happen. Some people call it luck. For example, suppose the psychology course you want to take is full, but when you check again you find that someone has dropped the course and you are able to register for it. You were in the right place at the right time.

The title of this book, *Write Time, Write Place*, is a play on these words. As you read this text, know that this is the right time to learn to write at the college level. The right place is the space where learning happens—in a classroom, online, in a discussion group, or at a lecture. It is also a place in your mind where you learn, think about, and analyze ideas and prepare to share them with others in your college community. You are in the right place at the right time.

But being in the right place at the right time is, according to Ray Kroc, only the first requirement for major success. The second part is "doing something about it." That means using *Write Time, Write Place* to learn and practice the most important skill associated with college success, **writing**. This text will prepare you for the writing assignments you will encounter in your college courses. It will help you to write well-developed paragraphs and essays using correct grammar and punctuation. It will also give you the opportunity to read material from college courses such as psychology, sociology, criminal justice, and business.

So, you are at the right place, and it's the right time. Now it's up to you to take advantage of this opportunity and achieve "major success" in your college career.

MIMI MARKUS

Preface for Instructors

How do you prepare your students for the demands of writing and reading assignments they will encounter in their college-level courses? This is the question I struggled with when choosing developmental writing textbooks and creating syllabi. Is teaching them basic writing, grammar, punctuation, and mechanics skills enough?

Through my experience teaching writing as part of a learning community team, I learned that this was not enough. The students were taking four classes: developmental writing, developmental reading, student success skills, and a college-level music appreciation course, and they frequently commented that their music course required more than they expected. For example, the textbook was hard to understand, and each chapter contained many new terms they had to learn. Writing assignments were challenging, too. They were asked to read about a composer in *The Grove Dictionary of Music and Musicians* and write a paper about the composer's contributions to the music of a particular time period.

I seized the opportunity to help students by going over passages from the music textbook and other academic reading assignments. We discussed these materials, and I asked them to respond with focused writing activities. These teachable moments made me realize that developmental writing students needed to be exposed to college-level reading material from a variety of college disciplines *as early as possible*. It was this experience that inspired me to write the *Write Time, Write Place* series.

Write Time, Write Place uses textbook excerpts from across the disciplines in instruction, exercises, and writing activities. These excerpts show students how academic writing is organized, give them practice reading and responding to college-level material, increase their general knowledge, and perhaps create an interest in enrolling in courses they might not have considered.

While introducing students to many college subjects, *Write Time, Write Place* also provides a highly structured approach to the writing process. The text takes students through the stages of writing using a step-by-step approach that shows them how to generate, plan, and organize their thoughts. To make it easier for students to plan their papers, a variety of graphic organizers are provided for students to use. Because students like to see examples of writing patterns they will be expected to produce, both student and textbook writing examples are provided. In addition, student writers benefit from writing frequently, so opportunities for writing both formally and informally are presented throughout the text.

To meet the needs of students with varying levels of knowledge of grammar, punctuation, and mechanics, *Write Time, Write Place* presents the conventions of academic English without devaluing students' own dialects or native languages. Instruction is simple and straightforward, and cross-discipline topics are used for practice exercises throughout these chapters. In addition, writing assignments direct students to apply chapter concepts in sentences or other writing activities.

A textbook can only do so much. It is up to us as instructors to bring the concepts and content to life in ways that will be meaningful to our students. *Write Time, Write Place* is a flexible resource that supports a variety of instructional techniques to engage students and promote effective learning and understanding.

MIMI MARKUS

Features of *Write Time, Write Place*

Write Time, Write Place includes all of the elements that students and instructors need to succeed in today's basic writing classroom (and beyond).

Write Time, Write Place Sets the Stage for College Success

An Introductory Chapter on College Writing The expectations of college professors and the nature of college assignments are introduced in Chapter 1, "Writing in College," along with the importance of writing in Standard English. The concept of code-switching helps students understand the need to adjust their written language for college assignments. These fundamentals are carried through in the rest of the text's instruction.

Differences between Spoken English and Standard Written English **3**

LO 1 Differences between Spoken English and Standard Written English

You may not realize it, but you already use many forms of spoken and written English. You choose the appropriate form of spoken or written English to use depending on the situation, the audience, and the topic. For example, you speak a certain way to your friends, another way to your family members, and still another way to your employer or teachers. You also use different forms of written English each day depending on your purpose, such as personal emails or other electronic communications, college assignments, or work-related messages.

However, as a beginning college writer, you may not realize that writing the same way you talk is not appropriate for most college writing assignments. Spoken English and Standard Written English are different with respect to audience, preparation, word choice, and sentence structure.

Differences in Audience

The **audience** is the person or group who listens to what you are saying or reads what you have written. Knowing your audience helps you decide what to say and how to say it. Speakers have an audience of listeners who give them immediate feedback through gestures, body movements, comments, and questions. On the other hand, college writers have an audience that is not present; they have to imagine that they are writing to a particular person or group. College writers have to wait for feedback from their readers.

Most of the time, the audience in your college English class will be your teacher or other classmates. Writing for your teacher may make you nervous because you know

---

English Success Tip: Keep a Learning Journal

A learning journal is a personal record of your notes and observations about a course you are taking. Keeping a learning journal will help you see how your knowledge and skills are developing over the semester. It will also help you focus on the course and practice writing. You can use a notebook or set up a file on a computer. Set aside at least ten minutes twice a week to write in your learning journal. Here are some topics to write about:

- information you learned and understand
- things that are difficult or hard to understand
- thoughts about material you have read
- ideas for papers
- connections with things you have learned in other classes

English Success Tips Each chapter concludes with suggestions for improving students' study skills, mastery of English, and their performance in English courses. Topics include guidelines for emailing instructors, manuscript formatting, use of spell-check software, writing improvement logs, learning journals, and portfolios.

Write Time, Write Place Provides a Framework for Learning

Learning Objectives Students learn better when they have a clear understanding of what they are expected to master. Learning objectives at the beginning of each chapter give students an overview of what they will accomplish by working through the chapter. To provide further guidance, each objective is keyed to a section of the chapter, and further resources for meeting the chapter objectives are provided in MyWritingLab.

CHAPTER

10

Comparison and Contrast

Learning Objectives

After working through this chapter, you will be able to:

LO 1 Define comparison and contrast as a pattern of writing that shows how two subjects are similar and/or different.

LO 2 Write a comparison and contrast paragraph.

LO 3 Write a comparison and contrast essay.

LO 1 What Is Comparison and Contrast?

Step-by-Step Clear Instruction Students learn more easily from concrete explanations; thus all instruction is carefully constructed to be clear and concise. The paragraph and essay chapters guide students step by step through the writing process for each pattern of development. The sentence, grammar, punctuation, and mechanics skill-building sections focus on easy-to-understand explanations of the essential points of each concept with color-coded examples. This step-by-step approach builds confidence as students complete and master each small increment.

Prewriting the Illustration Paragraph

Before you write, you must choose a suitable topic and develop it.

Decide on Your Topic and Purpose When deciding on your own illustration topic or responding to an assigned topic, consider the following:

1. **Choose a topic that is limited enough to be explained in one paragraph.** A topic like **modern day heroes** might bring to mind many different types of heroes such as people who perform courageous acts, like soldiers, fire fighters, or police officers, or people who are notable in a particular field like medicine or physics. Some people consider celebrities to be heroes. As you can see, it would not be possible to discuss all of those groups in a paragraph. Therefore, you could narrow to one group of heroes or even choose one modern day hero and write about his or her accomplishments.

2. **Choose a topic that can be supported with examples.** A topic such as **how to prepare for a job interview** has a different purpose, which is to give the steps in a process.

PRACTICE   Evaluating Topics for Illustration Paragraphs

6.3   Explain why each of the following topics would be acceptable or not acceptable for an illustration paragraph.

1. Careers

_____

Graphic Organizers As a complement to the step-by-step instruction, numerous graphic organizers provide visual tools for students to use in prewriting and planning their paragraphs and essays.

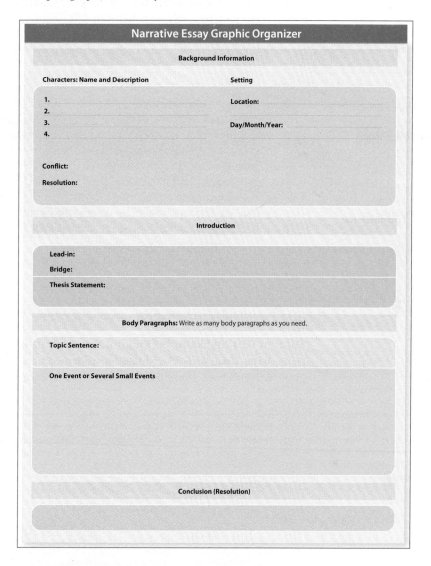

Narrative Essay Graphic Organizer

Background Information

Characters: Name and Description   Setting

1. _____   Location: _____
2. _____
3. _____   Day/Month/Year: _____
4. _____

Conflict:

Resolution:

Introduction

Lead-in:

Bridge:

Thesis Statement:

Body Paragraphs: Write as many body paragraphs as you need.

Topic Sentence:

One Event or Several Small Events

Conclusion (Resolution)

Other Graphic Elements Students are used to viewing graphic-rich Web pages, video game animation, and television and movie images. *Write Time, Write Place* incorporates graphic elements, such as charts, bulleted points, diagrams, and boxed items for instruction at-a-glance to increase the text's readability and ease of use. Other graphic elements include writing tips, checklists, cautions, and color-coded grammar examples.

The **simple sentence** is a group of words that has at least one subject and verb. It is an **independent clause** that expresses a complete thought. A simple sentence can contain one or more subjects and verbs, can be short or long, and can contain adjectives, adverbs, and prepositional phrases.

The manager plans.

The manager and the employees plan.

The manager plans and organizes.

The manager and the employees plan and organize.

Write Time, Write Place Provides Models of Writing

Academic Writing Examples To expose students to college writing and subject matter, many paragraph- and passage-length examples from textbooks are provided to illustrate the patterns of development. In addition, textbook excerpts are used as writing prompts and in grammar practices.

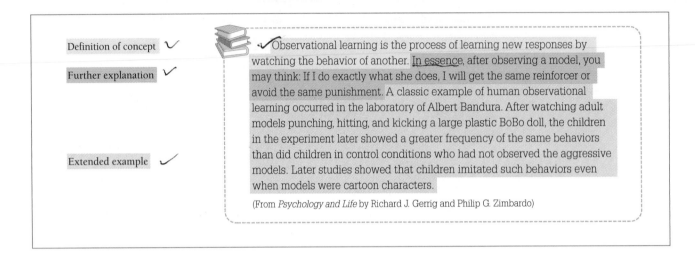

Definition of concept ✓

Further explanation ✓

Extended example ✓

Observational learning is the process of learning new responses by watching the behavior of another. In essence, after observing a model, you may think: If I do exactly what she does, I will get the same reinforcer or avoid the same punishment. A classic example of human observational learning occurred in the laboratory of Albert Bandura. After watching adult models punching, hitting, and kicking a large plastic BoBo doll, the children in the experiment later showed a greater frequency of the same behaviors than did children in control conditions who had not observed the aggressive models. Later studies showed that children imitated such behaviors even when models were cartoon characters.

(From *Psychology and Life* by Richard J. Gerrig and Philip G. Zimbardo)

Student Writing Examples Mindful that students like to read pieces written by their peers, *Write Time, Write Place* includes student-generated paragraph and essay examples in the writing chapters and in grammar, sentence structure, and punctuation exercises.

Swischuk 1

Barbara Swischuk

Professor Markus

College Preparatory Writing

30 Oct. 2010

My Fondness of Celebrity

1   Of all of the great opera tenors, Placido Domingo has always inspired me with his deep, rich voice. All of my friends knew of my passion for his work, so it was not too much of surprise when I got a phone call one day from a second editor-in-chief of a popular women's magazine who was a close friend from my journalist days. She offered me an opportunity to interview the **world-renowned** tenor. This was exciting because in the print business, most of the conversations with celebrities are held on the phone for time and money reasons. With only hours to plan, I managed to book a flight to Miami, hire a babysitter, and rush out the door. My short-notice assignment to interview Placido Domingo consisted of several mishaps including a late departure to the airport, a stressful confrontation with a police offi-cer, a forgotten credit card, and, finally, a face-to-face meeting with the star.

2   The first mishap of my short-notice assignment was my late departure to the airport. The babysitter was late, and the time that I had set aside to make the forty-minute ride to the Jacksonville airport got cut short. I arrived at my concourse thirty minutes before my departure time. On the way to the plane, I decided to stop by Starbucks to get a double espresso latte, which I spilled all over my blouse. "That is a great start," I thought and tried to figure out what to do about my coffee-stained blouse before my actual encounter with the celebrity. When the plane touched down in Fort Lauderdale, I had ninety minutes to the scheduled interview.

world-renowned
famous around the world

Write Time, Write Place Provides Many Opportunities to Practice and Write

Engaging and Various Writing Prompts Today's students need a variety of topics to write about. Although many enjoy writing about themselves, personal writing does not appeal to everyone, particularly those who are uncomfortable sharing their lives, whether for cultural or confidentiality reasons. Thus, in addition to providing suggestions for personal writing, *Write Time, Write Place* provides a variety of writing options:

- QUICK WRITES encourage spontaneous writing in response to a question or topic.
- PARAGRAPH PRACTICES provide step-by-step guidance for students for prewriting, planning, drafting, revising, and editing their own paragraphs.
- READING AND WRITING ACROSS THE CURRICULUM has students read a textbook paragraph and then write in response.
- COMMENT ON A CONTEMPORARY ISSUE offers topical prompts for persuasive writing.
- WRITE ABOUT AN IMAGE offers interesting photographs and other visuals as subjects for writing.
- WRITING PARAGRAPHS AND ESSAYS prompts provide general and academic topic suggestions for writing

Essay Writing Assignments

Write about an Image

What do you think happened in the photograph above? What was your first reaction to it? Choose the dominant impression, the one special quality or feature that stands out from all the others, that best describes the photograph. You may have many reactions to this photograph, but the dominant impression is the strongest.

Write an essay as if you were describing the scene for a major news network. Use vivid sensory and factual descriptive details to support your dominant impression.

Abundant and Varied Grammar Exercises Today's students need a variety of ways to practice new skills. To address the wide range of basic skills knowledge and learning styles, *Write Time, Write Place* offers different types of exercises for grammar, sentence skills, and punctuation. While identification and drills are useful at the beginning stages of learning, students need opportunities to make connections between the rules of Standard Written English and their application in their own writing. Therefore, this text goes beyond drills, using continuous discourses, editing in context, sentence combining, and original sentence generation. *Write Time, Write Place* emphasizes sentence building rather than error avoidance. There are several types of exercises:

- PRACTICES help students apply what they have just learned.
- HELP DESKS ask students to edit or improve the work of others.
- GROUP ACTIVITIES promote collaborative learning and writing.
- WRITING ASSIGNMENTS ask students to practice a grammar or sentence skill through original writing.

PRACTICE   Identifying Helping Verbs
18.7   Underline all of the helping verbs in the following sentences.

1. For years now, Southwest Airlines has been flying high in the short-trip, low-fare market.
2. Southwest's emphasis on reliability and customer service had kept the airline virtually unchallenged.
3. Most airlines have not managed to copy the operational success of Southwest.
4. Thanks to David Neeleman, JetBlue has become one of the most profitable new airlines in the United States.
5. David Neeleman had been working at Southwest for a short time.
6. He was fired from Southwest.
7. Neeleman had had extensive experience in the airline industry before his job at Southwest.
8. He did copy some of Southwest's strategies and lessons for JetBlue.
9. Neeleman must have used sound business practices and decisions.
10. Labor expenses could be kept down to 25 percent of earnings.
11. Younger workers were being hired for lower wages but with stock options.
12. JetBlue has been filling planes to capacity.

(Adapted from *Business Essentials* by Ronald J. Ebert and Ricky W. Griffin)

Write Time, Write Place Provides Additional Reading Selections

Reading Selections The end-of-book readings section provides lengthier selections on high-interest topics such as culture shock, peer pressure, video game design, and mind-body therapies. The readings section continues the text's emphasis on academic writing and reading by pairing a textbook passage with an essay or article on the same topic. Prereading and postreading activities help students understand and analyze the readings:

- VOCABULARY IN CONTEXT gives students an opportunity to learn new words.
- THINKING ABOUT AND RESPONDING TO THE READING asks students to respond to a reading through comprehension and critical thinking questions.
- WRITING ASSIGNMENTS present ideas for writing in response to readings
- CONNECTING THE READINGS asks students to compare, contrast, and/or synthesize elements of two readings on the same topic and organizational pattern.

NARRATION   Theme: *Sociology*

The Power of Peer Pressure: The Asch Experiment

The pressure to conform is motivated by the human need to be liked, to be correct, or to fit a social role. Changing your thinking or behavior to fit into a group can have positive or negative effects. As you read this textbook excerpt, think about how you would have reacted as a student in Dr. Asch's experiment.

Getting Ready to Read: Use the graphic organizer on page 530 to preview the reading.

Excerpt from *Essentials of Sociology*

James M. Henslin

1   How influential are groups in our lives? To answer this, let's look first at *conformity* in the sense of going along with our peers. Our peers have no authority over us, only the influence we allow.

2   Imagine that you are taking a course in social psychology with Dr. Solomon Asch and you have agreed to participate in an experiment. As you enter his laboratory, you see seven chairs, five of them already filled by other students. You are given the sixth. Soon the seventh person arrives. Dr. Asch stands at the front of the

How *Write Time, Write Place* Is Organized

Write Time, Write Place consists of eight parts that can easily be coordinated with your course's learning objectives. Parts 1 through 3 include writing college paragraphs, essays, and other writing assignments; Parts 4 through 6 include sentence skills, grammar and mechanics, Part 7 focuses on improving writing; and Part 8 covers active reading strategies and offers paired readings.

Part 1, Writing the College Paragraph and Essay, orients students to the language and structure of college writing. Instruction on the elements of the college-level paragraph is integrated with the stages of the writing process, including a student paragraph example in progress. This section also includes a separate chapter on the elements of the essay.

Part 2, Learning Paragraph and Essay Organization Plans, is the core of the text. It features a step-by-step process approach to guide students as they develop their own paragraphs and essays according to each organizational plan. Student examples and textbook excerpts serve as models for writing, and practice exercises are integrated with instruction.

Part 3, Learning Other College Writing Assignments, teaches students strategies for writing under pressure and for preparing source-based writing assignments including a summary and an essay enhanced with research. Students learn to find and evaluate library and Internet sources, take notes, and integrate and document source materials using Modern Language Association style.

Parts 4 through 7 provide a thematic, contextual approach to skills instruction. In each chapter, exercises and readings are based on content from a specific academic subject. As students learn to apply skills, they also learn about other disciplines. **Part 4, Building Powerful Sentences,** teaches students how to write simple, compound, and complex sentences. **Part 5, Building Grammar Skills,** provides basic grammar skills including subject-verb agreement, verb tenses, pronoun use, nouns and noun markers, and adjective and adverbs. **Part 6, Using Correct Punctuation, Mechanics, and Spelling,** teaches students to punctuate, spell, and capitalize. **Part 7, Improving Your Writing,** sharpens students' writing skills with word choice, consistency and parallelism, and sentence variety.

Part 8, Reading, teaches students to be active readers of textbooks and other college reading materials. Students learn and practice the stages of the reading process along with techniques for understanding, remembering, and reacting to a reading. The readings portion of this section presents a series of textbook excerpts, essays, and articles that are paired by theme and organizational pattern. Vocabulary development, critical thinking questions, and stimulating writing prompts supply abundant opportunities for building skills and expressing ideas.

Write Time, Write Place Links to MyWritingLab

At the end of each chapter, students are referred to specific resources of Pearson's MyWritingLab, www.mywritinglab.com, that will help them achieve the learning objectives of the chapter. MyWritingLab is an online learning program providing assessment, instruction, writing practice, and grammar exercises to help students meet the learning objectives of each chapter and improve their writing skills.

Developmental Writing Resources

Book-Specific Ancillary Material

Annotated Instructor's Edition for Write Time, Write Place: Paragraphs and Essays, 1/e (ISBN 0-205-64664-6). The Annotated Instructor's Edition for *Write Time, Write Place* includes general teaching tips, guidance on tailoring instruction for English language learners, and answers to the exercises, all on page for ease of reference.

Instructor's Resource Manual for Write Time, Write Place: Paragraphs and Essays, 1/e (ISBN 0-205-64663-8). Prepared by Caroline Seefchak, Edison State College, and Mimi Markus, the Instructor's Manual offers additional material to help instructors meet their course objectives. The manual follows the learning objectives established in the text, offers information on teaching developmental college students, includes material for quizzes, and provides graphic organizers in support of the various writing types and genres outlined in the text.

Additional Instructor Resources

The Pearson Writing Package Pearson is pleased to offer a variety of support materials to help make teaching writing easier for teachers and to help students excel in their coursework. Many of our student supplements are available free or at a greatly reduced price when packaged with *Write Time, Write Place: Paragraphs and Essays*. Visit www.pearsonhighereducation.com, contact your local Pearson sales representative, or review a detailed listing of the full supplements package in the *Instructor's Resource Manual* for more information.

Media Resources Where better practice makes better writers! **mywritinglab** www.mywritinglab.com

MyWritingLab, a complete online learning program, provides additional resources and better practice exercises for developing writers.

What makes the practice in MyWritingLab better?

- **Diagnostic Testing:** MyWritingLab's diagnostic test comprehensively assesses students' skills in grammar. Students are given an individualized learning path based on the diagnostic's results, identifying the areas where they most need help.
- **Progressive Learning:** The heart of MyWritingLab is the progressive learning that takes place as students complete the Recall, Apply, and Write exercises within each topic. Students move from literal comprehension (Recall) to critical understanding (Apply) to the ability to demonstrate a skill in their own writing (Write). This progression of critical thinking, not available in any other online resource, enables students to truly master the skills and concepts they need to become successful writers.
- **Online Gradebook:** All student work in MyWritingLab is captured in the Online Gradebook. Students can monitor their own progress through reports explaining their scores on the exercises in the course. Instructors can see which topics their students have mastered and access other detailed reports, such as class summaries, that track the development of their entire class and display useful details on each student's progress.
- **eText:** The *Write Time, Write Place: Paragraphs and Essays* e-text is accessed through MyWritingLab. Students now have the e-text at their fingertips while completing the various exercises and activities within MyWritingLab. Students can highlight important material in the e-text and add notes to any section for reflection and/or study throughout the semester.

Acknowledgments

Writing *Write Time, Write Place* has been a journey and the fulfillment of a dream, which would not have been possible without the many people who have helped, supported, and inspired me.

In particular, I appreciate the comments and suggestions offered by instructors who served as reviewers at various stages of the text's development:

Susan Achziger, Community College of Aurora

Gloria Bennett, Gainesville State College

Mary Anne Bernal, San Antonio College

Amy Boltrushek, Richland College

Chris Burdett, Georgia Perimeter College

April Carothers, Linn-Benton Community College

Christopher L. Costello, Reading Area Community College

Kate Cross, Phoenix College

Deborah Davis, Richland College

Marjorie Dernaika, Southwest Tennessee Community College

Rebecca Ferguson, Springfield College

Deborah Fuller, Bunker Hill Community College

Anthony C. Gargano, Long Beach City College

Alexandros Goudas, Darton College

Angela Lucas Green, Troy University

Bill W. Hall, St. Petersburg College

Jane Hasting, Cleveland State Community College

Matthew Horton, Gainesville State College

Mary Jenson, Hawkeye Community College

Cheryta Jones, Southwest Tennessee Community College

Laura Kingston, South Seattle Community College

Maria Garcia Landry, Palm Beach State College

Marilyn Lancaster, Tarrant County College, South

Angie Lazarus, Bevill State Community College (Sumiton)

Gina Mackenzie, Community College of Philadelphia

Peter M. Marcoux, El Camino College

Erin T. Martz, Northern Virginia Community College

James S. May, Valencia Community College

Judy McKenzie, Lane Community College

Catherine Moran, Bristol County Community College

Erin Nelson, Blinn College

Brit Osgood-Treston, Riverside Community College

Eldo Ostaitile, Volunteer State Community College

Marcus Patton, Sacramento City College

Paula Porter, Keiser University; Ashford University

Sharon Rinkiewicz, Broward College (Central)

Rebecca Samberg, Housatonic Community College

Desmond Sawyerr, Hillsborough Community College

Marcea Seible, Hawkeye Community College

Jeffrey Simmons, University of Maryland

Carmen Simpson, St. Petersburg College

Allyson Smith, North Georgia Tech College

Elizabeth Smith, State College of Florida—Sarasota, Manatee

Helen M. Smith (Higbee), Kentucky State University

John Stasinopoulos, College of DuPage

Trisha Travers, Penn State University (Abington)

Christine M. Tutlewski, University of Wisconsin-Parkside
Arnold Wood Jr., Florida State College at Jacksonville

I got helpful, specific feedback on the manuscript from my developmental English students:

Imtieas (Adrian) Amirbaksh
Valerie Bailey
Sevin Barnes
Tiffany Brown
Tori Brown
Desiree Carter
Joseph Chen
Jackie Cineus
Joshua Cummings
Tationa Freeman
Lenz Lamisere
Kenneth Lang
Michelle McGriff
Melissa Mendez
Dashka Milus
Urzule Renosa
William Runde
Dennis Su
Jemara Smith
George Vazquez
Natasha D. Wallace
Kia White
Justin Wright

I also benefited greatly from the contributions of Sally Gearhart, English as a Second Language specialist, who reviewed the manuscript, prepared the English Language Learner Tips, and offered suggestions that helped strengthen the instruction for English language learners.

I am grateful to my Pearson team, starting with sales representative Tracy Light, who has been my advocate over the years, especially for this project, and acquisitions editor Matt Wright, who believed in the concept for *Write Time, Write Place* and was instrumental in supporting it for publication. Matt's enthusiasm and encouragement kept our team positive throughout the process. Most importantly, I am indebted to Marion Castellucci, development editor, who with her expertise and knowledge of the field, skillfully guided me chapter by chapter. Her calm, steady demeanor and gentle nudging not only kept me on track, but also sustained me.

I also owe a debt of gratitude to the text's production team. Project editor Lake Lloyd guided me through each stage of the production process, and copy editor Dawn Adams checked the manuscript for clarity, consistency, and accuracy.

Many of my students deserve gratitude for their role in creating this text. First, I'm grateful to those who willingly gave me permission to use their paragraphs and essays as models and for activities; they are helping other students realize that they, too, can become effective writers. Finally, I thank all of my students who over the years have been and continue to be my greatest teachers.

MIMI MARKUS

Writing the College Paragraph and Essay

PART 1

CHAPTER 1

Writing in College

Learning Objectives

After working through this chapter, you will be able to:

LO 1 Explain the differences between Spoken English and Standard Written English.

LO 2 Choose the appropriate form of written English for different types of writing assignments.

LO 3 Describe the stages of the writing process.

Now that you are a college student, you will have to write many different kinds of papers in your courses to show what you know and how you think. For example, you may have to write essays and research papers in English class, lab reports in science class, and progress reports in a business course.

When you write at the college level, your teachers expect you to use **Standard Written English.** Standard Written English is the form of written English that is widely accepted as correct in education, publishing, government, science, and business. Standard Written English has some similarities with spoken English. However, it has its own set of rules for sentence and paragraph structure, word choice, punctuation, grammar, and spelling. You have probably learned many of these rules as you progressed through school before entering college. Your college textbooks use Standard Written English as in this example from an anthropology textbook. (**Anthropology** is the study of differences and similarities, both biological and cultural, in human populations.)

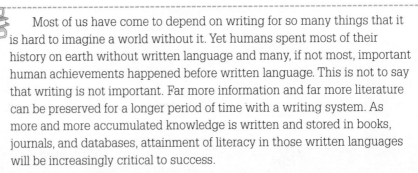

Most of us have come to depend on writing for so many things that it is hard to imagine a world without it. Yet humans spent most of their history on earth without written language and many, if not most, important human achievements happened before written language. This is not to say that writing is not important. Far more information and far more literature can be preserved for a longer period of time with a writing system. As more and more accumulated knowledge is written and stored in books, journals, and databases, attainment of literacy in those written languages will be increasingly critical to success.

(Adapted from *Anthropology* by Carol R. Ember, Melvin Ember, and Peter N. Peregrine)

Knowing how to use Standard Written English will help you succeed in college, get a job, and advance in the workplace. In fact, many employers consider writing ability an essential skill for hiring and for promotion. With the fast pace of electronic communications, the need for clear and correct writing is more important than ever before.

LO 1 Differences between Spoken English and Standard Written English

You may not realize it, but you already use many forms of spoken and written English. You choose the appropriate form of spoken or written English to use depending on the situation, the audience, and the topic. For example, you speak a certain way to your friends, another way to your family members, and still another way to your employer or teachers. You also use different forms of written English each day depending on your purpose, such as personal emails or other electronic communications, college assignments, or work-related messages.

However, as a beginning college writer, you may not realize that writing the same way you talk is not appropriate for most college writing assignments. Spoken English and Standard Written English are different with respect to audience, preparation, word choice, and sentence structure.

Differences in Audience

The **audience** is the person or group who listens to what you are saying or reads what you have written. Knowing your audience helps you decide what to say and how to say it. Speakers have an audience of listeners who give them immediate feedback through gestures, body movements, comments, and questions. On the other hand, college writers have an audience that is not present; they have to imagine that they are writing to a particular person or group. College writers have to wait for feedback from their readers.

Most of the time, the audience in your college English class will be your teacher or other classmates. Writing for your teacher may make you nervous because you know he or she is judging your writing and grading your performance. As you progress through the course, you will learn more about what the teacher expects of you.

Differences in Preparation

Preparation is the process of thinking about and planning what you will say or write. Speakers do not have to plan the way writers do. Speakers often do not plan at all. They may change their ideas, go off a topic, and repeat thoughts. In contrast, college writers plan what they are going to say. They organize their thoughts logically and use clear, concise details to support their points. College writers can revise and edit their papers before submitting them.

Differences in Word Choice

Word choice refers to the words you use to express your ideas. Many words that are appropriate in spoken English or electronic written English are not always appropriate in academic papers.

The Speaker's Word Choices Most spoken English is conversational. When you talk with someone, you use simple, conversational words and expressions, contractions, sounds, slang, and even nonstandard forms. Here is an example of one person talking to a friend:

> Well, I can't take you to school 'cause, like, I have to leave real early in the morning to make up a test, and, you know, like sometimes we have to rush because you always take like soooo long to get ready anyways. Call me, 'kay? Cool. Gotta go.

Slang is a popular feature of spoken English. **Slang** refers to words and expressions that are invented or whose meanings have been changed. Many popular slang terms come from television, music, and popular culture. Some slang terms are so popular that they become a permanent part of the language; others fade away over time as new ones are invented.

Another type of spoken English is a mixture of English and another language. For example, "Spanglish," as it is affectionately called, is a hybrid language that combines the words and grammar of Spanish and English. In the sentence, "If you see Jaime, dile that I can't to come esta noche" means, "If you see Jaime, tell him that I can't come tonight." The speaker mixes English and Spanish words; he also uses Spanish grammar with the verb form "to come" instead of the English form "come."

PRACTICE   Identifying Conversational Words and Expressions

1.1   Take a moment to identify the contractions, sounds, slang, and nonstandard forms in the example of conversation above.

_____

_____

PRACTICE   Listing Popular Slang Terms

1.2   Working in small groups of two to three students, make a list of some of popular slang terms and their meanings.

The Electronic Messager's Word Choices   With the increased use of cell phones and other handheld devices, a new form of written English has developed called "textspeak." **Textspeak** is an online screen language that consists of **acronyms** (abbreviations like TTYL for "talk to you later"), other abbreviations, numbers, and symbols. Instead of taking the time to type complete words and sentences on a tiny keyboard, texters can easily write and send a message in seconds. Texting is fun and convenient, but it has more in common with spoken English than with Standard Written English. Here is an example of textspeak:

This sentence says, "What's up? I'm so bored. Got to go. Teacher alert. Later."

Emoticons are another popular feature of conversational online language. **Emoticons** are symbols used to add humor, show emotion, or avoid misunderstandings. The most popular emoticons are smileys, representations of facial expressions created by using keyboard characters. Hundreds of these have been invented and listed on the Internet. You can read them by tilting your head to the side. These are examples:

:)	happy	:-)	happy with nose
:(	sad or frown	8-)	user wearing sunglasses

PRACTICE 1.3   Creating a Textspeak List

In groups of three to five, create a list of textspeak words, symbols, and expressions that you use in informal emails and text messages. Next to each one, give the meaning. Show how the word is used in a sentence. Then, share your list with the other groups in your class. Create and distribute the final list as a handout, a file, or a web posting for the class after eliminating any duplicate words.

The College Writer's Word Choices Contractions, slang, online and text message language, shortened words, and sometimes the pronoun "you" are not appropriate choices for college-level writing. College writers also do not use regional words or expressions that may be unfamiliar to their readers.

Style Reminder: To learn more about effective word choice for college writing, see Chapter 30.

In college you will be discussing, thinking, and writing about scholarly ideas from your academic courses. When you write a college-level paper, you choose the most effective words and expressions that convey your meaning clearly and concisely, unlike the conversational words you choose in spoken English and in electronic messaging.

Differences in Sentence Structure

Sentence structure is the arrangement of words in a sentence. Grammatical correctness and sentence variety are more important in writing than in speaking. Speakers are more interested in getting their message across quickly than in using correct grammar or sentence structure. Speakers use sentences that are short or incomplete. They may pause at any point.

Unlike speakers, college writers use sentences that are grammatically complete and follow Standard Written English rules of grammar and punctuation. In addition, they vary sentences through the use of simple, compound, and complex sentence structures to make the writing interesting.

PRACTICE 1.4   Using Standard Written English Words and Expressions

Find the conversational words and expressions in these sentences. Then revise each sentence by replacing those words and expressions with Standard Written English.

1. A very dumb driving distraction for guys is hot girls.

   girls are a distraction for guys.

2. On Friday night, I like to hang out with my friends._ On Friday night

   associate

Change the slang words

3. Boy, was I wrong.

_____

4. Whatever little chump change I have goes to burgers, pizza, or subs.

_____

5. Well, yes, getting my hair and nails done makes me feel happy.

_____

LO 2   College Writing Assignments

You can expect to have many different kinds of writing assignments in college, not only in your English composition classes but in your other classes, too. These writing assignments have specific purposes and can be divided into two general groups: informal and formal. In all assignments, you will be expected to use Standard Written English.

Informal Writing Assignments

Some writing assignments in college will be informal. These assignments are generally short, require less planning, and may be done in class or for homework. For instance, in your English course, your teacher may ask you to keep a journal or blog, review other students' writing, or participate in an electronic discussion. In other classes, informal writing assignments may include response papers, reading notes, interviews, or scenarios.

Informal writing assignments may not seem to be important because they may not be graded, or they may not be counted in your overall grade for the course; however, they have many benefits. Informal writing assignments help you become more comfortable with writing. They also give you an opportunity to apply what you already know and what you learned in class.

The following chart summarizes some of the types of informal writing assignments you may be asked to complete.

Informal College Writing Assignments	
Type	**Description**
Personal journal	Write about daily events, thoughts about personal beliefs or goals, assess real-life situations
Learning journal	React to readings, lectures, teachers' questions, prepare for tests, summarize information, observe your own learning process
Quick write	Respond to a teacher's question about concepts presented in a class or write to get ideas
Scenario	Apply knowledge and creativity to respond to an imaginary situation
Blog	Publish your thoughts on a blogging website for personal or class electronic discussions
Field notes	Write about what occurred during observation
Course notes	Take notes on important points given in class or from the textbook and outside readings

PRACTICE   Using a Learning Journal

1.5   Practice writing a learning journal entry by answering this question: What is the most important thing you learned from your English class discussion or lesson from Chapter 1 of this textbook?

_____

_____

Formal Writing Assignments

Most of your writing assignments in college will be formal and challenging. Your current English course is preparing you to tackle the different types of writing assignments through practice with writing the college-level paragraph, essay, and summary, and by reviewing grammar, punctuation, and mechanics.

As you take required courses for your major and optional courses (electives), you will learn the vocabulary, the content, and the style of writing needed to communicate in those subjects through your teacher's lectures, the textbook, and outside readings. The following chart summarizes a few of the types of formal writing assignments you may encounter in college.

Formal College Writing Assignments	
Type	**Description**
Summary	Select and present the most important points in a reading
Review	Summarize, analyze, and evaluate a book, article, film, or other work
Review of the literature in a particular field	Summarize and compare published information and research in a subject area
Argument	Take a position on an issue, present evidence to support your position, answer any opposing points of view, and convince your reader
Lab report	Write about a scientific experiment, describing the methods used, the results, and their significance
Proposal for research	Identify a topic to research, and develop a plan and method for researching it
Research paper	Read and select evidence from the writing of experts to support your topic through analysis or argument

> **PRACTICE**   Investigating Formal Writing for a Course
>
> **1.6**   Talk to a teacher at your school who teaches a college-level course in a field you are interested in to find out what types of formal writing assignments he or she gives. First, with your class or in small groups, create a list of questions to ask the teacher, such as the types of papers assigned, the average length, and the research, if any. After collecting your information, give a brief oral report to the class or write a paragraph about what you found.

LO 3   The Writing Process

Writing at the college level is challenging. It requires a conscious effort and lots of practice. Knowing how to use the writing process will help you manage any writing assignment.

Researchers who study the way people write have discovered that most writers go through a similar process. Th **writing process** consists of stages that writers use to compose: prewriting, organizing and drafting, revising, and proofreading and editing. The graphic below gives you an overview of these stages.

Stages of the Writing Process

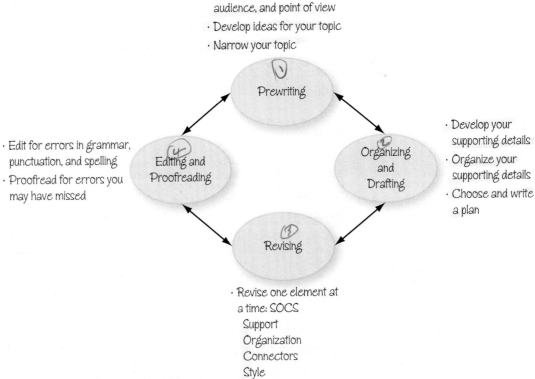

· Understand your topic, purpose, audience, and point of view
· Develop ideas for your topic
· Narrow your topic

Prewriting

· Develop your supporting details
· Organize your supporting details
· Choose and write a plan

Organizing and Drafting

· Edit for errors in grammar, punctuation, and spelling
· Proofread for errors you may have missed

Editing and Proofreading

Revising

· Revise one element at a time: SOCS
  Support
  Organization
  Connectors
  Style

The writing process is not a formula whose steps must be followed in order. Writers tend to switch back and forth through the various stages of the process. By learning about and practicing each stage in the process, you will discover what works best for you.

QuickWrite

Take a moment and write about the process you use when you write.

Writing Assignments

Help Desk

Noah wrote the following email and sent it to his teacher. Notice his use of English.

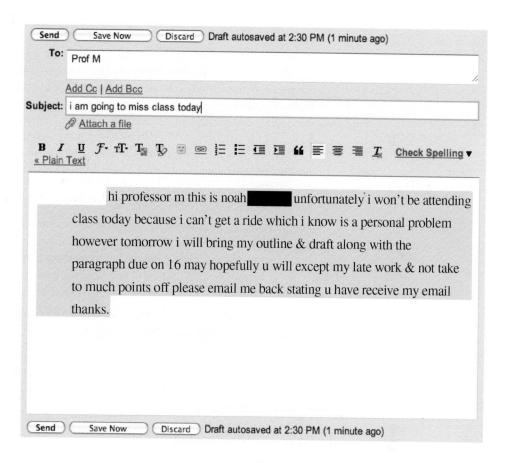

1. Has Noah considered his audience? What advice would you give him?

NO — His writing should be more formal, because he is writing to a Professor in education.

2. Rewrite the email. Dear Professor M,
This is noah, unfortunately I won't be attending class today because I don't have a ride. However I will bring in my outline & draft along with the Homework that is due on may 6th... I apologise for the late work and I hope you can overlook my reasons.

Reading and Writing across the Curriculum: Anthropology

Earlier in this chapter, you read a sentence in Spanglish, the combination of English and Spanish. Spanglish is an example of **codeswitching**, the use of more than one language in a conversation.

> Codeswitching involves a great deal of knowledge of two or more languages and an awareness of what is considered appropriate or inappropriate in a community. For example, in the Puerto Rican community in New York City, codeswitching within the same sentence seems to be common in speech among friends, but if a stranger who looks like a Spanish speaker approaches, the language will shift entirely to Spanish.
>
> (From *Anthropology* by Ember, Ember, and Peregrine)

Another example of codeswitching is to use "textspeak" to write to a friend but Standard Written English to write a paper. What codeswitching do you do? Observe yourself and others in conversation over a period of several days. You can include text messaging and instant messaging as a form of conversation. Write down who you spoke to, the situation, and the type of language you used. What did you notice?

Write a paragraph explaining how you change your word choice and speaking style depending on your situation. Use the examples that you noted from your own observations.

Comment on a Contemporary Issue

Many educators and parents are concerned that text messaging is hurting students' language skills. Others believe that it is actually increasing reading and writing skills. What do you think? Write a paragraph explaining your point of view.

English Success Tip: You Are What You Email: Guidelines for Emailing Your Teacher

Over the course of a semester, you may need to email your teacher. The informal style of emails and text messages you write to friends and family may not be appropriate in an email to the teacher. For example, Noah's email on page 9 shows how *not* to write an email to your teacher.

To give your teacher a good impression of you, keep the following guidelines in mind when emailing:

- **Subject line.** Write a specific subject including your course number, title, and meeting time.
- **Salutation.** Begin with the professor's name as written on your syllabus, such as "Hi Professor Benjamin."
- **Body of email.** Identify yourself as a student in your professor's class, and then present your problem or concern in an organized way. Be respectful and polite; do not use offensive language. Use proper spelling, grammar, and punctuation. Avoid abbreviations and emoticons if your professor does not like them.
- **Conclusion.** End with a sentence of appreciation, such as "I appreciate your time." Write your first and last name.

Finally, think about your reason for emailing. Use email for important issues; otherwise, wait to see your teacher in class.

For support in meeting this chapter's objectives, log in to www.mywritinglab.com, go to the Study Plan tab, click on **Writing in College** and choose **Standard and Non-Standard English and The Writing Process** from the list of subtopics. Read and view the videos and resources in the Review Materials section, and then complete the Recall, Apply, and Write exercises in the Activities section. You can check your scores and overall progress by using the Gradebook.

CHAPTER 2

Prewriting the Paragraph

Learning Objectives

After working through this chapter, you will be able to:

LO 1 Explain what an academic paragraph is and describe its three parts.

LO 2 Use prewriting strategies to explore a topic.

LO 3 Narrow your topic before writing.

LO 4 Write an effective topic sentence.

LO 1 What Is an Academic Paragraph?

The **academic paragraph** is a unit of writing with an organized group of sentences that logically develop one main point. The academic paragraph has a distinct appearance and specific parts.

Paragraph Appearance

When written or typed, the paragraph has a distinct form. The first sentence is indented. All sentences after that are written from the left margin to the right margin. Here is what a properly formatted paragraph assignment should look like:

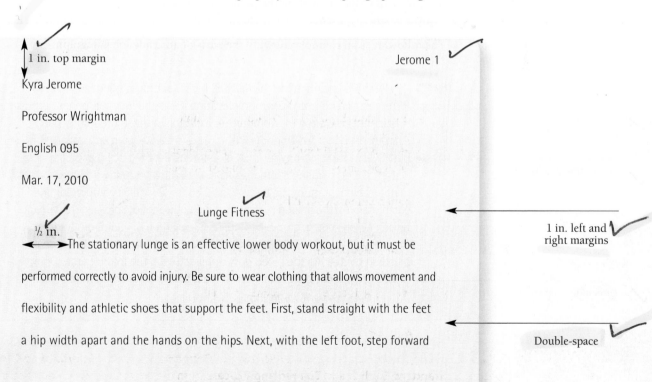

1 in. top margin

Jerome 1

Kyra Jerome

Professor Wrightman

English 095

Mar. 17, 2010

Lunge Fitness

½ in.

The stationary lunge is an effective lower body workout, but it must be

performed correctly to avoid injury. Be sure to wear clothing that allows movement and

flexibility and athletic shoes that support the feet. First, stand straight with the feet

a hip width apart and the hands on the hips. Next, with the left foot, step forward

1 in. left and right margins

Double-space

Jerome 2

about one foot. Third, lower the body until the left knee is over the left foot. To avoid injury, pay attention to form. Keep the chest up, shoulders back, and stomach muscles tight. Do not lean forward, which puts stress on the back. Be sure that the left knee does not extend past the toe. The right leg should be bent with the shin parallel to but not touching the floor. The right heel will lift so that the weight is on the toe, but the foot should stay in the same position. In step four, put the weight on the left heel and push the body up and back to the standing position. Last, repeat the lunge ten times stepping forward with the left foot. Then switch to the right foot and repeat the process ten times.

Parts of the Academic Paragraph

The academic paragraph has three parts:

1. **Topic Sentence** The topic sentence states the narrowed topic and the point the writer will prove.
2. **Supporting Details** The supporting details make up the body of the paragraph. Supporting details contain the specific information that the writer uses to explain, prove, describe, or analyze the point stated in the topic sentence.
3. **Concluding Sentence** The concluding sentence draws the paragraph to a close.

The following is an example showing the parts of an academic paragraph:

Topic sentence

Supporting details

Concluding sentence

First-aid treatment for virtually all personal fitness injuries involves RICE: rest, ice, compression, and elevation. Rest, the first component of this treatment, is required to avoid further irritation of the injured body part. Another aspect of treatment is ice, applied to relieve pain and constrict the blood vessels to stop any internal or external bleeding. Ice placed between a layer of wet toweling should be applied to the new injury for about twenty minutes every hour for the first 24 to 72 hours. The third component is compression of the injured body part, which puts indirect pressure to damaged blood vessels to help stop bleeding. Last, elevation of an injured hand or foot above the level of the heart also helps to control internal or external bleeding by making the blood flow uphill to reach the injured area. Doing all these parts together can help relieve pain and keep the area from swelling.

(Adapted from *Access to Health* by Rebecca J. Donatelle)

PRACTICE   Identifying the Parts of the Paragraph

2.1   Identify the three parts of student Sang-Don Lee's paragraph. Underline the topic sentence once, and the concluding sentence twice. Then circle the main supporting details.

Difficult grammar

Confusing

As a native speaker of Korean, learning English has been difficult. First of all, the Korean language does not have prepositions and articles. Therefore, I have no idea what they mean in sentences. For instance, when I took English class the first time, a teacher asked to see me after the class. I visited her office and asked her, "Why were you looking at me?" The teacher said, "I was not looking at you. I was looking for you, Don." She then explained the difference between "look for" and "look at." My face turned red as a beet, and I felt sorry because it was impolite. Also, the Korean language has characters, not an alphabet. English sounds f, p, r, v, x, and z do not exist. Often, people do not understand my pronunciation. For example, when I took a vision test for my driver's license, I could not pronounce the Z sound correctly. I told the officer I could not make that sound, but I drew the letter for him. He said, "Follow me! Z." That was how I learned the Z sound. Another problem is that English idioms are confusing. To illustrate, when I went to a restroom, my friend said, "Hey, Don, your fly is open!" I asked, "What! Is a fly open?" I did not understand. I thought he meant the fly as an insect. After I found out what he meant, I felt a bit ashamed. Learning English continues to be difficult, but I am improving.

Don't un.

LO 2 Prewriting

When you get your paragraph assignment, you need to understand what you are being asked to write about, who will read what you write, and what your purpose is for writing.

Understand Your Topic

Your teacher may assign a topic, give you a list of topics to choose from, or ask you to choose your own. The **topic** is the subject you have been asked to write about.

The topic can be assigned in the form of a question, a phrase, or several sentences.

Question	What are some money-saving ideas for college students?
Phrase	Money-Saving Ideas for College Students
Several Sentences	With rising costs of college tuition and living expenses, students do not have a lot of money. This makes managing money a challenge. To save money, students need to become aware of how they spend money every day. Write a paragraph about some ways students can save money.

Read your assigned topic carefully to be sure that you understand it. Look up any words you do not know. If you are not sure how to approach the subject, ask your teacher for some guidance. If you are asked to pick your own topic, find something that is interesting to you and relevant to your studies or your life.

✓ **PRACTICE**   Asking Questions about a Topic

2.2   Assume that you were assigned the topic Money-Saving Ideas for College Students on a Budget, but you have some questions about it. Write your questions as an email to your teacher.

Understand Your Purpose

The **purpose** is your reason for writing. Assignments have different purposes. For example, you may be asked to explain how something works, tell a story, give examples, or compare two things. In Part 2 of this textbook, you will be learning about the different purposes for writing and the patterns for organizing your writing.

Understand Your Audience

The **audience** is the person or group who will read your writing. Knowing your audience helps you decide what to say and how to say it. In your English class, most of the time you will be writing for your teacher and your classmates. When planning your writing, think about connecting with your readers by answering these questions:

- What does my audience already know about my topic?
- How can I organize my writing so that my audience will understand what I write?
- What do I want my audience to think of me?

PRACTICE   Learning about Your Audience

2.3   Try this activity to learn more about your audience: your teacher and the students in your class. On a small piece of paper or a 3" × 5" card, write four things that the people in your class do not know about you. Do not write your name on the paper or card. Form groups of four or five people. Choose one person to conduct the activity. That person will read one item on the card at a time to see if anyone in the group can guess who is being described. If no one can guess, then the person will self-identify.

Understand Your Point of View

Point of view is the approach you use: first, second, or third person. The following chart explains the three points of view:

Point of View		
Person	**Pronoun**	**When to Use**
First person	I, we	When writing about a personal experience or using a personal experience as a supporting detail
Second person	you	When giving directions or instructions
Third person	he, she, it, they	When writing about an object, idea, or someone other than yourself

You will write many academic paragraph assignments in third person; however, there are some writing situations in which other points of view can be used.

Prewrite to Develop Ideas for Your Topic

To get ideas for your topic, use a prewriting technique. **Prewriting** helps you think of ideas. Instead of staring at a blank piece of paper or computer screen for hours, you actively work with the topic until you feel comfortable enough to write about it.

The most commonly used prewriting techniques are questioning, freewriting, concept mapping, listing, and brainstorming.

Questioning **Questioning** is the process of asking questions about your topic and answering them. You can write your own list of questions and answers or use the set of six questions journalists use: Who? What? Where? When? Why? How?

Here is Jessica's list of questions and answers for our topic Money-Saving Ideas for College Students on a Budget:

Jessica's Questioning

Who needs to save money?	Most college students today
What is the problem?	Students buy stuff without thinking about what they're doing, spend too much money going out, on food, or shopping, charge every little thing on their credit card and run up bills, go over their talk minutes or texting limits, having to have the latest trend in clothing and hair styles, get nails done
Where can students save money?	Discount and dollar stores, online, work, sale days, student discounts
When can students save money?	Weekends by not hanging out with people who spend a lot, picking cheaper things to do when going out, going to an early movie, buy cheaper food at a restaurant, not driving around burning gasoline
How can students save money?	Don't run up credit card bills, don't eat out so much, buy used books, get a cheaper cell phone plan, don't buy expensive coffee drinks or smoothies, go to clubs on ladies night, buy bottled drinks and bring them along, make my own healthy snacks

PRACTICE 2.4   **Practicing Questioning**

Try the questioning prewriting strategy by answering the journalist's six questions about one of these topics or a topic of your own:

sports	jobs	music
studying	fashion	online communication

Freewriting **Freewriting** is a method that involves writing about any thoughts you have about a topic for five to fifteen minutes without stopping. You don't have to think about organizing ideas or making mistakes. If you get stuck, write about how you are feeling at that moment. Just keep writing. Soon the thoughts that distracted you will be gone, and you will be able to focus on the topic again.

The following freewrite shows how one student responded to the topic Money-Saving Ideas for College Students on a Budget:

Berenise's Freewrite

I have a lot of money problems. My family has always been poor. I am the first person in my family to go to college and everyone is proud of me but I have to work to help out the family expenses. So I have a job, I don't like it but I have to do it. After I give some money from my paycheck to my mother, I keep the rest for myself. I like to go out with my friends like go dancing. But lots of times I have to say no I can't go because then I won't have enough money to pay for things like my phone. I got so upset last month because my cell got cut off. I didn't have enough money to pay my bill which was really expensive from talking and texting to my boyfriend.

After reading her freewrite, Berenise realized that she wanted to focus her writing on ways she can manage her money.

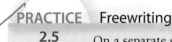

PRACTICE Freewriting

2.5 On a separate sheet of paper or on a computer, freewrite for five to fifteen minutes on one of these topics or on a topic of your own.

an activity you enjoy   your career goals   money

After reading your freewrite, choose ideas you would like to develop.

Concept Mapping **Concept Mapping** is a technique for placing ideas in a visual form. Concept maps help you picture your ideas and see the relationships among them. Some writers refer to this method as clustering, bubbling, or mind mapping. To make a concept map, follow these steps.

1. Write your subject in a circle in the center of a blank piece of paper.
2. Think of details and examples that relate to the subject (subtopics), and put them in circles around your center circle (your subject).
3. Draw lines from the center to each of the outer circles.
4. Continue to add more branches to your map as you think of ideas and examples that relate to each subtopic.

Here is an example of a student's concept map on Money-Saving Ideas for Students on a Budget. In his first attempt, Davon came up with five subtopics.

Davon's Concept Map

Clustering

Then, he added specific examples to each of the subtopics.

Davon's Revised Concept Map

PRACTICE   Concept Mapping

2.6   Using your own paper, prepare a concept map about one of these or your own topic:

shopping	travel	friends
Internet	restaurants	advertising

Listing **Listing** involves doing exactly that—making a list. Write your topic at the top of the page and list of all the words details, and examples that come to mind. Here are some of the ideas that Ermilie came up with for the topic Money-Saving Ideas for College Students on a Budget.

Ermilie's List

stop buying expensive drinks	free activities on campus
borrow textbook or buy used	shop at discount stores
take public transportation	get haircuts at cheaper salons
get financial aid	email instead of calling long distance
share music and DVDs	buy less makeup
no vending machine food	pay bills on time

When you have run out of ideas, take a look at your list for ideas that can be grouped and others that can be taken out. Ermilie noticed that she could group some of her ideas into categories: books, entertainment, personal items, and phone.

PRACTICE   Listing

2.7   Choose one of these topics and write a list on your own paper or on the computer:

traditions	food	transportation
family members	stress	computers

Brainstorming **Brainstorming** is an interactive group technique for thinking of ideas. Brainstorming helps you share your ideas and find new ideas you may not have thought of on your own. Small groups of two to five work well. Choose one person to record the group's ideas about a topic. As each person suggests an idea, the recorder writes it down in a list. Instead of a list, you can use a concept map or other graphic organizer for recording the ideas. Ten to fifteen minutes is usually enough time to brainstorm.

PRACTICE   Brainstorming

2.8   Form a group of two to five people. Together, choose one of the topics from the list below or a topic of your own. Ask one member to record the ideas, and then brainstorm together for ten to fifteen minutes.

| peer pressure | teachers | special events |
| success | credit cards | new products |

Now, look over the list for ideas that can be grouped together for development into a paragraph or essay. Then, discuss the advantages of brainstorming a topic with a small group.

LO 3 Narrow Your Topic

After prewriting on your topic, review all of your ideas. The topic should be narrow enough so that you can support your point in one paragraph.

In her list on the topic Money-Saving Ideas for College Students, Ermilie thought of items like books, entertainment, personal items, and phone. After looking at her list, she realized that she wanted to write about the ways students could save money as illustrated in the following diagram:

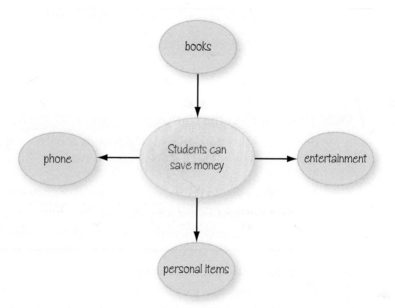

PRACTICE Narrowing a General Topic

2.9   Practice narrowing a general topic.

1. restaurants _____

2. fitness _____

3. an academic subject _____

4. relationships _____

5. clothing styles _____

LO 4 Write the Topic Sentence

Once you have narrowed your topic, you can write a topic sentence for your paragraph. The **topic sentence** controls the content of the paragraph. The topic sentence has two important parts:

1. It states your narrowed topic.

2. It states the point you will prove. ✔

Online shopping has several advantages.

Some energy drinks contain harmful ingredients.

The neighbors on my street have annoying habits. ✔

Hurricane Wilma taught me how to live without electricity.

Here is the topic sentence Ermilie wrote for Money-Saving Ideas for College Students.

College students can save money by making economical choices.

PRACTICE   Finding the Narrowed Subject and the Main Point
2.10   Underline the narrowed subject once, and the main point twice, in the following topic sentences. The first one is done for you.

1. Last week's tornado severely damaged the homes on my street.
2. Uncle Tai's Chinese Restaurant serves a variety of traditional Chinese dishes.
3. Cooking competition television shows present unusual challenges for the participants.
4. My customer service job at Target is helping me learn how to interact with people.
5. **Meditation** helps to manage stress.
6. LA Fitness has membership plans for people of all ages.
7. Quick weight loss diet supplements can have dangerous side effects.
8. New cars offer the latest technology.

meditation the act of giving your attention to only one thing, either as a religious activity or as a way of becoming calm and relaxed

Characteristics of a Good Topic Sentence

To better understand the elements that make a good topic sentence, let's look at some topic sentences written by students for the prewriting example topic Money-Saving Ideas for College Students.

1. The topic sentence makes one point.

> **Poor—Makes more than one point:** College students can save money by cutting back on unnecessary spending and setting long-term financial goals.
>
> Trying to support two topics will cause the paragraph to lose its focus.
>
> **Poor—Makes an incomplete point:** Making a budget to save money.
>
> This is not a complete sentence. The reader does not know who should make a budget.
>
> **Good—Makes one point:** College students can save money by cutting back on unnecessary spending.

2. The topic sentence states the point specifically.

> **Poor—Does not state point specifically:** As a college student, saving money is good.

> A word that is not specific may be misunderstood. The word *good* merely tells the reader that you like or do not like something.

> **Poor—Announces the topic:** I am going to discuss ways that college students can save money.

> Avoid announcing what you will do: "I plan to explain," "My paper is going to be about," This paper describes," "I am writing my paper on."

> **Poor—Asks a question:** Can college students save money?

> A topic sentence written as a direct statement makes the point clearly.

> **Good—States point specifically:** College students can save money by spending less on entertainment.

3. **The topic sentence is limited enough to be developed in a single paragraph.**

> **Poor—Too narrow:** College students can save money by cutting out expensive coffee drinks.

> This main point leaves little to explain after you tell the reader how much you spend on gourmet coffee each day.

> **Poor—Too broad:** College students' spending is out of control.

> This main point is too big for one paragraph.

> **Good—Limited:** College students can save money by setting up a budget.

4. The **topic sentence can be proved.**

> **Poor—Cannot be developed.** Fifty percent of all college students get financial aid to pay tuition.

> This statement is a fact and does not need additional proof.

> **Better—Can be proved:** College students can save money by limiting spending on personal items.

> This statement can be supported by examples.

TIPS | **Writing Good Topic Sentences**

Here are some tips for writing good, concise topic sentences.

1. Make one point about your narrowed topic.
2. State the point specifically.
3. Limit the point enough so it can be developed in a single paragraph.
4. Choose a point that can be proved.

PRACTICE Evaluating and Revising Topic Sentences

2.11   Identify the problems in the topic sentences below. Then revise them. If the sentence is good, write *G*.

1. In this paper, I am going to explain my opinion about the ways to avoid identity theft.   G

_____

_____

2. Moving to the United States by myself.

_____

_____

3. What are the benefits of hybrid cars?

_____

_____

4. The science museum is a great place to visit.

_____

_____

5. Students can be easily distracted in computer classrooms.

_____

_____

6. Despite all the health risks, people have been drinking alcohol for hundreds of years.

_____

_____

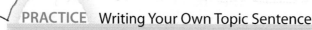

PRACTICE   Writing Your Own Topic Sentence

2.12   Write your own topic sentence based on one of your prewrites in this chapter. Underline the narrowed topic once and the main point twice.

Writing Assignments

Help Desk

One of your classmates, Valery, is an English language learner. She attended high school for two years in the United States. Now as a college student, she is not confident about her written English skills. Her grades on grammar tests are very good, but her grades on written assignments are barely passing. Valery has trouble understanding how to limit a topic and write a topic sentence. She is not comfortable about asking questions during class. What advice would you give Valery? Write your advice in an email to her.

Group Activity: Using Prewriting Strategies

Work in pairs or small groups of three or four. Choose questioning, concept mapping, listing, or brainstorming as your prewriting strategy for the following topic: Create a new, healthy drink targeted to college students and give it a name. Consider the important characteristics for selecting a brand name:

- Suggests something about the product's benefits and qualities
- Is easy to pronounce, recognize, and remember
- Is distinctive
- Does not infringe on existing brand names

(Adapted from *Marketing* by Gary Armstrong and Philip Kotler)

Write a paragraph about the steps your group went through to develop and name the new drink.

Reading and Writing across the Curriculum: Music

Read the following passage about music and culture from the textbook *Understanding Music*:

> It has often been said that music is a universal language, that it goes beyond the limits of nation and race. This is true, but only in a very specific sense. The fact that there is music seems to be universal: Every known human group has music. But for each culture, music has a different meaning. It takes different forms in different cultural groups. Even the definition of music differs from culture to culture. Some cultures don't even have a word for "music," because it is a part of their experience in the world, whereas others use different words to distinguish among several types of music.
>
> (Adapted from *Understanding Music* by Jeremy Yudkin)

What are some examples of different cultural groups in the United States? What types of music are associated with those groups? Select one cultural group and write a paragraph or essay about the music of that group, or write about your cultural group's music.

Comment on a Contemporary Issue

Using laptop computers in the college classroom has caused a controversy. Some professors feel that laptops distract students with temptations like surfing the Internet or going on social network sites. On the other hand, students say that laptops help them take more detailed notes. Do you think that laptop use is distracting or helpful? Choose a prewriting strategy and develop ideas for your position on the topic. Then, write a topic sentence that makes your point.

> ### English Success Tip: First Impressions: Appearance Does Count
>
> Did you ever think that the way your paper looks might affect your grade? Although content, organization, and correctness are most important, teachers may be influenced by your paper's appearance. Just as dressing appropriately for a job interview helps you make a good impression, submitting a neat, legible paper can give your teacher a positive first impression of your writing. Here are tips to improve your papers' appearance:
>
> - Word-process or type all your assignments if possible. If you must write a short assignment by hand, do so neatly.
> - Double-space your assignments unless instructed to do otherwise. Double-spaced text allows space for comments or corrections.
> - Use a standard 12-point font. A tiny font, such as 10 point, is hard for most to read.
> - Don't try to make your paper look longer than it is. Large fonts, large punctuation, triple spacing, and using wider margins are tricks that most teachers recognize.
>
> Handing in a presentable, legible paper doesn't take much effort and shows that you are proud of your work and that you care about your readers.

For support in meeting this chapter's objectives, log in to www.mywritinglab.com, go to the Study Plan tab, click on **Prewriting the Paragraph** and choose **Recognizing a Paragraph, Prewriting, and The Topic Sentence** from the list of subtopics. Read and view the videos and resources in the Review Materials section, and then complete the Recall, Apply, and Write exercises in the Activities section. You can check your scores and overall progress by using the Gradebook.

CHAPTER 3

Organizing and Drafting the Paragraph

Learning Objectives

After working through this chapter, you will be able to:

LO 1 Organize the supporting details of a paragraph.

LO 2 Draft a paragraph.

LO 1 Organizing

Once you have done your prewriting, narrowed your topic, and written your topic sentence, you are ready to organize your ideas and draft your paragraph.

Understand Supporting Details

Supporting details are sentences that contain specific information to back up the main point of the topic sentence. Supporting details are not statements of opinion.

The types of supporting details you use will depend on the purpose of your paragraph. For example, if you are writing about video games that are challenging, your details will be examples of those games. The five types of supporting details are examples, descriptions, steps or procedures, reasons, and facts and statistics.

Examples **Examples** are details that explain a point with a specific situation or instance. Examples can be written from your own personal observation or knowledge. In the following example, student Sang-Don uses a personal experience to explain his problem understanding prepositions in English:

> For example, during my first English class, the teacher asked to see me after class. I visited her office and asked her, "Why were you looking at me?" The teacher said, "I was not looking at you. I was looking for you, Don." Then she explained the difference between "look for" and "look at."

**PRACTICE
3.1** **Writing Examples to Support Topic Sentences**

Write three specific examples to support each of the following topic sentences.

1. My professor's office is a mess.

   ~~Because~~ there are books all over the
   office FLOOR.

Because she left trash on the floor.
Because nothing was organise, they were always out of place.

2. Some foods sold at fast food restaurants are healthy.

Food such as fresh salad, chicken salad (BLT) Bacon Lettuce and Tomato

3. My new cell phone has many convenient features.

Such as APP Store youTube,
Such as iTunes, Safari
Such as Stock,

Descriptions **Descriptions** are details that explain the characteristics of a person, place, object, or event. Descriptions often use sensory details, such as sight, smell, taste, touch, and hearing, to help the reader visualize the topic. In the following excerpt, Jason describes a few moments during a tense wrestling match:

> As I looked at the scoreboard to notice a tied game, eleven to eleven, the only thing I could hear was the pounding of my heart supporting my exhausted body and the faint sound of my coach and teammates offering me encouragement. As I approached the center of the mat, my eyes met my opponent's with an evil stare of determination and dominance.

PRACTICE **Writing Descriptive Details**

3.2   Write three descriptive details for each of the following topic sentences.

1. The severe thunderstorm damaged several houses on my street.

structure.

The wind threw roof from the House hitting
one house was severely damage to only its
other home have less damages, but were
still severely damage.

2. The mall was busy with shoppers the week before the holiday.

The

3. My family's car has many problems.

(handwritten: instructions)

Steps Steps are details that explain how to do something or how something happens. For example, if your purpose is to tell the reader how to study, your details will be a series of steps to accomplish the process. Allicyn, a massage therapist, explains the steps she follows to massage a client's head:

> Seated at the front of the table, I begin by holding the client's head in the palm of my hand and begin massaging the top of the head. This releases any tension in the tissue, which is the connective tissue that lies directly under the skin. Next, I move to the forehead, gently massaging the soft tissue of the face. By giving continuous pressure to fifteen pressure points on the face, I release any tension the client might have in this area. Then, I take the chin and massage along the jaw line. When I complete the face, I gently pull the ears toward the shoulders.

PRACTICE Writing Steps *(handwritten: What)*

3.3 Write three steps for each of the following topic sentences.

1. Students can get a student identification card by following these steps.

(handwritten: Student can register with the school for an academy course)
(handwritten: Student the college a nominal fee after registering with the)
(handwritten: Student make appointment with college to get ID made)

2. Using a search engine to find _____ sites is simple.

_____

_____

_____

3. Cooking _____ has several easy steps.

_____

_____

_____

Reasons *(handwritten: why)* Reasons are details that explain the cause for a belief, action, event, or opinion. For example, if you want to explain why you admire a particular person, you would provide reasons to support your opinion. Gabriel has chosen Oprah Winfrey as a person he admires and has chosen her financial support for education as one reason:

> One reason Oprah Winfrey is admirable is that she has given financial support to further education all over the world. Oprah built an academy for girls

from poor backgrounds in South Africa to give them the chance to become educated. Also, her scholars program gives money to students who will use their education to give back to their communities.

PRACTICE Writing Reasons

3.4   Write three reasons for each of the following topic sentences.

1. Being a full-time worker and full-time student is demanding.

_____

_____

_____

2. Participating in a study group can improve your test grades.

_____

_____

_____

3. Driving while talking on the phone is dangerous.

_____

_____

_____

Facts and Statistics **Facts and Statistics** are details that can be proved. They can be shown to be true, to exist, or to have happened based on evidence or experience. **Statistics** are facts that consist of numbers.

Here are some examples of facts and statistics:

- Ricardo moved from Colombia to the United States in 2007.
- Shawna has three sisters: Chantal, Keesha, and Tiffany.
- My boyfriend Brian drives a Honda Civic.
- I have completed 24 of the 60 credits required for my associate's degree in criminal justice.

*Research Reminder.
See Chapter 17 for
more information
about using information from
outside sources.*

Use facts that you know from your own life experience or from talking to people you know. If you want to use information from a source, such as magazine, book, television or radio news report, or website, either put that information in your own words or quote the information in your paragraph. You must give credit to your source.

PRACTICE Writing Facts

3.5   Write three facts about the students in your English class for each of the following topic sentences. You may want to interview your classmates for information.

where

1. The students in my English class come from different places (or countries).

_____

_____

_____

2. Some students in my English class are studying _____.

_____

_____

_____

3. Many students in my English class have a job.

_____

_____

_____

Avoiding Opinions **Opinions** are statements of beliefs or feelings. You can use an opinion as a main point in a topic sentence, but your supporting details must be examples, descriptions, steps or procedures, reasons, and facts and statistics.

The following sets of sentences show the differences between opinions and specific supporting details.

Opinion	Specific Supporting Details
My friend Tina is a great friend.	I left my wallet on my desk at home last Tuesday, so Tina gave me five dollars for lunch at Burger King on College Avenue.
Dupree always looks tired.	Dupree works as a forklift operator Mondays through Thursdays from 3 a.m. to 7 a.m.

QuickWrite

Write your opinion about your college, a friend, a movie you just saw, or something you just bought.

PRACTICE Fact or Opinion?

3.6 Identify each sentence below as either a fact or opinion. Write *F* for fact and *O* for opinion in the blank next to each sentence.

_____ 1. There is too much violence on television.

_____ 2. When NBC first aired all its programs in color on February 17, 1961, only 1 percent of American homes had color TV sets.

_____ 3. In the United States, men and women are supposed to be equal—at least that is the stated ideal. (From *Human Communication*, Joseph A. DeVito)

_____ 4. Aaron "T-Bone" Walker is generally credited with being the first blues guitarist to use an electric guitar and his influence on subsequent musicians was tremendous. (From *Crossroads* by Elizabeth F. Barkley)

_____ 5. Attitudes towards gambling in America probably became less negative beginning in the early 1960s when a legal lottery introduced in New Hampshire proved wildly popular. (From *Travel and Tourism* by Paul S. Biederman)

_____ 6. In 1933, Mexican artist David Alfara Siqueiros painted a mural, *America Tropical*, on Olvera Street, the historic center of Chicano and Mexican culture in Los Angeles. (From *A World of Art* by Henry M. Sayre)

_____ 7. The use of fingerprints in identifying offenders was popularized by Sir Francis Galton and was officially adopted by Scotland Yard in 1901. (From *Criminal Justice Today* by Frank Schmalleger)

_____ 8. Designers with a love of computer work and a minimum need for client contact may enjoy becoming specialists in computer-aided design and drafting. (From *Designing Your Future* by Cindy V. Beacham)

Develop Supporting Details

Developing your supporting details is the next step in the writing process. One strategy you can use is to go back to the prewriting notes you made when you narrowed your topic and wrote your topic sentence. Another strategy is to prewrite a second time.

In Chapter 2, you saw Ermilie's prewriting list for money-saving ideas for college students (page 18). Ermilie reviewed her list, crossing out the weaker points and adding some new supporting details.

Ermilie's Supporting Details

Stop buying expensive drinks	~~Free activities on campus~~
Borrow textbook or buy used	Shop at discount stores
~~Take public transportation~~	~~Get haircuts at cheaper salons~~
~~Get financial aid~~	~~Share music and DVDs~~
~~Don't buy so much makeup~~	No vending machine food
~~Pay bills on time~~	Email instead of long distance calls

Here are the details she added:

Change cell phone plan	Bring snacks from home to school
Buy textbooks online	No eating at expensive restaurants
Text message less often	Keep same phone longer

Next, Ermilie grouped the items from her list into three major supporting points and explained each point with details from her list:

Ermilie's Supporting Points and Details

1. Books and school supplies

   Buy textbooks online, borrow a textbook, buy a used book, buy school supplies at discount stores

2. Cell phone

   Change to a cheaper plan, make shorter calls, text message less, keep same phone longer, email instead of making long distance calls

3. Food

   Make healthy snacks and bring them to school, avoid buying expensive coffees and smoothies, avoid buying drinks from vending machines—buy large quantities and bring from home, stay away from expensive restaurants

---

PRACTICE   Developing Supporting Details

3.7   Using the details from a topic you used in the prewriting activities in Chapter 2 or from the supporting details exercises in this chapter, develop supporting details.

Organize Supporting Details

Organizing your paragraph before you write will keep you on track as you write your first draft. Your organization plan lists all of the supporting points and the details that explain those points. Three methods you can use to organize your ideas are **time order**, **spatial order**, and **order of importance**.

As you read through the explanation and sample paragraph for each method, you will notice that some words are boldfaced. These words are called connectors and transitions. **Connectors and transitions** are words and phrases used to alert the reader that you are beginning a new point. Without these words, the reader may not be able to tell where one point ends and the next one begins. You will find a list of connectors and transitions for each method after the sample paragraph.

Time Order **Time Order**, also called chronological order, is the arrangement of details in the order they happened. Time order is most commonly used when writing about the events of a story or a period in history, or when describing how something happens or works.

The paragraph that follows uses time order by describing the process of checking out of a hotel:

The traditional method of guest checkout at hotels involves five stages of customer activities. **First,** the departing guest walks from the room to the front desk in the lobby for checkout. The guest **next** waits in line for desk service. **Then,** upon reaching the front desk, the guest reviews the bill before payment. **At this point,** the guest can question items on the bill or request changes. **When** the bill is approved, the guest makes payment. **Finally,** the guest leaves the front desk to resume activities. Because this checkout method can be time consuming, improved methods are being developed.

(Adapted from *Business Essentials* by Ronald J. Ebert and Ricky W. Griffin)

Common Connector/Transition Words for Time Order

then	afterward	next	subsequently
previously	first	second	at last
meanwhile	in the meantime	today	soon
at length	yesterday	during	tomorrow
eventually	immediately	while	later
before	after		

Spatial Order **Spatial order** is the arrangement of details according to their position in physical space. Spatial order is most commonly used when describing a place, an object, or a person. Your details should follow an order so that the reader can visualize the physical position of the subject. For example, you can describe something in any number of ways:

- front to back or back to front
- inside to outside or outside to inside
- left to right or right to left

The paragraph below uses spatial order.

There are four taste experiences: sour, sweet, bitter, and salty, plus a recently discovered fifth sense, called *umami,* which tastes glutamates. Each of these four taste types is experienced in a specific area of the tongue that contains taste buds with specialized functions. Taste receptors for all tastes are located **in a narrow area surrounding the entire tongue**. Sweet, salty, and sour taste receptors are **in a region just inside the outer edge of the tongue**. Salty and sour receptors are located **in a small region toward the back of the tongue**. Sour-only receptors are located approximately **in the center of the tongue**. There is an area **toward the center and front of the tongue** where no sensation of taste is experienced. Sweet and sour taste receptors are located just **in front of this region**, with bittersweet and sour tastes being experienced **near the tip of the tongue just inside** the area containing the receptors for all tastes.

(Adapted from *The Pharmacy Technician* by Mike Johnston)

Common Connector/Transition Words for Spatial Order

above	along the edge	on top	behind
on the side	beneath	under	around
below	over	straight ahead	at the top
at the bottom	surrounding	opposite	at the rear
at the left	at the right	in the center	at the front

next to	nearby	within sight	beyond
in the forefront	in the foreground	near	out of sight
across	down	up	adjacent
in the background	beside		
in front of	in the distance		

Order of Importance **Order of importance** is the arrangement of details according to how interesting, significant, or memorable they are. Order of importance is most commonly used when your supporting details are facts, examples, causes and effects, and comparisons and contrasts.

The following paragraph uses order of importance:

People who abuse their partners or their children share some common characteristics. **First of all**, most batterers have low self-esteem and tend to blame everyone else for their behavior. They are **also** typically extremely jealous and often use sex as their weapon of aggression and ultimate instrument of control. **Moreover**, while violence is the way they express their anger or frustration, they underestimate or even deny that their behaviors are "really that violent" or harmful. **Most importantly**, batterers have the need to control and dominate, and they become master manipulators—they can manipulate their partner's weaknesses and their strength. Recognizing these characteristics of abusers can minimize the risk of encountering abuse in a relationship.

(From *Family Life Now* by Kelly J. Welch)

Common Connector/Transition Words for Order of Importance

most important	least important	first	second
third	next	in addition	also
furthermore	moreover	another	first of all, etc.

Choose a Plan

After reading about the three methods of organization, you are ready to choose the plan that will work best for your supporting points. Ermilie decided that **order of importance** would work best for her paragraph about ways college students can save money. She decided to put the least important point first and end with the most important because the last point is the one that readers will remember best.

Ermilie's Paragraph Plan

1. Food

   Make healthy snacks and bring them to school, avoid buying expensive coffees and smoothies, avoid buying drinks from vending machines—buy large quantities and bring from home, stay away from expensive restaurants

✓ 2. Cell phone

Change to a cheaper plan, make shorter calls, text message less, keep same phone longer, email instead of making long distance calls

✓ 3. Books and school supplies

Buy books online, borrow a book, buy a used book, buy school supplies at discount stores

PRACTICE   Organizing Details

3.8   Each of the following sets of sentences has supporting details that are not in the correct order. Put the details in order and tell which method of organization you used.

Sentence Group 1

Topic sentence: The cruise industry line faces seasonal variation by demand.

3 _____   The off-season runs from mid-August through the first week of January and accounts for about 25 percent.

2 _____   The period between April and mid-August, known as the normal period, also garners 35 to 40 percent of all business, but over a period twice as long as the wave season.

1 _____   The so-called wave season runs from the second week of January through the end of March and accounts for 35 to 40 percent of annual passengers.

(From *Travel and Tourism* by Paul S. Biederman)

Method of Organization: _____

Sentence Group 2

Topic sentence: Music Television (MTV) came into existence in 1981 for several reasons.

3 _____   Next, MTV was less subject to censorship than was mainstream television, which was not prepared to air some of the rock that contained lyrics or video gestures that might be considered offensive to the general television audience.

1 _____   Most important were the technological developments in the film and sound recording industry, which presented a vehicle for the production of music videos.

4 _____   Finally, the development of a network directed toward the teenage market so-lidified the success of such a venture.

2 _____   Second, network television was not prepared to air some of the rock that con-tained lyrics or video gestures that might be considered offensive to the gen-eral television audience.

(Adapted from *Musical Encounters* by David C. Nichols)

Method of Organization: _____

Sentence Group 3

Topic sentence: Four distinct communities of birds and mammals feed from the top to the bottom of a lowland tropical forest of the Far East.

_____ The zone of tree trunks includes a world of flying mammals, birds, squirrels, and insect-eating bats.

_____ The forest floor is occupied by large herbivores, such as the gaur, tapir, and elephant, which feed on ground vegetation and low hanging leaves.

_____ The group feeding above the treetops is made up mostly of birds, fruit bats, and other species of mammals.

_____ Small ground and undergrowth animals, birds, and small mammals feed at the lower portion of the tree trunks.

(From *Elements of Ecology* by Robert Leo Smith and Thomas M. Smith)

Method of Organization: _____

PRACTICE Choosing a Method of Organization

3.9 Using the details for your own paragraph from Practice 3.7, choose a method of organization for your ideas.

Write a Plan

After you have decided how you want to organize your supporting points, your next step is to write a plan for your first draft. Written plans keep you from getting lost or going off the topic while you are writing. Two types of written plans are a scratch outline and a graphic organizer.

Scratch Outline A **scratch outline** is a written plan in which you jot down each of your supporting points in logical order. Under each of those points, add details to back them up. Here is how a scratch outline might look. This particular outline has three supporting points with one detail for each support, but you may have more.

Scratch Outline

Topic Sentence:

Supporting point 1:

    Detail(s) for supporting point 1

Supporting point 2:

    Detail(s) for supporting point 2

Supporting point 3:

    Details(s) for supporting point 3

Concluding Sentence:

Ermilie put her details into the following scratch outline, which helped her tighten her organization.

Ermilie's Scratch Outline

Topic Sentence: College students can save money by making economical choices.

  Supporting Point 1: Food

    Detail: Make healthy snacks and bring them to school instead of using vending machines

    Detail: Bring drinks instead of buying expensive coffees, smoothies, and other drinks

    Detail: Eat out at inexpensive restaurants

  Supporting Point 2: Cell phone

    Detail: Change to a cheaper plan

    Detail: Spend less time using phone—shorter calls, fewer text messages

    Detail: Keep same phone longer

    Detail: Email instead of making long distance calls

  Supporting Point 3: Books and school supplies

    Detail 1: Save on books: buy online, borrow, buy used

    Detail 2: Buy school supplies at discount stores

PRACTICE   Making a Scratch Outline

3.10   Make a scratch outline based on the following paragraph.

High technology equipment is used to search cargo and conveyances without having to perform the costly and time-consuming process of unloading cargo or drilling through containers. One type is trace-detection technology. It focuses on cargo, luggage, packages, containers, and vehicles. Trace detection devices gather and analyze the small amounts of vapors given off and microscopic particles left behind from drugs and explosives. Another type is radiation-detection equipment. It is used at border crossings and ports to detect radioactive materials being smuggled into the U.S. Finally, the Remote Video Inspection System (RVIS) is designed to speed up the clearance of low-risk travelers and enhance security at remote border areas. RVIS transmits images of a driver, vehicle, documents, and passengers to an inspector located miles away at a port of entry monitored twenty-four hours a day.

(Adapted from *Criminal Justice Today* by Frank Schmalleger)

Scratch outline

_____

_____

_____

_____

_____

_____

_____

_____

_____

_____

✓PRACTICE   Writing Your Own Scratch Outline

3.11   Write a scratch outline for the paragraph you have been working on in this chapter.

Graphic Organizer A graphic organizer is a visual, such as a chart, web, or diagram, used to arrange your thoughts in an organized way. See the facing page for a graphic organizer for a standard academic paragraph.

✓PRACTICE   Using the Paragraph Graphic Organizer

3.12   Using the paragraph graphic organizer, organize the details of the paragraph you have been working on.

✓ LO 2 Drafting

Once you have a plan for your paragraph, you are ready to draft it. **Drafting** is the process of putting your plan into sentences that explain and support your topic sentence. The purpose of drafting is to get your ideas down in rough form, not to write a perfect paragraph. Ermilie used her scratch outline to guide her as she wrote her rough draft.

Ermilie's Rough Draft

College students can save money by making economical choices. Instead of buying that bag of Doritos or Snickers candy bar at vending machine prices, save money by bringing snacks from home. Healthy snacks like home made trail mix, fruit, or cut up vegetables are inexpensive and portable. Cutting down on expensive gourmet coffees or fruit smoothies can save students almost five dollars a day. Most companies offer more than one cell phone plan, students can do research to find the cheapest plan. Spending less time on the phone with friends at peak times and keeping text messaging to a minimum will help reduce phones expenses. Also,

Paragraph Graphic Organizer

Topic Sentence

Supporting Point 1   **Details**

Supporting Point 2   **Details**

Supporting Point 3   **Details**

Concluding Sentence

students do not have to buy the latest phone every six months. Books are the biggest expense for college students. Buy books online. Some online companies will even ship for free. Buying used books is cheaper than buying new. Students can even make money by selling their used books for less than the bookstore. Avoid the bookstore for supplies; the big discount stores have better prices.

Note that Ermilie's paragraph is not perfect. There are mistakes in it, but she can correct them later. Furthermore, the paragraph just stops; it doesn't come to a satisfying end.

TIPS **Drafting Your Paragraph**

1. **Follow your plan, but don't be upset about making changes.** If an idea comes to you as you are writing, put it in the margin or in brackets on the computer.
2. **Don't stop writing to correct errors in grammar, punctuation, or spelling.** You will correct these errors later, during the editing and proofreading stages.
3. **Know what to do if you get stuck.** If you get stuck on a word, leave a space and come back to it later. If you get stuck for ideas, use a prewriting strategy.
4. **Don't worry about the length of your paper.** You can always add or remove ideas later.
5. **Take a break when you need one.** Taking a break will help keep you alert and free up your thoughts.
6. **Get an early start on your assignment.** Writing your rough draft in a hurry at the last minute will make more work for you at the revision stage.

 PRACTICE Drafting Your Paper

3.13 Draft the paragraph you have been working on in this chapter.

Write the Concluding Sentence

The concluding sentence is the last sentence of the paragraph, the final statement. It shows the reader that the writer has finished supporting the main point and brings the ideas of the paragraph together. The concluding sentences in the following examples make the point of the paragraph:

Topic Sentence	Concluding Sentence
The traditional method of guest checkout at hotels involves five stages of customer activities.	Because this traditional checkout method can be time consuming, improved methods are being developed.
People who abuse their partners or their children share some common characteristics.	Recognizing these characteristics of abusers can minimize the risk of encountering abuse in a relationship.

Here is the concluding sentence that Ermilie wrote for her paragraph about how college students can economize:

> Students who spend economically can avoid money problems and may end up with some money in the bank.

TIPS | **Writing the Concluding Sentence**

1. **Write your concluding sentence to fit the purpose of the paragraph.** For example, if you are contrasting two computers, you could state your preference for one over the other in your concluding sentence. In a paragraph giving a set of instructions on how to plan a party, you could conclude with your opinion about the results of following your instructions. Avoid repeating your topic sentence.
2. **Make sure that your concluding sentence signals the end of the paragraph.** Adding another supporting detail or starting a new topic will make the reader think that you are not done.
3. **State your sentence directly.** You do not need to address your reader with phrases such as these: *As I have said, As you can see, As I have proved,* or *In conclusion.*

PRACTICE   Writing a Concluding Sentence

3.14   Write a concluding sentence for the following paragraph:

> Establishing relationships online has many advantages. For example, online relationships are safe in terms of avoiding the potential for physical violence or sexually transmitted diseases. Another advantage is that Internet communication reveals your inner qualities first rather than your physical appearance. Computer talk is also a benefit for shut-ins and extremely shy people who have trouble meeting others in traditional ways. Finally, online relationships are empowering for those with physical deformities or disabilities.
>
> (Adapted from *Human Communication* by Joseph A. DeVito)

Not only does online relationship reveal your inner qualities but it builds communicatnip practices which will shows your strength and weakness as a person

PRACTICE   Writing Your Own Concluding Sentence

3.15   Write a concluding sentence for your draft paragraph.

Write the Title

The title is the last thing that you write, but it is the first thing the reader sees. The title is the name you give your paragraph. The title of a paper is like the title of a song or movie. It gives a brief idea of what the paper is about.

important

TIPS | **Writing the Title**

1. **Catch the reader's interest.** Use your imagination to write a title that will attract the reader. The titles " Descriptive Paragraph" or "Writing Assignment" are uninteresting.
2. **Make it informative.** Your title should give the reader an idea of what your paper is about. Look back over your paper for some key words.
3. **Apply the rules for capitalizing titles.**

   - Capitalize the first and last words.
   - Capitalize all other words except the following:

     Articles: a, an, the
     Coordinating conjunctions: for, and, nor, but, or, yet, so
     Prepositions: at, on, to, in, after, with, off, by, etc.

Grammar Reminder. See Chapter 21 for a longer list of prepositions.

PRACTICE **Capitalizing Titles**

3.16   Capitalize these Oscar-winning movie titles:

1. *to kill a mockingbird* _To Kill a Mockingbird_
2. *the fellowship of the ring* _The fellowship of the Ring_
3. *no country for old men* _NO country for old Men_
4. *the silence of the lambs* _The science of the Lambs_
5. *harry potter and the half-blood prince* _Harry Potter and the half-blooded Prince_

PRACTICE **Writing Your Own Title**

3.17   Write a title for your draft paragraph.

Writing Assignments

Help Desk

Howard was unhappy about the low grade he received on his paragraph about Jamaica. His teacher told him that he did not support his topic sentence. What suggestions would you give him?

> A place people should visit is Jamaica. Through the years, Jamaica has been famous for its beauty. It is also one of the favorite destinations for travelers. I was born in Jamaica, so I can say no one will regret his or her visit to the island. As a Jamaican, I appreciate my country, and I think others will too.

Reading and Writing across the Curriculum: Student Success

College students are expected to have academic integrity. However, many students do not have a clear understanding of what academic integrity is and how to avoid carrying out dishonest acts.

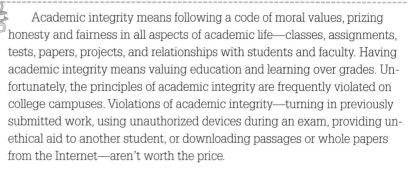

> Academic integrity means following a code of moral values, prizing honesty and fairness in all aspects of academic life—classes, assignments, tests, papers, projects, and relationships with students and faculty. Having academic integrity means valuing education and learning over grades. Unfortunately, the principles of academic integrity are frequently violated on college campuses. Violations of academic integrity—turning in previously submitted work, using unauthorized devices during an exam, providing unethical aid to another student, or downloading passages or whole papers from the Internet—aren't worth the price.
>
> (Adapted from *Keys to Success*, 6th ed., by Carol Carter et al.)

Find out your school's policy for academic integrity. Write a paragraph explaining that policy in your own words. If your school does not have such a policy, look for samples on the Internet and write one for your school.

Comment on a Contemporary Issue

The Internet has had an enormous influence on relationships. For example, many people use the Internet to find friends or romantic partners. They also join communities or discussion groups for a variety of special interests, such as work, child rearing, video games, music, and socializing. The paragraph in Practice 3.14 points out some of the advantages to online relationships. What are some of the disadvantages? Write a paragraph explaining the disadvantages of online relationships in general or of a particular group that you are familiar with such as Facebook.

English Success Tip: Paragraph Length

Many students want to be told the exact number of sentences that a paragraph should have. Requiring a specific number of sentences, a percentage of a page, or a word count does not address the purpose of a paragraph: to make a point and support it fully.

A paragraph of two or three sentences is likely to be too short and does not give enough support. On the other hand, a paragraph can be too long. This can happen when the topic is too broad, when the writer offers too many details, or the writer repeats details.

A successful paragraph will be the right length when it supports a narrowed topic with adequate and relevant details.

For support in meeting this chapter's objectives, log in to www.mywritinglab.com, go to the Study Plan tab, click on **Organizing and Drafting the Paragraph** and choose **Developing and Organizing a Paragraph and Getting Started** from the list of subtopics. Read and view the videos and resources in the Review Materials section, and then complete the Recall, Apply, and Write exercises in the Activities section. You can check your scores and overall progress by using the Gradebook.

CHAPTER 4

Revising, Editing, and Proofreading the Paragraph

Learning Objectives

After working through this chapter, you will be able to:

LO 1 Revise your papers for SOCS: Support, Organization, Connectors and transitions, and Style.

LO 2 Edit and proofread your papers.

The purpose of writing a first draft is to put your ideas in rough form. The next important and necessary stages in the writing process are revising, editing, and proofreading.

LO 1 Revising

Revising is the process of taking another careful look at your writing and making changes to improve your topic sentence and supporting details. You may have beliefs about revising that stop you from making valuable changes to your writing. For example, you may feel that you worked hard on your draft and like it the way it is or that you don't have the time to revise your paper. However, even professional writers revise their drafts.

QuickWrite

What process do you use to revise your papers?

Checking the Assignment

Before beginning to revise your draft, first make sure that you have fulfilled the requirements of your assignment:

- The paragraph is written about the assigned topic.
- The paragraph has a topic sentence with a narrowed subject and main point.
- The paragraph is written for a college audience.

PRACTICE 4.1 Checking Requirements of a Paragraph Assignment

Read the following student paragraph written in response to an assignment about the reasons for wanting (or not wanting) to go to the senior prom. Then answer the questions about whether or not the student has done the assignment properly.

> [1]It's my turn to live out a dream like people do in movies. [2]I really could care less about going to **prom**, I see no reason to spend money that would do better going for something else. [3]How much the prom is going to cost is a good question, but it doesn't matter because I don't want to go. [4]Anyway, I don't want to spend money I don't have. [5]Another reason why I refuse to go is, I have to work late and I can't call in sick. [6]My mom starts an argument because I don't want to go to the senior prom. [7]She gives me money to rent a suit, buy two tickets, and get the car cleaned. [8]So my mother makes me go through all this unnecessary stuff just for one evening I do not want. [9]I ended up going. [10]As the night begins our parents meet. [11]We took pictures right before we left for the stupid prom. [12]I wondered if it would turn out to be as dumb as I thought. [13]As the night came to an end, I watched the sun rise as I pulled into my driveway where my mother, along with my grandparents, met me at the door to ask how it was. [14]I told them it was okay. [15]Then my mother told me it was the moment she had been waiting for.

prom a formal dance for high school students

1. Is the paragraph written on the assigned topic?

_____

_____

2. Does the paragraph have a topic sentence with a narrowed subject and main point?

_____

_____

3. Is this paragraph written appropriately for a college audience?

_____

_____

PRACTICE   **Checking Requirements of Your Paragraph Assignment**

4.2   Look over the draft paragraph that you wrote in Chapter 3 to be sure that you have fulfilled the requirements of your assignment:

Have you written about the assigned topic?
Does your paragraph have a narrowed subject and main point?
Is the paragraph written for a college audience?

Revising One Element at a Time: SOCS

Revising can seem like an overwhelming task. To help you revise effectively and use your time efficiently, go over your paper one element at a time. The four elements you need to check when revising are Support, Organization, Connectors-Transitions, and Style.

You can easily remember the elements for revising by putting the first letter of each word into the acronym **SOCS**.

Support   The first element in SOCS revision is Support. When you revise for support, you look at your details to make sure that they are adequate and relevant. **Adequate** means that your supporting points give enough information to support your points. **Relevant** means that all of your details directly support the main point of the paragraph. They stay on the topic and are not repetitious.

1. **Adequate supporting points give enough information to prove the main point.**
    The student's paragraph below does not give enough information to prove the main point.

> ¹As an employee of Starbucks Coffee, I encounter some sloppy customers. ²For example, last Sunday morning, a customer purchased a large coffee and a banana walnut muffin. ³When he finished, he left his used napkins, spilled coffee and sugar, and muffin crumbs all over the table assuming that it was my job to clean up after him.

She writes about just one sloppy customer, but additional examples would provide more adequate support and be more convincing to her readers.

PRACTICE   Supporting a Main Point

4.3   Write two more examples to support the main point, "encounter some sloppy customers."

_____

_____

2. **Adequate supporting points are specific.**
    The student who wrote the following paragraph attempts to describe the special qualities of the beach, but she does not give specific details.

> ¹The beach has many special qualities. ²If you ask me, they are endless, but I will name a couple. ³The most obvious is its beauty. ⁴I have never seen such a mesmerizing, attractive, gorgeous place in my life. ⁵Another special quality is its profound peacefulness. ⁶To me it is the ideal example of peace. ⁷The sand and water are therapeutic enough to give me peace of mind for the rest of my life. ⁸The special quality I hold to my heart is all the priceless memories of me and my friends growing up on the beach.

Note that the writer has not given specific details about the beach. The writer does not specify a particular beach and does not give specific details. For example, she uses opinion words, such as "mesmerizing," "captivating" and "gorgeous" to support "beauty." Another vague quality she mentions is peacefulness/peace.

PRACTICE   Writing Supporting Points with Details
4.4   Write two supporting points with details about the special qualities of a beach. If you have never been to a beach, look at a picture or online video for ideas or talk with a classmate who has been to the beach.

_____

_____

3. **Adequate supporting points often have details to explain them.**
   Sometimes you need to add details to your supporting point to help the reader understand it. Read this student paragraph on the reasons people drink alcohol:

> [1]People drink alcohol for several reasons. [2]The first is that they believe that there is no risk in consuming alcohol. [3]The second is that most individuals enjoy the immediate effects. [4]In addition, alcohol, unlike drugs, is accepted. [5]Last, alcohol is available everywhere.

This paragraph has four supporting points, but the writer did not provide any information to help the reader understand each of them.

PRACTICE   Adding Explaining Details
4.5   Write one explaining detail for sentences 2, 3, 4, and 5.

_____

_____

_____

_____

4. **Relevant details stay on the topic.**
   In this paragraph, the student writer goes off his topic, "pumping iron."

> [1]Lifting weights is an activity that helps me improve my health. [2]It helps me to burn fat and to increase the strength of my bones. [2]I can lift weights alone at any time I choose. [3]I mostly lift weights at the gym. [4]My favorite time to go to

the gym is early morning or late at night when there is less of a crowd. ⁵I enjoy

the burn of the muscle. ⁶While I work out, I get to do other things, like read a

book between sets, watch television, or listen to music on my iPod. ⁷When I work

out, I enjoy the feeling of doing something to improve my health.

The writer's main point, stated in the first sentence, is that lifting weights helps him improve his health. However, only sentences 2 and 7 are relevant to this main point. The rest of the paragraph is not relevant to the main point.

PRACTICE Adding Relevant Details

4.6   Provide two additional relevant details that support the topic sentence of the paragraph on lifting weights.

_____

_____

5. **Relevant details are not repetitious.**

In the paragraph you read on the beach, the writer repeated herself in sentences 5 and 6:

⁵Another special quality is its profound peacefulness. ⁶To me it is the epitome

of peace.

Here is another example of repetitious details in a section of a student's paragraph on the reasons she likes working at a travel agency:

¹One of the reasons I like working at the travel agency is because of the peo-

ple I meet on a daily basis. ²People from all over the country come to the office

on a daily basis. ³Every day I meet different people. ⁴Some are regular customers

who come in to visit almost every day.

The word choices are repetitious and the writer repeats the same point.

PRACTICE Revising for Repetition and Adding Details

4.7   Revise this part of the student's paragraph on working in a travel agency, omitting the repetition and adding specific details.

_____

_____

_____

_____

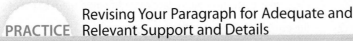

PRACTICE
4.8

Revising Your Paragraph for Adequate and Relevant Support and Details

Revise your own draft paragraph to make sure your supporting points and details are adequate and relevant.

Organization   The second element in SOCS revision is Organization. When you revise for organization, you check to see that your ideas are expressed in a logical order and that each point is equally developed.

1. **Express ideas in a logical order.**

   In Chapter 3, you learned about the three methods of logical order: time order, spatial order, and order of importance. When you wrote the plan for your draft, you chose an order to present your supporting points. During the drafting process, you might have drifted away from the plan. Now you can take another look at your paper to check its organization.

   Read Katie's draft about her jealous friend Alyce, paying attention to logical order.

Main idea — *Supporting Detail*

¹My friend Alyce is the most jealous person I know. ²For example, she does not want her boyfriend to talk to on the phone when she is with him. ³Last weekend, the three of us were spending time together when his mother called his cell phone. ⁴Alyce's whole mood changed from happy to angry. ⁵She interrupted his conversation by telling him that he should talk to her later. ⁶As a result, he makes his phone calls short to avoid a fight. *second supporting detail* ⁷Another example of her jealousy is that she cannot stand it when her friends make new friends. ⁸A few weeks ago, I met a girl at work, and I started spending time with her. ⁹Alyce insisted on knowing every detail about my new friend and accused me of not wanting to spend time with her anymore. ¹⁰Alyce called me every day to make plans so I would not have any time for my friend. *minor detail* ¹¹The most obvious example of her jealousy is her negative way of reacting when she thinks other girls have nicer figures than she does. ¹²When Alyce sees a girl whom she believes looks better, she criticizes her. ¹³She says things like "Her nose is so big," "Her shoes do not match," or "Her pants are out of style." *Conclusion* ¹⁴It is a good thing jealousy is not a crime because Alyce would definitely be in jail.

Katie uses order of importance to organize her paragraph, but it's difficult to check this just by reading. Reverse outlining is a technique that will help you check a paper's organization. **Reverse outlining** is the process of outlining your paper after you have written it. You can use the scratch outline covered in Chapter 3 for this process.

Here is a reverse outline of Katie's paragraph.

Topic sentence:	[1]My friend Alyce is the most jealous person I know.
Supporting point 1	Does not want boyfriend to talk on phone when with her.
Detail(s)	Boyfriend's mom called on cell phone; she got angry and interrupted conversation.
Supporting point 2	Does not like it when her friends make new friends.
Detail(s)	Met girl at work. Alyce insisted on knowing every detail; accused me of not wanting to be with her; called every day to make plans.
Supporting point 3	Negative reactions to girls who have better figures.
Detail(s)	Says "Her nose is big," "Her shoes do not match," "Her pants are out of style."
Concluding sentence:	[14]It is a good thing jealousy is not a crime because Alyce would definitely be in jail.

With this reverse outline, you can see that Katie's supports and details all prove the main point of the paragraph. However, sentence 6 is an effect and could be eliminated.

PRACTICE Preparing a Reverse Outline for Your Draft Paragraph

4.9   Prepare a reverse outline of your draft paragraph and check its organization. Revise the paragraph's organization if necessary.

2. **Develop each point equally.**

When each point is equally developed, your paper will be balanced. Read this student's paper on ways he enjoys soccer now that he does not have time to play on a team. As you read, check for equal development of the points, which are highlighted.

[1]Now that I am living in the United States and do not have time to play on a soccer team, I enjoy soccer in other ways. [2]One thing I do is watch soccer games on television. [3]I bought a special sports package so I can watch games between leagues from all over the world, even the league from my country, Colombia. [4]Another thing that I do is get together with my friends and play soccer for fun on Sundays. [5]My group of friends comes from all many countries around the world. [6]Not everyone speaks English, but we communicate with the soccer ball. [7]I also enjoy soccer by talking about it with my friends and family. [8]I enjoy soccer now as much as I used to as a young boy in a different country, but in different ways.

There are three main points in this paragraph, and the first two are supported with details. The last point, expressed in sentence 7, is not supported at all, so the paper is not balanced.

PRACTICE   Revising Your Paragraph for Balance

4.10   Reread your draft paragraph and make sure all your points are balanced. If they are not, revise the paragraph to balance them.

Connectors and Transitions   The third item in a SOCS revision is Connectors and transitions. To help the reader follow your ideas in a logical, understandable order, make sure you have used connectors and transitions to join ideas. Also, use synonyms and pronouns to avoid repetition and add variety.

1. **Use connectors and transitions.**

   Connectors and transition words and phrases tell the reader that you are introducing new ideas and adding details as well as showing relationships between them.

   In Chapter 3, you learned about connectors and transition words for time order, spatial order, and order of importance. Another group of words is used to add details to supporting points.

> **Common Transition Words for Added Points and Information**
>
> | also | another | finally | furthermore |
> | additionally | as well | for example | in addition |
> | along with | besides | for instance | moreover |

The following paragraph about the leading reasons managers waste time shows how addition transitions help you follow the writer's ideas. Notice how they introduce supporting points and add information to the supporting points. The transitions are boldfaced.

> To manage time effectively, managers must address four leading causes of wasted time. The **first** cause is paperwork. **For example**, some managers spend too much time deciding what to do with letters and reports. **Another** cause of wasted time is telephone calls. **For instance**, experts estimate that managers get interrupted by the telephone every five minutes. **Also**, the explosive use of cell phones seems to be making this problem even worse for many managers. The **third** cause of wasted time is meetings. Many managers spend up to four hours a day in meetings. Often these meetings are not focused on the agenda and do not end on time. The **last** cause of wasted time is email. Managers are relying heavily on email and other forms of electronic communication. **Moreover**, time is wasted when managers have to sort through spam and a variety of electronic folders, in-boxes, and archives.
>
> (Adapted from *Business Essentials* by Ronald J. Ebert and Ricky W. Griffin)

PRACTICE Adding Transitions to a Paragraph

4.11 Revise the following paragraph, adding transitions to help your reader follow the ideas. Remember to change a capital letter to a lowercase letter when it no longer is the first word of a sentence.

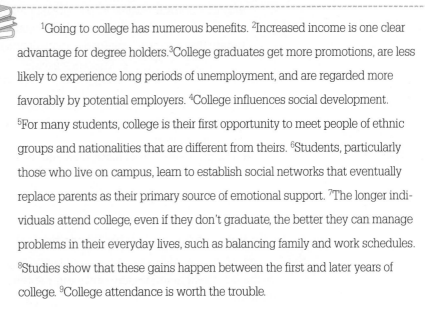

¹Going to college has numerous benefits. ²Increased income is one clear advantage for degree holders.³College graduates get more promotions, are less likely to experience long periods of unemployment, and are regarded more favorably by potential employers. ⁴College influences social development. ⁵For many students, college is their first opportunity to meet people of ethnic groups and nationalities that are different from theirs. ⁶Students, particularly those who live on campus, learn to establish social networks that eventually replace parents as their primary source of emotional support. ⁷The longer individuals attend college, even if they don't graduate, the better they can manage problems in their everyday lives, such as balancing family and work schedules. ⁸Studies show that these gains happen between the first and later years of college. ⁹College attendance is worth the trouble.

(Adapted from *The World of Psychology* by Samuel E. Wood et al.)

PRACTICE Revising Your Paragraph for Connectors and Transitions

4.12 Revise your draft paragraph to improve the use of connectors and transitions.

2. **Use synonyms and pronouns.**
   Synonyms and pronouns help to avoid repetition and add variety.
   - A **synonym** is a word that means the same as another word. For example, some synonyms for the word *revise* are *change, alter,* or *rethink.*

     When you **revise** your paragraph, you **alter** its meaning.
   - A **pronoun** is a word that replaces a noun. In this sentence, the pronoun **it** replaces the word **family**.

     The **family** is the most important consumer buying organization in society, and **it** has been researched extensively.

   The following paragraph shows how synonyms and pronouns add variety.

¹Country music emerged out of the rural American South from the folk traditions of the **British immigrants**, who settled in the New England colonies in the eighteenth century. ²In the nineteenth century, many of the **settlers** moved to the cities, but **others**, especially **those** in the poorer Southeast areas, such as the Appalachian mountains, did not. ³**They** lived in

the backwoods without indoor plumbing and other modern conveniences. ⁴Although **they** were poor, **their** lives were rich with music. ⁵**They** kept the old folk music traditions. ⁶Each generation passed down the songs and instrumental music that **they** had learned from the previous generation. ⁷These **poor white folks** with simple country ways were disrespectfully called "hillbillies" when **they** came into town to look for work or buy supplies. ⁸"Billy" is the name for a male goat, and "hill" described the locations of **their** homes deep in the mountains. ⁹"Hillbilly" was also the term used to describe **their** old-time mountain music. ¹⁰It is from **this music** that "country" emerged as type of music in the 1920s.

(Adapted from *Crossroads* by Elizabeth F. Barkley)

- The synonym *settlers* replaces *British immigrants. Poor white folks* replaces *settlers* who did not move to the cities. *This music* refers to the old-time mountain music.
- The pronouns *others, those, they,* and *their* refer to settlers who lived in the backwoods.

PRACTICE   Revise a Paragraph for Repetitious Words

4.13   The following sentences from a student's paragraph repeat some words unnecessarily. Revise the sentences by replacing the repetitious words with synonyms and pronouns.

1. In the Bahamas, people can travel the island in different ways. People can travel the island by taxi, scooter, or jitney bus. People can notice that when traveling in the Bahamas by taxi, scooter, or jitney bus that driving is done on the left side of the road.

   _____

   _____

2. The straw market in the Bahamas is a famous attraction for tourists to experience. The vendors at the straw market in the Bahamas sell many items. The vendors in the straw markets sell handcrafted straw items like hats, baskets, mats, and bags. The straw market vendors also sell t-shirts, fabric, woodcarvings, and homemade guava jelly.

   _____

   _____

   _____

3. Tourists can enjoy the traditional foods that the people who live in the Bahamas eat. Some of the traditional foods are conch fritters, rice, peas, plantains, curried goat, and oxtail. Tourists can eat the traditional foods cooked in the Bahamian style in many different restaurants. Tourists can eat authentic food from take-out places to five-star restaurants.

   _____

   _____

PRACTICE Analyzing Your Paragraph for Repetitious Words

4.14   Analyze your draft paragraph for repetitious words and replace them with synonyms, pronouns, and descriptive words.

Style   The last element of a SOCS revision is Style. **Style** is the way you express yourself in writing, the way you put a sentence or a group of sentences together. Two stylistic elements you can use are tone and sentence variety.

1. **Use a more serious, formal tone.**

   Tone is your attitude toward your subject. The tone of a paper can be serious or funny, formal or informal, or sincere or sarcastic, depending on the words you choose and the arrangement of your ideas. College writing is usually serious and formal, not conversational. Choose Standard Written English words that your readers are familiar with.

   Read the following student's paragraph, paying attention to its tone.

   > My life as a college student is not easy because I have many things going on. For example, I have temptations. I mean like there are a lot of parties open to me. Then I have the temptation to skip class because most of my teachers don't have an attendance policy. Second, I have a lot of pressure in college. It could be my friend telling me to do the next best thing. My English teacher gets on my back about the grammar of my papers. The last thing I want to touch on is relationships. My relationship with my girlfriend conflicts with school. I'm tempted to hang out with her instead of studying. And when I am not with her she is all I can think about instead of the stuff I'm supposed to be learning in my classes. My life as a college student is a very difficult one.

   The writer's tone is too informal and conversational. His informal word choices include *things going on, I mean, parties open to me; skip class, do the next best thing, gets on my back, to touch on, hang out, stuff.* In addition, the writer uses the contractions *don't* and *I'm* and overuses *a lot.*

PRACTICE Revising a Paragraph for Tone

4.15   Revise the paragraph about life as a college student, making its tone more serious, formal, and sincere.

PRACTICE Revising Your Draft for Tone

4.16   Revise your draft paragraph to improve its tone.

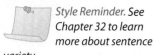

Style Reminder. See Chapter 32 to learn more about sentence variety.

2. Use sentence variety.

Sentence variety is the use of sentences that differ in type and length. Varying your sentences keeps the reader interested. If you use too many short sentences, your writing will sound immature. On the other hand, if all of your sentences are too long, your writing will be hard to read and understand.

Here is an excerpt of a student paper that illustrates how short sentences can make writing sound elementary:

> [1]I hated my job at Wal-Mart because the managers did not respect the workers. I worked four to eleven every weekday. [2]That was fine for me. [3]Then they had me working from two to eleven on weekends. [4]That was a problem. [5]I went to the manager. [6]I told her that I wanted to talk. [7]She was busy. [8]I waited until she was done. [9]She was helping a customer. [10]She kept ignoring me. [11]She did other things. [12]Those things were not important. [13]She never called me into the office. [14]She did not respect me. [15]I quit.

PRACTICE   Revising a Paragraph for Sentence Variety

4.17   Revise the paragraph about the student's job at Wal-Mart. You can take some words out and rewrite some of the short, choppy sentences by combining them.

_____

_____

_____

_____

_____

_____

PRACTICE   Revising Your Own Paragraph for Sentence Variety

4.18   Revise your own paragraph for sentence variety.

TIPS | **Revising Your Paragraph**

1. **Give yourself time away from the paper.** Take at least an hour's break. When you return, you will be able to see the paper from a new perspective.
2. **Focus on one element at a time.** Remember SOCS: support, organization, connections and transitions, and style.
3. **If you are using a computer, print your paragraph.** Printing a copy will help you see the entire paper rather than a portion of it.

4. **Get someone else to read your paragraph.** Peer review is the process of reading another writer's paper and giving practical suggestions to help the writer revise. Peer review can be done in pairs or in a group. Here are some guidelines:

- Choose someone you know you can work with.
- Make a copy of the paper so that both of you have one to read.
- Read the paper out loud while the other person listens closely.
- Offer helpful suggestions without criticizing the writer.
- Focus on the revision strategy of one element at a time: SOCS: structure, organization, connections and transitions, and style.

Peer Review Response Sheet for Revision Stage

Your Name _____   Date _____

Title of Paper Reviewed _____

Directions: Please give careful thought and complete answers to each of these questions. If time permits, do a reverse scratch outline of this paper to see the writer's supporting points and organizational pattern more easily.

1. What is this paper about?

_____

_____

2. Do any of the supporting points need more explanation? Which ones?

_____

_____

3. Do all supporting points prove the main idea? Which supporting points do not?

_____

_____

4. Are any points out of order? Where do they belong?

_____

_____

5. Does the writer use transitions? Give some examples.

_____

6. What tone does the writer use?

_____

7. Were any sentences hard to understand? Write them here.

_____

_____

_____

Ermilie's Revised Paragraph

In Chapter 3, page 36, you read Ermilie's draft for the topic Money-Saving Tips for College Students. Below is her revised paragraph.

Ermilie's Revision

One way to save money is to spend less on food.

College students can save money by making economical choices. Instead
~~a~~   ~~a~~   *students*

of buying ~~that~~ bag of Doritos or Snickers candy bar at vending machine prices~~.~~
can   *healthy*   *S*

save money by bringing snacks from home. ~~Healthy~~ snacks like home made trail
a piece of   *more nutricious than vending machine treats.*

mix, fruit, or cut up vegetables are ~~inexpensive and portable~~. Cutting down on
                                                                  close to

expensive gourmet coffees or fruit smoothies can save students ~~almost~~ five dollars
Cell phone costs can also be reduced to save money. Most companies offer discounted rates
for students, so its worth the time to research rates and plans to find the cheapest one.

a day. ~~Most companies offer more than one cell phone plan, students can do~~

~~research to find the cheapest plan.~~ Spending less time on the phone with friends at

peak times and keeping text messaging to a minimum will help reduce phone
                although new phones come out every few months, students can save money by
not giving in to the temptation to buy a new one.

expenses. Also, ~~students do not have to buy the latest phone every six months.~~
                        , so find ways to spend less on books is worth the effort.

Books are the biggest expense for college students. ~~Buy books online. Some~~
                For example, buying

~~online companies will even ship for free. Buying~~ used books is cheaper than
                ones.

buying new~~.~~ Students can even make money by selling their used books for less
                charges. In addition, students can buy books online and spend one-third less.

than the bookstore~~. Avoid the bookstore for supplies; the big discount stores have~~

~~better prices.~~ Student who make economical choices can avoid money problems

and may end up with some money in the bank.

LO 2 Editing and Proofreading

Editing and proofreading are the last steps in the paragraph writing process. **Editing** is the process of reading your paper for errors in grammar, punctuation, and spelling. **Proofreading** is the process of checking your final draft for errors you may have missed.

Editing

Editing involves looking at your paper very closely, sentence by sentence. Look for sentences that may be vague or confusing. In addition, check for errors in grammar, punctuation, and spelling.

TIPS | **Editing Your Paragraph**

1. **Focus on areas of weakness.** If you already know that you tend to make mistakes in a specific area, such as comma placement, you can check for those. Check one type of mistake at a time.
2. **Read your paper out loud.** By using more of your senses, you may be able to hear a part that needs to be revised that you were not able to see while reading silently.

3. **Get someone else to read your paper.** You may not be able to find your errors because you do not realize that you have made them or know how to fix them. Find someone in your class or a tutor at your campus writing center who can point out errors that you do not see.

4. **Read your paper backwards.** When you read your paper from beginning to end, you may miss errors because you are caught up in the flow of ideas. Start at the end and read backwards to the beginning.

5. **If you are writing on a computer, use a spell-checker and grammar checker.** The spell-checking feature can automatically correct spelling and typographical errors. However, the program cannot tell whether you have used a word correctly such as *to, two,* or *too* correctly. Also, the program may not recognize some names or technical words. Grammar and style checkers cannot pick up all the errors or variations of meanings in your writing and may make inaccurate suggestions and point out errors that are actually correct.

Ermilie's Edited Paragraph

College students can save money by making economical choices. One way to save money is to spend less on food. Instead of buying a bag of Doritos or a Snickers candy bar at vending machine ~~prices. Students~~ prices, students can save money by bringing healthy snacks from home. Snacks like home made trail mix, a piece of fruit, or cut up vegetables are portable and more nutritious than vending machine treats.

Also, ~~Cutting~~ cutting down on expensive gourmet coffees or fruit smoothies can save students close to five dollars a day. ~~Cell~~ phone costs. Another way to save money is to cut cell ~~can also be reduced to save money.~~ Most companies offer discounted rates for students, so, its worth the time to research rates and plans to find the cheapest one. Spending less time on the phone with friends at peak times and keeping text messaging to a minimum will help reduce phones expenses. Also, although new phones come out every few months, students can save money by not giving in to the temptation to buy a new one. Finally, books ~~Books~~ are the biggest expense for college students, so ~~find~~ finding ways to spend less on books is worth the effort. For example, buying used textbooks is cheaper than buying new ones. Students can even make money by selling their used books for less than the bookstore charges. In addition, students can buy books online and spend one-third less. Student who make economical choices can avoid money problems and may end up with some money in the bank.

PRACTICE   Editing a Paragraph

4.19   Practice editing by finding and correcting the errors in the following paragraphs. Each paragraph has two errors.

¹Hikari Oe was born with his brain extended beyond his skull. ²Doctors said that the surgery was dangerous. ³They tell his parents about the possibility of the child's retardation and other nervous system difficulties. ⁴Hikaris parents decided to go ahead with the surgery.

⁵When Hikari was about six years old, his parents noticed that he could memorize and sing songs although his ability to speak and understand language was quiet limited. ⁶They decided to give him a piano lessons and found a teacher who was willing to take on the challenging student. ⁷As the teacher worked with Hikari, it became clear that the child had remarkable musical gifts. ⁸Within months, he was playing difficult classical pieces easily; moreover, he began to play his own arrangements of classical forms to create his own pieces.

⁹Though she did not think that the effort would be successful, Hikari's piano teacher decided to try to teach him musical notation so he could write down his compositions. ¹⁰To her surprise, he mastered the difficult skill of writing classical musics in a short time. ¹¹Today, as a middle-aged man, Hikari Oe is an accomplished and celebrated composer. ¹²Of classical music.

(Adapted from *The World of Psychology* by Samuel E. Wood et al.)

Proofreading

Proofreading is your final step before submitting your paper. By reading your paper one last time, you may find a mistake that you missed while editing. Here are some proofreading tips:

TIPS	Proofreading Your Paragraph

1. **Make sure that your paper is neatly written or typed to make it easy for your teacher to read.**
2. **If your teacher has given you format guidelines, be sure that you have followed them.** Format guidelines may include the following: positioning of your name, course, and date and title; skipping lines (or double spacing if typing); and writing in ink.
3. **Read your paper one last time** for grammar, spelling, and punctuation errors you may have missed while editing.

Ermilie's Final Paragraph

College students can save money by making economical choices. One way to save money is to spend less on food. Instead of buying a bag of Doritos or a Snickers candy bar at vending machine prices, students can save money by bringing healthy snacks from home. Snacks like home made trail mix, a piece of fruit, or cut up vegetables are portable and more nutritious than vending machine treats. Also, cutting down on expensive gourmet coffees or fruit smoothies can save students close to five dollars a day. Another way to save money is to cut cell phone costs. Most companies offer discounted rates for students, so it is worth the time to research rates and plans to find the cheapest one. Spending less time on the phone with friends at peak times and keeping text messaging to a minimum will help reduce phones expenses. Also, although new phones come out every few months, students can save money by not giving in to the temptation to buy a new one. Finally, textbooks are the biggest expense for college students, so finding ways to spend less on books is worth the effort. For example, buying used textbooks is cheaper than buying new ones. Students can even make money by selling their used books for less than the bookstore charges. In addition, students can buy books online and spend one-third less. Students who make economical choices can avoid money problems and may end up with some money in the bank.

Writing Assignments

Help Desk

Brianna feels that she does not need to revise her papers. She says it takes too much time. Also, she does not like to write and does not want to take the time to revise. For Brianna, writing one draft and copying it over to make it look neat is adequate. In a paragraph, explain to Brianna why revision is important.

Reading and Writing across the Curriculum: Western Civilization

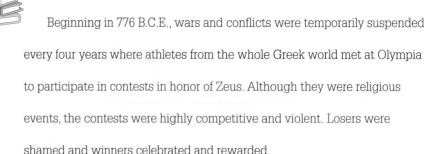

Beginning in 776 B.C.E., wars and conflicts were temporarily suspended every four years where athletes from the whole Greek world met at Olympia to participate in contests in honor of Zeus. Although they were religious events, the contests were highly competitive and violent. Losers were shamed and winners celebrated and rewarded.

The most celebrated hero of the <u>pankration</u>, which combines wrestling and boxing, was Arrichion, who won but died in victory. Although his opponent was slowly strangling him, Arrichion managed to kick in such a way as to horribly dislocate his adversary's ankle. The extreme pain caused the opponent to signal defeat just as Arrichion died, victorious.

(Adapted from *Civilization in the West* by Mark Kishlansky et al.)

Write a paragraph about the importance of winning, not just in sports but in any type of activity. Give examples of situations in which winning was important.

Comment on a Contemporary Issue

What you do on the Internet tells more about you than you think. Companies track your searches and collect information about you. For example, if you search for information about cars, the websites you visit are tracked and sorted. Soon after, when you go to your favorite websites, you may see an advertisement for one of the cars you researched.

Some consumers feel that the companies doing the tracking are secretly spying on them. Write a paragraph about either the benefits or the disadvantages of tracking people's searching behavior.

English Success Tip : Ewe Can Knot Rely on You're Spell-Checker

Computer spell-checkers search for misspelled words in a sentence. A spell-checking program uses its own dictionary to recommend or correct words it identifies as misspelled.

While spell-checker can catch many errors, they are not 100 percent perfect, spell-checkers may miss the following errors, as shown by the title of this tip.

Error that spell check misses	Example
Misspellings of proper names or other words that may not be in the spell-checker's dictionary	*Ewe* should be *You*. An ewe is a female sheep.
Typographical errors that create other words that are correct	*Knot* should be *Not*. Both are correctly spelled words, but *knot* is wrong here.
Wrong use of a correctly spelled word	*You're* should be *Your*. *You're* means you are, but the possessive pronoun *Your* is the correct form in this sentence.
Words that sound the same but differ in meaning	*Can Knot* should be *Cannot*.

For support in meeting this chapter's objectives, log in to www.mywritinglab.com, go to the Study Plan tab, click on **Revising, Editing, and Proofreading the Paragraph** and choose **Revising the Paragraph and Editing the Paragraph** from the list of subtopics. Read and view the videos and resources in the Review Materials section, and then complete the Recall, Apply, and Write exercises in the Activities section. You can check your scores and overall progress by using the Gradebook.

Writing the College-Level Essay

LO 1 What Is the College-Level Essay?

The college-level essay is a form of writing that consists of multiple paragraphs, which prove, discuss, or argue a central idea or thesis. Each of the paragraphs in the essay has a function: to introduce, to support, or to conclude the essay. The length of a college-level essay varies depending on the writing assignment.

In the college-level essay, you may not be asked to write about how you feel, to give "where and when" facts, or to repeat information you learned. Instead, you will be asked to use critical-thinking skills to express your point of view, support it, and present your evidence logically. In addition, you will be expected to use correct grammar and mechanics and to take responsibility for editing and revising on your own.

QuickWrite

Describe the kinds of papers you were asked to write in school or in the workplace.

Parts of the College-Level Essay

The essay consists of three main parts: the introduction, the body, and the conclusion. The illustration on page 63 shows the purpose and content of each of these types of paragraphs. The number of paragraphs in an essay will vary depending on the topic and purpose.

College-Level Essay Example

Writing Reminder. See Chapter 11 to learn more about using the classification pattern.

The student essay titled "Frequent Flyers" on the next page is an example of the college-level essay. It is based on a narration paragraph that the student wrote about her first parachute jump (see Chapter 7, Narration, page 106). The writer developed this essay using the classification pattern.

Parts of the Essay

Introduction
- **Lead-in:** Gain reader interest
- **Bridge:** Connect the lead-in to the thesis statement
- **Thesis statement:** Present main idea of essay

Body Paragraphs
- **Topic sentence:** Present a point to explain or prove the thesis statement
- **Evidence:** Provide details to support the point

Concluding Paragraph
- **Concluding thoughts:** Provide final comments based on the point you have made in the essay

McGee 1

Melinda McGee

Professor Markus

College Preparatory Writing

12 Apr. 2010

Frequent Flyers

The sound of propeller engines accelerating down the runway echoed through the open hanger as I practiced my next skydive move by move. Lying face down, I got onto a board with wheels meant to give me the weightless feeling I would experience once I was in the air. I waited for the list of passengers to be called to board the plane. It was an unusually busy day at this drop zone, the official drop zone for Team USA and home to about twenty teams that compete on the national circuit. It also has the most new jumpers per day than any other drop zone in Florida. Of the two hundred or so jumpers I watched that day, I noticed that they could be classified according to their unique approaches towards jumping, such as the nervous newcomers, the adrenaline junkies, and the freefall flyers.

The most obvious group, the nervous newcomers, approaches jumping with fearful excitement. They are easy to notice because they wear the obviously rented equipment from the drop zone: matching jumpsuits and helmets bearing the Skydive Deland logo. The unmistakable oversized pack on their backs signals a large parachute that is required for student jumpers. The most telling sign, however, is the look on their faces. This is the look that every skydiver has had when jumping for the first time: the nervous stare. Although this look is common when newcomers are strapping on their parachutes or boarding the plane for the first time, it is most evident at 12,500 feet when the airplane door opens. The most memorable were two friends who wanted to make their first jump together. They took their positions at the doorway, each strapped to his instructor in a tandem harness, their toes right to the edge. Suddenly, that nervous look came over their faces. The first friend and his instructor stepped out into the deep blue, but the other froze and refused to go. Then, suddenly, without warning, the second instructor leaned back, and out the door they went.

Unlike the nervous newcomers, the adrenaline junkies are experienced jumpers who approach jumping with an uncontrollable hunger for **white-knuckle** adventure. Their gear consists of the lightest, smallest packs they can buy to be more streamlined while in freefall and to reach higher speeds. Many have made modifications to their jumpsuits, helmets, and parachutes to try to go faster or farther than in previous jumps. Modifying something as complex as a parachute can be dangerous and often the parachute does not open properly. While most skydivers are fearful of this possibility, the adrenaline junkies seem to enjoy the

white-knuckle
causing great fear

extra challenge. Their daring tricks brand them as dangerous because they show off during landings in winds that are unsteady at less than 200 feet. I have seen them doing spirals and hook turns just feet off the ground. Adrenaline junkies try jumping out of hot air balloons, helicopters, and illegally off of buildings and bridges. They are intense skydivers who push the boundaries of the sport.

Neither nervous like the newcomers nor extreme risk takers like the adrenaline junkies, the freefall flyers approach skydiving as a sport. Freefall flyers are the most dedicated group of jumpers; they spend hours practicing to perfect their maneuvers, try new ones, and often enter competitions. These skydivers perform during freefall, the first stage of the jump in which the skydiver exits the plane and falls towards earth before opening the parachute. Dropping at the speed of 160 to 170 miles per hour, the diver has about a minute in which to perform one or more maneuvers. For example, some people fly in on their back, with their head down, on their belly, sitting or standing—any position one can think of. Others enjoy acrobatic maneuvers such as loops, spins, twists, and poses. I have often seen groups jump together to build formations on their bellies, sometimes gripping each other's arms or legs. Freefall flyers take the sport seriously and often complete.

Skydiving has become a popular sport with facilities opening up all over the country. Although it appears dangerous, proper training and modern equipment have made it safe. In addition, almost anyone over eighteen can participate without a concern for physical conditioning. Because skydiving delivers excitement and challenge, as well as the chance to fly like a bird, people continue to come back for more as do the nervous newcomers, the adrenaline junkies, and the freefall flyers.

PRACTICE   Analyzing a College-Level Essay
5.1

1. What does the writer do to get the reader's attention in the first paragraph?

   _____

2. Underline the main idea sentence of the essay twice. What does the writer intend to explain in her essay?

   _____

3. Underline the topic sentence of each body paragraph. How does the writer connect the main idea sentence with each topic sentence?

   _____

   _____

4. What does the writer talk about in the concluding paragraph?

   _____

   _____

LO 2 Writing the College-Level Essay

To write a successful college-level essay, it is essential to understand the purpose and contents of each part: the introduction, the body, and the conclusion.

The Introduction

The introduction is the first paragraph of the essay. The purpose of the introduction is to get the readers interested in your topic and state the point of your paper. The parts of the introduction are the lead-in, the bridge, and the thesis statement.

The Lead-in: Get the Readers Interested   The introduction begins with a lead-in. The **lead-in** is a technique used to get the readers interested so that they will want to continue reading the rest of your essay.

A lead-in that captures the readers' interest may take some time and creative thinking to develop. You can experiment by trying several of the methods suggested in this section to find one that works best. If you have trouble thinking of an interesting lead-in, try writing the body of the essay first; as you write, an idea for the lead-in is likely to emerge. Techniques can be combined as long as you keep each of them brief.

1. **Tell a brief story.** A brief story, also called an anecdote, explains an event that is funny, interesting, or emotional. The story should be related to your topic. It can come from your own or someone else's personal experience. Because most readers enjoy reading a story, this technique is likely to get them involved right away.

Psychology Text Chapter Introduction Using a Brief Story

Jonathan I. was a painter who, throughout his successful artistic career, produced abstract canvases with great mixtures of vivid colors. At age 65, he suffered brain damage that left him completely colorblind. When he looked at his own artwork, all he could see was gray, black, and white; where formerly he had seen colors with rich personal associations, now he saw splotches that were "dirty" or "wrong." And it wasn't just his art. In his day-to-day life, for example, he began to limit his diet to black foods and white foods—black olives and white rice still looked right to him, whereas colored foods now appeared disturbingly gray and unpalatable. Over time, as he recovered from his initial sense of confusion, Mr. I began to explore painting in black and white. Despite his loss of color vision, Mr. I's sensory processes still provide him with a version of the world he can appreciate and transform as art. Mr. I's story illustrates how the senses involve a remarkably complicated group of mechanisms. The body and the brain work together to make sense of sensory stimulation.

(Adapted from *Psychology and Life* by Richard J. Gerrig and Philip G. Lombardo)

2. **Give background.** Background consists of facts, history, or other information that helps the reader understand your topic.

Art Appreciation Textbook Chapter Introduction Using Background

Cameras record the world around us, and the history of the camera is a history of technologies that record our world. These technologies are becoming more advanced and skillful. Photography began with images that did not move and then later added motion. To the silent moving image was added sound called a "talkie." To the "talkie" was added color. Film developed in its audience a taste for "live" action, a taste satisfied by live television transmission, video images that allow us to view anything happening in the world as it happens. These technologies are becoming more advanced and skillful. The study of the history of camera arts not only shows how these technologies developed over time but also the way the artists used them to explore time.

(Adapted from *The World of Art* by Henry M. Sayre)

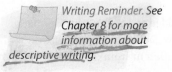

Writing Reminder. See Chapter 8 for more information about descriptive writing.

3. **Use description.** Description can bring actions, places, people, and objects to life. Use subjective description to express your personal impressions through colorful word pictures. Use objective description to give a realistic, unemotional view by using facts that describe without personal opinion.

Student Introduction Using Subjective Description

The sun, clearly above near midday, pierces through the trees of the mountain range like a skilled **archer** shooting target practice. Just as a well conducted orchestra plays its musical arrangement, so does the forest. Water bounces off rocks as it

archer person who shoots with a bow and arrow

crescendo a gradual increase in loudness

trickles down its path, leaves dance their way down to the forest floor, and rocks tumble as they race at the mercy of gravity's will. But they do not play silently. The wind rhythmically whooshes through the trees while the creek bubbles enthusiastically. Twigs snap and pop in a forceful **crescendo**. The music of these mountains creates a lasting impression on those who appreciate nature's splendor. However, observing nature is not the only way to enjoy this area. For people who find pleasure in outdoor activities, the Blue Ridge Mountains are the perfect place for white water rafting, horseback riding, and hiking.

Punctuation Reminder. See Chapter 28 for more information about punctuating quotations.

4. **Use a quotation.** A thought-provoking, profound, or powerful quotation can make the reader think more deeply about your topic. Quotations can come from a variety of sources such as a newspaper, magazine, book, or a song. Slogans, popular sayings, proverbs, and favorite family expressions are other sources.

When using a quotation, be sure to tell the reader the source of the statement. Also, punctuate the statement with quotation marks.

Sociology Textbook Chapter Introduction Using Quotation

In a discussion in a sociology class at Bronx Community College in New York, the instructor explains that people have changed the way they think about race and ethnicity. When he asked students how they would describe themselves, Eva Rodriguez was quick to respond. She said, "This is hard for me to answer. Most people think of race as black and white. But it's not. I have both black and white ancestry in me, but you know what? I don't think of myself in that way. I don't think of myself in terms of race at all. You can call me Puerto Rican or call me Hispanic. I prefer the term 'Latina.' Calling myself Latina says I have mixed racial heritage, and that's what I am. I wish more people understood that race is not clear cut." There are now millions of people in the United States who, like Eva Rodriguez, do not think of themselves in terms of a single category but as having a mix of ancestry. This chapter examines the meaning of race and ethnicity.

(From *Society* by John J. Macionis)

5. **Define a term.** A definition can helpful when it is added to the introductory paragraph to explain a word that the readers do not know. Define a word when you have your own personal meaning of a word that is different from one that people usually think of.

In some cases, defining a word is not helpful. Defining words that readers already know will bore them. Also, using a dictionary definition in the first sentence, such as "According to *Webster's College Dictionary* . . . " is an overused, unimaginative method.

> ### Student Introduction Using Definition
>
> On April 20, 2010, an explosion and fire on the Deepwater Horizon offshore oil-drilling rig in the Gulf of Mexico caused the death of eleven workers and the injury of seventeen others. The sea floor oil gusher that resulted from the explosion has been responsible for what is now considered the largest oil spill in United States history. British Petroleum (BP) has been blamed for the accident and held accountable for cleanup costs and other damages. An oil spill is an accidental or intentional discharge of oil into the environment. The term is often used when oil is released into the ocean or coastal waters. Many attempts were made to contain and control the oil while millions of gallons of crude oil poured into the Gulf of Mexico. Unfortunately, this disaster has had many negative effects. The Gulf oil spill has resulted in an extensive environmental disaster that has impacted marine and wildlife habitats, human health, and the United States economy.

6. **Use other techniques.** One other commonly used technique is the funnel method. This method is named after an object called a funnel, which has a wide opening at the top that slopes into a narrow tube at the bottom. The funnel method starts with a broad, general sentence and narrows the topic sentence-by-sentence, ending with the thesis.

You do not have to limit yourself to the techniques explained in the previous section. You can develop your own unique lead-in or explore some others such as stating a surprising fact or statistic, asking an intriguing or controversial question, or expressing an opposing point of view.

The Bridge: Connect the Lead-in to the Thesis Statement In order for the readers to see the connection between your lead-in and your thesis statement, you should include a bridge sentence. Avoid directly telling the reader what you are going to do as in this example:

> Now that I have given some background about my topic, I am going to tell you what I will prove in this paper.

PRACTICE   Identifying Bridge Sentences

5.2   Find and underline the bridge sentences in the example introductory paragraphs you read on pages 67–69.

EXAMPLE: Bridge sentence from student's brief story example: <u>When my friend died, I realized that associating with my friends and being influenced by their unlawful actions would only lead me down the same path as my late best friend.</u>

The Thesis Statement The **thesis statement** is a sentence that tells the readers the main point of your essay, that is, what you want them to know, believe, or understand. The lead-in and bridge of the introduction prepare the readers with information about the subject of the essay, and the thesis tells them specifically what you plan to discuss. Although the placement of the thesis statement may vary, a good place is at the end of the introductory paragraph.

The thesis statement can be written in one of two ways: with a narrowed topic and main point or with a narrowed topic, main point, and a list of supporting points. The thesis statement that lists the supporting points not only tells the reader the points you plan to cover, but also serves as a helpful organizer to keep you on track as you write.

Thesis with Narrowed Topic and Main Point

Students who take a class in a computer classroom are easily tempted to use the computer for other activities rather than classwork.

Thesis with Narrowed Topic, Main Point, and List of Supporting Points

Students who take a class in a computer classroom are easily tempted to use the computer for other activities rather than class work such as surfing the Internet, instant-messaging friends, or playing games.

TIPS | **Writing Thesis Statements**

1. **Choose specific words.**

    Not specific: Soccer is a great sport.

    Specific: Soccer promotes healthy development in children for several reasons.

    Specific with listed supporting points: Soccer promotes healthy development in children because it promotes good sportsmanship, develops inner resources, and provides aerobic exercise.

2. **Make a point about your topic rather than state a fact.**

    States a fact: The Mall of America, located in Bloomington, Minnesota, opened in 1992 and has over 500 stores in its four-story building.

    Makes a point: The Mall of America offers a variety of entertainment options under one roof.

    Makes a point with listed supporting details: The Mall of America offers a variety of entertainment options under one roof, such as Nickelodeon Universe, Underwater Adventures Aquarium, and Moose Mountain Golf Adventures.

3. **Make a point that is neither too broad nor too narrow.**

    Too broad: Moving from one country to another is difficult.

    Too narrow: When I came to this country I had trouble understanding the news on television.

    Adequate: When I moved from Medellin, Colombia, to Victory Gardens, New Jersey, I had a difficult time.

    Adequate with listed supporting details: When I moved from Medellin, Colombia, to Victory Gardens, New Jersey, I had a difficult time learning how to speak English, making new friends, and understanding the laws.

4. **State your point directly.** Avoid announcing what you plan to do or what you think or believe.

    Announcement: In this paper, I plan to discuss the different ways students who take a class in a computer classroom are easily tempted to use the computer for other activities rather than for class work.

Belief: In my opinion, I believe that students who take a class in a computer classroom are easily tempted to use the computer for other activities than for class work.

Direct statement: Students who take a class in a computer classroom are easily tempted to use the computer for other activities rather than for class work.

5. **If you list supporting points in the thesis statement, decide on the most effective order to discuss them and make them grammatically parallel.** Parallelism, also called parallel structure, is the use of the same forms of words, phrases, or clauses when they appear in pairs, in groups, or in lists. Notice the difference between the two pairs of sentences that follow.

Style Reminder. See Chapter 31 for more information about parallelism.

Not Parallel	**Parallel**
During my first semester in college, I learned **to have more self-confidence, time management,** and **my study habits improved.**	During my first semester in college, I learned **to have more self-confidence, to manage my time,** and **to improve my study habits.**
Driving habits that put the driver and others at risk are **speeding, to tailgate,** and **text messaging.**	Driving habits that put the driver and others at risk are speeding, **tailgating,** and **text messaging.**

PRACTICE Evaluating Thesis Statements

5.3

Explain what is wrong with each of the following thesis statements.

1. The benefits of having a part-time job while being enrolled in college are gaining work experience, I can make extra money, and to deal with a diverse group of people.

_____

2. I am going to talk about football and how it has affected my life.

_____

3. Auto enthusiasts come in all shapes, sizes, and forms.

_____

4. The restaurants in my area are Italian, Mexican, Hispanic, Greek, French, Japanese, and Chinese.

_____

5. Our economy and our environment can use a lot of help at this point when every bit counts and everything you participate in could make such a difference.

_____

The Body

The **body** of the essay consists of paragraphs that support the thesis statement. Each body paragraph is an academic paragraph, an organized group of sentences that logically supports one main point of the thesis statement. See the following page for a review of the parts of a paragraph.

Parts of the Body Paragraphs

Topic Sentence
- Connects the point of the paragraph to the thesis statement
- May include words or phrases from the thesis statement

Evidence
- Evidence supports the main point of the topic sentence
- Supporting points are connected with transitions
- Evidence may include reasons, examples, causes, effects, comparisons, contrasts, types or groups, steps, or points of an argument depending on the purpose of the essay
- Supporting points are arranged by time order, spatial order, or order of importance

Concluding Sentence
- Sums up in a new way

Ordering Body Paragraphs Paragraph order will depend on the purpose of the essay or the organizational pattern, such as comparison and contrast, cause and effect, or process. If you have written a thesis statement that lists the supporting points, each body paragraph will discuss one of those points in the order that they appear in the list.

Connecting Body Paragraphs A transition topic sentence helps readers see the connection between the thesis statement and the main point of the body paragraph. Notice the wording of the following topic sentences.

> **Thesis statement**: Students who take a class in a computer classroom are easily tempted to use the computer for other activities rather than class work.
> **Topic sentence**: One activity that tempts students is surfing the Internet.
> **Topic sentence**: In addition to surfing the Internet, students are tempted to play online games.
> **Topic sentence**: Not only are students tempted to surf the Internet and to play on-line games, but also they visit social networking sites.

The Conclusion

The **conclusion** is the last paragraph of the essay. Its purpose is to remind the readers of the main point of the essay and make final comments. The conclusion is your last chance to connect with the readers and say something that leaves them with a lasting impression. Your goal is to hold the readers' attention to the very end.

The conclusion does not have to be organized in a specific way, nor does it have required parts as the introduction does. However, the conclusion should be as strong as the other paragraphs in the essay.

There are a number of techniques that you can use to create an effective conclusion. Most often, your technique will depend on the purpose of your essay. For example, if you have written a narrative essay, your conclusion will explain how the conflict was resolved and what the narrator learned from the experience. The conclusion for an argument essay will try to convince readers that your position on the issue is the best.

Some of the techniques that are suggested for introductions can also be used for conclusions. For instance, you can end with a thought-provoking question, brief story, or a surprising fact or statistic.

Try to avoid techniques that have been overused and are, therefore, no longer interesting or others that are simply not appropriate as in the following list:

1. Beginning with phrases like these: *In conclusion, In summary, So you can see,* or *In closing*
2. Including each of the topic sentences of the body paragraphs
3. Repeating the introduction
4. Retelling the reader what you have already written: *I have tried to show, I have discussed, I have presented*
5. Apologizing for not being able to give more information

Here are several techniques for effective conclusions and examples of each written by students or college textbook authors:

Use a Quotation: Student Example

"Be all that you can be" has a special meaning for U.S. Army soldiers. The message is simple yet important; the U.S. Army offers a unique opportunity to realize one's potential. Although I exited the service to pursue my education, I credit Army life with transforming me into a mature, responsible individual. Most importantly though, my four-year experience as a soldier blessed me with a sense of bravery to overcome obstacles, the power of determination to succeed, and a newly discovered ability to understand the suffering of all human beings.

Make a Recommendation: Student Example

Becoming a single parent at sixteen quickly transformed me from a carefree adolescent to an adult with more responsibility than I could handle. Rather than enjoying high school, going to parties, and planning my future education, I was changing diapers and losing sleep. I was not prepared for the many challenging changes that took place in my life: working full-time at a low-paying job, not being able to go out with my friends, and being deserted by the baby's father. Through this difficult, life-changing experience, I had to grow up fast. Although I would not change my decision to bring my daughter into the world, I suggest that teenage girls plan for the care and costs of raising a child before getting pregnant.

Project into the Future: Student Example

The many advantages that Facebook offers, such as long distance communication, new friends, and business advertising, will most probably continue to make it a popular site for many years to come. However, because of the potential employer rejection after reading applicants' pages, attacks by sexual predators, and security breaches, users need to be careful about the amount of personal information they share on the site. Even with improvements to privacy settings, security holes are found on a regular basis, and the site is under constant attack by hackers. Facebook users need to understand that their personal information will be accessed and used for purposes that are not always beneficial.

Project into the Future: Textbook Example

The United States has been, and will remain, a land of immigrants. Immigration has brought cultural diversity and stories of hope, struggle, and success told in hundreds of languages. Like those of an earlier generation, today's immigrants try to blend into U.S. society without completely giving up their traditional culture. Some still build racial and ethnic groups in a community, so that in many cities across the country, the little Havanas and Koreatowns of today stand alongside the Little Italys and Chinatowns of the past. In addition, new arrivals still carry the traditional hope that their racial and ethnic diversity can be a source of pride rather than a source of inferiority.

(From *Society* by John J. Macionis)

Call for Action: Student Example

Animal and human research studies have given the scientific society a foundation for the possible health hazards of **radio frequency energy** from cell phones. However, scientists who oppose the findings of these studies criticize the research methods that were used. Other researchers have claimed that current studies do not provide absolute proof. More research along with better research methods are needed to prove unquestionably that cell phones present health hazards to humans.

radio frequency energy cell phones give their signals through radio waves, which are comprised of radio-frequency (RF) energy, a form of electromagnetic radiation

> Add to the Significance of the Topic: Student Example
>
> The effects of the Gulf oil spill of 2010 makes it obvious that the United States should move away from its dependence on oil as an energy source. Clean energy fuel technologies must be developed. Automobile manufacturers have responded by producing alternative fuel vehicles that use electricity, hydrogen, fuel cells, and hybrid technology. As more methods to produce alternative fuels are found, the economy and environment will benefit.

Peer Review Reminder. For feedback on your writing, have someone read your paper and make comments on the Peer Review Response sheet in Chapter 4, page 55.

Finally, you may include a restatement of your thesis using different words to avoid repeating the same sentence.

The Essay Graphic Organizer

The Essay Graphic Organizer on the following page will help you organize the parts of your essay.

Writing Assignments

Help Desk

Rose-Marie admits that she has trouble writing introductions. Read her introduction to an essay about her native country, Haiti, and offer her some suggestions to improve it by answering the questions that follow her introduction.

> [1]Haiti is known to be one of the poorest countries in the world. [2]People do not know that although we might be poor, we are very nice people. [3]I would like to teach you about Haiti, the people, their food, and their culture. [4]I hope you are willing to learn about it.

1. Does Rose-Marie's lead-in get your attention? What strategy would you suggest that she use?

   _____

   _____

2. Underline the thesis statement. What is the main point? How could she be more specific?

   _____

   _____

   _____

3. Circle the numbers of the sentences that make the mistake of directly addressing the reader.

Essay Graphic Organizer

Introduction

Lead-in:

Bridge:

Thesis Statement:

Body Paragraphs: Write as many body paragraphs and supporting details as you need.

Topic Sentence:

Supporting Detail 1:

Supporting Detail 2:

Supporting Detail 3:

Conclusion

Group Activity: Developing a Thesis Statement and Supporting Points

Many new websites are being developed to help college students. One site offers students money to upload their class notes, essays, research papers, and study guides. Every time a file is viewed, the person who posted the information earns money. Another feature of the site is an option to form study groups. Students can communicate with each other and form networks such as study groups about any topic anywhere in the world. The site is also available to teachers.

Along with the benefits of a site such as this one are the potential problems. In small groups of three or four, brainstorm some of the problems that a site like this could have. For example, how would students know if the notes or papers they were downloading were accurate and of good quality? Does a website that provides notes encourage laziness among students? Would students be more likely to skip class and download notes? What would prevent students from copying others' work and using it as their own?

Develop a thesis statement about the possible problems of this type of student information-sharing and networking website. Then, develop three supporting points for each problem you identified using the essay graphic organizer.

Reading and Writing across the Curriculum: Political Science

reasonable accommodation any change in the workplace that enables a qualified individual with a disability to enjoy equal employment opportunities

The Americans with Disabilities Act of 1990 (ADA) requires employers and public facilities to make "**reasonable accommodations**" for people with disabilities. It also prohibits discrimination against these individuals in employment. In 1998, the Supreme Court ruled that the ADA offers protection against discrimination to people with AIDS. Unfortunately, Americans with disabilities continue to suffer from discrimination. Stereotypes of the disabled are still common in our culture, especially in the media.

Brainstorm how the media represents the disabled. Choose three ways and support them with examples, using movies, television images, or advertisements.

Comment on a Contemporary Issue

With advances in technology and increased commuting costs, teleworking is quickly becoming popular. **Teleworking** is an arrangement in which companies allow employees to perform their work away from a central office. Teleworkers can work from home, telework centers, or satellite offices.

Telework has both advantages and disadvantages. Some employers report that teleworking actually increases communication and productivity. In addition, more jobs are open to disabled workers as well as single parents. Workers can save money by not having to commute or buy clothing to wear to work. On the other hand, some workers feel the need to be around other people or feel socially and professionally isolated.

Comment about the advantages and disadvantages of teleworking. Would you like this arrangement? Why or why not?

Write about an Image

If you have ever been pulled over by a police officer for speeding, you know that your actions can affect the charges that can be made against you. (See the photo on the next page.) Write an essay in which you advise someone about what to do when being pulled over for speeding. If you come from another country, advise someone from the United States about the actions to take when pulled over in your home country.

Here are some ideas to consider telling the reader:

- what to do when you see the police car
- how to talk to the officer
- how to act towards the officer
- whether or not to give excuses to get out of the ticket
- whether or not to agree to a search without a **search warrant**
- whether or not to answer questions without an attorney

search warrant an official document which gives police officers the authority to search for stolen property, illegal goods, or information which might help to solve a crime

English Success Tip: The Perils of Padding

Have you ever tried to make an essay longer by adding unnecessary words or material? This may seem like a good way to meet the length requirements of an assignment. However, using this technique, also known as **padding**, makes your writing less effective and does not impress your teacher.

When revising your paper, look for evidence of padding:

- using unnecessary adjectives and adverbs, repetitious words, and wordy expressions which make writing less precise and clear
- adding unnecessary information
- including details that do not prove your main idea or details that repeat the same point

Style Reminder. See Part 7 for help with improving your writing style.

For support in meeting this chapter's objectives, log in to www.mywritinglab.com, go to the Study Plan tab, click on **Writing the College-Level Essay** and choose **Recognizing the Essay, Essay Introductions, Conclusions, and Titles, Thesis Statements, and Essay Organization** from the list of subtopics. Read and view the videos and resources in the Review Materials section, and then complete the Recall, Apply, and Write exercises in the Activities section. You can check your scores and overall progress by using the Gradebook.

Learning Paragraph and Essay Organization Plans

CHAPTER 6

Illustration

Learning Objectives

After working through this chapter, you will be able to:

LO 1 Explain that illustration is a form of writing that supports a point with examples.

LO 2 Write an illustration paragraph.

LO 3 Write an illustration essay.

LO 1 What Is Illustration?

Illustration is a form of writing that supports a point with examples. For instance, if you wanted to write about rude people at your workplace or in college, you would give specific examples of rude behavior to back up your opinion.

QuickWrite

Take a few moments to jot down one or more examples of knowledge you learned in a college course.

Illustration in College Writing

Illustration is used in many college writing assignments where explanations and examples are needed. For example, in a biology class, you may be asked to explain the stages of cellular respiration; in a social science course, you may be asked to give examples to show how the news media influenced an election. Illustration is often used in textbooks to explain difficult concepts. Here is an excerpt explaining a concept in psychology called *observational learning*:

Definition of concept

Further explanation

Extended example

> Observational learning is the process of learning new responses by watching the behavior of another. In essence, after observing a model, you may think: If I do exactly what she does, I will get the same reinforcer or avoid the same punishment. A classic example of human observational learning occurred in the laboratory of Albert Bandura. After watching adult models punching, hitting, and kicking a large plastic BoBo doll, the children in the experiment later showed a greater frequency of the same behaviors than did children in control conditions who had not observed the aggressive models. Later studies showed that children imitated such behaviors even when models were cartoon characters.
>
> (From *Psychology and Life* by Richard J. Gerrig and Philip G. Zimbardo)

LO 2 The Illustration Paragraph

Main points in illustration paragraphs can be supported in two ways: by using either multiple examples or one extended example. The following paragraphs show the two methods.

Multiple Examples

The following illustration paragraph is called "Lessons from the Mat". Jason Duarte, a student, uses several examples to support his main point.

[handwritten annotations: main idea ✓, 3 major supports ✓, main point 1st, 2nd, 3rd, Conclusion]

¹My participation in high school wrestling taught me valuable lessons. ²The first lesson I learned was to be responsible. ³For example, one day, when I was late for practice and I had no good excuse for it, the coach made me run two extra miles and then wrestle the whole team, one person after another for one minute each. ⁴There were over twenty people on our team, which meant I had to wrestle over twenty minutes nonstop. ⁵I was never late to practice again after that day. ⁶Wrestling also taught me to eat foods that promote good health. ⁷Many of the foods I enjoyed eating were not nutritious and did not give my body the fuel it needed, but I had a hard time not eating them. ⁸One of my worst practices was after a big meal at a fast food restaurant. ⁹I felt slowed down and nauseated. ¹⁰After that experience, I realized that I had to make better food choices to feel energetic at practice. ¹¹As a result, I added more fruit and vegetables into my diet and ordered healthy items when eating fast food. ¹²The most valuable lesson wrestling taught me was to be a good sportsman. ¹³Wrestlers must be able to control their aggression once the match is over. ¹⁴At one competition, I saw a wrestler who had just lost a contest start a fight by attacking his opponent. ¹⁵Because of his poor sportsmanship, he was temporarily not allowed to go to school for three days. ¹⁶When I step onto the mat with my opponent, my goal is to win the match, but when the match is over, I shake my opponent's hand, and the intensity of the battle gradually disappears. ¹⁷Even though my wrestling days are long over, the lessons I learned from this sport still remain fresh in my mind.

PRACTICE	Analyzing an Illustration Paragraph with a Series of Examples
6.1	Answer the questions about the paragraph you just read, Lessons from the Mat.

1. Underline the topic sentence.

2. What is the main point of the paragraph?

_____

3. What are the three examples Jason uses to support his main point?

_____

4. Do the examples use factual information or personal experiences?

[handwritten] personal experien...

_____

5. What is the method of organization?   *[handwritten] Chronological order*

_____

6. Which verb tense does the writer use?   *[handwritten] Past verb tense*

_____

One Extended Example

The following paragraph shows how student writer Jessica Vilca's illustration paragraph called "A Simple Act of Honesty" uses one extended example to support her main point.

[1]A simple act of honesty can provide personal satisfaction. [2]For example, last semester, at the end of my last class of the day, chemistry, I observed a small canvas bag lying on top of the desk behind me. [3]I waited for almost ten minutes for the owner of the bag to come back for it, but no one showed up. [4]I decided to take the bag home with me and try to find the owner the next time the class met. [5]Curious about what was inside the bag, I opened it and found an iPod, headphones, and a pencil. [6]At the beginning of the next chemistry class, I asked the boy who sat in the same chair where I found the bag if he had left something in class that day. [7]He said he had and listed the three items I had seen in the bag. [8]When I returned his bag, he was surprised and happy, and I felt gratified. [9]Approximately two weeks after that incident, I found one hundred dollars that I thought I had misplaced two months ago. [10]The money was in a shoebox where I had placed it for safekeeping. [11]Perhaps the universe smiled down in favor of my good deed.

PRACTICE   Analyzing an Illustration Paragraph with One Extended Example

6.2   Answer the questions about the paragraph you just read, "A Simple Act of Honesty".

1. Underline the topic sentence.   *[handwritten] Honesty*
2. What is the main point of the paragraph?

[handwritten] A simple act of honesty can provide personal satisfaction

3. What example does the writer give to support her main point?

[handwritten] Honesty is self gratifying

4. What are the main events of the narrative example?

when she return the bag she felt gratified

ILLUSTRATION PARAGRAPH ESSENTIALS

The purpose of the illustration paragraph is to help the reader understand your main point through the use of specific, interesting, accurate examples. An effective illustration paragraph has these essential elements:

1. The illustration paragraph makes a point about a broad statement or belief.
2. The supporting details are multiple examples or an extended example to illustrate the main point.
3. The supporting details are equally developed and sufficient in number.
4. The methods of organization can be order of importance, chronological order, or spatial order, depending on the purpose of the paragraph.
5. Words are specific and accurate.

Prewriting the Illustration Paragraph

Before you write, you must choose a suitable topic and develop it.

Decide on Your Topic and Purpose When deciding on your own illustration topic or responding to an assigned topic, consider the following:

1. **Choose a topic that is limited enough to be explained in one paragraph.** A topic like **modern day heroes** might bring to mind many different types of heroes such as people who perform courageous acts, like soldiers, fire fighters, or police officers, or people who are notable in a particular field like medicine or physics. Some people consider celebrities to be heroes. As you can see, it would not be possible to discuss all of those groups in a paragraph. Therefore, you could narrow to one group of heroes or even choose one modern day hero and write about his or her accomplishments.
2. **Choose a topic that can be supported with examples.** A topic such as **how to prepare for a job interview** has a different purpose, which is to give the steps in a process.

PRACTICE Evaluating Topics for Illustration Paragraphs

6.3   Explain why each of the following topics would be acceptable or not acceptable for an illustration paragraph.

1. Careers

2. How to design a web page

_____

3. Inaccurate ideas that people who visit or move to the United States have about its culture

_____

4. Economic problems in the United States

_____

5. An admirable quality of an individual

_____

Develop Ideas for Your Topic Prewriting for an illustration paragraph involves developing a strong series of examples or an extended example. Developing ideas by using your preferred prewriting technique will help you discover whether or not you have enough information to support your topic.

Jason chose to write about lessons he learned as a high school wrestler. Here is his concept map:

Jason's Concept Map

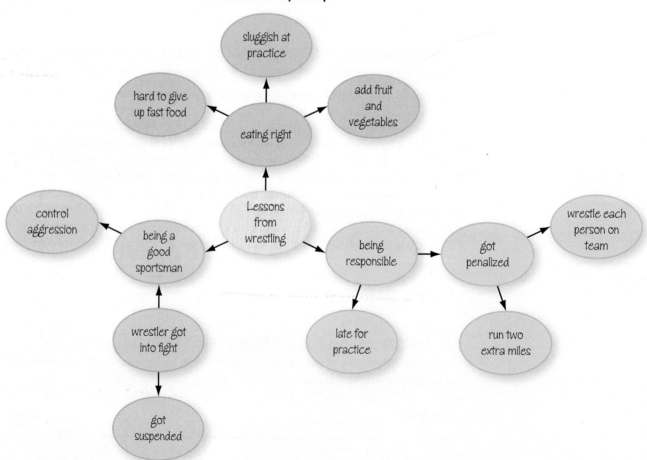

Paragraph Practice: Prewriting to Develop Ideas

Using your preferred prewriting technique, develop ideas for three of these illustration topics. You can develop a topic with multiple examples or an extended example.

General Topics

advice for new college students
important lessons you have learned
annoying driving behaviors
effective parenting practices
body modifications (i.e., tattoos, piercing)

Writing across the Curriculum Topics

Environmental Science: energy-saving strategies for the home
Film: minorities in movies
Sociology: cultural traditions
Marketing: disturbing print, Internet, or television advertisements
Travel and Tourism: places for tourists to visit in your city or town

Narrow Your Topic and Write the Topic Sentence The topic sentence of the illustration paragraph includes your narrowed topic and your main point. Your main point can be your opinion about a topic, which will be proved, or an informative statement about a topic, which will be explained.

Opinion as Main Point   An **opinion** is a statement of belief or feeling about a topic. The following topic sentences have the writer's opinion as the main point of a narrowed subject.

Students taking online courses need to have self-discipline.

My grandfather was the most generous leader of the village in Tai Shang City in China.

Informative Statement as Main Point   An informative statement tells the reader what the writer will explain about the topic. Each of the following topic sentences has an informative statement as its main point.

Nurses wear gloves to protect themselves from exposure to potentially infective materials.

Throughout history, police departments have adapted to technological advances.

TIPS | **Writing Illustration Topic Sentences**

1. **Choose only one topic and one main point.** Only one topic and one main point can be adequately explained in one paragraph. The following chart illustrates incorrect topic sentences and their corrections.

Type of error	Poor topic sentence	Corrected topic sentence
One topic with two main points	Moving out of my parents' home taught me independence and self-discipline.	Moving out of my parents' home taught me self-discipline.

(Continued)

(Continued)

Type of error	Poor topic sentence	Corrected topic sentence
Two topics with one main point	Working out and monitoring food choices have become common practices for people who want to improve their health.	Monitoring food choices has become a common practice for people who want to improve their health.

2. **Choose a specific word or phrase for your topic and main point.** A word that is not specific may be misunderstood. The following topic sentences show the difference between a vague and specific topic and main point.

Vague	Specific
Sedona, Arizona, is a wonderful place to visit.	Sedona, Arizona, known for its red rock canyons and surrounding forests, offers numerous options for outdoor exploration.
The word *wonderful* in this topic sentence is not specific enough, and your readers may not interpret the word the same way you do.	This topic sentence is more specific. Also, a few descriptive words about Sedona provide information for readers unfamiliar with the city.

3. **Avoid using a fact as your main point.** A fact may be used to briefly describe your topic but should not be used as your main point. Facts can be examples that support your main point. Notice how the first topic sentence below is a fact while the second topic sentences uses a fact to describe the topic but uses an informative idea as the main point.

Fact as a main point	Pesticides are used to get rid of insects.
Informative idea as a main point	Instead of fulfilling the purpose of eradicating insects, pesticides have created a wide range of problems.

PRACTICE   Writing Topic Sentences For an Illustration Paragraph

6.4   Write a main point for each of the following narrowed topics. The resulting topic sentence should be suitable for an illustration paragraph.

1. Joslyn's fear of heights

_____

2. The food in the college cafeteria

_____

3. My brother's daring personality

_____

4. Although online shopping can save time and money

_____

5. People can save energy

_____

Paragraph Practice: Writing a Topic Sentence

Look over the details you developed for your illustration paragraph (page 85) and write a topic sentence for each topic about which you developed ideas.

Organizing and Drafting the Illustration Paragraph

Develop Supporting Details Supporting details for the illustration paragraph can come from personal experience, personal observation, or discussions in class or with friends and family. As you develop your details, make sure that they support the main point and are specific. Cross out details that do not support your main point. You may need to do some additional prewriting to develop more details or add information to the ones you have.

PRACTICE   Eliminating Details that Do Not Support the Main Point

6.5   In each group of sentences, underline the main point in each of the topic sentences. Then circle any details that do not support the main point.

1. Topic sentence: Staying up late is a bad habit I would like to change.

    a. Every night I play games online until 2 a.m.

    b. I know that time should not be wasted.

    c. Instead of turning my cell phone off at night so that I can get some sleep, I cannot resist talking to my friends who call me at 3 or 4 a.m.

2. Topic sentence: My job as a stock clerk keeps me busy.

    a. One of my duties is to put groceries in their proper places on the shelves.

    b. I also help customers find products that they cannot locate on their own.

    c. Last summer I worked in a summer job program in Puerto Rico where I washed patrol cars at a police station.

    d. At the end of the night, my co-workers and I organize the items that have been misplaced and straighten the items on the shelves.

3. Topic sentence: My best friend Jennifer participates in many extracurricular activities.

    a. Jennifer is a senior in high school and all of her classes are advanced placement (AP).

    b. Jennifer volunteers and teaches a Bible study class at her church.

    c. Three days a week, she has choir practice at school.

    d. She also coaches cheerleaders in her town's Optimist cheerleading program.

Paragraph Practice: Selecting Details

Look back at your prewriting for your illustration paragraph (page 85), and choose one of the topics you worked on. Then evaluate the details to see which ones support your main point. Cross out the details that you do not plan to use. Prewrite to add more details if you need them.

Organize Your Supporting Details

After collecting all of the details to support your main point, you are ready to organize them into a plan for your paragraph. An illustration graphic organizer can help you identify your examples and the details that support them and can help you put your ideas into a logical order.

Identifying the Example and Explaining Details An illustration paragraph presents each example and explains it. A paragraph that does not explain each example is merely a list of sentences.

The following student paragraph lists examples without explaining them.

> Being a college student can be stressful. One source of stress is the pressure to earn high grades. Another stress is being a student and an employee at the same time. In addition, my friends put pressure on me. Finally, my family gives me more responsibilities than I can handle.

PRACTICE   Providing Details for Each Example

6.6   Revise the student's paragraph about college stress by giving an explaining detail for each example.

1. One source of stress is the pressure to earn high grades.

_____

_____

2. Another stress is being a student and an employee at the same time.

_____

_____

_____

3. In addition, my friends put pressure on me.

_____

_____

4. Finally, my family gives me more responsibilities than I can handle.

_____

_____

Using an Illustration Graphic Organizer An illustration graphic organizer can help you organize your examples and explanations. Here is the graphic organizer Jason completed to plan the paragraph you read at the beginning of the chapter, "Lessons from the Mat".

Jason's Illustration Paragraph Graphic Organizer

Topic Sentence: My participation in wrestling taught me valuable lessons.

Example/Evidence 1: To be responsible

Explanation
- Late for practice
- Had to run two extra miles
- Had to wrestle 20 team members, 1 minute each
- Always on time to practice

Example/Evidence 2: To eat healthy foods

Explanation
- Sluggish and nauseated at practice after meal at fast-food restaurant
- Added more fruit and vegetables to diet
- Ordered healthy items when eating at fast-food restaurant

Example/Evidence 3: To be a good sportsman

Explanation
- Wrestler lost a contest and started a fight with opponent
- Student was suspended
- Shake opponent's hand after contest

Paragraph Practice: Using a Graphic Organizer to Plan

Choose one of illustration graphic organizers (see pages 90 and 91) and fill it in with your illustration paragraph details. The first one is arranged for a series of examples, which has space for each example and the information that explains, illustrates, or proves the example. Add examples and explanations to extend the organizer as needed. The second organizer is arranged for an extended example, which has space to list the events of the story.

Illustration Graphic Organizer for Multiple Examples

Topic Sentence:

Example/Evidence 1: _____

Explanation

Example/Evidence 2: _____

Explanation

Example/Evidence 3: _____

Explanation

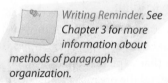

Writing Reminder. See Chapter 3 for more information about methods of paragraph organization.

Putting Your Ideas into a Logical Order   The method you use to organize your examples depends on your purpose. Three methods you can choose from are order of importance, time order, or spatial order.

Illustration Graphic Organizer for an Extended Example

Topic Sentence:

Extended Example (List events or describe)

Paragraph Practice: Organizing the Details

Check the order of details in your illustration graphic organizer to see if you have used a method of organization that fits your purpose. Make changes if necessary.

Write the First Draft

Use your illustration graphic organizer to guide you as you write the first draft. Check off each example as you complete it. In addition, consider the following elements.

Writing Reminder. See Chapter 3 for lists of transition words used for order of importance, time order, and spatial order.

Add Connectors and Transitional Words and Expressions Illustration paragraphs use specific transition words and expressions to give a signal to the reader that you are introducing examples or that you are giving an explanation of the example. Be sure to choose the transition that is appropriate for the type of supporting detail you are presenting. Illustration, order of importance, time order, or spatial order transition words can also be used to introduce examples depending on the purpose of your paragraph.

The following illustration transitions can be used to introduce examples:

An example of this is	As an illustration,	For instance,	To demonstrate,
An instance of this is	For example,	One example is	To illustrate,
Another example is	Equally important is	The most important example is	The next example is (the second, the third, etc.)

PRACTICE   Adding Connectors and Transitions to an Illustration Paragraph
6.7   Add transitions to the following paragraph.

¹As a rich nation of people who value convenience, the United States has become a disposable society. ²_____, Fast food is served in cardboard, plastic, and Styrofoam containers that we throw away within minutes. ³_____, Countless other products, from film to fishhooks, are elaborately packaged to make them more attractive to the customer and to discourage damage and theft. ⁴_____, Countless items are designed to be disposable: pens, razors, flashlights, batteries, even cameras. ⁵_____, Other goods, from light bulbs to automobiles, are designed to have a limited useful life after which they become unwanted junk. ⁶_____, Manufacturers market soft drinks, beer, and fruit juices in aluminum cans, glass jars, and plastic containers, which not only use up limited resources but also create mountains of solid waste. ⁷The high level of consumption in the United States generates most of the world's refuse, which ends up in dump sites that will be an unwelcome **legacy** for future generations.
(From *Society* by John J. Maconis)

legacy anything handed down from the past

Paragraph Practice: Writing the First Draft

Write a first draft of your illustration paragraph, using the graphic planner you prepared. Be sure to choose a suitable method of organization and verb tense.

Revising, Editing, and Proofreading

Revise your draft by looking at one element at a time: Support, Organization, Connectors and transitions, and Style.

REVISION CHECKLIST FOR AN ILLUSTRATION PARAGRAPH

Element	Revision Checkpoints
Topic	☐ The topic is significant and memorable.
	☑ The topic is limited enough to be described in one paragraph.
	☐ The topic can be supported with multiple examples or an extended example.
Topic Sentence	☑ The topic sentence contains the narrowed topic and the main point.
	☐ The narrowed topic is expressed specifically and concisely.
	☐ The main point contains an opinion to be proved or a general statement about information to be explained.

Support	☐ The supporting details are multiple examples or an extended example.
	☐ The supporting details are adequately explained.
	☑ All details support the main point.
Organization	☑ The paragraph follows order of importance, time order, or spatial order depending on the purpose of the paragraph.
Connectors and transitions	☐ Appropriate connectors and transitions for illustration, order of importance, time order, or spatial order provide coherence.
Style	☐ Writing is clear, concise Standard Written English.
	☐ Tone is appropriate for a college audience.
	☑ Specific details create reader interest through the use description, narration, and illustration.
	☐ Sentences are varied.

Paragraph Practice: Revising

Revise your illustration paragraph draft using the checklist above.

Peer Review Reminder. For feedback on your writing, have someone read your paper and make comments on the Peer Review Response sheet in Chapter 4, page 55.

Check Grammar, Punctuation, and Spelling

As you reread your paper to check for grammar, punctuation, and spelling errors, pay special attention for possible errors that may arise in illustration paragraphs. For example, be sure that you have used present or past tense verb forms consistently throughout the paragraph. Another area to look over is word choice. Use specific words to help the reader understand your examples. Finally, check your use of commas after transition words and phrases when introducing each example.

PRACTICE Revising, Editing, and Proofreading an Illustration Paragraph
6.8   Read and edit this illustration paragraph written by student Ryan Olkowski, and answer the questions below.

¹At Publix Supermarket, office cashiers have demanding responsibilities that they may be assigned each day. ²One of these responsibilities is front-end coordinator (FEC). ³Front-end coordinators supervise the employees who work in the front end of the store, this includes cashiers, office cashiers, and front-end service clerks. ⁴The FEC makes sure that the floors and bathrooms get cleaned and that the parking lot is free of carts. ⁵At the end of the day, the FEC who closes the store has additional duties. ⁶Having employees arrange items on shelves, clean

registers, refill bags, empty trash, and sweeping and mopping floors. [7]Another responsibility is working in the back office, known as the money room. [8]Part of this duty is counting and balancing cashier tills as well as making sure cashiers get their breaks or finish their shifts on time. [9]In addition, back office personnel deposit cash and order change for the next day. [10]The most challenging responsibility is working in customer service. [11]On top of the list is handling customer returns and dealing with customer complaints. [12]Other tasks are issuing rain checks, directing phone calls, and processing money orders. [13]Lottery is self-serve now. [14]Although the job as office cashier is rigorous, the benefits are excellent, and there are many opportunities for advancement.

Questions on Revising

1. Underline the topic sentence. What is the narrowed topic and main point?
   Narrowed topic: _____

   Main point: _____

2. Show that the writer has adequate and relevant support by filling in the illustration graphic organizer on the next page.

3. Which sentence is not relevant and can be removed?

   _____

Questions on Editing and Proofreading

4. Which sentence is a fragment? Find and correct it.

   _____

5. Which sentence has a comma splice error? Find and correct it.

   _____

Paragraph Practice: Editing and Proofreading

Edit and proofread your illustration paragraph. Check that your final draft is complete, accurate, and error-free.

Illustration Graphic Organizer

Topic Sentence:

Example/Evidence 1: _____

Explanation

Example/Evidence 2: _____

Explanation

Example/Evidence 3: _____

Explanation

Paragraph Writing Assignments

Help Desk

James was asked to revise the content of his illustration paragraph about the lessons he learned from his grandmother. He thought that his paper had fulfilled the assignment. Read James' paragraph on page 96 and write him an email suggesting some specific things he can do to improve the content.

¹Growing up with my grandmother was a good learning experience for me. ²I love my grandmother so much. ³I do not know what I would do without her. ⁴My grandmother taught me to appreciate life. ⁵She also gave me the faith that I could do whatever I wanted to in my life. ⁶She taught me how to love my family. ⁷My grandmother showed me how to stand up for myself and be a man. ⁸I would not trade this experience for anything in this world.

Group Activity: Identify Cultural Behaviors

As a college student, you are beginning a new stage of your life. You will meet many new people from this and other countries. Some students' cultures will be unfamiliar to you. This activity will give you an opportunity to learn about other cultures.

In small groups of three to four, identify the cultures represented in your group. Discuss and list behaviors that are required, recommended, or not necessary in each culture. For example, in your culture, do you leave a tip at a restaurant? Do you accept a gift? Do you take your shoes off before entering someone's house? You may find that even if each person in your group is from the same culture that there are differences.

Write a paragraph with your group or individually, giving examples of the behaviors that are required, recommended, or not necessary in each culture.

Reading and Writing across the Curriculum: Psychology

You have probably heard the noun *hassle* as an informal term meaning an annoying difficulty or a source of trouble. Psychologist Richard Lazarus uses *hassles* to mean the little stressors that seem to crop up every day:

Hassles cause more stress than major life events do. Daily hassles include irritating, frustrating experiences such as standing in line, being stuck in traffic, waiting for an appliance or utility repair technician to come to your home, and so on. Relationships are another frequent source of hassles, such as when another person misunderstands us or when coworkers or customers are hard to get along with.

Back in 1981, DeLongis and his colleagues found that the ten hassles most frequently reported by college students they surveyed were as follows:

1. Troubling thoughts about the future
2. Too many things to do
3. Not getting enough sleep
4. Misplacing or losing things
5. Wasting time
6. Not enough time to do things you need to do
7. Inconsiderate smokers
8. Concerns about meeting high standards
9. Physical appearance
10. Being lonely

(Adapted from *The World of Psychology* by Samuel E. Wood et al.)

Do you think the listed items are still relevant today? Prewrite about the hassles (little stressors) you experience. Choose the most significant hassles in your life and write an illustration paragraph explaining of each of them.

Comment on a Contemporary Issue

U.S. culture places a strong emphasis on body image. The popular media—television, magazines, movies, and the Internet—present images of thin, physically fit women and trim, muscular men. This focus on weight, fitness, and beauty has influenced the way people, especially adolescents, feel about themselves. According to the National Institute on Media and the Family, exposure to soap operas, music videos, fashion magazines, and video games has been associated with a drop in self-esteem in young people.

Comment on this emphasis on weight, fitness, and beauty.

Write about an Image

Today, t-shirts are a means of personal self-expression. They display designer logos, advertisements, political messages, and humor. You can find just about anything written on a t-shirt, and if it has not been written, you can have your message printed on one.

Write a paragraph giving examples of t-shirt messages that fit into a particular category, such as politics, advertisements, designer, environment, music, and so on. Describe each of them to give the reader a mental image.

LO 3 The Illustration Essay

Writing Reminder. For more help with writing an essay, including introductions and conclusions, see Chapter 5.

The illustration essay has the same purpose as the illustration paragraph: to support a main point with specific examples. The illustration essay uses the same organizational patterns as the illustration paragraph. Each body paragraph gives either multiple examples or an extended example to support the thesis statement.

The illustration essay graphic organizer on page 103 can be used to plan your essay. It will help keep you organized as you prewrite, draft, and revise.

The Thesis Statement

The thesis statement for an illustration essay makes a point that can be supported with specific examples. The thesis statement can be expressed in one of two ways:

Two-part thesis: The narrowed topic + the main point.

Many new consumer products that looked promising have ended as failures.

Three-part thesis: The narrowed topic + the main point + the examples.

Many new consumer products that looked promising have ended as failures, such as unusual cars, food, and electronics.

The Body Paragraphs

Each of the body paragraphs in the illustration essay can provide multiple examples or an extended example.

Multiple Examples Organization	**Extended Example Organization**
Support 1: Cars Example: DeLorean Example: Edsel	Support 1: Cars Extended Example: DeLorean
Support 2: Beverages Example 1: New Coke Example 2: Thirsty Dog/Thirsty Cat Example 3: Surge	Support 2: Beverages Extended Example: New Coke
Support 3: Electronics Example 1: BetaMax Example 2: WebTV Example 3: Apple Newton	Support 3: Electronics Extended Example: WebTV

Each body paragraph can be organized by order of importance, chronological order, or spatial order, depending on the purpose of the paragraph.

Illustration Essay Example

The following essay uses a series of examples of the unfortunate events a student encountered on her trip to interview the world-renowned tenor Placido Domingo.

Swischuk 1

Barbara Swischuk

Professor Markus

College Preparatory Writing

30 Oct. 2010

My Fondness of Celebrity

1   Of all of the great opera tenors, Placido Domingo has always inspired me with his deep, rich voice. All of my friends knew of my passion for his work, so it was not too much of surprise when I got a phone call one day from a second editor-in-chief of a popular women's magazine who was a close friend from my journalist days. She offered me an opportunity to interview the **world-renowned** tenor. This was exciting because in the print business, most of the conversations with celebrities are held on the phone for time and money reasons. With only hours to plan, I managed to book a flight to Miami, hire a babysitter, and rush out the door. My short-notice assignment to interview Placido Domingo consisted of several mishaps including a late departure to the airport, a stressful confrontation with a police officer, a forgotten credit card, and, finally, a face-to-face meeting with the star.

2   The first mishap of my short-notice assignment was my late departure to the airport. The babysitter was late, and the time that I had set aside to make the forty-minute ride to the Jacksonville airport got cut short. I arrived at my concourse thirty minutes before my departure time. On the way to the plane, I decided to stop by Starbucks to get a double espresso latte, which I spilled all over my blouse. "That is a great start," I thought and tried to figure out what to do about my coffee-stained blouse before my actual encounter with the celebrity. When the plane touched down in Fort Lauderdale, I had ninety minutes to the scheduled interview.

world-renowned
famous around the world

3   The nerve-wracking race to the airport was matched by my stressful

encounter with a police officer. With only ninety minutes to get to the interview,

I stepped hard on the accelerator of my midsize rental vehicle and sped onto the

highway. I had turned up the radio to distract me from the onset of stage fright

that accompanies every meeting with a famous person. As I was exiting the Julia

Tuttle Causeway to race onto Alton Road in Miami Beach, I noticed that behind me

was an officer in a police car with its lights flashing and siren blaring, which I did

not hear because the music on the radio was playing noisily. After pulling over at

his request, the officer came up to my window, and by that point I was extremely

nervous. "You were driving sixty in a thirty mile per hour zone," he said as he looked

at me with disapproval. I explained that I was in a hurry to make it in time to an

interview with the great Placido Domingo for a German magazine. I told him that

I was very nervous and probably should not be driving at all. Feeling sorry for me, he

let me off without a ticket and urged me to calm down if I wanted to get there at all.

4   If my hectic race to the airport and confrontation with a police officer

were not enough, I realized that I had forgotten my credit card when trying to

buy a new blouse to look presentable for my interview. Even though I was running

late and did not know the area, while driving through the heart of South Beach,

I found a department store with a parking garage located conveniently next to it.

After quickly trying on a few, I chose a sporty-looking blouse tailored at the waist.

I kept it on, went to the counter, and realized that I did not have my credit card with

me. After digging into my purse searching for cash, I could only produce twenty

dollars, not enough to pay for the blouse I was now wearing. Fortunately, the sales

associate offered to use my license to look up my account. Her phone call seemed

to take forever as I watched the minutes fly by. After finally being approved and

Swischuk 3

with the sale now complete, I now felt adequately suited to meet the multiple

Grammy award winner.

5   The hectic travelling to the location of the desirable assignment paid off as I

finally met Placido Domingo face-to-face. A press agent met me in the foyer of the

Eden Roc Hotel and led me to a suite on the tenth floor. I sat down in a postmodern

armchair with a view of the turquoise blue water of the ocean below, read over my

questions, and rehearsed my introductory words. With arms stretched out in an all-

embracing gesture, he entered the room as if it were a stage. He walked in a cloud

of charm, his eyes sparkling, a warm smile on his face. My nervousness fell away as

soon as we sat down. I asked about his new album, his future plans, and his

humanitarian work. After an hour, his assistant took an interview photo of the two

of us. When it was time to say goodbye, Placido kissed my hand in a gentlemanly

manner. After he left the room, I was still overwhelmed by his presence.

6   In retrospect, my fondness for Placido Domingo resulted in a day that went

extremely well for me: I made my flight, I did not get a ticket for speeding, I bought

a new blouse to stock my wardrobe, and I met the very memorable and charming

opera singer whom I have always admired. Ever since that day, every time I hear his

moving voice, I feel like an old friend is singing to me, and the picture of the two of

us is still gracing my wall.

PRACTICE   Analyzing an Illustration Essay

6.9

Answer the following questions about "My Fondness of Celebrity."

1. Underline the thesis statement in the first paragraph.
2. What technique does the writer use for her lead-in?

3. Underline each of the topic sentences in the body paragraphs. Circle the main idea of each one.

4. In each body paragraph, does the writer support the thesis by using multiple examples or an extended example?

_____

5. In addition to referring to the thesis, what point does the writer make?

_____

Peer Review Reminder. For feedback on your writing, have someone read your paper and make comments on the Peer Review Response sheet in Chapter 4, page 55.

Illustration Essay Graphic Organizer

Using an illustration graphic organizer will help you place your details in the appropriate pattern. The sample graphic organizer shown on page 103 can be changed to suit your needs by adding paragraphs, examples, and evidence.

Essay Paragraph Writing Assignments

Write about an Image

Electronic communications help keep people connected and make our lives run more smoothly, but they also create distractions. The constant interruptions keep us from completing our work. Write an essay giving examples of digital distractions that prevent people from getting important things accomplished.

Illustration Essay Graphic Organizer

Introduction

Lead-in:

Bridge:

Thesis Statement:

Body Paragraph for Multiple Examples

Topic Sentence:

Example 1 with Evidence/Explanation:

Example 2 with Evidence/Explanation:

Example 3 with Evidence/Explanation:

OR Body Paragraph for Extended Example

Topic Sentence:

Extended Example with Evidence/Explanation:

Conclusion

Choose Effective Closing Technique.

Writing Topics for an Illustration Essay

For your illustration essay, choose one of these options:

- from paragraph to essay: expand the paragraph you wrote in the paragraph section of this chapter
- any of the writing topics in the paragraph section of this chapter
- any topic from the following list:

General Topics

challenges facing college students
responsibilities of a particular job
risk-taking behaviors
qualities of a public figure whom you admire
values taught by a specific sport or game

Writing across the Curriculum Topics

Sociology: products that show the people of United States value convenience
Psychology: examples of observational learning as defined in on page 80 of this chapter (the process of learning new responses by watching the behavior of another)
Health: problems college students face when trying to eat the right foods
Education: successful or unsuccessful teaching techniques
Family: advantages or disadvantages of being the youngest, middle, oldest, or only child

English Success Tip: Getting Help with Writing

If you are having problems thinking of or organizing ideas, or noticing and correcting errors, take action and ask for help. Look for free tutoring opportunities or ask a classmate or friend to work with you.

When working with a writing tutor, classmate, or friend, you may want that person to correct every problem for you. In the end, relying on someone else to do your revising, editing, and proofreading will not make you a stronger writer; it will make you weak and dependent. Have the person work with you to help you find, understand, and correct your own errors.

For support in meeting this chapter's objectives, log in to www.mywritinglab.com, go to the Study Plan tab, click on **Illustration** and choose **Paragraph Development—Illustrating and Essay Development—Illustrating** from the list of subtopics. Read and view the videos and resources in the Review Materials section, and then complete the Recall, Apply, and Write exercises in the Activities section. You can check your scores and overall progress by using the Gradebook.

CHAPTER 7

Narration

Learning Objectives

After working through this chapter, you will be able to:

LO 1 Explain that narration is a form of writing that tells a story or gives an account of a significant experience or event.

LO 2 Write a narrative paragraph.

LO 3 Write a narrative essay.

LO 1 What Is Narration?

Narration is a form of writing that tells a story or gives an account of a significant experience or event. Narratives are used in a variety of writing situations. A text message to a friend about something that just happened, a news story recounting the capture of a criminal, and a history book's explanation of a Civil War battle are all narratives. Fiction writers also use the narrative form to tell their stories.

QuickWrite

Have you heard a good story in the past few days? Take a moment and write a brief account of the story.

Narration in College Writing

Narratives are frequently used in college writing assignments. For example, you may have an assignment in a history course in which you recount an important event or a discovery someone made. In a business-related course, you might write about the growth of a company, hotel, store, or restaurant. Courses in health care fields often assign medical histories. In the social sciences, narrative writing projects include case studies.

Textbooks frequently explain events through the use of narratives. The following story of a "shaming" custom that took place in England in the 1600s is an example:

Thomas Mills suffered the personal humiliation of a shaming custom called *skimmington* that was directed against husbands whose wives had been unfaithful. On May 27, 1618, the peace of the small village of Quemerford, in the west of England, was shattered by the appearance of a large crowd from the neighboring market town of Calne. Men marched with guns to the unpleasant noise of drums, clanging pots, whistles, and shouts. Among them, on a red horse, rode a man wearing a strange costume. He wore a loose shirt covering his body. A nightcap with two long shoehorns was tied to his ears. The horns were a universal symbol of adultery. On his face, he wore a false beard made from a deer's tail. The crowd escorted the rider to his home and stopped. Guns were discharged into the air and the rough music got louder. When Mills opened his door, members of the crowd waved the horns of goats or rams mounted on sticks. Then a few strong men entered the house and grabbed hold of his wife Agnes. They dragged her to a village mud hole where she was ducked and covered in dirt. Through the use of skimmingtons, men attempted to restore the dominance of husbands over wives by shaming men into discipline and warn women to remain obedient.

(Adapted from *Civilization in the West* by Mark Kishlansky et al.)

LO 2 The Narrative Paragraph

The following is an example of a student narrative paragraph called "My First Jump."

[1]My first jump from an airplane taught me that I could overcome my fear of skydiving. [2]On a clear, sunny spring day, I was about to fulfill the dream I had had since I was a young girl. [3]I was one of the thirty jumpers and instructors riding in the biggest airplane at the Skydive Deland drop zone, an air van. [4]Strapped to the front of my instructor waiting to take my first **tandem jump**, I watched those before me confidently and happily take a large jump out of the plane. [5]When I realized that my turn was approaching, I felt my fear in the pit of my stomach. [6]Preparing for the **freefall**, the instructor and I took our position at the edge of the open doorway. [7]Suddenly, I threw my hands above my head, grabbed hold of the doorway, and locked my knees. [8]For a moment I stayed there as if I were a cat about to get a bath, pushing and clawing against the weight of my instructor strapped to my back. [9]We both stood motionless, I at the opening and the instructor behind me suspended outside the plane. [10]Calmly and quietly, the instructor leaned over my shoulder and spoke to me. [11]Finally, I let go of the doorway, and we stepped back into the plane. [12]I thought that we were going to walk to the front of the airplane to take the long, slow ride back down. [13]Just then, the instructor smiled as he grabbed my arms and leaned back towards the door. [14]Completely unaware of what was about to happen, I found myself going out the door of the plane. [15]My fear melted into excitement and happiness as we fell through the air and floated down watching the parachute billow above us. [16]Once safely on the ground, I grinned and told my friends who were waiting for me about the jump as if that moment of fear had never happened.

(Adapted from a paragraph by Melissa McGee, student)

tandem jump a type of skydiving where the student skydiver is strapped to the instructor so that they skydive together

freefall falling through the air before opening a parachute

PRACTICE Analyzing a Narrative Paragraph
7.1 Answer the questions about the paragraph you just read, "My First Jump."

1. What is the topic sentence of the narrative? *Fear of Jumping*

2. Where does the incident of the paragraph take place? *Skydive Deland Drop Zone*

3. Who are the people involved in the events of the story? *30 jumpers and Instructors.*

4. What is the conflict in the paragraph? *Fear — happiness ✓ cause and affect*

5. How is the conflict resolved? *After she jump she felt excitement after the jump*

6. Which logical order does the writer use? *time order*

7. Which verb tense does the writer use? List the verbs in sentence 7. *Past verb tense*

NARRATIVE PARAGRAPH ESSENTIALS ✓

The purpose of the narrative paragraph is to make a point about the meaning or importance of an event or experience. The story happens at a specific time and place and focuses on a person or people who want something but experience a **conflict**, which is the problem or struggle in the story. At the end of the story, the conflict is resolved.

An effective narrative paragraph has these essential elements:

1. The narrative makes a point about the meaning or significance of an event or experience.
2. The event or experience has a conflict that is resolved.
3. The supporting details that help the reader understand the story include the setting, the characters, the conflict, the events, and the resolution.
4. The events are presented in time order. ✓
5. The event or experience is told in the past verb tense.

Prewriting the Narrative Paragraph

Before you write, you must choose a suitable topic and develop it.

Decide on Your Topic and Purpose When deciding on your own narrative topic or responding to an assigned topic, consider the following:

1. **Choose an incident that is significant enough so you can make a point about its meaning or importance.** Writing about an encounter with a rude person at work that taught you to control your temper is more meaningful than writing about a smooth day at work when nothing out of the ordinary happened.

2. **Choose an incident that took place in a short period of time.** For example, you can write about your high school graduation ceremony, which took place in a few hours, rather than your entire senior year in high school.

3. **Choose an incident that has only one conflict.** The conflict is the heart of your story and keeps your reader focused and interested in the outcome of your story.

PRACTICE Evaluating Topics for Narrative Paragraphs
7.2
Explain why each of the following topics would be suitable or unsuitable for a narrative paragraph.

✗ 1. a fun two-week summer vacation in the city

_____

✓ 2. passing the road test for a driver's license

_____

✗ 3. shopping at the mall

_____

✓ 4. throwing the winning touchdown in the last seconds of a playoff game

_____

Develop Ideas for Your Topic Prewriting for a narrative paragraph involves writing a rough sketch of the story you want to tell. Freewriting or listing work well for narratives. For example, Daniel was asked to write about an event that changed his life. Here is part of his freewrite about an experience in the United States Navy.

> I will never forget how I felt when I saw the news on September 11, 2001. I was in the United States Navy onboard a ship in Norfolk, Virginia. I saw what happened on the news. I was in total shock. One of my cousins worked in one of the towers. I had so many emotions running through me. My time in the navy was coming to an end. I wasn't sure what to do.

Paragraph Practice: Prewriting
Using your preferred prewriting technique, develop ideas for three of these narrative topics.

✓ an embarrassing experience
a moment of failure or success ✓
the breakup of a relationship
a difficult decision ✓
a misjudgment of someone or something

Writing across the Curriculum Topics

History: an account of an important event
Psychology: an experience with discrimination
Education: understanding a new idea, skill, or concept in a course
Biology: an experience of learning about animal behavior
Literature: a character in a story, movie, or television episode who overcame an
   experience with adversity

Narrow Your Topic and Write the Topic Sentence   The topic sentence of the narrative paragraph includes your narrowed topic, which is the incident, and the meaning or importance of the incident. The student whose paragraph you read about her first jump from an airplane was responding to the topic

Write about a time when you overcame a fear.

   [1]My first jump from an airplane taught me that I could overcome my fear of sky-diving.

TIPS | **Writing Narrative Topic Sentences**

1. **Express your narrowed topic as specifically and concisely as possible.** In a few words, summarize what happened in the incident.

Not specific	Specific
Getting a ticket taught me to be a more responsible driver.	Getting my first ticket for violating a traffic light taught me to be a more responsible driver.
I made a mistake that taught me a valuable lesson.	Misplacing a customer's credit card taught me a valuable lesson.

2. **Make a point about the meaning or importance of the incident.** Your point should tell the reader what the experience taught you or how it changed you.

Does not make a point	Makes a point
On May 3, 2005, I learned that I was not going to graduate from high school.	Learning that I was not going to graduate from high school taught me the importance of taking school seriously.
I have always been afraid of lightening and thunder.	Saving my niece's life during a thunderstorm showed me that I could conquer my fear of lightening and thunder.

3. **Choose a specific word or phrase to describe the meaning or importance of the incident.** Avoid words like *fun, exciting, wonderful,* and *good.* These words show that you do or do not like something, which does not give your incident meaning or importance.

Nonspecific	Specific
Attending cosmetology school instead of college was not good.	Attending cosmetology school instead of college made me realize that I should have taken my parents' advice.

PRACTICE 7.3   Analyzing Narrative Topic Sentences

Explain what is wrong with each of the following topic sentences. If a topic sentence is good, write "good."

1. The craziest thing happened to me last Saturday night.   *no good*

_____

2. We all make decisions in life; some are positive and some are negative.   *good*

_____

3. It was the morning of June 3, and my mom asked me if I had heard about the eighteen-year-old girl who had been in a car accident.   *good*

_____

4. Being embarrassed by tripping and falling on stage did not ruin my fifth grade graduation.   *good*

_____

PRACTICE 7.4   Writing Main Points for Narrative Topics

Each of the following topic sentences has a narrowed topic for a narrative paragraph, but the main point has been left blank. Write a main point, which is the meaning or importance, for each narrowed topic.

Example: Getting pulled over for violating a traffic light taught me to drive more carefully.

1. When I almost lost my life in a car accident, I learned *the true sense of safety*

_____

2. Being caught in a lie made me realize *that honesty is the be policy*

_____

3. My parents' divorce taught me *not to take life for granted*

_____

Paragraph Practice: Writing Topic Sentences

Write topic sentences for the three topics that you prewrote about in Paragraph Practice on page 108.

Organizing and Drafting the Narrative Paragraph

Using your topic sentence as a guide, the next steps are to develop and organize supporting details and write the first draft.

Develop Supporting Details To help your reader to fully understand your narrative, you need to include all the important details of the story:

- **Setting:** the time and place of your story
- **Characters:** the people in the story
- **Conflict:** the problem or struggle in the story (e.g., a disagreement, a choice to be made, an obstacle to overcome, or a person who is difficult to deal with)
- **Events:** the series of actions that happen in the story from beginning to end
- **Resolution:** the solution to the problem, the way found to deal with the situation

Organize Your Supporting Details After collecting all of the information for your story, you are ready to organize the details into a plan for your paragraph.

The pattern used to organize the events in a narrative paragraph is called chronological or time order. **Chronological order** is the organization of events presented in time order from beginning to end.

Melinda's list of events from her paragraph "My First Jump" is shown in her graphic organizer.

Melinda's Narrative Graphic Organizer

Topic Sentence: My first jump from an airplane taught me that I could overcome my fear of skydiving.

Characters: Name and Description	Setting
1. Me (Melinda)	**Location:** Skydive Deland drop zone and an air van
2. My instructor	
3. Other jumpers and instructors	**Day/Month/Year:** A sunny spring day

Conflict: The jumper is afraid to jump out of the plane.

(Continued)

Events

1. Watched others jump out of the airplane

2. Felt fear as my turn approached

3. Stood at the door opening with instructor

4. Threw my hands above my head and grabbed hold of the door

5. Stood at the open door while instructor spoke to me

6. Let go of the door and we went back into the plane

7. Suddenly, instructor pulled my arms and pulled me out of the plane

8. Felt exhilaration falling through the air

Resolution

The instructor tricks the young woman by leading her back into the plane and then suddenly pulling her out the door.

PRACTICE   Placing Events in Time Order

7.5   The events in the next two paragraphs are out of order. Number the sentences to put the events in their proper time order.

Paragraph 1

___*1*___ 1. Young children's emotions develop according to a biological schedule for a specific age.

___*4*___ 2. Laughter appears somewhere between 3 and 4 months.

___*2*___ 3. Somewhere between 18 months and 3 years, children begin to show first empathy, envy, and embarrassment, followed by shame, guilt, and pride.

___*5*___ 4. Between the ages of 4 and 6 months, the emotions of anger and surprise emerge.

_3_   5. By 3 months of age, babies can express happiness and sadness.

_1_   6. By about 7 months, infants show fear.

(Adapted from *The World of Psychology* by Samuel E. Wood et al.)

Paragraph 2

_1_   1. John Schnatter, founder of Papa John's, fulfilled his dream to open a pizza chain that delivered superior quality traditional pizza delivered to the customer's door.

_2_   2. To help his father, Schnatter sold his car, used the money to purchase $1,600 of used restaurant equipment, knocked out a broom closet in the back of his father's tavern, and began selling pizzas to the tavern's customers.

_5_   3. Shortly after graduating from Ball State University with a business degree, he faced his first business challenge.

_3_   4. After the success of the pizza in the tavern, Schnattner officially opened the first Papa John's restaurant in 1985 and opened as many stores as the market would bear.

_6_   5. The challenge was that his father's tavern was $64,000 in debt and failing.

_4_   6. Schnatter worked his way through college making pizzas, improving the techniques and tastes that would some day become Papa John's trademark.

_6_   7. Soon the pizza became the tavern's main attraction and helped turn the failing business around.

(Adapted from *Business in Action* by Courtland Bovee, John V. Thill, and Barbara E. Schatzman)

Paragraph Practice: Planning the Paragraph

Choose one of the topics from the Your Narrative Paragraph activity on page 108 or your own topic, and using the narrative graphic organizer on page 114, fill in the events and other important information for your narrative paragraph.

Narrative Graphic Organizer

Topic Sentence: _____

Characters: Name and Description   **Setting**

1. _____   **Location:** _____

2. _____

                                          Day/Month/Year: _____

3. _____

Conflict: _____

Events

1. _____

2. _____

3. _____

4. _____

5. _____

Resolution

_____

Paragraph Practice: Placing Events in Time Order

Looking back at your graphic organizer, check your list of events. If you have left any events out, add them now.

Write the First Draft As you write your first draft, consider these elements: dialogue, description, transitional words and expressions, and verb tense.

Add Dialogue When telling a story, you may want to include a few lines of dialogue. <u>Dialogue is a written conversation</u>. The purpose of using dialogue in your narrative is to give your reader an idea of what your character sounds like. Spoken words need to be punctuated with quotation marks.

Punctuation Reminder.
See Chapter 28 for
more information
on punctuating
direct quotations.

Use brief dialogue only at an important moment in your story. Too much dialogue breaks the flow of the narrative and sounds like a conversation, not a story. The student who wrote the following paragraph uses dialogue to tell his story:

> ¹During my first day of high school in the United States, I discovered that the English I had learned in my country did not help me understand slang expressions. ²As I entered the building that morning, I realized that I did not know where any of my classrooms were. ³I stopped a student to ask him for directions, and instead, I got my first slang lesson. ⁴I said, "Hi." ⁵He answered, "What's up, man?" ⁶A little confused, I replied, "Nothing. You?" ⁷"Chillin" was his response. ⁸Without knowing what that word meant, I said, "No, thank you." ⁹He gave me a strange look, so I quickly asked him how to get to my class. ¹⁰After he gave me directions, he added, "Got it, dawg?" ¹¹At that moment, I did a 360-degree spin looking for a dog. ¹²After thanking him for his help, he said, "Fa sho," which I spent the rest of the day trying to figure out.

PRACTICE   Evaluating the Use of Dialogue
7.6   Look back at the paragraph you just read and answer this question:
Did the writer break the flow of the story with too much dialogue? Explain your answer.

_____

Add Description   Use vivid details to create word pictures to help the reader visualize the setting, people, and events. This student paragraph helps the reader visualize the event:

> ¹The wind was hitting my Honda Civic a bit harder than usual from the speed I was picking up on the curvy back roads. ²My favorite song came on the radio, and I sang along and danced to the beat. ³Looking ahead, I saw a stop sign on a side road. ⁴This was the famous Shotgun Road where many of my friends had wrecked their cars. ⁵If they had not been such careless drivers, I thought, they would not have had accidents. ⁶Pushing on my brakes slowly, I stopped my car. ⁷Looking right, I saw a few cars in the distance. ⁸On my left, I saw a tall wood telephone post covered with bushes. ⁹I could not see the left side of the road. ¹⁰As I looked right again, I could see cars coming closer, so I decided to make a speedy turn and just go for it. ¹¹Making my left turn, not paying attention, I saw an enormous Mack truck about to hit me. ¹²At that moment, I realized that death was right in front of me.

PRACTICE   Identifying Vivid Details

7.7   Reread the student paragraph and underline parts that help you form a mental image of the event.

Add Connectors and Transitional Words and Expressions   Narratives use time order connectors and transition words and expressions to help the reader follow the sequence of events. The following is a list of transitions commonly used for narratives:

after	eventually	once
afterward	finally	one day
after a while	first	previously
after that	immediately	soon
as soon as	in the meantime	the next day
at first	in the past	then
at last	later	today
at that time	last	until
before	meanwhile	when
before this	next	while
during	not long after	yesterday
earlier	now	

PRACTICE   Using Narrative Connectors and Transition Words

7.8   In the following student paragraph by student Denise Eyssalem, fill in the blanks with an appropriate transition word or expression from the list. Avoid repeating the same word or expression more than once.

¹Attempting to be on time to my first class as a new college student was stressful. ²I wanted to be on time to my 9:30 a.m. class, but dropping my children off at school and slowing down through school zones were making me late. ³_____ I got to the college, I found a parking spot right away, and I still had fifteen minutes to get to class. ⁴_____ on my way out of the parking lot, I was stopped by a security guard who told me that I had parked in a staff lot and would have to move my car. ⁵_____ I drove out of the staff lot, carefully steering my car around the crowds of students entering and leaving the college grounds in their cars. ⁶_____ I found a parking spot, but it was far from my classroom. ⁷Thinking I was late, I rushed to class. ⁸_____ I arrived at my classroom and saw that no one was there. ⁹I thought I had gone to the wrong building. ¹⁰_____ I realized that my watch was ten minutes fast and, to my amazement, I was actually early. ¹²Now I make sure that my watch is set to the right time and that I park in the student lot.

Grammar Reminder.
See Chapters 22 and 23 for more information about verb tenses.

> **TIP** When writing a narrative, be sure to use the appropriate past tense forms and avoid shifting your verbs back and forth from the past tense to the present tense.

Revising, Editing, and Proofreading

Revise your draft by looking at one element at a time: Support, Organization, Connectors and transitions, and Style. The following Revision Checklist contains the SOCS elements as they apply to narrative paragraphs.

REVISION CHECKLIST FOR A NARRATIVE PARAGRAPH

Element	Revision Checkpoints
Topic	☐ The event is significant and memorable.
	☐ The event tells about an event that takes place in a short period of time.
	☐ The event has one conflict.
Topic Sentence	☐ The topic sentence contains the narrowed topic and the meaning or importance of the event.
	☐ The narrowed topic is expressed specifically and concisely.
	☐ The meaning or importance is described with a specific word or phrase.
Support	☐ The supporting details include the setting, characters, conflict, events, and resolution.
	☐ All supporting details are relevant and adequate.
Organization	☐ The paragraph follows chronological order to show story events from beginning to end.
Connectors and Transitions	☐ Time order connectors and transitions provide coherence.
Style	☐ Writing is clear, concise Standard Written English.
	☐ Tone is appropriate for a college audience.
	☐ Dialogue and vivid details create reader interest.
	☐ Sentences are varied.

Paragraph Practice: Revising

Using the revision checklist, revise the first draft of your narrative paragraph.

Peer Review Reminder.
For feedback on your writing, have someone read your paper and make comments on the Peer Review Response sheet in Chapter 4, page 55.

Check Grammar, Punctuation, and Spelling As you reread your paper to check for grammar, punctuation, and spelling errors, pay special attention for possible errors that may arise in narrative paragraphs. Be sure that you have used past tense verb forms. Also, check punctuation and capitalization of dialogue.

PRACTICE

7.9 Revising and Editing a Narrative Paragraph

Revise and edit Daniel Koffer's paragraph called "Eight More Years." Then answer the questions below.

¹The September 11, 2001, attacks on the Twin Towers of the World Trade Center in New York City compelled me to reenlist in the United States Navy. ²That day, I was in Norfolk, Virginia, onboard the USS Porter DDG-78. ³We had just began a fire fighting drill. ⁴Thirty minutes into the drill, our commanding officer came over the ship's public address system to tell us that a plane had just hit one of the World Trade Center towers. ⁵He wanted everyone to assemble on the mess decks to watch the news. ⁶When I saw that one tower was gone, I was in total shock. ⁷I realized that one of my cousins worked in one of the towers. ⁸Many emotions went through me. ⁹Later that day, when I tried calling my family members to find out if my cousin was okay and to see if anyone else I knew had been injured in the city area, I was unable to reach them. ¹⁰The next day, I was scheduled for my separation physical because my navy contract was almost up. ¹¹As I was waiting to be seen, I realized that getting out of the navy would be the wrong thing to do, so I reenlisted for another eight years to serve my country.

Questions on revising

1. Underline the topic sentence. What is the narrowed topic and the main point?
   Narrowed topic: _____

   _____

   Main point: _____

2. Show that the writer has adequate and relevant support by filling in the information on setting, characters, conflict, and resolution.
   Setting: _____

   Characters: _____

   Conflict, problem, or struggle: _____

   Resolution: _____

3. What order do the events of the story follow?

   _____

4. Does the writer tell the story in the first or third person?

   _____

Questions on editing and proofreading

5. One sentence in this paragraph has a problem with a verb form. Find the error and write the corrected sentence here.

_____

6. In sentence 1, the word _navy_ is capitalized, but it is not capitalized in sentence 10. Is the use of capitals correct? If yes, tell why. If not, make the correction.

_____

Paragraph Practice: Editing and Proofreading

Edit and proofread your narration paragraph. Check that your final draft is complete, accurate, and error-free.

Paragraph Writing Assignments

Help Desk

Enrico is having a problem keeping the verbs in the past tense in his narrative paragraph. He tends to shift from past verb forms to present verb forms. Circle the verbs that are in the present tense and change them to the appropriate past verb forms.

> [1]One cold winter's day, I cheated death by avoiding a serious accident.
>
> [2]I was driving home from college during a snowstorm. [3]I have never driven in the snow before, and I was worried about how my old Nissan Maxima will manage. [4]The snow-covered roads made driving hazardous. [5]One road is especially curvy and slippery. [6]As I approached an especially steep turn, I put my foot on the brake to slow down. [7]Unexpectedly, my tires lock, and the car begins to skid. [8]My hands started to perspire, and my heart was beating rapidly. [9]I thought I was going to crash and die. [10]In a split second, the car suddenly stops. [11]Luckily, there were no other cars on the road. [12]When I realized that I was not hurt and that the car was not damaged, I am happy to be alive.

Group Activity: Working Together to Tell a Story

In this exercise, you will tell a story through photographs. During class time, form groups of two or three, and choose a busy location, such as the library, a lab, advisement/student services, or a place where students get together to socialize on campus, such as the cafeteria, student center, or courtyard. Take a camera, cell phone, or other electronic device that takes pictures and photograph an event that takes place. Then, view the photos and select the ones that best represent the event. If possible, print the photos or upload them to a photo sharing website and arrange them in chronological order. Finally, write a narrative paragraph about the event.

Reading and Writing across the Curriculum: American History

Family stories are memorable stories from our lives and our family's lives. Read the following family story about immigrating to America.

> In 1894, Mary Antin, a 13-year-old Jewish girl from Russia, and her mother and sisters made a perilous journey from persecution in tsarist Russia to the ship that would take them from Hamburg, Germany, to join her father in faraway America. Mary and her family were removed from the train at the Russian-German border by Russian police because of improper documents. Once her mother had settled the issue with the help of a local Jewish family, they reboarded the train to Berlin. Outside that city, they were once again removed from the train. Though they did not immediately understand what was happening, German authorities had arranged for a thorough cleansing and health inspection, since a cholera epidemic was raging in Russia. They took their things away, took their clothes off, rubbed them with disinfectant, and forced them to find their clothes thrown in a pile with everyone else's. Then, worried that they would miss the train, they hurried to get back on the train, realizing that they would not be murdered. Finally, Mary and her family boarded a ship for the United States, the place that lay beyond the horizon.
>
> (Adapted from *The American Journey* by David Goldfield et al.)

Write a narrative paragraph about one of your family's stories. The paragraph could be about a holiday celebration, arrival in the United States, a marriage, a vacation, a cherished object, an event that is often recounted, or the funny or strange behavior of a relative.

Comment on a Contemporary Issue

> We live in a time of rapid advances in technology and product development. While we like these advances, the products we buy today may be **obsolete** (not used anymore) within several years or less. Critics call this technological obsolescence. For example, USB drives have now replaced disks and CDs as storage devices. Cell phone models change so rapidly that a cell phone purchased a year ago is considered an old model, and chargers for it are no longer available. Some people who have video cameras can no longer buy the tapes needed to record videos.
>
> (Adapted from *Marketing* by Gary Armstrong and Philip Kotler)

Comment on an experience you had with a product was no longer used or was out-of-date even though it was still working or usable. Consider clothing fads, electronics, kitchen items including appliances, software, cars, grooming products, video games, toys, workout equipment, and so on.

Write about an Image

A photo can tell a story about an object, person, place, or situation. Look at the details in the photo below. In a paragraph, tell the story of what may have happened.

LO 3　The Narration Essay

Writing Reminder. For more help with writing an essay, including introductions and conclusions, see Chapter 5.

The narration essay has the same purpose as the narration paragraph: to make a point about the meaning or importance of a single, significant experience or event. The narration essay uses the same organizational pattern, chronological order, as the narration paragraph. The narration graphic planner on page 123 can also be used to plan your essay and keep you organized as you prewrite, draft, and revise.

Thesis Statement

The thesis statement makes a point about the meaning or importance of an experience or event. The thesis statement consists of the event + the meaning or importance of the event.

The night I was brutally attacked, I learned that the justice system is not always fair.

Body Paragraphs

The body paragraphs in the narrative essay are organized by chronological (time) order, the order in which the events happened. Each of the body paragraphs develops the events of the story. A body paragraph can develop one event or several smaller events. Notice how the events are listed in the planning notes shown on the next page. Each event will be developed into a body paragraph.

Thesis Statement: The night I was brutally attacked, I learned that the justice system is not always fair.

Characters: Name and Description	Setting
1. Me, Imtieas	Location: Duval Street, Key West, Florida
2. The attackers: a stocky, drunk, white male in his thirties; small, blond woman in her late twenties	Day/Month/Year: 1 a.m., April 2009
3. People at a local hotel	
4. Police officers	

Conflict: My story of the incident versus my attacker's story

Events

1. Walking home, saw two drunk adults riding toward me on bicycles on the sidewalk
2. The male ran into me with his bicycle, then kept punching me and telling me, "You do not belong here. Go back to your country." Then the two individuals rode off.
3. Went to nearby hotel and yelled for help.
4. Told police officers what happened and gave them a description of attackers.
5. Several hours later, police officers arrested the couple.

Resolution

The police officers had to let the couple go because there were no witnesses, and they said they had not done anything.

Narrative Essay Example

Student Myriam Alexandre recounts the events of a frightening night in which she and her family escape persecution.

Alexandre 1

Myriam Alexandre

Professor Markus

College Preparatory Writing

21 Nov. 2010

The Power of Words

¹   When I was five years old, freedom of speech in my country, Haiti,

was taboo. The government in power was falling, creating chaos and fear. People

were afraid for their lives because the government agents reported anyone who

spoke against those in power, and with no warning, in the middle of the night, the person was arrested, never to be seen again. During one long, frightening night, I learned that the misuse of the simplest words could be dangerous and destructive.

2   My father, a well-known preacher, teacher, and department director for the board of education, was one of those who criticized the government's actions when he preached and when he spoke with his friends. My mother encouraged him to stop, fearful of what might happen to him. Even though my father had friends in the government who had power, they also told him to stop speaking negatively because they could not protect him from the people who were unhappy with his sermons. However, my father said he would not stop this preaching until the situation in the country changed.

3   The population wrongly believed that my father was one of the government's spies or one of the agents who was giving orders to kill citizens. Therefore, they planned to kill him once the government fell from power. For months, the priest, the governor, and the other teachers of the town made a secret plan to kill my father. They were superstitious and believed that to overcome evil, they had to ask their god for permission to kill an evil, in this case, my dad. Most of the people in our town agreed to kill him. They wanted to decapitate him because they said he was the devil in human form, so if he lost his head, he would not be able to come back from the dead.

4   On a rainy night at the end of January, a countless number of people carrying heavy rocks came to our two-story house, which was on a plantation with a field of sugar cane in front of the house. The crowd wanted to destroy my father completely, so it did not matter if his children got hurt in the process. One group of people threw rocks at every glass window we had. At the time, I was in a deep sleep, and my bed was situated under the window. I never woke up or heard the voices of the

crowd until my window and the bricks that surrounded it fell on my bed. It was a miracle

that I had rolled over to the only safe spot on my bed and was not hurt. While one group

was throwing rocks, another was breaking into the main entrance of the house. At the

back of the house, still another group broke into the storage room full of food we had

saved for the poor. Others set fire to part of the sugar cane field.

5   While all of this destruction was happening, my father came into the

bedroom and grabbed me and my other sisters who had been awakened by the

crowd's violent activities. My father decided to get all of us, my sisters, my three

brothers, and my mother, out of the house to safety. We could hear the crowd

downstairs calling my dad's name, waiting for him to come out so that they could

decapitate him.

6   My mother wrapped my two-year-old brother in a white sheet, and we

all left by the back door in such a hurry that we forgot our shoes and without food or

objects to help us survive. We walked for approximately thirty minutes into the forest

before we stopped under a tree and sat on the wet ground. My siblings and I were

shaking; we did not understand what was going on. In the distance, we could hear

the crowd singing, cursing, and yelling, and we cold see the flames from the burning

sugar cane.

7   Half asleep on the ground, I could hear my mother singing and praying.

I began to think about what had happened. I wondered why the crowd hated us until

I remembered the last sermon my dad had given the previous week. Suddenly,

everything made sense. He said that he could say whatever he wanted because

he had the power, so no one could hurt him. That night in the forest, I swore that

I would never make the mistake my dad did. I would never speak words that would

not have a positive impact on my life or my loved ones.

PRACTICE   Analyzing a Narrative Essay

7.10   Answer the following questions about "The Power of Words."

1. Underline the thesis statement. What is the writer's main point?

   _____

2. What technique does the writer use in the lead-in?

   _____

3. What was the conflict of the story?

   _____

   _____

4. What are the main events of the story?

   _____

   _____

5. In addition to referring to the thesis, what point does the writer make in the conclusion? Underline the sentence.

   _____

Narrative Essay Graphic Organizer

Using a narrative essay graphic organizer will guide you as you list the important elements of your story: the setting, time, characters, conflict, events, and resolution. The sample graphic organizer on page 126 can be changed to suit your needs by adding body paragraphs to describe events.

Narrative Essay Graphic Organizer

Background Information

Characters: Name and Description

1. _____
2. _____
3. _____
4. _____

Setting

Location: _____

Day/Month/Year: _____

Conflict:

Resolution:

Introduction

Lead-in:

Bridge:

Thesis Statement:

Body Paragraphs: Write as many body paragraphs as you need.

Topic Sentence:

One Event or Several Small Events

Conclusion (Resolution)

Essay Writing Assignments

Write about an Image

 Peer Review Reminder. For feedback on your writing, have someone read your paper and make comments on the Peer Review Response sheet in Chapter 4, page 55.

As human beings evolved and transportation and technology improved, people risked going further from original locations, and this natural search for new places and experiences continues to this day. Humankind's seemingly endless series of migrations seems to be an inborn trait of the human species. People travel for a variety of reasons, for example, to visit friends and relatives, to relocate, to do business, to relax, to experience an adventure, and to see places of historical or cultural interest.

(Adapted from *Travel and Tourism* by Paul S. Biederman)

Write a narration essay telling the story of a travel experience that had a significant impact on you or someone you know.

Writing Topics for a Narration Essay

For your narrative essay, choose one of these options:

- from paragraph to essay: expand the paragraph you wrote in the paragraph section of the chapter
- any of the writing topics in the paragraph section of this chapter
- any topic from the following list:

General Topics

facing a fear
meeting or not meeting a customer's or patient's needs
standing up for a belief
a conflict over money
a difficulty with a new technology

Writing across the Curriculum Topics

Business: a business success or failure
Foreign Language: an experience with a foreign language
Family: a family conflict
Culinary Arts: a memorable experience while preparing or eating food
Anthropology: a rite of passage in your culture (a ceremony or informal activity
that marks an important life stage or occasion, especially becoming an adult)

English Success Tip: Learn from Your Mistakes with a Writing Improvement Log

Keeping the papers you wrote and the tests you took in your English course can provide you with valuable information about your progress. Comparing results on papers and tests will show you areas of strength and weakness. Record your problems in a writing improvement log like the one below. Write down grammar, punctuation, and sentence structure errors. Also, list problems with content such as weak supporting details. An example entry has been made to the log to show how to use it.

Writing Improvement Log

Item	Type of Error or Weakness	Correction
In high school, students are tested on small amounts of material. Whereas in college students are tested on much more information.	Fragment	In high school, students are tested on small amounts of material, whereas in college students are tested on much more information.

For support in meeting this chapter's objectives, log in to www.mywritinglab.com, go to the Study Plan tab, click on **Narration** and choose **Paragraph Development—Narrating and Essay Development—Narrating** from the list of subtopics. Read and view the videos and resources in the Review Materials section, and then complete the Recall, Apply, and Write exercises in the Activities section. You can check your scores and overall progress by using the Gradebook.

CHAPTER 8 Description

Learning Objectives

After working through this chapter, you will be able to:

LO 1 Explain that description is a form of writing that creates a clear mental picture of a topic.

LO 2 Write a descriptive paragraph.

LO 3 Write a descriptive essay.

LO 1 What Is Description?

Description is a form of writing that creates a clear mental picture of a topic. Description is used in a variety of writing situations. Fiction writers bring characters, scenes, and events to life with description. Technical writers describe objects and mechanisms for instruction manuals, while journalists describe people and events. Menus, catalogs, and travel brochures all use description. Description is often used with other writing patterns, such as narration, illustration, process, and comparison.

QuickWrite

 Think about a food that you enjoy eating. Take a moment and write a brief description of it.

Description in College Writing

In academic writing, description is often factual. For example, in a chemistry class, you may be asked to write a lab report that describes the experiment you performed, the method used, and a chemical reaction. In a computer science class, you may write a plan for a website describing its content, design, and structure. Writing up an experiment for a psychology class involves describing how and why you performed the experiment and what you discovered.

LO 2 The Descriptive Paragraph

Descriptive paragraphs can be objective, subjective, or a combination of the two. An **objective description** is based on real facts, while a **subjective description** is based on personal beliefs or feelings. A blended description is based on real facts and includes personal beliefs or feelings.

Objective Description Example

The following paragraph is an example of an objective description. Notice how the student writer uses factual details without offering an opinion yet still effectively creates an image for the reader.

The Bic Matic grip 0.7mm number 2 mechanical pencil is a tool that is used for writing. The pencil consists of two main components: a black plastic outer tube and a black plastic inner tube filled with lead. The pencil measures 8" from the top of the eraser to the pencil opening at the bottom. The 5⅝" shatter-resistant outer tube is a hollow cylinder, open at both ends. A purple plastic 1¼" clip is attached to the outer tube 1" from the top of the pencil. This clip allows the user to clip the pencil to a pocket or notebook. A 1½" thick, contoured, purple rubber grip is placed one half inch above the pencil opening for the writer's comfort. The inner tube, which is also cylindrical and the same length as the outer tube, contains the lead. At the top end is a white eraser that fits snuggly into a cup-like holder. At the other end is a claw. When the eraser is pressed, the claw opens to allow the lead to drop through the opening of the outer cylinder. When the eraser is released, the claw closes and keeps the lead from falling out or going back up into the pencil.

Subjective Description Example

In 1826, artist Thomas Cole described a storm in the Catskills, the mountains of Eastern New York and Western Connecticut. Colorful sensory images and actions draw the reader into the stormy scene in this subjective description example.

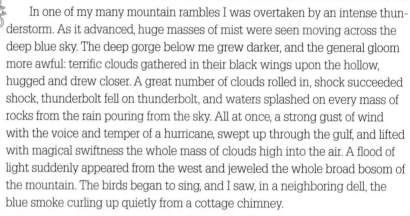

In one of my many mountain rambles I was overtaken by an intense thunderstorm. As it advanced, huge masses of mist were seen moving across the deep blue sky. The deep gorge below me grew darker, and the general gloom more awful: terrific clouds gathered in their black wings upon the hollow, hugged and drew closer. A great number of clouds rolled in, shock succeeded shock, thunderbolt fell on thunderbolt, and waters splashed on every mass of rocks from the rain pouring from the sky. All at once, a strong gust of wind with the voice and temper of a hurricane, swept up through the gulf, and lifted with magical swiftness the whole mass of clouds high into the air. A flood of light suddenly appeared from the west and jeweled the whole broad bosom of the mountain. The birds began to sing, and I saw, in a neighboring dell, the blue smoke curling up quietly from a cottage chimney.

(Adapted from *A World of Art* by Henry M. Sayre)

Blended Objective-Subjective Description Example

The following is an example of student Mariella's description paragraph called "Winter's Desolation":

¹Wellington Beach, a small village located on the shores of Lake Ontario, was **desolate** in the winter. ²The sting of cold, northern air replaced summer's breeze that smelled like the scent of suntan lotion, seaweed, and French fries. ³In the

desolate having an unpleasant emptiness

center of town, shops were boarded up, and bars and restaurants drew few patrons. ⁴Emptied of the large groups of vacationing tourists, Main Street became a lonely road for a handful of residents braving the cold and snow to pick up groceries or to stop at the local post office. ⁵Along the sidewalk, dried up, brittle leaves surrendered to being tossed aimlessly with sudden gusts of wind. ⁶Peeking up through the snow that blanketed the ground were dried flower stems, a stark reminder of the splendid color that had once graced the frozen bed beneath the drift. ⁷Beyond the town, the beaches were deserted, left to stray dogs and washed up trash. ⁸Jutting out into the lake, the empty fishing piers became resting spots for migrating birds. ⁹The wind howled eerily through the pillars and walkway boards. ¹⁰Lapping around the piers and across the lake, tiny white-capped waves formed as the wind pushed against the icy water. ¹¹With boats laid to rest in dry docks, the horizon seemed without end. ¹²Winter had etched itself on the town, bringing desolation with it.

PRACTICE 8.1   Analyzing a Descriptive Paragraph

Answer the questions about the paragraph you just read, "Winter's Desolation."

1. Underline the topic sentence.
2. What is the dominant impression, the distinctive feature that describes the topic?

   _____

3. List three details that support the dominant impression.

   _____

4. List one detail that is a fact and one detail that is a personal impression.

   Factual detail: _____

   Personal impression detail: _____

5. What is the method of organization?

   _____

- -

DESCRIPTIVE PARAGRAPH ESSENTIALS

The purpose of the descriptive paragraph is to present a clear picture of a person, place, event, object, or concept. In a subjective or blended descriptive paragraph, the main point is called the *dominant impression*, which is the one distinctive feature that best describes the topic. All of the details support the dominant impression. An effective descriptive paragraph has these essential elements:

1. The description focuses on a dominant impression, which is the one distinctive feature that best describes the topic.

2. The supporting details work together to present a clear picture of the dominant impression.
3. The supporting details are both factual and sensory (related to the physical senses of touch, smell, taste, sight, and hearing).
4. The method of organization is either spatial order or order of importance.
5. Words show instead of tell.

Prewriting the Descriptive Paragraph

Decide Your Topic and Purpose When deciding on your own description topic or responding to an assigned topic, consider the following:

1. **Choose a topic that can be described in one paragraph.** For example, a description of a shopping mall would require more than one paragraph.
2. **Choose a topic that will achieve one of these purposes:**
   - to make a scene memorable
   - to cause the reader to experience an emotion
   - to create a mood or atmosphere
   - to bring someone or something to life
3. **Choose a topic that you have a strong reaction to.** Your strong physical or emotional reaction to a topic will add intensity to your description.

PRACTICE Evaluating Topics for Description Paragraphs
8.2
Explain why each of the following topics would be suitable or unsuitable for a descriptive paragraph.

1. paintings in a large museum

_____

2. a disorganized workplace

_____

3. the snowy evening as viewed through a window

_____

4. a restroom in a service station

_____

5. a soccer game

_____

Understand the Dominant Impression The main point in a descriptive paragraph is called the dominant impression. The **dominant impression** is the one special quality or feature of the topic being described that stands out from all the others. For example, in the paragraph about the thunderstorm in the beginning of this chapter, the writer chose the word *intense* as his dominant impression because it was the feature that stood out the most for him.

You may have many reactions to a topic, but the dominant impression is the strongest. Because the dominant impression is personal, two writers who describe a waiting room in a doctor's office may choose very different dominant impressions. One may describe the waiting room as peaceful, while the other may describe it as frightening.

PRACTICE Developing Dominant Impressions

8.3 Think of a dominant impression for each of the following topics.

1. a home that is in poor condition

_____

2. a fast-food restaurant at dinnertime

_____

3. a car in a junkyard

_____

4. a young child who is lost in a large store

_____

5. traffic

_____

Develop Ideas for Your Topic Prewriting for a descriptive paragraph involves developing factual and sensory details. Factual details are words that explain things such as physical characteristics, names, dates, locations, and numbers. Sensory details are words and phrases that help the reader see, feel, hear, smell, taste, and touch the topic. Both factual and sensory details are necessary in a descriptive paragraph.

Factual Details Factual details provide the framework for the descriptive details. The objective description of the Bic Matic mechanical pencil that you read on page 130 contains many factual details.

The following chart contains suggestions for ways to develop the factual descriptions of people, places, and objects:

People	physical features, such as facial features (eyes, hair, mouth, facial hair), coloring, height, build, age, clothing, posture, speech; mannerisms (things that a person does repeatedly with face, hands, or voice that the person may not be aware of)
Places	location, size, weather, scenery, buildings/structures, objects, life forms, design
Objects	color, shape, size, texture, material, amount, pattern/design, ingredients, age, components, or parts

PRACTICE Developing Factual Details

8.4 Write three factual details for each of the following topics:

1. walking outside on a very hot or very cold day

_____

2. taking a shower or a bath

3. lying in your bed in the dark

Sensory Details Sensory details help the reader experience the topic through the five senses: sight, hearing, taste, smell, and touch. The paragraph describing the thunderstorm that you read on page 130 is filled with sensory details.

PRACTICE Developing Sensory Details
8.5
Write three sensory details for each of the same topics that you used in Practice 8.4, which are listed again here:

1. walking outside on a very hot or very cold day

2. taking a shower or a bath

3. lying in your bed in the dark

Paragraph Practice: Prewriting

Using your preferred prewriting technique, develop ideas for three of these description topics.

General Topics

an object used in a workplace
the interior of a vehicle
a worn out object
a child having a tantrum
a room at your college or your online classroom

Writing across the Curriculum Topics

Fashion: an article of clothing, accessory, or shoes
Biology: an insect or plant
Marketing: a print or online advertisement for a product or service
Music: a musical instrument
Literature: a fictional character

Use a Descriptive Details Graphic Organizer Using a descriptive details graphic organizer can be a helpful prewriting and organizing tool because it provides a place to write both subjective and objective details.

On the next page is an example of Mariella's descriptive detail graphic planner for her paragraph "Winter Desolation" in which she describes Wellington Beach, a small village located on the shores of Lake Ontario, Canada.

Mariella's Descriptive Details Graphic Organizer

Type		Details
Sensory	**See**	**Places:** boarded-up shops, deserted beaches **People:** a few people walking to post office or grocery store **Things:** waves on lake, snow on ground covering dead plants, trash on shore, leaves blowing in wind **Animals, etc.:** birds sitting on pier, stray dogs **Colors:** white snow, steel-gray sky, brown wooden boards and posts of piers, white or brown/black birds, brown, dried out plant stems, white caps on waves
	Feel	**Snow:** soft, cold, wet, solid **Air:** cold, biting, dry **Lake:** icy cold **Plants, leaves:** dry, brittle, easily broken
	Smell	**French fries:** oily, potatoes **Suntan lotion:** coconuts; seaweed, fishy **Snow and ice:** like ice cubes **Stray dogs:** wet-dog odor
	Taste	**French fries:** salty **Ice and snow:** cold and dull **Air:** tasting like metal
	Sound	**Wind:** whistles, howls like a hurt animal **Birds:** high pitched squeals (long, high sound) **Dogs:** barks, whimpers (small sounds expressing pain) **Waves:** lapping against shore **Leaves:** scraping against objects
Factual: people, places, things, and their location		Wellington Beach, small village located on the shores of Lake Ontario, Canada, shops, bars and restaurants, snow on ground, winter, stray dogs, debris, beaches, piers, Lake Erie, sidewalk, dead plants, few residents at grocery store or post office, suntan lotion, French fries, seaweed

Paragraph Practice: Developing Details

Choose one of the topics from Practices 8.4 and 8.5, and arrange the details you developed in the graphic organizer on the next page.

Descriptive Details Graphic Organizer

Type	Details	
Sensory	**See**	
	Feel	
	Smell	
	Taste	
	Sound	
Factual: people, places, things, and their location		

Narrow Your Topic and Write the Topic Sentence The topic sentence of the descriptive paragraph includes the narrowed topic, which is the person, place, or object you want to describe, and the dominant impression word or phrase.

The student whose descriptive paragraph you read about the winter scene at Wellington Beach was responding to the topic "Describe your favorite place during one season of the year." After completing her graphic planner, Mariella noticed that the details showed how deserted and lifeless Wellington Beach looked in the winter. She chose the dominant impression "desolate." When writing her topic sentence, Mariella added the physical location to her subject to make it more specific:

Wellington Beach, Ontario, a small village located on the shores of Lake Ontario, was desolate in the winter.

| TIPS | Writing Descriptive Topic Sentences |

1. **Choose only one dominant impression.** The dominant impression guides your selection of supporting details. Writing about more than one dominant impression would be confusing to the reader.

> **Two dominant impressions**: During the dinner hour, the local supermarket was full of energetic activity and was crowded.

> **One dominant impression**: During the dinner hour, the local supermarket was full of energetic activity.

2. **Choose a *specific* dominant impression word or phrase.** Choosing a vague dominant impression will not help the reader picture the topic or share the writer's experience.

> **Vague dominant impression**: The English classroom in Building 48 was small.

> **Specific dominant impression**: The English classroom in Building 48 was cramped.

3. **Avoid using a fact as the dominant impression.** A place's location, a person's name or relationship to you, a physical feature, or an object's owner or origin are facts, not distinctive features.

Fact	Dominant Impression
On March 18, 1925, the deadliest tornado in United States history killed 689 people and injured 2000.	The tornado's destructive force was devastating.
The *Mona Lisa* is a portrait of a woman painted by Leonardo DaVinci in the sixteenth century.	The *Mona Lisa* is a portrait of a woman whose facial expression is mysterious.
The Galapagos Islands are located in the eastern Pacific Ocean, 604 miles off the west coast of South America.	The abundant plants that grow on the Galapagos Islands are unique.

PRACTICE   Evaluating Descriptive Topic Sentences

8.6   Explain what is wrong with each of the following descriptive topic sentences. If a topic sentence is good, write "good." The first one has been completed for you.

1. Dr. Martin Cooper is considered the inventor of the first portable handset and the first person to make a call on a portable cell phone in April 1973.

_____

2. Tom O'Brien's abandoned meat packing plant on Federal Street is old.

_____

3. The equipment in Iron Man Gym is rusty and old-fashioned.

_____

4. County Youth Detention Center in Alligator Bay is a demoralizing place.

_____

5. The economy airplane seat was uncomfortable.

_____

Paragraph Practice: Writing a Topic Sentence

Look over the details for your descriptive paragraph (see page 136), and write a topic sentence. Be sure your topic is specific and the sentence includes a dominant impression.

Organizing and Drafting the Descriptive Paragraph

Develop Details that Support the Dominant Impression All of the details for the descriptive paragraph must support the dominant impression. Therefore, you need to carefully evaluate your details. Remove those details that are vague or unrelated. You may discover that you need to do some additional prewriting to develop new sensory and descriptive details so that you will have enough information to support your dominant impression.

PRACTICE   Choosing Details that Support the Dominant Impression

8.7   For each of the topic sentences, circle the dominant impression. Then circle the letters of the detail sentences that support the dominant impression.

1. **Topic sentence:** My child's daycare classroom is a colorful environment.

   a. The yellow-green walls are covered with children's paintings hung with masking tape.

   b. On the left side of the room, a big blue plastic bucket holds trucks, wooden puzzles, dolls, and bright-colored boxes of board games.

   c. Cartoon character sheets and pillowcases cover the mattresses and pillows on the three cribs in the back of the room.

   d. The child-care workers are very caring people.

   e. The children put their backpacks in a locker.

2. **Topic sentence:** Ever since my son was born, my bedroom has become a messy scene.

   a. Piles of shoe boxes, some empty and others with missing lids, have accumulated behind the door so that it cannot open all the way.

   b. Squeezed against the left wall is my big king-size bed.

   c. The baby wakes up two to three times a night.

   d. Right next to the bed is the baby's crib filled with stuffed animals and clothes that need to be folded and put away.

   e. The sight of the colorful clothes scattered across the floor looks like the result of a storm.

3. **Topic sentence:** The removal of the grand old oak tree outside my high school brought about a sentimental remembrance of the past.

   a. The tree, taller than the three-story school it shaded, had a trunk so thick that a person could hide behind it and never be seen.

   b. To make way for new housing developments, builders have cleared the land of native plants and trees.

c. In a storm, the branches banged on the walls and windows so loudly that we could hardly hear the teacher.

d. The fall season was the best time for sitting under that tree, for the leaves would fall into piles on top of our books.

e. In the spring and summer, during our lunch break, we sat comfortably shaded under that wonderful tree with our shoes off while studying or listening to music.

Paragraph Practice: Choosing Details that Support Your Dominant Impression

Looking back at your descriptive paragraph graphic organizer, evaluate the sensory and factual details to see whether any of them support the dominant impression in your topic sentence. Circle the details that should be included. You may find it helpful to create a list of only the details that are relevant so that you will not be distracted by those details that you do not plan to use. Prewrite to add more details if you need them.

Organize Your Supporting Details After collecting all of the supporting details to support your dominant impression, you are ready to organize the details into a plan for your paragraph.

Choose one of three patterns to organize the details in a descriptive paragraph: spatial order, order of importance, or the five senses.

- **Spatial order**: arrangement according to their position in physical space, for example left to right, top to bottom, front to back, outside to inside, and so on. For example, if you were describing the inside of a store, you could start at the entrance and end up at the back of the store.
- **Order of importance**: arrangement according to how interesting, significant, or memorable they are. Instead of describing the inside of a store from front to back, you could describe it by starting with the most impressive feature and end with the least impressive feature.
- **Order by five senses**: arrangement according to each sense. For example when describing an ice cream sundae, you could start with how it looks (sense of sight) and proceed through each of the senses.

Writing Reminder. For more on scratch outlines, see Chapter 3.

Once you decide on a plan, you may want to write a scratch outline to keep you on track when you write.

Mariella used spatial order for her paragraph "Winter's Desolation." She started her description at the center of town and ended at Wellington Beach. The following is her scratch outline.

Mariella's Scratch Outline

Topic sentence: Wellington Beach, Ontario, a small village located on the shores of Lake Ontario, was desolate in the winter. was desolate in the winter.

1. In the air

    —sting of cold air

2. In the center of town

    —boarded up shops

    —few patrons at bars and restaurants

—no tourists

—snow covered sidewalk

—withered, brittle leaves tossed in wind

—dried flower stems

3. At the beaches

—deserted

—stray dogs, washed up debris

4. At the fishing piers

—empty except for migrating birds

—eerie sound of wind

5. Across the lake

—white capped waves

6. On the horizon

—no boats, endless horizon

Write the First Draft

Use Memorable Images Using memorable images will bring your description to life for the reader. Here are three ways to spice up your writing.

1. **Use images that appeal to the five senses.** In the prewriting section of this chapter, you explored your topic by thinking of words and phrases for each of the five senses: see, feel, smell, taste, sound. Kristin uses several senses in her description:

   FEEL   SEE

   As the sun slowly heats under the clear blue morning sky, the clean, crisp

   SMELL

   morning air smells of freshly cut grass and tree sap.

2. **Use strong, active verbs to show movement.** Describing actions with strong verbs helps the reader feel a part of the scene.

   The tires screeched and two cars slammed into each other, metal striking metal. Smoke exploded from the air bag, filling the car's interior and causing me to cough and gasp for breath.

3. **Make comparisons.** Making comparisons is another way to bring description to life. Comparisons show how two things that may not seem to be alike are similar in one way. A **simile** is a comparison that uses the words *like* or *as*. Notice the comparisons in the following similes:

   The overcooked rice tasted *like* coarse pebbles.

   The newly washed floor is *as* slippery *as* an ice-covered road.

PRACTICE   Writing Similes

8.8   Use each of the words below to write a sentence containing a simile. Compare the word to something that relates and conveys a picture in the reader's mind.

1. river _____

2. cloud _____

3. eyes _____

4. candy _____

Add Connectors: Transitional Words and Expression   Descriptive paragraphs use either spatial order or order of importance connectors and transition words and expressions to help the reader visualize the topic. The following charts list common transitions for spatial order.

Common Transition Words for Spatial Order

above	along the edge	at the right	up
on the side	beneath	on top	in the center
below	over	under	behind
at the bottom	surrounding	straight ahead	around
at the front	in front of	opposite	at the top
next to	nearby	beside	at the rear
in the forefront	in the foreground	in the distance	beyond
across	under	within sight	out of sight
in the background	down	near	adjacent
at the left			

PRACTICE   Describing Spatial Order

8.9   Study the photograph of a Japanese garden.

For each of the objects from the photograph listed on page 142, write a sentence describing its location. Use the chart of transitional words for spatial order to describe location.

1. waterfall

_____

2. pond

_____

3. rocks

_____

4. flowers

_____

5. trees

_____

Paragraph Practice: Writing the First Draft

Using the topic sentence and details you developed, write a first draft of your descriptive paragraph.

Revising, Editing, and Proofreading

Revise your draft by looking at one element at a time: Support, Organization, Connectors and transitions, and Style. The following Revision Checklist contains the SOCS elements as they apply to descriptive paragraphs.

REVISION CHECKLIST FOR A DESCRIPTIVE PARAGRAPH

Element	Revision Checkpoints
Topic	☐ The topic is meaningful and memorable.
	☐ The topic is limited enough to be described in one paragraph.
	☐ The topic achieves one of these purposes: creates a mood, brings someone or something to life, conveys an emotion, or makes the topic memorable.
Topic Sentence	☐ The topic sentence contains the narrowed topic and the dominant impression.
	☐ The narrowed topic is expressed specifically and concisely.
	☐ The dominant impression is described with a specific word or phrase.
Support	☐ The supporting details are factual.
	☐ All supporting details describe the dominant impression.
Organization	☐ The paragraph follows spatial order or order of importance.
Connectors and Transitions	☐ Appropriate transitions for either spatial order, order of importance, or by five senses provide coherence.
Style	☐ Writing is clear, concise Standard Written English.
	☐ Tone is appropriate for a college audience.
	☐ Specific details create reader interest through the use of sensory images, comparisons, and active verbs.
	☐ Sentences are varied.

Peer Review

Reminder. For feedback on your writing, have someone read your paper and make comments on the Peer Review Response sheet in Chapter 4, page 55.

Paragraph Practice: Revising

Using the Revision Checklist for a Descriptive Paragraph, revise your descriptive paragraph.

Check Grammar, Punctuation, and Spelling As you reread your paper to check for grammar, punctuation, and spelling errors, pay special attention to possible errors that may arise in descriptive paragraphs. For example, be sure that you have not shifted verb forms. Another area to look over is word choice. If you have used a thesaurus, be sure that you know the meanings of words and that you have used and spelled these words correctly. Finally, check your use of commas when using two or more adjectives in front of a word to describe it.

PRACTICE Revising and Editing a Descriptive Paragraph

8.10   Revise and edit Roslyn's paragraph. Then answer the questions below.

¹My brother's experience of almost dying was a nightmare brought to life. ²In the sunlit kitchen, as I poured freshly squeezed orange juice into a glass. ³I heard my mother scream as if someone had just stab her in the heart and twist the knife. ⁴Dropping the glass and leaving the broken pieces in the orange liquid pooled around it. ⁵I ran into the living room to find my brother, blue-faced with foam coming from his mouth. ⁶His eyes were lifeless. ⁷With tears burning my cheeks like acid, I lie my brother on the floor. ⁸My mother's screaming suddenly sounded far away and mufled compared to the extremely loud drumbeat of my heart. ⁹I stuck my hand down his throat and pulled three marble out. ¹⁰As I raised my hand, I felt his saliva streaming down my hand and dripping off of the marbles. ¹¹I looked at those marbles and realized that I had just beaten death.

Questions on Revising

1. Underline the topic sentence. What is the narrowed topic? What is the dominant impression?

2. What method of organization does the writer use?

3. Show that the writer has used memorable details by giving an example of a sensory image, a comparison, and an active verb.

4. What verb tense does the writer use?

_____

Questions on Editing and Proofreading

5. Two sentences in this paragraph have verb tense problems. Find the sentences and write the corrected sentences here.

_____

6. Two sentences are fragments. Correct each fragment by adding it to the sentence before or after.

_____

_____

_____

_____

_____

7. One sentence contains a spelling error. Write the corrected word here.

_____

8. One sentence contains an error with plurals. Write the corrected form here.

_____

Paragraph Practice: Editing and Proofreading

Edit and proofread your descriptive paragraph. Check that your final draft is complete, accurate, and error-free.

Paragraph Writing Assignments

Help Desk

Rodney's description paragraph assignment was to write about a place that he would not like to return to. He chose the detention center. Read Rodney's rough draft and give him some specific suggestions about how he can improve the paragraph.

> [1]The juvenile hall unit is a degrading place for youths facing criminal charges. [2]The guard station is in the middle of the room. [3]Some cells have as many as three people crowded into them. [4]The cells are eight feet by ten feet. [5]In the cells are a toilet, a sink with no running water, and mattresses to sleep on. [6]On the left and right sides of the room are cells. [7]Gang symbols have been carved into the walls. [8]The cells on one side of the room face the cells on the other side of the room. [9]The cells stink; they smell like sweat, stale food, and urine. [10]The segregation unit is in the back of the room where there are a group of six cells. In those cells are youths who are dangerous or that have diseases. [11]Boredom and anger are common when people are locked up for more than sixteen hours a day.

Group Activity: Working Together to Write an Objective Description

In small groups of two or three, choose an object belonging to one person in the group such as a stapler, a cell phone, a lipstick, an item with a zipper, a calculator—any object that has more than one part. For example, a simple ballpoint pen consists of an outer plastic casing, a tube of ink, and a cap to keep the tube in place. Your assignment is to write an objective physical description of the object in one paragraph.

Reading and Writing across the Curriculum: Art

The paragraph describing a thunderstorm in the beginning of this chapter is reflected in Thomas Cole's 1836 painting *The Oxbow*. Cole painted it ten years after he had written about the storm. The following is a description of the painting:

The Oxbow captures the Catskill Mountains scene after the storm by presenting themes of light and dark. In the left side of the painting, Cole depicts the wilderness. The two trees at the left have been blasted by lightning. The forest is dense and frightening, and a thunderstorm rolls across the mountainous landscape. This wild scene contrasts dramatically with the civilized valley floor on the right. Here, bathed in serene sunlight, are cultivated fields, hillsides cleared of timber, and farmhouses from whose chimneys rise gentle plumes of smoke. The Connecticut River itself flows in a giant arc that reinforces the tranquility of the scene. Cole's umbrella juts out across the river from the rock at the right. Just below it, to the left, is Cole himself, now at work at his easel. The furious forces of nature have moved on, and the artist captures the scene just as civilization would tame the wild.

(Adapted from *A World of Art* by Henry M. Sayre)

Write a description of Thomas Cole's painting below, *The Fountain of Vaucluse*. Before writing, spend some time looking at the painting.

What is your immediate impression? What is distinctive about it? Choose a prewriting strategy or graphic organizer to write down both subjective and objective details. Once you have picked a dominant impression, follow the steps in this chapter to complete your paragraph.

Write about an Image

Study this photograph that was taken after the devastating Hurricane Katrina in 2005. Fleeing to safety, many people had to abandon their pets. What feeling or feature stands out the most to you? Write a descriptive paragraph from one of these points of view: one of the dogs, a representative from Animal Rescue, or an owner of one of the dogs.

Comment on a Contemporary Issue

Did you ever buy a product that promised more than it delivered? What descriptive information convinced you to try the product? Now that you have had a disappointing experience with the product, think of a dominant impression to describe it. Write a paragraph describing the product as you see it now.

LO 3 The Descriptive Essay

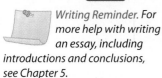

Writing Reminder. For more help with writing an essay, including introductions and conclusions, see Chapter 5.

The description essay has the same purpose as the description paragraph: to create a clear mental picture of a person, place, event, object, or concept. It uses objective details, subjective details, or a combination of the two. The description essay follows the same organization patterns as the description paragraph: spatial order, order of importance, or five senses order. The description graphic organizers on pages 136 and 151 can also be used to prewrite, plan, and draft your essay.

Thesis Statement

The thesis statement for a descriptive essay expresses a dominant impression about a narrowed topic. The thesis statement can be expressed in either of two ways:

Two-part thesis: The subject to be described + dominant impression.

The massive January 2010 earthquake, centered in Port-au-Prince, Haiti, brought considerable destruction.

Three-part thesis: The subject to be described + dominant impression + details describing the dominant impression.

The massive January 2010 earthquake, centered in Port-au-Prince, Haiti, brought considerable destruction to buildings, roads, and people.

Body Paragraphs

The body paragraphs in the descriptive essay can be organized by using spatial order, order of importance, or five senses order as illustrated in the chart below.

Spatial Order	Order of Importance	Five Sense Order
1. National Palace	1. Displacement	1. Sound: of buildings crumbling, people screaming, shouting, crying; glass breaking
2. City Hall	2. Injuries	2. Sight: dust and debris
3. Port-au-Prince Cathedral	3. Death	3. Feeling: wobbly ground, shaking buildings, blood
4. Homes		4. Taste: dust
		5. Smell: smoke

Description Essay Example

Student Amy Kahn describes damage to her family's home after Hurricane Wilma.

Amy Kahn

Professor Markus

College Preparatory Writing Skills

2 April 2010

The Aftermath

[1]   The outer fringes of the hurricane arrived, bringing with it waves of heavy rain that thrashed against the windows. The wind suddenly increased its speed, lifting and hurling tree limbs and debris into the air. Concrete tiles were torn from neighboring roofs, assaulting the roof and rear of the home with loud thumps as it stood defenselessly. Suddenly, breaking glass and a change in air pressure indicated that the storm entered the house. The family members rushed into the only windowless room in which a full-size washer and dryer occupied most of the space. They huddled together for the duration of the storm, listening to the storm's progress on their portable radio. After several frightening hours, the winds and rain died down, and the weatherman reported that the worst was over. When the family opened the laundry room door, they discovered their house had been severely damaged by the hurricane.

[2]   The master bedroom suffered the worst damage. The glass in the two-panel sliding doors had been shattered into hundreds of tiny pieces and strewn across the large room. The curtain rod dangled from one corner of the window, and the curtains lay bunched together in a tangled, wet lump on the floor. Next to the doors, an antique brass lamp lay on its side, dented and dripping water onto the wood night table, which was swelling from having taken in so much water. Rain had soaked the carpet near the window and was quickly spreading to the dry areas in the room. Leaves, branches, and palm fronds lay across the once-pristine white bedding. In the middle of the king-size bed, a large roof tile rested quietly now after its destructive flight through the window. Across from the bed was a deep gash in the wall.

3   The other rooms in the house had sustained damage as well. Some of the windowpanes in the bathroom had broken, and pieces of glass had fallen into the tub and were now floating in several inches of rainwater. Next to the bathroom, the college student's room did not escape the hurricane's fury either. Rain poured in through yet another broken window. The recently completed research paper lay on the desk in a pool of water next to the laptop, a gift from his grandparents. Torn wall posters hung precariously, curling from the dampness, and clothing that had been left in a huge pile on the floor was wet and covered with debris, creating an unpleasant odor within the room.

4   The storm's fury not only damaged the interior of the house, but also the exterior. The pale yellow stucco exterior had been a target for flying debris. Cracks, gaping holes, and a variety of roof tile imprints were evident on the back wall. The roof itself had lost thirty percent of its tiles; some looked as if they had slid from their original places while others balanced precariously at the edges of the roof. Scattered in disarray round the perimeter of the house was a collection of stones, roofing materials, and other unidentifiable objects. In the front of the house, the large ficus tree, which had once provided shady relief from the sun's intense heat, had been uprooted and had fallen across the driveway, imprisoning the family's car in the garage. The screening from the patio had been torn from its frame and flapped like shredded ribbons in the wind.

5   The hurricane's unusual path had surprised everyone in the town. The storm, which had travelled across the Caribbean Sea into the Gulf of Mexico, made an unexpected turn and moved quickly across the state. Although their house had sustained considerable damage, the cleanup process would take some time, and the power would be down for several weeks, the family felt fortunate to be alive.

PRACTICE   Analyzing a Description Essay

8.11   Answer the following questions about "The Aftermath."

1. Underline the thesis statement. What is the dominant impression?

_____

2. What technique does the writer use for the lead-in?

_____

3. Underline the topic sentences for each of the body paragraphs. How does each one connect to the thesis statement?

_____

4. The writer uses sensory details. List examples for sight, smell, and sound.

_____

_____

_____

_____

5. In addition to referring to the thesis, what point does the author make in the conclusion? Underline the sentence.

_____

Descriptive Essay Graphic Organizer

Using a description graphic organizer will help you place your details in the appropriate order. The descriptive essay graphic organizer shown on page 151 can be changed to suit your needs by adding body paragraphs and details.

Descriptive Essay Graphic Organizer

Introduction

Lead-in:

Bridge:

Thesis Statement with Dominant Impression:

Body Paragraphs: Write as many body paragraphs as you need.

Topic Sentence:

Support: Spatial order, order of importance or sense order

Descriptive Details:

Conclusion

Use Effective Closing Technique.

Essay Writing Assignments

Write about an Image

What do you think happened in the photograph above? What was your first reaction to it? Choose the dominant impression, the one special quality or feature that stands out from all the others, that best describes the photograph. You may have many reactions to this photograph, but the dominant impression is the strongest.

Write an essay as if you were describing the scene for a major news network. Use vivid sensory and factual descriptive details to support your dominant impression.

Writing Topics for a Descriptive Essay

For your descriptive essay, choose one of these options:

- from paragraph to essay: expand the paragraph you wrote in the paragraph section of this chapter
- any of the writing topics in the paragraph section of this chapter
- any topic from the following list:
    a place where a sporting or entertainment event is held
    a home appliance
    an electronic communication or gaming device
    a piece of equipment used in a workplace
    a crowd of people

Writing across the Curriculum Topics

Ecology: plant or animal life in an area you are familiar with
Fashion Design: elements used to show clothing on display at a store, such as tables, wall décor, posters, banners, light effects, and video
Hospitality Management: an unusual vacation spot
Architecture: a building from any period in history
Computer Science: your college or university website or the website of one you would like to attend

Peer Review Reminder. For feedback on your writing, have someone read your paper and make comments on the Peer Review Response sheet in Chapter 4, page 55.

English Success Tip: Using a Thesaurus

Descriptive writing creates a clear mental picture of a topic in the reader's mind. Finding the right words to create a mental image or to avoid repeating the same word can be challenging. Using a thesaurus can help. A **thesaurus** is a dictionary of synonyms, words that have the same meanings. *Roget's Thesaurus* is one of the most widely used thesauruses and can be found in print and online at Bartleby.com.

1. Use synonyms that match your writing style. Unusual, long, or impressive-sounding words are not necessarily better choices than simple ones.
2. Choose synonyms that are Standard English, not slang or informal.
3. Be sure to know the meanings of both the original word and the word you want to use to replace it. The synonym may not have the same meaning. Check the definitions in a dictionary.

For support in meeting this chapter's objectives, log in to www.mywritinglab.com, go to the Study Plan tab, click on **Description** and choose **Paragraph Development—Describing and Essay Development—Describing** from the list of subtopics. Read and view the videos and resources in the Review Materials section, and then complete the Recall, Apply, and Write exercises in the Activities section. You can check your scores and overall progress by using the Gradebook.

CHAPTER 9

Process

Learning Objectives

After working through this chapter, you will be able to:

LO 1 Describe process as a form of writing that explains how to do something, or how something happens or works.

LO 2 Write a process paragraph.

LO 3 Write a process essay.

LO 1 What Is Process?

Process is a form of writing that explains how to do something or how something happens or works. The two types of process writing are the How-to Process and the How Something Happens or Works Process.

The **How-to Process** paragraph, also called *directional process*, gives step-by-step instructions so that the reader can perform the process. Examples of this type of process writing are how to do a chemistry experiment, how to use a piece of equipment, or how to get to a particular location.

The **How Something Happens or Works Process**, also called *informational process*, explains a process rather than giving step-by-step instructions. The reader does not have to perform it. The purpose is to explain, analyze, or inform the reader about the process. Examples of this type of process writing are explaining how a computer central processing unit (CPU) functions or how a U.S. President is elected.

QuickWrite

What is a process you do every day? Brush your teeth? Text a friend? Cook a meal? Take a moment and list the steps in that process.

Process in College Writing

Process is used in many kinds of college writing assignments. For example, a How-to Process paper in nursing may explain the procedure for cleaning a wound. In biology, you may write about how breathing supplies oxygen to our cells. How-to Process is also frequently used in culinary arts, for example, how to remove scales from a fish. How Something Happens or Works Process writing is useful in a criminal justice course, such as explaining how electronic evidence is collected. An assignment in a pharmacy technician course might be to describe how drugs are absorbed in the body.

LO 2 The Process Paragraph

The two types of process paragraphs, the How-to Process and the How Something Happens or Works Process, are illustrated in the two examples on the same topic that follow.

How-to (Directional) Process Example

¹To satisfy customers' needs as a restaurant server, follow these steps. ²First, greet the guests. ³After greeting the guests, introduce and suggestively sell beverages and appetizers. ⁴Next, bring the guests their beverages. ⁵Give the guests time to make selections from the menu. ⁶Then, return to the table to take the entrée orders. ⁷Begin at a specific point at the table and take the orders **clockwise**. ⁸When the entrées are ready, bring them to the table. ⁹After the guests have taken a few bites of their entrées, check to see that everything is to their liking. ¹⁰At this time, ask if the guests would like another drink. ¹¹As soon as the guests are finished with their entrees, clear the entrée plates. At the same time, suggestively sell desserts. ¹³Recommend, describe, or show the desserts. ¹⁴Also, offer after-dinner drinks and coffee. ¹⁵Following these steps will make customers happy and increase the possibility of a generous tip.

(Adapted from *Hospitality Management* by John R. Walker)

clockwise in the direction that the hands of a clock move on an analog clock face

---

PRACTICE 9.1   Analyzing a How-to Process Paragraph

Answer the following questions about the paragraph you just read.

1. Underline the topic sentence.
2. How does the reader know that the paragraph is a How-to Process?

_____

3. Three of the steps in the paragraph take more than one sentence to explain. Which steps are they?

_____

_____

4. Which sentences command the reader to do something? What are the subjects of those sentences?

_____

_____

5. What method of organization is used for the supporting details?

_____

How Something Happens or Works (Informational) Process Example

¹Serving guests in a restaurant is a process that is designed to satisfy customers' needs. ²First, the server introduces himself or herself, offers a variety of beverages and/or specials, or invites guests to select form the menu. ³This is known as suggestive selling. ⁴The server then takes the entrée

orders. ⁵Often, when taking orders, the server begins at a designated point at the table and takes the orders clockwise from that point. ⁶In this way, the server will automatically know which person is having a particular dish. ⁷When the entrees are ready, the server brings them to the table. ⁸He or she checks a few minutes later to see if everything is to the guests' liking and perhaps asks if they would like another beverage. ⁹Good servers are also encouraged, when possible, to help clear tables. ¹⁰Busers and servers may clear the entrée plates, while servers suggestively sell desserts by describing, recommending, or showing the desserts. ¹¹Coffee and after-dinner cocktails are also offered.

(Adapted from *Hospitality Management* by John R. Walker)

PRACTICE 9.2   Analyzing a How Something Works Process Paragraph

Answer the following questions about the paragraph you just read.

1. Underline the topic sentence.
2. How do you know that the paragraph is a How Something Happens or Works paragraph?

   _____

3. What is the difference between the sentences used to explain the processes in the two example paragraphs?

   _____

   _____

4. What method of organization is used for the supporting details?

   _____

5. Which of the two example paragraphs could be used to train a new restaurant server? Why?

   _____

PROCESS PARAGRAPH ESSENTIALS

An effective process paragraph has these elements:

1. A process paragraph makes a point about the process to explain how the process is useful, why it is important, or assure readers that they can perform it.
2. The supporting details work together to give all the necessary steps in the process or the appropriate amount of information to understand the process.
3. The process lists any necessary equipment or materials.
4. The process is presented in chronological order or order of importance, depending on the type of process and its purpose.
5. The process gives advice about possible problems and suggests how to resolve them.
6. The process is explained in the present or past tense depending on the type of process and its purpose.

Prewriting the Process Paragraph

Decide Your Topic and Purpose When deciding on your own process topic or responding to an assigned topic, consider the following:

1. **Choose a process that you know well.** Having mastered or understood the process, you will be able to explain it, knowing that your instructions work.
2. **Choose a process that can be explained in a single paragraph.** Some topics are too narrow. For example, how to save a file on a computer can be explained in just one or two sentences. On the other hand, some topics require too many steps to be explained completely in one paragraph. Giving a health care worker instructions for bathing an adult sounds like a simple process, but it involves many steps that must be followed carefully.
3. **Choose a process that can be easily explained without being too technical.** You may have the knowledge and ability to perform a process that may seem easy to you but may be too technical for your reader. Installing a home security system, for example, requires knowledge of electrical terminology and circuitry, which a general reader will not have.
4. **Choose a topic that many people do not know how to do.** Writing about a process that most people are familiar with, like how to brush your teeth, may not interest the reader.

PRACTICE   Evaluating Topics for a Process Paragraph

9.3   Explain why each of the following topics would be suitable or unsuitable for a process paragraph.

1. how to boil water in a microwave

_____

2. how a tornado forms

_____

3. how to pack a suitcase

_____

4. how to play soccer

_____

5. how to rebuild a car engine

_____

Develop Ideas for Your Topic Prewriting for a process paragraph involves listing the steps in order from start to finish. Kyra decided to write her paragraph on how to do an exercise called a stationary lunge. Here is her list of steps:

> Kyra' List of Steps
>
> 1. Stand comfortably with the feet slightly apart and the hands on the hips.
>
> 2. With one foot, step forward until the knee is over the top of that foot and is in
>
>   a vertical line with the ankle. When lowering into the lunge, the front knee

should not extend past the toe. Only the tip of the toe should be visible. The lower knee gets close to the ground but does not touch. Don't let knee roll inward or outward. Keep the weight on the heel of the extended foot. Keep the back straight and the shoulders back. Don't let the body roll forward. If you can't lower to 90 degrees, lower as much as you can.

3. Put the weight on the heel and use the front leg to push the body up and back to the standing position.

4. Repeat the lunge 10 times stepping forward with the same foot and pushing the body up and back.

5. Using the opposite foot, follow the same process of stepping forward into a lunge and pushing the body up and back 10 times.

Paragraph Practice: Developing Ideas

Practice developing ideas by listing the steps for two of these How-to process paragraph topics.

General Topics

improve a grade in a specific course
operate a simple, useful device found around the home
perform a simple task at home, school, or work
choose the best plan for cell phone, cable television, or Internet service
improve the appearance of a car interior or exterior or a room in the home
or workplace

Writing across the Curriculum Topics

Fashion: dress to impress in personal life or at work
Reading: improve a reading skill using a technique
Communication: convince someone to do something
Fitness: do a particular exercise with or without weights
Finance: save or spend money carelessly

Narrow Your Topic and Write the Topic Sentence The topic sentence of the process paragraph identifies the process and makes a point about it. Your point will express what you want to tell the reader about the process. Below are the topic sentences from the two example paragraphs you read at the beginning of the chapter.

How-to Process Topic Sentence
To satisfy customers' needs as a restaurant server, follow these steps.

How Something Happens or Works Process Topic Sentence
Serving guests in a restaurant is a process that is designed to satisfy customers' needs.

> **TIPS** | **Writing Process Topic Sentences**
>
> 1. **State the process specifically and concisely.**
>
> | Process not specifically stated | Braids are fashionable and very popular today. |
> | --- | --- |
> | Process stated specifically | Braiding hair takes practice but can be learned by following these steps. |
>
> 2. **Make a point about the process.** The reader needs to know what he or she will be able to do or why the process is important.
>
> | What the reader should be able to do | Why the process is important |
> | --- | --- |
> | No point: Bathing a dog involves six steps. | No point: Follow these simple rules to perform a chemistry lab experiment. |
> | With a point: The frustration of bathing an uncooperative dog can be avoided by following these steps. | With a point: Follow these simple rules to guarantee a safe chemistry lab experiment. |

PRACTICE   Evaluating Process Topic Sentences

9.4   Explain what is wrong with each of the following topic sentences. If a topic sentence is good, write "good." The first one has been completed for you.

1. Follow these steps to find online sources.

   _____

2. These steps must be followed carefully.

   _____

3. To get the most meat from a turkey, follow these simple carving directions.

   _____

4. Here is how to clear a paper jam in a copier.

   _____

Paragraph Practice: Writing Topic Sentences

Look over your details for the two topics you worked on in Paragraph Practice: Developing Ideas (page 158) and write a topic sentence for each.

Organizing and Drafting the Process Paragraph

Develop Supporting Details   The reader may not know the process you are writing about; therefore, present all steps or parts of the process clearly and concisely. Keep the following points in mind:

- Include all the steps in order from the beginning of the process to the end.
- Include any equipment or materials needed.

- Tell the reader about possible difficulties or problems with any of the steps.
- Leave out obvious steps.

Using a Process Graphic Organizer Using a process graphic organizer can help you list all of the steps in order. Kyra's process graphic organizer for her topic "How to Perform a Stationary Lunge" is shown on the next page.

Paragraph Practice: Planning

Choose one of the processes you have been working on in the Paragraph Practice exercises. Using the graphic organizer on page 162, fill in the steps and other information for the process paragraph you will write. Add or subtract steps as needed.

Organize Your Supporting Details After listing all of the steps for your topic, you are ready to organize them into a plan for your process paragraph. You may want to turn your list into a scratch outline to keep you on track when you write.

Use Chronological Order or Order of Importance To organize the steps in a process paragraph, you can use either chronological order or order of importance, depending on the process you are explaining. How-to paragraphs require chronological order because the reader must perform the steps in order. In the How Something Happens or Works paragraph, you may use either pattern of organization.

PRACTICE Analyzing a How Something Happens or Works Process Paragraph

9.5 The following How Something Happens or Works paragraph explains a process in stages. Underline each sentence that states a stage in the process. Then circle the number(s) of the sentence(s) that explain each stage.

¹Fashion styles pass through a four-stage process that occurs over time. ²The cycle begins with the introduction stage when a style is introduced into the marketplace. ³At this point there is no way of knowing if the style will be popular with retail buyers and the consumer public. ⁴Therefore, due to the cost of materials and production, the styles are usually expensive. ⁵The growth stage is next. ⁶If the style is generally accepted and successful, copies are marketed at many different prices in the marketplace. ⁷During the maturity stage, the style achieves its greatest sales volume. ⁸The time of maturity might be one season or many. ⁹Not knowing when maturity will happen can leave manufacturers and sellers with merchandise that the public no longer considers fashionable. ¹⁰The final stage is the decline stage. ¹¹The style has lost its popularity. ¹²Left-over pieces are drastically reduced to prices that will sell quickly to get rid of unwanted merchandise. ¹³It is urgent to rid the inventory of such items before they are no longer desired at any price.

(Adapted from *Fashion Apparel, Accessories, and Home Furnishings* by Jay Diamond and Ellen Diamond)

Kyra's Process Graphic Organizer

Topic Sentence: The stationary lunge is an effective lower body workout, but it must be performed correctly to avoid injury.

Equipment/materials: Clothing allowing for movement and flexibility, athletic shoes to support feet.

Step 1

- Stand straight with the feet hip-width apart and the hands on the hips.

Step 2

- With one foot, step forward until the knee of that foot is over the top of the foot and is in a vertical line with the ankle.
- When lowering into the lunge, the front knee should not extend past the toe.
- Keep the front shin perpendicular to the ground.
- Also, do not lean forward on the way down, which puts stress on the back.
- During the lunge, continue to keep the back straight.

Step 3

- Put the weight on the heel of the left foot and push the body up and back to the standing position.

Step 4

- Repeat the lunge 10 times stepping forward with the same foot and pushing the body up and back.

Step 5

- Using the opposite foot, repeat the same process 10 times.

Process Graphic Organizer

Topic Sentence:

Equipment/materials:

Step 1

Step 2

Step 3

Step 4

Step 5

PRACTICE   Distinguishing between Steps and Details

9.6   The following is a set of directions for putting on a surgical face mask in a health care setting. Some of the sentences are steps and others are details. Put an "S" next to the sentences that are steps and a "D" next to sentences that are details that explain the steps.

1. Locate the top edge of the mask.

2. The mask usually has a narrow metal strip along the edge.

3. Hold the mask by the top two strings or loops.

4. Place the upper edge of the mask over the bridge of the nose, and tie the upper ties at the back of the head or secure the loops around the ears.

5. If glasses are worn, fit the upper edge of the mask under the glasses.

6. With the edge of the mask under the glasses, clouding of the glasses is less likely to occur.

7. Secure the lower edge of the mask under the chin, and tie the lower ties at the back of the neck.

8. To be effective, a mask must cover both the nose and the mouth because air moves in and out of both.

9. A secure fit prevents both the escape and the inhalation of microorganisms around the edges of the mask and the fogging of eyeglasses.

10. Wear the mask only once, and do not wear any mask longer than the manufacturer recommends or once it becomes wet.

11. A mask should be used only once because it becomes ineffective when moist.

12. Do not leave a used face mask hanging around the neck.

(Adapted from *Essentials of Nursing* by Audrey Berman et al.)

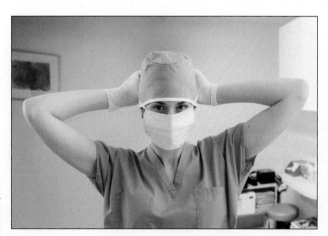
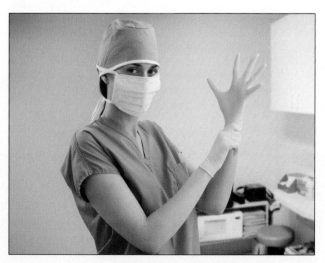

Double-Check the Steps and Details   Kyra looked at her process graphic organizer to check the accuracy of the steps. She performed the exercise several times to make sure that each step was easy to understand. Kyra also reorganized the details in Step 3. Here is her scratch outline:

Kyra's Scratch Outline

Topic sentence: The stationary lunge is an effective lower body workout, but it must be performed correctly to avoid injury.

Equipment/materials: Clothing allowing for movement and flexibility, athletic shoes to support feet

Step 1: Stand straight with the feet hip-width apart and the hands on the hips.

Step 2: With the left foot, step forward about one foot.

Step 3: Lower the body until the left knee is over the top of the left foot.

Detail 1. Keep the chest up, shoulders back, and abdominal muscles tight.

Detail 2. Do not lean forward on the way down, which puts stress on the back.

Detail 3. The left knee should not extend past the toe.

Detail 4. The right leg should be bent with the shin almost parallel to but not touching the floor.

Detail 4. The right leg should be bent with the shin parallel to but not touching the floor.

Step 4: Put the weight on the heel of the left foot and push the body up and back to the standing position.

Step 5: Repeat the lunge 10 times stepping forward with the left foot and pushing the body up and back.

Step 6: Using the opposite foot, repeat the same process 10 times.

Write the First Draft   As you write the first draft consider these elements: definitions of technical words, verb tense, and transitions and connectors.

Define Words   If your process includes technical terms or words that your reader may not know, be sure to define them. Note the two terms and the way the writer defined them in the following process paragraph on how wind makes waves:

Wind generates waves on large lakes and open seas. The frictional drag of the wind on the surface of smooth water causes it to move in small waves. Frictional drag is the rubbing of one surface against another. As the wind continues to blow, it applies more pressure to the steep side of the small wave, and wave size begins to grow. As the wind becomes stronger, short, choppy waves of all sizes appear; and as they absorb more energy, they continue to grow. When the waves reach a point at which the energy supplied the wind is equal to the energy lost by the breaking waves, they become whitecaps, waves that are white at the top. Up to a certain point, the stronger the wind, the higher the waves.

(From *Elements of Ecology* by Robert Leo Smith and Thomas M. Smith)

Choose Commands or Statements   The How-to Process uses commands. Commands are used to give orders or make requests. The subject of a command is not stated but is understood to be second person "you." The How Something Happens or Works paragraph uses statements. Statements are used to express facts and opinions.

Commands	Statements
Greet the guests.	First, the server greets the guests.
Return to the table to take entrée orders.	Then the server takes the entrée orders.

TIP   Present tense is used for How-to process paragraphs. Present or past tense is used for How Something Happens or Works process paragraphs.

PRACTICE   Editing Sentence Subjects in a Process Paragraph

9.7   After the topic sentence, each sentence in the following paragraph uses commands. Change the sentences into statements using "the student" or "he or she" as the subject. Vary the subjects of the sentences to avoid repetition. The topic sentence does not have to be changed.

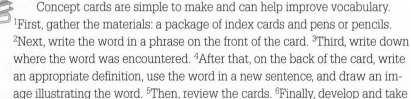

Concept cards are simple to make and can help improve vocabulary. [1]First, gather the materials: a package of index cards and pens or pencils. [2]Next, write the word in a phrase on the front of the card. [3]Third, write down where the word was encountered. [4]After that, on the back of the card, write an appropriate definition, use the word in a new sentence, and draw an image illustrating the word. [5]Then, review the cards. [6]Finally, develop and take a quiz to test learning.

(Adapted from *Bridging the Gap* by Brenda D. Smith)

Example:

1. First, the student gathers the materials: a package of index cards and pens or pencils.

_____

_____

_____

_____

_____

Add Connectors: Transitional Words and Expressions How-to process paragraphs use sequence transitional words and expressions in chronological order to label the steps and connect them.

> **Numerical sequence words**: first, second, third, next, last, the first step, the second step, etc.
>
> **General sequence words**: after this, as soon as, at the same time, during, finally, last, meanwhile, soon after, then, while

PRACTICE Adding Transitions to a Process Paragraph

9.8 Add the following transitions to the paragraph below. Use each transition once.

Following this, The next stage, The first stage, The final stage, The second stage

The conversation process consists of stages that require a choice as to what is said and how it is said. _____ is the opening, which initiates and begins the conversation. It usually starts with some kind of greeting to establish a connection between two people. _____ is feedforward. Feedforward gives the other person a general idea of the conversation's focus. _____ is the business. This is the focus of the conversation and the reason for starting the first and second stages. _____ is the feedback stage. The purpose of the feedback stage is to summarize or show that the business of the conversation is completed. _____ is the closing, which brings the conversation to an end. The way people follow these stages will depend a number of factors such as their personalities, culture, and purpose.

(Adapted from *The Interpersonal Communication Book* by Joseph A. DeVito)

Paragraph Practice: Writing a First Draft

Using your topic sentence and paragraph organizer (page 162), write a first draft of your process paragraph.

Revising, Editing, and Proofreading

Revise your draft by looking at one element at a time: Support, Organization, Connectors and transitions, and Style. The following Revision Checklist contains the SOCS elements as they apply to process paragraphs.

Revision Checklist for a Process Paragraph

Element	Revision Checkpoints
Topic	☐ The process is one that you have done before or seen many times.
	☐ The process can be explained in a single paragraph.
	☐ The process can be easily explained without being too technical.
	☐ The process is one that many people do not know how to do.
Topic Sentence	☐ The topic sentence identifies the process and makes a point about it.
	☐ The process is stated specifically and concisely.
	☐ The point explains how the process is useful, why it is important, or assures readers that they can perform it.
Support	☐ All the steps are included from the beginning of the process to the end.
	☐ Any equipment or materials are listed.
	☐ Difficulties or possible problems with any of the steps are explained.
	☐ Obvious steps are left out.
Organization	☐ The How-to process follows chronological order.
	☐ The How Something Happens or Works follows chronological order or order of importance.
	☐ Smaller steps may be grouped into larger steps.
	☐ Some steps may have details to help the reader understand or perform the step.
Connectors and Transitions	☐ Chronological order or order of importance transitions provide coherence.
Style	☐ Writing is clear, concise Standard Written English.
	☐ Tone is appropriate for a college audience.
	☐ Commands or statements are used consistently.

Paragraph Practice: Revising

Using the Revision Checklist for a Process Paragraph, revise the first draft of your process paragraph.

Peer Review Reminder.
For feedback on your writing, have someone read your paper and make comments on the Peer Review Response sheet in Chapter 4, page 55.

Check Grammar, Punctuation, and Spelling As you reread your paper to check for grammar, punctuation, and spelling errors, pay special attention for possible errors that may arise in narrative paragraphs. For example, be sure that you have not shifted from commands to statements.

PRACTICE   Revising and Editing a Process Paragraph

9.9   Revise and edit Kyra's paragraph called "Lunge Fitness". Then answer the questions below.

¹The stationary lunge is an effective lower body workout, but it must be performed correctly to avoid injury. ²Dress comfortably in clothing that allows movement and flexibility and athletic shoes that support the feet. ³First, stand straight with the feet a hip width apart and the hands on the hips, next, with the left foot, step forward about one foot. ⁴Third, lower the body until left knee is over the top of the left foot. ⁵To avoid injury while doing the third step. ⁶Pay attention to form. ⁷Keep the chest up, shoulders back, and abdominal (stomach) muscles tight. ⁸Do not lean forward on the way down, which puts stress on the back. ⁹Be sure that the left knee do not extend past the toe. ¹⁰The right leg should be bent with the shin parallel to but not touching the floor. ¹¹The heel of the right leg will lift so that the weight is on the toe, but the foot should stay in the same position. ¹²In step four, put the weight on heel of left foot and push the body up and back to the standing position. ¹³Last, repeat the lunge ten times stepping forward with the left foot and pushing the body back up. ¹⁴Switch to the opposite foot and repeat the process ten times. ¹⁵Doing stationary lunges on a regular basis will burn calories and strengthen all the major muscle groups in the legs.

Questions on Revising

1. Underline the topic sentence. What are the process and the main point?

_____

2. Does the writer uses transitions throughout the paragraph? If not, where are transitions needed and which ones would you use?

_____

_____

3. What order does the process follow?

_____

4. Does the writer use commands or statements?

_____

Questions on Editing and Proofreading

5. One sentence is a fragment and another is a comma splice. Find the sentences and write the corrections here.

_____

6. One sentence has a verb error. Find the error and write the correction here.

_____

7. One sentence is missing the article *the* in two places. Find the sentence and write the correction here.

_____

Paragraph Practice: Editing and Proofreading

Edit and proofread your process paragraph. Check that your final draft is complete, accurate, and error-free.

Paragraph Writing Assignments

Help Desk

Mizuki's teacher told her that she left out essential words in her process paragraph, which made the instructions confusing and hard to read. This problem is called **telegraphic writing**. Here is her paragraph. Revise it by filling in words that she has left out.

> [1]Processing patient at Dr. Hernandez's office must be done correctly to avoid errors. [2]First, print out patient appointment schedule for day. [3]Next, when patient comes into doctor's office, ask patient to sign name and time of arrival on patient intake sheet. [4]Confirm patient's name, address, phone number, and insurance coverage to be sure that information is up-to-date and correct. [5]Then, collect patient's co-pay. [6]Finally, put patient's chart in rack and ring bell notifying nurses and doctor that patient's chart is ready.

Group Activity: Working Together to Plan a Multicultural Event

In a group of three or four students, plan a multicultural three-hour event at your campus. To prepare for this event, complete these writing tasks:

1. Write a set of directions to the location on campus.
2. Write a schedule of events in the order in which they will take place.
3. Write the recipes with instructions for several traditional dishes that you plan to serve.

Reading and Writing across the Curriculum: Communications

Presentation aids are used in education and real world situations to clarify ideas and concepts, to reinforce messages, to stimulate the audience, and to be culturally sensitive.

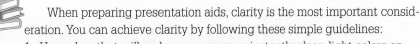

When preparing presentation aids, clarity is the most important consideration. You can achieve clarity by following these simple guidelines:
1. Use colors that will make your message instantly clear; light colors on dark backgrounds or dark colors on light backgrounds provide the best contrast. Be cautious about using yellow, which is often difficult to see.

2. Use direct phrases, not complete sentences and use bullets to highlight your points. Make sure the meaning is clear.
3. Use the aid to highlight a few essential points; don't clutter it with too much information. Four bullets are as much information as you should include.
4. Use typefaces that can be read easily from all parts of the room.
5. Give the slide or chart a title to further guide your listeners' attention and focus.

(From *Human Communications* by Joseph A. DeVito)

Prepare three presentation aids for the process paragraph you have written or for another one of the process writing topics on page 158.

Comment on a Contemporary Issue

Campus safety has become a major issue on college campuses across the United States. You can take responsibility for your own safety by knowing what to do and which resources are available. Comment about the steps students at your school can take to stay safe while driving or walking around campus or to protect personal property.

Write about an Image

Take the role of a police officer and write a report about this automobile accident. Write a paragraph explaining how the accident happened.

LO 3 The Process Essay

The process essay supports its thesis by explaining the steps for performing a process or for understanding a process.

Thesis Statement

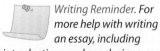
Writing Reminder. For more help with writing an essay, including introductions and conclusions, see Chapter 5.

The thesis statement makes a point about a process to tell the readers how the process is useful, explain why it is important, or assure readers that they can perform it. The thesis can consist of two or three parts:

Two-part thesis: The process + why it is important or what the reader will be able to do.

At Moki's Vegan Garden restaurant, several challenging steps are involved to train a new employee to be a knowledgeable cook.

Three-part thesis: The process + why it is important or what the reader will be able to do + the main steps in the process.

At Moki's Vegan Garden restaurant, several challenging steps are involved to train a new employee to be a knowledgeable cook: prepare, tell, show, do, and review.

Body Paragraphs

Each of the body paragraphs supports the thesis by explaining all the necessary steps in the process. Each may discuss one large step or a group of small steps. The body paragraphs guide the reader by accomplishing the following:

- include a topic sentence that indicates which step or group of steps will be explained in the topic sentence.
- are organized by chronological order or order of importance.

The following is an example of body paragraphs that consist of groups of small steps organized in chronological order.

Prepare

Explain why skill is important.

Explain hazards or problems and how to deal with them.

Answer questions.

Tell

Explain task by breaking into smaller steps.

Show

Demonstrate how the task should be done.

Ask trainee to explain in his or her own words.

Do

Trainee performs the task.

Trainer watches and directs when necessary.

Review

Trainer provides feedback on performance.

Process Essay Example

In the following essay, student Allicyn Vaupel explains the process for giving a back and neck massage.

Vaupel 1

Allicyn Vaupel

Professor Markus

College Preparatory Writing Skills

21 Oct. 2010

Giving a Back Massage

1   When I was growing up, I always wanted to work in the medical field. However, I knew that attending college for twelve years was not for me. Instead, I decided to become a licensed massage therapist and earned my license after taking the required courses and passing a certification exam. This occupation gives me a chance to work directly with people and help them feel better. One complaint many people have is back pain, and they often request a massage of this area. When I give a back massage, I begin by preparing the room and end with thanking my client.

2   Preparing the room is the first step in making a massage enjoyable for the client. I always dress the massage table with a clean set of sheets. I prepare the massage oil by adding some lavender essential oil, which is known for its relaxing effects. To set the mood, I play soothing music and light several candles placed on small tables around the room.

3   Once the room is ready, I welcome and prepare the client for the massage. After introducing myself, I make sure that the client does not have any medical conditions that I should be aware of such as first trimester pregnancies, cancer, or heart disease. I also explain what to expect during the massage and ask if there is a particular area that may be painful or may need more attention. After the preliminary questions have been answered, I step out of the room, giving the client sufficient time to get ready and lie on the massage table face down. When the client is ready, I re-enter the room and dim the lights.

4   First, I start massaging the upper back, isolating and working each muscle group. I take a few pumps of massage gel and spread it across the upper shoulders. Included in this region is the trapezius muscle, which is a large muscle spanning from the shoulders and partway down the back. Muscle strain or tension can cause these muscles to tighten, causing pain. I gently squeeze the trapezius muscles, following them to the tops of the shoulders. I gradually increase the pressure, avoiding discomfort to the client.

5   Next, I move to the shoulder blades and work down to the middle and lower back. Placing my fists between the shoulder blades, I apply even pressure down the spine to the lower back. Sometimes I use my elbows to get deep into the muscle. I manipulate both sides of the shoulder blades in great detail. If the client has indicated any particular area of the back that needs more work than others do, I will spend a majority of the time massaging that area. With closed fists, I work the lower back. Last, I do some effleurage strokes, which are long, continuous strokes.

6   When I have finished the massage, I take the opportunity to give the client final instructions to get feedback about the massage. I leave the room to give the client a few moments to relax and then to dress. After the client is dressed, I reenter the room. We discuss what was beneficial and whether the client would like to devise a treatment plan. I give the client a glass of water and him or her to drink lots of water throughout the day to flush out any toxins that were released from the muscles during the massage. After thanking the client for coming, I clean my room and wait for my next client to arrive, knowing that I have helped someone feel better by relieving pain and reducing stress.

PRACTICE 9.10 Analyzing a Process Essay

Answer the following questions about "Giving a Back Massage."

1. Underline the thesis statement. What process will the writer explain?

2. What technique does the writer use for the lead-in?

3. Underline the topic sentences of each of the body paragraphs. What does each topic sentence do?

4. Circle the transition word in each topic sentence.
5. How many steps does each of the body paragraphs contain?
   a. single step   b. series of steps
6. What point does the writer make in the concluding paragraph?

Process Essay Graphic Organizer

Using a process graphic organizer will help you place your steps in order. The sample graphic organizer shown on page 175 can be changed to suit your needs by adding body paragraphs. Include any necessary equipment or materials where appropriate.

Writing Assignments

Write about an Image

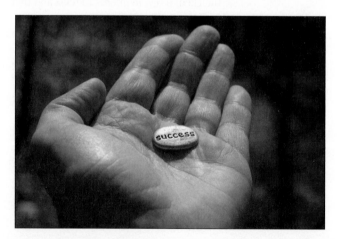

"There are no secrets to success. It is the result of preparation, hard work, and learning from failure."—Colin Powell

Think about a time when you achieved a desired goal or success in school, in your personal life, or at work. Although you may not have realized it then, you followed a series of steps or strategies to reach your goal. Write an essay in which you describe your process for achieving a specific goal or success.

Process Essay Graphic Organizer

Introduction

Lead-in:

Bridge:

Thesis Statement with Point about the Process:

Body Paragraphs: Use as many paragraphs as you need.

Step 1

Step 2

Step 3

Conclusion

Use Effective Closing Technique.

Writing Topics for a Process Essay

For your process essay, choose one of these options:

■ from paragraph to essay: expand the paragraph you wrote in the paragraph section of this chapter
■ any of the writing topics in the paragraph section of the chapter
■ any topic from the following list:

collaborate with others on a project in school, work, or personal life
find an affordable apartment, house, or condo
maintain a vehicle, home, or equipment
find a reliable source on the Internet for an academic subject
survive a physical or emotional challenge

Writing across the Curriculum Topics

Physical Science: prepare for a severe weather event
Health: plan an exercise program for a beginner
Psychology: stop harassment or bullying
Business: get out of debt
Computer Science: design a website

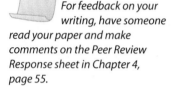

*Peer Review Reminder.
For feedback on your
writing, have someone
read your paper and make
comments on the Peer Review
Response sheet in Chapter 4,
page 55.*

English Success Tip: Keep a Learning Journal

A learning journal is a personal record of your notes and observations about a course you are taking. Keeping a learning journal will help you see how your knowledge and skills are developing over the semester. It will also help you focus on the course and practice writing. You can use a notebook or set up a file on a computer. Set aside at least ten minutes twice a week to write in your learning journal. Here are some topics to write about:

• information you learned and understand
• things that are difficult or hard to understand
• thoughts about material you have read
• ideas for papers
• connections with things you have learned in other classes

For support in meeting this chapter's objectives, log in to www.mywritinglab.com, go to the Study Plan tab, click on **Process** and choose **Paragraph Development— Process and Essay Development—Process** from the list of subtopics. Read and view the videos and resources in the Review Materials section, and then complete the Recall, Apply, and Write exercises in the Activities section. You can check your scores and overall progress by using the Gradebook.

chapter 10

Comparison and Contrast

Learning Objectives

After working through this chapter, you will be able to:

LO 1 Define comparison and contrast as a pattern of writing that shows how two subjects are similar and/or different.

LO 2 Write a comparison and contrast paragraph.

LO 3 Write a comparison and contrast essay.

LO 1 What Is Comparison and Contrast?

Comparison and contrast is a form of writing that shows similarities and differences. **Comparison** shows how two subjects are alike, whereas **contrast** shows how two subjects are different. You use comparison and contrast when deciding which course and teacher to sign up for or where to go on a Saturday night. Examples of workplace comparing and contrasting are reports that recommend the purchase of new equipment or suggest alternate ways of doing business.

Comparing and contrasting involve more than developing two different sets of ideas on two different subjects. You will also be analyzing the relationship between them.

QuickWrite

Think about two courses you are taking (or have taken). Write about their similarities and/or differences.

Comparison and Contrast in College Writing

Academic writing assignments often ask you to compare and contrast topics. For instance, in an education course, you may be asked to write about the differences between a teacher-centered and a student-centered classroom. A writing assignment in a music course may involve comparing and contrasting music of the Renaissance and Baroque periods. Comparing and contrasting men's and women's management styles in a business course is yet another example.

LO 2 Comparison and Contrast Paragraph

The following paragraphs on probation and parole illustrate the different methods of organizing comparison and contrast paragraphs. The first paragraph illustrates the point-by-point method and the second illustrates the subject-by-subject method.

Point-by-Point Paragraph Example

The **point-by-point method** of organization explains both subjects together for each point of comparison and/or contrast.

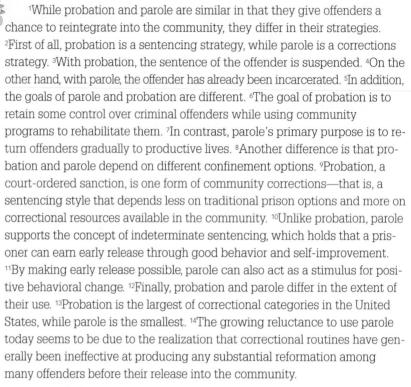

¹While probation and parole are similar in that they give offenders a chance to reintegrate into the community, they differ in their strategies. ²First of all, probation is a sentencing strategy, while parole is a corrections strategy. ³With probation, the sentence of the offender is suspended. ⁴On the other hand, with parole, the offender has already been incarcerated. ⁵In addition, the goals of parole and probation are different. ⁶The goal of probation is to retain some control over criminal offenders while using community programs to rehabilitate them. ⁷In contrast, parole's primary purpose is to return offenders gradually to productive lives. ⁸Another difference is that probation and parole depend on different confinement options. ⁹Probation, a court-ordered sanction, is one form of community corrections—that is, a sentencing style that depends less on traditional prison options and more on correctional resources available in the community. ¹⁰Unlike probation, parole supports the concept of indeterminate sentencing, which holds that a prisoner can earn early release through good behavior and self-improvement. ¹¹By making early release possible, parole can also act as a stimulus for positive behavioral change. ¹²Finally, probation and parole differ in the extent of their use. ¹³Probation is the largest of correctional categories in the United States, while parole is the smallest. ¹⁴The growing reluctance to use parole today seems to be due to the realization that correctional routines have generally been ineffective at producing any substantial reformation among many offenders before their release into the community.

(Adapted from *Criminal Justice Today* by Frank Schmalleger)

PRACTICE   Analyzing a Point-by-Point Comparison and Contrast Paragraph
10.1
Answer the following questions about the paragraph you just read.

1. Underline the topic sentence in the paragraph above. What is the point of the topic sentence?

_____

2. What do the two subjects have in common?

_____

3. What is the purpose of the paragraph?

_____

4. What are the main points of contrast?

_____

_____

5. Circle the transitional words and expressions used to move readers from point to point.

Subject-by-Subject Paragraph Example

The **subject-by-subject method** of organization explains all the points of comparison and contrast for one subject and then explains the same points for the other subject in the same order. This example paragraph covers the same information about probation and parole as the point-by-point example but uses the subject-by-subject method.

¹While probation and parole are similar in that they give offenders a chance to reintegrate into the community, they differ in their strategies. ²First of all, probation is a sentence of imprisonment that is suspended. ³Its goal is to retain some control over criminal offenders while using community programs to rehabilitate them. ⁴In addition, probation, a court-ordered sanction, is one form of community corrections—that is, a sentencing style that depends less on traditional prison options and more on correctional resources available in the community. ⁵Finally, probation is the largest of correction categories used in the United States. ⁶Parole differs from probation in that parolees, unlike probationers, have been incarcerated. ⁷Parole is the conditional early release of a convicted offender from prison. ⁸It is a corrections strategy whose primary purpose is to return offenders gradually to productive lives. ⁹Parole depends more on traditional confinement options by supporting the concept of indeterminate sentencing, which holds that a prisoner can earn early release through good behavior and self-improvement. ¹⁰By making early release possible, parole can also act as a stimulus for positive behavioral change. ¹¹Unlike probation, parole is the smallest category of corrections used in the United States. ¹²The growing reluctance to use parole today seems to be due to the realization that correctional routines have generally been ineffective at producing any substantial reformation among many offenders before their release into the community.

(Adapted from *Criminal Justice Today* by Frank Schmalleger)

**PRACTICE
10.2** **Analyzing a Subject-by-Subject Comparison and Contrast Paragraph**

Answer the following questions about the paragraph you just read.

1. Match the points of contrast for probation with those of parole. Some points may include more than one sentence. Write the sentence numbers here:

    _____

    _____

2. Circle the transition words and expressions used to move the readers from point to point.

3. Which of the two example paragraphs uses more contrast transitional words and expressions? Why?

    _____

    _____

4. Which of the two paragraphs is more understandable for the reader?

_____

COMPARISON AND CONTRAST PARAGRAPH ESSENTIALS

The purpose of the comparison and contrast paragraph is to compare and/or contrast two things and make a point about them. An effective comparison and contrast paragraph has these elements:

1. The paragraph makes a point about the similarities and/or differences between two subjects by informing, persuading, or showing understanding.
2. The two subjects being compared and/or contrasted must have something in common.
3. The supporting details for each subject are relevant and complete. Both subjects are explained equally, and the same points are covered.
4. The supporting details are organized either point by point or subject by subject.
5. The supporting details in the point-by-point or subject-by-subject patterns are arranged according to their importance or their difficulty.
6. Comparison and contrast transitional words or expressions are used to show the movement from one point to another or from one subject to another.

Prewriting the Comparison and Contrast Paragraph

Before you write, you must choose a suitable topic and develop it.

Decide Your Topic and Purpose When deciding on your own comparison and/or contrast topic or responding to an assigned topic, consider the following:

1. **Choose two subjects that have some characteristics in common.** For example, you might decide to compare or contrast two cars. It would make sense to select two cars from the same group such as two economy cars rather than an economy car and a luxury car. While an economy car and a luxury car are both cars, they are in different classes.
2. **Choose two subjects that can be compared and/or contrasted in a single paragraph.** If you decided to compare or contrast two ballpoint pens, you would quickly run out of points to discuss. On the other hand, if you wanted to compare or contrast two colleges, you would need to cover such subjects as programs, fees and tuition, faculty, extra-curricular activities, and entrance requirements. A single paragraph would not give you the chance to cover the features of each subject in any depth.
3. **Choose two subjects that readers do not already know about.** Most readers know the difference between a landline telephone and a cell phone. The similarities and differences are obvious. Therefore, unless you can offer the reader new information or a new way of looking at the subjects, it is best to avoid obvious topics.

PRACTICE   Evaluating Topics for a Comparison and Contrast Paragraph
10.3   Explain why each of the following topics would be suitable or unsuitable for a comparison contrast paragraph.

1. two homes where you have lived

_____

2. a fast-food restaurant and a five-star restaurant

3. a manual toothbrush and an electric toothbrush

Develop Ideas for Your Topic Prewriting for a comparison and contrast paragraph involves creating a list of your subjects' similarities and differences in a side-by-side chart. To see how this is done, take a look at Natasha's graphic organizer comparing and contrasting her two dogs, Sabra Lee and Butch.

Natasha's Prewriting Graphic Organizer for Sabra Lee and Butch

Similarities

Sabra Lee and Butch

Five-year old males
Brought up together as puppies
Raised and live in Natasha's house
Eat the same dog food
Given love and attention
Given preventive care

Differences

Sabra Lee	Butch
Responds to commands	Does not respond to commands, just "Food"
Protective watch dog	Passive
Chases monkeys, scares people	Lies around, timid
Affectionate, likes to be hugged, kissed, petted, meet and greet	Does not like affection, runs away and hides
Seeks attention	Does not seek attention
Sleeps on driveway by front door	Sleeps on secluded back patio

Your Comparison and Contrast Paragraph: Prewriting

Choose one of the following topics for a comparison and contrast paragraph, or choose your own topic. Then create a comparison and contrast prewriting graphic planner of their similarities and differences.

two jobs (preferably ones you have experienced)

two memorable people (friends, relatives, teachers, bosses, sports fans, athletes, movie or television personalities)

two popular brands of an item

the personalities of two pets that you lived with or knew well

two places where you have lived

Writing across the Curriculum Topics

Music: two musicians, singers, or musical groups

Education: an online class and a traditional face-to-face class

Health: two types of diets (i.e., two types of diets for general health or two types of weight-loss diets)

Marketing: two methods of advertising (ways of persuading people to buy a product or service)

Anthropology: two different cultural views on a topic such as money, treatment of older people, or marriage

Comparison and Contrast Prewriting Graphic Organizer

Similarities

Subject A _____ and Subject B _____

Differences

| Subject A _____ | Subject B _____ |

Narrow Your Topic and Write the Topic Sentence   Narrowing your topic involves looking at your prewriting graphic organizer to see whether your subjects have more similarities or differences. Decide whether to write about similarities or differences or both. Finally, think about the point you want to make about the two subjects. Then you will be ready to write the topic sentence of your paragraph.

The topic sentence for comparison and contrast will do the following:

1. State the two subjects that you will compare and/or contrast.
2. State the purpose, to discuss similarities and/or differences.
3. State the point of the comparison and/or contrast.

Natasha wrote this topic sentence contrasting her two dogs:

> Although Sabre Lee and Butch were brought up in the same home in South Africa, their personalities are vastly different.

Notice how Natasha mentions the similarities briefly and then moves on to the point, the difference between their personalities. She chose to acknowledge the similarities, but her point is to discuss differences.

TIPS | **Writing Comparison and Contrast Topic Sentences**

1. **Make a point by giving the reason for the comparison and/or contrast.** Without this, the reader will not know why you are writing.

   No point: The Guatemala City where I grew up is different from the Guatemala City of today.

   With a point: Guatemala City, where I grew up, has been transformed into a modern city since I moved away.

It is not enough to say that two subjects are different. The point the writer wants to make is that Guatemala City has changed into a modern city.

   No point: Food grown on organic farms is different from food grown on traditional farms.

   With a point: Food grown on organic farms is more nutritious than food grown on traditional farms.

The point is that organic food is more nutritious. The writer intends to persuade the reader.

2. **State your purpose: to compare and/or to contrast.** This tells the reader what to expect from your paragraph.

   No purpose: I took math in high school and in college.

   Purpose: My high school math class differed from my college math class with respect to the demands it placed on students.

The purpose is to explain the differences between high school and college math classes.

PRACTICE   Evaluating Comparison and Contrast Topic Sentences

10.4   Explain what is wrong with each of the following topic sentences. If a topic sentence is good, write "good."

1. My friend and I have a lot in common, but we also have a lot of differences.

_____

2. A laptop computer is different from a desktop computer.

_____

3. I am taking both English and reading classes in school this semester.

_____

4. China Buffet is a better restaurant than China Palace because of the variety of food served.

_____

Your Comparison and Contrast Paragraph: Writing a Topic Sentence

Write a topic sentence for the topic about which you have been freewriting. Label the two subjects, the purpose, and the point of the comparison and/or contrast as illustrated in the example below.

Subjects	Purpose	Basis of contrast

Example: Touch screen and keyboard cell phones differ with respect to ease of use.

_____

Organizing and Drafting the Comparison and Contrast Paragraph

Using the topic sentence as a guide, the next steps are to develop and organize supporting details and write the first draft.

Develop Supporting Details   Look back at your prewriting graphic organizer and choose the details that will support the point you make in your topic sentence. As you choose the details, see if you can group them into categories.

Using a comparison contrast graphic organizer can help you organize your details by matching details to each category. This tool will help you keep your points organized.

Here is Natasha's contrast graphic organizer. It shows how she grouped her details.

Natasha's Contrast Graphic Organizer

Points of Contrast	Subject A Sabre Lee	Subject B Butch
Obedience	Responds to commands	Does not respond to commands, turns away Responds only to "Food."
Protectiveness	Alert watch dog Sits in front of house and roams on driveway Chases monkeys Scares people passing by Sleeps on driveway by front door	Timid Lies around Scared of everything Sleeps on secluded back patio
Affection	Loves to be hugged, kissed, begs for attention Meet and greet	No desire for affection, runs and hides

Your Comparison and Contrast Paragraph: Selecting Supporting Details

Choose the details that will support the point you made in the topic sentence you wrote. Then, group your details into categories and fill in the graphic organizer on page 186.

Organize Your Supporting Details   There are two methods of organization for a comparison/contrast paragraph: point by point or subject by subject. Once you have selected the method, you can arrange your supporting details within the pattern using order of importance.

Comparison and Contrast Graphic Organizer

Point of Comparison and/or Contrast	Subject A	Subject B

Point-by-Point The point-by-point method of organization explains both subjects together for each point of comparison or contrast (see the diagram at the top of the next page).

Subject-by-Subject The subject-by-subject method of organization explains all the points of comparison or contrast for one subject and then explains the same points for the other subject in the same order. The second diagram on page 187 shows this method.

Order of Importance Arranging your points in order of importance—from most to least or least to most—shows the reader how you view them. In the point-by-point method, you can choose to put the most important point first or last. In the subject-by-subject method, you can arrange the points in order of importance for the first subject and use that same order for the second subject.

Point by Point Organization

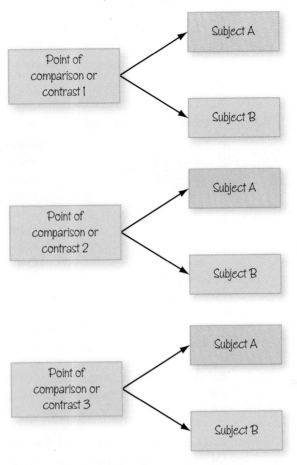

Subject by Subject Organization

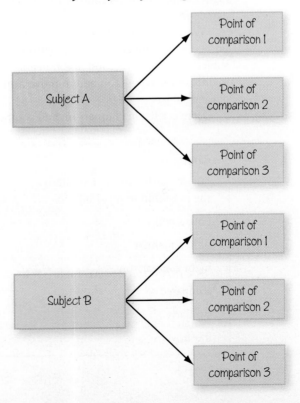

Your Comparison or Contrast Paragraph: Outlining

Choose a method of organization for your comparison or contrast paragraph. You may find it helpful to write a scratch outline. The following chart shows the two models.

Point-by-Point Outline	Subject-by-Subject Outline
Point 1	Subject A
Subject A	Point 1
Subject B	Point 2
Point 2	Point 3
Subject A	Subject B
Subject B	Point 1
Point 3	Point 2
Subject A	Point 3
Subject B	

Write the First Draft As you write your first draft, consider these elements: balance, transitional words and expressions, and verb tense.

Balance Your comparison and contrast paragraph should be balanced in both content and in organization. As you write, follow the same organizational pattern throughout the paragraph.

Add Connectors: Transitional Words and Expressions Following the details of a comparison and contrast paragraph can be confusing to the reader because you are writing about two subjects and explaining matching points about each. To help the reader follow your method of organization, you need to add transitional words and expressions.

When using the point-by-point method, use transitions to introduce each new point and to connect one explanation to another within each point. When using the subject-by-subject method, use transitions to switch from one subject to another in the middle of the paragraph and to move from one point to another within the discussion of each subject

Here is a list of comparison and contrast transitions that are most commonly used:

Comparison	Contrast
one similarity, another similarity, the most important similarity	one difference, another difference, the most important difference
both *x* and *y*	whereas *x*, *y*
in like manner	on the other hand
by/in comparison	by/in contrast
compared to	contrasted to
similarly	conversely
like *x*, *y*	unlike *x*, *y*

PRACTICE   Analyzing Transitions in a Contrast Paragraph

10.5   Stephen used the subject-by-subject method of organization for his paragraph Violence in "*Donkey Kong*" and "*Metal Gear Solid*". Read the paragraph and answer the questions about transitional words and expressions that follow.

¹Although the original versions of the video games *Donkey Kong* and *Metal Gear Solid* were landmark games for their times, they differ with respect to violence they contain. ²In the era of Atari 2600, just about all video games were designed to entertain children and adults alike. ³*Donkey Kong* is a prime example of that decade's family-friendly games. ⁴In *Donkey Kong*, there is no physical violence between hero and villain. ⁵Throughout the game, Donkey Kong throws barrels and teacups at Mario, the hero, but he never once lays a finger on him. ⁶As a matter of fact, in the entire game, Mario has only one obtainable weapon, a hammer to smash barrels and teacups. ⁷Even if Mario does get hit by anything, he does not bleed. ⁸ On the other side of the spectrum, *Metal Gear Solid* is a game designed specifically for mature game player because of its violent content, rated "M" by the video game rating system. ⁹In this game, the hero, Solid Snake, is forced to kill every Fox-Hound henchman that he comes in contact with because each villain does not hesitate to shoot at the hero. ¹⁰Unlike Mario in *Donkey Kong*, who has only a hammer at his disposal, Solid Snake has dozens of weapons that he can use, some of which are a sniper rifle, a bazooka, a handgun, a machine gun, and hand grenades. ¹¹While *Donkey Kong's* characters do not bleed, *Metal Gear Solid* has enough blood to satisfy action-loving adults and scare little children. ¹²The video game industry continues to produce violent video games to satisfy gamers' demands; however, *Donkey Kong* provides hours of excitement and, unlike *Metal Gear Solid*, does not need physical violence to be entertaining.

1. Circle the transition that is used to switch from one subject to another in the middle of the paragraph.
2. Underline the transitional expression and related words that contrast *Metal Gear Solid* with *Donkey Kong*.
3. What is the purpose for the transitions in sentences 10 and 11?

_____

Your Comparison or Contrast Paragraph: Writing the First Draft

Using your outline and graphic organizer, write the first draft of your paragraph.

Revising, Editing, and Proofreading

Revision is best done by looking at one element at a time: Support, Organization, Connectors and Transitions, and Style. The following Revision Checklist contains the SOCS elements as they apply to comparison and contrast paragraphs.

REVISION CHECKLIST FOR A COMPARISON AND CONTRAST PARAGRAPH

Element	Revision Checkpoints
Topic (2 subjects)	☐ The subjects have some characteristics in common.
	☐ The subjects can be fully discussed in a single paragraph.
	☐ The similarities or differences between the two subjects are explained clearly.
Topic Sentence	☐ The topic sentence includes three elements: ■ states the two subjects to be compared or contrasted. ■ states the purpose, to discuss similarities or differences. ■ makes a point about the two subjects.
Support	☐ The supporting details are grouped into categories for each subject.
	☐ All supporting details are relevant and adequate.
Organization	☐ The paragraph follows one of two methods of organization consistently: point-by-point or subject-by-subject.
	☐ The point-by-point method explains both subjects together for each point of comparison or contrast.
	☐ The subject-by-subject method explains all the points of comparison or contrast for one subject and then explains the same points for the other subject in the same order.
	☐ Points are arranged in order of importance.
	☐ The paragraph is balanced in both content and in organization.
Connectors and Transitions	☐ Comparison or contrast connectors and transitions provide coherence.
	☐ Connectors and transitions are used to introduce each new point, to connect one explanation to another within each point, and to change subjects.
Style	☐ Writing is clear, concise Standard Written English.
	☐ Tone is appropriate for a college audience.
	☐ Sentences are varied.

Your Comparison and Contrast Paragraph: Revising

Using the Revision Checklist for a Comparison and Contrast Paragraph, revise the first draft of your paragraph.

Peer Review Reminder. For feedback on your writing, have someone read your paper and make comments on the Peer Review Response sheet in Chapter 4, page 55.

Check Grammar, Punctuation, and Spelling As you reread your paper to check for grammar, punctuation, and spelling errors, pay special attention for possible errors that may arise in comparison and contrast paragraphs.

1. Avoid using *but* in sentences beginning with *although, even though,* or *while.*
   Incorrect: Although Sabre Lee and Butch were brought up in the same home in South Africa, **but** their personalities are vastly different.
   Correct: Although Sabra Lee and Butch were brought up in the same home, their personalities are vastly different.

2. When using the word *despite*, add the phrase *the fact that.*
   Incorrect: Despite he was raised with affection, as an adult Butch runs away and hides when I try to pet him.
   Correct: Despite the fact that he was raised with affection, as an adult Butch runs away and hides when I try to pet him.

3. Avoid creating a fragment when using *whereas.*
   Incorrect: Whereas Butch turns his back and walks away.
   Correct: Sabra Lee obeys commands, whereas Butch turns his back and walks away.

Grammar Reminder.

For more on correcting sentence fragments, see Chapter 20.

PRACTICE 10.6 Revising and Editing a Comparison and Contrast Paragraph

Revise and edit Natasha's paragraph. Then answer the questions below.

¹Although Sabre Lee and Butch were raised together as puppies in the same home in South Africa, their personalities are vastly different. ²The most notable difference is their obedience. ³Sabre Lee immediately obeys commands given to him. ⁴Butch, on the other hand, turns just turns his back and walks away when a command is given. ⁵The only statement Butch responds to is "Food!" ⁶Another difference between the dogs is their protectiveness. ⁷Sabre Lee is an alert watchdog, always on the lookout. ⁸When outside, he sits in front of the door to the house or roams around on the driveway, chasing wild monkeys and scaring people passing by on the road. ⁹He even prefers to sleep outside by the front door to protect the house. ¹⁰Unlike Sabre Lee. ¹¹Butch is timid and would rather spend his time lying around rather than chasing intruders. ¹²He sleeps much of the time on his comfortable blanket on the secluded patio in the back of the house. ¹³The dog's personalities also differed in their display of affection toward people. ¹⁴Whenever a family member comes home, Sabre Lee does his "meet and greet," which

consists of wagging his tail vigorously while rubbing his body against the individual, begging to be petted. [15]In contrast, Butch has no desire to give or to get affection. [16]He runs away and hides when anyone tries to pet him. [17]Although Sabre Lee and Butch have different personalities, both dogs are treasured members of the family.

Questions on Revising

1. Underline the topic sentence. What are the two subjects, the focus, and the main point?

2. List the main points of contrast.

3. Does the writer use point by point or subject by subject as her method of organization? Is it effective?

4. How does the writer introduce each major point of contrast?

Questions on Editing and Proofreading

5. The paragraph has one fragment error. Find and correct it.

6. Identify and correct the one verb shift error.

7. The paragraph has one error in apostrophe use. Find and correct it.

Your Comparison and Contrast Paragraph: Editing and Proofreading

Edit and proofread your comparison or contrast paragraph. Check that your final draft is complete, accurate, and error-free.

Paragraph Writing Assignments

Help Desk

Earl has written his rough draft paragraph about the differences between his two friends Diego and Joe. Read Earl's paper and suggest how he can improve its balance.

Diego and Joe have many differences in their lifestyle. To begin, Diego enjoys working out on a regular basis. He runs four to five miles every morning and then goes to the gym where he spends two hours working out. As a result, he is in great physical shape. Joe rarely works out. Another difference is their eating habits. Diego is careful about what he eats. He eats a lean protein, a starchy carbohydrate, and a complex carbohydrate at each meal. In contrast, Joe eats fast food every day. The final difference is their study habits. Diego spends his free time studying because he wants to maintain his 3.5 grade point average. When his friends ask him to go out, even though he is tempted, he tells them that he needs to spend time doing homework or studying. He has joined a math study group for extra help in his college algebra course. Unlike Diego, Joe does not spend much time studying for his courses. If Joe continues with his current lifestyle, he will not be successful like Diego.

Reading and Writing across the Curriculum: Interior Design

Throughout history, humans have arranged and improved their surroundings to meet their physical and psychological needs. Today, interior design is a profession that creates spaces and furnishings to meet the needs of people of all ages and abilities, including the elderly, children, and those who are temporarily or permanently disabled.

Interior designers use **anthropometrics** to determine how much space people need to function in an environment. Anthropometrics is the science of measuring the physical sizes and shapes of the human body in various activities. Designers use this information to plan for the comfort, size, and usefulness of space and furnishings.

(Adapted from *Beginnings of Interior Environments* by Lynn M. Jones and Phyllis Sloan Allen)

Write a paragraph comparing and/or contrasting how well two restaurants meet the needs of the customer in the way they use their physical space. Choose two restaurants that are similar in the type of food served, the size of the restaurant, and the prices. For example, you could choose two fast-food restaurants or two coffee shops.

When developing your details, use these points of comparison and/or contrast:

- Size: Is the restaurant too big, too small, or adequate?
- Furniture: Is the furniture user-friendly? Is it easy to move, rearrange, and clean? Does it fit all sizes? How comfortable is it? Is the furniture arranged for usefulness?

■ Accessibility: Does the restaurant accommodate children, elderly, and people with disabilities?

■ Ease of use: Is the restaurant easy to enter, exit, order food, and pay?

Comment on a Contemporary Issue: Going Green

"Going green" refers to actions people can take to change their habits as consumers to conserve and improve the natural environment. Many people are becoming aware of their lifestyle's impact on the environment and are making changes. On the other hand, others are resistant to giving up their comfortable lives. Write a paragraph contrasting two people or families, one going green and the other not making lifestyle changes. Some possible categories for your points of contrast could be recycling, pest control, energy use (electricity, water, gasoline), chemical product use (for cleaning, pest control), and vehicle choices.

Write about an Image: Two Paintings

Both of these paintings have the same title, *Mother and Child*, but the images the artists use to show a mother and child are very different. Write a paragraph in which you compare and/or contrast these paintings.

Writing Reminder.
For more help with writing an essay, including introductions and conclusions, see Chapter 5.

LO 3 The Comparison and Contrast Essay

The comparison and contrast essay has the same purpose as the comparison and contrast paragraph: to explain how two subjects are alike and/or different. The comparison and contrast essay uses the same organizational patterns as the comparison and contrast paragraph: point by point or subject by subject. The comparison and contrast graphic organizers on pages 199 and 200 can also be used to plan your essay. They will help keep you organized as you prewrite, draft, and revise.

Comparison and contrast essays can inform or persuade. For example, in writing a comparison and contrast essay about the differences between two notebook computers, you could provide factual information about the differences in features, storage, and size. On the other hand, if you wanted to persuade the reader that one notebook computer was the better choice, you would explain how the features, storage, and size of one are better than those of the other.

Thesis Statement

The thesis statement for a comparison and contrast essay makes a point about how two subjects are similar and/or different. The thesis statement can be expressed in either of two ways:

Two-part thesis: The two subjects to be compared and/or contrasted + the main point.

Although the video games *Donkey Kong* and *Metal Gear Solid* were ahead of their time when they were released to the public, they differ considerably.

Three-part thesis: The two subjects to be compared and/or contrasted + the main point + the points of comparison and/or contrast.

Although the video games *Donkey Kong* and *Metal Gear Solid* were ahead of their time when they were released to the public, they differ considerably with respect to their story lines, game play, and violent content.

Body Paragraphs

The body paragraphs in the comparison and contrast essay follow one of two patterns: point by point or subject by subject. The plans below have two or three body paragraphs; however, you can use as many paragraphs as necessary to support your thesis statement.

Point-by-Point Organization

Point 1: Story line
 Subject A: *Donkey Kong*
 Subject B: *Metal Gear Solid*
Point 2: Game play
 Subject A: *Donkey Kong*
 Subject B: *Metal Gear Solid*
Point 3: Violent content
 Subject A: *Donkey Kong*
 Subject B: *Metal Gear Solid*

Subject-by-Subject Organization

Subject A: *Donkey Kong*
 Point 1: Story line
 Point 2: Game play
 Point 3: Violent content
Subject B: *Metal Gear Solid*
 Point 1: Story line
 Point 2: Game play
 Point 3: Violent content

Comparison and Contrast Essay Example

Student Kathryn Butler explains the differences between the styles of two softball coaches.

Butler 1

Kathryn Butler

Professor Markus

College Preparatory Writing Skills

29 Nov. 2010

Two Coaching Styles

1   The score is tied. There are two outs. Coach L.D. says, "Come on girls.

You can do it! Make the play at first base." The next batter steps up to the plate. Coach

Slaughter screams, "You girls better make the play or you're going to be hearing from me!" The ball leaves the pitcher's hand and floats toward the batter with a slight arch. The ball is hit. The shortstop fields the ball and throws it to first base. The third out is made. The proud softball team hustles into the dugout. Coach L.D. congratulates the team for the great play, while Coach Slaughter tells the team that the play meets his expectations. Coach L.D. and Coach Slaughter have different, but effective attitudes toward our performance, techniques for motivating the team, and approaches to winning.

2   One striking difference between Coach L.D. and Coach Slaughter is their attitudes toward our performance. Coach L.D. always speaks in a calm voice. He never gets upset during the games when the team makes bad plays. He keeps a smiling face waiting for us when the team comes back into the dugout. When our team played the Johnson's team, we could not make a decent play. We were overthrowing the ball, missing easy catches, and hitting ground balls to the pitcher. Coach L.D. encouraged us by saying, "Come on girls. You have what it takes. You just need to concentrate. We can pull out of this slump of bad plays and win this game." His positive attitude and consistent encouragement helped us achieve the positive state of mind we needed to win the game. In every losing situation, Coach L.D. remains calm and cheers us up. On the other hand, Coach Slaughter is always yelling. When our team makes bad plays during a game, he yells that we should be making the outs and winning the game. Every time we return to the dugout after an inning, he lectures us about what we are doing wrong and what we should be doing. When we played the Devils, we were making every play and hitting the ball into the outfield. When we returned to the dugout after an excellent inning for our team, Coach Slaughter said, "This is the type of fielding and hitting I expect from you girls. Don't slack off tonight." His expectations for us help us stay focused on playing well. In every game situation, Coach Slaughter expects perfection and corrects imperfection.

3 Another difference between Coach L.D. and Coach Slaughter is their techniques for motivating the team. Coach L.D. technique is to be positive. He only expects average plays and hits from us; anything more is a bonus. Coach L.D. motivates us by giving rewards for superior plays. At our last game, he announced that he would give anyone who hit a homerun five dollars and anyone who hit a grand slam ten dollars. In contrast, Coach Slaughter's technique is to be negative. He expects homeruns and good plays from us. If we do not play perfectly, he is disappointed in us. He wants perfect double plays and homeruns, and if we do not meet his standard, he is upset; anything less is a disappointment. When Mandi, our shortstop, hit a homerun, she returned to the dugout, only to hear further batting tips from Coach Slaughter. According to him, there is always room for improvement. He motivates us by telling us that we will not get a lecture after the game if we play flawlessly.

4 The most important difference between Coach L.D. and Coach Slaughter is their approach to winning. Coach L.D. just wants us to have fun, and, therefore, he is understanding and willing to compromise. For example, Melissa was not happy playing center field, so she explained her reasons to Coach L.D. He decided that she would also make a good second baseman, so he made the switch, and we have never seen a better second baseman than Melissa. Unlike Coach L.D., Coach Slaughter's believes winning is life or death. For instance, during a game, Kim made a bad play. When Coach Slaughter criticized her, she gave the excuse that her ankle injury was bothering her, but he did not want to hear it. No matter what the excuse, he will not accept it.

5 Although Coach L.D. and Coach Slaughter have such different coaching styles, they work well together because they complement one another. Some of the

Butler 4

more sensitive girls on the team need Coach L.D.'s encouragement and lack of

criticism in order to feel confident and do their best. However, some of the

unmotivated girls need Coach Slaughter's "wake-up calls." When the girls who have

been lectured by Coach Slaughter feel that their egos have been bruised, Coach L.D.

restores their self-esteem. When the girls who are not trying their best are

complimented by Coach L.D., they are brought back to reality by some sharp

observations voiced by Coach Slaughter. The combination of these two coaches, who

have such opposite philosophies, adds up to a winning situation for all the players on

the team.

PRACTICE   Analyzing a Comparison and Contrast Essay
10.7
Answer the following questions about "Two Coaching Styles."

1. Underline the thesis statement. What are the differences the writer will discuss?

_____

2. What technique does the writer use for the lead-in in the introductory paragraph?

_____

3. Underline the topic sentences of the body paragraphs. What is the point of each of the topic sentences?

_____

4. Circle the transition words used to introduce each difference in each of the topic sentences.

5. Which organizational plan does this essay use?

a. Point-by-point   b. Subject-by-subject

6. In addition to referring to the thesis, underline the point(s) the writer makes in the concluding paragraph.

Comparison and Contrast Essay Graphic Organizers

Using a point-by-point or subject-by-subject graphic organizer will help you place your details in the appropriate pattern. The sample graphic organizers shown on pages 199 and 200 can be changed to suit your needs by adding paragraphs, points, and supporting evidence.

Point-by-Point Compare/Contrast Essay Graphic Organizer

Introduction

Lead-in:

Bridge:

Thesis Statement: Narrowed subject A + B + main point (+ list of supporting points)

Body Paragraphs

Topic Sentences: First, second, third, etc, point for subjects A + B

Subject A:
    Supporting Evidence

Subject B:
    Supporting Evidence

Concluding Paragraph

Effective Closing Technique:

Subject-by-Subject Compare/Contrast Essay Graphic Organizer

Introduction

Lead-in:

Bridge:

Thesis Statement: Narrowed subject A + B + main point (+ list of supporting points)

Body Paragraph 1

Topic Sentence: Subject A

First Point:
Supporting Evidence

Second Point:
Supporting Evidence

Third Point:
Supporting Evidence

Body Paragraph 2

Topic Sentence: Subject B

First Point for Subject B:
Supporting Evidence

Second Point for Subject B:
Supporting Evidence

Third Point for Subject B:
Supporting Evidence

Concluding Paragraph

Effective Closing Technique:

Essay Writing Assignments

Write about an Image: Men, Women, and Shopping

This photograph illustrates a common belief that men and women feel differently about shopping. Write an essay in which you contrast two shoppers of the same or different genders.

Writing Topics for a Comparison and Contrast Essay

For your comparison and contrast essay, choose one of these options:

- from paragraph to essay: expand the paragraph you wrote in the paragraph section of this chapter
- any of the writing topics in the paragraph section of this chapter
- any topic from the following list:

  two websites on the same subject
  beliefs you had that have changed now that you are older
  living at home and living away from home
  two individuals, one who is a positive and the other who is a negative role model
  a product you would like to own and the same type of product you own now
  (such as a car, home, electronic equipment, etc.)

Writing across the Curriculum Topics

History: the time period you are living in and the time period that a parent, relative, or other older person grew up in

Education: teaching styles of two college instructors or high school teachers

Communications: face-to-face communication and electronic communication

Business: being self-employed or working for someone else

Cooking: foods of two different cultural groups (two different regions of a country or two different countries)

Peer Review Reminder. For feedback on your writing, have someone read your paper and make comments on the Peer Review Response sheet in Chapter 4, page 55.

English Success Tip: Keeping a Portfolio of Your Writing

A writing portfolio is a collection of the best examples of your written work over the entire semester. You can save your papers in print or in electronic format.

Some teachers require a writing portfolio as part of the course grade. However, if the portfolio is not a course requirement for you, consider keeping one on your own. Keeping a portfolio is a good way to monitor your progress and showcase your achievements. After the course is over, you will have a record of the writing you have completed.

You can choose the papers you want to include:

- papers written in class
- timed writing assignments
- papers written out of class

You can also include prewriting, rough drafts, and final drafts of writing assignments. To keep organized, create a table of contents or list of assignments as shown.

Table of Contents for Portfolio

Date	Type of Writing Assignment	Title

For support in meeting this chapter's objectives, log in to www.mywritinglab.com, go to the Study Plan tab, click on **Comparison and Contrast** and choose **Paragraph Development—Comparing and Contrasting and Essay Development—Comparing and Contrasting** from the list of subtopics. Read and view the videos and resources in the Review Materials section, and then complete the Recall, Apply, and Write exercises in the Activities section. You can check your scores and overall progress by using the Gradebook.

Learning Objectives

After working through this chapter, you will be able to:

LO 1 Define classification as a form of writing that arranges items into groups based on a single characteristic.

LO 2 Write a classification paragraph.

LO 3 Write a classification essay.

LO 1 What Is Classification?

Classification is a form of writing that arranges items within a topic into groups based on a single characteristic. Key words that show how a topic is classified are *types, categories, groups, kinds,* or *components.*

You use classification when you decide to listen to a type of music, such as rap, hip hop, top 40, country, salsa, reggae, and so on, for your own enjoyment. Retail stores use different types of music to influence sales. For example, people spend more money in restaurants that play slow music, while they spend less but leave sooner in restaurants that play fast music. Stores that want to sell to teenagers play loud music because teens like to feel and hear the music.

QuickWrite

Write about the types of music played in stores and restaurants you are familiar with.

Classification in College Writing

Classification is often used to present material in college courses and in textbooks. In a music appreciation course, the types of instruments in an orchestra or the six main periods in music history are examples of classification. In a criminal justice course, examples of classification are strategies of police work and methods of interrogating a suspect.

LO 2 The Classification Paragraph

There are two types of classification paragraphs that you can write:

- A **formal classification** paragraph explains categories that already exist, such as classifying animals in biology or types of movies.
- An **original classification** paragraph explains categories that the writer makes up, such as types of behaviors among toddlers.

A Classification Paragraph Example

The following paragraph is an example of the formal classification paragraph.

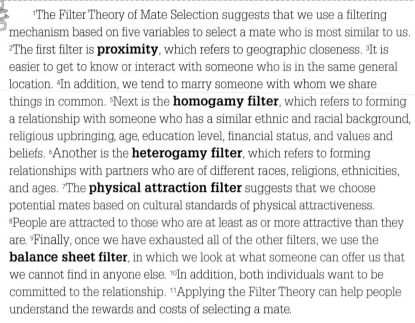

¹The Filter Theory of Mate Selection suggests that we use a filtering mechanism based on five variables to select a mate who is most similar to us. ²The first filter is **proximity**, which refers to geographic closeness. ³It is easier to get to know or interact with someone who is in the same general location. ⁴In addition, we tend to marry someone with whom we share things in common. ⁵Next is the **homogamy filter**, which refers to forming a relationship with someone who has a similar ethnic and racial background, religious upbringing, age, education level, financial status, and values and beliefs. ⁶Another is the **heterogamy filter**, which refers to forming relationships with partners who are of different races, religions, ethnicities, and ages. ⁷The **physical attraction filter** suggests that we choose potential mates based on cultural standards of physical attractiveness. ⁸People are attracted to those who are at least as or more attractive than they are. ⁹Finally, once we have exhausted all of the other filters, we use the **balance sheet filter**, in which we look at what someone can offer us that we cannot find in anyone else. ¹⁰In addition, both individuals want to be committed to the relationship. ¹¹Applying the Filter Theory can help people understand the rewards and costs of selecting a mate.

(Adapted from *Family Life Now* by Kelly J. Welch)

PRACTICE   Analyzing a Classification Paragraph

11.1   Answer the questions about the paragraph you just read about the Filter Theory of Mate Selection.

1. Underline the topic sentence.
2. What is the topic that is being classified?

_____

3. Circle the names of the five filters.
4. What kind of support details are used for each of the filters?

_____

5. Underline the transition words.
6. Why is the balance sheet filter the last one to be covered in the paragraph?

_____

CLASSIFICATION PARAGRAPH ESSENTIALS

The purpose of a classification paragraph is to explain a topic by dividing it into groups according to something the groups have in common. A classification paragraph may achieve any of the following:

- inform the readers about a topic they are not familiar with
- show knowledge about a course concept to a teacher
- persuade readers by applying a rating system
- give readers a new way of looking at a topic

An effective classification paragraph has these essential elements:

1. The paragraph makes a point about what the items in the topic have in common—the basis of their classification.
2. The groups are complete, fit under the same classification principle, and do not overlap.
3. The supporting details explain each group in a similar way and are developed with the same amount of detail. They can be examples, descriptions, short narratives, and facts.
4. The groups are organized in order of importance.
5. Classification transitional words or expressions help readers see the movement from one point to another or from one subject to another.

Prewriting the Classification Paragraph

Decide Your Topic and Purpose When deciding on your own classification topic or responding to an assigned topic, consider the following:

1. **Choose a topic that is not too complicated or technical for your readers to understand.** Consider your readers' background knowledge when selecting a topic. For example, many readers do not know about auto engines and might have a hard time understanding a paper classifying them.
2. **Choose a topic that will interest your readers.** For instance, most people know the various types of electronic communication, so the topic would not be interesting. However, you could take a more original approach, such as classifying text messagers.
3. **Choose a topic that can be explained completely in one paragraph.** If your topic is classified into too many groups or categories, you will not be able to include all the information needed to explain each one.

PRACTICE   Evaluating Topics for a Classification Paragraph
11.2   Explain why each of the following topics would be suitable or unsuitable for a classification paragraph.

1. types of transportation

   _____

2. duties of uniformed police officers

   _____

3. types of expenses you have

   _____

4. seasons of the year

   _____

5. types of poisonous spiders.

   _____

Develop Ideas for Your Topic Prewriting for a classification topic involves finding details for your topic, identifying what the details have in common (the basis of classification), and then putting the details into groups based on that common feature.

Understand the Basis for Classification   The **basis for classification** is the common feature used to classify or group the details for your topic. For example, each of the items in the following list shows a different basis for classifying chocolate:

- varieties of chocolate
- types of chocolate candies
- health benefits of chocolate
- movies about chocolate
- countries famous for chocolate production

Student Sue chose the topic "college students" for her classification paragraph. She thought of six different ways to classify college students: by gender, major, age, marital status, reasons for attending, and irritating behaviors. She decided to classify students according to their irritating behaviors. As a student who recently returned to college, Sue found the behavior of some students in her environmental science class irritating, and she knew that she could think of several behaviors to write about.

PRACTICE   Developing Classification Principles
11.3   Find three different ways to classify each of the following topics.

1. relationships

_____

2. cars

_____

3. games

_____

Paragraph Practice: Choosing a Basis for Classification

Prewrite to choose a basis for classification for one of the following topics.

    clubs, organizations, or teams at your college or in your community
    unhealthy weight loss or exercise programs
    jobs in your career choice
    your personal rating system for video games, movies, websites, or television shows
    unpleasant or pleasant chores or responsibilities at home or at work

Writing across the Curriculum: Topics

Business: customers or clients
Fashion: clothing, accessories, or shoes for a specific activity or occasion
Environmental Science: endangered species
Culinary Arts: cooking methods or styles
Art Appreciation: music, art, or literary forms of a particular culture

Grouping Ideas   When you have chosen your basis for classification for your topic, you are ready to find groups or categories. For example, the topic "Chocolate" can be grouped according to health benefits, one of the bases for classification listed above.

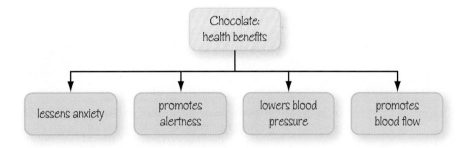

The topic "Chocolate" can also be grouped according to another basis for classification, movies in which chocolate plays a role:

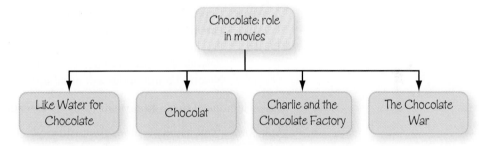

When choosing your basis for classification and groups for your topic, check for these possible problems:

1. **Group overlap.** Overlap happens when one group fits into more than one category. The next diagram shows some groups for the basis for classification *driver distractions.*

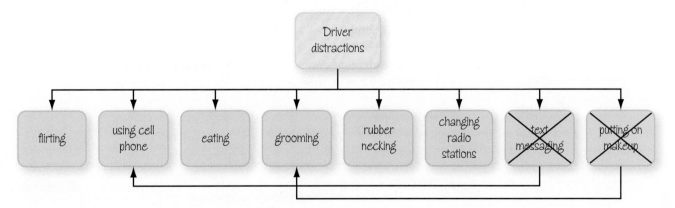

Four of these potential groups overlap.

- The group "text messaging" belongs in "using the cell phone" group. Text messaging is just one way of using a cell phone. Using the cell phone could also include making a call or taking a photo.
- The "putting on makeup" group fits into the "grooming" group. Grooming includes putting on makeup as well as styling hair, shaving, and so on.

2. **Groups all belong to the same classification principle.** If one or more of the groups do not fit, the classification will not be logical. Look at the groups on the next page for the basis of classification, types of test questions.

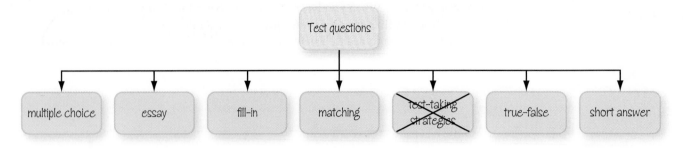

The group "test-taking strategies" is not a type of test question and does not belong to the basis of classification.

3. **Groups are complete.** All of the groups should be included, particularly when writing about groups that are well known. For example, to classify movies according to their content suitability for certain audiences, you would need to include all of the groups:

G   General audience; material appropriate for all ages
PG   Parental guidance recommended
PG-13   Parental guidance recommended for children under 13
R   Restricted; children under 17 must be with a parent
NC-17   No one 17 and under will be admitted

If you left one of these groups out, your classification would not be complete.

Sometimes, you will have more groups than you can discuss in a paragraph. If this happens, you may need to take a different approach to your topic. You may be able to take one of the groups and use it as your topic, then find a new basis for classification, and develop new groups. For example, you could choose PG-13 movies as your topic and then classify the types of movies that are PG-13.

PRACTICE   Identifying Classification Errors

11.4

Find the grouping error for each topic and tell why it is wrong.

O Overlaps with other groups   D Does not belong with this topic
I   Incomplete list of groups

Example:

1. sports: a. indoor   b. outdoor   c. competitive
c. competitive, O. Both indoor and outdoor sports can be competitive.

2. sneakers: a. leather   b. vinyl   c. canvas   d. synthetic

3. computers: a. notebook   b. laptop   c. handheld

4. teaching styles: a. good-looking   b. strict   c. not strict

5. natural bodies of water: a. seas   b. oceans   c. dams   d. lakes

6. dog breeds: a. German Shepherd   b. Chihuahua   c. Doberman Pinscher   d. Akita

Develop Your Groups   A classification graphic organizer can be a helpful tool for developing groups according to your basis for classification.

Using the classification graphic organizer, Sue created four groups for her topic "college students" using *irritating behaviors* as her basis for classification. As you can see in the figure below she gave each group an original name.

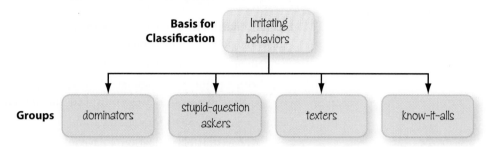

Paragraph Practice: Developing Groups

Using the classification graphic planner, develop at least three groups for the basis for classification you selected for one of the topics on page 206. Then check your groups to see that they do not overlap, are clearly different from one another, and are complete.

The classification graphic organizer shown here has four boxes. However, the planner is flexible. You can add as many boxes as you need.

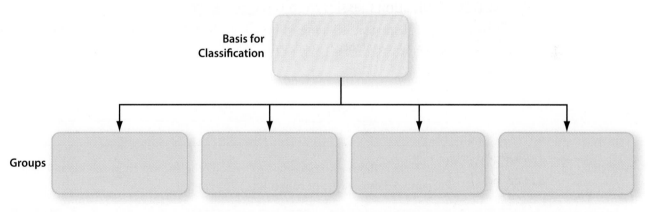

Narrow Your Topic and Write the Topic Sentence At this point, you have chosen a topic, selected a basis for classification, and developed groups. Writing the topic sentence involves putting all of these pieces together.

The topic sentence for a classification paragraph can be written in two ways:

1. Including the narrowed topic and the basis for classification:

> Movies can be classified according to their content appropriateness for certain audiences.

2. Including the narrowed topic, the basis for classification, and the list of groups:

> Movies can be classified according to their content appropriateness for certain audiences: G, PG, PG-13, R, and NC-17.

Here is Sue's topic sentence:

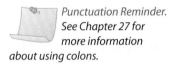

Punctuation Reminder. See Chapter 27 for more information about using colons.

> The students in my environmental science course can be classified by their irritating behaviors: the dominators, the stupid-question askers, the texters, and the know-it-alls.

TIPS | **Writing Classification Topic Sentences**

1. **Include a narrowed topic and basis for classification.** You need both parts to make the point of your paragraph.

   No point: I lived with eighty-seven women for ten weeks during naval training.

   With a point: My roommates in navy boot camp can be classified by their personalities as the easily controlled, the militants, and the rebels.

2. **Include a specific basis for classification.**

   No basis for classification: I have four kinds of tattoos on my body.

   With specific basis for classification: My tattoos can be classified according to their style: portraits, tribal pieces, script, and art.

It is not enough to give the number of groups that you are classifying. You need the basis for classification to make your groups specific.

PRACTICE   Evaluating Classification Topic Sentences

11.5   Explain what is wrong with each of the following classification topic sentences. If a topic sentence is good, write "good."

1. The employees in the music section of Borders Books have worked together for two years.

   _____

   _____

2. As a working mother who has had to rely on others to watch my children, I have encountered three types of babysitters.

   _____

   _____

3. My friends can be classified according to their personality types: the pleaser, the perfectionist, and the nonconformist.

   _____

   _____

4. At my high school, students had many annoying rules of conduct to follow.

   _____

   _____

Paragraph Practice: Writing a Topic Sentence

Write a topic sentence for the topic and groups you developed in the Paragraph Practice on page 209.

Organizing and Drafting the Classification Paragraph

Develop Supporting Details Developing supporting details for the classification paragraph involves deciding how to explain each of the groups. The supporting details for each group can be examples, descriptions, short narratives, and facts.

Each of the groups should be developed in a similar way. Also, the amount of detail should be the same for each group. For example, if you were writing about toy terrier dog breeds, you would explain the same points for each breed, such as size, coat, and temperament.

Using a side-by-side graphic organizer will help keep you organized as you develop your details. Fill in the names you have given to each of the groups. The side-by-side graphic organizer below shows Sue's details for her paragraph about the irritating behaviors of the students in her environmental science class. First, she describes the behavior of each of the groups and then gives an example.

Sue's Classification Graphic Organizer

Topic Sentence: The students in my environmental science course can be classified by their irritating behaviors: the dominators, the stupid-question askers, the texters, and the know-it-alls.

Groups: dominators | stupid-question askers | texters | know-it-alls

Details:

dominators	stupid-question askers	texters	know-it-alls
Behavior Take control of the class by talking	**Behavior** Ask questions that have already been answered	**Behavior** Text message from cell phones	**Behavior** Know the material, feel and act superior
Details Ryan made a 15-minute speech about environmental problems from coal mining.	**Details** Laurie asked what to bring the day of the test after the teacher had told the class.	**Details** Jackson texts from phone on his lap, never listens, takes notes, takes part in discussion.	**Details** Eugene laughs with disrespect when someone cannot answer a question.

Paragraph Practice: Developing Details

Using the side-by-side graphic organizer on the next page or another method, develop details for the topic you have been working on. Add or remove boxes as needed.

Organize Your Supporting Details Classification paragraphs are usually organized by order of importance, but they can be in spatial order or time order, depending on your topic. The most commonly used method is order of importance. Using your side-by-side graphic organizer, rank your groups from most to least important or least to most important.

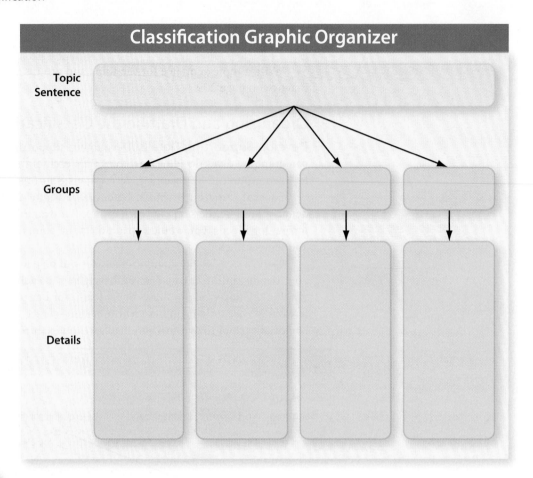

Classification Graphic Organizer

Topic Sentence

Groups

Details

Paragraph Practice: Organizing Supporting Details

Organize your groups by order of importance, spatial order, or chronological order, and check that you develop each group in the same way with the same amount of detail.

Write the First Draft As you write your first draft, consider balance and transitional words and expressions.

Balance Your classification paragraph should be balanced in both content and in organization. As you write, follow the same organizational pattern throughout the paragraph. Keep the following points in mind to avoid potential problems:

- Develop each group in the same way with the same amount of detail.
- Organize the points for each group in the same order.
- Cover each group completely before moving on to the next one.

Add Connectors: Transitional Words and Expressions Classification is similar to comparison and contrast in that you are writing about more than one subject. However, in classification, you explain the groups without comparing or contrasting them. Transitions for order of importance and for adding information are used most frequently.

Order of importance	the most important group, the least important type, equally important, even more important, another group, the final group
Add information	also, another example, equally important, furthermore, moreover, next, the next (the second, the third), yet another

Writing Reminder. For more information on transitional words and expressions, see Chapter 3.

Paragraph Practice: Writing the First Draft

Using your graphic organizer and topic sentence, write the first draft of your classification paragraph.

Revising, Editing, and Proofreading

Revise your draft by looking at one element at a time: Support, Organization, Connectors and transitions, and Style. The following Revision Checklist contains the SOCS elements as they apply to classification paragraphs.

REVISION CHECKLIST FOR A CLASSIFICATION PARAGRAPH

Element	Revision Checkpoints
Topic	☐ The topic can be classified.
	☐ The topic can be fully discussed in a single paragraph.
Topic Sentence	☐ The topic sentence includes these elements:
	▪ states the subject that you will be classifying.
	▪ states the point, which is the basis for classification.
	▪ may list the groups.
Support	☐ The groups are complete, fit under the same basis of classification, and do not overlap.
	☐ Supporting details for each group are developed in the same way.
	☐ The supporting details for each group can be examples, descriptions, short narratives, and facts.
	☐ All supporting details are relevant and adequate.
Organization	☐ Each group is discussed completely, one at a time.
	☐ The groups are arranged in order of importance, spatial order, or chronological order.
	☐ The paragraph is balanced in both content and in organization.
Connectors and Transitions	☐ Connectors and transitions provide coherence.
	☐ Transitions are used to introduce each new point and to connect details within each point.
Style	☐ Writing is clear, concise Standard Written English.
	☐ Tone is appropriate for a college audience.
	☐ Sentences are varied.

Peer Review Reminder.
For feedback on your writing, have someone read your paper and make comments on the Peer Review Response sheet in Chapter 4, page 55.

Paragraph Practice: Revising

Using the Revision Checklist for a Classification Paragraph, revise your classification paragraph.

Check Grammar, Punctuation, and Spelling As you reread your paper to check for grammar, punctuation, and spelling errors, pay special attention for possible errors that may arise in classification paragraphs. For example, be sure that you do not shift verb tenses or pronouns.

PRACTICE Revising and Editing a Classification Paragraph
11.6 Revise and edit Sue's paragraph. Then answer the questions that follow.

¹The students in my environmental science course can be classified by their irritating behaviors: the dominators, the stupid-question askers, the texters, and the know-it-alls. ²The first irritating group is the dominators. ³These students like to be the center of attention, so they take control of the class by monopolizing the discussion. ⁴For example, Ryan, the worst of the dominators, took over the discussion of worldwide cooperation to decrease global warming by giving a fifteen-minute speech expressing his opinion about environmental problems created by coal mining. ⁵Another irritating group is the stupid-question askers. ⁶For some reason, they ask questions that the teacher has already answered. ⁷Last week, for instance, the teacher told the students that they would need to bring a pencil and a scantron for our first major test. ⁸Not ten minutes after this announcement, Laurie, well-known for asking obvious questions, asked the teacher, Do I need to bring a pencil? What else do I need? What happens if I forget them? ⁹The next group, the texters, is a quiet bunch because they are busy using their cell phones to text message instead of paying attention to what is going on in class. ¹⁰Jackson's eyes are never on the teacher. ¹¹He is always looking down at his cell phone hidden in the folds of his baggy t-shirt and typing text messages nonstop from the beginning of class to the end. ¹²The most irritating group, though, is the know-it-alls. ¹³These bright students have read and studied the assigned chapters in the textbook and know all the answers to the teacher's questions, so they feel and act superior. ¹⁴Eugene is the poster child for the know-it-all group. ¹⁵He has no tolerance for the other students. ¹⁶Slumping back in his chair, he laughs and snickers with disrespect when someone answers a question incorrectly or makes a comment that he thinks is stupid. As an older, returning student, I realize that I have to ignore those who are irritating and focus on learning.

Questions on Revising

1. Underline the topic sentence. What are the narrowed topic, the basis for classification, and the groups?

_____

_____

2. The paragraph is missing a concluding sentence. Write an interesting concluding sentence that does not just restate the main idea of the paragraph.

_____

_____

3. Sentence 10 is missing a transitional word or expression. Add an appropriate transition.

_____

Question on Editing and Proofreading

4. Quotation marks are necessary to show that someone is speaking, but they are missing in this paragraph. Add quotation marks where they are needed.

Paragraph Practice: Editing and Proofreading

Edit and proofread your classification paragraph. Check that your final draft is complete, accurate, and error-free.

Paragraph Writing Assignments

Help Desk

Tyson has written his rough draft paragraph classifying the rules he had to follow in high school. Read Tyson's paper and suggest how he can classify his details into groups.

internal suspension a form of punishment where students must stay in a room away from other students where they work on school assignments

detention a punishment in which students must stay in school after regular school hours

Central High School had many frustrating rules that the students had to follow. For example, students had to always wear their picture IDs. In addition, passes were needed to show security guards that you had permission to be in the hallways. If we didn't have an ID and a pass, we would be sent to **Internal Suspension**. Also, we couldn't wear hats in class because the teachers felt it was disrespectful. We had to be in class by the second bell or we would get a **detention**. There was also a dress code. For example, we couldn't wear gang colors. No shirts with offensive words printed on them. There was also the rule that you could not show your cell phone on school grounds, and it had to be turned off at all times. We couldn't listen to iPods or have them out. No food was allowed in class. Chewing gum, juice, chips, and sunflower seeds are all considered food. Many students did not like the rules, and it's a relief to now be in college where we have more freedom.

Group Activity: Working Together to Classify

In small groups of three or four, classify the types of entertainment available in the city or town in which you live. Some ideas for the basis of classification could be as follows:

> type: sports, music, movies, dancing, car shows, dining, etc.
> cost: cheap, moderate, and expensive
> age group: children, teens, adults, etc.

Write a classification paragraph for an audience that is not familiar with the area where you live.

Reading and Writing across the Curriculum: Marketing

Read this paragraph classifying shopping centers and choose one of the writing assignments that follow.

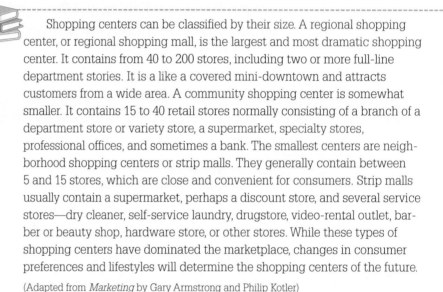

Shopping centers can be classified by their size. A regional shopping center, or regional shopping mall, is the largest and most dramatic shopping center. It contains from 40 to 200 stores, including two or more full-line department stories. It is a like a covered mini-downtown and attracts customers from a wide area. A community shopping center is somewhat smaller. It contains 15 to 40 retail stores normally consisting of a branch of a department store or variety store, a supermarket, specialty stores, professional offices, and sometimes a bank. The smallest centers are neighborhood shopping centers or strip malls. They generally contain between 5 and 15 stores, which are close and convenient for consumers. Strip malls usually contain a supermarket, perhaps a discount store, and several service stores—dry cleaner, self-service laundry, drugstore, video-rental outlet, barber or beauty shop, hardware store, or other stores. While these types of shopping centers have dominated the marketplace, changes in consumer preferences and lifestyles will determine the shopping centers of the future.

(Adapted from *Marketing* by Gary Armstrong and Philip Kotler)

Write a classification paragraph about one of the following topics:

- Classify the types of shopping centers in the area where you live or an area that you are familiar with.
- Classify the types of stores in one shopping center in the area where you live or an area that you are familiar with.

Comment on a Contemporary Issue

Do brands matter to you? How important is it for you to have the latest, best cell phone, the most popular sneakers, or a particular clothing line? The following writing activity may give you some insight about how status conscious you are.

Think of three easily recognizable brand-name items that you own or would like to own. Write a paragraph classifying those three items according to what they say about you. For each item, describe it and tell whether or not the brand name is noticeable. Then explain what using or wearing each item says about you. Does it give a positive or negative message?

Write about an Image

The Saffir-Simpson Hurricane Scale is a rating of 1 to 5 based on a hurricane's intensity. It gives an estimate of damage to property or flooding expected along the coast. The factor determining the potential damage is wind speed.

Using the information from the chart below, write a paragraph classifying hurricanes according to their intensity.

SAFFIR/SIMPSON HURRICANE SCALE

CATEGORY 1
Surge: 4–5 feet   Winds and Effects: 74–95 mph *(64–82 kt)*
No real damage to building structures. Damage primarily to unanchored mobile homes, shrubbery, and trees. Also, some coastal flooding and minor pier damage.

CATEGORY 2
Surge: 6–8 feet   Winds and Effects: 96–110 mph *(83–95 kt)*
Some roofing material, door, and window damage. Considerable damage to vegetation, mobile homes, etc. Flooding damages piers and small craft in unprotected moorings may break their moorings.

CATEGORY 3
Surge: 9–12 feet   Winds and Effects: 111–130 mph *(96–113 kt)*
Some structural damage to small residences and utility buildings, with a minor amount of structural failures. Mobile homes are destroyed. Flooding near the coast destroys smaller structures with larger structures damaged by floating debris. Terrain may be flooded well inland.

CATEGORY 4
Surge: 13–18 feet   Winds and Effects: 131–155 mph *(114–135 kt)*
More extensive structural failures with some complete roof failure on small residences. Major erosion of beach areas. Terrain may be flooded well inland.

CATEGORY 5
Surge: 19 feet + Winds and Effects: 156 mph+ *(135+ kt)*
Complete roof failure on many residences and industrial buildings. Some complete building failures with small utility buildings blown over or away. Flooding causes major damage to lower floors of all structures near the shoreline. Massive evacuation of residential areas may be required.

LO 3 The Classification Essay

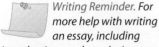

Writing Reminder. For more help with writing an essay, including introductions and conclusions, see Chapter 5.

The classification essay has the same purpose as the classification paragraph: to explain a topic by sorting it into groups according to something the groups have in common. Like the classification paragraph, the classification essay can inform or persuade. For example, in writing an essay classifying your teachers according to their teaching styles, you could explain their choices of activities, classroom policies, and attitudes toward students. On the other hand, if you wanted to persuade, you would develop a rating system for their choices of activities, classroom policies, and attitudes toward students.

Thesis Statement

The thesis statement for a classification essay makes a point about a topic by classifying it into groups according to a common feature called the basis for classification.

The thesis statement can be expressed in either of two ways:

Two-part thesis: The topic + basis for classification.
Electronic payment systems can be classified according to the process they use.

Three-part thesis: The topic + basis for classification + list of groups.
Electronic payment systems can be classified according to the process they use: electronic checks, blink credit cards, debit cards, and smart cards.

Body Paragraphs

Each of the body paragraphs in the classification essay explains one of the groups. Each group is developed in a similar way with the same amount of detail, as shown in the example below.

Body Paragraph: electronic checks	**Body Paragraph: blink credit cards**	**Body Paragraph: debit cards**	**Body Paragraph: smart cards**
Point 1. Description: substitute check for payment	**Point 1. Description:** credit card that uses radio frequency signals	**Point 1. Description:** plastic card allowing transfer of money from account for payment	**Point 1. Description:** credit-card-size plastic card programmed with electronic money
Point 2. Process used: receiving bank makes electronic image of paper check and sends image to the paying bank for instant payment	**Point 2. Process used:** consumers wave card in front of merchant's terminal or gas pump; computer chip sends customer information, and transaction is authorized	**Point 2. Process used:** consumers swipe card to make retail purchases	**Point 2. Process used:** consumers swipe card to make purchases
Point 3. Advantage: faster check clearing	**Point 3. Advantage:** replaces swiping and signing, waiting in line	**Point 3. Advantage:** replaces check writing	**Point 3. Advantage:** convenient for prepaid phone service, ATMs, vending machines, gas pump

(Adapted from *Business Essentials* by Ron Ebert and Ricky Griffin)

Classification Essay Example

Student Nadine Brown classifies babysitters based on their unusual character traits.

Brown 1

Nadine Brown

Professor Markus

College Preparatory Writing Skills

18 Oct. 2010

The Misses

1   When my husband, two sons, and I moved to the United States from Jamaica, we both found full-time jobs and needed a babysitter. We thought that finding a babysitter who was right for our family would be a simple process, but our experience proved the opposite to be true. The babysitters my husband and I employed over a two-year period can be classified according to their unusual character traits such as Miss Magnetic Fingers, Mrs. Heavenly Bound, and Miss Never Satisfied.

2   Miss Magnetic Fingers, the first babysitter we employed, created havoc in my life with her deceptive character. I had hired this young woman because she had two children, spoke excellent English, and needed a temporary job. I was told that she was honest and hardworking, so I took her in without reservations. When my world began to turn upside down, I had second thoughts about her. Her sticky magnetic fingers held on to all of my possessions that interested her. My necklaces and earrings disappeared from my jewelry boxes, and my clothing disappeared from my drawers. I had to start counting my money. At first I thought I had just misplaced these items. Then, I started to suspect Miss Magnetic Fingers and decided to do some detective work. If she had stolen my jewelry, she would certainly want to show it off at the local dance club. One Saturday night, I headed to her favorite club, and to my utter amazement, she was swirling on the dance floor wearing my jewelry and my engagement dress. When I confronted her, she admitted her theft and begged for forgiveness, but she was a con artist, and she had to go.

3   The next babysitter who replaced Miss Magnetic Fingers was Mrs. Heavenly Bound, who imposed her interpretations of the Bible on the family. Mrs. Heavenly Bound was highly recommended to us by a family member. This fifty-six-year-old married woman had raised four children and was looking for a babysitting position not merely for monetary gains, but also because, in her words, "All children belong to her." She seemed to be the mother I never had and the grandmother my children needed. Suddenly, our days were filled with messages from the Bible. She brought us religious magazines and books and placed them in every room of the house. Mrs. Heavenly Bound made recommendations about how I should dress, where I should go, and which occasions I should celebrate. She insisted that we follow her religious beliefs, which differed from ours. Her overly controlling behavior was like a dark cloud nestled over my house. Mrs. Heavenly Bound and I agreed that things were not working out.

4   The last babysitter, Miss Never Satisfied, seemed happy at first but later turned out to be a constant complainer. Like Mrs. Heavenly Bound, she had been recommended to us by a family member. She was a devoted member of our church who seemed pleased with the pay and the job itself. The days went by smoothly until I heard Miss Never Satisfied gossiping on the phone about how poorly she was being paid when learning about her friend's salary. She said, "These Jamaicans want you to overwork, but they don't want to pay. I will never work for a Jamaican again." I realized that although she had seemed happy, she really was not. From then on, her personality changed. She complained that we did not have food in the house though I had just shopped two days before. She complained that she was tired eating chicken and beef, that my children were spoiled and had too many toys, that the house was cold, and that the neighborhood was boring. I had to send her home.

Brown 3

5   After having had problems with Miss Magnetic Fingers, Mrs. Heavenly

Bound, and Miss Never Satisfied, I had no choice but to quit my job to stay home with

my children. This decision turned out to be one of the best decisions of my life. The dark

clouds above my home suddenly disappeared. The experience I had with the babysitters

taught me that my family, above all things, came first even if it meant firing someone

and quitting my job.

PRACTICE   Analyzing a Classification Essay
11.7   Answer the following questions about "The Misses."

1. Underline the thesis statement. What is the writer's organizing principle?

_____

2. What technique does the writer use in the lead-in?

_____

3. Underline the topic sentences of each of the body paragraphs. What is the point of each body paragraph?

_____

4. Circle the transition words used to introduce each difference in each of the topic sentences.

5. Which patterns of development does the writer use in his body paragraphs?

_____

6. What is the point(s) the writer makes about her experience with babysitters?

_____

Classification Essay Graphic Organizer

Using a classification essay graphic organizer will help you place your details in the appropriate pattern. The sample graphic organizer shown on the following page can be changed to suit your needs by adding paragraphs with supporting details.

Classification Essay Graphic Organizer

Introduction

Lead-in:

Bridge:

Thesis Statement:

Body Paragraphs: Write as many body paragraphs as you need.

Topic Sentence

Supporting Details

Conclusion

Thesis Statement Reminder:

Effective Closing Technique:

Essay Writing Assignments

Write about an Image

We all have many different roles in our lives. We are workers, teammates, music listeners, students, parents, and so on. We choose clothing styles that match those roles. For example, many workers wear uniforms, and teenagers often dress in the style of celebrities they admire.

Write an essay in which you classify your clothing styles according to the different roles that you play.

Writing Topics for a Classification Essay

For your classification essay, choose one of these options:

- from paragraph to essay: expand the paragraph you wrote in the paragraph section of this chapter
- any of the writing topics in the paragraph section of this chapter
- any topic from the following list:

> computer programs or websites you use for school, work, or entertainment
> memory strategies
> vehicles
> groups of people, such as sports fans, church goers, college students, and so on
> living arrangements

Writing across the Curriculum: Topics

Biology: insects and bugs found in your area
Family Studies: types of families
Sociology: forms of racism
Pharmacy: nonprescription drugs
Criminal Justice: crimes

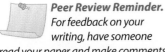 ***Peer Review Reminder.*** *For feedback on your writing, have someone read your paper and make comments on the Peer Review Response sheet in Chapter 4, page 55.*

English Success Tip: Strategies to Reduce Writing Anxiety

Many students experience anxiety when they have a writing assignment. Some worrying is good, but too much writing anxiety can lead to procrastination. You can help yourself gain control of the situation by trying the following strategies:

1. **Pick a place.** Find a comfortable place to write, make it your own space, and use it when you have a writing assignment. Your mind and body will associate that place with the task of writing.

2. **Choose a time.** Set time limits for writing and accomplish what you can in that time frame. If possible, write at the same time every day to establish a routine.

3. **Perform a ritual.** A ritual is a pattern of behavior performed in a set way. Before you start writing, do something that puts you in the mood to write. Here are some ideas: take a walk, have a snack, clear your desk, or listen to relaxing music.

For support in meeting this chapter's objectives, log in to www.mywritinglab.com, go to the Study Plan tab, click on **Classification** and choose **Paragraph Development—Division / Classification and Essay Development—Division / Classification** from the list of subtopics. Read and view the videos and resources in the Review Materials section, and then complete the Recall, Apply, and Write exercises in the Activities section. You can check your scores and overall progress by using the Gradebook.

Cause and Effect

Learning Objectives

After working through this chapter, you will be able to:

LO 1 Define cause as a form of writing that explains why something happened and effect as a form of writing that explains the results of something that happened.

LO 2 Write a cause and effect paragraph.

LO 3 Write a cause and effect essay.

LO 1 What Is Cause and Effect?

Cause and effect is a form of writing that shows the relationship between the reasons and results of a situation. **Cause** explains why something happened. **Effect** explains the results of something that happened. A cause and effect paragraph can explain causes or effects or both.

Some causes and effects are obvious. For example, think about what might cause a student to cheat on a final exam. The most obvious reason is that the student does not know the correct answers. However, other underlying reasons might be that the student did not study or is under pressure to get a good grade. The diagram at the top of page 226 shows possible causes and effects of cheating on a final exam.

Sometimes cause and effect can form a causal chain. One action has an effect, which becomes the cause for another effect, and so on as shown on page 226.

You use cause and effect to analyze situations in everyday life. For example, you may try to convince a friend to stay in school or to justify why you need to buy an expensive pair of sneakers you have been wanting. At work, a company may have penalties for employees who show up late.

QuickWrite

Write about a situation in which you saw someone cheat in school, at work, or in everyday life. What were the causes and/or effects?

Cause and Effect in College Writing

Cause and effect is often used in college writing. In a college humanities class, for example, you may study why ancient Egypt fell to the Romans or the effects of the introduction of sound on the film industry. In an advertising or business class, you may study the effects of the newer media, such as email, the Internet, podcasts, video games, product placement, and video on demand (VOD), on a company's communication about its products.

LO 2 The Cause and Effect Paragraph

The main point in a cause and effect paragraph can be developed by giving causes, effects, or both. The following paragraphs are examples of cause or effect writing.

Causes and Effects of Cheating

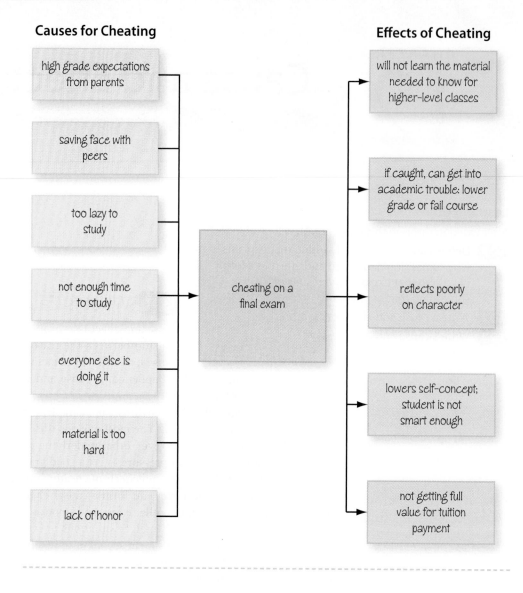

Causes for Cheating

high grade expectations from parents

saving face with peers

too lazy to study

not enough time to study

everyone else is doing it

material is too hard

lack of honor

cheating on a final exam

Effects of Cheating

will not learn the material needed to know for higher-level classes

if caught, can get into academic trouble: lower grade or fail course

reflects poorly on character

lowers self-concept; student is not smart enough

not getting full value for tuition payment

Causal Chain

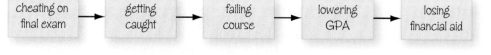

cheating on final exam → getting caught → failing course → lowering GPA → losing financial aid

Effects Paragraph Example

The effects of using a cell phone while driving are explained in this paragraph.

[1]Experiments have shown that cell phone use clearly affects drivers' behavior. [2]One effect is that drivers tend to slow down when talking on the phone. [3]Another effect is that they also have slower reaction times. [4]For example, drivers are slower to hit the brakes and take longer to resume normal speed. [5]A third effect is that they often drift outside the lines of the lane in which they are driving. [6]Using a cell phone also affects drivers' judgment. For instance, they may stop at green lights. [7]The last effect is that drivers miss

stop signs and red lights. ⁸Some slam on their brakes when they notice they are part of the way through an intersection at which they were supposed to stop. ⁹These effects have been observed just as often in studies using hands-free phones as conventional hand-held models. ¹⁰Thus, experimental studies show definitively that, on average, cell phone use weakens driving ability.

(Adapted from *The World of Psychology* by Samuel E. Wood et al.)

PRACTICE Analyzing an Effects Paragraph

12.1 Answer the questions about the effects paragraph you just read about cell phone use.

1. Underline the topic sentence. What is the point of the topic sentence?

_____

2. Find and list three effects from the paragraph.

_____

_____

3. Underline the transition words.

Cause Paragraph Example

The following paragraph explains the causes of criticism of cell phone studies.

¹Critics have attacked cell phone use studies for many reasons. ²First, they say other attention-demanding tasks impair driving behaviors just as much as cell phone use does. ³One study found, for example, that searching for a radio station while driving produced the same kinds of harmful effects on drivers' behavior as cell phone use. ⁴Another reason is that the same kinds of effects on driving behavior occurred whether a person was talking on a cell phone or talking to a passenger in the car. ⁵Additional criticism involves the nature of the cell phone task itself. ⁶In most studies, participants do not have real conversations on their cell phones. ⁷Instead of trying to create real-world conversations, experimenters transmitted math problems to drivers that they were supposed to solve in their heads within a limited time frame. ⁸A fourth reason critics attack cell phone use studies is their failure to consider the effects of practice. ⁹Critics say that people become more efficient at multi-tasking with practice, a factor that is not thought about in most experiments. ¹⁰Finally, critics note that real-world drivers often take actions to reduce distraction and that they are well aware of the potentially risk-enhancing effects of behavior changes caused by distractions, so they work to manage the number of demands on their attention while driving.

(Adapted from *The World of Psychology* by Samuel E. Wood et al.)

PRACTICE   Analyzing a Cause Paragraph

12.2   Answer the questions about the reasons paragraph you just read.

1. Underline the topic sentence. What is the point of the paragraph?

_____

2. Underline the transition words and expressions used in the paragraph.

3. How many causes (reasons) are given in the paragraph? List the sentence numbers that introduce each one.

_____

4. Do you think the reasons given in the paragraph are convincing? Why?

_____

CAUSE AND EFFECT PARAGRAPH ESSENTIALS

A good cause and effect paragraph has these essential elements:

1. The topic sentence makes a point about the causes and/or effects of a situation.
2. The causes and effects are logical, are complete, and show a clear relationship.
3. The supporting details are organized by order of importance, spatial order, or chronological order.
4. The supporting details are explained with descriptions, examples, short narratives, comparisons, and facts.
5. Cause and effect connectors and transitions help readers see the movement from one cause or effect to another.

Prewriting the Cause or Effect Paragraph

Before you write, you must choose a suitable topic and develop it.

Decide Your Topic and Purpose   The purpose of your cause and effect paragraph can be to inform or to persuade. For example, you could inform the reader by giving the reasons your college redesigned the computer lab in the Writing Center. On the other hand, you could persuade the reader that the redesigning of the computer lab was beneficial for students.

When deciding on your own cause or effect topic or writing about an assigned topic, consider the following:

1. **Choose a topic that you know well.** Writing about a topic that you know about or have studied is essential. Cause and effect writing requires that you logically think through the causes and effects of a situation to avoid errors in reasoning. For example, if you do not know the reasons for economic inflation, then you will end up with nothing to say.

2. **Choose a topic that can be explained completely in one paragraph.** Some topics have multiple causes or effects or both and cannot be covered in a single paragraph. Explaining the causes or effects of global warming would be difficult to accomplish in one paragraph because there are many theories about this topic.

Cause and Effect Graphic Organizer

Causes   **Effects**

Narrow Your Topic and Write the Topic Sentence Narrowing your topic involves deciding whether you want to write about causes, effects, or both. You may find it easier to focus your paragraph on causes or effects rather than on both. Look at the causes and effects you listed for one of the topics in the prewriting exercise. Choose the one that has enough details to support in a paragraph.

The topic sentence for a cause and effect paragraph includes the narrowed topic and the main point, which will be a cause or effect or both.

Cause	People choose to move to the United States for many reasons.
Effect	Some scientists believe that frequent online social networking has negative effects on the brains of young users.
Cause and Effect	Because hurricanes bring together destructive kinds of weather, they can have devastating effects.
Causal Chain	My daughter's birth caused my personal journey that started with seeking counseling and ended with achieving **sobriety**.

sobriety state of not being
intoxicated on alcohol or drugs

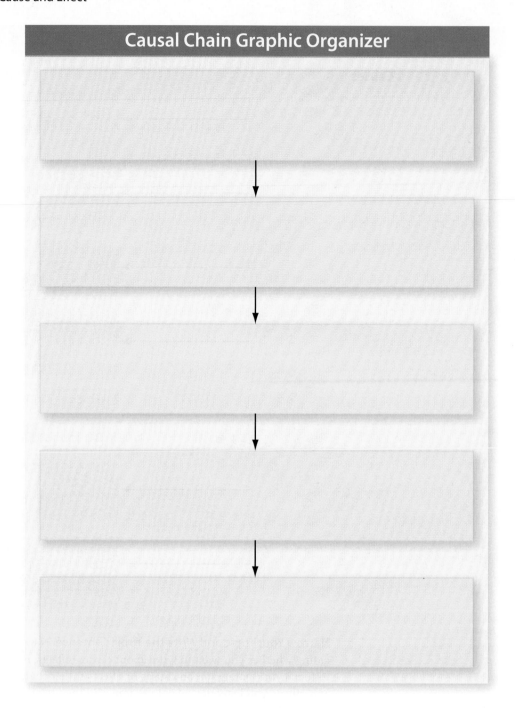

Causal Chain Graphic Organizer

Royce's topic sentence focuses on the effects of quitting smoking:

> Quitting smoking has had many positive effects on my life.

TIPS | **Writing Cause or Effect Topic Sentences**

1. Indicate your focus: cause, effect, cause and effect, or causal chain.

   No focus: Taking advantage of a good shopping deal may be the reason for **impulse buying** although there are other factors too, but not all people who look for good deals are impulse buyers.

   Focused: Impulse buying is caused by many factors.

impulse buying buying something suddenly without thinking about it

2. Clearly state the cause and/or effect relationship.

> **Not clear:** College students can learn a lot in a psychology course.
>
> **Clear:** Taking a psychology course in college can change students' views on human relationships.

PRACTICE Evaluating Cause and Effect Topic Sentences

12.4   Explain what is wrong with each of the following cause effect topic sentences. If a topic sentence is good, write "good."

1. More young adults voted in the past presidential election than in previous elections.

_____

2. The birth of my son positively affected every aspect of my life.

_____

3. Alcoholism has several serious health effects.

_____

4. Having a credit card can be good or bad.

_____

5. My goal is to be self-employed.

_____

Paragraph Practice: Writing a Topic Sentence

Write a topic sentence for the topic about which you have been prewriting. Label the narrowed topic and the focus as in the previous topic sentence examples.

Organizing and Drafting the Cause and Effect Paragraph

Develop Supporting Details Developing supporting details for the cause or effect paragraph involves finding relevant, logical causes and/or effects and providing explanations for them.

From your prewriting graphic organizer, choose the causes and/or effects that will support the point of your topic sentence. You may need to do some additional prewriting to develop more details.

Writing Reminder.
To learn more about errors in logic for cause and effect, see the English Success Tip at the end of this chapter.

Find Relevant, Logical Causes and/or Effects   Your causes and effects must be based on sound, logical reasoning. One error in logic is called "false cause," which means that just because one thing happened before another does not mean that it caused the other. An example is that a person got a cold because she got caught in the rain. Colds are caused by a person's coming in contact with cold viruses, not by rain.

Provide Explanations   Support each cause and/or effect with a thorough explanation to help the reader understand the relationship between the causes and effects. You can use facts, examples, short narratives, comparisons, and descriptions.

For example, Royce decided to write about the positive effects he experienced by quitting smoking. One of the effects he listed was that his parents no longer nag him to stop smoking. To further explain this, Royce could tell the reader his relationship with his parents has improved to the point where they enjoy having dinner together every night, discussing their day's activities and their opinions about current events.

Paragraph Practice: Selecting Supporting Details

Select the causes and/or effects that you would like to include in your paragraph from your cause and effect graphic organizer. Put a checkmark next to each one you select.

Organize Your Supporting Details Organizing your supporting details includes choosing an order for presenting them and if needed, grouping them. As you organize, analyze your causes and effects and add, remove, and arrange details as needed.

Choosing an Order   Choose the most appropriate order to present your details: order of importance, spatial order, or chronological order.

Order of importance	to rank causes or effects, such as the most important to least important reasons for your decision to attend college
Spatial order	to explain causes or effects that occur in a specific location, such as the effects of a tsunami on various parts of an island
Chronological order	to explain causes or effects that occur in a sequence, such as events that led to World War II

Grouping Causes and Effects   Grouping causes and/or effects can help you tighten your organization. For instance, Royce grouped his details as health, financial, and emotional effects.

Royce's Effects Grouped	
Group	**Effect**
Health effects	Stamina has improved, don't get short of breath when doing physical activities Chances of getting smoking-related diseases like my aunt and uncle are decreased No more bad breath; can get teeth whitened and they will stay white Appetite increased, am at a normal weight No frequent colds or bronchitis
Financial effects	Saving the money that I would have spent on cigarettes to pay for school
Emotional effects	Parents happy, no more nagging

Paragraph Practice: Organizing Supporting Details

Group any causes or effects and choose the pattern and order you want to use for your paragraph. You may find it helpful to use a graphic organizer as student Royce did to list the groups and put them in your preferred order.

Write the First Draft As you write your first draft, explain each cause and/or effect thoroughly and add connectors and transitional words and expressions.

- *Explain each cause and effect thoroughly.* Causes and effects are usually related. Therefore, each one must be thoroughly explained so that the reader can understand the connection between them. Use your planning materials to guide you while writing.
- *Add connectors: transitional words and expressions.* The following transitional words and expressions can be used in cause and effect paragraphs.

Cause and Effect Connectors and Transitions	
Cause Connectors and Transitions	**Effect Connectors and Transitions**
because, because of	as a result, as a result of
due to	consequently
for	as a consequence
for this reason	one effect (result) is, another effect (result) is, etc.
if ... then	therefore
one reason (cause) is, another reason (cause) is, etc.	thus
since	

Revising, Editing, and Proofreading

Revise your draft by looking at one element at a time: Support, Organization, Connectors and transitions, and Style. The following Revision Checklist contains the SOCS elements as they apply to cause or effect paragraphs.

REVISION CHECKLIST FOR A CAUSE AND EFFECT PARAGRAPH

Element	Revision Checkpoints
Topic	☐ The topic addresses causes and/or effects.
	☐ The topic can be fully discussed in a single paragraph.
Topic Sentence	☐ The topic sentence states includes the narrowed topic and the point, which focuses on one of the following: cause, effect, or both.
Support	☐ Supporting details consist of causes and/or effects.
	☐ The causes and effects are based on logical reasoning.
	☐ The explanations for each cause or effect can be examples, descriptions, comparisons, short narratives, and facts.
	☐ All supporting details are relevant and adequate.

Element	Revision Checkpoints
Organization	☐ Each cause and/or effect is discussed completely, one at a time.
	☐ Points are arranged in order of importance, spatial, or chronological order.
Connectors and Transitions	☐ Cause and effect and addition connectors and transitions provide coherence. Spatial or chronological order transitions are used when appropriate.
	☐ Connectors and transitions are used to introduce each new point and to connect details within each point.
Style	☐ Writing is clear, concise Standard Written English.
	☐ Tone is appropriate for a college audience.
	☐ Sentences are varied.

Your Cause and Effect Paragraph: Revising

Using the Revision Checklist for a Cause and Effect Paragraph, revise your cause and effect paragraph.

Peer Review Reminder. For feedback on your writing, have someone read your paper and make com - ments on the Peer Review Response sheet in Chapter 4, page 55.

Check Grammar, Punctuation, and Spelling As you reread your paper to check for grammar, punctuation, and spelling errors, pay special attention for possible errors that may arise in cause and effect paragraphs.

Words Easily Confused: Affect and Effect It is easy to confuse these two words because they sound similar. However, they are used differently. **In cause and effect writing, *affect* is a verb meaning to have an influence on, while *effect* is a noun meaning a result.**

Affect **as a verb** Moving into my own apartment affected my life in many ways.

Effect **as a noun** Moving into my own apartment had many effects on my life.

Repetition When writing a sentence giving a reason, avoid writing **the reason why is because**. This phrase has three reason words when only one is needed. Instead, begin your sentence **the reason is**.

Grammar Reminder. For more information on fragments, comma splices, and run-ons, see Chapters 19 and 20.

Sentence Errors Fragments may occur when you begin sentences with words such as *because* or *since*. Comma splice and run-on errors may occur when you use words such as *for* (meaning *because*), *therefore*, or *consequently* to connect two sentences. In addition, check the meanings of these connecting words to ensure that you use them correctly.

PRACTICE Revising and Editing an Effect Paragraph

12.5 Revise and edit Royce's paragraph. Then answer the questions that follow.

[1]Quitting smoking has had many positive effects on my life. [2]The first effect was financial. [3]I used to smoke about a pack a day and more than that when I went out with friends. [4]I had been spending about twenty-five dollars a week on cigarettes. [5]My yearly expense was twelve hundred dollars. [6]When I stopped smoking, I realized that I could save the money I spent on cigarettes by opening a money market account to pay for college. [7]Another effect was emotional. [8]My parents criticized me every day about my smoking. [9]They had both quit smoking several years ago. [10]They complained about the second hand smoke they had to suffer with when I smoked in the house or in their car. [11]The lingering odor of cigarette smoke irritated them too. [12]I felt like an outcast in my own home. [13]When I stopped smoking, my parents stopped complaining; and we developed a friendly relationship. [14]During dinner, we discussed the events of our day and other issues rather than arguing. [15]My dad was so happy that he rewarded me with tickets to an NFL football game. [16]The final and most important effect of my quitting smoking was that my health improved, I could now run five miles without getting chest pains or out of breath. [17]In addition, my appetite increased, and I went from being ten pounds underweight to my normal weight. [18]I also noticed that I did not get sick; those frequent colds and bronchitis that I used to suffer from were no longer a problem for me. [19]Finally, by quitting smoking, I have reduced my chances of dying from lung cancer like my aunt and uncle did. [20]Quitting smoking was not easy, and I still want a cigarette now and then, but I am proud that I conquered my addiction.

Questions on Revising

1. Underline the topic sentence. What are the narrowed topic and the focus?

   Narrowed topic: _____

   Focus: _____

2. Which sentence is the least relevant to the passage? Circle the number of the sentence.

3. What transitions would be best for sentences 14 and 15?

   Sentence 14: _____

   Sentence 15: _____

Questions on Editing and Proofreading

4. Which sentence uses the semicolon incorrectly? Write the corrected sentence here.

_____

_____

5. Which sentence has a comma splice error? Write the corrected sentence here.

_____

_____

_____

Paragraph Practice: Editing and Proofreading

Edit and proofread your cause or effect paragraph. Check that your final draft is complete, accurate, and error-free.

Paragraph Writing Assignments

Help Desk

Javier has written a cause paragraph on the reasons he enjoys baseball. Read the paragraph and answer the questions below.

> ¹Baseball, which I have been playing ever since I was five years old, is a sport that I enjoy for many reasons. ²One reason is that baseball keeps me active. ³If it was not for baseball, I would not be the person I am today. ⁴Another reason I enjoy baseball is it is a team sport. ⁵I love to cheer on my teammates when they make a good play or get a great hit. ⁶I always cheer them on because I want to make them feel good about themselves, which will give them the confidence to make another play or get another hit. ⁷The most important reason is that playing baseball can make me some money in the future. ⁸In a couple of years, if I am good enough, a major league team will draft me, and I could become very rich just for playing the sport I love.

1. Each reason in a paragraph must be explained with adequate and specific details. Which reason(s) need to be revised by adding more specific details?

_____

_____

2. What details could Javier add to make his supporting points convincing?

_____

_____

Group Activity

You have been asked to develop a list of convincing reasons to solve a problem on your campus or in your community. For example, your college may need additional parking or an improved registration-advisement process. Your community may need a stop light at a specific location or additional law enforcement at a local mall.

In groups of three or four, identify a problem, decide on a solution, and develop a minimum of four strong, logical reasons and explanations for your solution. Then, put these ideas into a paragraph for your school or local newspaper.

Reading and Writing across the Curriculum: Health

Noise is one of the common causes of stress and hearing loss in the United States. If you have ever sat close to speakers during a concert, you may have experienced a temporary hearing loss or ringing in your ears hours after the concert was over. Even using headphones or earbuds with the volume up high can cause damage. The following paragraph explains the physical effects of noise:

dilate become wider

> Physically, our bodies respond to noise in a variety of ways. Blood pressure increases, blood vessels in the brain **dilate**, and vessels in other parts of the body constrict. The pupils of the eyes open wider. Cholesterol levels in the blood rise, and some endocrine glands secrete additional stimulating hormones, such as adrenaline, into the bloodstream. Noise-related problems include disturbed sleep patterns, headaches, and tension. Hearing can be damaged by varying lengths of exposure to sound, which is measured in decibels. If the duration of allowable daily exposure to different decibel levels is exceeded, the sensitive hair cells of the inner ear and the hearing nerve become damaged, and hearing loss will result.
>
> (Adapted from *Access to Health* by Rebecca J. Donatelle and ASHA.org, American Speech-Language-Hearing Association)

Write a paragraph about the effects of noise on you in school, at work, or in every day life (including entertainment).

Comment on a Contemporary Issue

generalization an idea based on limited facts that may be partly true but not always true

> Prejudice is an inflexible and unfair **generalization** about an entire category of people. Prejudice is unfair because such attitudes are supported by little or no direct evidence. Prejudice may target people of a particular social class, sex, sexual orientation, age, political affiliation, race, or ethnicity.
>
> (Adapted from *Society* by John J. Macionis)

Write a paragraph about the causes and/or effects of prejudice.

Writing about an Image

Prewrite possible causes and effects that this image suggests to you. Then, write a cause and/or effects paragraph using the details from your prewriting activity.

LO 3 The Cause and Effect Essay

The cause and effect essay has the same purpose as the cause and effect paragraph: to show the relationship between the causes and/or effects of a situation. **Cause** explains why something happened. **Effect** explains the results of something that happened.

The cause and effect essay uses the same organization pattern as the cause and effect paragraph, focusing on causes, effects, causes and effects, or a causal chain. The cause and effect graphic organizers on pages 231, 232, and 244 can also be used to plan your essay. They will help keep you organized as you prewrite, draft, and revise.

Cause and effect essays can inform or persuade. For example, in writing a cause and effect essay about a car accident, you could give the reader a factual account of the causes and effects. The drivers of two cars were both attempting to pull into the same parking space when they collided. On the other hand, you could persuade the reader by explaining why one of the drivers was at fault for the crash.

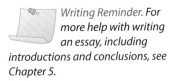

Writing Reminder. For more help with writing an essay, including introductions and conclusions, see Chapter 5.

Thesis Statement

The thesis statement for a cause and effect essay makes a point about the causes and/or effects of a situation. The thesis statement can be expressed in either of two ways:

Two-part thesis: Narrowed topic + main point about causes, effects, or both. Jay's underage drinking and driving had many life-changing effects.

Three-part thesis: Narrowed topic + main point about causes, effects, or both + list of specific causes, effects, or both.

Jay's underage drinking and driving had many life-changing effects; he was arrested, he was fired, and his parents took his truck away.

Body Paragraphs

The body paragraphs in the cause and effect essay are arranged according to whether you are writing about causes, effects, or both. Each cause and effect can be supported with evidence such as facts, examples, short narratives, or descriptions. The essay plans below have two or three body paragraphs; however, you can use as many paragraphs as necessary to support your thesis statement.

All Causes Plan

Paragraph 1: Cause
Paragraph 2: Cause
Paragraph 3: Cause

All Effects Plan

Paragraph 1: Effect
Paragraph 2: Effect
Paragraph 3: Effect

Causal Chain Plan

Paragraph 1: Cause and Effect
Paragraph 2: Cause and Effect
Paragraph 3: Cause and Effect

Cause and Effect Plan A

Paragraph 1: Cause Cause Cause
Paragraph 2: Effect Effect Effect

Cause and Effect Plan B

Paragraph 1: Cause Effect
Paragraph 2: Cause Effect
Paragraph 3: Cause Effect

Cause and Effect Essay Example

Student Royce Bonta had previously written a paragraph about the positive effects he experienced after he quit smoking. He decided to develop his paragraph into an essay. In his introduction, Royce explains his attempts and final success at quitting. Each of the body paragraphs identifies one or more effects on himself or on his family.

Royce Bonta

Professor Markus

College Preparatory English

22 Oct. 2010

Clean Living

1   Several years ago, I took up the bad habit of smoking cigarettes. I never considered myself to be a heavy smoker at one pack a day compared to my friends, who smoked two to three times as many cigarettes a day as I did. At first, I only smoked socially, but slowly I became addicted. I began to realize how smoking affected my life and tried to quit but failed each time. I tried using the nicotine patch, but it gave me nightmares. Nicotine gum tasted awful. I realized that quitting cold turkey was the best solution and the most difficult one, but I succeeded. Quitting smoking had many positive effects on my life such as improving my health, saving me money, making my parents happy, and getting the disgusting smell of cigarette smoke out of my car.

2   The most important effect of quitting smoking was that my health improved. I can now run five miles without getting chest pains or out of breath. In addition, my appetite increased, and I am no longer ten pounds underweight. My sense of taste is no longer impaired by the chemicals from cigarettes, and now I actually enjoy my favorite foods. I also noticed that I did not get sick; those frequent colds and bronchitis that I used to suffer from were no longer a problem for me. Finally, although my health had not been seriously affected, I was not

willing to take any more risks. By quitting smoking, I have reduced my chances of

dying from lung cancer like my aunt and uncle did. As a side benefit, I no longer

have smoker's breath, and the nicotine stains on my teeth are fading.

3   Quitting smoking not only improved my health, but also saved me

money. I decided not to pay Phillip Morris to kill me any longer. When I started

smoking, a pack of cigarettes was around three dollars, but when I quit, the cost was

five dollars a pack. After calculating what I was spending per year on cigarettes, I

determined that I could save around two thousand dollars a year, money that I could

be putting towards my education. I realized that I could have gone to Home Depot

and purchased the materials to construct an elaborate coffin for the price I was

paying to slowly dig my grave. In addition, the cost of my health insurance decreased

since I was no longer considered high risk.

4   Another positive effect of quitting smoking besides improving my health

and saving me money was that I made my parents happy. My mother, a former

smoker, has tried repeatedly to get me to stop smoking. She complained about the

second-hand smoke both she and my father had to put up with when I smoked in

the house. My father, who lost his mother, sister, and brother-in-law to lung cancer

from smoking, did not want me to follow in their footsteps and offered me money to

quit, but I had refused. When I finally stopped smoking, my parents were delighted. I

did not want to take the money my father offered me, but he insisted. I was no

longer a person who was rejected in my own home and my relationship with my

parents improved.

5   Getting rid of the disgusting smell of cigarette smoke from my car, while

not as significant as the other positive effects, was the final benefit of quitting

smoking. I realize now how overpowering the smell of cigarette smoke was in the

Bonta 3

enclosed space of a car and how difficult it is to eliminate the strong, unpleasant smell from the interior after being exposed to it for so long. My new car no longer smelled like a rolling chimney, and I did not have to worry about burning a hole in the interior, lowering its resale value.

6   Quitting smoking was not easy, and I still get cravings for a cigarette now and then, but I am proud that I conquered my addiction. I no longer have to feel like an outcast at restaurants, work, and other public places where smoking is not allowed. Most importantly, I no longer worry about my health, I have been able to save money, my parents are happy, and my car smells fresh and clean.

PRACTICE 12.6   Analyzing a Cause and Effect Essay

1. Underline the thesis statement. What is the writer's main point?

   _____

2. What technique does the writer use in the lead-in?

   _____

3. Underline the topic sentences of each of the body paragraphs. What is the point of each body paragraph?

   _____

4. Circle the transition words used to introduce each difference in each of the topic sentences.

5. Which body paragraphs include multiple effects?

   _____

6. In addition to referring to the thesis statement, underline the point the writer makes in the conclusion.

Cause and Effect Essay Graphic Organizer

Using a cause and effect graphic organizer will help you place your details in the appropriate pattern: causes, effects, or both. It will also help you see the relationship between the causes and effects. The sample graphic organizer shown on page 244 can be changed to suit your needs by adding paragraphs, points, and supporting evidence.

Cause and Effect Essay Graphic Organizer

Introduction

Lead-in:

Bridge:

Thesis Statement:

Body Paragraph for Cause or Effect Plan

Topic Sentence:

Cause or Effect 1 with Evidence/Explanation:

Cause or Effect 2 with Evidence/Explanation:

Cause or Effect 3 with Evidence/Explanation:

Body Paragraph for Cause and Effect Plan

Topic Sentence:

All Causes or All Effects with Evidence/Explanation or
One Cause and Effect with Evidence/or Explanation

Conclusion

Choose Effective Closing Technique.

Essay Writing Assignments

Write about an Image

The message in the fortune cookie in this photograph expresses the outcome that college students expect when they earn their degree. Many students choose a major because it will get them a job that pays well after graduation. Others choose a major that they love even though they may not find a good job right away.

Write an essay explaining the reasons you chose your major. If you have not selected a major yet, write about the reasons for one you are considering.

Writing Topics for a Cause and Effect Essay

For your cause and effect essay, choose one of these options:

- from paragraph to essay: expand the paragraph you wrote in the paragraph section of this chapter to an essay
- any of the writing topics in the paragraph section of this chapter
- any topic from the following list:

  an accident
  participation in an activity or group
  a particular college course
  popularity of shows about actual crimes
  a troublesome habit

Peer Review Reminder. *For feedback on your writing, have someone read your paper and make comments on the Peer Review Response sheet in Chapter 4, page 55.*

Writing across the Curriculum Topics

Anthropology: preserving a particular cultural heritage
Environmental Science: human activity on the environment
Health: a particular illness or disease
Humanities: a particular work or movement in art, music, film, or literature
Psychology: over-concern with weight or physical appearance

English Success Tip: Avoiding Common Cause and Effect Errors

Several errors in logic can occur when writing cause and effect papers. Four of the most common errors are explained in the following chart. Be sure to avoid them.

Error in Logic	Example	Explanation
Thinking that one event caused another just because it happened first (mistaking sequence for cause)	Student Manfredo bought a new calculator. As a result, he received an A on his math test.	While Manfredo may have done well on his test when using new calculator, the calculator did not cause the A.
Thinking that because two things happened at the same time that one of those things caused the other.	While Manfredo was taking his math test, it was raining. Therefore, the rain caused him to get a low grade on the test.	Even though it rained at the same time Manfredo was taking his test, the rain was not responsible for his low grade.
Not looking at underlying causes	Manfredo believes that he received an A on his math test because he studied the night before.	Manfredo did much more than study the night before. A week before the test, he joined a math study group where students practiced solving and explaining solutions to problems from class and ones they made up. After every math class, he went over the homework problems and solved them until he could get them right with no difficulty.
Including insignificant causes	Manfredo earned an A on his math test because he turned in all of his homework assignments.	Turning in homework assignments certainly contributed to his good grade, but it was not a significant reason.

For support in meeting this chapter's objectives, log in to www.mywritinglab .com, go to the Study Plan tab, click on **Cause and Effect** and choose **Paragraph Development—Cause and Effect and Essay Development—Cause and Effect** from the list of subtopics. Read and view the videos and resources in the Review Materials section, and then complete the Recall, Apply, and Write exercises in the Activities section. You can check your scores and overall progress by using the Gradebook.

CHAPTER 13 Definition

Copyright © 2011 Pearson Education, Inc.

Learning Objectives

After working through this chapter, you will be able to:

LO 1 Explain that definition is a form of writing that discusses what a word, expression, or concept means.

LO 2 Write a definition paragraph.

LO 3 Write a definition essay.

LO 1 What Is Definition?

Definition is a form of writing that explains what a word, expression, or concept means. Definitions are used in many writing situations. In the workplace, definition is used in proposals, memos, reports, technical documents, and instructions. In addition, many fields have their own specific terms. For instance, the computer field has hundreds of special words, such as *application, backup, browser, database,* and *software.*

QuickWrite

Write your own definition of a word or expression that you use in college, at work, or in everyday life.

Definition in College Writing

Knowing how to define a word is an important skill to develop in college. Every course you take has specialized terms that you must learn. For example, nursing students must learn the definitions of various diagnoses, called diagnostic labels. There are over 170 labels for clinical use and testing. To show your knowledge of words for your courses, you may be asked to recognize the definitions of specific terms on objective tests or to write a sentence definition or an in-depth explanation of a word.

LO 2 The Definition Paragraph

There are two types of definitions that you may be asked to write: formal and extended.

- A **formal definition** is a concise, brief statement of a word's meaning, usually in a sentence.
- An **extended definition** is a one- to several-paragraph explanation of a word using a variety of writing patterns.

Formal Definition Examples

The following are examples of formal definitions you might find in your college textbooks. Each consists of three parts: the word, the group it belongs to, and its features.

Bulimia nervosa is an eating disorder that is characterized by binge eating followed by measures to get rid of the excess calories by vomiting or emptying the bowels.

A *business* is an organization that provides goods and services to earn profits.

Greenhouse effect is the buildup of carbon dioxide in the Earth's atmosphere that allows light to enter but inhibits the release of heat.

Culture shock is a feeling of confusion that people experience when they visit or move to a fundamentally different culture.

PRACTICE   Identifying the Parts of Formal Definitions

13.1   Using a dictionary or personal knowledge, for each of the definition examples that you just read, write the group it belongs to, and the word's features in the space provided. The first one is done for you.

Word	Group	Features
bulimia nervosa	eating disorder	binge eating followed by measures to get rid of the excess calories by vomiting or emptying the bowels.
business		
greenhouse effect		
culture shock		

Extended Definition Paragraph Example

The following is an example of an extended definition of the word *contamination* as used in the food service industry.

[1]**Contamination** is the introduction of harmful organisms or substances into a food. [2]When eaten in sufficient quantities, contaminants from food can cause illness or injury, long-lasting disease or even death. [3]The contamination can be biological, chemical, or physical. [4]Contamination occurs in two ways: direct contamination and cross contamination. [5]Direct contamination occurs in raw foods or the plants or animals from which they come. [6]For instance, bacteria and fungi are present in the air, soil, and water, so foods can be easily contaminated by their general exposure to the environment. [7]In addition, grains can be contaminated in the field by pesticides sprayed to kill pests, while shellfish can be contaminated when they

eat toxic marine algae. [8]The second way is called cross contamination. [9]It can occur when humans, rodents, or insects carry the chemicals and microorganisms to foods and food contact surfaces. [10]People are the major cause of this. [11]For example, food handlers can transfer contaminants to food while processing, preparing, cooking or serving it. [12]Side towels are an especially common source of cross contamination. [13]If a cook uses a side towel to wipe a spill off the floor and then uses that same towel to dry his hands after visiting the restroom, he has recontaminated his hands with whatever bacteria or dirt was on the floor. [14]Cross contamination also occurs when raw foods come in contact with cooked foods and from smoking, eating, or drinking unless hands are properly washed. [15]Therefore, food service workers should try to reduce direct contact with prepared food by using single-use gloves, clean **tongs**, tasting spoons, and other appropriate tools when possible.

(Adapted from *On Cooking* by Sarah R. Labensky and Alan M. Hause)

tongs a device used for picking up objects

PRACTICE 13.2 Analyzing an Extended Definition Paragraph

Answer the questions about the paragraph you just read about contamination.

1. Underline the topic sentence.
2. Which sentence or sentences tell the reader about the causes and/or effects of contamination?

_____

3. Which sentence or sentences tell the reader of the types of contamination?

_____

4. Which sentence or sentences explain how direct contamination happens? Which explain how cross contamination happens?

_____

5. Circle the transition words.

DEFINITION PARAGRAPH ESSENTIALS

An effective extended definition paragraph has these essential elements:

1. The topic sentence makes a point by giving the formal definition of a word.
2. The paragraph makes the meaning of the word understandable to the reader.
3. A variety of writing patterns or methods are used as supporting details such as descriptions, examples, causes and effects, comparison and contrast, and process.
4. The supporting details are organized to clearly explain the meaning of the word.
5. Transitional words and expressions connect the different methods used to define the word.

Prewriting the Extended Definition Paragraph

Decide Your Topic and Purpose The purpose of an extended definition paragraph can be to inform or persuade. You may be asked define a word that is an idea such as *prejudice* or a word that has a standard definition such as *earthquake*. Another type of assignment might be to come up with your own original definition of a word.

When deciding on your own word, expression, or concept to define or responding to one that has been assigned, consider the following:

1. **Choose a word that you understand and can explain.** You need to know enough about the word that you can explain it in several different ways through examples, description, and causes and effects to name a few.

2. **Choose a word that can be defined in a single paragraph.** If you choose a word that is too broad or too general, you will not be able to narrow it down to a single definition. For example, the word *park* is a broad term, which includes a variety of different kinds, such as a water park, a park to walk dogs, a state park, a national park, and so on.

PRACTICE Evaluating Topics for Definition Paragraphs
13.3
Explain why each of the following topics would be suitable or unsuitable for an extended definition paragraph.

1. volcano

_____

2. Civil Rights Movement

_____

3. spider

_____

4. abuse

_____

5. geologist

_____

6. personality disorder

_____

7. team

_____

8. philosophy

_____

Develop Ideas for Your Topic Developing ideas for an extended definition paragraph involves first understanding the methods for defining a word and then prewriting.

Patterns of Development for Writing an Extended Definition An extended definition paragraph does not have one specific pattern of development. You can use several different patterns in the same paragraph. For example, many writers begin with a formal definition of the word and then explain it by giving examples, descriptions, or causes and effects.

Student writer Josh decided to define *video game* for his extended definition paper. His extended definition graphic organizer is shown on page 251. Although Josh used all the patterns, you do not need to use them all.

Josh's Extended Definition Graphic Organizer

Formal Definition

Word	Group	Features
A video game	is a computerized activity	that is played by moving images on a video display or computer screen.

Etymology/Origin: What language did the word come from? What did it mean originally? What is the word's history?

Old English gamen meaning joy, fun, amusement. Video comes from Latin videre, to see.

First video game table tennis developed in 1958 by physicist Willy Higinbotham, played on oscilloscope. First video game available to public was video arcade game Computer Space. In 1972, Atari founded by Bushnell and Dabney. Atari's first game Pong, video version of ping-pong.

Negation: What the word is not

A video game is not a board game.

Description/Process: Describe the word. Explain how it works or happens if applicable.

Fictional story line, activities for fun, education, or training, graphics to create setting and involve player in game's fantasy, risks and rewards to challenge player, rules.

The electronic device makes the game go, sets the pace, and determines when the player reaches the goal.

Cause/Effect: Give the causes and/or effects of the word.

People like to play because it's fun and challenging to perform game action like fly a plane, shoot a rifle, design clothing, build a castle, or sing and dance; lets players do a lot of things that are expensive or impossible to do in real life; can be educational

Example/Narrative: Give an example of the word.

Super Mario, Lara Croft (Tomb Raider), Donkey Kong, Pac Man, Link (The Legend of Zelda), Max Payne, Pokemon, Grand Theft Auto Series, Halo, and Blanka (Street Fighter)

Comparison/Contrast: Compare or contrast the word to another word.

A video game is not like a traditional game.

Point of Comparison	Video Game	Conventional Game
Rules	Not written but machine makes players obey	Written and players obey
Time	Timed by the electronic device	If timed, controlled by players

Synonym: Give a word similar in meaning.

Contest, competition, amusement.

Research and Extended Definition   You may need to do some research in the library or on the Internet. A good dictionary will give the word's pronunciation, meanings, uses, and history. You can also find specialized dictionaries or encyclopedias for information. The *Oxford English Dictionary* contains almost every word in the English language as well as each word's history. Additional information about a word can be found in many print and online sources. Don't forget to cite information that is not your own.

Research Reminder. For more information about citing sources, see Chapter 17.

Your Extended Definition Paragraph: Prewriting

Prewriting for an extended definition paragraph involves gathering supporting details to help define your word or expression. The extended definition graphic organizer on page 253 lists the types of details you can use in your paragraph and provides space for you to write them. Choose one of the words from this list and prewrite by filling in the graphic organizer.

> a popular slang term
> a specific food
> an emotion, such as fear, anger, guilt, happiness, pride, shame
> a term from one of your courses
> an item of clothing or apparel

Writing across the Curriculum: Words

Music Appreciation: a specific type of music, such as jazz, rock, blues, rap, and so on
Sociology: gang
Biology: a specific plant, fish, bird, reptile, amphibian, or mammal
Criminal Justice: a particular crime, such as robbery, DUI, hate crime, identity theft, child abuse, drug trafficking
Pharmacy: a particular medication or drug

Narrow Your Topic and Write the Topic Sentence   After prewriting to develop ideas, you are ready to write your topic sentence. The topic sentence for an extended definition paragraph is most often the formal definition of the word you have selected. The formal definition is made up of the word + the group the word belongs to + the features of the word that make it different from others in the group.

Use italics or underline the word you are defining.

Hypnosis is an altered state of awareness characterized by deep relaxation induced by suggestions and changes in perception, memory, motivation, and self-control.

Student Josh's definition: A *video game* is a computerized activity that is played by moving images on a video display or computer screen.

Extended Definition Graphic Organizer

Formal Definition

Word	Group	Features

Etymology/Origin: What language did the word come from? What did it mean originally? What is the word's history?

Negation: What the word is not

Description/Process: Describe the word. Explain how it works or happens if applicable.

Cause/Effect: Give the causes and/or effects of the word.

Example/Narrative: Give an example of the word.

Comparison/Contrast: Compare or contrast the word to another word.

Point of Comparison

Synonym: Give a word similar in meaning.

TIPS	Writing Definition Topic Sentences

1. **Write your own definition.** Your paper will express your definition of a word. Avoid copying the dictionary definition. In addition, many dictionary definitions do not provide the group and features of a word.
2. **Write a complete definition.** Do not leave out the group or the features.
3. **Use a word that does not repeat the word or a form of the word you are defining.**

Repeats Word	A *waiter* is a person employed to **wait** on people.
Revised	A *waiter* is a person employed to **bring food and beverages** to people, usually in a restaurant.

4. **Avoid defining your word using "is when" or "is where."**

Is When	A *test* **is when** a person or group answers questions to show a skill or knowledge.
Revised	A *test* is a set of questions or exercises that measures the skill or knowledge of an individual or a group.

PRACTICE Evaluating Topic Sentences for an Extended Definition Paragraph

13.4 Explain what is wrong with each of the following formal definition topic sentences. If a topic sentence is good, write "good."

1. A paralegal performs legal work that requires knowledge of legal concepts.

_____

2. A factory outlet is when a store sells manufacturers' extra merchandise directly to consumers.

_____

3. Meditation is a relaxation technique.

_____

4. Wildlife tourism is tourism to observe animals, birds, and fish in their native habitats.

_____

5. An obsession is a persistent, involuntary thought, image, or sudden wish that invades consciousness and causes great discomfort.

_____

Paragraph Practice: Writing a Topic Sentence

Write a topic sentence for the word about which you have been prewriting. Remember, the topic sentence is the formal definition.

Organizing and Drafting the Definition Paragraph

Develop Supporting Details Looking back at your definition graphic organizer, choose the details that you want to use in your paragraph.

For his extended definition of *video game*, student Josh chose the formal definition, description/process, cause/effect, and examples.

Paragraph Practice: Selecting Supporting Details

Select the information that you would like to include in your paper from your extended definition graphic organizer on page 253.

Organize Your Supporting Details Once you have chosen your supporting details, you are ready to organize them. Unlike other types of paragraphs, the extended definition paragraph does not follow a specific pattern of organization. As you look at the details you have chosen, organize them in a way that will make the meaning of the word clear and understandable to your readers. Here is an example of one possible organization plan:

Topic sentence: Formal definition
1. Origin/history
2. Description
3. Examples

Write the First Draft As you write the first draft, consider using connectors and transitions.

Writing Reminder. For a complete list of connectors and transitions, see the inside of the back cover.

Add Connectors: Transitional Words and Expressions   Most of the writing chapters in this book focus on one pattern of organization and include specific connectors and transitions. In contrast, for extended definition, several patterns of organization are often used in the same paragraph to define the word. Therefore, a variety of connectors and transitions can be used. Use addition transitions to add new points and order of importance transitions to put points in a particular order.

Paragraph Practice: Writing the First Draft

Using the details you selected from your graphic organizer, write the first draft of your extended definition paragraph.

Revising, Editing, and Proofreading

Revise your draft by looking at one element at a time: Support, Organization, Connectors and transitions, and Style. The following Revision Checklist contains the SOCS elements as they apply to extended definition paragraphs.

- -

REVISION CHECKLIST FOR A DEFINITION PARAGRAPH

Element	Revision Checkpoints
Topic	☐ The topic addresses an extended definition of a word, concept, or expression.
	☐ The topic can be fully discussed in a single paragraph.
Topic Sentence	☐ The topic sentence states the formal definition of the word and consists of the word, the group, and the features.

Element	Revision Checkpoints
Support	☐ Supporting details consist of information that makes the meaning of the word understandable to the reader.
	☐ The supporting details are developed using several methods such as descriptions, examples, causes and effects, comparison and contrast, and process.
	☐ All supporting details are relevant and adequate.
Organization	☐ The paragraph is logically organized in a way that makes the definition understandable.
	☐ The paragraph is balanced in both content and in organization.
Connectors and transitions	☐ Connectors and transitions provide coherence between each pattern of organization used to define the word.
Style	☐ Writing is clear, concise Standard Written English.
	☐ Tone is appropriate for a college audience.
	☐ Sentences are varied.

 *Peer Review Reminder.* For feedback on your writing, have someone read your paper and make comments on the Peer Review Response sheet in Chapter 4, page 55.

 Your Extended Definition Paragraph: Revising

Using the Revision Checklist for a Definition Paragraph, revise the first draft of your extended definition paragraph.

Check Grammar, Punctuation, and Spelling As you reread your paper to check for grammar, punctuation, and spelling errors, pay special attention for possible errors that may arise in definition paragraphs. For example, review the section in this chapter, Tips for Writing Definition Topic Sentences, to avoid grammar errors in your formal definition, such as using *is when* or *is where.*

PRACTICE Revising and Editing an Extended Definition Paragraph

13.5 Read and edit Josh's extended definition paragraph and answer the questions that follow.

> [1]A video game is a computerized activity that is played by moving images on a video display or television screen. [2]Video games appealed to players of all ages because they let players do a lot of things that are expensive or impossible to do in real life. [3]A video game can include imaginary people, places, and situations. [4]Many games incorporate some kind of story as part of the entertainment to make the players think that they are inside the story affecting the flow of events.

⁵To produce the total play experience, graphics and gameplay work together, the graphics create the setting, which makes the gamer want to play and involves the player in the game's imaginary story. ⁶Risks and rewards raise the level of stress and make success or failure more meaningful to the player. ⁷Rewards can give the player something like money that helps him play or something else that is still valuable. ⁸The computer determines when the player reaches the goal; it also sets the speed and makes the game go. ⁹Some of the most popular video games are: *Super Mario, Lara Croft (Tomb Raider), Donkey Kong, Pac Man, Link (The Legend of Zelda), Max Payne, Pokemon, Grand Theft Auto, Halo,* and *Blanka (Street Fighter).*

Questions on Revising

1. Underline the topic sentence. Does the topic sentence contain all the parts of a formal definition? What, if anything, is missing?

_____

2. List the methods of extended definition Josh uses to provide adequate and sufficient supporting details.

_____

3. The paragraph is missing a concluding sentence. Write an interesting concluding sentence for it.

_____

_____

Questions on Editing and Proofreading

4. One sentence is a run-on. Find the error and rewrite the sentence correctly.

_____

_____

5. One sentence misuses the colon. Find the error and rewrite the sentence correctly.

_____

_____

6. One sentence has a verb shift. Find the error and rewrite the sentence correctly.

_____

_____

Paragraph Practice: Editing and Proofreading

Edit and proofread your extended definition paragraph. Check that your final draft is complete, accurate, and error-free.

Paragraph Writing Assignments

Help Desk

Luigi has written an extended definition paragraph on **crowd surfing** at a rock concert. Read Luigi's paper and review his paper by answering the questions below.

> [1]Crowd surfing is where teens are basically carried over the top of a sea of people. [2]It is a popular activity at rock concerts. [3]However, crowd surfers are susceptible to being dropped. [4]When crowd surfers are dropped during a show, it is a general rule that the people around them help them up and protect them from being stepped on. [5]I remember two summers ago during a summertime music festival, where a young female was dropped while crowd surfing. [6]She landed on her head and was knocked out. [7]The people around her acted quickly to get her off the ground safe from being trampled. [8]A good Samaritan picked her up and brought her out of the crowd to a waiting medical unit. [9]Crowd surfing is considered dangerous, but it is really fun to do. [10]Most people only end up with bruises. [11]Females need to be careful when crowd surfing because some people may try to touch them in ways that are not appropriate as they are being passed around. [12]Crowd surfing is illegal in some countries.

Formal Definition of Crowd Surfing		
Word	Group	Features
Crowd surfing		

1. Underline the formal definition. Fill in the chart to identify the parts of the formal definition and then advise Luigi how to correct it.
   What is wrong?

   _____

   Rewrite the formal definition, correcting it.

   _____

   _____

2. List the methods Luigi uses to develop his extended definition.

   _____

3. Which sentence needs more development?

   _____

   _____

4. If you could move sentences 9, 10, and 11, where would you place them?

   _____

Group Activity

Success is an abstract word. Abstract words refer to concepts or ideas instead of physical things that we can experience with our five senses. Abstract words can mean different things to different people. Some famous people have commented on the meaning of success:

- "Success in life consists of going from one mistake to the next—without losing your enthusiasm."—*Winston Churchill*
- "There are no secrets to success. It is the result of preparation, hard work, and learning from failure."—*Colin Powell*
- "Eighty percent of success is showing up."—*Woody Allen*

In small groups of three or four, plan and write an extended definition paragraph for the word *success*. You may include one of the quotations listed above in your paragraph.

Write about an Image

Emblems are body gestures that directly translate into words or phrases. Emblems are culture specific. In other words, hand gestures do not mean the same thing in every culture. Choose one of the gestures pictured below and write an extended definition paragraph explaining what the gesture means in the United States culture or another culture that you are familiar with.

Reading and Writing across the Curriculum: Sociology

> In society, a *subculture* is a group that has some kind of trait—social, economic, ethnic, or other traits—distinctive enough to make it different from others within the same culture or society. Subcultures consist of people whose experiences have led them to distinctive ways of looking at life or some aspect of it.
>
> The United States society contains tens of thousands of subcultures. Some examples are "chopper" motorcyclists, New England "Yankees," Ohio State football fans, the southern California "beach crowd," and wilderness campers. Some ethnic groups in the United States also form subcultures; their values, foods, religion, language, and clothing may set them apart. Occupational groups formed by police officers or fire fighters are other subculture examples.
>
> (Adapted from *Essentials of Sociology* by James M. Henslin)

Choose a subculture that you are familiar with. Write an extended definition paragraph about that group, explaining their characteristics.

Comment on a Contemporary Issue

> Although the form of a family varies from one society to another and even within societies, all societies have families. The U.S. Census Bureau, which collects data about the nation, its people, and the economy, says a *family* "consists of two or more people related by birth, marriage, or adoption residing in the same unit." Thus, according to the federal government, a married couple and their children are considered to be family, while unmarried couples who live together make up a household.
>
> (Adapted from *Family Life Now* by Kelly J. Welch)

Your definition of *family* is probably different from that of the government. How do you define *family*? Write an extended definition paragraph in which you define *family* based on your own unique experiences.

LO 3 The Definition Essay

Writing Reminder.
For more help with writing an essay, including introductions and conclusions, see Chapter 5.

The definition essay has the same purpose as the extended definition paragraph: to explain what a word, expression, or concept means. An extended definition essay can explain the meaning of a word in greater depth than the paragraph version.

An extended definition can inform or persuade. You may want to define a word to show your understanding or to motivate people to accept a point of view. For example, you could inform by defining the word *family* through an explanation of its traditional definition and changes in its meaning over time. On the other hand, through your definition of *family*, you could persuade readers that the definition of family must change as society's needs change.

Like the extended definition paragraph, the essay version uses a variety of patterns of development to support the main idea. The extended definition graphic organizer on page 253 can be used to help you prewrite your ideas for your essay. The graphic organizer on page 265 will help you organize the parts of your essay.

Writing Reminder. **To review** *writing formal definitions, see page 248.*

The extended definition essay also includes the formal definition of the word, which gives the meaning of a word in a single sentence. The formal definition includes the word, the group the word belongs to, and the features of the word that make it different from others in the group.

Thesis Statement

The thesis statement of the extended definition essay gives the significance or importance of the term being defined. The thesis can consist of two or three parts:

> **Two-part thesis**: Narrowed word + the significance or importance of the word being defined.
>
> The term *dude* has a traceable history that has helped to mold its modern definition.
>
> **Three-part thesis**: Narrowed word + significance or importance of the word being defined + aspects or characteristics of the word to be defined.
>
> The term *dude* can be better understood by examining its etymology and origin, its changes in meaning over time, and its uses in contemporary writing and speech.

You may want to include the formal definition in the introductory paragraph as part of your lead-in.

Body Paragraphs

The body paragraphs of an extended definition essay use a variety of patterns of organization, such as narration, example, comparison, contrast, cause, effect, description, process, and classification. You can also give the word's history and origin, any misconceptions about it, and a synonym.

Begin each body paragraph with a topic sentence that guides the reader by giving the aspect or characteristic of the word that will be discussed. Since you may use a different pattern of organization for each body paragraph, organize the supporting details in each of them according to the pattern you used, such as order of importance, chronological order, or spatial order.

Definition Essay Example

In the following essay, student Jones Howard writes an extended definition of the term *slam dancing*.

Howard 1

Jones Howard

Professor Markus

College Preparatory English

12 Nov. 2010

Slam Dancing

1   If dancing leads to bloodshed, is it still considered dancing? It is hard to imagine that the fans of heavy metal rock music like to dance, but what they call dancing many would call violence. Unlike ballet, salsa, or hip hop, the style of

dancing that these rock fans do often results in serious injuries, or, in worst-case scenarios, death. Slam dancing, also known as moshing, is an aggressive style of dance with movements that consist of shoving or violently throwing one's body against another dancer.

2   In both slamming and moshing, participants dance in an area called a pit or mosh pit. The pit is an open, circular area in front of the concert stage or in the middle of a crowd. During a concert, fans create mosh pits to show their appreciation for the music and to give dancers room to dance. Usually, the dancers move in a clockwise motion around the pit.

3   Slam dancing began in the 1970s and early 1980s as part of the punk rock subculture. Punk rockers, who did not like the commercialism of the popular forms of music at that time, such as rock, disco, and heavy metal, developed their own music. Punk music was easy to play; the songs used simple guitar chords. Because punk rockers were against society's values, their songs were often loud and angry; their lyrics were about politics, sex, and boredom.

4   Slam dancing is fast-paced and has several forms. One form is the pogo, in which dancers jump up and down in the same spot, as if they were pogo sticks. They keep their legs close together, their arms at their sides and their body stiff. The slam is similar to pogo, but dancers intentionally try to bump into other pogo dancers. Fast arm swinging and kicking in time to the music is another variety of slamming.

5   Moshing developed in the 1980s and 1990s with grunge, a type of alternative rock that was a cross between punk and heavy metal music. Grunge appealed to those who did not like punk or heavy metal rock. Athough the popularity of grunge has long since faded, moshing has not. Its popularity continued in the 2000s, especially with heavy metal rock fans.

6   Slamming moves can still be seen in a mosh pit, but slamming evolved into moshing, a more violent form. Just as slamming has variations, so does moshing. Some moshers randomly bash into each other with the specific intentions of either hurting someone or getting hurt. Another popular move is the windmill where the dancers swing their arms in a 360-degree motion. The motion looks like a spinning windmill. Stage diving is a favorite with daring fans. Those who manage to avoid security get up on stage, and with a running start, they fling their bodies into the crowd of moshers in the pit. The goal is for the people in the crowd to catch them and pass them around from one person to another on top of the moshing audience. Stage divers risk getting trampled or suffering broken bones or concussions if the people in the crowd do not catch them. In addition, crowd surfers risk having personal items stolen or removed as they are passed around, and females risk being groped and grabbed.

7   Those who slam or mosh enjoy it for many reasons. Some find the danger of dancing in a mosh pit exciting, while others enjoy the physical release of pent up energy and emotions. There can be no denial of the dangers of these dances, but they are no more devastating than the possible results of a competitive football game.

PRACTICE Analyzing a Definition Essay
13.6

1. Underline the thesis statement. What term does the writer plan to define?

_____

2. What technique does the writer use in the lead-in?

_____

3. Underline the topic sentences of each of the body paragraphs. What is the point of each body paragraph?

_____

_____

4. Which methods of definition are used in each of the body paragraphs?

_____

5. In addition to referring to the thesis statement, what points does the writer make in the conclusion?

_____

Extended Definition Essay Graphic Organizer

Using an extended definition graphic organizer will help you structure your writing. The sample graphic organizer on page 265 can be changed to suit your needs by adding paragraphs, points, and supporting evidence.

Essay Writing Assignments

Write about an Image: Standards of Beauty

Beauty is the combination of qualities that are pleasing to the senses or mind. Most people view beauty as a pleasing physical appearance. Write an essay defining the standards of beauty for the group or culture you most identify with.

Definition Essay Graphic Organizer

Introduction: You may want to include the formal definition of the word in the introduction.

Lead-in:

Bridge:

Thesis Statement:

Body Paragraph(s): Patterns of development will vary.

Topic Sentence:

Evidence/Explanation:

Conclusion

Choose Effective Closing Technique.

Writing Topics

For your definition essay, choose one of these options:

- from paragraph to essay: expand the paragraph you wrote in the paragraph section of this chapter
- any of the writing topics in the paragraph section of this chapter
- any topic from the following list:

    an unexplained phenomenon such as a UFO, ghost, miracle, near death experience, crop circles, ESP, intuition

    an adjective describing a personal quality, such as compassionate, honest, loyal, imaginative, resourceful, patient, jealous

    an electronic or computing device

    gender

    a job, such as administrative assistant, restaurant server, nurse, teacher, social worker, psychologist, events planner, fashion stylist

Writing across the Curriculum: Words

Psychology: a specific mental disorder, such as psychosis, schizophrenia, depression, anorexia or bulimia, bipolar disorder

Game Design: a type of video game, such as action, strategy, role playing, sports, or vehicle simulation

Hospitality: a form of entertainment (an activity performed for the enjoyment of others) such as foodservice, amusement or theme park, campground, arcade, cruise, nightclub

Marketing: advertisement

History: genocide

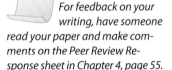

Peer Review Reminder. For feedback on your writing, have someone read your paper and make comments on the Peer Review Response sheet in Chapter 4, page 55.

English Success Tip: A New Word Every Day

If you want to improve your vocabulary, try learning one new word every day. Finding new words is as simple as looking in a dictionary; open it to any page and find a word you do not know. Another way to learn new words is by reading something that is a bit more difficult than what you are accustomed to. As you come across a word you do not know, try to figure out what it means, and then look it up to find out if you were right. To keep track all of those new words you are learning, create a word list including the correct spelling and the definition; include your own sentence using the word. Make a commitment to increasing your vocabulary.

For support in meeting this chapter's objectives, log in to www.mywritinglab.com, go to the Study Plan tab, click on **Definition** and choose **Paragraph Development— Definition and Essay Development—Definition** from the list of subtopics. Read and view the videos and resources in the Review Materials section, and then complete the Recall, Apply, and Write exercises in the Activities section. You can check your scores and overall progress by using the Gradebook.

CHAPTER 14

Argument

Learning Objectives

After working through this chapter, you will be able to:

LO 1 Define argument as a form of writing that states a point of view on an issue and supports it with evidence in order to persuade readers.

LO 2 Write an argument paragraph.

LO 3 Write an argument essay.

LO 1 What Is Argument?

Argument is a form of writing that states the writer's point of view on an issue and supports it by giving evidence. The purpose of argument is to persuade readers to agree with the writer's point of view or to take action.

You experience argument in all aspects of life. As a child, you have probably tried to convince a relative or caregiver to let you stay up a little later or to buy you a special toy you felt you could not live without. As you matured, you argued for more important things, such as being allowed to stay out late on weekends or for purchasing a new laptop. In the workplace, you may convince your employer to give you a raise or to try a new way of conducting business.

QuickWrite

Take a few moments to write about a time when you convinced someone to do something or believe something. Explain the situation and the strategy you used to persuade that person.

Argument in College Writing

Much of the information you learn in college has been argued at some point. For example, in the field of psychology, researchers have done studies to prove their hypotheses about the causes of mental problems, the stages of child development, and the process of learning. In the field of environmental science, researchers have presented evidence on both sides of the global warming issue.

Most writing you will do in college is a form of argument. For instance, each of the writing patterns you study in this text asks you to make and support a point, whether you are describing, giving causes and effects, defining, narrating, or comparing and contrasting. In a political science course, for example, you may be asked to write about whether people, especially children, should be forced to repeat the Pledge of Allegiance if it violates their beliefs.

LO 2 The Argument Paragraph

It is possible to make a brief argument in a paragraph as the following example shows.

Argument Paragraph Example

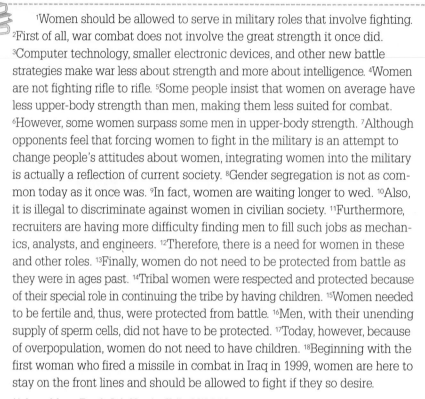

¹Women should be allowed to serve in military roles that involve fighting. ²First of all, war combat does not involve the great strength it once did. ³Computer technology, smaller electronic devices, and other new battle strategies make war less about strength and more about intelligence. ⁴Women are not fighting rifle to rifle. ⁵Some people insist that women on average have less upper-body strength than men, making them less suited for combat. ⁶However, some women surpass some men in upper-body strength. ⁷Although opponents feel that forcing women to fight in the military is an attempt to change people's attitudes about women, integrating women into the military is actually a reflection of current society. ⁸Gender segregation is not as common today as it once was. ⁹In fact, women are waiting longer to wed. ¹⁰Also, it is illegal to discriminate against women in civilian society. ¹¹Furthermore, recruiters are having more difficulty finding men to fill such jobs as mechanics, analysts, and engineers. ¹²Therefore, there is a need for women in these and other roles. ¹³Finally, women do not need to be protected from battle as they were in ages past. ¹⁴Tribal women were respected and protected because of their special role in continuing the tribe by having children. ¹⁵Women needed to be fertile and, thus, were protected from battle. ¹⁶Men, with their unending supply of sperm cells, did not have to be protected. ¹⁷Today, however, because of overpopulation, women do not need to have children. ¹⁸Beginning with the first woman who fired a missile in combat in Iraq in 1999, women are here to stay on the front lines and should be allowed to fight if they so desire.

(Adapted from *Family Life Now* by Kelly J. Welch)

PRACTICE   Analyzing an Argument Paragraph
14.1

1. Underline the topic sentence. What is the issue being argued?

_____

2. How many reasons does the writer give? Briefly list each reason.

_____

_____

_____

_____

3. Circle the transition words and expressions.
4. Which two opposing arguments does the writer acknowledge?

_____

_____

_____

_____

5. Which of the arguments is least convincing to you?

_____

_____

- -

ARGUMENT PARAGRAPH ESSENTIALS
The purpose of the argument paragraph is to persuade readers to agree with the writer's point of view or to take action. An effective argument paragraph has these essential elements:

1. The argument paragraph expresses the writer's point of view on an issue and supports it by giving evidence.
2. The supporting evidence consists of facts, statistics, examples, personal experience, expert testimony, and consequences.
3. The supporting evidence is logical, adequately developed, and convincing.
4. The method of organization is order of importance.
5. Word choices should be neutral and fair-minded.

- -

Prewriting the Argument Paragraph

Decide Your Topic and Purpose Argument paragraphs are designed to persuade the readers. The paragraph may present a view with no opposition from the audience; persuade an audience to agree with your view; or persuade an audience to take action.

Argument is more complicated than other types of writing. Therefore, you need to choose your topic carefully and analyze how your audience will react to it. Your topic is an issue that can be argued. An issue is a current subject or problem people are thinking and talking about.

Choosing an Issue for Argument   When choosing an issue or responding to an assigned issue for your argument paragraph, consider the following:

1. **Choose an issue that you know well.** In order to write a convincing argument paragraph, you need to know your issue well. Your knowledge can come from personal experience or your own knowledge.
2. **Choose an issue that you care about.** When you have strong feelings about the issue in general or about one side of an issue, you will be more likely to influence the reader to consider your point of view.
3. **Choose an issue for which more than one point of view is possible.** The issue should be one that provokes different opinions. You should be able to identify at least two sides of the issue.
4. **Choose an issue that can be argued.** A fact is not an issue; it cannot be debated because it has already been proven. Some personal opinions cannot be argued with evidence.
5. **Choose an issue that can be argued in a single paragraph.** Some issues are too large to be argued in one paragraph, such as the following: The federal government should provide health care for all citizens who cannot afford their own. While this issue does provoke different opinions, it cannot be adequately argued in one paragraph because there are too many points to argue.

PRACTICE Evaluating Issues for Argument Paragraphs

14.2   Explain why each of the following issues would be suitable or unsuitable for an argument paragraph.

1. Making English the official language of the United States is ridiculous.

   _____

   _____

2. High school graduates should take a year off before entering college.

   _____

   _____

3. Marijuana should be a medical option.

   _____

   _____

4. The military should be allowed to recruit in high schools.

   _____

   _____

5. Students should not be allowed to use *Wikipedia.com* as a source for research papers.

   _____

   _____

6. The mass media, including television, radio, and the Internet, have a negative influence on the younger generation.

   _____

   _____

Develop Ideas for Your Issue Prewriting for an argument paragraph involves taking a position on an issue and exploring both sides of it. Sometimes your position on an issue is so strong that you can only see one side. By looking at the other side, you allow yourself to be more open-minded in your thinking. In addition, you will be able to respond to opposing arguments.

Using an argument For/Against graphic organizer will help you look at both sides of your issue and show you whether or not you can support your point of view. To see how this is done, take a look at Roxanne's For/Against graphic organizer on page 271 that explores both sides of the argument for relocating the Muscovy ducks on her campus.

Paragraph Practice: Prewriting to Develop Ideas

Using the For/Against Argument Graphic Organizer (page 272), develop ideas for one of these issues or any other issue mentioned in the paragraph section of this chapter:

   a requirement in your college or one of your classes
   grade inflation
   academic dishonesty
   influence of celebrities
   workplace dating

Roxanne's For/Against Argument Graphic Organizer

Issue: The Muscovy ducks on our campus should or should not be relocated.

For: Should be relocated	**Against:** Should not be relocated
There are greenish-black, watery droppings all over campus—unhealthy and disgusting. Walking is not pleasant because students have to avoid stepping in duck droppings.	Just walk around the duck droppings.
They interfere with the flow of traffic by standing in the middle of the roads. We have to wait while they waddle from one side of the road to the other.	The ducks don't take so long to cross the street. It's fun to watch them.
They take up parking spaces by sitting in them. Parking spaces near classrooms are hard to enough to find. Even honking won't get them to move.	There are parking spaces on the other side of campus far from the buildings and the ducks. Walking is good for one's health anyway.
They destroy native plants and wildflowers. Newly planted flowers were completely uprooted.	Flowers can be replanted. Ducks help the environment. They eat algae that destroy the lakes. Also, they help control pests by eating mosquitoes, roaches, ants, and spiders.
Because people feed them, they have learned to depend on students and employees for food.	It is enjoyable and gratifying to feed them.
They beg for food. They stand around when we're eating looking up at us and snorting. They jump on people's laps or beg at vending machines. Their aggression is frightening.	The ducks have learned to trust people and are being friendly.

Writing across the Curriculum Issues

Health: cosmetic surgery
Family Studies: single-parent families
Education: home schooling
Culinary Arts: organic food
Communications: online dating

Narrow Your Topic and Write the Topic Sentence

After you have explored both sides of your topic, decide which side of the issue you want to argue.

The topic sentence for an argument paragraph expresses your stand on an issue. It includes the issue and your position on the issue.

Smoking should be restricted to specific areas on campus.

An introductory computer course should not be required for all students.

People who move to the United States from other countries should try to fit into American culture.

Roxanne decided to argue that the Muscovy ducks should be relocated:

The Muscovy ducks on our campus should be relocated.

For/Against Argument Graphic Organizer

Issue:

For:	Against:

TIPS | **Writing Argument Topic Sentences**

1. Take a strong stand on the issue.

   Weak: Having designated smoking areas on campus seems like a good idea.

   Weak: Designated smoking areas on campus might or might not work depending on a person's point of view.

   Weak: My campus is considering designated smoking areas.

   Strong: The campus should establish designated smoking areas.

2. Use verb forms that signal argument such as *should, should not, could, could not, must, must not, needs, requires, must have.*

3. **Avoid using a fact as your topic sentence.** Your topic sentence will state your position, which is your opinion.

   Fact: Secondhand smoke contains over 4,000 chemicals, including over 40 cancer causing agents and 200 known poisons.

   Position: The campus should establish designated smoking areas.

PRACTICE   Evaluating Argument Topic Sentences

14.3

Explain what is wrong with each of the following argument topic sentences. If a topic sentence is good, write "good."

1. A lawsuit filed by David Reynard against NEC blamed his wife's death from a brain tumor on her cell phone.

_____

_____

2. Stricter handgun laws should be enacted to save lives.

_____

_____

3. Teaching sex education in middle/junior high school is not such a good idea.

_____

_____

4. Cheating is out of control.

_____

_____

5. Requiring students to pass a proficiency test to receive a high school diploma will not improve academic achievement.

_____

_____

Paragraph Practice: Writing a Topic Sentence

Look over the details you developed for your argument paragraph in your For/Against Argument Graphic Organizer, decide on your position, and write a topic sentence for it.

Organizing and Drafting the Argument Paragraph

Develop Supporting Details After stating your position in your topic sentence, the next step is to understand and develop the kinds of evidence that can be used to support the points of your argument. In addition, you need to think about opposing points of view.

Evidence   The types of evidence you can use are facts, statistics, expert authority, example, anecdote, and personal observation. Each of these is defined and explained with examples for the topic "The campus should establish designated smoking areas."

Type of Evidence	Example
Facts or Statistics *Facts* are pieces of information that can be shown to be true. *Statistics* are pieces of information that are represented in numbers.	**Reason using facts:** Second hand smoke has been classified by the Environmental Protection Agency as a known cause of cancer. **Reason using statistics:** According to the American Lung Association, secondhand smoke causes approximately 3,400 lung cancer deaths and 22,700–69,600 heart disease deaths in adult nonsmokers in the United States each year.
Expert authority *Expert authority* is information from someone who has personal experience with the issue or who is an expert in the field. The information is sound and based on facts.	**Reason using expert authority:** Dr. Thomson, President of the college's Center for Health Science, says the college has a responsibility for the health and safety of all students. Recognizing the risks of smoking, the college should be persistent in its efforts to achieve a campus-wide restricted smoking area policy.
Example *Examples* illustrate the point you are making. You can use personal examples from your experience or the experience of people you know.	**Reason using example:** Being around secondhand smoke triggers asthma in individuals who have the condition. For example, when my friend Terrell is in an area where people are smoking, his asthma acts up and he coughs and has difficulty breathing.
Anecdote An *anecdote* is a brief story, often a personal experience.	**Reason using an anecdote:** Cigarette smoke residue attaches itself to hair and clothing of anyone around the smoke, not just the smokers. After classes the other day, I picked up my son from the daycare center. I went to give him a big hug and he backed away from me saying, "Mommy, you smell smoky!" As we drove home in the car, the odor irritated his eyes and caused his nose to run.
Personal Observation Descriptive details or examples based on *personal observation*.	**Reason using personal observation:** Restricting smoking to designated areas will decrease cigarette litter thus making the campus cleaner. Many smokers carelessly drop cigarette butts wherever they want to on campus, creating litter on the walkways and entrances to buildings. Also, workers will not have to spend extra time cleaning up after smokers. Having restricted areas for smokers will also reduce the risk of fire started from discarded cigarettes.

PRACTICE Developing Convincing Evidence

14.4 Provide one convincing piece of evidence for each of the following arguments. In addition, identify the type of evidence you used.

1. Students should study in groups to learn more effectively.

Your evidence: _____

Type of evidence: _____

2. High schools should do a better job of preparing students for college.
Your evidence: _____

Type of evidence: _____

3. People under 18 should be required to have parental permission to get tattoos and piercings.
Your evidence: _____

Type of evidence: _____

4. Playing a game is only fun when you win.
Your evidence: _____

Type of evidence: _____

5. To reduce accidents, all young drivers should complete a safe driver education course before being licensed to drive.
Your evidence: _____

Type of evidence: _____

Paragraph Practice: Developing Details

Look back at your prewriting For/Against argument graphic organizer. Evaluate the points and place a checkmark next to the ones that strongly prove your position. Add new points that may occur to you as you give more thought to your argument.

Organize Your Supporting Details After analyzing your supporting points, you are ready to organize them into a plan for your paragraph. A point-by-point argument graphic organizer will help you identify each of the points of your argument and add supporting evidence both for and against each point.

Roxanne's point-by-point argument graphic organizer is shown on page 276. She used the ideas from her for/against argument graphic organizer and developed the points and support for her argument, choosing only those that were the most convincing.

Paragraph Practice: Using a Point-By-Point Argument Graphic Organizer to Plan

Fill in the point-by-point argument graphic organizer shown on page 277.

Putting Your Ideas into a Logical Order To be effective, your points should be arranged in a way that builds the argument in the most convincing way, which will depend on your purpose. State your points or reasons with supporting evidence. Organize them in order of importance for maximum impact.

Write the First Draft Use your argument graphic organizer to guide you as you write the first draft. In addition, consider these elements: connectors and transitions and argument errors.

Roxanne's Point-by-Point Argument Graphic Organizer

Topic Sentence: The Muscovy ducks on our campus should be relocated.

Point 1: Ducks destroy the campus environment
Support: Droppings create a health hazard on campus.

- Ducks have bowel movements on sidewalks—unpleasant to walk on campus

- Their droppings are wet and slimy; a person could slip, fall and get injured.

The ducks destroy native plants and wildflowers.

- They uprooted all the wildflowers that had just been planted by the environmental restoration committee.

Point 2: The ducks are aggressive toward people.
Support: Bold, unwanted approaches annoy and occasionally frighten students, especially when ducks want food.

- When someone sits outside on a bench to eat a snack or socialize, groups of snorting ducks gather around, pushing their beaks against the individual's leg to beg for a handout.

- Aggressive ducks have attacked students. On one occasion, a duck jumped on my friend's lap while she was snacking on some chips. The duck tried to bite her face in an attempt to be fed.

Add Connectors: Transitional Words and Expressions In an argument paragraph, you are offering reasons and supporting evidence that may consist of examples, anecdotes, expert opinion, facts, statistics, and personal observation. Finally, you will be organizing your arguments in their order of importance.

> **Transitions to introduce examples**: *an example of this is, for example, for instance, one example is, to illustrate,* and so on.

> **Transitions to add information**: *also, another point is, furthermore, moreover, in addition, the next point is, the first, second, third point is,* and so on.

Argument Errors To make your argument effective, be aware of possible argument errors writers make.

1. **Hasty Generalization.** A **hasty generalization** is an argument based on insufficient evidence or no evidence at all. Using words like *everyone* and *all* can create this error.

Hasty generalization	Everyone knows how to use a computer nowadays, so students should not have to take a computer literacy course.
Improved	Colleges should survey incoming students' computer knowledge to determine whether they should be required to take a computer literacy course.

Point-by-Point Argument Graphic Organizer

Topic Sentence:

Point 1 of Argument:
Support:

Point 2 of Argument:
Support:

Point 3 of Argument:
Support:

2. **Circular Reasoning. Circular reasoning** is an attempt to support a statement by repeating it in a different way. In the example, the words *advantageous* and *beneficial* are similar in meaning.

Circular reasoning	College computer literacy classes are beneficial because they are advantageous.
Improved	College computer literacy classes are beneficial because students need to continually upgrade their computer knowledge with rapid advances in technology.

3. **Attack on Character.** Also known as *ad hominem*, this error attacks the person rather than his or her arguments.

Ad hominem The college president wants all students to take a computer literacy course because he is greedy and just wants the college to make money off students.

Improved The college president believes that students should take a computer literacy course because computer capabilities are essential for success in the business world.

Paragraph Practice: Writing the First Draft

Write a first draft of your argument paragraph using the point-by-point argument graphic organizer you prepared.

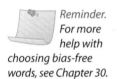

Reminder.
For more
help with
choosing bias-free
words, see Chapter 30.

Revising, Editing, and Proofreading

Revise your draft by looking at one element at a time: Support, Organization, Connectors and transitions, and Style. The following Revision Checklist contains the SOCS elements as they apply to argument paragraphs.

- -

REVISION CHECKLIST FOR AN ARGUMENT PARAGRAPH

Element	Revision Checkpoints
Topic	☐ The issues can be argued.
	☐ The issue provokes differing opinions.
	☐ The issue can be fully discussed in a single paragraph.
	☐ You have strong feelings about the issue.
	☐ You are familiar with the issue.
Topic Sentence	☐ The topic sentence states includes two elements: the issue and your position on the issue.
	☐ The sentence uses verb forms that signal argument: *should, should not, could, could not, must, must not, needs, requires, must have.*

Element	Revision Checkpoints
Support	☐ The support consists of the following types of evidence: facts, statistics, expert authority, example, anecdote, and personal observation.
	☐ The support appeals to readers' logic, and ethics.
	☐ All supporting details are relevant and adequate.
	☐ Argument errors are avoided.
Organization	☐ Each reason is discussed completely, one at a time.
	☐ The reasons in the argument are arranged in a way that is most convincing: most-to-least or least-to-most important method of organization.
	☐ The paragraph is balanced in both content and in organization.
Connectors and Transitions	☐ Connectors and transitions are used to introduce, add, and argue points.
Style	☐ Writing is clear, concise Standard Written English.
	☐ Tone is appropriate for a college audience.
	☐ Sentences are varied.

Peer Review Reminder.
For feedback on your writing, have someone read your paper and make comments on the Peer Review Response sheet in Chapter 4, page 55.

Paragraph Practice: Revising

Revise your argument paragraph draft using the Revision Checklist for an Argument Paragraph.

Check Grammar, Punctuation, and Spelling As you reread your paper to check for grammar, punctuation, and spelling errors, pay special attention for possible errors that may arise in argument paragraphs. If you use an embedded question, be sure to use the correct word order.

Embedded Questions An embedded question is a question within a sentence. Questions written within a sentence should not use question word order.

Error: Some students wonder <u>why do they have to take a computer literacy course?</u>

Corrected: Some students wonder <u>why they have to take a computer literacy course.</u>

PRACTICE   Revising, Editing, and Proofreading an Argument Paragraph

14.5   Read and edit Roxanne's argument paragraph and answer the questions below:

> ¹The offensive Muscovy ducks that have taken up residence on our campus should be relocated. ²The first reason is that they destroy the campus environment, for example, the ducks go to the bathroom wherever they please, so the walkways are frequently littered with fresh feces. ³People have to always watch where you are walking to avoid slipping and possibly getting injured. ⁴The Muscovy ducks also destroy the native plants and wildflowers on campus. ⁵To illustrate, last month some of the ducks uproot all of the flowers that had just been planted by the campus environmental restoration committee. ⁶Another reason the ducks should be relocated is that they are aggressive toward people. ⁷Their bold, unwanted approaches annoy and occasionally frighten students, especially when the ducks want food. ⁸For instance, when someone sits outside on a bench to eat a snack or to socialize with other students, groups of snorting ducks gather around that person, pushing their beaks against the individual's legs to beg for a handout. ⁹Specifically, on one occasion, a duck jumped on my friend's lap while she was snacking on some chips; the duck tried to bite her face in an attempt to be fed. ¹⁰For the benefit of the campus, the Muscovies are an annoyance and should be caught and relocated.

Questions on Revising

1. Underline the topic sentence. What is the issue? What is the point of view?

_____

2. List the two main reasons that support the topic sentence.

_____

3. Circle the transitions. Which ones introduce reasons or points and which ones introduce examples?

_____

Questions on Editing and Proofreading

4. Find the sentence that contains a comma splice and correct it.

_____

5. Find the sentence that contains a verb shift and correct it.

_____

6. Find the shift in pronoun and correct it.

_____

Paragraph Practice: Editing and Proofreading

Edit and proofread your argument paragraph. Check that your final draft is complete, accurate, and error-free.

Paragraph Writing Assignments

Help Desk

Kate was asked to write an argument paper on one of the topics listed in this chapter. She chose the topic "People should/should not drop out of high school." Kate argues that people should not drop out of high school. Read Kate's paper and answer the questions below.

> [1]People should not drop out of high school. [2]Dropping out of high school is one of the biggest mistakes many people make. [3]Every day I see my friends experience difficulty. [4]For example, my boyfriend struggles because he is limited to certain jobs. [5]Whether you have an education or not really makes a difference when looking for a job. [6]My boyfriend is limited to certain jobs. [7]Many places do not hire without at least a high school diploma. [8]When he does find a job, there are always negativities like the hours he gets and the amount he gets paid hourly. [9]Most places pay minimum wage if the person lacks an education. [10]He has no future to look forward to because of his lack of education. [11]Not having an education also makes your life pretty boring. [12]It makes someone feel like they are spending much of their life at home. [13]Most people think that not finishing high school and not going to college would not be boring because they think they will have their friends to hang out with during the day. [14]In most cases, though, the reality is that most people work or go to school, so no one is around to hang out with. [15]My boyfriend spends most of his day at home without much to do. [16]He sleeps in late and watches television all day. [17]As the day goes by and there is not much to do, it gets boring for him. [18]People who drop out of high school will never have an easy future.

1. What are Kate's reasons for not dropping out of high school?

_____

2. Is Kate's argument convincing? Explain.

_____

_____

3. List some other reasons for not dropping out of high school.

_____

_____

Group Activity

Many consumer products are either wasteful or difficult to open. For example, in fast-food restaurants, almost every item is wrapped and has a restaurant advertisement or logo on it. Disposable shaving razors use a lot of packaging for such a small product. Some products that are difficult to open include electronic devices, dolls, toothbrushes, and food containers.

In groups of three or four, choose a product whose packaging is either wasteful or impossible to open. Design an improved package that is less wasteful and environmentally friendly. Then write an argument paragraph as a proposal to the company explaining why it should use your new and improved package.

Reading and Writing across the Curriculum: Criminal Justice

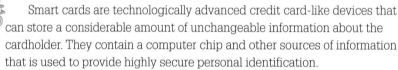

Smart cards are technologically advanced credit card-like devices that can store a considerable amount of unchangeable information about the cardholder. They contain a computer chip and other sources of information that is used to provide highly secure personal identification.

Smart cards can be used for a variety of purposes. They can store detailed records of a person's medical history or banking transactions. They can enable the holder to purchase goods and services, to enter restricted areas, or to perform other operations. Today, most smart cards are set up for a variety of limited uses. For example, colleges and universities have adopted modified versions for use as student identification cards.

Currently, U.S. government offices have mandated the use of a Personal Identification Verification (PIV) smart card containing chips that store personal information and **biometric data**, including two digitized fingerprints and a photograph. As personal identification technologies continue to develop, some people are concerned that eventually, all citizens will have to carry a national ID smart card.

(Adapted from *Criminal Justice Today* by Frank Schmalleger)

biometric data detailed information about someone's body, such as the patterns of color in their eyes, which can be used to prove who they are

Would requiring all citizens and others living in the United States to carry a national ID smart card provide greater security or invade personal privacy? Write an argument paragraph in which you take a stand on whether or not a national ID smart card should be required.

Comment on a Contemporary Issue

The ability to use computer technology is essential in college and in the workplace. Many colleges require students to take a basic computer literacy course that cover skills that students already know. Do you think that these courses are necessary?

Comment about whether students should or should not be required to take a computer literacy course in college.

Write about an Image

This poster was designed to be persuasive. Write an argument paragraph about animals in shelters that makes the same point as the poster does.

LO 3 The Argument Essay

The argument essay has the same purpose as the argument paragraph: to express the writer's point of view on an issue and support it by giving evidence to persuade readers to agree with the writer's point of view or to take action. The argument essay explores several sides of an issue. In order to be convincing, the arguments and evidence supporting the point of view must be strong.

The argument essay may use the same patterns of development as the paragraph version. However, since the essay discusses the topic in greater depth and includes more evidence and opposing viewpoints, other patterns of development are possible.

You may want to do some research on your topic to find out what experts say. To avoid plagiarism, take careful notes by labeling paraphrases, summaries, and direct quotations. Write down all the publication information from the sources you use. When you include material from your sources in your paper, follow the MLA format.

Research Reminder. For more information about taking notes and using research, see Chapters 16 and 17.

Thesis Statement

The thesis statement states the writer's point of view about an issue. The thesis can consist of two or three parts:

Two-part thesis: Narrowed issue + point of view.

Social network websites should not be trusted.

Three-part thesis: Narrowed issue + point of view + supporting arguments.

Social network websites should not be trusted because they leave users vulnerable to security attacks, harassment by friends or strangers, and invasion of privacy by advertisers.

Body Paragraphs

The body paragraphs in an argumentation essay include the reasons for your point of view with evidence. They may also include the arguments against your point of view with your rebuttal of—or answer to—the arguments against. When arranging your reasons and arguments against, you can begin with the strongest and end with the weakest or begin with the weakest and end with the strongest. You can use the point-by-point arrangement, or you can give all your points and evidence first, then follow with the arguments against and rebuttal. The figure below shows a basic organization for an argument essay.

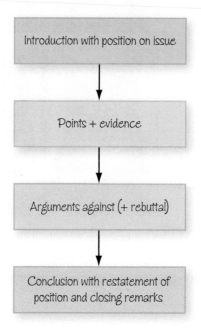

Concluding Paragraph

The concluding paragraph has an important role in your argument essay. Your goal is to convince the reader that your position on the issue is the strongest. After restating your position, you can add any of the following: suggest results or consequences, end with a warning, discuss the future of the subject, or suggest that more research on the subject is needed. No new arguments should be presented in the conclusion.

Argument Essay Example

The following essay was developed from a paragraph on the same issue. Student Roxanne Byrd argues that the Muscovy ducks on her campus should be relocated.

Byrd 1

Roxanne Byrd

Professor Markus

College Preparatory English

20 Nov. 2010

The Duck Problem

1   Muscovy ducks are a common sight on our college campus, which has a

big lake on its border. They are large birds with feathers that can be white, greenish

black, blue, brown, or a combination. Their most distinctive characteristics are a crest

on the top of their heads and large areas of red, bumpy skin around their eyes and

bill. Native to Central and South America, Muscovies were imported to North

America and are raised on farms for their eggs and meat. Unfortunately, many have

escaped into the wild. As a result, large numbers of wild, breeding Muscovies can be

found near local waters. So many of these ducks have taken up residence on our

campus that they have become a nuisance. The Muscovy ducks should be relocated

because they spoil the campus environment, they are aggressive towards people, and

they cause accidents.

2   One reason to relocate the Muscovy ducks is that they spoil the campus

environment. First of all, their droppings create a health hazard. One Muscovy duck

creates a large amount of droppings a day. The droppings carry bacteria that can

make humans sick. Since the ducks have bowel movements wherever they please, the

walkways are frequently littered with their droppings, making people watch every

step while walking across campus. In addition, their greenish-black, watery droppings

are slippery when stepped on; therefore, someone could slip, fall, and get injured.

Another way they spoil the campus is by destroying native

Muscovy duck

Byrd 3

sustainable landscape policy
one which causes little or no damage to the environment and therefore able to continue for a long time

plants and wildflowers. Our campus has a **sustainable landscape policy** where we install native plants to reduce the use of fertilizer and pesticides and conserve water. Both students and faculty have worked to install gardens across campus. However, last month, some of the ducks uprooted all of the rare, native wildflowers that had just been planted by the environmental science classes. Duck lovers argue that the Muscovies benefit the campus environment because they control pests by eating mosquitoes, roaches, ants, and spiders. However, the benefit of creating our sustainable gardens is to attract beneficial insects that control other pests and keep a natural balance.

3   Not only do the Muscovy ducks spoil the campus environment, but also they are aggressive toward people. Their bold, unwanted approaches annoy and occasionally frighten students, staff, and visitors, especially when the ducks want food. For instance, when someone sits outside on a bench to eat a snack or to socialize with other students, groups of hissing, snorting ducks quickly rush toward and gather around that person, pushing their beaks against the individual's legs to beg for a handout. On one occasion, a duck jumped on my friend's lap while she was snacking on some chips. The duck pecked at her face and in an attempt to get some of her food, bit her on the lip. Duck supporters claim that people are misinterpreting the ducks' intentions. They say that the Muscovies have learned to be unafraid of approaching people because so many students and staff members are friendly towards them and frequently feed them. Nevertheless, the supporters do not realize that many individuals are either fearful of wild creatures or do not want to feel as if they are in a petting zoo.

4   The most important reason for relocating the Muscovy ducks is that their presence on campus roads and in parking spaces endangers both people and ducks.

Although the campus is bordered by a lake, the ducks do not limit themselves to that location, roaming the campus grounds for food. For instance, they often sit in empty parking spaces preening their feathers or sleeping. At popular class times, competition for parking spaces is intense, so when a space opens up, students pull in quickly, unaware that a duck may also be occupying it. If a duck is lucky enough to avoid its death in this situation, it may not avoid being run over or causing an accident. Although the campus is small, there are two entrances from the main street with roads leading to student parking areas near classroom buildings. Traffic can get heavy on these roads when students are arriving and leaving. On many occasions, one or more ducks have interfered with the flow of traffic while attempting to cross the road, halting traffic in both directions. The worst problem is that accidents have occurred because of duck crossings. Last semester, one student saw a duck crossing the road and, stopped short, and caused a three-car pile up. Those who support the ducks' right to live on campus believe that drivers should be aware that ducks may be in parking spaces and on the roads and should drive accordingly. However, students should not have to worry about running over a duck or having a car accident because of one.

5   The Muscovy ducks are a non-native species; they are not considered wildlife. Therefore, they cannot be protected by any state or federal law. In addition, they cannot be relocated to public lands. While the law does not prohibit their capture and humane killing, this is not the solution being suggested. In order to prevent the ducks from destroying the campus environment, being aggressive towards people, and causing accidents, the Muscovy ducks should be moved to a confined environment where they cannot escape or come into contact with wild birds or people who do not want to interact with them.

PRACTICE   Analyzing an Argument Essay
14.6

1. Underline the thesis statement. What point does the author plan to argue?

_____

2. What technique does the writer use in the lead-in?

_____

3. Underline the topic sentences of each of the body paragraphs. What is the point of each body paragraph?

_____

4. Circle the transition words used to introduce each difference in each of the topic sentences.

5. Each body paragraph contains an opposing point and answer to that point. Double-underline the point of opposition and answer in each body paragraph.

6. In addition to referring to the thesis statement, underline the additional argument the writer makes in the conclusion.

For more help with writing an essay, including introductions and conclusions, see Chapter 5.

Argument Essay Graphic Organizer

Using an argument essay graphic organizer will help you arrange your reasons, arguments against, and rebuttals. The graphic organizer on page 288 shows a pattern that can be used for your argument essay. You can change it to suit your needs by adding paragraphs, points, and reasons, arguments against, and rebuttals.

Writing Assignments

Write about an Image: Is a College Degree Necessary?

Argument Essay Graphic Organizer

Introduction

Lead-in:

Bridge:

Thesis Statement: Your position on the issue

Body Paragraph(s) with Points and Evidence

Topic Sentence:

Point 1 of Argument with Evidence:

Point 2 of Argument with Evidence:

Point 3 of Argument with Evidence:

Body Paragraph(s) with Arguments Against (and Rebuttal)

Topic Sentence:

Argument Against (and Rebuttal):

Argument Against (and Rebuttal):

Argument Against (and Rebuttal):

Conclusion

Choose Effective Closing Technique.

In the United States, a college degree has been considered the ticket to success. However, Professor Richard Vedder has a different point of view. Dr. Vedder has taught economics at Ohio University for forty-four years and has written extensively about the connection between higher education and the work force. He believes that not everyone has the interest, ability, or need to go to college. In addition, many of the fastest growing jobs do not require a college degree.

What do you think? Write an argument essay for or against getting a college degree.

Writing Topics for an Argument Essay

For your argument essay, choose one of these options:

- from paragraph to essay: expand the paragraph you wrote in the paragraph section of this chapter
- any of the writing topics in the paragraph section of this chapter
- any topic from the following list:
    vegetarianism
    moral values in the United States
    illegal immigration
    a law that should be changed
    media violence

Writing across the Curriculum: Topics

Peer Review Reminder. For feedback on your writing, have someone read your paper and make comments on the Peer Review Response sheet in Chapter 4, page 55.

Business: self-employment
Sociology: cultural diversity
Biology: choosing the sex of your children
Education: school violence
Criminal Justice: police brutality

English Success Tip: **Improve Your Writing by Reading**

Students often ask how they can improve their writing. Most often, the advice is to study grammar, mechanics, punctuation, and sentence structure. However, reading can help you become a better writer.

Reading stimulates your language development in a number of ways.

- You unconsciously absorb the author's style of writing.
- You learn how different writers express their thoughts.
- You see how writers handle complex ideas.

Reading is especially helpful for English language learners. In addition to the benefits already discussed, by reading in English, you increase your exposure to the language and the way it is used in writing.

Set aside at least fifteen minutes each day to read. Read newspapers, magazine articles, and novels that interest you. You will be amazed at the improvement in your writing skills, and will enjoy the entertainment and stress relief that reading can offer.

For support in meeting this chapter's objectives, log in to www.mywritinglab.com, go to the Study Plan tab, click on **Argument** and choose **Paragraph Development—Argument and Essay Development—Argument** from the list of subtopics. Read and view the videos and resources in the Review Materials section, and then complete the Recall, Apply, and Write exercises in the Activities section. You can check your scores and overall progress by using the Gradebook.

Learning Other College Writing Assignments

Writing under Pressure

LO 1 What Is Timed Writing?

Timed writing is a writing activity that must be completed within a limited time period. The purpose of a timed writing activity is to test your ability to think and write under pressure. Learning how to write well in a limited time period will help you handle the pressures of writing in college and in the workplace. For example, writing tasks such as reports, proposals, memoranda, and training materials are done on the spot at work.

Timed Writing in College

In college, a variety of writing activities may be timed. The most common is the essay question or exam. In writing courses, you may be asked to write a paragraph or essay in class to show that you can apply the writing skills you have been practicing and studying. Some colleges have students do a timed-writing sample for placement into certain courses or for exiting from a particular program.

How Is Timed Writing Evaluated?

Timed writing is usually graded differently from traditional writing assignments. First, instructors or other graders understand that writing within a limited time puts enormous pressure on the writer. In addition, they take into consideration that the writer has not had much time to think about, plan, and support the topic. They consider the paper to be a first draft; however, they expect a well-organized essay that follows a method of development appropriate to the topic.

- -

TIMED WRITING ESSENTIALS

Good timed writing has these characteristics:

- The main idea is clearly stated.
- The main idea is supported with specific details.
- A clear pattern of organization is used.
- Ideas are expressed logically.
- Transitional words and expressions show connections between ideas.
- Vocabulary is used effectively.
- Different sentence types give variety to the writing.

- -

LO 2 How to Approach Timed Writing: The 5 Ps

Although timed writing can be challenging, understanding and applying five basic steps will give you a feeling of control over the process, thus building your confidence. The five steps are as follows: *(1) understand the Prompt, (2) make a Point, (3) form a Plan, (4) Produce the essay, and (5) Proofread.*

Step 1. Understand the Prompt

What is a prompt? The **prompt** is the topic that you are being asked to write about. Prompts can be written in many ways. Here are some examples.

- **Incomplete sentence:** The most valuable item you own that was not bought in a store
- **Statement:** Sports stars should or should not bear responsibility for being role models.
- **Question:** What childhood experience taught you something about life?
- **Quotation:** "Success is doing ordinary things extraordinarily well."—Jim Rohn
- **Scenario:** Many young adults read very little. They get most of their news and information from the Internet, television, and the movies. They would rather read a magazine than a novel. Write an essay in which you explain the reasons for this situation.

Read the Prompt Carefully Take the time to read the prompt carefully to understand what you are being asked to write about. If you do not respond to the prompt or you respond only to part of it, your score could be lowered. Look for key words that may tell you how to develop your essay. For instance, in the scenario example in the previous section, the last sentence tells you that the essay should explain the reasons young adults do not read much. That means you can use the cause and effect pattern of development. The following are some key words that are commonly used in essay prompts:

Key Words in Prompts	What to Do
Argue, take a position	State a point of view on an issue and support it by giving evidence.
Cause, effect, give reasons or results, why	Make a point about the reasons for and/or results of a situation
Classify, categorize, group	Make a point by arranging items within a topic into groups based on a single characteristic.
Compare, contrast, explain similarities or differences	Make a point about how two subjects are similar or different.
Define, explain the meaning	Make a point by explaining what a word, expression, or concept means.
Describe, give details of characteristics or features	Make a point by creating a clear mental picture in the reader's mind.
Illustrate, give examples	Make a point and support it with examples.
Narrate, tell the story of	Make a point by telling a story or giving an account of a significant experience or event.
Process, explain how	Make a point by explaining how to do something or how something happens or works.
Explain, discuss	Make a point by using any of the methods.

If you cannot find key words, you may be able to choose from several different approaches. For example, the topic "A place that people should visit" does not include any key words. Here are some possible approaches:

- Reasons people should visit a particular place
- Examples of what people will see while visiting a historical place of interest
- Description of a location of natural beauty
- Types of things to do or see in a specific place

PRACTICE 15.1 Choosing a Method of Development for Timed Writing Prompts

For the example prompts 1 through 4, choose an appropriate method of development for a paragraph or essay. More than one type may be acceptable.

1. The most valuable item you own that was not bought in a store
   a. argument   b. causes   c. description   d. classification
2. Sports stars should or should not bear responsibility for being role models.
   a. narration   b. process   c. description   d. argument
3. What childhood experience taught you something about life?
   a. narration   b. classification c. contrast   d. definition
4. "Success is doing ordinary things extraordinarily well."—Jim Rohn
   a. narration   b. illustration   c. process   d. cause and effect

Step 2. Make a Point

Once you have figured out what the prompt is asking you to do, spend a few minutes prewriting. Your goal is to come up with the main point you want to make—your topic sentence for a paragraph or your thesis statement for an essay.

When developing your topic sentence or thesis statement, include some words from the prompt. Including words from the prompt will show the reader that you are addressing the topic and will keep you on track when you are writing.

Here are some examples of essay exam prompts and thesis statements that respond to them. Note how the thesis statements include words from the prompt and the main point. The supporting points are optional and are in parentheses in the examples.

Prompt: A well-known discount store chain is proposing to build a store in your neighborhood. Do you support or oppose this plan? Give specific reasons for your answer.

Thesis statement: The plan to build a discount store in my neighborhood should be opposed (because the store will cause an increase in traffic, theft, and noise).

Prompt: What are some important qualities of a good manager?

Thesis statement: Some important qualities of a good manager are the ability to communicate, to lead, and to have faith in employees.

PRACTICE 15.2 Writing Thesis Statements for Timed Writing Prompts

After thinking about the following prompts, write a thesis statement for each one. Include some of the words from the prompt.

1. Students who do not want to write their own essays can find dozens of websites on the Internet that sell essays on many different topics. Argue against buying essays on the Internet.

_____

_____

2. Discuss the ways you have changed as a result of your experience in college.

_____

_____

3. Many schools employ security guards or police officers and have installed security equipment such as video cameras or metal detectors in buildings. Write about security measures that are provided on your college campus or security measures that should be provided on your campus.

_____

_____

Step 3. Form a Plan

Once you have written your thesis statement, take a few minutes to jot down some supporting ideas. Write a brief description of the points you want to make. Developing a scratch outline will help to keep you on track as you write. Here is a scratch outline for the thesis statement: "To maintain good health, I eat nutritious foods, exercise five times a week, and meditate every morning".

> ✓1. Eat nutritious foods
> —fruits and vegetables
> —low-fat dairy and fish
> —grains and nuts
> ✓2. Exercise five times a week
> —lift weights
> —jog
> —cycle
> ✓3. Meditate every morning
> —mindfulness meditation practice

Step 4. Produce the Essay

Most of your time should be devoted to writing the essay. Because you are writing within a time limit, you will not be able to support your main ideas with the same amount of detail that you would in a take-home essay. However, you will be expected to complete the essay with enough specific development to prove your main point.

> TIPS | **Producing the Essay**
>
> 1. Avoid changing your topic and starting over when you will not have enough time to fully develop another one.
> 2. Avoid focusing on errors in grammar, punctuation, or spelling while you are drafting.
> 3. If you cannot think of an attention-getting introduction, either skip it and return to it later or write an introduction that takes a more general approach.
> 4. Don't spend too much time developing any one supporting paragraph only to discover that you have little time to work on the others.
> 5. If you get stuck, skip to another paragraph. You can always return to it later.
> 6. Don't forget a conclusion, even if you have time to write only one sentence.
> 7. If you are writing your essay by hand, write legibly. If you decide that you want to remove material, neatly draw a line through it.

Step 5. Proofread

In timed writing, proofreading and editing are very important. Save five to ten minutes of your total writing time to read your paper carefully for grammar, punctuation, and spelling errors. If you know that you have a problem with commas, pay specific attention to them as you proofread.

LO 3 How to Manage Your Time

When writing under pressure, you may forget to keep track of the time and end up with an unfinished paper. To avoid running out of time, budget your time and pay attention to the clock. For example, if you are given 60 minutes, divide your time in the way shown here.

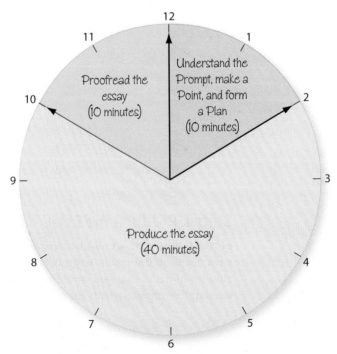

Pay attention to the clock. Sit where you can see it or wear a watch to monitor your time.

Timed Writing Examples

The two student timed-essay examples presented here were written on the same topic: "A business that provides excellent goods or services". Read the essays and answer the questions that follow each one. These examples may contain vocabulary and spelling errors as well as grammar and sentence errors.

PRACTICE   Evaluating Timed Essay Example 1

15.3   Using the timed writing essentials on page 292, what are the strengths and weaknesses of this essay?

---

[1]The Starbucks in Wilton Manors provides excellent services. [2]For example, I am there often sometimes three or four times a week. [3]I like to go there because it is convenient located, comfortable, and they know me by name.

[4]My friends and I live in different neighborhoods, so we decided to choose a place that was conveniently located. [5]This Starbucks is located in a neighborhood that we are familiar with, it was a good choice for us. [6]Starbucks furniture is soft, comfortable, and modern. [7]There is plenty of space to move around. [8]At Starbuck there is wheelchair access from the outside courtyard and from the parking lot. [9]In addition to being conveniently located, and comfortable, they know their customers and they treat them well. [10]Whenever I am there I do not have to wait in line for a long time. [11]Scott, Brian, Dale, Jessica and Bonnie knows me by my name. [11]They know what I like to drink and eat. [12]They also knows how I like my beverage. [13]I get the same drink, a medium mocha frappucino without the whipped cream, and my usual a piece of the Bluberry Crumb coffee cake. [14]One of these days I will try something different just to see their reactions. [15]I like and enjoy going to this Starbucks because they provide excellent customer service. [16]You can tell that just by driving by. [17]The parking lot is always full, and there is a long line of people waiting. [18]This is usually a good sign that it's a good place.

Strengths _____

_____

Weaknesses _____

_____

PRACTICE   Evaluating Timed Essay Example 2

15.4   Using the timed writing essentials on page 292, what are the strengths and weaknesses of this essay?

[1]There are many different types of coffee shops in my neighborhood, but my favorite is Starbuck's coffee. [2]I am a frequent customer there and they always provide excellent customer service, coffee and food.

[3]One noticeable quality of Starbucks is their excellent customer service. [4]The baristas are always dressed well and are smiling. [5]When I walk in they also greet me by name, making the visit a more personal experience. [6]Sometimes they even have my drink ready by the time I get to the front counter. [7]The baristas always make the environment in the store warm and friendly.

[8]Another great thing Starbucks serves is coffee. [9]They import their coffee beans from all over the world and keep them sealed fresh in bags until it is time to grind and brew them. [10]Their coffee is always hot and fresh as they brew a new pot every thirty minutes. [11]I can also add a variety of flavors into my drink such as vanilla, caramel or hazelnut. [12]My drink is always personalized and made exactly how I like it.

[13]Finally, there is their very tasty food. [14]Each morning a bakery delivers fresh pastries to be sold in the store. [15]The pastries come in a large variety from muffins to scones and are very delicious. [16]The baristas also prepare fresh fruit cups and breakfast sandwiches in the morning for customers. [17]The display case for the pastries and food is also kept clean and full of fresh product.

[18]I have loved going to Starbucks since my first initial visit. [19]They always have excellent customer service and goods in nearly every store. [20]I would reccomend for everyone to visit a Starbucks coffee shop at least once.

Strengths _____

_____

Weaknesses _____

_____

Writing Assignments

Help Desk

Micky has been having difficulty writing timed essays. He wrote the following timed essay on this topic: "An activity people participate in despite the risk". When he got his paper back, he was disappointed to see that he had failed. Read Micky's essay and answer the questions that follow.

[1] People enjoy harsh activities despite the risk. Whether it is to have fun or take their mind off problems they are having, they still participate. Drinking and driving is the most common mistake one can ever make. This act not only harms yourself, but it also harms others. Drinking and driving can have several risks such as you can harm innocent people and or yourself, go to jail, and it can also interfere with your brain system.

[2] One of the most common risk of drinking and driving is the harming of innocent victims and or yourself. Driving drunk is not responsible. The majority of highway accidents is the cause of a drunk driver. Thousands of innocent people are dying every year to a drunk driver. They have not been under the influence of alcohol but, still have to face consequences of someone eles. When driving drunk you are not only hurting others but, most of all you are hurting yourself.

[3] Another risk of drinking and driving, is the possibility you might go to jail.

1. What are some of the weaknesses of this essay?

_____

_____

2. What tips can you offer Micky?

_____

_____

Reading and Writing across the Curriculum: Sociology

Sociologists study how groups influence people, especially those who share a culture and physical location.

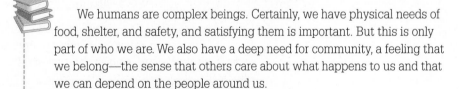

We humans are complex beings. Certainly, we have physical needs of food, shelter, and safety, and satisfying them is important. But this is only part of who we are. We also have a deep need for community, a feeling that we belong—the sense that others care about what happens to us and that we can depend on the people around us.

(From *Essentials of Sociology* by James M. Henslin)

Some people find a sense of community in the city, while others find it in the suburbs (communities located just outside a city), or rural areas. In a timed 60-minute paper, write about why you would prefer to live in a city, a suburb, or a rural area.

Topics for Timed Writing

Set a time limit for writing about one of these topics—45 or 60 minutes.

If you had the power to change three things in your community or in the world, what would you change and why?

Giving a gift to a child, such as a pet, a camera, or a bicycle, can contribute to a child's development. What gift would you give to a child and how would it help him or her develop?

What advice would you give to students who are just entering college?

The Dalai Lama, Tibetan spiritual leader, once said, "In the practice of tolerance, one's enemy is the best teacher." Give examples of times when you learned tolerance from people you did not like or did not agree with.

Explain the effect of a particular invention on the family.

Writing across the Curriculum Topics

Environmental Science: Some people believe that human activity is harming the Earth. Others feel that the Earth is a better place to live because of human activity. Which do you believe?

Psychology: Explain the differences between the male and female approaches to solving relationship problems.

Music Appreciation: Many of us like music from our own generation. Convince someone who is not in your generation that your music is worth listening to.

Literature: What book, poem, or story should be required reading for everyone?

Sociology: Many people from other countries come to live in the United States because they believe that it is better than their native country. What features make the United States desirable?

 Peer Review Reminder. For feedback on your writing, have someone read your paper and make comments on the Peer Review Response sheet in Chapter 4, page 55.

✔ **English Success Tip: Build Timed Writing Confidence with Practice**

Many students experience stress when writing under pressure. Practicing will reduce your anxiety and build your confidence. Here are some things you can to do prepare for timed writing.

1. Make a list of writing prompts that you can use for practice.
2. Expand your knowledge of current events by reading reliable materials or following news reports.
3. Understand the criteria that will be used to grade your paper.
4. Recreate the testing situation. Choose a topic and apply the 5 Ps: *understand the Prompt, make a Point, form a Plan, Produce the essay, and Proofread.*
5. Make note of the parts of the timed-writing process that were most troublesome for you. Work on these when you practice.
6. Get an objective point of view by asking another student or an assistant in your campus writing center to read your completed paper and evaluate it using the criteria.
7. Practice often.

Taking Source Notes and Writing a Summary Essay

Learning Objectives

After working through this chapter, you will be able to:

LO 1 Identify outside sources.

LO 2 Take proper notes on sources and avoid plagiarism.

LO 3 Explain what a summary is.

LO 4 Write a summary essay presenting a brief version of a passage's main idea and supporting points in your own words.

LO 1 What Are Outside Sources?

Many college course assignments include reading, viewing, or listening to material from outside sources in addition to reading a textbook. Outside sources can take many forms such as books, articles, interviews, websites, television shows, or podcasts. Your teachers will expect you to show that you can read, understand, use, and respond to these sources.

A variety of academic writing activities also involves the use of outside sources. One type of paper is the summary, which you will learn about in this chapter. Another type is the research paper, discussed in Chapter 17. Critiques, reports, business plans, and literature reviews are other examples of academic writing that use outside sources.

This chapter will show you how to put information from outside sources in the appropriate forms and how to write a summary paper.

LO 2 Taking Source Notes to Avoid Plagiarism

When you take notes from outside sources that you would like to include in a paper, you should prepare that information in acceptable forms that show the reader that the information has been borrowed from other sources. By preparing your source information properly, you will avoid **plagiarism**, which is copying the words and ideas of others and presenting them as if they were your own ideas. Western cultures consider a writer's work as his or her own property; in other words, the writer owns his or her expression of an idea. Therefore, a writer's ideas must be used properly and given recognition in your paper.

The acceptable forms for using other writers' ideas are paraphrases, direct quotations, and summaries.

Direct Quotation, Paraphrase, and Summary

The chart below explains direct quotation, paraphrase, and summary and gives examples of each. The examples are based on the following passage from *Game Design and Development* by Ernest Adams and Andrew Rollings, pages 120–21. Each of the examples shows the Modern Language Association (MLA) style of documenting sources in the body of a paper.

[1]Video game designers establish a game's morality. [2]They tell a player which actions should be performed to win the game and define those actions as good or desirable. [3]Likewise, they tell the player to avoid certain actions; these are defined as bad or undesirable. [4]The players who come into the world must adopt the game standards, or they will lose the game. [5]Game designers are strongly discouraged from creating games that reward or even allow the player to do truly hateful things. [6]Games that expect a player to participate in sexual assault, torture, or child abuse tarnish the reputation of the game industry as a whole.

(Adapted from *Game Design and Development* by Ernest Adams and Andrew Rollings)

Direct Quotation, Paraphrase, and Summary

Form	When to Use It	Example
Direct Quotation A **direct quotation** is the use of the exact words of a source. The direct quotation matches the original word for word. ■ Quotation marks are used at the beginning and at the end of the quoted material to show that the information is copied word for word. ■ Use a signal phrase to show readers that you are using a source. Place the page numbers of the quotation in parentheses at the end.	Use a direct quotation when the source is recognized as an authority, the writer's words are memorable or especially clear, or the material is complex.	Adams and Rollings state, "Games that expect a player to participate in sexual assault, torture, or child abuse tarnish the reputation of the game industry as a whole" (121).
Paraphrase A **paraphrase** is the use of your own words to restate the words or ideas of another. ■ No quotation marks are needed. ■ A paraphrase should be about the same length as the original source. The organization, wording, and sentence structure should be your own. ■ Use a signal phrase or place the author's name and page(s) of the source in parentheses.	Use a paraphrase when you want to make a short passage clearer.	Paraphrase of sentence 5: Designers should not include morally offensive activities in their games (Adams and Rollings 121).

Punctuation Reminder
To learn more about punctuating direct quotations, see Chapter 28.

Research Reminder. For more information about how to document sources, see Chapter 17.

Summary

A **summary** is the use of your own words to give a shortened version of another writer's words or ideas.

■ A summary gives the most important point of the original source, leaving out examples and explanations.

■ No quotation marks are needed.

■ Use a signal phrase or place the author's name and page(s) of the source in parentheses

Use a summary when you want to present the main points of a longer passage.

Game designers set up the moral standards that players must adopt to win the game. These standards should be ethically responsible (Adams and Rollings 120–21).

Identifying Your Source

When you include a direct quotation, paraphrase, or summary from an outside source in your paper, you need to identify the source. This is called documentation, which you will learn more about in Chapter 17. In the examples in this section, notice how the author's name is provided as well as the page(s) of the source.

A good way to tell the reader where an outside source comes from and to introduce it is to use a **signal phrase**, also called an attributive tag. A signal phrase can be a word, a phrase, or a sentence. It can be placed before or after the source material. It often includes the author's name and a verb that fits what the author is saying. You can use the author's full name or last name, but not the first name by itself.

Example:

Ernest Adams and Andrew Rollings emphasize, "Computer games are about bringing fantasies to life, enabling people to do things in make-believe that they could not possibly do in the real world. But make-believe games are dangerous when played by people for whom the line between fantasy and reality is not clear, especially children under the age of eight" (124).

TIPS | **Using Verbs to Introduce Source Material**

■ **Choose the verb that shows the author's point of view.** For example, if the author is giving a point of view, use a verb such as *argues*.

■ **Vary the verbs you choose to introduce a source.** Using a variety of appropriate verbs helps the reader understand each of the source author's meanings. Using the same verb, such as *states*, each time is repetitious and uninteresting. Here are some verbs you can use when introducing source material.

Neutral	Shows Opposition	Agrees	Suggests or Implies	Questions
comments	argues	admits	concludes	asks
describes	complains	agrees	implies	inquires
explains	disagrees		predicts	questions
illustrates	insists		speculates	
observes			suggests	
points out				
reports				
says				
shows				
thinks				
writes				

Avoiding Plagiarism

Plagiarism is copying the words and ideas of others and presenting them as your own. The word *plagiarism* originally meant "to kidnap." When you plagiarize, you are stealing someone else's ideas.

Plagiarism is a serious form of academic dishonesty. Most teachers and colleges do not tolerate plagiarism and enforce severe penalties for students who are caught. Although plagiarism has become easy with instant access to information on the Internet, and the ease of cutting and pasting, with the help of plagiarism detection software, teachers can type in a suspicious phrase or sentence and find proof of cheating.

Plagiarism can take many forms. Here are a few examples:

- copying someone else's paper and submitting it as your own
- submitting a research paper purchased online from a research paper service
- copying information from outside sources in your paper without documenting them
- paraphrasing or summarizing information from outside sources in your paper without documenting them

Sometimes, students accidentally plagiarize because they do not understand how to put their source information into an acceptable form and document it properly. Common examples of these errors are copying, substituting words, and rearranging words, phrases, and sentences. Read the following passage from page 48 of the college text *The Interpersonal Communication Book* by Joseph A. DeVito and then compare it to the plagiarized examples.

[1]A common barrier to intercultural communication occurs when you assume that similarities exist and that differences do not. [2]This is especially true of values, attitudes, and beliefs. [3]You might easily accept different hairstyles, clothing, and foods. [4]In basic values and beliefs, however, you may assume that deep down all people are really alike. [5]They aren't. [6]When you assume similarities and ignore differences, you'll fail to notice important distinctions and when communicating will convey to others that your ways are the right way and that their ways are not important to you. [7]Consider this example. [8]An American invites a Filipino coworker to dinner. [9]The Filipino politely refuses. [10]The American is hurt and feels that the Filipino does not

want to be friendly. [11]The Filipino is hurt and concludes that the invitation was not extended sincerely. [12]Here, it seems, both the American and the Filipino assume that their customs for inviting people to dinner are the same when, in fact, they aren't. [13]A Filipino expects to be invited several times before accepting a dinner invitation. [14]When an invitation is given only once, it's viewed as insincere.

Copying the Exact Words of the Original The most common form of plagiarism is copying the exact words of the original without using quotation marks. The parts of the sentences that are copied word for word are highlighted in this example:

In *The Interpersonal Communication Book,* Joseph A. DiVito states that a common barrier to intercultural communication occurs when you assume that similarities exist and that differences do not. You should not think that all people are alike because they are not. If you do not pay attention to differences, you will communicate to others that your ways are the right way and that their ways are not (48).

Substituting Words Another form of plagiarism is replacing some of the words in the original passage with **synonyms**, which are words that have the same or similar meanings as another. In this example, the word replacements are highlighted in this example:

In *The Interpersonal Communication Book,* Joseph A. DiVito states that a usual barrier with intercultural communication happens when you think that likenesses have an existence and that dissimilarities do not. When you presume likenesses and ignore differences, you will be unable to see important differentiations and will make known to others that your methods are the correct way and their methods are not significant to you (48).

Rearranging Words, Phrases, and Sentences Using the same words, phrases, and sentences but placing them in a different order from the original passage is another form of plagiarism. In the following example, the exact words of the main idea of the passage from sentences 1 and 6 are rearranged:

In *The Interpersonal Communication Book,* Joseph A. DiVito states that when you assume that all people are really alike and that differences do not exist, a common barrier to intercultural communication occurs. You will convey that their ways are not important to you and that your ways are the right ways to others (48).

An Acceptable Summary The following example is an acceptable summary of the passage. The writer uses his own words to summarize the content.

> In *The Interpersonal Communication Book,* Joseph A. DiVito points out that problems communicating with people of different cultures arise when you mistakenly think they have the same beliefs and values that you do. If you do not recognize the differences when communicating, you will give others the impression that you do not consider their customs to be correct or important (48).

PRACTICE Detecting Plagiarism in Paraphrases

16.1 Read the following textbook selection about McDonald's and then the paraphrases that follow. Identify the paraphrases that are plagiarized. Also, write the type of error the writer made: copying exact words, substituting words, or rearranging words, phrases, and sentences.

[1]McDonald's has become an international icon of the fast-food industry. [2]With 30,000 restaurants in over 100 countries, the golden arches have become synonymous with American culture. [3]Yet in recent years, McDonald's seems to have lost its competitive edge both at home and abroad. [4]In the United States, for example, its stores are outdated and its customer service skills seem to be slipping. [5]Moreover, concerns about health have driven many customers away from Big Macs and French fries. [6]McDonald's no longer leads in technology, with rivals inventing new processing and cooking technologies. [7]Profits have dropped, forcing McDonald's to expand aggressively into foreign markets, especially Europe and Asia.

(Adapted from *Business Essentials* by Robert J. Ebert and Ricky W. Griffin)

1. Ebert and Griffin point out that McDonald's does not have its competitive edge both in the United States and abroad (19).

_____

2. McDonald's has been forced to expand aggressively into foreign markets, especially Europe and Asia because their profits have dropped (Ebert and Griffin 19).

_____

3. McDonald's used to be in the forefront of food preparation, but now, competitors have improved upon McDonald's older technology (Ebert and Griffin 19).

_____

4. Ebert and Griffin state that McDonald's has become an international icon of the fast-food industry (19).

_____

PRACTICE   Practicing Paraphrasing, Summarizing, and Quoting
16.2
Read the following passage, which was taken from the textbook *Crossroads* by Elizabeth F. Barkley, a multicultural study of America's popular music, page 280. Then answer the questions that follow.

turntable a piece of equipment used in record players and having a flat, round surface that turns the record around while it is being played

[1]Hip Hop was originally used to refer to the background music for rap. [2]Several techniques developed to make this background music more interesting. [3]For example, an early technique called "scratching" involved playing a record on a **turntable** but changing the direction of rotation back and forth rapidly to create a rhythmic beat. [4]A variation was to use a second turntable to play the same record straight through while one scratched the record in a different rhythm on the first turntable. [5]In addition to "scratching," another technique used multiple turntables to insert sections from one recording into another called "cutting." [6]A related technique was to move between recordings. [7]If the recordings had different tempos or speeds, the player used a mechanism that controlled the speed to keep a constant beat pattern to blend the different song. [8]These are just some of the techniques that evolved to create the background music.

(Adapted from *Crossroads* by Elizabeth F. Barkley)

1. Write a summary of the passage.

_____

_____

2. Make sentence 5 a direct quotation. Introduce the quotation with an appropriate verb.

_____

_____

3. Paraphrase sentence 3.

_____

_____

LO 3   What Is a Summary Essay?

A **summary essay** is a paper that restates the essential points of an article, a web page, a chapter in a book, or a whole book. A summary essay takes the place of an original source, and, therefore, must be accurate and complete.

SUMMARY ESSENTIALS

An effective summary has these elements:

1. The summary presents a brief version of a passage's main idea and supporting point in your own words.
2. The first sentence of the summary expresses the main idea of the original passage and gives the author and the title of the work being summarized.
3. The body of the summary includes only the supporting points and omits minor points and examples.
4. The details of the summary are written in the same order as they appear in the original passage.
5. The summary does not include your personal opinions or thoughts.

LO 4 Writing the Summary

Writing an effective summary includes three main steps: (1) read to understand the passage, (2) take notes that identify the main idea and supporting points, and (3) write the summary.

Step 1. Read to Understand the Passage

You must understand what you read in order to summarize it. First, read the passage to find out what it is about. Then, read the passage again, but more carefully this time. Annotate each section of a passage *after* reading it. **Annotating** is a method for marking main ideas and supporting details. You mark the passage using a system that will be the most helpful to you. For example, you may want to circle words that you need to look up. You can also underline important details and cross out unimportant ones. For multiple paragraph passages, choosing a few words that summarize each paragraph and writing them in the margins will help you remember key points.

Step 2. Take Notes to Identify the Main Idea and Supporting Points

After you have found the main idea and supporting points of the passage, write those points down in your own words. Be sure to take the notes in the same order as they appear in the passage. Using a note-taking graphic organizer on the next page will help you keep your notes from the original passage separate from the notes you put into your own words.

Using Direct Quotations in a Summary On occasion, you may find a word or phrase that cannot be written in your own words, for example, a specific term or a technical description. In this situation, put quotation marks around the word or phrase to show that it was taken directly from the original passage. Quote words or phrases only when absolutely necessary. Read the following passage and see how a quotation is used in the summary that follows.

Note-taking Graphic Organizer

Title of Passage:

Author:

Page Number(s):

Direct Quotation

Paraphrase

Summary

nurturing through avoidance
choosing an addictive behavior to avoid unpleasant feelings or situations

Addiction is a process that evolves over time. It begins when a person repeatedly seeks the illusion of relief to avoid unpleasant feelings or situations. This pattern is known as **nurturing through avoidance** and is not an appropriate way of taking care of emotional needs. As a person becomes increasingly dependent on the addictive behavior, relationships with family, friends, and coworkers; performance at work or school; and personal life become worse. Eventually, addicts do not find the addictive behavior pleasurable but consider it preferable to the unhappy realities they are seeking to escape.

(From *Access to Health* by Rebecca J. Donatelle)

> Summary
>
> Rebecca J. Donatelle, in *Access to Health*, says that the process of addiction, called "nurturing through avoidance," is a cycle that starts when a person uses a substance or activity to avoid troublesome emotions or conditions and becomes dependent on it even though it does not give them pleasure (352).

Step 3. Write the Summary

Writing the summary is the last step. Write a rough draft first. Using your notes, write the author's main idea and important supporting points in your own words in the same order as they are presented in the passage. If the passage has a conclusion, summarize it. If it does not, leave a conclusion out.

After you have written your rough draft, you may need to make revisions. Compare your version against the original and use the Summary Checklist below to make sure you have written your summary correctly.

TIPS | **Writing Summaries**

1. Be sure that you have not given your opinion or ideas in the summary. The summary is your objective reporting of a passage's main points.
2. When summarizing someone else's writing, give the author's name, the title of the piece, and the main idea in the first sentence, not just the author and title.

> **Incomplete:** *Crossroads* is written by Elizabeth F. Barkely.
>
> **Incomplete:** "Country Music in a Historical and Social Context" is about the music traditions of immigrant groups and the development of these musical styles into uniquely American music.
>
> **Complete:** In *Crossroads,* Elizabeth F. Barkley writes about the music traditions of immigrant groups and the development of these musical styles into uniquely American music.

SUMMARY CHECKLIST

☐ 1. I have used my own words.

☐ 2. I have identified the source.

☐ 3. I have included the passage's main idea and important supporting details, leaving out examples and other nonessential descriptive details.

☐ 4. I have followed the order of the passage.

☐ 5. My summary does not include my personal opinions or thoughts.

Writing Assignments

Help Desk

Barry was asked to write a summary for this passage from *On Cooking* by Sarah R. Labensky and Alan M. Hause. Read his summary and give Barry some feedback by answering the questions that follow.

Chicken has become increasingly popular in recent years, in part because it is inexpensive, adaptable and considered healthier than meat. Indeed more than 100 million chickens are processed weekly in this country. To meet an ever-increasing demand, chickens are raised indoors in huge chicken houses that may contain as many as 20,000 birds. They are fed a specially developed mixture composed primarily of corn and soybean meal. Animal protein, vitamins, minerals and small amounts of antibiotics are added to produce quick growing, healthy birds.

Many consumers feel that chickens raised this way do not have the flavor of chickens that are allowed to move freely and search for food. Some consumers are concerned about the effects on people of the vitamins, minerals and antibiotics added to the chicken feed. To meet the demand for chickens raised the old-fashioned way, some farmers raise (and many fine establishments offer) free-range chickens.

Although the USDA has not standardized regulations for free-range chicken, generally the term *free-range* applies to birds that are allowed unlimited access to the area outside the chicken house. Often they are raised without antibiotics, fed a vegetarian diet (no animal fat or by-products), processed without the use of preservatives and raised under more kinder growing methods than conventionally grown birds. They are generally more expensive than conventionally raised chickens.

(Adapted from *On Cooking* by Sarah R. Labensky and Alan M. Hause)

Barry's Summary

[1]In this passage, it says that chicken has become very popular lately because it is inexpensive and healthier than meat. [2]To meet the demand, chickens are raised inside big chicken houses. [3]They are fed mostly corn and soybean meal. [4]They also get animal protein, vitamins, minerals, and small amounts of antibiotics to make them grow fast. [5]Many people think that chickens raised in chicken houses do not taste as good as chickens that are allowed to move around and find their own food. [6]People are also worried that some of the vitamins, minerals, and antibiotics stay in the chicken and could affect people. [7]Chickens raised the old-fashioned way are called "free range." [8]Most of them are not fed antibiotics and are fed a vegetarian diet. [9]They are more expensive.

---

1. Has Barry copied from the original passage? Underline the words, phrases, or sentences that are copied.
2. Has Barry replaced words in the original with his own? Circle any words that have been substituted.
3. What other errors does Barry make in his summary?

_____

_____

4. Has Barry included only the major supporting points? Is there anything that should be added or removed?

_____

_____

5. Write your own summary of the passage on a separate sheet of paper.

Reading and Writing across the Curriculum: Marketing

To practice working with longer pieces, write a summary of this passage from the textbook *Marketing* by Gary Armstrong and Philip Kotler. Use the note-taking graphic organizer on page 309.

[1]About ten years ago, GEICO was a little-known company in the auto insurance industry. Thanks in large part to an industry-changing advertising campaign, GEICO has become a major industry player. GEICO started out as an insurance company that targeted a select customer group of government employees and noncommissioned military officers with exceptional driving records. For nearly 60 years, the company relied mostly on direct-mail advertising and telephone marketing.

[2]In 1996, billionaire Warren Buffet bought the company and told the newly hired Martin Agency, a marketing group, to increase the advertising. In the beginning, the Martin Agency faced a tough task—introducing a little-known company with a funny name to a national audience. Like all good advertising, the GEICO campaign began with a simple but long-lasting theme, one that emphasizes the convenience and savings advantages of GEICO's direct-to-customers system. Every single one of the commercials produced in the campaign so far drives home the now-familiar tagline: "15 minute could save you 15 percent or more on car insurance."

[3]What really set GEICO's advertising apart was the inspired way the company chose to bring its customer benefits to life. At the time, competitors were using serious and emotional appeal advertisements: "You're in good hands with Allstate" or "Like a good neighbor, State Farm is there." To help make its advertising stand out, GEICO decided to deliver its punch line with humor. The creative approach worked and sales began to climb.

[4]As the brand grew, it became apparent that customers had difficulty pronouncing the GEICO name (which stands for Government Employees Insurance Company). Too often, GEICO became "gecko." Enter the charismatic green lizard. In 1999, GEICO ran a 15-second spot in which the now-famous, British-accented gecko calls a press conference and pleads: "I am a gecko, not to be confused with GEICO, which could save you hundreds on car insurance. So stop calling me." The ad was supposed to be a "throwaway." Consumers thought it was funny, and they quickly flooded the company with calls and letters begging to see more of the gecko.

[5]The rest, as they say, is history. Not only has the gecko helped people to pronounce and remember GEICO's name, it's become a pop culture icon. The unlikely lizard has become so well known that it was recently voted one of America's top two favorite icons by attendees of Advertising Week in New York, one of the ad industry's largest and most important gatherings.

[6]Although the gecko ads remain a fixture, one lizard could take the company only so far. GEICO told the Martin Agency, "Make people understand that GEICO.com is simple." The agency responded with the "Caveman" minicampaign, designed to bring younger buyers to the GEICO website by showing them how easy it is to purchase insurance online. In the campaigns, a group of cavemen, having somehow eluded extinction while developing a taste for racquet sports, and plasma televisions, is insulted by the company's advertising slogan, "It's so easy to use GEICO.com, even a caveman can do it." The indignant cavemen have a large group of fans. They've starred in a large number of ads and have their own GEICO-created website where you can visit one of the cavemen at home.

[7]Not only have the gecko and cavemen helped GEICO grow, they've changed the face of the auto insurance industry. Many analysts credit GEICO with changing the way insurance companies market their products in this traditionally boring category. Rising from being unknown only a dozen years ago, the company now serves more than eight million customers, making it the fourth-largest insurance company.

Peer Review Reminder. For feedback on your writing, have someone read your paper and make comments on the Peer Review Response sheet in Chapter 4, page 55.

✔

English Success Tip: **Summarize to Learn**

Summarizing a chapter in a textbook is one of the best ways to learn and understand new material or to study for a test. It also helps you manage long chapters of information more easily.

1. Read the entire chapter to get an idea of what it is about. Notice how the chapter is organized by looking at headings, subheadings, and the topic sentences that follow the headings.
2. Read each section or paragraph and figure out its main idea. Write the main idea in your own words so that it makes sense to you. Leave out minor details.
3. Put all of your sentences together into a summary.

Summarizing textbook material takes practice, but as you become better at it, your reading comprehension will improve as well.

For support in meeting this chapter's objectives, log in to www.mywritinglab.com, go to the Study Plan tab, click on **Taking Source Notes and Writing a Summary Essay** and choose **Summary Writing** from the list of subtopics. Read and view the videos and resources in the Review Materials section, and then complete the Recall, Apply, and Write exercises in the Activities section. You can check your scores and overall progress by using the Gradebook.

CHAPTER 17

Using Research in College Writing

Learning Objectives

After working through this chapter, you will be able to:

LO 1 Explain how research can be used to strengthen an essay.

LO 2 Find library and Internet resources.

LO 3 Evaluate sources.

LO 4 Cite the sources you use in your paper.

LO 5 Prepare a Works Cited list in Modern Language Association (MLA) style of all of the sources referred to in your paper.

LO 1 What Is Research?

Research is the process of finding information about something to learn more about it. In your daily life, for example, you may want to learn about a health issue, find out more about a product or service, or discover career options. Based on your findings, you can make an informed decision or develop a belief.

Research in College Writing

Academic research is done to gather and evaluate information about a subject. This type of research involves reading material in sources that include magazines, newspapers, books, journal articles written by researchers and professionals in a particular field, and websites. Through your reading, you learn what experts in a particular field have learned and written about the subject and then develop your own informed opinion.

One type of college writing assignment is the formal research paper. This paper includes an in-depth study of a topic through reading, taking notes, developing your own idea, and supporting it with evidence from experts.

Not all college writing assignments are formal research papers. For example, you can use research to support points in an argument essay. In this chapter, you will learn basic research skills and how to add research to an essay.

Research in Context

To illustrate how research makes an argument essay more convincing, read the next two paragraphs. The first one is taken from student writer Roxanne Byrd's argument essay in Chapter 14. Her purpose was to persuade college administrators to relocate the annoying Muscovy ducks on campus. In the second example paragraph, Roxanne adds information she found in outside sources through her research on the subject.

Paragraph without Research

> The Muscovy ducks are a non-native species; they are not considered wildlife. Therefore, no state or federal law protects them. In addition, they cannot be relocated to public lands. While the law does not stop people from capturing

them and killing them in a humane way, this is not the solution being suggested. In order to prevent the ducks from spoiling the campus environment, being aggressive towards people, and causing accidents, the Muscovy ducks should be moved to a captive environment where they cannot escape or come into contact with wild birds or people who do not want to interact with them.

Paragraph with Research   In this paragraph, the information from the sources Roxanne used is highlighted.

The Muscovy ducks are a non-native species, originally imported to the United States from South and Central America to be raised as food. They were also released into lakes and parks by various organizations, businesses, and residents to make those areas more inviting to the public (Schaefer). Now that the duck population has expanded, they have become a problem. Since they are not considered native to any state, the Muscovies cannot be protected by any state or federal law, according to the federal Migratory Bird Treaty Act ("Nuisance Muscovy Ducks"). For example, in Florida, they are considered exotic and cannot be released into the wild because they can transmit disease to native water birds. The only possible solution is to move them to a captive environment where they cannot escape and wander into the wild or public waters (Schaefer). Although no state or federal law forbids someone from capturing these ducks and humanely killing them ("Nuisance Muscovy Ducks"), this is not the solution being suggested. Therefore, in order to prevent the ducks from spoiling the campus environment, being aggressive toward people, and causing accidents, the Muscovy ducks on campus should be relocated to a place where they can be confined and cared for by individuals interested in raising them for food or keeping them as pets.

Notice how Roxanne added source information to strengthen her argument for relocating the Muscovy ducks. For example, she included specifics about state and federal laws that control relocation and other options. Roxanne put the information from the sources in her own words, but she showed readers where the information came from by citing the author or title in parentheses. At the end of her essay, Roxanne included a list of sources she used in her paper, called a Works Cited list. This list contains the complete publication information for each source mentioned in her paper. It is shown on page 332.

There are several styles used in college for citing and documenting sources. In this chapter, you will learn how to document your sources and put together a Works Cited list in Modern Language Association (MLA) style.

LO 2 Finding Sources

With so much information available on the Internet, you may not know where to start looking for good sources. Most students begin with what they are familiar with and know how to use, which is usually an Internet search engine such as Google or Yahoo!. However, the most direct route to academic sources is your college library. Most college libraries have materials and databases that you cannot find on the Internet. Thus, you must learn how to use both the library and the Internet search engines to locate the best information for your papers.

Internet Research

Internet search engines can provide many web sources on a topic. However, not all websites are scholarly, accurate, or reliable. Also, with so many results possible for one search term, sorting through them can be a time-consuming, frustrating process.

To save time and avoid frustration, learn how to use search engines effectively. Here are some tips for using general search engines like Google, Yahoo!, or Bing.

TIPS | **Doing Internet Searches**

- Be as specific as possible when entering search terms: *ducks* instead of *birds*.
- Put the main subject first. Many search engines first list the matches for the first search word: *ducks pests*.
- Spell the search terms correctly.
- Use a phrase of two or more words in the exact order. Nouns work best: *muscovy ducks*.
- Put quotations marks around words or phrases to find the exact word or phrase on the page: *"Migratory Bird Treaty Act."*
- Use AND between words when you want pages that contain all the words: *ducks AND pests*.
- Use OR between words when you want pages with either of the words: *muscovy ducks OR non-native ducks*.
- If one search term does not get results, try different terms.

Some search engines will give you better results than others. Choose the search engine that will give you the type of information you want. The following chart lists some helpful Internet sites.

Internet Search Engines and Other Useful Sites

Type of Information	Where to Look	Internet Address (URL)
General information	Google	www.google.com
	Yahoo!	www.yahoo.com
	Bing	www.bing.com
Academic information	Google Scholar	scholar.google.com
	Find Articles	www.findarticles.com
	Infomine	www.infomine.ucr.edu
	HighWire Press	www.highwire.stanford.edu
	Directory of Open Access Journals	www.doaj.org
	Internet Public Library/ Librarians Internet Index	www.ipl2.org

(Continued)

Internet Search Engines and Other Useful Sites

Type of Information	Where to Look	Internet Address (URL)
Magazines and news	Google News	news.google.com
	Newspapers.com	www.newspapers.com
	MagPortal	www.magportal.com
Statistics	FedStats	www.fedstats.gov
	U.S. Census Bureau	www.census.gov
	Bureau of Labor Statistics	www.bls.gov

PRACTICE Using Search Engines

17.1 Choose one of the websites from each of the four types in the chart above and look for one reputable source for the topic "Cyber Abuse" from each. Write down the information about the source such as the author, the title of the article and/or website, the owner or sponsor of the website, and the date of publication; then write the reason you selected it.

Source Information	Reason for Selection
Academic information site	
Magazine and/or news site	
Statistics site	
General information site	

Library Research

Your college library is essential for academic research. While search engines may seem easier and more convenient, the fastest way to find reliable academic resources is through your library's online catalog and databases. Take advantage of the resources your college library offers both online and in the library itself.

Visit the Library Online Most modern libraries offer electronic catalogs, library networks, and databases. These resources are available from any computer with an Internet connection. Each of them allows you to search for sources by author, title, subject, or key words.

Online Library Resources

Electronic databases	An **electronic database** is a collection of journals, magazines, and newspapers from many subject areas. Many of these items are not available on the Internet.
	Your library pays to subscribe to databases. As a student, you can use them for free. They will meet most of your academic research needs.
	Examples of databases are *InfoTrac Expanded Academic*; *LexisNexis Academic*; *ProQuest Research Library*, *Wilson Databases*, and *EBSCOhost Academic Search*.

(Continued)

Online Library Resources	
Electronic catalog	The **electronic catalog** lists all the materials the library owns or subscribes to: books, reference works, magazines, newspapers. Your library's electronic catalog may have a special name.
Electronic library network	An **electronic library network** gives you access to the resources of other libraries in your area or state. This service allows you to borrow materials from another library.

PRACTICE Practice Using Your College Electronic Library

17.2   Using your college electronic library, find a book, magazine, and academic journal article on the topic "Cyber Abuse." For each source, write down the author's name(s), the title of the article or book, the name of the magazine or journal, and the date each source was published. Then, give your reason for choosing it.

Author, Title, and Other Publication Information	Reason for Selection
Book	
Magazine article	
Academic journal article	

Roxanne's Research Process   Roxanne first went on the web and used Google to get some general information about Muscovy ducks. Then, she checked a few online encyclopedias and looked at the references linked from those sites. She learned that some people considered the ducks to be a nuisance, while others kept them as pets or raised them for their delicious meat, which helped her see both sides of her argument. Roxanne then went to her college library for help using the online databases *Academic OneFile* and *Expanded Academic*. Roxanne made sure that she copied all of the publication information for each source.

LO 3 Evaluating Sources

Knowing how to evaluate the quality of the information you have found is another important research skill. You want to be sure that the information is accurate and can be trusted. Articles from scholarly journals, books, and other academic resources in your college library have already been evaluated by other scholars, publishers, or librarians.

On the other hand, newspaper and magazine articles have not been evaluated in the same way as scholarly resources. Some articles do not include an author or references. In this case, you will need to evaluate them carefully. Does the article show that the subject has been researched? Is the information fact or opinion? Is the author trying to persuade you to his or her point of view? Can the facts presented be found in another source?

The Internet offers information from all over the world. Much of that information has not been evaluated or checked for accuracy. Anyone can publish on the Internet or copy someone else's work and put it on his or her website. Also, the person or organization that set up the site may not be qualified to give information on the topic or may try to influence your beliefs. Some sites can be hateful or harmful or give incorrect information about such topics as health, science, and business; or imitate someone or something in a humorous way. Therefore, it is important for you to evaluate the information you find on websites before considering it as a source for a paper and citing it in your writing.

To help you evaluate the sites you find on the Internet, use the Q&A Checklist for Evaluating Online Sources. This involves asking six questions about each site: Who, What, Where, When, Why, and How.

Q&A CHECKLIST FOR EVALUATING ONLINE SOURCES

The Question	What to Look For

Credibility: Who published the site?	☐ Find the part of the web address (URL) that tells who is responsible for the site. Often, it is at the end of the URL:
	  .edu = higher education
	  .gov = government agencies
	  .mil = military
	  .org = nonprofit, charitable, research organizations, lobbying
	  .com, .net, .biz = commercial business, entertainment, news
	  .net = Internet service provider
	  country codes such as .ca for Canada
	  .name = personal pages
	☐ If the page is on someone's personal account, use caution. A personal page will have ~ or % followed by a personal name or *users, members* or *people.*
	☐ Look for *About Us, Mission Statement, Contact Us.*

Authority: What are the author's credentials?	☐ Check for information about the author, such as experience, education, or training. ☐ Use a database or search engine to find out what else the author has written or what has been written about the author.
Accuracy: Where is the information from?	☐ Check for list of sources. ☐ Look for errors in spelling or grammar.
Currency: When was the site published?	☐ Find the date the page was first published. ☐ Find the most recent update. ☐ Look for other clues to help identify the date, such as copyright notice.
Purpose: Why was the site developed?	☐ Decide whether the purpose is to inform, teach, persuade, sell, or entertain. ☐ Look for ways the site may try to influence the reader. ☐ Check facts on a fact-checking site. ☐ Look up the author or group in a search engine.
Presentation: How is the information presented?	☐ Look for a format that is easy to read. ☐ Check for how well pages are organized. ☐ Decide if advertisements interfere with the page's purpose. ☐ See if graphics are not distracting.

Here is an evaluation of the Federal Bureau of Investigation's Cyber Investigations website using the Q&A checklist:

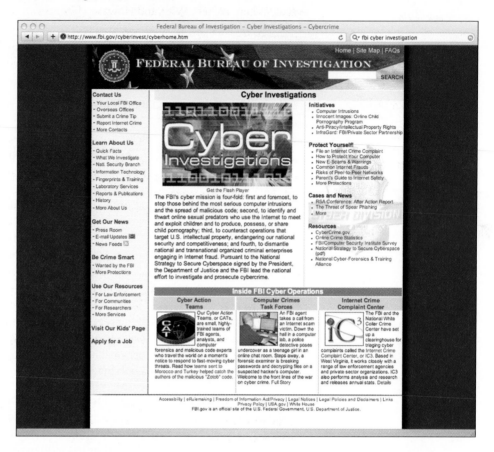

Credibility: Who published the site? This is a U.S. government website. The FBI is a government branch.

Authority: What are the author's credentials? No author is indicated. If no author is mentioned, assume that the content is written by FBI staff writers with appropriate credentials. From the home page, link to "Reports and Publications" or "Get Our News."

Accuracy: Where is the information from? From the Cyber Investigations department and other FBI departments. No errors in spelling or grammar.

Currency: When was the site published? No specific date is listed. News updates and press releases updated daily. Link to "Cases and News" or "Get Our News" from the FBIs main site. All links work and are up to date.

Purpose: Why was the site developed? The site was developed to inform and educate the public about the cyber investigations arm of the FBI. All of the categories of information provided can be viewed from the home page, for example, Initiatives, Protect Yourself, Cases and News, Resources, and Inside FBI Cyber Operations.

Presentation: How is the information presented? The format is easy to read. Pages and links are well organized. There are no advertisements to interfere with the content. Graphics are purposeful, not distracting.

PRACTICE Evaluating Websites

17.3 Evaluate a website that you found for Practice 17.1 on cyber abuse using the Q&A Checklist.

Research Reminder.

As you learned in Chapter 16, **plagiarism** is copying the words and ideas of others and presenting them as your own. For more information on using paraphrases, summaries, and direct quotations, and avoiding plagiarism, see Chapter 16.

Roxanne's Source Evaluation Roxanne found information on several websites and articles through her college's online databases. After evaluating her sources using the Q&A Checklist, she realized that some of her websites did not have the credibility or authority she needed. For example, one site consisted of a duck lover's pictures and personal notes about the Muscovy ducks and their hatchlings in her neighborhood. After discarding the sources that were not credible, she had four strong sources that she could use in her paper.

Saving Information

When you find information you would like to use or refer to, use a system to keep the materials organized. One method is to download all the information to your computer or storage device. Create a specific folder where you can easily find the materials when you need them. Also, always make a backup copy on a device of your choice. If you prefer to work from print or photocopies, keep a separate folder for them.

Taking Notes

When you have identified information from your sources that you want to use in your paper, you are ready to write it down. To avoid copying information directly into your paper, take notes. Use any of these three forms for your notes: paraphrases, summaries, or direct quotations.

You can write the notes in computer files, on paper, or on index cards (notecards). Whichever method you use, be sure to write down the author, title, and page number of your source next to each note.

Roxanne's Note-Taking Roxanne used note cards to write her paraphrases, summaries, and direct quotations from her sources that she wanted to use in her paper. Here is an example of one of her note cards.

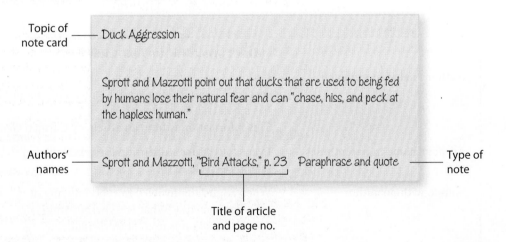

LO 4 Adding Source Information and Giving Credit

When you have paraphrased, summarized, or quoted the information you want to use, you are ready to add it to your paper. In this section, you will learn how to use source information in your paper and give credit to the authors. Giving credit is called **documentation**.

The Modern Language Association (MLA) format for documenting the sources you use in your paper consists of two parts: connecting the information to the point you are making and identifying the source.

TIPS | **Identifying Common Knowledge**

Some information that is generally known and accepted by most people, not just experts, does not need to be documented. This information is considered **common knowledge**. Examples of common knowledge are dates of holidays, names of presidents, and capitals of states or countries. When in doubt, document the source.

Connect the Source Information to Your Own Point

Each time you add source information, you must connect it to the point you are making. Making a connection helps the reader understand what the source is adding to your paper. It also tells the reader that the information is from a source and not your own idea. Use the author's name and if appropriate, the author's credentials to show that he or she is an authority as in the following paraphrase:

> Dr. Robin M. Kowalski, a psychology professor at Clemson University, explains that cyberbullying and schoolyard bullying are not the same and that the people who participate in each type are not the same group.

Research Reminder.
See Chapter 16 for more on how to use signal words to introduce a source.

Identify the Source in the Text of Your Paper

You must give a brief **citation**, the information necessary to identify each source in your paper, where it is used. This brief citation information is usually the author and page. Because some sources do not have authors or pages, the source information may vary. Here are examples of several ways to identify sources using parenthetical citations. Note that what goes in the parentheses depends on whether you have mentioned the author's name in the text. If the reader wants to find your source, he or she can check the full citation at the end of the paper.

MLA Format for In-Text Citations	
Author's name in sentence	Carmen Gentile reported that high school senior Katherine Evans was suspended for writing negative statements about her English teacher on Facebook (A20). This information is from an article by Carmen Gentile, section A page 20.
Author's name in parentheses	Evans fought her suspension for cyberbullying by suing the principal of her school (Gentile A20).
Source with no author	When adults are involved in cyberbullying, it is called cyberstalking or cyberharassment ("What Is Cyberbullying?"). This information is from *Stopcyberbullying.org*.
Source with no page numbers Many Internet sources do not have page numbers.	"Cyberbullying refers to the new, and growing, practice of using technology to harass, or bully, someone else" (McDowell). This information is from "Dealing with Cyberbullies" at *us-cert.gov*.

Roxanne's Adding and Documenting Sources in the Text of Her Paper Using her note cards, Roxanne added her paraphrases, summaries, and direct quotations into her paper. She made sure that her source information was not plagiarized and that it was accurate. As she added the information, she referred to Chapters 16 and 17 to be sure that she connected her sources and cited them properly.

LO5 Listing Sources: MLA Works Cited

At the end of your paper, the **Works Cited** is a list of all of the sources you referred to in your paper. This list gives the reader full publication information about each source. The reader should be able to find every source used in the text of your paper in your Works Cited list.

You may have read other sources while doing your research but later decided not to use them. You do not need to list any of the sources that you did not refer to in your paper.

The Modern Language Association (MLA) has specific guidelines for where to put the Works Cited, how to order the sources on the Works Cited list, and how to format the information for each source.

Placement of the Works Cited

The list of the works you have cited is the last page of your paper. If possible, make your list before you add your in-text citations so you will know what information to put in them. Roxanne's Works Cited list is shown on page 332.

- Begin the Works Cited list on a new page.
- Number the page as the next page of your paper. For example, if the paper ends on page 3, then the Works Cited list will begin on page 4.
- Center the title, Works Cited, one inch from the top of the page. Capitalize only the first letter of each word: Works Cited. Use the same size font as the rest of the paper. Do not underline, boldface, or use quotation marks for Works Cited.

Order of the Sources in the Works Cited

- List the sources in alphabetical order by the author's last name. Do not number the sources.
- If the source does not have an author, alphabetize by the first major word in the title. Ignore *A, An,* or *The,* if any of those are the first word of the title. For example, for the article, "The Danger of Cyberbullies," alphabetize by "Danger."
- Type the first line of each source beginning at the left-hand margin. If you need more than one line for all of the information about the source, indent the second and all other additional lines five spaces (1/2 inch).
- The publication information for each source consists of various parts. Each part has a punctuation mark. Put one space after each punctuation mark.
- Double-space the entire list. Do not double-space twice between entries.

Common Works Cited Formats

MLA style for the most common sources and their Works Cited forms is explained in this section. These types are grouped into categories: print sources, electronic sources, and other sources. No matter what type of source you use, there are common rules for listing authors' names and for capitalizing titles.

Listing Authors in Any Source The name of the author is always the first piece of information you give for the source unless the source does not have an author. Below are models for a single author, two authors, or three or more authors.

One author	Last name, First name.	Willard, Nancy E.
Two or three authors	Last name, First name, and First name Last name.	Hinduja, Sameer, and Justin W. Patchin.
Four or more authors	Last name, First name, et al.	Corbett, Patrick E., et al.

If the author has a middle initial, place it after the first name. A suffix like *Jr.* or a roman numeral appears after the first name and middle initial if there is one (e.g., Martin, John D., III.

Capitalizing Titles in Any Source The MLA has specific rules for capitalizing titles. To simplify the rules, here are the words that are NOT capitalized when they are in the middle of a title:

- Articles: *a, an, the*
- Prepositions: e.g., *in, of, to, on, between*
- Coordinating conjunctions: *and, but, or, nor, for, so, yet*
- The "to" in infinitives: *How to Stop Cyberbullying*

Print Sources

Print sources include books, magazines, newspapers, and journals that are not online.

Books (Print)

Author Name(s). *Title of Book*. Place of publication: Publisher, year of publication. Medium of publication (Print).

Example

Hinduja, Sameer, and Justin W. Patchin. Bullying beyond the School Yard. Thousand Oaks: Corwin, 2009. Print.

If the book does not have an author, begin with the title of the book. Write the title in italics. Include the subtitle if the book has one. Leave out *A, An,* or *The* before the publisher's name. If the publisher has more than one name, list the first name only. Leave out *Inc., Press, Publishers, Books,* etc.

Essay, Short Story, or Other Work in an Anthology (Print)

A work in an anthology gives information about the work being cited, the editor of the anthology, and the publication information of the anthology.

Author Name. "Title of part of the book being cited." *Title of Book*. Ed. Editor's name. Place of publication: Publisher, year. Page numbers. Medium of publication (Print).

Example

Hoff, Diane, and S. N. Mitchell. "Gender and Cyberbullying: How Do We Know What We Know?" *Truths and Myths of Cyber-bullying: International Perspectives on Stakeholder Responsibility and Children's Safety*. Eds. Andrew Churchill and Shaheen Shariff. New York: Lang, 2009. 76–188. Print.

Encyclopedia or Dictionary (Print)

Author name. "Title of entry." *Title of Encyclopedia or Dictionary*. Edition. Year of publication. Medium of publication (Print).

If no author is provided, begin with the title of the entry. The edition may not be stated. If the reference is specialized, such as *Encyclopedia of Criminology*, give full publication information.

Example

Humphreys, R.A. Laud. "Crime and Criminology." *Encyclopedia Americana*. 2009 ed. Print.

Magazine Articles (Print)

Author Name(s). "Title of Article." *Name of Magazine* day month year: page number(s). Medium of publication (Print).

Example

Groc, Isabelle. "Taunting with Tech: Cyberbullying Is on the Rise in America's Schools." *PC Magazine* 4 Sept. 2007: 20. Print.

Newspaper Articles (Print)

Author Name(s). "Title of Article." *Name of Newspaper* day month year, ed.: page number(s). Medium of publication (Print).

Example

Gentile, Carmen. "Student Fights Record of 'Cyberbullying.'" *New York Times* 8 Feb. 2009, late ed.: A20. Print.

- Leave out *The* in the title of the newspaper. If the city is not included in the name of a local newspaper, add the city in brackets.
- Abbreviate all months except for May, June, and July. If the edition is listed, place a comma after the year and then provide the edition. If no edition is listed, leave it out.
- Include all of the page numbers of the article. If the article is not printed on consecutive pages, write only the first page number and a + sign and follow it with a period. Sometimes the article is in a section of the newspaper that has its own page numbers. Write the section and page number like this: B1.

Scholarly Journal Articles (Print)

Author Name(s). "Title of Article." *Name of Journal.* volume number. issue number (year of publication): page numbers(s). Medium of publication (Print).

Example

Kowalski, Robin M. "Cyber Bullying: Recognizing and Treating Victim and Aggressor." *Psychiatric Times* 25.11 (2008): 45. Print.

- Some journals have volume and issue numbers, and some have only volume numbers. Write the year of publication in parentheses followed by a colon.
- Include all of the page numbers of the article. If the article is not printed on consecutive pages, write only the first page and a + sign followed by a period.

Electronic Sources

Electronic sources include information published on the Internet. These sources might be websites or online databases.

Basic Website Sources   Web publications can be challenging to document. Web pages often have many links, making it hard to figure out where one ends and another begins.

Author Name(s). "Title of Web Page." *Title of Website.* Publisher or sponsor of site, date of publication, revision, or update. Medium of publication (Web). Date of access.

Example

"Cyberbullying." *Stop Bullying Now.* U.S. Department of Health Resources and Services Administration, n.d. Web. 20 Nov. 2010.

- Give the name of the author, compiler, editor, narrator, etc., if available. If no author is given, begin with the title.
- Sometimes the title of the web page is the same as the title of the overall website. If they are the same, put quotation marks around the name of the page and omit the name of the website.
- The publisher or sponsor could be an educational institution, a company, or a nonprofit organization. You can usually find it at the bottom of the home page. If not available, write N.p.
- Write the day, month, and year or the most recent update of the publication. The date is often listed at the bottom of the web page. If there is only a copyright date or year, write that. If nothing is available, write n.d.
- Date of access is the date you found it on the web. Write the day, month, and year (31 Dec. 2010).

Online Databases   If your source came from a library database or subscription service, follow the guidelines for the print source (book, magazine, newspaper, journal), and after that, give information about the database you used.

Example

Mishna, Faye, Alan McLuckie, and Michael Saini. "Real-world Dangers in an Online Reality: A Qualitative Study Examining Online Relationships and Cyber Abuse." *Social Work Research* 33.2 (2009): 107+. *Academic One File.* Web. 16 Nov. 2010.

After giving the information for the print source, add the name of the database in italics, medium of publication (Web.), and date of access.

Additional Common Sources

Other sources you may cite include television or radio shows, films, videos, interviews, or podcasts.

Television or Radio Show

"Title of the episode or segment." *Title of the Program Series.* Name of network (if any). Call letters, city of the local station (if any), date of broadcast. Medium of reception (e.g., Television or Radio).

Example

"Cyberbullying." *The Tyra Banks Show.* CW. WTVX, West Palm Beach, 4 Feb. 2008. Television.

Film, Video, DVD

Title. Director. Distributor. Year of release. Medium (Film, Video, DVD).

Example

Playing It Safe Online. Dir. Anson W. Schloat. Human Relations Media. 2008. DVD.

Online Podcast

Speaker(s) if available. "Title of Podcast Episode." *Title of Podcast.* Publisher or Sponsor, Date of publication or posting. Title of Larger Site. Medium consulted (Web). Date of access.

Reynolds, Matthew, Dr. Corrine Fendon, and Marci Hertz. "Electronic Aggression."
    Podcasts at CDC. National Center for Injury Prevention and Control, Division of
    Violence Prevention. 28 Nov. 2007. Center for Disease Control and Prevention.
    Web. 6 July 2010.

Personal Interview   A personal interview is one that you, the researcher, conducted.
Name of person interviewed. Kind of interview (Personal or Telephone). Date of
    interview.

Example
Williams, Marya. Personal interview. 19 Nov. 2010.

Roxanne's Works Cited List   Roxanne referred to the guidelines and examples in this
chapter to provide the publication information for each source that she used in her paper.
Her Works Cited on page 332 lists the sources in alphabetical order, double-spaced according to MLA style.

PRACTICE   Practicing with Works Cited Entries

17.4   The following sources were selected for use in a research paper on cyberbullying.
Use the MLA guidelines explained in this section to arrange the publication informa-
tion for each source in a Works Cited list. Then put the sources in alphabetical order.
Write your list in the space provided or on your own paper.

Source: A scholarly journal article in print
The title is "Sticks and Stones Can Break My Bones, but How Can Pixels Hurt Me?"
The article was written by Wanda Cassidy, Margaret Jackson, and Karen N. Brown. It
was published in 2009 in *School Psychology International,* volume 30, pages 383–402.

Source: A newspaper article on an electronic database
The article was written by Jon Boone in the April 11, 2007, page 2 of the *Financial
Times.* The title is "Google Urged to Join Team Tackling Cyber-bullying." The article
was retrieved from the *Academic OneFile* database on November 21, 2010.

Source: A book in print.
The book was published in 2007 by Research Press in Champaign, Ill. The author
is Nancy E. Willard. The title of the book is *Cyberbullying and Cyber Threats.*

Source: A website.
The article appeared on the CNET News website on August 19, 2009. The title
is "Missouri Woman Charged with Cyberbullying" and was written by Lance
Whitney. The article was found on the Web on November 22, 2010.

Works Cited

_____

_____

_____

_____

_____

_____

_____

_____

_____

MLA Model Research Essay

The following is Roxanne's research essay using the MLA style.

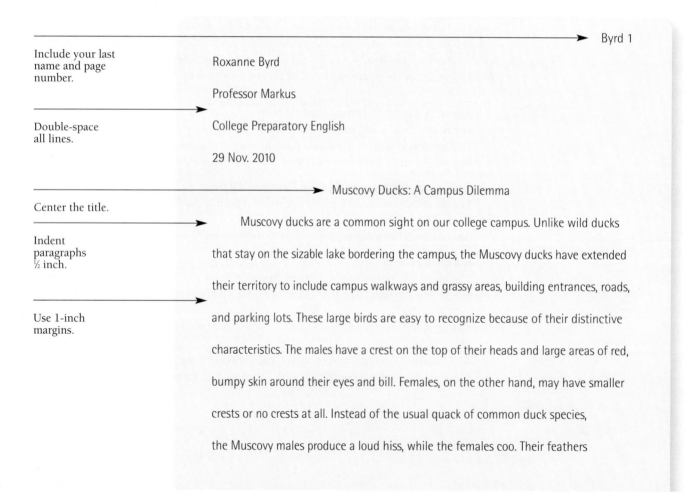

Byrd 1

Include your last name and page number.

Roxanne Byrd

Professor Markus

Double-space all lines.

College Preparatory English

29 Nov. 2010

Center the title.

Muscovy Ducks: A Campus Dilemma

Indent paragraphs ½ inch.

Muscovy ducks are a common sight on our college campus. Unlike wild ducks that stay on the sizable lake bordering the campus, the Muscovy ducks have extended their territory to include campus walkways and grassy areas, building entrances, roads,

Use 1-inch margins.

and parking lots. These large birds are easy to recognize because of their distinctive characteristics. The males have a crest on the top of their heads and large areas of red, bumpy skin around their eyes and bill. Females, on the other hand, may have smaller crests or no crests at all. Instead of the usual quack of common duck species, the Muscovy males produce a loud hiss, while the females coo. Their feathers

Byrd 2

can be white, greenish black, blue, brown, or a combination of these colors. Because

of their ability to lay eight to ten eggs three times a year, their population has

increased to the point that the ducks have become a nuisance to students, staff, and

visitors. The Muscovy ducks should be relocated because they spoil the campus

environment, are aggressive towards people, and get in the way of cars, causing

accidents.

The college takes pride in keeping the campus clean and green; however,

the Muscovy ducks have spoiled the campus environment. First of all, the daily

manure production of the freely roaming ducks creates a hazardous mess.

According to Joe Schaefer of the University of Florida, one adult duck produces

one-third of a pound of manure. Since the ducks defecate wherever they please, the

areas where people walk are frequently fouled, creating an unsanitary obstacle

course. In addition, their greenish-black, watery droppings are slippery when stepped

on, which could cause someone to slip, fall, and get injured. The Muscovy ducks also

destroy native plants and wild flowers. The campus has a sustainable landscape

policy. Native plants have been installed to reduce the use of fertilizer and pesticides

and to conserve water. Students and faculty have worked together to plant native

plant gardens across the campus. However, last month, some of the ducks

uprooted all of the rare, native wildflowers that had been newly planted by the

environmental science classes. Duck advocates argue that Muscovies benefit the

campus environment because they control pests by eating bugs and insects

such as mosquitoes, roaches, ants, and spiders, eliminating the need for pesticide

use. In fact, Muscovies were originally called "Musco Ducks" because they were

known for controlling mosquito populations on farms (Maynard). An experiment

conducted by Surgeoner and Glofcheskie at the University of Guelph in Ontario

Note the author
tag and
paraphrase.

Paraphrase.

Byrd 3

to determine the use of Muscovy ducks to control flies on farms showed that "ducks

Paraphrase with
quotation.
are better than flypaper" ("Waiter, There's a Duck"). However, the campus is not a

farm, and insect control is less of a problem than the destruction of the beauty and

cleanliness of the campus.

Not only do the Muscovy ducks spoil the campus environment, but also they

Paraphrase.
are aggressive toward people. When people feed them on a regular basis, ducks

Paraphrase and
quotation.
come to expect being fed and can become aggressive (Johnson and Hawk). Sprott

and Mazzotti point out that the ducks who are used to being fed by humans lose

their natural fears and can "chase, hiss, and peck at the hapless human." Because

some duck-loving students and staff regularly feed the ducks, they think all people

will do the same. As a result, they boldly beg for food in a way which frightens

students, staff, and visitors. For instance, when someone sits outside on a bench to

eat a snack or to socialize with other students, groups of hissing, snorting ducks rush

toward and gather around that person, pushing their beaks against the individual's

legs to beg for a handout. On one occasion, a duck jumped on my friend's lap while

she was snacking on some chips. The duck pecked at her face, and in an attempt to

get a chip, bit her on the lip. Duck supporters claim that Muscovy ducks are friendly

birds and that people misinterpret the ducks' intentions. Those who have been

attacked by a Muscovy duck would heartily disagree.

The most important reason for relocating the Muscovy ducks is that they get

in the way of cars and cause accidents. Unaware of the danger, the ducks tend to

roost wherever they please, which includes campus roads and parking spaces. For

instance, they frequently sit in empty or occupied parking spaces, preening their

feathers or sleeping. When students arrive for class, they are focused on hunting for

available parking spaces, not for ducks that may be in those spaces. If a duck is lucky

Byrd 4

enough to avoid its demise in this situation, it may not be able to avoid being run over on the roads. During peak class times, traffic builds on the two narrow roads used as entrances and exits to the campus. The Muscovies also use these roads to waddle from the lake to the campus. On a good day for the ducks, kind-hearted drivers stop to ensure that the ducks get across safely; however, the wait for them to complete their slow journey across the road causes a huge backup of impatient student drivers. Not all duck crossings end successfully, unfortunately. For example, last semester, a student driver stopped short to avoid hitting a duck while exiting the campus and caused a multiple collision. Those who support the ducks' right to live on campus believe that drivers should watch out for ducks in parking spaces and on the roads. If the ducks were relocated to a safe place, they would have a better chance of survival, and drivers would not have to be concerned about harming them while driving.

The Muscovy ducks are a non-native species, originally imported to the United States from South and Central America to be raised as a source of food. They were also released into canals and lakes by various organizations, businesses, and residents for ornamental purposes. (Schaefer). Because they are not native to any state, Muscovies cannot be protected by any state or federal law, according to the federal Migratory Bird Treaty Act ("Nuisance Muscovy Ducks"). For example, in Florida, they cannot be released into the wild because they can transmit disease to native water birds. The only possible solution is to move them to a captive environment where they cannot escape and wander into the wild or public waters (Schaefer). Therefore, in order to prevent the ducks from spoiling the campus environment, being aggressive toward people, and causing accidents, the Muscovy ducks on campus

Paraphrase.

Paraphrase.

Byrd 5

should be relocated to a place where they can be confined and cared for by individuals

interested in either raising them for food or as pets.

Works Cited

Begin Works Cited on a new page, and center the title.

Johnson, Steven Albert, and Michelle Hawk. "Florida's Introduced Birds: Muscovy Duck."

EDIS. University of Florida IFAS Extension, Mar. 2009. Web. 29 Oct. 2010.

Maynard, Pam. "Raising Chickens and Poultry for Home Pest Control." *Grit.com*. Ogden

Indent each line after the first line ½ inch.

Publications, May/June 2009. Web. 21 Nov. 2010.

"Nuisance Muscovy Ducks." *MyFWC.com*. Florida Fish and Wildlife Conservation

Commission, 2009. Web. 21 Nov. 2010.

Schaefer, Joe. "Domestic Duck Problems in Urban Areas." *EDIS*. University of Florida IFAS

Double-space the entire list.

Extension, Mar. 1999. Web. 29 Oct. 2010.

Sprott, Patricia, and Frank J. Mazzotti. "Bird Attacks." *EDIS*. University of Florida IFAS

Extension, June 1991. Web. 22 Nov. 2010.

"Waiter, There's a Duck in My Soup." *Economist* Nov. 1989: 101. *Academic One File*. Web.

29 Oct. 2010.

Writing Assignments

Add Research to an Essay

Enhance a paper you have already written by adding research. Choose a paper that you wrote this term that has a topic that can be researched. Read through the paper to find places where you could add details from outside sources. Think about adding statistics, expert opinions, facts, and examples. Add the sources to your paper using the MLA format and include a Works Cited list.

Reading and Writing across the Curriculum: Criminal Justice

 Cybercrime, sometimes called *computer crime* or *information-technology crime*, uses computers and computing technology as tools in crime commission. Computer criminals manipulate the information stored in computer systems in ways that violate the law.

(From *Criminal Justice Today* by Frank Schmalleger)

Research and write a paragraph or an essay giving examples of *one* type of cybercrime. Find three (or more) reliable sources, take notes, add the information to your paper, and create a Works Cited list. Some examples of cybercrime are credit card fraud, identity theft, child pornography, indecent chat-room behavior, software and media piracy, website vandalism, release of viruses and worms, spam marketing, invasion of privacy, cyber-spying, and most forms of hacking.

Writing Topics for Researching

For further practice with research and creating a Works Cited list, choose one of the following topics:

> aviation and airport security
> paranormal phenomena
> impact of social networking sites
> alternative energy
> celebrity culture

Writing across the Curriculum Topics

 Peer Review Reminder. For feedback on your writing, have someone read your paper and make comments on the Peer Review Response sheet in Chapter 4, page 55.

Biology: endangered species
Journalism: the future of print media, such as newspapers
Education: standardized testing
Pharmacy: performance-enhancing drugs
Psychology: cheating

✔ **English Success Tip: Signaling the Author**

When you are introducing the author and title of someone's work, avoid the following common errors:

1. Drop the "in" and the "it."

Incorrect: In the passage by Elizabeth F. Barkley, it explains how country music came from the folk music of the rural American South and over the years was shaped by the commercial entertainment industry.

Correct: The passage by Elizabeth F. Barkley explains how country music came from the folk music of the rural American South and over the years was shaped by the commercial entertainment industry.

2. Avoid repetition.

Repetitious: In the passage "Country Music in a Historical and Social Context" by Elizabeth F. Barkley, the author explains how country music came from the folk music of the rural American South and over the years was shaped by the commercial entertainment industry.

Correct: In the passage "Country Music in a Historical and Social Context," Elizabeth F. Barkley explains how country music came from the folk music of the rural American South and over the years was shaped by the commercial entertainment industry.

For support in meeting this chapter's objectives, log in to www.mywritinglab.com, go to the Study Plan tab, click on **Using Research in College Writing** and choose **Research Process** from the list of subtopics. Read and view the videos and resources in the Review Materials section, and then complete the Recall, Apply, and Write exercises in the Activities section. You can check your scores and overall progress by using the Gradebook.

Building Powerful Sentences

PART

4

Simple Sentences

Theme: *Business*

Learning Objectives

After working through this chapter, you will be able to:

LO 1 Define a simple sentence.

LO 2 Identify the subject(s) of a sentence.

LO 3 Identify prepositional phrases.

LO 4 Identify the verb(s) of a sentence.

LO 1 What Is a Simple Sentence?

The **simple sentence** is a group of words that has at least one subject and verb. It is an **independent clause** that expresses a complete thought. A simple sentence can contain one or more subjects and verbs, can be short or long, and can contain adjectives, adverbs, and prepositional phrases.

The manager plans.

The manager and the employees plan.

The manager plans and organizes.

The manager and the employees plan and organize.

Yesterday, during the weekly meeting, the manager and the employees developed a new strategy for the sales staff and divided the staff into teams.

Subjects and Verbs in Context

In the following passage about workplace design, the subjects are highlighted in tan and the verbs are highlighted in green.

Some workplaces have a large number of workers in a very large space. Human factors psychologists, those who combine psychology and product design, call the large space an open design. Sometimes there are partitions or other kinds of barriers between workers. With this kind of arrangement, organizations can use large spaces flexibly. Individual workspaces can be rearranged. Further, open designs are cheaper. They have few walls and doors. However, many workers do not like open designs. For one thing, these workplaces are noisier than those with individual workspaces. Workers sometimes complain about interruptions and lack of privacy. Moreover, a private office is perceived as a status symbol. Employees in management positions expect to have rooms with doors. They want privacy for meetings with employees. Consequently, most open designs include at least a few private spaces, usually managers' offices and conference rooms.

(Adapted from *The World of Psychology* by Samuel E. Wood et al.)

LO 2 Finding the Subject

The **subject** tells who or what the sentence is about. The subject is usually a noun or pronoun.

Noun Subjects

Grammar Reminder.
*A **noun** is the name of a person, place, thing, idea, or activity. For more information about nouns, see Chapter 25.*

Singular or Plural Subjects can be **singular**, meaning one, or **plural**, meaning more than one.

   Singular subject: An employee is happier in a healthy work environment.

   Plural subject: Employees are happier in a healthy work environment.

Compound Subjects A compound subject consists of two nouns connected with any of these words: *and*, *or*, *either … or*, *neither … nor*, or *not only … but also*.

   Work responsibilities *and* child-care duties often cause stress.

   Either my health *or* my job performance can be affected.

   Neither my boss *nor* my teachers understand my child-care problems.

Noun Subjects Ending in *-ing* Some subjects end in *-ing* and look like verbs. They are called **gerunds**, which act as nouns.

   Working in a large company gives me good experience.

Numbers, Fractions, Percentages, and Money Amounts Amounts can be the subject of a sentence.

   Ninety-five percent of workplace desks and chairs can be adjusted for comfort.

   Forty dollars was deducted from my paycheck for health care.

PRACTICE   Identifying Noun Subjects

18.1   Underline the noun subjects in each of the following sentences. To find the noun subject, ask who or what is or does something.

Example: Interstate banking is a fairly new development. *— adjective*

1. A law was passed in 1994.
2. Interstate banking is the operation of banks or branches across state lines.
3. Government agencies regulate these banks.
4. Thirty percent is the most business an interstate bank can control per state.
5. Deposits and credit services must be offered to meet the needs of the community.

compound   *adjective*

Grammar Reminder.
*A **pronoun** is a word that is used in place of a noun. For more information about pronouns, see Chapter 24.*

Pronoun Subjects

Personal Pronouns

   I   you   he   she   it   we   they

   He has his own computer workstation.

Possessive Pronouns

| mine | yours | his | hers | its | ours | theirs |

Mine is the last workstation in the row.
Hers is the office on the left with the large window.

Indefinite Pronouns **Indefinite pronouns** refer to nouns that are not named or specific.

all	each, each one	more	one
another	either	most	other, others
any	everybody	much	several
anybody	everyone	neither	somebody
anyone	everything	nobody	someone
anything	few	no one	something
both	many	nothing	such

Everyone in the office stayed late today.
Most of the workers earned overtime pay.

Compound Pronouns A compound pronoun subject consists of two pronouns connected with any of these words: *and, or, either ... or, neither ... nor,* or *not only ... but also.*

He *and* I always prepare the meeting agenda.

PRACTICE **Identifying Pronoun Subjects**

18.2   Underline the pronoun subjects in each of the following sentences. To find the pronoun subject, ask who or what is or does something.

Example: Almost everyone can benefit from electronic banking.

1. You and others should know about changes to payment by check.
2. Eventually, most of the checks will be replaced in banks by electronic images.
3. They will use a substitute check for payment.
4. All of us should appreciate the amount of time and energy saved by the process.
5. No one will have much time to put money in an account to cover a check.

LO 3 Identifying Prepositions and Prepositional Phrases

Knowing how to recognize prepositions and prepositional phrases makes finding the subject of a sentence easier because the subject is never in a prepositional phrase.

Prepositions

A **preposition** is a word that shows time, place, or direction. The following is a list of the most commonly used prepositions.

Commonly Used Prepositions

aboard	at	concerning	of	to
about	before	down	off	toward
above	behind	during	on	under
across	below	except	onto	underneath
after	beneath	for	out	up
against	beside	from	outside	upon
along	besides	in	over	with
amid	between	inside	past	within
among	beyond	into	since	without
around	by	like	through	
as		near	throughout	

Like **Can Be a Preposition or a Verb.** Some words have more than one job. The preposition *like* can also be a verb.

Preposition: Tyrone looks like his Uncle Reggie.
Verb: Tyrone and Uncle Reggie like to go fishing.

Prepositional Phrases

A **prepositional phrase** is a group of words that begins with a preposition and ends with a noun or pronoun. It does not have a subject and a verb.

Five employees walked into the manager's office.
They brought their reports with them.
They wrote their reports about recycling.

⚠️ **Prepositional Phrase or Infinitive.** The word *to* is sometimes used with the simple form of a verb. This is called an **infinitive.** The infinitive is not a prepositional phrase.

Infinitive: Employees are not permitted to make personal phone calls during business hours.

The infinitive is not a verb, so it will not have a verb ending (-s, -es, -ed, -ing).

Employees are not permitted to makes make personal phone calls.

Do not use the preposition *for* before the infinitive: Employees are not permitted for to make personal phone calls during business hours.

PRACTICE Identifying Prepositional Phrases
18.3   Circle the prepositional phrases in the following sentences.
     Example: McDonald's has become an icon of the fast food industry.

1. McDonald's seems to have lost its competitive edge at home and in other countries.
2. Many of its stores are outdated.
3. Concerns about health have driven customers away from Big Macs and French fries.

4. McDonald's has had to expand into foreign markets, especially in Europe and Asia.

5. To appeal to consumers in foreign countries, McDonald's serves popular local foods like salmon sandwiches in Scandinavia and beer in Germany.

PRACTICE Writing Sentences with Prepositional Phrases

18.4 Write ten sentences that describe the office workers in the photograph shown here. Use at least one prepositional phrase in each sentence. Underline all of your prepositional phrases.

LO 4 Finding the Verb

Grammar Reminder.
*A **verb** is a word or word group that expresses action, movement, or mental condition or state. See Chapters 22 and 23 for more on verbs.*

A **verb** gives information about the subject by expressing what the subject does (the action) or what the subject is (a state of being). The three kinds of verbs are action, linking, and helping.

Action Verbs

An **action verb** expresses what the subject of the sentence does. The action can be a physical or mental activity.

Franz decorated his office with family photos and his college diploma.
Jen arranges her files in alphabetical order.
The manager makes the schedule for the week on Fridays.

PRACTICE Identifying Action Verbs

18.5 Circle the action verbs in the following sentences.

Example: A modern cruise ship carries an average of 2,000 passengers and 1,000 crewmembers.

1. Three thousand people generate a lot of waste.

2. On a typical day, a ship of this size produces seven tons of solid garbage.

3. The ship dumps fifteen gallons of highly toxic chemical waste and 30,000 gallons of sewage.

4. Cruise ships also collect ballast water while on the ocean.

5. Later they discharge the water, with living things and pollution, in other parts of the world.

Pronoun

(Adapted from *Business Essentials* by Ronald J. Ebert and Ricky W. Griffin)

Linking Verbs

A **linking verb** connects or "links" the subject and a word that describes the subject or further identifies it. The linked information can be in the form of a noun, a pronoun, or an adjective.

The company is a strong competitor in the automotive industry.
The company is his.
The company became successful.

Learn the linking verbs so that you can recognize them.

am	were	become	look	sound
is	being	feel	remain	taste
are	been	get	seem	turn
was	appear	grow	smell	

 Some Verbs Have More Than One Job. Here are some linking verbs that can also do the job of action verbs depending on how they are used in a sentence:

| appear | get | look | smell | taste |
| feel | grow | remain | sound | turn |

Linking verb: The computer technician looks tired.
Action verb: The computer technician looks for the problem on the hard drive.

PRACTICE Identifying Linking Verbs

18.6 Circle the linking verbs in the following sentences.

1. Attitudes are our beliefs and feelings about ideas, situations, and people.

2. Job satisfaction is an important attitude in the workplace.

3. A satisfied employee seems happy about performing his or her job.

4. Dissatisfied employees appear more stressed out.

5. Job security and fair treatment remain important to employee satisfaction.

Helping Verbs

A **helping verb** is a verb form that "helps" the action verb or linking verb to express time, necessity, or possibility. One or more helping verbs can be placed in front of an action or linking verb. Together they make a **verb phrase**. The action or linking verb is called the **main verb**.

Helping verbs are placed before the action or linking verb (except in questions):

Technology has influenced the flow of information in a company.

Helping Verb

Everyday social interactions could have created a positive work environment. In June, Ms. Ritchey will have been working for the company for three years.

> **TIP** | Another Name for Helping Verb is *Auxiliary Verb*

Helping Verbs That Express Time The helping verbs *be, do, and have* are placed before action or linking verbs to express time:

Forms of the verb *be*   am, is, are, was, were, be, being, been
Forms of the verb *do*   do, does, did
Forms of the verb *have*   has, have, had

No two companies are organized exactly the same way.

Most businesses have developed organization charts of a company's jobs and structure.

The organization chart does not show the two new jobs in the finance department.

 Be, do, and have can also function as helping verbs and as main verbs:

Have **as main verb:** Many managers have a large number of employees.

Have **as helping verb:** Many managers have had meetings with their employees this week.

Helping Verbs That Express Necessity or Possibility The following helping verbs show that an action or state is necessary or possible:

can	may	shall	will
could	might	should	would
must	ought to		

A manager can delegate work to others.
Managers should recognize the benefits of effective delegation.

PRACTICE   Identifying Helping Verbs

18.7   Underline all of the helping verbs in the following sentences.

1. For years now, Southwest Airlines has been flying high in the short-trip, low-fare market.
2. Southwest's emphasis on reliability and customer service had kept the airline virtually unchallenged.
3. Most airlines have not managed to copy the operational success of Southwest.
4. Thanks to David Neeleman, JetBlue has become one of the most profitable new airlines in the United States.
5. David Neeleman had been working at Southwest for a short time.
6. He was fired from Southwest.
7. Neeleman had had extensive experience in the airline industry before his job at Southwest.
8. He did copy some of Southwest's strategies and lessons for JetBlue.
9. Neeleman must have used sound business practices and decisions.
10. Labor expenses could be kept down to 25 percent of earnings.
11. Younger workers were being hired for lower wages but with stock options.
12. JetBlue has been filling planes to capacity.

(Adapted from *Business Essentials* by Ronald J. Ebert and Ricky W. Griffin)

[Handwritten margin notes: Adverbs / Discribe How often, / To what Extent / when, where]

Adverbs between Main and Helping Verbs Adverbs are sometimes placed between a helping verb and action or linking verb. The adverb is not part of the verb. Examples of these adverbs are as follows:

almost	not	only	seldom	usually
always	now	rarely	sometimes	
never	often	recently	soon	

Gossip in companies can often distort information.

Informal groups in the workplace should not interfere with employees' work responsibilities.

Office gossip isn't permitted in our company.

> **TIP** | To avoid confusion in finding verbs, cross out the adverbs. Be aware of *not* in contractions.

PRACTICE Identifying Verbs and Adverbs

18.8 Underline the verbs and circle any adverbs that come between the main and helping verbs.

1. The euro was first introduced in 2002.
2. It has now replaced other currencies, such as the German deutsche mark and the French franc.
3. The euro will soon become as important as the dollar and the Japanese yen in international commerce.
4. Companies with international operations must always watch exchange-rate changes.
5. These changes can sometimes affect overseas demand for their products.

Compound Verbs

A compound verb consists of two separate verbs connected by *and* or *or*.

Agreeable workers have a high level of understanding and cooperate well with others.

A worker with a low level of agreeableness becomes irritable easily and is often uncooperative.

PRACTICE Identifying Compound Verbs

18.9 Underline the compound verbs in the following sentences.

1. On-the-job training occurs during work and is done informally.
2. For example, an employee may explain and demonstrate the use of the photocopier.
3. Off-the-job training is done away from the work site and gives workers place to study.
4. Educational improvement will give workers more skills and will motivate them to work towards higher-level jobs.

5. Vestibule training takes place in a pretend work environment and makes the off-the-job training more realistic.

(Adapted from *Business Essentials* by Ronald J. Ebert and Ricky W. Griffin)

PRACTICE 18.10 Identifying Subjects and Verbs

Circle the subjects and underline the verbs in the following sentences.

1. Sales promotions increase product recognition and sales.
2. Most consumers have participated in a variety of sales promotions.
3. Free samples allow customers to try products without risk.
4. A coupon promotion gives a person savings off regular prices.
5. Premiums are free or reduced-price items, such as pencils or coffee mugs.
6. Low-interest credit cards can be given to consumers in return for buying a product.
7. In addition, consumers may win prizes by entering contests.
8. Displays near checkout counters will often grab customers' attention.
9. A computer-interactive display provides people with information about services.
10. Bank lobbies and physicians' waiting rooms sometimes have computer-interactive areas.

Simple Sentences with Harder-to-Find Subjects and Verbs

Some subjects and verbs may be harder to find, as in sentences with inverted word order, prepositional phrases, commands, and appositives.

Sentences with Inverted Word Order

Not all sentences begin with a subject followed by a verb. Sometimes the subject and verb are inverted; in other words, the subject comes after the verb.

Questions In a question, the subject usually follows the verb or is between a helping verb and a main verb.

Will you copy these files for me?

Where is the key to the supply room?

TIP	To help find the subject and verb, try changing the question into a statement. Find the subject and place it first. Then follow it with the verb(s).

Question: Will someone get tablets and pens from the supply room?

Statement: Someone will get tablets and pens from the supply room.

Sentences Starting with *Here/There* In a sentence starting with **here** or **there**, the subject usually follows the verb. Neither *here* nor *there* can be subjects.

There are two forms of flexible scheduling in the workplace.

> **TIP** | To help find the subject and verb, cross out *here* or *there*. Look for the subject after the verb.
>
> ~~Here~~ is the schedule for the flextime program.

Sentences with Prepositional Phrases

Sentences can begin with prepositional phrases or have prepositional phrases placed between the subject and the verb.

In the workplace, work sharing allows two people to share a single full-time job.

An increased sense of freedom and control in flexible schedules reduces stress.

> **TIP** | To avoid confusing the noun in a prepositional phrase with the subject of the sentence, circle or cross out the prepositional phrases to set them apart from the subject.
>
> A growing number ~~of United States workers~~ do a large portion of their work by telecommuting.

Commands

A command expresses a direction or instruction. The subject, *you*, is not stated.

(You) Press the enter key after inputting the data.

Sentences with Appositives

An **appositive** is a noun or noun phrase that renames the word in front of it.

Lowell Karo, an accountant with a large clientele, has an office in his home.

> **TIP** | To avoid confusing the noun in the appositive with the subject of the sentence, circle or cross out it out to set it apart from the subject.
>
> Tania Chen, ~~consultant to a large telecommunications company,~~ can choose her own schedule.

PRACTICE Identifying Subjects and Verbs

18.11   Circle the subjects and underline the verbs in the following sentences.

1. Have you ever shopped online?
2. Electronic retailing, also called e-retailing, has become very popular.
3. There are millions of small businesses with their own websites.
4. Through e-retailing, consumers can buy many different kinds of products.
5. In place of traditional mail catalogs, electronic displays give millions of users pages of product information.
6. How does e-retail help the seller?
7. There are no costs for printing and mailing catalogs or advertisements.

8. Use a chat room to talk securely about a product with a service operator. You

9. For answers to specific questions, an online shopper can have a one-on-one chat.

10. Also, cybermalls, a collection of business websites, represent a variety of products and stores for online shopping in one place.

Review: The Simple Sentence

The following paragraphs contain all simple sentences. Circle the subjects, underline the verbs, and bracket the prepositional phrases in each sentence.

[1]Radio Frequency Identification (RFID) is a powerful new technology. [2]This technology can be used in nearly every civilian industry. [3]One way to use RFID is to track store inventory. [4]An RFID code number is assigned to each item at the time of manufacturing. [5]The code contains information about the item such as the time and place of manufacture and the product's location. [6]The code is stored on an RFID label. [7]The label has a microchip and tiny antenna. [8]That label is attached to a piece of tape and placed on a product. [9]It communicates by radio signals with RFID scanners. [10]The scanner gets the product's information, such as its current location and price. [11]A computer updates the information about the product from stage to stage.

[12]RFID is much faster than barcode scanning. [13]Radio waves from RFID scanners can communicate with many tags at the same time. [14]Barcodes can only scan one at a time with laser beams. [15]Imagine a loaded grocery cart under an overhead scanner. [16]That scanner would read all items at the same time. [17]Then, at the checkout stand, an itemized total would be ready for you. [18]The RFID information instantly reorders the items for replacement in the store.

(Adapted from *Business Essentials* by Ronald J. Ebert and Ricky W. Griffin)

Writing Assignments

Write a paragraph describing a place where you have worked or where business is conducted. Circle the subjects, underline the verbs, and bracket the prepositional phrases.

English Success Tip: Remembering Word Lists

Remembering lists of words such as helping verbs, linking verbs, and prepositions can be challenging. Try using a memory aid: creating an acronym from the words, putting the words into a familiar song, or writing a catchy poem or rap.

- **Create an acronym.** An **acronym** is a word created from the first letters of each word in a series of words. An acronym that you can use for indefinite subject pronouns is *famos ben.* The acronym consists of the first letters of the pronouns.

  F: few
  A: anyone, anything, anybody, all, another, and any
  M: many, more, most, much
  O: one, other, others

S: several, somebody, someone, something, such
B: both
E: each, each one, either, everybody, everyone, everything
N: neither, no one, nobody

- **Put the words into a familiar song.** Find a song that you know well and replace the original words with the word list you need to remember.
- **Write a catchy poem or rap.** Rhyming words makes them easier to remember. Add an electronic beat in the background or accompany your rhyme with clapping or stomping.

For support in meeting this chapter's objectives, log in to www.mywritinglab.com, go to the Study Plan tab, click on **Simple Sentences** and choose **Sentence Structure, Subjects and Verbs, and Prepositions** from the list of subtopics. Read and view the videos and resources in the Review Materials section, and then complete the Recall, Apply, and Write exercises in the Activities section. You can check your scores and overall progress by using the Gradebook.

Joining Ideas Using Compound Sentences

Theme: *Communication*

Learning Objectives

After working through this chapter, you will be able to:

LO 1 Explain what a compound sentence is.

LO 2 Combine two independent clauses to make a compound sentence.

LO 3 Avoid the comma splice error.

LO 4 Avoid the run-on error.

LO 1 What Is a Compound Sentence?

A **compound sentence** consists of two or more independent clauses that are connected with appropriate connecting words and punctuation. An **independent clause** is a group of words with at least one subject and verb that makes sense on its own. An independent clause is also called a simple sentence, as you learned in Chapter 18. In this chapter, you will learn three ways to combine independent clauses to build compound sentences:

[handwritten margin note: An independent clause is a sentence subject & verb]

Comma + Coordinating Conjunction:

[handwritten note: so = coordinating conjunction]

I want to improve my verbal skills, **so** I am taking a human communications course.

Semicolon:

I want to improve my verbal skills; I am taking a human communications course.

Semicolon + Transition Word or Phrase + Comma:

I want to improve my verbal skills; **therefore,** I am taking a human communications course.

[handwritten note: or period]

Compound Sentences in Context

In the following passage about how the media influences people, the compound sentences are highlighted. Notice how the compound sentences are connected in three different ways.

¹Media messages have effects on readers, listeners, and viewers. ²Some messages seek to influence people in obvious ways; for example, there are advertisements on television or on the Internet and editorials in the newspaper. ³Other media messages use indirect ways through dramas and sitcoms.

⁴Researchers have proposed three theories of media influence. ⁵An early theory is called the one-step theory. ⁶The media influences people in one step, for it is direct and immediate. ⁷This theory sees people as passive and easily influenced. ⁸Another theory views media influence as a two-step process. ⁹First, the media influences opinion leaders; then, these opinion

leaders influence the rest of the people. [10]The multistep theory is a more current one. [11]The media may influence an individual on a specific issue. [12]The individual then interacts with others; as a result they influence the individual to change his or her opinion.

(Adapted from *Human Communication* by Joseph A. DeVito)

LO 2 Building Compound Sentences

Two or more independent clauses can be connected in three ways: with a comma and coordinating conjunction; with a semicolon; or with a semicolon, a transitional expression, and a comma.

Connect Independent Clauses Using a Comma and a Coordinating Conjunction

Two independent clauses can be connected with **a comma and a coordinating conjunction**.

INDEPENDENT CLAUSE + , **COORDINATING CONJUNCTION** + INDEPENDENT CLAUSE.

Emotions are often revealed through words, but a large part of the emotional experience is nonverbal.

A **coordinating conjunction** is a word used to connect two or more words, phrases, or sentences. Here are the seven coordinating conjunctions:

| but | or | yet | for | and | nor | so |

| TIP | To remember these words, use an acronym like BOYFANS or FONYABS. These acronyms are made from the first letter of each of the coordinating conjunctions. |

Each of the coordinating conjunctions has a specific meaning. Choose the coordinating conjunction that best expresses the meaning you want to convey.

Coordinating Conjunctions and Their Uses

Coordinating Conjunction	Use	Example
for	to give a reason	A person's home decorations are a form of nonverbal communication, for they tell something about that person.
and	to add ideas or to show similarities	The cost of the furnishings may communicate wealth, and their coordination may communicate a sense of style.
nor	to show a negative choice	Many teenagers do not choose their own decorations, nor do they choose their own furniture.
but	to show the difference between ideas	Bookcases lining the walls reveal the importance of reading, but the absence of books may communicate the opposite.

or	to show a choice or alternative	Office furnishings can communicate high status with a mahogany desk and oriental rugs, or they can show lower status with a metal desk and bare floor.
yet	to show an un-expected difference between ideas	People may know nothing about you, yet they will form opinions about you on the basis of room decorations.
so	to show the result	Watching television is important to some people, so they arrange their chairs around their television.

(Sentences adapted from *The Interpersonal Communication Book* by Joseph A. DeVito)

! **Do not place a comma after the coordinating conjunction.**
Incorrect: Bookcases lining the walls reveal the importance of reading but, the absence of books may communicate the opposite.

Correct: Bookcases lining the walls reveal the importance of reading, but the absence of books may communicate the opposite.

PRACTICE 19.1   Identifying Simple and Compound Sentences   *2 Independent clauses*

For each sentence below, write *S* next to any simple sentences and *C* next to any compound sentences.

Example: Colors can influence our perceptions and behaviors. S

 my lab

1. Color communication takes place on many levels, and the English language is filled with color symbolism. C   *Coordinating conjunction*

2. Breathing increases in the presence of red light, and it decreases in the presence of blue light. C

3. Eye blinks increase with exposure to red light but decrease with exposure to blue light. S

4. "In the red" means a person is in debt, but "being in the black" means a person is making a profit. C   *Coordinating conjunction*

5. People described coffee from a yellow can as weak, yet they identified coffee from a brown can as strong and from a red can as rich. C

(Adapted from *The Interpersonal Communication Book* by Joseph A. DeVito)

PRACTICE 19.2   Using Coordinating Conjunctions in Compound Sentences

For each of the following sentences, fill in a coordinating conjunction that best expresses the meaning of the sentence. Each conjunction is used one time: *but, or, yet, for, and, nor, so.*

1. Clothing protects people from the weather and from injury in sports, _but_ it conceals parts of your body.

2. Clothing also serves as a form of cultural display, _for_ it communicates your ethnic group.

3. Jewelry communicates messages about people, _for_ men with earrings will be judged differently from men without earrings.

4. People wearing piercings jewelry may wish to communicate their own messages, _but_ these messages infer an unwillingness to conform.

5. In a study on attraction, male and female models without glasses were rated positively, _yet_ the same models with glasses were rated more negatively.

6. Tattoos can communicate the name of a loved one or a symbol of affiliation, _or_ they can communicate to the wearers themselves a more adventurous and creative image.

7. Nose-pierced job applicants did not receive high scores on character and trust, _but_ were they given high scores on sociability and hirability.

(Adapted from *The Interpersonal Communication Book* by Joseph A. DeVito)

PRACTICE   Writing Your Own Compound Sentences

19.3   Write five compound sentences about the following photograph of two men applying for a job. Consider what each one communicates in the way he dresses.

Use the coordinating conjunctions *and, but, or, so,* and *yet* one time. Remember to place a comma in front of the coordinating conjunction.

Example: One man is wearing baggy jeans, and the other man is wearing suit pants.

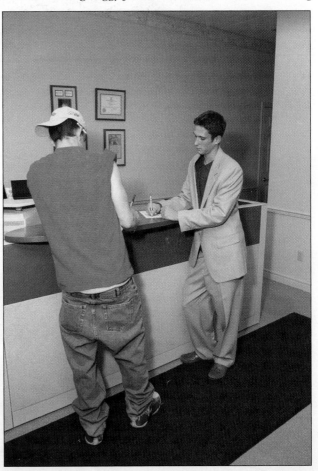

Connect Independent Clauses Using a Semicolon

Another way to connect two independent clauses is to place a semicolon (;) between them.

INDEPENDENT CLAUSE + ; + INDEPENDENT CLAUSE.

At times, a person may say the wrong thing; the most common way to explain it is with an excuse.

 Do not add a coordinating conjunction after the semicolon.

Incorrect: The main reason for making an excuse is to project a positive image; and it also represents an effort to reduce stress.

Correct: The main reason for making an excuse is to project a positive image; it also represents an effort to reduce stress.

PRACTICE   Using a Semicolon in Compound Sentences

19.4   Insert the semicolon between each pair of simple sentences.

Example: A good excuse can be accepted; it will reduce the negative reaction.

1. Good excuse makers use excuses in moderation; bad excuse makers rely on excuses too often.
2. Good excuse makers avoid blaming others; blaming is characteristic of bad excuse makers.
3. Accepting responsibility for an excuse will make a person seem more credible; those denying responsibility seem less believable.
4. Denial is the worst of all excuses; these excuses do not accept responsibility.
5. Effective excuses vary from one culture to another; they depend on a culture's values and beliefs.

(Adapted from *The Interpersonal Communication Book* by Joseph A. Devito)

PRACTICE   Writing Compound Sentences with Semicolons

19.5   Write five compound sentences about the couple in the following photograph. Use a semicolon to connect each of your two related simple sentences.

Example: Marlon wants to apologize; Kara does not want to listen.

[handwritten margin notes: "& — comma", "& so coordinating conjunction", "; semicolon", "; ,"]

Connect Independent Clauses Using a Semicolon and a Transitional Word or Phrase

A semicolon and a transitional word or phrase can also be used to connect two independent clauses.

> INDEPENDENT CLAUSE + ; **TRANSITION WORD OR PHRASE**, + INDEPENDENT CLAUSE.

Physical space is an important factor in interpersonal communication; **however,** people rarely think about it.

Like coordinating conjunctions, transitional words and phrases have specific meanings. In the sentence above, the transitional word *however* shows a contrast between the two independent clauses. Always choose the transition that best expresses the relationship between two independent clauses.

The following chart lists the most commonly used transitional words and phrases according to the relationship they show. If you are not sure of the meaning of the word, look it up in a dictionary and see how it is used in a sentence.

Transitional Words and Phrases and Their Uses

Use	Transitional Words and Phrases
to add information (meaning *and*)	also, at the same time, besides, in addition, moreover, furthermore, equally important Public distance ranges from twelve to more than twenty-five feet; **furthermore,** it can further be divided into the close phase and the far phase.
to give an example	as an illustration, for example, for instance, to illustrate In the close phase, a person seems protected by space; **for example,** you might keep this distance from a drunk on a public bus or train.
to make a contrast or give an alternative (meaning *but*)	however, in contrast, on the contrary, on the other hand, otherwise, nevertheless, nonetheless You lose the fine detail of a person's face or eyes in the close phase; **however,** you are still close enough to monitor that person.
to express an effect or result (meaning *so*)	as a result, consequently, therefore, thus The far phase is the distance of actors on stage from their audience; **consequently,** their actions and voices have to be exaggerated.
to clarify a point	in fact, in other words People automatically create a large space of about thirty feet around important public figures; **in fact,** they do this with or without guards to keep them away.
to make a comparison	in the same way, likewise, similarly You will maintain short distances with familiar people; **similarly,** you will keep a closer distance to people you like.
to express time	afterward, in the meantime, later, meanwhile, subsequently Edward T. Hall pioneered the study of spatial communication; **later,** the area was called proxemics.

(Sentences adapted from *The Interpersonal Communication Book* by Joseph A. DeVito)

Do not place a comma before the transitional expression and a semicolon after it:

Incorrect: People like to keep a certain physical distance between themselves, **in fact;** it is a form of protection.

Correct: People like to keep a certain physical distance between themselves; **in fact,** it is a form of protection.

PRACTICE Using Transitional Words and Phrases in Compound Sentences
19.6

Write the transitional word or phrase that best expresses the relationship between each of the following compound sentences. Use each one of these transitions one time: *in fact, for example, in contrast, moreover, therefore*.

Example: Throughout your life, you will meet many people __; however,__ you will develop few friendships.

1. Friendships develop over time _____ they develop in stages.

2. At one end of the friendship progression are new acquaintances _____ at the other end are intimate friends.

3. Communications increase as you progress from the initial contact stage to intimate friendship _____ you talk about issues that are closer and closer to your inner core.

4. In a developing friendship, people are torn between revealing and not revealing personal information _____ friendships do not always follow a straight path.

5. Friendships become stable at a comfortable level for each person _____ some will remain casual and others will remain close.

(Adapted from *The Interpersonal Communication Book* by Joseph A. DeVito)

PRACTICE Punctuating Compound Sentences
19.7

Insert the proper punctuation in each of the following sentences.

mentoring helping and advising someone at work about how to do a job

networking meeting people who might be useful to know, especially in your job

Example: All forms of communication take place at work; in addition, all forms of relationships may be seen such as romantic, **mentoring**, and networking.

1. **Networking** is often viewed as a technique for getting a job; however, it actually has other uses.

2. Informal networking is sharing information with someone at work or school; for example, a new student might ask about the best places to eat or about the best English teachers.

3. Formal networking is more organized and planned; therefore, you choose people with specialized knowledge for help in many different ways.

4. Networking gives you access to a wealth of specialized information; at the same time, you can get that information from others instead of on your own.

5. Networking relationships should benefit both people; in other words, you help others, and in return, they will help you.

(Adapted from *The Interpersonal Communication Book* by Joseph A. DeVito)

PRACTICE Combining Independent Clauses
19.8

Combine each pair of sentences below. First, figure out the relationship between the first and second independent clause. Next, choose a transition that best expresses that relationship. Then join the two independent clauses. Remember to punctuate your sentence with a semicolon before the transition and a comma after it.

Example:

a. In television shows, workers move in and out of romantic relationships with little difficulty.

b. Real-life office romance can be complicated.

difficulty; however, in Real life office romance can be complicated.

1a. Some organizations have rules against workplace romantic relationships.

1b. Members can be fired for such relationships.

Romantic relationships, for members can be fired for such relationship.

2a. On the positive side, the work environment seems a perfect place to meet a romantic partner. *; because,*

2b. You work in the same office, have similar training, and spend a great deal of time together.

_____

_____

3a. Many Americans are marrying later in life.

3b. Work seems the logical place to meet possible partners.

_____

_____

4a. An office relationship may be good for the two individuals.

4b. It may not be good for other workers.

_____

_____

5a. Other workers may be jealous of the romance.

5b. They may make up destructive office gossip.

_____

_____

(Adapted from *The Interpersonal Communication Book* by Joseph A. DeVito)

PRACTICE   Writing Your Own Compound Sentences

19.9   Write five compound sentences about the photograph on the next page. Use a different transitional expression in each sentence. Be sure to punctuate sentences correctly.

Example: Someone at Tanya's workplace likes her; furthermore, he emails her romantic **e-cards** every day.

e-card a digital greeting card

LO 3 Avoiding Comma Splices

A common punctuation error in compound sentences is the comma splice. The **comma splice** happens when two independent clauses are connected with a comma.

Hate speech is offensive and degrading to a particular group of people, it can take many forms.

To correct a comma splice, use any of the three methods explained in this chapter to connect the independent clauses.

COMMA + COORDINATING CONJUNCTION

Hate speech is offensive to a particular group of people, and it can take many forms.

SEMICOLON

Hate speech is offensive to a particular group of people; it can take many forms.

SEMICOLON + TRANSITION WORD OR PHRASE + COMMA

Hate speech is offensive to a particular group of people; in addition, it can take many forms.

PRACTICE Correcting Comma Splices

19.10 Correct the following comma splices using the method suggested for each sentence.

1. The term *girl* should only be used to refer to a very young female, it should not be used for a female over thirteen or fourteen.
   Use a semicolon.

2. *Lady* has a meaning of the prim and proper woman, *woman* or *young woman* is preferred.
   Use a transitional expression.

3. *Older person* is preferred for anyone over 65, *elder, elderly,* or *senior citizen* should be avoided.
   Use a coordinating conjunction.

4. *Hispanic American* refers to United States residents with ancestry in a Spanish culture, the term includes Mexicans, Caribbeans, and Central and South Americans.
   Use a semicolon.

5. The term is inaccurate, it leaves out the large numbers of people in the Caribbean and in South America with African, Native American, French, or Portuguese ancestry.
_____Use a transitional expression.

(Adapted from *The Interpersonal Communication Book* by Joseph A. DeVito)

LO 4 Avoiding Run-Ons   *no Punctuation*

Another common punctuation error in compound sentences is the run-on. The **run-on** happens when two independent clauses are combined into one sentence without any punctuation between them.

Most people have some degree of fear of giving a speech it is perfectly normal.

To correct a run-on, use any of the three methods explained in this chapter to connect the independent clauses:

COMMA + COORDINATING CONJUNCTION

Most people have some degree of fear of giving a speech, **so** it is perfectly normal.

SEMICOLON

Most people have some degree of fear of giving a speech; it is perfectly normal.

SEMICOLON + TRANSITION WORD OR PHRASE + COMMA

Most people have some degree of fear of giving a speech; therefore, it is perfectly normal.

TIP | To check your sentence to see if it is a run-on, try changing the sentence from a statement to a yes/no question or a tag question. If the sentence is a run-on, you will not be able to do it.

yes/no question	Do most people have some degree of fear of giving a speech is it perfectly normal?
	You cannot make the sentence into one question because it has two separate sentences in it. You have to split the sentence into two questions.
tag question	Most people have some degree of fear of giving a speech it is perfectly normal, isn't it?
	You cannot make the sentence a tag question because it contains two separate sentences; therefore, you can see that your original sentence is a run-on.

PRACTICE Correcting Run-On Sentences

19.11   Correct the following run-on sentences using the method suggested for each sentence.

although

1. Fear of public speaking is not necessarily harmful fear can motivate you to work harder.
   Use a transitional expression.

2. The audience cannot see your nervousness; they do not notice your shaking hands or dry throat.
   Use a semicolon.

3. Taking a drug to reduce stress may create problems because they may keep you from remembering the parts of your speech.
   Use a transitional expression.

4. Physical movement can lessen anxiety, but showing a visual aid can help your body relax.
   Use a coordinating conjunction.

5. Much of your fear is fear of failure, however extra preparation will build your confidence.
   Use a transitional expression.

(Adapted from *The Interpersonal Communication Book* by Joseph A. DeVito)

Review: Correcting Compound Sentences

In the following paragraph, some of the sentences are simple and some are compound. Find the compound sentences that are not punctuated correctly and insert the correct punctuation. The first error has been corrected for you.

[1]Cultures differ in a wide variety of ways. [2]The most obvious difference is language; other differences are nonverbal signals. [3]Each culture has its own rules and customs for communicating. [4]For example, in American culture, you would call a person for a date three or four days in advance in contrast in some Asian cultures you might call the person's parents weeks or even months in advance. [5]In some cultures people show respect by avoiding direct eye contact with the person being spoken to however in other cultures this same eye avoidance would signal disinterest. [6]Men walk arm in arm in some European cultures but in American culture, this is considered inappropriate.

[7]Learning about other cultures is the best preparation for intercultural communication. [8]You can see a movie or documentary with a realistic view of the culture or you can read material about the culture. [9]Another way to learn is to read magazines and websites from a particular culture. [10]Talking with members of the culture will also help furthermore you can chat in an international chat room. [11]Being aware of cultural differences will build your cultural sensitivity in fact cultural sensitivity is crucial for interpersonal communication. [12]Without it, there can be no communication between people of different gender, race, or nationality so you need to be mindful of cultural differences.

(Adapted from *The Interpersonal Communication Book* and *Human Communication* by Joseph A. DeVito)

Writing Assignments

Write a paragraph about the advantages or disadvantages of dating someone with whom you work. Include three compound sentences in your paragraph, one for each method for joining simple sentences. Here is a review of the methods:

INDEPENDENT CLAUSE + , **COORDINATING CONJUNCTION** + INDEPENDENT CLAUSE.

INDEPENDENT CLAUSE + ; + INDEPENDENT CLAUSE.

INDEPENDENT CLAUSE + ; **TRANSITION WORD OR PHRASE**, + INDEPENDENT CLAUSE.

English Success Tip: Relate, Don't Ramble

Using a variety of sentences makes your writing interesting and easier to read and understand. Connecting simple sentences using coordination is one way to add variety. However, connecting too many simple sentences can hurt rather than help your writing.

A rambling sentence is made up of many simple sentences added together with coordinating conjunctions. The sentence is very long and continues on and on without direction. The following is an example of a rambling sentence. It is made up of ten independent clauses connected with coordinating conjunctions.

> Heavy traffic from a major accident this morning made me late to school, and I saw that the parking lot near my class was full, so I had to drive around for twenty minutes to find a space, so I was a half hour late for class, and I had to walk past the teacher and the other students, and I was embarrassed, and then I could not find my essay, for I had left it at home on my desk, and my teacher refuses to accept late papers, so now I have a zero for that assignment.

To avoid sentences that ramble, connect sentences that show a relationship to one another. The following is a revision of the rambling sentence. Notice that the compound sentences are made up of two simple sentences that are related to each other.

> Heavy traffic from a major accident this morning made me late to school. I saw that the parking lot near my class was full, so I had to drive around for twenty minutes to find a space. I was a half hour late for class. I had to walk past the teacher and the other students, and I was embarrassed. Then I could not find my essay, for I had left it at home on my desk. My teacher refuses to accept late papers, so now I have a zero for that assignment.

For support in meeting this chapter's objectives, log in to www.mywritinglab.com, go to the Study Plan tab, click on **Joining Ideas Using Compound Sentences** and choose **Parts of Speech, Phrases and Clauses, Combining Sentences and Run-Ons** from the list of subtopics. Read and view the videos and resources in the Review Materials section, and then complete the Recall, Apply, and Write exercises in the Activities section. You can check your scores and overall progress by using the Gradebook.

Joining Ideas Using Complex Sentences

Theme: *Health and Wellness*

Learning Objectives

After working through this chapter, you will be able to:

LO 1 Identify the parts of a complex sentence: the independent clause and dependent clause.

LO 2 Write complex sentences using subordinating conjunctions to begin dependent clauses.

LO 3 Write complex sentences using relative pronouns to begin dependent clauses.

LO 4 Identify and correct dependent clause fragments.

LO 1 What Is a Complex Sentence?

A **complex sentence** includes an independent clause and a dependent clause. The independent clause expresses a complete idea, but the dependent clause does not. The dependent clause "depends" on the independent clause for its meaning and is not a complete sentence by itself.

> People have become conscious of their lifestyles because the media focuses on health problems.
>
> People who want to make healthy lifestyle choices need to be informed consumers.

Complex Sentences in Context

In the following passage about vegetarianism, the dependent clauses are highlighted.

Today, between 5 and 15 percent of all Americans identify themselves as vegetarians. The term *vegetarianism* means different things to different people. Strict vegetarians, or *vegans*, avoid all foods of animal origin, including dairy products and eggs. Vegans must be careful to obtain all of the necessary nutrients. Far more common are *lacto-vegetarians*, who eat dairy products but avoid flesh foods. Their diet can be low in fat and cholesterol but only if they consume skim milk and other low-fat or non-fat products. *Ovo-vegetarians* add eggs to their diet, while *lacto-ovo-vegetarians* eat both dairy products and eggs. *Pesco-vegetarians* eat fish, dairy products, and eggs, while *semivegetarians* eat chicken, fish, dairy products, and eggs. Some people in the semivegetarian category prefer to call themselves "non-red meat eaters." Although in the past vegetarians often suffered from vitamin deficiencies, the vegetarian of today is usually good at combining the right types of foods to ensure proper nutrient intake. The strictest vegetarians who eat a full variety of grains, legumes, fruits, vegetables, and seeds each day can be in excellent health.

(Adapted from *Access to Health* by Rebecca J. Donatelle)

LO 2 Building Complex Sentences with Subordinating Conjunctions

One way to build a complex sentence is by starting one of the independent clauses with a subordinating conjunction. Adding the subordinating conjunction changes the sentence to a dependent clause.

> Our bodies cannot produce certain essential nutrients. We must get them from the foods we eat.
>
> **Because** our bodies cannot produce certain essential nutrients, we must get them from the food we eat.

Understanding Subordinating Conjunctions

Subordinating conjunctions are connecting words that you can use to start a dependent clause. They show cause and effect, time, contrast, condition, or location. The following chart explains each of the types of subordinating conjunctions.

Subordinating Conjunctions

Purpose	Subordinating Conjunctions	Sentence Examples
Cause and Effect gives reasons or results	*because, now that, since*	**Because** you are hungry, the brain tells the stomach to churn. You feel hunger pangs **since the stomach muscles have nothing to churn,**
Time tells when	*after, as, as long as, as soon as, before, by the time, every time, once, since, until, when, whenever, while*	**As** you think about food, you begin to produce saliva. Digestion begins **when you chew your food.**
Contrast shows one idea is in contrast to another	*although, even though, though, while, whereas*	**Although** you have just eaten a meal, your stomach takes two to six hours to empty. Some chemical digestion starts in the stomach, **whereas most of it occurs in the small intestine.**
Condition explains that an action can only take place if a certain condition is fulfilled	*even if, if, in case, in the event that, only if, so that, unless, whether or not*	Stomach acid will not be released **unless you see, smell, or taste food. If** some stomach acid flows back up into the esophagus, you may experience heartburn.
Location tells where	*where, wherever*	Food passes from the stomach to the small intestine, **where nutrients are absorbed.**

PRACTICE   Identifying Subordinating Conjunctions and Dependent Clauses

20.1   Circle the subordinating conjunctions and underline the dependent clauses in each of the following sentences.

Example: Although *serving size* and *portion* are often used interchangeably, they actually mean very different things.

1. A serving is the recommended amount a person should consume, while a portion is the amount a person chooses to eat at any one time.
2. When most people select a portion, it is usually much bigger than a serving.
3. A serving size of meat, poultry, or fish is three ounces, whereas a serving size of cheese is one ounce.
4. Experts have developed some tips so that people can judge how big a serving size should be.
5. Since most people have trouble visualizing a true serving size, experts suggest relating it to an everyday item.
6. For example, a small baked potato is considered a serving if it is the size of a computer mouse.
7. Imagine a deck of cards to determine a serving of meat, poultry, or fish even though the serving appears to be small.

depen

PRACTICE   Analyzing Complex Sentences

20.2   In each of the sentences, underline the dependent clause and write the kind of relationship between the two clauses:

cause and effect   condition   contrast   time   location

Example: When someone eats too quickly or does not chew food thoroughly, he or she may choke. time

1. Unless breathing is restored within minutes, brain damage or death may result.
   time

2. In 1974, American surgeon Henry J. Heimlich devised a new method to help choking victims because slapping a person's back did not unblock the airway.
   Cause & effect

3. The Heimlich Maneuver can be performed as long as the victim is conscious.
   Condition

4. A person can perform the Heimlich Maneuver wherever the choking incident occurs. _Location_

5. The process is carried out so that the foreign object can be removed from the throat to get air flowing. _Contrast_

6. Although the procedure is usually used for choking victims, it can also be performed on drowning victims. _Contrast_

7. When no one is around to help, you can use the Heimlich Maneuver on yourself.
   Location

Using Subordinating Conjunctions to Write Complex Sentences

A dependent clause that begins with a subordinating conjunction can often be placed at the beginning or end of the complex sentence as long as the intended meaning of the sentence does not change.

Begin with the independent clause and add the dependent clause.

> The amount of sugar in one's diet can be hard to control **because** it can be hidden in certain foods.

Begin with the dependent clause and add the independent clause.

> **Because** it can be hidden in certain foods, the amount of sugar in one's diet can be hard to control.

, Punctuating Dependent Word Groups with Subordinating Conjunctions

Apply the following rules for using commas with dependent clauses.

> INDEPENDENT CLAUSE + **NO COMMA** + DEPENDENT CLAUSE.
>
> Experts recommend eating whole fruit and avoiding fruit products with corn syrup **since** they are often high in added sugar.
>
> DEPENDENT CLAUSE + , + INDEPENDENT CLAUSE.
>
> **Since** they are often high in sugar, experts recommend eating whole fruit and avoiding fruit products with corn syrup.

TIP | Always use a comma before a dependent clause that begins with *while* or *whereas*.

> Simple sugars provide short-term energy, **whereas** complex carbohydrates provide sustained energy.

A comma is not needed after a subordinating conjunction.

Incorrect: Although, proteins in the body are certainly important, carbohydrates give people energy to sustain normal daily activity.

Correct: Although proteins in the body are certainly important, carbohydrates give people energy to sustain normal daily activity.

PRACTICE   Punctuating Complex Sentences

20.3   Underline the subordinating conjunctions in the following complex sentences. Add commas where they are needed. Some of the sentences are correct.

Example: The feeling of anxiety before a test can be useful <u>because</u> it can make you more careful or alert. Correct. ✓

1. <u>When</u> a person's anxiety does not go away and gets worse over time, he or she has an anxiety disorder.
2. With an anxiety disorder, the body triggers the person's alarm system <u>even though</u> there is no danger.
3. <u>Although</u> feelings of anxiety are scary, they do not hurt the person.
4. Some people have a general feeling of worry, <u>whereas</u> others have a sudden attack of panicky feelings.
5. <u>If</u> a person feels worried over personal finances, this worry does not mean that the person has an anxiety disorder.
6. <u>Whenever</u> people worry about something for hours every day and cannot sleep or perform usual tasks, they are suffering from more than normal anxiety.
7. Men and women are both affected by general anxiety disorder <u>though</u> women are twice as likely to be affected.

PRACTICE   Using Subordinating Conjunctions

20.4   In the following sentences, fill in the subordinating conjunction that best expresses the relationship between the two word groups. Use each of the following subordinating conjunctions once.

since	whereas	while	now that
if	when	because	even though

Example: ____Now that____ the United States is considered one of the fattest nations on Earth, the health of the population is at risk.

1. Obesity is a label used to refer to individuals _____ their body fat is beyond normal for a person based on age, sex, and body type.
2. One way to measure overweight and obesity is a standard height-weight chart, _____ another measurement is the body mass index (BMI) formula, which is based on the relationship of weight to height.
3. Some people, such as lean, muscular athletes, would be considered overweight according to BMI charts _____ these individuals do not have excess body fat.
4. Men's bodies should contain between 11 and 15 percent total body fat, _____ women should be within a range of 18 to 22 percent body fat.
5. Generally, _____ men exceed 20 percent body fat and women exceed 30 percent body fat, they have slipped into obesity.
6. _____ men's and women's body structures and sex hormones differ, their desirable body fat ranges differ.
7. Too much fat and too little fat are both potentially harmful _____ a certain amount of fat is needed to insulate the body, cushion body parts, and maintain good body functions.

(Adapted from *Access to Health* by Rebecca J. Donatelle)

PRACTICE   Writing Complex Sentences

20.5   The obesity problem in this country has made some people concerned about their weight. Write five complex sentences about the photo shown here. Use a different subordinating conjunction in each sentence. Be sure to write a subject after the subordinating conjunction:

Example:
Incorrect: High rates of obesity concern health professionals because can cause long- and short-term health effects.
Correct: High rates of obesity concern health professionals because **obesity** can cause long- and short-term health effects.

LO 3   Building Complex Sentences with Relative Pronouns

Another way to build a complex sentence is by starting one of the independent clauses with a relative pronoun. Adding the relative pronoun changes the sentence to a dependent clause.

Athletes must train to increase stamina and muscle strength. Athletes compete in physically strenuous sports.
Athletes **who** compete in physically strenuous sports must train to increase stamina and strength.

Understanding Relative Pronouns

A relative pronoun is a word that refers to a noun. When a relative pronoun begins a dependent clause, the clause adds information to the word it refers to.

Relative Pronouns		
Relative Pronoun	Use	Sentence Example
who	Use *who* or *whom* to refer to people. *Who* is sometimes used to refer to animals possessing special intelligence.	The average adult who does not sweat profusely requires only about one-fourth of a teaspoon of salt per day.
whom		People for whom high blood pressure is a problem should cut back on sodium.
that	Use *that* refer to places, things, ideas, activities, animals. *That* gives specific information that is necessary to the meaning of the sentence.	The majority of sodium in our diet comes from highly processed foods that contain added sodium to enhance flavor and preserve food.
which	Use *which* to refer to places, things, ideas, activities, and animals. Use *which* for information that is not necessary to the meaning of the sentence.	Examples of high sodium foods which contain several hundred milligrams of sodium per serving are pickles, fast foods, salty snack foods, processed cheeses, smoked meats and sausages, and breads and bakery products.
whose	Use *whose* to show ownership for people, places, things, ideas, activities, animals.	People whose goal is to reduce sodium intake can choose low-sodium or salt-free products.

PRACTICE   Identifying Relative Pronouns and Dependent Clauses

20.6   In each of the following sentences, circle the relative pronoun and underline the dependent clause. Then draw an arrow to the word that the dependent clause is describing.

Example: As of 2002, any food that is sold as organic has to meet the criteria set by the United States Department of Agriculture under the National Organic Rule.

1. Farmers who label their food 100 percent organic must grow and manufacture their products without the use of added hormones, pesticides, and synthetic fertilizers.

2. Also, a crop that can be called organic cannot have been treated with synthetic products for three years.

3. Organic products appeal to people who are concerned about food safety.

4. They want to avoid non-organic food grown with chemicals that cause cancer, immune system problems, and many other ailments.

5. The market for organics has been increasing by over 20 percent per year, which is five times faster than food sales in general.

6. It is difficult to determine if people who eat only organic food are healthier.

7. Many farmers are choosing organic farming, which is better for the environment.

(Adapted from *Access to Health* by Rebecca J. Donatelle)

Using Relative Pronouns to Write Complex Sentences

Writing complex sentences with a dependent clause that begins with a relative pronoun involves two steps: (1) forming the dependent clause and (2) placing it next to the word it describes in the independent clause.

The dependent clause with relative pronouns follows one of two patterns:

Dependent Clause Pattern	Example Sentence
Pattern 1 RELATIVE PRONOUN + SUBJECT + VERB	Recreational physical activities that you enjoy provide health benefits.
Pattern 2 RELATIVE PRONOUN AS SUBJECT + VERB	Adding more physical movement to your day, which might include parking farther from your destination, can contribute to overall health.

TIP

When forming a dependent clause using pattern 2, remember to take out the subject the pronoun is replacing.

Some **people** can still be physically active and benefit from physical exercise. Some **people** have physical limitations.

Some **people** who ~~people~~ have physical limitations can still be physically active and benefit from exercise.

PRACTICE   Combining Simple Sentences to Create Complex Sentences
20.7

Combine each pair of sentences into a complex sentence. Use a relative pronoun to change the second sentence into a dependent clause. Underline the dependent clause. Use *who, which, that,* or *whose.*

Example: The term *aerobic* describes any type of exercise. The exercise increases heart rate.

The term *aerobic* describes any type of exercise <u>that increases heart rate.</u>

1. A person is described as being in good shape. The person has an above-average aerobic capacity.

   _____

2. Aerobic capacity is a term. The term is used to describe the function of the heart, lungs, and blood vessels.

   _____

3. The most beneficial aerobic exercises are total body activities. These activities involve all the large muscle groups of the body.

   _____

4. There are three main components of an aerobic exercise program. The three components are frequency, intensity, and duration.

   _____

5. People will need to vigorously exercise at least three times a week. People want to improve their cardiovascular endurance.

_____

6. A person can make improvements by doing less intense exercise more days a week. A person is a newcomer to exercise.

_____

7. A person should begin at a low intensity and progress slowly. A person's lifestyle has not involved physical activity.

_____

(Adapted from _Access to Health_ by Rebecca J. Donatelle)

Using _Who_ and _Whom_ to Start Dependent Clauses Follow these rules to use _who_ and _whom_.

Rule	Sentence Example
whom	
When the dependent clause has a subject, use _whom_. WHOM + SUBJECT + VERB	Dr. Murray E. Jarvik, **whom scientists admired for his contributions to smoking cessation**, helped invent the nicotine patch.
who	
When the dependent clause does not have a subject, use _who_. WHO + VERB	Dr. Murray E. Jarvik, **who helped invent the nicotine patch**, was admired for his contributions to smoking cessation.

PRACTICE Using _Who_ and _Whom_

20.8 In each of the following complex sentences, fill in the blank with _who_ or _whom_.

Example: Dr. Murray Jarvik, __who__ was a professor at the University of California, was a leader in the study of how drugs affect human behavior.

1. Jarvik, _____ always wondered why people smoked, discovered that nicotine was the key addictive component in tobacco.

2. Tobacco harvesters, _____ Jarvik and his colleague Jed Rose studied, became sick with green tobacco sickness.

3. The workers _____ became ill were absorbing nicotine from the tobacco through their skin.

4. Their discovery led Jarvik and Rose, _____ realized that small doses of nicotine might help people stop smoking, to invent the nicotine patch.

5. They could not get permission to try the nicotine patch on people _____ they had chosen as testers.

6. Jarvik and Rose, _____ were nonsmokers, decided to try the patch on themselves.

7. The patch gave them the same effects that people _____ smoke experience.

8. Smokers, for _____ the patch was invented, were able to get nicotine patches by prescription in 1992 and over the counter in 1996.

Punctuating Dependent Clauses with Relative Pronouns

To decide whether to use commas or not, you must decide if the dependent clause is essential or nonessential to the meaning of the sentence. Then follow the rules explained in the chart below.

- **Essential** means that the information in the dependent clause is needed to make the noun specific. *That* is generally used to introduce essential dependent clauses although *which* can also be used.
- **Nonessential** means that the information in the dependent clause is not needed because the noun it describes is already specific. The dependent clause adds extra information that could be omitted. *Which* is used to introduce nonessential information.

Dependent Word Group	Comma Rule	Sentence Example
Essential	**No commas** before or after the dependent clause	An echocardiogram is a test that uses sound waves to create a moving picture of the heart.
Nonessential	**Commas** before and after the dependent clause	An echocardiogram, which causes no discomfort, allows doctors to see the heart beating and to see the structures of the heart.

PRACTICE   Punctuating Essential and Nonessential Word Groups

20.9   Underline the dependent clause in each sentence. Add commas to the nonessential dependent clauses.

Example: Techniques <u>that allow physicians to see the organs and organ systems without surgery</u> are constantly improving. Essential, no commas

1. Computed tomography (CT) which is a noninvasive X-ray produces a three-dimensional image of the organ or structure.

2. A CT scan is a procedure that distinguishes minor differences in the density of tissues.

3. The CT scans produce high-resolution images of cross-sections of the body which can be studied.

4. Magnetic resonance imaging (MRI) which is also a noninvasive technique is commonly used to make images of the brain, spine, limbs, joints, heart, blood vessels, abdomen, and pelvis.

5. During an MRI, the patient lies very still on a platform that moves into a scanner.

6. The platform can move into either a narrow, closed, high-magnet scanner, or into an open, low-magnet scanner which may cause people to feel closed in.

7. Earplugs are offered to the client to reduce the discomfort from the loud noises that occur during the test.

(Adapted from *Fundamentals of Nursing* by Barbara Kozier and Glenora Erb)

PRACTICE Writing Complex Sentences

20.10 Write five complex sentences using relative pronouns about the picture shown here. You can write about your own personal experience with X-rays or other imaging technologies. You can also write about people you know who work in the field or about any medical procedure you know about.

Example: The X-ray that was taken after the accident showed a fracture in my leg.

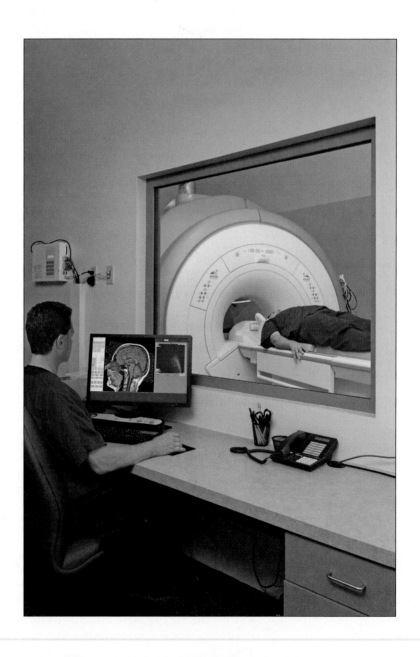

LO 4 Avoiding Dependent Clause Fragments

When a dependent clause is not connected to an independent clause, the dependent clause is called a **fragment**. A fragment is an error.

Fragment Error	Correction
Today, people are looking for alternatives. That are safer and more effective ways of getting and staying healthy.	Today, people are looking for alternatives that are safer and more effective ways of getting and staying healthy.
Choosing a health care professional is challenging for people. Who want to use an alternative medical approach.	Choosing a health care professional is challenging for people who want to use an alternative medical approach.
Although alternative treatments have become popular. Their safety and effectiveness have not been proven.	Although alternative treatments have become popular, their safety and effectiveness have not been proven.

PRACTICE Correcting Dependent Clause Fragments

20.11   Underline the dependent clause fragments in the following items. Revise each of the items by creating a complex sentence. Add commas when needed.

Example: Although the United States has been slow to accept plant remedies as standard treatment. Twenty-five percent of all modern pharmaceutical drugs come from herbs.

Revision: Although the United States has been slow to accept plant remedies as standard treatment, twenty-five percent of all modern pharmaceutical drugs come from herbs.

1. Medicines made from plants were used widely in the United States until World War II. When FDA-tested drugs took over in the later part of the twentieth century.

   _____

2. Many of these earlier treatments have become popular in the twenty-first century. Because people have grown dissatisfied with medications that have side effects.

   _____

3. Even though herbal medicines are milder than chemical drugs. They are still drugs.

   _____

4. Herbal medicines contain some of the same chemicals. That are in chemical drugs.

   _____

5. Some herbs and dietary supplements pose risks to consumers. Who may be taking prescription drugs.

   _____

[Handwritten margin note: Add a comma when the subordinating conjunction is before the Dependent clause]

6. On the other hand, many people take dietary supplements. So that they get the nutrients they need to be healthy.

_____

7. People should learn about its positive and negative effects. Who want to take a prescription drug or a dietary supplement.

_____

Writing Assignments

Review: Complex Sentences

Correct any fragment or comma errors in the following sentences.

Example: The heart is a muscular, four-chambered pump. Which is roughly the size of your fist.

The heart is a muscular, four-chambered pump, which is roughly the size of your fist.

1. It is a highly efficient, extremely flexible organ, that contracts 100,000 times each day.

_____

2. Each day, the heart pumps the equivalent of 2,000 gallons of blood to all areas of the body. Although the human body contains only six quarts of blood.

_____

3. The heart's four chambers work together, so that blood is recirculated constantly throughout the body.

_____

4. The atria are the two upper chambers of the heart. Which receive blood from the rest of the body.

_____

5. The two lower chambers which are called ventricles pump the blood out again.

_____

6. When blood flows between chambers. Small valves regulate the steady, rhythmic flow of blood and prevent it from washing backwards.

_____

7. All four chambers must beat in an organized manner, if the heart is to function properly.

_____

(Adapted from *Access to Health* by Rebecca J. Donatelle)

Comment on a Contemporary Issue

Human activities are causing problems for the environment. Write five complex sentences about the human activities that you believe cause problems for the Earth's plants, animals, and people.

Example: Many of our rivers and lakes that have been used for waste disposal are no longer clean.

English Success Tip: Complex but Not Confusing

Scholarly writing, such as the material you read in textbooks and journals, includes many sentences with dependent clauses. Some sentences can contain four or five dependent clauses.

Complex sentences will add variety to your writing. However, some complex sentences lose their effectiveness when dependent clauses are overused. The following student's sentence contains eight dependent clauses.

> When I lost my job at the company where I had worked for a year, I was not able to make my car payments, which were $250 a month, until I found another job where I could earn enough to pay the monthly payment while having extra money to cover the payments that I missed.

Here is a revision that groups the ideas into time relationships.

> When I lost my job at the company where I had worked for a year, I was not able to make my $250 a month car payments. Two months later, I found another job where I earned more than enough to cover my car payment. With the extra money that I made, I paid back the payments that I had missed.

For support in meeting this chapter's objectives, log in to www.mywritinglab.com, go to the Study Plan tab, click on **Joining Ideas Using Complex Sentences** and choose **Parts of Speech, Phrases and Clauses, Combining Sentences and Fragments** from the list of subtopics. Read and view the videos and resources in the Review Materials section, and then complete the Recall, Apply, and Write exercises in the Activities section. You can check your scores and overall progress by using the Gradebook.

Building Grammar Skills

PART 5

Subject-Verb Agreement

CHAPTER
21

Theme: *Sociology*

Learning Objectives

After working through this chapter, you will learn to:

LO 1 Identify singular and plural subjects and verbs.

LO 2 Make present tense verbs agree with their subjects.

LO 3 Make verbs agree with singular subjects.

LO 4 Make verbs agree with plural subjects.

LO 5 Make verbs agree with indefinite pronoun, collective noun, and inverted subjects.

LO 1 What Is Subject-Verb Agreement?

Subject-verb agreement is a grammar rule that states that a subject and verb must agree in number. The subject and the verb must both be either singular or plural. The subject of the sentence determines whether the verb is singular or plural.

- If the subject of a sentence is **singular**, the verb must have a **singular ending**.
- If the subject is **plural**, the verb must have a **plural ending**.

A **singular subject** is one person, place, thing, idea, or activity. A **plural subject** is more than one of those items. In each of the following sentences, the subjects are highlighted in yellow and the verbs in green. Notice how both the subjects and verbs change from singular to plural.

Singular and Plural Subjects and Verbs	
Singular subject and singular verb form	Plural subject and plural verb form
A sociologist studies society and human behavior.	Sociologists study society and human behavior.
A person learns acceptable behavior from his or her experiences in society	People learn acceptable behavior from their experiences in society.
An image on television makes society's expectations about gender stronger.	Images on television make society's expectations about gender stronger.

Subject-Verb Agreement In Context

In the following passage from a sociology text, the subjects and verbs in each sentence are highlighted.

[1]In society, males and females are sorted into different roles. [2]This is called gender socialization. [3]Different attitudes and behaviors are expected

from males and females. ⁴We get these gender messages from our family and from the mass media.

⁵We first learn our gender role from our family or caretakers. ⁶The lessons begin in infancy and continue throughout childhood. ⁷Parents let their preschool sons roam farther from home than their preschool daughters. ⁸They encourage rough-and-tumble play in boys. ⁹They also urge them to get dirtier and be more defiant.

¹⁰Other influences come from the mass media, especially television. ¹¹Television reinforces stereotypes of the sexes. ¹²For example, there are more male characters than female characters. ¹³Male characters have higher-status positions. ¹⁴Sports news also maintains traditional stereotypes. ¹⁵Women athletes receive little coverage. ¹⁶Also, male newscasters give women's achievements less importance.

(Adapted from *Essentials of Sociology* by James M. Henslin)

LO 2 Subject-Verb Agreement and the Present Tense

Tense is the form of the verb that shows when an action or state happens. **Present tense** is a verb form used to write about an action or state that is (1) happening now, (2) happens all the time, or (3) is a fact.

Happening now

Past   Present   Future

Video games are more popular than ever before.

Happens all the time, is repeated or habitual

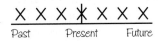

Past   Present   Future

Many male college students relieve stress by escaping into video games.

Max usually plays video games after dinner.

Is a fact (always true)

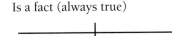

Past   Present   Future

A video game is an electronic computerized activity.

The present tense form changes to match the subject in person and number. The present tense has two forms, the base form or the *-s/-es* form.

Subject	Base form of verb
I, you, we, they plural nouns	enjoy
Subject	*-s* or *-es* form of verb
he, she, it, singular and noncount nouns	enjoys

 Many nouns that end in -s are plural. A verb with an -s ending is singular. If you are not sure if a noun with an -s ending is singular or plural, consult a dictionary.

Incorrect: The boys plays a video game.

Correct: The boys play a video game.

See page 380 for examples of singular subjects that end in -s.

PRACTICE 21.1 Making Subjects and Present Tense Verbs Agree

Write the correct present tense form of each verb in the parentheses.

Example: Video games <u>expose</u> players to action. (expose)

1. They also _____ players powerful ideas and images about gender. (give)
2. Some video games _____ gender stereotypes. (show)
3. Many video games _____ females passive or background characters. (make)
4. Lara Croft *breaks* the stereotypical gender role. (break)
5. Digital fantasy girl Lara Croft *stars* in *Tomb Raiders* and its many sequels. (star)
6. With both guns blazing, Lara *conquer* her enemies with intelligence and strength. (conquer)
7. Lara Croft *reflect* women's changing role in society. (reflect)

Irregular Present Tense Verbs: *Be, Have, Do*

Some verbs are irregular and form the present tense differently. *Be, have,* and *do* are three verbs that have their own forms. The following chart shows the present tense forms of each of these verbs.

Present Tense Forms of *Be, Have,* and *Do*			
	Be	*Have*	*Do*
Singular Subject			
First person	I am.	I have.	I do.
Second person	You are.	You have.	You do.
Third person	He is.	He has.	He does.
Singular and noncount nouns	She is.	She has.	She does.
	It is.	It has.	It does.
Plural Subject			
First person	We are.	We have.	We do.
Second person	You are.	You have.	You do.
Third person and plural nouns	They are.	They have.	They do.

TIP	When forms of *be* are used as linking verbs, they must agree with their subjects.
	Darren's favorite activity is video game competitions.

PRACTICE 21.2 Writing the Correct Present Tense Form of *Be, Have,* and *Do*

Write the correct present tense form of <u>be, have,</u> or <u>do</u> as indicated in the parentheses for each sentence.

Example: Gender __is__ the behaviors and attitudes for males and females in a society. (be)

1. Each human group _has_ its ideas of "maleness" and "femaleness." (have)
2. A person's sex _is_ inherited, but his or her gender is learned. (be)
3. Society _has_ a role in teaching people about gender. (have)
4. Ideas of gender _are_ different from one culture to another. (be)
5. Each gender group _does_ what is expected. (do)
6. They _are_ also given different privileges in their society. (be)
7. Society's gender rules _are_ responsible for opening or closing doors to property and power. (be)

Be, Have, and *Do* as Helping Verbs

Forms of *be, do,* and *have* are used as helping verbs to form other verb tenses. Notice how the subjects and helping verbs agree in each of the sentences below:

Subject-Verb Agreement with Helping Verbs	
Be helping verbs: *am, is, are, was, were*	I am working on my sociology project right now.
	Jose is working on his sociology project right now.
	The students are working on their sociology projects right now.
	Sara was typing her sociology paper when the power went out.
	Last night the students were preparing their PowerPoint presentation when the power went out.
Have helping verbs: *has, have*	Sara has studied about social organizations in her sociology class.
	Some sociologists have studied social organizations.
Do helping verbs: *does, do*	Sara does want to major in sociology.
Do can add emphasis to the main verb or can form a negative sentence.	Sara does not want to specialize in medical sociology.
	Many students do not know much about sociology.

Agreement rules do not apply to *has* or *have* when it is the second of two helping verbs or with *can, could, shall, should, will, would, may, might,* or *must.*

Marci could have decided to live at home after graduation.

Marci could decide to live at home after graduation.

Agreement rules also do not apply to past tense verb forms that do not have helping verbs.

Marci decided to live at home after graduation.

> **TIPS** | Avoid common errors with *be*.
>
> *is*
> Jose ~~be~~ working on his sociology project.
>
> *is*
> Jose working on his sociology project.

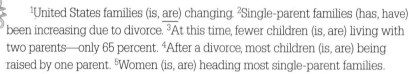

PRACTICE   Choosing the Correct Helping Verbs

21.3   Underline the correct forms of the helping verbs in the next selection.

¹United States families (is, <u>are</u>) changing. ²Single-parent families (has, have) been increasing due to divorce. ³At this time, fewer children (is, are) living with two parents—only 65 percent. ⁴After a divorce, most children (is, are) being raised by one parent. ⁵Women (is, are) heading most single-parent families.

⁶Divorce (do, does) present difficulties for children. ⁷Adjustment problems (is, are) known to continue into adulthood. ⁸Many divorced fathers (does, do) not maintain ongoing relationships with their children. ⁹Also, financial difficulties (is, are) known to be greater for the former wives. ¹⁰Usually, single female parents (is, are) not able to earn as much as their former husbands. ¹¹For single mothers, poverty (have, has) become the primary strain.

(Adapted from *Essentials of Sociology* by James M. Henslin)

LO 3 Subject-Verb Agreement with Singular Subjects

Singular subjects take singular verbs. Usually, a singular subject is easy to figure out. For example, words like *school*, *education*, *student*, and *college* are clearly singular.

The college offers many degree and certificate programs.

Some subjects do not seem to be singular, but they are singular. Study the following chart to learn about them.

Singular Subjects that May Not Seem Singular	
Singular subject	**Example**
-ing subjects: writing, studying, teaching	Teaching has many rewards.
Companies and organizations: ■ Honda, Nintendo, Starbucks, Walgreens ■ Environmental Protection Agency, Disabled American Veterans, Mothers Against Drunk Driving	Mothers Against Drunk Driving (MADD) has a mission to stop drunk driving and to help victims of this violent crime.
Singular nouns ending in *-s*: ■ athletics, economics, politics, mathematics ■ measles, AIDS, news ■ United States, Paris, Buenos Aires	Mathematics is Pat's best subject.
Titles: *Joy Luck Club*, *Kite Runner*, *Fundamentals of Nursing*, "The Star-Spangled Banner"	*Kite Runner* tells the story of a young boy from Kabul who betrays his best friend and lives his life regretting it.
Hours, minutes when considered units of time: three hours, ten minutes	Sixty minutes is not enough time to write a polished essay.
Two subjects that express a single idea: spaghetti and meatballs, peanut butter and jelly, red beans and rice	Spaghetti and meatballs makes a delicious meal.

PRACTICE   Identifying Correct Verb Forms for Singular Subjects

21.4   Circle the correct form of the verb that agrees with the subject in each of the following sentences. You may want to cross out prepositional phrases to help you find the subjects.

*Grammar Reminder.
For more help with
finding subjects and
verbs, see Chapter 18.*

Example: Self-knowledge (help, helps) a person make choices.

1. Self-knowledge about your areas of ability (help, helps) you explore majors and choose careers.
2. The theory of multiple intelligences (was, were) developed by Howard Gardner in 1983.
3. Gardner's first book on multiple intelligences (was, were) called *Frames of Mind.*
4. Ten years of research (was, were) reported in this first book.
5. *Multiple Intelligences* (is, are) his latest book, which includes the most recent developments and research.
6. Gardner's definition of intelligence (take, takes) the concept of intelligence beyond what a standard IQ test can measure.
7. His theory (state, states) that people have a different range of intelligences for solving different kinds of problems.

LO 4 Subject-Verb Agreement with Plural Subjects

Plural subjects take plural verbs. Many plural subjects such as *schools, students, classes,* and *colleges* are easy to identify.

The students in my sociology class like to study for tests in study groups.

Compound Subjects

Some sentences have more than one subject, called a **compound subject**. A compound subject is joined by any of these words: *and, or, nor, either/or, neither/nor,* and *not only/but also.*

Compound Subjects Joined by *And*

Compound subjects joined by *and* take plural verbs.

Two singular compound subjects	A high school diploma and a college degree open doors of opportunity.
Two plural compound subjects	In high school, ability groupings and educational tracks affect students' educational opportunities.

> **TIP** | To check the verb form, substitute the pronoun *they* for the compound subject.

PRACTICE   Choosing the Correct Verbs for Plural and Compound Subjects
21.5   Circle the correct verbs in the following sentences.

Example: Some U.S. high schools (place, places) students into one of three tracks.
  1. General, college prep, and honors (is, are) the three tracks.
  2. Students on the lowest track (tends, tend) to go to work after high school.
  3. Sometimes, these high school graduates (takes, take) vocational courses.
  4. The honors groups usually (attends, attend) well-respected colleges.
  5. Local colleges and regional universities (attracts, attract) students in the middle track.
  6. Jobs, income, and lifestyle (is, are) affected by tracking.
  7. Schools now (assigns, assign) students to ability groups.
  8. Researchers (disagrees, disagree) on the benefits of ability grouping.
  9. Labeling and segregation (creates, create) problems for students' self-esteem.
  10. Emphasis on cooperation and sharing in the classroom (contributes, contribute) to learning and (is, are) a better alternative to ability grouping.

(Adapted from *Essentials of Sociology* by James M. Henslin)

Compound Subjects Joined with *Or, Nor, Either/or, Neither/nor, Not only/but also*

When two subjects are joined with *or, nor, either/or, neither/nor,* or *not only/but also,* the verb agrees with the subject closest to the verb.

Either/or   Either Professor Thorner or Professor Calle is going to teach the film as literature course.

Neither/nor   Neither the professor nor the students come to the college on Fridays.

Intervening Phrases

Prepositional phrases and phrases like *along with, as well as, together with,* and *in addition to* usually do not affect subject-verb agreement.

Each student in my English class at the college wants to succeed.

The teachers at my college help students succeed.

Patriotism as well as national identity is taught in U. S. schools.

Plural Subjects That Seem Singular

Some single-word subjects seem like one thing but are considered plural.

Plural Subject	Example
Single things with parts: binoculars, glasses, scissors, tweezers, shorts, jeans, pants	Jeans are a popular wardrobe item.
Sports teams: New York Giants, Miami Heat, Utah Jazz, Philadelphia Phillies	The Miami Heat were formed in 1988 and won the 2006 NBA finals.
Decades: 1930s, 1960s	The 1960s are known in popular culture as the decade of social revolution.

PRACTICE   Identifying Correct Verb Forms
21.6
Circle the correct verb in each of the following sentences.

Example: Over one million children (is, are) currently being home schooled.

1. The 1950s (is, are) the decade when home schooling started.
2. Two of every 100 students across the United States (is, are) being taught at home.
3. Home schoolers (receives, receive) an intense, one-on-one education.
4. Mothers (teaches, teach) 90 percent of the students.
5. Most fathers of home schooled students (is, are) in the labor force.
6. Neither behavior issues nor isolation (is, are) a problem for home schoolers.
7. Sports programs or physical education through the public schools (is, are) available to home schooled children.
8. **Peer pressure**, bullies, and competition (does, do) not harm a home schooler's self-esteem.
9. Neither teenage trends nor dangerous experimentation (influences, influence) their lives.
10. Mothers and fathers (has, have) to sacrifice a loss in income because one parent must stay home, but they feel that the sacrifice is worth it in the long run.

(Adapted from *Essentials of Sociology* by James M. Henslin)

peer pressure social pressure on somebody to adopt a type of behavior, dress, or attitude in order to be accepted as part of a group

LO 5   Subject-Verb Agreement with Other Subjects
Indefinite Pronoun Subjects

Indefinite pronouns are words that refer to nonspecific people or things. Some indefinite pronoun subjects are always singular or always plural, while others can be singular or plural.

Singular Indefinite Pronouns as Subjects

anyone	someone	no one	everyone
anybody	somebody	nobody	everybody
anything	something	nothing	everything
another	one	other	each
either	neither		

Everyone wants to be a part of a group.

One meets that need by being a member of a group.

One of the sociologists says that the group we choose influences our behavior.

Anyone gets messages about conformity and deviance from their group.

Plural Indefinite Pronoun Subjects

both	few	many
	others	several

Many of the researchers say that family is important for teaching values.

Others point out that delinquents often come from families that get in trouble with the law.

Singular or Plural Indefinite Pronoun Subjects Some indefinite pronouns can be singular or plural. To decide if the indefinite pronoun subject is singular or plural, look at the noun or pronoun in the phrase that follows it. If the word in the phrase is singular, then the verb is singular; if the word in the phrase is plural, then the verb is plural. This rule also applies to fractions and percentages.

> all   any   most
>   none   some

Most of us have strong inner desires to do things that get us in trouble.

Most of this desire gets stifled.

All of our behavior is based on our inner and outer controls.

Some of our inner controls include conscience and ideas of right and wrong.

Twenty percent of teenagers know someone in a gang.

TIP	A helpful way to remember the indefinite pronouns that can be singular or plural is by the acronym **SANAM**, **s**ome, **a**ny, **n**one, **a**ll, **m**ost.

Collective Noun Subjects

Some words refer to a group of people or things. They are called **group** or **collective nouns**. They can describe the group as a whole (only one) or the individuals in the group (more than one).

Common Collective Nouns

army	class	crowd	group	senate
audience	club	family	jury	society
band	committee	gang	public	team

When the word describes the group as a whole, then it is singular. All members of the group are acting as one, all doing the same thing or thinking the same way. The verb is singular.

    The international student club meets on Monday afternoons.

When the word describes the individuals in the group, then it is plural. The members of the group are acting individually. The verb is plural.

    The international student club disagree on the way to raise money.

PRACTICE **Editing for Subject-Verb Agreement with Indefinite**
21.7   **Pronouns and Group Words**

Circle any verbs that do not agree with their subjects and write the correct verb. Write *C* if the sentence is correct.

Example: One of the best examples of deviant groups are motorcycle gangs. is

1. One of the studies are the result of sociologist Mark Watson's living with and observing outlaw bikers.

2. Each of the outlaw bikers see the world as hostile and weak.

3. Everyone prides himself on looking dirty and mean.

4. No one get in their way.

5. Many treat women as lesser beings.

6. The gang devalue women.

7. Few thinks of themselves as winners in life.

8. Ninety-five percent of the bikers believes they are losers.

9. All of them takes pleasure in shocking people with their appearance.

10. The police has been having more trouble going undercover in the biker gangs.

(Adapted from *Essentials of Sociology* by James M. Henslin)

Inverted Subjects

In some sentences, the subject does not come first. Notice the position of the subjects and verbs in the following sentences.

Sentences Beginning with *Here/There* In most sentences that begin with *here* or *there*, the subject comes after the verb. Neither *here* nor *there* is the subject of the sentence.

> **There** are many groups that make up our society.

Sentences Beginning with Prepositional Phrases In some sentences that begin with one or more prepositional phrases, the subject may follow the verb.

> Among the important groups in our lives is our family.

Questions In questions that begin with verbs, the subject follows the verb or comes between the helping verb and the main verb.

> Are friendship groups important to our well-being?
>
> Do friendships offer a sense of belonging?

Sentences with Dependent Clauses Beginning with *Who, Which*, or *That* *Who, which*, and *that* are relative pronouns that take the place of subjects when they begin dependent clauses. The verb in the dependent clause should agree with the word that the relative pronoun refers to.

> As humans, we have an intense need for face-to-face interaction that gives us feelings of self-esteem.

PRACTICE Identifying Subjects and Correct Verbs When
21.8 Subjects Do Not Come First

Underline the subjects and circle the correct verbs in the following sentences.

Example: There (is, are) six types of groups that make up society.

1. Primary groups, which (offers, offer) us a feeling of belonging, are our family and friends.

2. From family's and friends' values (comes, come) the way we view life.

3. (Is, Are) you a member of many secondary groups?

4. The secondary group that (base, bases) its membership on a common interest or activity is the second type.

5. (Do, Does) the people in your group (feels, feel) loyal to each other?

6. There (is, are) groups that we use as standards to evaluate ourselves.

7. The social network group (refer, refers) to people who (is, are) linked to one another.

8. People within social networks (form, forms) groups that are called cliques.

9. There (has, have) been a new group that was discovered in the late 1990s called the electronic community.

10. (Do, Does) you or your friends (belongs, belong) to any electronic social networking sites?

(Adapted from *Essentials of Sociology* by James M. Henslin)

Writing Assignments

Review: Subject-Verb Agreement

Correct the nine subject-verb agreement errors in the following passage.

Example: [1]Why do people in poverty-stricken countries <u>has</u> so many children? [have]

[2]To understand this, we must understand why Celia and Angel are so happy about having their thirteenth child. [3]We must take the role of the other to understand how they see it. [4]Celia and Angel's culture tell them that twelve children ~~is~~ *are* not enough for three reasons.

[5]The first reason is the status of parenthood. [6]In the least industrialized nations, motherhood ~~is~~ *are* the most prized status a woman achieve. [7]The more children a woman ~~give~~ *given* birth to, the more she is thought to have achieved the purpose for which she was born. [8]Similarly, <u>a man prove his manhood by fathering children</u>. [9]The more children he fathers, especially sons, the better because through them, his name live on.

[10]Second, the community support this view. [11]The last reason is that for poor people, children are economic assets. [12]They begin contributing to the family income at a young age. [13]Their government do not provide social security or medical and unemployment insurance. [14]This motivate people to bear more children so that the children can take care of them when they become too old to work or when no work is to be found.

(Adapted from *Essentials of Sociology* by James M. Henslin)

Write about an Image

The photograph shows groups of dried fruit and nuts that are alike. Most of us have belonged to groups at some point in our lives. Practice subject-verb agreement by writing five sentences about one or several of the groups you have belonged to in your lifetime. The group could be associated with school, athletics, dance, teams, religion, music, vehicles (cars, trucks, bikes, etc.), self-help, charity, and so on. If you prefer, write your sentences about the food groups in the photo below.

1. Use a compound subject.
2. Use a group word subject.
3. Use an indefinite pronoun subject.
4. Use a dependent clause starting with who, which, or that.
5. Write a yes/no question.

English Success Tip: Something Doesn't Have to Sound Right to Be Right

Some of the grammar forms you are learning in this book may sound different from the ones that you use or hear every day. For example, which of the following sentences seems right to you?

A. Him and I like to learn about other cultures.
B. Him and me like to learn about other cultures.
C. He and I like to learn about other cultures.

If you picked sentence C, you were correct. C is the correct Standard Written English form, the accepted form for written English. To be successful in college writing and beyond, you need to know how to write using the accepted form.

You may have heard A or B in conversation, so one of those sentences sounded right to you. However, conversational English is informal, so many forms of English are acceptable. Most people do not speak the way they write.

Sometimes a sentence that sounds right is right, but to be sure, check the rules for Standard English.

For support in meeting this chapter's objectives, log in to www.mywritinglab.com, go to the Study Plan tab, click on **Understanding Subject-Verb Agreement** and choose **Subject-Verb Agreement** from the list of subtopics. Read and view the videos and resources in the Review Materials section, and then complete the Recall, Apply, and Write exercises in the Activities section. You can check your scores and overall progress by using the Gradebook.

CHAPTER 22

Past Tense

Theme: *Humanities*

Learning Objectives

After working through this chapter, you will be able to:

LO 1 Define past tense.

LO 2 Form the past tense for regular and irregular verbs.

LO 3 Form questions and negative statements in the past tense.

LO 1 What Is the Past Tense?

The **past tense** is a verb form that expresses an action or state that began and ended at one specific time in the past. The diagram shows when a past tense action or state occurred.

Past · · · · X | · · · · Future
Past   Present   Future

Thomas Edison and W. K. Laurie Dickson invented the Kinetoscope in 1889. The kinetoscope was the first continuous-film motion-picture viewing machine.

Past Tense in Context

In the following passage about silent movies, the past tense verb forms are highlighted.

> Before movies had sound, movies were by no means "silent." Every theater had a piano or organ to provide musical accompaniment to the films it projected. This made cinema a multimedia event. A live musician or orchestra reacted to and participated in the presentation of the film.
>
> The introduction of sound radically changed the motion-picture industry. For one thing, theaters everywhere had to be wired, a process that took several years to accomplish. For another, putting sound into the film itself changed the culture of film viewing. In the 1920s, the cinema was the world's largest employer of musicians. Then, just as the Great Depression hit in 1929, thousands of cinema musicians found themselves out of work.
>
> Sound also changed the nature of acting in the cinema. Before sound, communication with the audience depended on facial expression and physical gesture, often exaggerated. Now actors had to rely on speech to communicate, and many silent-era stars simply lacked a powerful voice. Dialogue writing became important, so **playwrights** gained influence. Finally, sound brought foreign languages into the theaters.
>
> (Adapted from *The Humanities*, Book 6, by Henry M. Sayre)

playwright someone who writes plays

LO 2 Past Tense Forms

Past tense verb forms can be regular or irregular. Regular verbs form the past tense by adding a -*d* or -*ed* to the end, while irregular verbs do not follow this pattern. Past tense verbs **do not** change form to agree with singular and plural subjects.

I enjoyed the movie, and my parents enjoyed it, too.

TIP	*Was* or *were* is not added to the verb to form the past tense.
	He ~~was go~~ home last night.

went (above "was go")

Regular Past Tense Verb Forms

Regular verbs are so named because they always form the past tense by adding a -*d* or -*ed* to the end of the base form of the verb. The base form is the verb without any endings added to it.

I, he, she, it watched the film.

We, you, they watched the film.

Spelling of Regular Past Tense Verbs Some verbs change their spellings when adding -*d* or -*ed* endings. The spelling rules are explained in the following chart:

Spelling Rules for Regular Past Tense Verbs			
If the verb ends in	**Make the past tense**	**Example**	
-*e*	Add -*d*	change	changed
consonant + *y*	Change -*y* to -*i* and add -*ed*	apply	applied
one vowel + one consonant (not *w* or *y*)	Double the consonant and add -*ed*	clap	clapped
-*c*	Add -*ked*	panic	panicked
all other endings	Add -*ed*	react	reacted

PRACTICE Writing Correct Regular Past Tense Verbs

22.1   Write the past form of the each verb in parentheses. Don't forget to check the spelling.

Example: In 1888, George Eastman (invent) ____invented____ celluloid film for a new camera called the Kodak.

1. W. K. Laurie Dickson (devise) _____ a wheel with teeth to move the roll of film.

2. Thomas Edison (decide) _____ on a 35-millimeter width for the film strip of his new motion-picture camera.

3. To see the film, only one person at a time (watch) _____ through a small hole.

4. Each film (stop) _____ after about twenty seconds.

5. People (enjoy) _____ these short movies in viewing parlors.

6. The first movies shown to a large audience (occur) _____ on December 28, 1895.

7. That night, August and Louis Lumière (show) _____ the audience ten films that lasted for about twenty minutes.

8. Another famous Lumière brothers' film (depict) _____ a single train arriving at a station.

9. The audience (panic) _____ as the train got closer to the camera because it seemed so real to them.

10. The first comedy was a two-second movie in which a boy (step) _____ on a gardener's hose, stopping the flow of water. When the boy got off the hose, the water (spray) _____ all over the gardener, who chased the boy.

(Adapted from *The Humanities* by Henry Sayre)

Irregular Past Tense Verb Forms

Irregular verbs do not form the past tense by adding *-d* or *-ed*. There are about 200 irregular verbs in English. The following chart lists the most commonly used irregular verbs in the past tense. The base form is given first, and next to it is the past tense form.

Irregular Past Tense Verbs			
Base verb	**Past form**	**Base verb**	**Past form**
arise	arose	do	did
awake	awoke	drink	drank
be	was, were	drive	drove
beat	beat	eat	ate
become	became	fall	fell
begin	began	feed	fed
blow	blew	feel	felt
break	broke	fight	fought
bring	brought	find	found
build	built	fit	fit
burst	burst	fly	flew
buy	bought	forbid	forbade
catch	caught	forget	forgot
choose	chose	forgive	forgave
come	came	freeze	froze
cut	cut	get	got
deal	dealt	give	gave

(Continued)

Irregular Past Tense Verbs (*Continued*)

Base verb	Past form	Base verb	Past form
go	went	seek	sought
grow	grew	sell	sold
have	had	send	sent
hear	heard	set	set
hide	hid	shake	shook
hit	hit	shine	shone
hold	held	sing	sang
hurt	hurt	sit	sat
keep	kept	sleep	slept
know	knew	speak	spoke
lay	laid	spend	spent
lead	led	spring	sprang
leave	left	stand	stood
let	let	steal	stole
lie	lay	swim	swam
lose	lost	swing	swung
make	made	take	took
meet	met	teach	taught
pay	paid	tear	tore
quit	quit	tell	told
read	read	think	thought
ride	rode	throw	threw
ring	rang	understand	understood
rise	rose	wake	woke
run	ran	wear	wore
say	said	win	won
see	saw	write	wrote

PRACTICE   Writing Irregular Past Tense Verbs

22.2   Fill in the correct past tense form of each irregular verb in the parentheses.

Example: [1]At the end of the 1800s, motion pictures (be) _____were_____ merely an interesting novelty.

²That changed when businessmen (understand) _____ their real motion picture audience. ³At that time, thousands of immigrants (come) _____ to the United States mostly from southern and central Europe. ⁴They lived in overcrowded apartment houses in city slums and (do) _____ not have much money to pay for entertainment. ⁵However, they (have) _____ a nickel (approximately $1 in today's money) to pay for a movie.

⁶In 1905, the nickelodeon theater (bring) _____ motion pictures to the masses. ⁷By 1910, the number of nickelodeon theaters (grow) _____ to 10,000 in the United States. ⁸The nickelodeon (begin) _____ to offer a variety of films. ⁹Most films (run) _____ for ten to fifteen minutes.

¹⁰Vitagraph, an early movie producer, (give) _____ viewers a military film, a drama, a Western, a comedy, and a special feature each week. ¹¹Working-class immigrants who did not know much English (feel) _____ comfortable watching these silent films because language was not an obstacle.

(Adapted from *The Humanities* by Henry Sayre)

Easily Confused Past Tense Forms

The Irregular Verb *Be* Past tense verbs usually have one form with the exception of the past tense of the irregular verb *be*, which has two forms: *was* and *were*.

Subject	Singular	Plural
First person subject	I was	We were
Second person subject	You were	You were
Third person subject	He was She was It was The student was	They were The students were

TIP Some languages and dialects omit forms of *be*, but Standard English does not.

Vernacular	Standard English
He be early. (meaning temporarily)	He was early this morning.
We early. (meaning habitually)	We are early every day.

PRACTICE Using the Past Tense of *Be*

22.3 For each of the following sentences, write *was* or *were* in the space provided. Use *was* for first and third person subjects (I, he, she, or it).

Example: [1]The early nickelodeon films _____ were _____ short.

[2]Most _____ on one reel; they held 1,000 feet of film and ran ten to fifteen minutes. [3]Audiences wanted to see movies that _____ longer. [4]D. W. Griffith _____ the person who met the demand. [5]He _____ the foremost single-reel director at that time. [6]His film *The Birth of a Nation* had its first public showing in 1915 and _____ a big success. [7]*The Birth of a Nation* _____ about the Civil War and Reconstruction, a period in United States history; the film _____ controversial because of its racist elements. [8]The film's box office receipts _____ the largest in film history.

[9]An important aspect of *The Birth of a Nation* _____ the number of camera shots Griffith invented to create visual variety in film. [10]Some of these _____ the full shot, the medium shot, the close up, and the long shot. [11]Griffith's film techniques _____ responsible for influencing every film since then; however, the film is a painful record of racist views in America in 1915.

(Adapted from *The Humanities* by Henry Sayre)

LO 3 Questions and Negative Sentences

To write a question or a negative sentence in the past tense, add the helping verb **did**. Do not add a *-d* or *-ed* to the base verb. The helping verb shows the verb tense of the sentence.

Past	Question	Negative Sentence
The students took a humanities course.	Did the students take a humanities course?	The students did not take a humanities course.
They learned about art, history, and philosophy.	Did they learn about art, history, and philosophy?	They did not learn about art, history, or philosophy.

When the main verb is *was* or *were*, no helping verb is needed to form a question or a negative sentence in the past tense.

Past	Question	Negative Sentence
The course was enjoyable.	Was the course enjoyable?	The course was not enjoyable.

> **TIP** | In college writing assignments, write out the verb form and the word *not*. Although contractions are acceptable in spoken English, they are not preferred in academic writing.
>
> did not
> The students ~~didn't~~ take a humanities course.

PRACTICE 22.4 Forming Questions and Negative Sentences

Part A Forming Questions

Change the sentence into a question:

Example: Leonardo da Vinci was a famous artist.

Was Leonardo da Vinci a famous artist? _____

1. Da Vinci lived from 1452 to 1519.

_____

2. Da Vinci liked to show the personality of the people he painted.

_____

3. He was famous for his painting the *Mona Lisa*.

_____

mysterious referring to something that has not yet been explained or understood

4. The woman in the painting had a **mysterious** smile.

_____

5. For many years, people wanted to know the reason for her smile.

_____

Part B Forming Negative Sentences

Make each of the sentences in Part A untrue by changing them to negative sentences.

Example: Leonardo da Vinci was not a famous artist.

1. _____
2. _____
3. _____
4. _____
5. _____

Writing Assignments

Review: Past Tense

Write the correct past tense form for each of the verbs in the parentheses.

Example: In 1914, nearly 90 percent of all African Americans (live) _____lived_____ in the South.

boll weevil infestation the spread of a beetle pest in the cotton crop

¹As millions of men in the North (go) _____ to fight in Europe during the First World War, a huge demand for labor followed. ²Because of the demand for labor, Southern blacks (begin) _____ to move north—between 200,000 and 350,000 in the years 1915 to 1918 alone. ³Also, in the 1920s, a **boll weevil infestation** (hurt) _____ the cotton crop industry, causing more people to move North. ⁴Many others (leave) _____ to escape racial discrimination and segregation.

⁵The African-American population (grow) _____ 40 percent in the Northern states, mostly in the largest cities like Detroit, Chicago, and New York City. ⁶Many educated and socially conscious African Americans (choose) _____ to settle in Harlem, a neighborhood in New York City. ⁷Harlem (become) _____ a center for culture and politics for black America.

⁸A movement called the Harlem Renaissance (arise) _____. ⁹This movement (bring) _____ up major issues that affected the lives of African Americans at that time. ¹⁰People (give) _____ expression to the issues of racism and social inequality. ¹¹Through art, literature, music, drama, painting, sculpture, movies, and protests, people (communicate) _____ the most essential part of the African-American experience.

¹²The Harlem Renaissance affirmed that African Americans (have) _____ a unique cultural heritage. ¹³The movement (be) _____ a celebration of heritage and racial pride. ¹⁴The influence of the Harlem Renaissance (spread) _____ throughout the nation.

(Adapted from *The Humanities* by Henry M. Sayre)

Write about an Image

Find a photograph of yourself when you were younger. If you do not have a picture, imagine how you looked at a time in your past or write about one of the children in the photo. Practice using the past tense verb forms you learned about in this chapter by writing at least five original sentences describing yourself at the time the photo was taken. You can write about your height, weight, hair and eye color, clothing style, hairstyle, jewelry, tattoos, and so on.

English Success Tip: **Avoiding Verb Tense Shifts**

When writing about events that happened in the past, avoid shifting your verb tense to the present. Shifting from past to present makes it difficult for readers to understand when events happened. Shifts from past to present are most likely to happen in papers that give story examples, give the details of an event in history, or discuss lab results.

Here is an example from a student's paper. The story is about the past, but the writer shifts into the present. The verb shifts to the present are highlighted:

> My relationship with my ex-boyfriend taught me not to be a jealous girlfriend. For example, on our six-month anniversary, we went to a nightclub to celebrate. As we walk into the club, I see him walk up to another girl that I do not even know. He stands there talking to her for about ten minutes and leaves me in a corner all by myself. I got upset and angry. We ended up fighting the entire time we were at the club.

To avoid verb shifts from past to present, underline each verb to check that it is in the right tense.

For support in meeting this chapter's objectives, log in to www.mywritinglab.com, go to the Study Plan tab, click on **Past Tense** and choose **Tense and Regular and Irregular Verbs** from the list of subtopics. Read and view the videos and resources in the Review Materials section, and then complete the Recall, Apply, and Write exercises in the Activities section. You can check your scores and overall progress by using the Gradebook.

Past Participles

Theme: *Criminal Justice*

Learning Objectives

After working through this chapter, you will be able to:

LO 1 List the uses of past participles.

LO 2 Form regular and irregular past participles.

LO 3 Use the present perfect tense.

LO 4 Use the past perfect tenses.

LO 5 Use passive voice.

LO 6 Use past participles as adjectives.

LO 1 What Is a Past Participle?

A **past participle** is a verb form that is used to make the present perfect and past perfect tenses, to form passive voice, and to describe nouns.

Present perfect tense *HAS/HAVE* + PAST PARTICIPLE	The number of students studying criminal justice has grown.
Past perfect tense *HAD* + PAST PARTICIPLE	Police departments had increased their recruiting efforts before the county cut taxes.
Passive voice FORM OF *BE* + PAST PARTICIPLE	People who speak a foreign language are given bonuses by police recruiters.
To describe nouns (as adjectives)	Many police departments have job openings for interested candidates.

Past Participles in Context

¹A mere 200 years ago, before people were imprisoned, convicted law breakers were routinely subjected to physical punishment that often resulted in death. ²Physical punishment fit the doctrine of *lex talionis*, the law of retaliation. ³Under *lex talionis,* the convicted offender was sentenced to a punishment that was close to the original injury. ⁴This rule of "an eye for an eye, a tooth for a tooth" generally duplicated the offense. ⁵If a person had blinded another, he was blinded in return. ⁶Murderers were executed, sometimes by the same method they had used in committing the crime. ⁷In an important historical development, around the year 1800, the purpose for imprisonment changed. ⁸Prisoners were no longer imprisoned to be physically punished; instead they were imprisoned as punishment.

⁹Since that time, the effort has been to humanize the treatment of offenders. ¹⁰However, previous attempts at rehabilitation had failed because large numbers of offenders returned to crime and to prison. ¹¹By 1995, the prison system had focused completely on the concept of just deserts. ¹²This

concept bases the amount of punishment on how bad the crime is. [13]"Get tough" actions have resulted in longer mandatory prison sentences, increased use of life without parole, and increased development of maximum-security prisons. [14]Many states have also adopted "three strikes you're out" laws, which mandate long prison terms for criminal offenders convicted of a third violent crime or felony.

(Adapted from *Criminal Justice Today* by Frank Schmalleger)

LO 2 Regular and Irregular Past Participles

Past participles are either regular or irregular. Regular past participles are formed by adding -d or -ed to the base verb. The base verb is the verb without any endings added to it.

The Internet has changed the way people break the law.

Irregular past participles end in a variety of ways.

Law enforcement teams have found it difficult to keep up with Internet crime, but they have made progress.

The following chart lists the past forms and past participles of commonly used irregular verbs.

Irregular Past Participles		
Base Verb	Past Tense	Past Participle
Verbs with All Forms the Same		
burst	burst	burst
cut	cut	cut
fit	fit	fit
hit	hit	hit
hurt	hurt	hurt
let	let	let
quit	quit	quit
read	read	read
set	set	set
Verbs with the Same Base and Past Participle Forms		
become	became	become
come	came	come
run	ran	run
Verbs with the Same Past Tense and Past Participle Forms		
bring	brought	brought
build	built	built
buy	bought	bought
catch	caught	caught
deal	dealt	dealt
		(Continued)

Irregular Past Participles (*Continued*)

Base Verb	Past Tense	Past Participle
Verbs with the Same Past Tense and Past Participle Forms		
feed	fed	fed
fight	fought	fought
find	found	found
get	got	got/gotten
have	had	had
hear	heard	heard
hold	held	held
keep	kept	kept
lay	laid	laid
lead	led	led
leave	left	left
lose	lost	lost
make	made	made
meet	met	met
pay	paid	paid
say	said	said
seek	sought	sought
sell	sold	sold
send	sent	sent
shine	shone	shone
sit	sat	sat
sleep	slept	slept
spend	spent	spent
stand	stood	stood
swing	swung	swung
teach	taught	taught
tell	told	told
think	thought	thought
try	tried	tried
understand	understood	understood
win	won	won
Verbs with All Forms Different		
arise	arose	arisen
awake	awoke	awoken
be	was, were	been
begin	began	begun
blow	blew	blown
break	broke	broken
choose	chose	chosen
do	did	done
drink	drank	drunk
drive	drove	driven
eat	ate	eaten
fall	fell	fallen

(*Continued*)

Irregular Past Participles (Continued)		
Base Verb	Past Tense	Past Participle
Verbs with All Forms Different		
fly	flew	flown
forbid	forbade	forbidden
forget	forgot	forgotten
forgive	forgave	forgiven
freeze	froze	frozen
give	gave	given
go	went	gone
grow	grew	grown
hide	hid	hidden
know	knew	known
lie	lay	lain
ride	rode	ridden
ring	rang	rung
rise	rose	risen
see	saw	seen
shake	shook	shaken
sing	sang	sung
speak	spoke	spoken
spring	sprang	sprung
steal	stole	stolen
swim	swam	swum
take	took	taken
tear	tore	torn
wake	woke	woken
wear	wore	worn
write	wrote	written
Verbs with the Same Base and Past Form		
beat	beat	beaten

TIP | Many of the irregular past tense and past participle forms are different. The past participle must have a helping verb in front of it, but the past tense does not.

> *gone*
> He could have ~~went~~ to the police academy for training.

> *did*
> He ~~done~~ well on his entrance test.

PRACTICE Using Past Participles

23.1   Fill in the past participle forms of the base verb in the parentheses.

Example: In 2005, the World Health Organization (WHO) discovered that Meridian Bioscience of Cleveland, Ohio, had _____lost_____ (lose) some samples of a potentially dangerous flu virus.

¹The company had _____ (send) samples to over four thousand laboratories in eighteen countries. ²The Bio-kits contained the influenza A (H2N2) virus, which had _____ (cause) the flu pandemic of 1957–1958. ³These kits were _____ on behalf of several U.S. organizations that had _____ (set) testing standards for laboratories.

⁴The organizations had _____ (want) to test the labs' ability to identify flu viruses. ⁵Most of the laboratories were in the United States with some in South America, but the few that were sent to the Arab world had _____ (raise) fears. ⁶The WHO feared that Islamic terrorists had _____ (get) hold of the viral material and had _____ (plan) to use it to spread the disease, creating a worldwide epidemic. ⁷On May 2, 2005, the scare had _____ (end). ⁸The CDC announced that it had _____ (find) the last remaining sample of the virus at the American University of Beirut in Lebanon. ⁹A local delivery service had _____ (misplace) the sample. ¹⁰Someone had _____ (discover) it in a warehouse at the Beirut airport. ¹¹Although the incident had _____ (come) to a successful conclusion, it had _____ (increase) concerns about the spread of contagious flu viruses and possible crimes committed through the use of these substances.

(Adapted from *Criminal Justice Today* by Frank Schmalleger)

PRACTICE   Editing Past Participles

23.2   The past participles are underlined in each of the following sentences. Circle any incorrect past participles and write the correction above them.

led

Example: ¹Research in the area of nutrition has [lead] to the development of biocriminology, a field of study that links violent or disruptive behavior to eating habits, vitamin deficiencies, and other conditions that affect body tissues.

²In one early study in 1943, researchers had tried to find out if chemical imbalances could be a cause of crime. ³Authors of the study had linked murder to hypoglycemia (low blood sugar), which is caused by too much insulin in the blood or by poor nutrition.

⁴A number of studies have report that allergic reactions to common foods have cause violence and homicide; for example, people who have ate foods that they are allergic to can have swelling of the brain and brain stem. ⁵Other studies have prove that food additives, such as monosodium glutamate, dyes, and artificial flavorings, have produce criminal behavior. ⁶The amount of coffee and sugar prisoners have drank is greater than that of the outside population, leading researchers to connect excessive coffee and sugar intake to crime.

[7]Hormones have also <u>came</u> under investigation as having a role in criminal behavior. [8]Some studies of the levels of the male sex hormone, testosterone, have <u>showed</u> a link to aggressive behavior. [9]Sex offenders with high levels of testosterone have <u>became</u> more violent with their victims. [10]In 2007, researchers at the University of Michigan proved young men with higher blood levels of testosterone had <u>enjoy</u> making others angry. [11]Steroid abuse among body-builders has <u>be</u> responsible for destructive urges and psychosis.

LO 3 The Present Perfect Tense

The **present perfect tense** is formed by combining *has* or *have* with the past participle. The present perfect is neither the present nor the past. It connects an action that started in the past and continues to the present. The time it happened is not specific.

Steve has decided to major in criminal justice.

The present perfect tense has several uses, which are explained in the following chart.

Uses of Present Perfect Tense	
Use	**Example**
An action started in the past and is continuing now.	Steve has worked as a prison officer since last January.
	Steve has had his job for six months.
	Use *for* and the amount of time or *since* and the start of the action.
An action repeats in the past and is continuing now. More repetition may occur.	He has found a dozen illegal cell phones in inmates' cells this week.
	Cell phone smuggling into prisons has become a serious problem in the past several years.
	Use words like *this week, today, so far, already*.
An action happened at some nonspecific time in the past.	Steve has witnessed violence among inmates several times.
	Use words like *many, once, several times, recently*.

Comparing Present Perfect to the Past and Present Tenses

The present perfect tense is sometimes confused with the past tense or with the present tense. The following chart explains the differences.

Present Perfect	Present	Past
Steve has worked as a prison officer since last January.	Steve works as a prison officer.	Steve worked as a prison officer.
The action began in the past and continues to the present.	*The action occurs at this moment.*	*The action is completed.*

> **TIP** | Use the past tense, not the present perfect, to state the exact time something happened.
>
> Steve ~~has~~ worked as a prison officer two years ago.

PRACTICE Using the Past and Present Perfect Tenses

23.3   Use the correct form of the past or present perfect tense of the verb in the parentheses to complete this student's paragraph.

¹Today, my college friends think that I am a well-behaved, respectful person. ²However, in high school, I _____ (be) the opposite. ³I never _____ (obey) my teachers, I _____ (curse) at people, and I _____ (write) on desks. ⁴I _____ (do) not respect anyone. ⁵About five years ago, my math teacher _____ (give) me advice. ⁶He _____ (teach) me that respecting others would help me succeed in life. ⁷Since then, I _____ (change) my behavior. ⁸I _____ (learn) to be quiet when my classmates take tests. ⁹After a classmate assaulted me for disrespecting him, I _____ (become) polite when greeting people. ¹⁰In addition, instead of being rude to my teachers, I _____ (be) courteous. ¹¹I am proud to say that I _____ (grow) into a righteous man.

LO 4 The Past Perfect Tense

The **past perfect tense** is formed by combining **had** with the past participle. The past perfect tense is used to talk about two actions that happened in the past. One action finished before the other in the past.

In the following sentence, both actions took place in the past.

Steve had worked as an interrogator in the army before he became an officer at the state prison.

Use the past perfect tense to talk about the earlier event in the past. Use the past tense to talk about the later event in the past.

Past   Present   Future

The past perfect tense is often used in complex sentences. The dependent clauses in the following sentences use the past perfect tense, while the independent clauses use the past tense.

Steve decided to become a state prison guard because he had served as a prison officer during his tour in the army.

After he had taken a few criminal justice courses, he chose law enforcement as his career path.

> **TIP** | When you write about one action in the past that does not include an earlier action, use the past tense, not the past perfect tense.
>
> He ~~had~~ registered for a criminal justice course last semester.

Comparing Past Perfect to Past Tense

Past Perfect

After an inmate's friend had sent him legal research downloaded from the Internet, prison officials seized it.

Two actions happened in the past. One happened before the other in the past.

Past

The prison prohibited prisoners from receiving printed material downloaded from the Internet.

The action was completed in the past.

> **TIP** | Avoid using past tense for two actions in the past when one came before the other.
>
> Steve decided to become a state prison guard because he *had* worked with prisoners in the army.

PRACTICE Using Past and Past Perfect Tenses

23.4 Circle the correct past or past perfect verb form in each of the following sentences:

Example: In 2002, a jury (convicted, had convicted) Andrea Pia Yates for the drowning murders of her five young children.

1. The judge (ordered, had ordered) Yates to serve life in prison.
2. She (wanted, had wanted) to save her children from the devil, so she killed them one at a time.
3. Before she killed her children, Yates (attempted, had attempted) suicide twice.
4. After she (gave, had given) birth to her last child, she suffered from postpartum depression.
5. At the trial, both the prosecution and the defense (agreed, had agreed) that she was severely mentally ill.
6. Yates' attorneys did not convince the jury that their client (killed, had killed) her children by reason of insanity.
7. The legal definition of insanity asks what a person (knew, had known) at the time of the crime.
8. Jurors (learned, had learned) of her history of mental illness, but they reasoned that she knew that what she was doing was wrong.

9. They believed this because she (called, had called) the police immediately after she had killed the children.

10. In a new trial in 2006, the jury (found, had found) Yates not guilty by reason of insanity.

(Adapted from *Criminal Justice Today* by Frank Schmalleger)

LO 5 Passive Voice

Past participles are also used to make passive voice. **Voice** is a grammar category for verbs. English verbs have two voices: active and passive. When writing, if you want to focus on the subject of the sentence, use the active voice. If the goal is more important than the subject, then use passive voice.

The passive voice consists of a form of the verb *be* and the past participle. Notice the difference between active and passive voice and their verb forms in the following examples:

Active Voice	Performer	Action	Goal
The active voice focuses on the subject that performs the action.	The police officer	caught	the car thief.
Passive Voice	**Goal**	**Action**	**Performer**
Be + past participle			
The passive voice focuses on the receiver of the action. The subject of the sentence is not the performer.	The car thief	was caught	by the police officer.

Passive voice can be used with many verb tenses. Here are examples of how *be* is used with the past participle to form both active and passive voice:

Verb Tense	Active	Passive *be* + past participle
Simple present	Criminal justice agencies use computer-based training.	Computer-based training is used by criminal justice agencies.
Present progressive	Criminal justice agencies are using computer-based training.	Computer-based training is being used by criminal justice agencies.
Future	Criminal justice agencies will use computer-based training.	Computer-based training will be used by criminal justice agencies.
Simple past	Criminal justice agencies used computer-based training.	Computer-based training was used by criminal justice agencies.
Present perfect	Criminal justice agencies have used computer-based training.	Computer-based training has been used by criminal justice agencies.
Other helping verbs: *can, could, would, should, might, must*	Criminal justice agencies can use computer-based training.	Computer-based training can be used by criminal justice agencies.

TIP	The *by* phrase can be omitted when the doer of the action is understood.
	Police-pursuit driving **simulators** are widely used training programs ~~by police training divisions~~.

simulator a computerized system that imitates real conditions.

PRACTICE   Identifying Active and Passive Voice

23.5   Read the following sentences and decide if the underlined verb is active or passive. Write *A* for active and *P* for passive.

DNA profiling the process used to help police identify someone suspected of committing a crime, which involves testing human bodily fluids, bones, hair, and teeth found at the scene of a crime and comparing it with the DNA of the accused person

Example: **DNA profiling** <u>uses</u> human DNA for identification. A

1. DNA <u>is</u> a nucleic acid found in the center of cells.
2. A large role <u>is played</u> by DNA in criminal cases throughout the country.
3. DNA <u>can convict</u> or <u>can clear</u> a suspect.
4. DNA <u>is considered</u> highly reliable by the U.S. Department of Justice.
5. Originally, DNA <u>was used</u> by laboratories as a test to determine paternity.
6. The first use of DNA in criminal cases <u>began</u> in 1986 in England.
7. DNA testing <u>has been called</u> one of the most important technological breakthroughs in criminology.
8. DNA profiling <u>requires</u> only a few human cells for comparison.
9. Sufficient genetic material <u>is provided</u> by one drop of blood, a few hairs, a small amount of skin, or a trace of body fluid.
10. Because DNA is stable, genetic tests <u>can be conducted</u> on evidence taken from crime scenes for a long time after fingerprints have disappeared.

(Adapted from *Criminal Justice Today* by Frank Schmalleger)

PRACTICE   Using Active and Passive Voice

23.6

Part A

Change the underlined verb from the active to passive form in each of the sentences, and rewrite each sentence in the space provided. The first sentence is done for you.

Example: A defendant <u>offers</u> some type of defense. Some type of defense is offered by a defendant.

1. The defendant <u>gives</u> evidence and arguments.

_____

2. The U.S. legal system <u>recognizes</u> four categories of defense.

_____

3. The alibi defense <u>claims</u> that the defendant is innocent.

_____

alibi an excuse used to show that a person could not have committed a crime

4. Witnesses and documentation <u>supports</u> an **alibi**.

_____

Part B

Change the underlined verb from the passive to active form in each of the sentences below.

self-defense justification when the person claims that it was necessary to harm an attacker for his or her own safety from injury or death.

5. The self-defense justification <u>can be used</u> by a person who harms an attacker.

_____

6. This defense <u>should be used</u> by a person only when cornered with no path of escape.

_____

outweigh is more important than something else.

7. The protection of property <u>is **outweighed**</u> by the protection of human life.

_____

8. Reasonable, non-deadly force <u>can be applied</u> by a property owner to prevent others from unlawfully taking or damaging it.

_____

LO 6 Past Participles as Adjectives

Past participles can be used as adjectives. When past participles are used as adjectives, they show how someone feels.

Participle before a noun	He is a frightened man.
Participle after a linking verb	The man seemed frightened by the thief.

TIP | A past participle cannot be used to describe an object. The *-ing* verb form must be used.

The movie was frightening. **Not:** The movie was frightened.

PRACTICE Identifying Participles as Adjectives or Verbs
23.7   For each of the following sentences, indicate whether the underlined word is a past participle adjective or past participle verb form.

Example: On April 20, 1999, twelve Columbine High School students and a teacher were <u>killed</u> by two students. Verb

outcasts people not accepted by the others

1. Eric Harris and Dylan Klebold were <u>seen</u> as **outcasts** at Columbine.
2. The community was <u>horrified</u>.
3. A year before the murders, Harris and Klebold were <u>caught</u> with stolen tools by Littleton, Colorado, police.
4. In the months before the attacks, two 9 millimeter firearms and two 12-guage shotguns were <u>bought</u> for them by a friend, Robyn Anderson.
5. On the day of the attacks, their plan to set off bombs in the cafeteria was <u>spoiled</u> when the bombs failed to explode.
6. Harris and Klebold were <u>disappointed</u> that the bombs did not explode.

7. They were <u>armed</u> with guns, knives, and bombs as they entered the school's cafeteria at around 11:20 a.m.

8. They walked through the hallways, into classrooms, and into the library shooting at students and teachers, many who were <u>hurt</u> or <u>killed</u>.

9. All students and employees were <u>terrified</u>.

10. Shortly after 12 p.m., Harris and Klebold were <u>finished</u> shooting others and committed suicide.

Review: Past Participles

Decide whether each of the underlined items in the following passage is correct or has an error in the use of past participles or perfect tenses. Write the correction above the error. If the item is correct, write a *C* above it.

Example: [1]The famous *Miranda v. Arizona case* of 1966 <u>has established</u> the well-known **Miranda warnings**. established

Miranda warnings You have the right to remain silent. Anything you say can be used against you in a court of law. You have the right to speak to an attorney and to have an attorney present while you are being questioned. If you cannot afford to hire an attorney, one will appointed to represent you at government expense.

[2]The case involved Ernesto Miranda, whom police <u>have arrested</u> in Phoenix, Arizona. [3]Miranda was accused of having kidnapped and raped a young woman. [4]At police headquarters, the victim <u>identified</u> him. [5]After police <u>had question</u> him for two hours, Miranda signed a confession that formed the basis of his later conviction on the charges.

[6]His conviction <u>was overturn</u> on appeal. [7]The U.S. Supreme Court ruled that Miranda's conviction <u>had been</u> unconstitutional. [8]Interrogators <u>have</u> not <u>warned</u> him of his rights during questioning. [9]Therefore, evidence police <u>had receive</u> as a result of questioning could be used against him. [10]Later, Miranda was convicted after the court <u>had gave</u> him a fair trial. [11]As a result of *Miranda v. Arizona*, suspects eighteen years or older who are in custody <u>are advise</u> of their Miranda rights before any questioning begins.

(Adapted from *Criminal Justice Today* by Frank Schmalleger)

Writing Assignments

Write about an Image

Part A Write five sentences about some things that have changed since you became a college student. Use the present perfect tense.

Example: I have learned some good test-taking strategies.

Part B Imagine that a teenager had a party while his or her family members were on vacation. When they came home, they were upset at the condition of the house. Write five sentences about what had happened during the party. Use the past perfect tense.

Example: Someone had spilled a can of grape soda on the rug and did not clean it up.

English Success Tip: Using Passive Voice Wisely

Many writing teachers tell students to avoid passive voice. Sentences are usually more effective and direct when the subject is performing the action.

Less Direct	More Direct
I was told by my friend to meet him at the library.	My friend told me to meet him at the library.
An investigation was conducted by the FBI.	The FBI conducted an investigation.

However, passive voice is not wrong. It is often used in legal, scientific, and technical fields to be unbiased. Passive voice is more acceptable in these situations:

Situation	Passive Voice Example
Performer of action is unknown or kept secret	A body was discovered at the crime scene.
Not necessary to know the performer	The evidence was collected and transported to the lab.
To make an authoritative statement	Cell phone use is prohibited in this area of the hospital.
To stress the outcome	Budget cuts have eliminated twenty positions.

For support in meeting this chapter's objectives, log in to www.mywritinglab.com, go to the Study Plan tab, click on **Past Participles** and choose **Regular and Irregular Verbs, Misplaced or Dangling Modifiers, and Adjectives** from the list of subtopics. Read and view the videos and resources in the Review Materials section, and then complete the Recall, Apply, and Write exercises in the Activities section. You can check your scores and overall progress by using the Gradebook.

CHAPTER 24

Pronouns

Theme: *Music*

LO 1 What Is a Pronoun?

A **pronoun** is a word that is used to refer to another noun or pronoun or to replace a noun or pronoun. Writers use pronouns so that they do not have to keep repeating the same noun:

Repetitious: Workers around the world have found ways of singing together to help workers work, lighten workers' loads, and give workers a feeling of togetherness.

Improved: Workers around the world have found ways of singing together to help them work, lighten their loads, and give them a feeling of togetherness.

Pronouns have other uses as well. They can be used as adjectives and to form questions. The following chart shows how pronouns can be used in sentences.

How Pronouns Are Used	
To refer to another noun or pronoun	Almost all people sing whether they can carry a tune or not.
To replace a noun or pronoun	Some people sing in the shower, while others sing in the car. Others replaces *people*.
To modify a noun	Their voices sound better in enclosed spaces. My brother sings that song every day.
To ask a question	Who likes to sing in the car?

Pronouns in Context

In the following passage about the influences of rock and roll music, the pronouns are highlighted.

The early influences on rock and roll were many and varied. First and most important was the mixture of slow blues singing with a harder, more rhythmic background sound that became known as rhythm and blues (R&B). Early R&B artists included singers such as Muddy Waters, who grew up on a Mississippi plantation and moved to Chicago. Most were black. Rhythm and blues mixed two sounds. One was the rural sound of the blues, and the other was the electrified edge and rhythms of the city streets. The personal sound of one man with a guitar was expanded in R&B to include a group of musicians.

Also important to the early growth of rock and roll were the hard-driving sounds of Little Richard and Chuck Berry. Little Richard was from the South, and he pounded the piano and screamed his lyrics like a wild man. He and his group were responsible for some of the early hits of rock and roll, such as "Tutti Frutti" and "Rip It Up." Chuck Berry wrote all of his own music. His songs spoke directly to teens who were sitting in class but ready to party.

Another of the early influences on rock and roll was country music. Before the term "rock and roll" was widely used, the early sound was known as "rockabilly" ("rock" + "hillbilly"). It combined the drive of rhythm and blues with the elements of country and western, a style popular in the rural South for its fiddle playing, guitar picking, and warm vocal harmonies. Rockabilly stars who scored big hits at this time were Jerry Lee Lewis and Johnny Cash. All of these artists were white, poor, and from the rural South.

(Adapted from *Understanding Music* by Jeremy Yudkin)

LO 2 Pronoun Case

Case is the form personal pronouns take to show how they function in a sentence: as a subject, as an object, or as a possessive.

Pronouns as Subjects

The following pronouns are used as subjects: *I, you, he, she, it, we, they, who, whoever.*
Subject pronouns are used as subjects of verbs and after linking verbs.

Subject Pronouns	
Subject of a verb	She likes to sing the latest pop hit song. *She* is the subject of the verb *likes*.
Compound subject of a verb	She and I like to sing together. *She* and *I* are both subjects of the verb *like*.
Pronoun combined with a noun as subject	We singers plan to form a group. *We singers* is the subject of the verb *plan*.
After a linking verb	The singer is she. *She* follows the linking verb *is*.

TIP | To be sure that you are using the correct pronoun(s) in a compound subject, use this process: omit one half of the compound and check it.

Example: Him and me had a band.
            Him ~~and me~~ had a band. ~~Him and~~ me had a band.
Correction: He and I had a band.

Pronouns as Objects

The following pronouns are used as objects: *me, him, her, it, us, you, them, whom, whomever.*
Object pronouns are used as objects of verbs and objects of prepositions.

Object Pronouns	
Object of a verb	The panel of judges heard me sing. *Me* is the object of the verb *heard*.
Compound object of a verb	The panel of judges heard her and me sing. *Her* and *me* are both objects of the verb *heard*.
Pronoun combined with a noun as object	The panel of judges heard us singers perform. *Us singers* is the object of the verb *heard*.
Object of a preposition	The judges had a good opinion of me. *Me* is the object of the preposition *of*.

TIP
To be sure that you are using the correct pronoun(s) in a compound object, use this process: omit one half of the compound and check it.

Example: The panel of judges heard he and I sing.
The panel of judges heard he ~~and I~~ sing. The panel of judges heard ~~he and~~ I sing.

Correction: The panel of judges heard him and me sing.

PRACTICE Using Subject and Object Pronouns
24.1
Circle the correct pronoun in each of the following sentences.

Example: ¹My friend Jenna and (I, me) had to attend an orchestral concert for our music appreciation class.

²We asked two of our friends from our class to go with (we, us). ³Neither (them, they) nor (us, we) knew what to expect. ⁴Our professor gave (we, us) students some advice. ⁵Since most people get dressed more formally for the concert, my friends and (me, I) could not wear tee shirts and jeans. ⁶(They, Them) are not appropriate clothes for an orchestral concert. ⁷(My teacher she, She) told us to arrive at the concert hall early.

⁸To become more familiar with the pieces on the program, Jenna and (me, I) watched videos of those pieces on YouTube. ⁹Jenna, (me, I), and our friends also looked for information about the composers on the Internet. ¹⁰While the musicians were warming up, Darvins and (me, I) named the instruments (us, we) had learned about in class. ¹¹None of (we, us) students thought that the concert would be so inspiring and memorable.

Pronouns as Possessives
Pronouns showing ownership are called possessives. The following are possessive pronouns: *my, mine, his, hers, its, our, ours, your, yours, their, theirs, whose.*

Some possessive pronouns are used as adjectives and others are used in place of nouns.

Possessive Pronouns	
Before nouns	Jazz singers use their voices in special ways.
In place of nouns	Theirs are used in special ways. (their voices)

 Possessive pronouns do not require an apostrophe. Avoid confusing possessive pronouns with contractions.

Possessive pronouns: *its, their, your*

Contractions: *it's = it is; they're = they are; you're = you are*

 Word Reminder. For more information about confusing word pairs, see Chapter 30.

A small group of pronouns can be changed to possessives by adding an -'s:

anybody's, anyone's, everybody's, everyone's,
nobody's, no one's, one's, somebody's, someone's

Someone's instrument is out of tune. Everyone's comments about the performance were positive.

 Possessive pronouns do not have plural forms, such as **everybodies**, **somebodies**, or **nobodies**.

PRACTICE   Using Possessive Pronouns

24.2   Circle the correct possessive pronoun or possessive adjective.

Example: That mp3 player is (my, mine).

1. Jack did not bring his music; he listened to (her, hers).
2. Saika is one of (his, his') best friends.
3. (Our, ours) friends have a huge music collection.
4. Some friends of (our, ours) plan to share (their, they're, there) music with us.
5. We are going to download some songs onto (your, you're) computer.
6. How many songs do you have on (your, yours)?
7. My favorite group just released (its, it's) latest song.
8. That new song is going to be (everyones, everyone's) favorite.

Reflexive and Intensive Pronouns

Reflexive pronouns and **intensive pronouns** are formed by adding -*self* or -*selves* to the end of a personal pronoun. Although the reflexive and intensive pronouns have the same forms, they are used differently.

Reflexive and intensive pronouns have singular and plural forms:

Singular forms: *myself, yourself, himself, herself, itself, oneself*

Plural forms: *yourselves, ourselves, themselves*

 Hisself, ourself, theirself, and *theirselves* are not Standard English forms. Do not use them in college writing.

Reflexive pronouns refer to the subject and are used as objects.

Object of a verb	He watched himself in the video.
Object of a preposition	He made a video of himself.

Intensive pronouns add emphasis to the noun they refer to.

The performers themselves are responsible for their own actions.

They will take responsibility themselves.

Use a subject pronoun as the subject, not a reflexive pronoun.

Incorrect: Bryan and **myself** are members of the marching band.

Correct: Bryan and **I** are members of the marching band.

PRACTICE **Using Reflexive and Intensive Pronouns**

24.3 Fill in the correct reflexive or intensive pronoun. Choose from the following singular and plural forms: *myself, yourself, himself, herself, itself, ourselves, yourselves,* or *themselves.*

Example: In the nineteenth century, members of the middle class bought <u>themselves</u> sheet music.

1. After dinner, a woman would give a piano performance by _____

2. During that time, many composers made a good income for _____ from their music.

3. Before this, the church _____ dictated the style or content composers had to use.

4. Pianos became much cheaper, so you could own one _____

5. The Romantic era brought with it a new sound from larger orchestras, which I _____ enjoy listening to.

Comparisons

Comparisons are formed by using word groups that begin with *than* or *as . . . as.* A sentence expressing a comparison may end in a pronoun but omit the rest of the comparison. The end of the sentence is not completed. To decide whether to use a subject or object pronoun, finish the sentence and use the pronoun that would be correct if the sentence were completed.

Incomplete sentence: Jamal has been studying piano longer **than she.**

Completed sentence: Jamal has been studying piano longer **than she has been studying piano.**

If you complete the sentence with the incorrect pronoun, the error will be obvious:

Jamal has been studying piano longer **than her has been studying piano.**

Sentences with incomplete comparisons can be confusing to readers. Instead, revise the sentence. Notice how confusion can occur in the following sentences when they are not completed:

Incomplete comparison	Complete comparison
Jamal likes playing the piano **better than she.**	Jamal likes playing the piano **better than she likes playing the piano.**
Jamal likes playing piano **better than her.**	Jamal likes playing the piano **better than he likes her.**

Who and Whom

Who and *whom* are called relative pronouns. They appear in questions and in dependent word groups. *Who* is a subject pronoun and is used as the subject in a question or a dependent clause. *Whom* is an object pronoun and is used as an object of a verb or object of a preposition in a dependent word group. The following chart shows how to use *who* and *whom*.

How to Use *Who* and *Whom*	
Questions	
subject	Who is the most famous musician of all time?
object of the verb	Whom should I choose?
object of the preposition	About whom are you speaking?
Dependent clauses in sentences	
subject of the dependent clause	The composer who **started to compose at age six** was Mozart.
object of the verb in the dependent clause	The composer whom **I admire** is Mozart.
object of the preposition	For whom did young Mozart play?

TIP If you have trouble figuring out whether to use *who* or *whom*, substitute a personal pronoun for *who* or *whom* to help you decide which one to use:

he or *she* = *who*   *him* or *her* = *whom*

Who/Whom plays an instrument?   **He** plays an instrument. ***Who*** is correct.
Who/Whom do you admire?   You do admire **him**. ***Whom*** is correct.
Who/Whom did you meet yesterday?   You did meet **him** yesterday. ***Whom*** is correct.

PRACTICE 24.4 Using Pronouns Correctly

Part A

Circle the correct pronoun in the following comparisons.

Example: Andrew practices as hard as (me, I).

1. She is a better performer than (he, him).
2. We have been writing songs longer than (them, they).
3. He practices more with you than (me, I).
4. Andrew spent more money on his guitar than (me, I).
5. They are less talented than (us, we).

Part B

Circle the correct form (*who* or *whom*).

Example: Michael Jackson, (who, whom) was called the "King of Pop," died on June 25, 2009.

5. (Who, Whom) became famous for his spins, kicks, anti-gravity lean, and moonwalk?
6. Jackson was one of the few artists (who, whom) was inducted into the Rock and Roll Hall of Fame twice.
7. Jackson, to (who, whom) many awards had been given, had a great impact on world music and culture.

8. Quincy Jones, (who, whom) made the elaborate video *Thriller* with Jackson, said that Jackson changed the music business.

9. Jackson, with (who, whom) Jones shared a Grammy award for Album of the Year, also won a Grammy for "Billy Jean," a hit from that album.

LO 3 Pronoun-Antecedent Agreement

An **antecedent** is a word or phrase that a pronoun refers to.

ANTECEDENT   PRONOUN   PRONOUN

Jimi Hendrix used his guitar to play his highly original music.

The basic rule for pronoun-antecedent agreement is that a pronoun must agree with its antecedent.

A singular pronoun must have a singular antecedent.	Hendrix had to make changes to his Stratocaster guitar so he could play it. A left-handed guitar was rare, so Jimi had to swap the strings and turn it upside down to play it.
A plural pronoun must have a plural antecedent.	Hendrix's guitar changes were creative, and they made him famous. He was known for his jet engine and dive-bomb effects, and many guitar players copied them.
The pronoun must be in the same gender as the antecedent.	Currently, a left-handed musician can easily find a Stratocaster for him or her to play.

> **TIP** | If you are not sure if the third person singular antecedent is male or female, use the word group *he or she* for subject pronouns or *him or her* for object pronouns.

PRACTICE Identifying Pronouns and Antecedents

24.5 Circle the antecedent of each underlined pronoun. Then draw an arrow from the pronoun to the antecedent.

Example: Jimi Hendrix was fascinated with guitars when he was a child.

1. Jimi's father bought Jimi his first real guitar; however, it was made for a right-handed player.

2. Jimi was left-handed, so by reversing the strings on the guitar, Jimi could play it.

3. Hendrix never learned to read music, but he trained his ear by listening to other guitarists and observing their style.

4. He had to watch other guitarists play a song and then figure out how to play it left-handed.

5. In the 1960s, Hendrix went to London where he introduced many new guitar techniques, and they impressed audiences and guitarists.

6. Electronics whiz Roger Mayer worked with Hendrix, and they created effects that helped Hendrix create his heavy psychedelic sound.

7. Hendrix's musical sounds are as fresh today as they were when he first played them.

Compound Subject Antecedents

Special rules apply with compound subjects.

1. When the antecedent is a compound subject joined by *and*, the pronoun that refers to them is always plural. It does not matter if one or both of the antecedents is plural.

   The attitudes of teenagers and parents affect their choice of music.

2. When the compound subject antecedents are joined by *or, neither … nor, either … or,* or *not only … but also,* the pronoun agrees with the second antecedent.

   A teenager or his parent has his or her own music preferences.

   A teenager or his parents often have their own music preferences.

> **TIP** | To decide which pronoun to use with *or, neither … nor, either … or,* or *not only … but also,* cross out the part of the compound subject before the *or, nor,* or *but also.*
>
> A teenager or his parents often have their own music preferences.

PRACTICE   Using Correct Pronoun–Compound Antecedent Agreement
24.6   Circle the connecting words *and, or, either/or,* or *neither/nor.* Then underline the compound antecedent and circle the correct pronoun.

Example: Denmark, South America, and Asia had (its, their) version of flutes dating from the Stone Age.

1. Bone, wood, or ivory determined (its, their) sound.

2. In wind instruments, the tube and sound determine (its, their) tone.

3. Open-holed instruments or beaked instruments go by (its, their) generic term "flute."

4. Both a flute and a whistle produce (its, their) sound when a player blows an air stream into the open hole of the instrument.

5. Either cymbals or a drum makes (its, their) sounds by striking (it, them).

6. Sticks or tubes are played by banging (it, them) on a hard surface.

7. Both the harp and the lute were used in ancient customs and have kept (its, their) popularity.

8. Either the piano or the violin is played when (its, their) strings are plucked, bowed, or struck.

Collective Noun Antecedents

A **collective noun** is a word that refers to a group of people or things. It can describe the group as a whole (only one) or the individuals in the group (more than one). The following are common collective nouns:

army	class	crowd	group	senate
audience	club	family	jury	society
band	committee	gang	public	team

A group noun can be singular or plural depending on the meaning.

■ If the members of the group are acting as one, doing the same thing or thinking the same way, the pronoun that refers to the noun is singular.

> The group agreed to perform its hit songs at the concert.

■ If the members of the group are acting as individuals, doing different things or thinking differently, the pronoun that refers to the noun is plural.

> The group gave their individual opinions about which songs to play.

PRACTICE 24.7 Using Correct Pronoun–Collective Noun Antecedent Agreement

Underline the antecedents and circle the correct pronoun.

Example: The <u>orchestra</u> will rehearse (its, their) musical pieces several days a week.

1. An orchestra spends more time rehearsing (its, their) music before a concert than playing (it, them) at a concert.
2. The audience expressed (its, their) appreciation of the performance with a **standing ovation**.
3. The audience showed (its, their) disappointment by walking out or talking.
4. The band left the stage when (it, they) saw the curtain catch fire from the fireworks display.
5. The Alvin Ailey dance troupe will begin (its, their) international tour in July.
6. The American Ballet Company temporarily disbanded in 1938 because (it, they) disagreed on the dance arrangements.
7. The group broke up to develop (its, their) own solo careers.

standing ovation an action where an audience stands up and claps for a long time to show appreciation

---

 Antecedents and Prepositional Phrases. Sometimes a prepositional phrase comes between the pronoun and the antecedent. In most cases, the antecedent is not found in the prepositional phrase.

> A group's image in the world of pop and rock and roll is important to its success. Groups in the current commercial market must also have their unique style.

Indefinite Pronoun Antecedents

Indefinite pronouns are words that replace nouns but do not refer to any specific person or thing. Indefinite pronouns are often used as subjects and antecedents. Some indefinite pronouns are always singular or plural, but other pronouns can be either singular or plural. This chart will help you learn the singular and plural indefinite pronouns.

Singular Indefinite Pronouns When the subject is a singular indefinite pronoun, the antecedent will be singular. These indefinite pronouns are always singular:

anyone	someone	no one	everyone
anybody	somebody	nobody	everybody
anything	something	nothing	everything
another	one	other	each
either	neither		

> Anyone can improve his or her enjoyment of music by becoming an experienced listener.

> Everyone has his or her music preference.

Plural Indefinite Pronouns When the subject is a plural indefinite pronoun, the antecedent will be plural. These indefinite pronouns are always plural:

both   few   many   others   several

Many like to listen to their favorite music while studying.

Others keep their radio playing in the background at home all the time.

Singular or Plural Indefinite Pronouns A few indefinite pronouns can be singular or plural:

some   any   none   all   most

These indefinite pronouns are often followed by prepositional phrases that modify them. If the object of the preposition is plural, then the subject pronoun is considered plural. Therefore, the antecedent should be plural.

Some of the composers use repetition in their pieces.

If the object of the preposition is not plural, then the subject pronoun is considered singular. Therefore, the antecedent should be singular.

All of Mozart's music has its classical style elements.

TIP | A helpful way to remember these pronouns is by the acronym SANAM: some, any, none, all, most.

PRACTICE Using Correct Pronoun-Antecedent Agreement

24.8   Underline the indefinite pronoun antecedent and circle the correct pronoun that refers to it.

Example: <u>Some</u> of the folk music passed down through the generations had (its, their) words changed.

1. No one may know the age of (his or her, their) folk song.
2. Each of the folk singers gives (his or her, their) personal interpretation of a song.
3. Anyone can change the tempo or melody of (his or her, their) song.
4. One does not have to train (his or her, their) voice to be a folk singer.
5. All of the Native American cultures have used music to teach (its, their) oral history.
6. Most of the tribe's music reflects (its, their) use of drums, rattles, and other percussion instruments.
7. None of the singers try to match (its, his or her) notes with the other singers.
8. One of the vocal traditions of the Xhosa South African culture is (its, their) overtone singing.
9. Someone could train (his or her, their) voice to learn this skill.

Plural Antecedents with Singular Meaning

Some antecedents have plural forms, but they are considered singular.

Plural antecedent	Example
Titles of single entities: books, organizations, countries	*Musical Encounters* gives its readers a multicultural approach to music study.
Singular nouns ending in -s: news, mathematics, economics, measles, athletics	The news directs its delivery to gain viewers.

Avoid Problems with Pronoun Shifts

A pronoun shift is an error that happens when the writer switches from one pronoun to another. One shift occurs when a pronoun and antecedent do not agree.

> **Shift**: If a person works hard, you can be successful.

> **Correct**: If a person works hard, he or she can be successful.

Another common error is a shift in person. This happens when the writer shifts pronouns when talking about the same person.

> **Shift**: Learning about music helps us develop the skills you need to evaluate it.

> **Correct**: Learning about music helps us develop the skills we need to evaluate it.

PRACTICE Correcting Pronoun Shift Errors
24.9 Underline the pronoun that is shifted and write your correction above it.

they
Example: When people hear Tejano, you may remember the pop star of the 1990s, Selena Quintanilla-Perez.

1. She brought Tejano to the U.S. culture, and they brought attention to Mexican musical traditions.
2. Mexican-American farm workers took Mexican music, and he blended it with music of other immigrant groups that lived in the community.
3. Selena spoke English, but her father insisted that you needed to learn to speak Spanish to be successful in both the United States and Mexico.
4. Abraham, Selena's father, believed that you should stay true to her Mexican roots.
5. Selena gave Mexican-Americans ethnic pride while they also highlighted Mexican language, music, and culture.

LO 4 Pronoun Reference

The following guidelines will help you use pronouns clearly.

A pronoun should refer to one specific antecedent in a sentence.	**Unclear:** It says in the newspaper that the concert was rescheduled for tomorrow night.
	Clear: The newspaper reporter said that the concert was rescheduled for tomorrow night.

A pronoun should have an antecedent.	**Unclear:** The outdoor concert was rained out, so they gave everyone a refund. **Clear:** The outdoor concert was rained out, so the ticket company gave everyone a refund.
A pronoun should refer to only one antecedent.	**Unclear:** The drummer asked the guitarist where he performed last week. **Clear:** The drummer asked the guitarist where the guitarist performed last week. **Better:** The drummer wanted to know where the guitarist performed last week.
A pronoun should refer to a specific antecedent, not one that is implied (not stated outright).	**Unclear:** Shauna's singing was so loud that she did not need a microphone. **Clear:** Shauna sang so loudly that she did not need a microphone.
Pronouns such as **this** and **which** should refer to a specific noun, not a group of words that explain an idea or a situation.	**Unclear:** Christa did not go to rehearsal, which was not considerate of her. **Clear:** Christa was inconsiderate by not going to rehearsal. **Unclear:** Christa called Sam late last night to explain why she was not at rehearsal yesterday. This made Sam angry. **Clear:** Christa called Sam late last night to explain why she was not at rehearsal yesterday. Her late night call made Sam angry.

PRACTICE   Correcting Pronoun Use

24.10   Underline the vague pronoun in each sentence and correct it. You may need to rewrite the sentence.

                                                                 Chante

Example: Shireen took Chante to the college's multi-cultural festival so <u>she</u> could enjoy dance, music, and food from different cultures.

1. They say that the festival attracts many students each year.

2. Chante took her student ID and her ticket out of her wallet and showed it to the security guard at the entrance to the festival.

3. Shireen called the day care center to see how her son was doing, but they did not answer.

4. Chante could not decide which booth to visit first, so Shireen complained about it.

5. Shireen explained to Chante that she would enjoy the Jamaican booth.

6. On the center stage, they heard a reggae band playing and saw students dancing to the music. This was fun to watch.

7. Someone stepped right in front of Chante and blocked her view. It upset her.

8. Shireen and Chante listened to the music for a half hour before she decided to try some jerk chicken, rice and peas.

9. While Shireen was holding her plate of food and her cell phone, she dropped it.

10. They had run out of food, so Shireen had to go without it, but she had a good time anyway.

Writing Assignments

Review: Pronoun Use

Underline any incorrect pronouns and correct them. One sentence is correct.

Example: [1]Robert Schumann ~~he~~ was an early Romantic composer whose music was inspired by literature.

[2]His father was a bookseller, so he had unlimited access to the popular writings of the day. [3]As a young man Schumann hisself wrote poems and novels. [4]He studied law but was not interested in it; instead he drank heavily and spent their money on having a good time. [5]Schumann met Friedrich Wieck, a famous piano teacher, and Schumann took lessons from he.

[6]When Schumann heard Paganini, whom was a famous Italian violinist, play a concert, he was impressed and decided to become a master of the piano. [7]Schumann took a room in Wieck's house so Wieck and him could devote all they time to practice. [8]Clara, Wieck's daughter, was half Schumann's age, but she could play piano better than him. [9]Schumann practiced constantly and permanently damaged his hand. [10]This ended his piano playing career.

[11]He turned from performing to composing and fell in love with Clara, who was fifteen years old at the time. [12]Wieck saw that Schumann barely made a living, and he did not want his daughter with someone as poor as him. [13]Wieck took his daughter away on long tours and would not let the two of them be in each others' company. [14]While apart, Schumann and Clara they wrote secret letters to each other. [15]Finally, Clara and him had to go to court to get freedom to marry.

[16]In they're home, both of them had a music room. [17]The first year they were married, Schumann wrote 140 songs, and in the four years that followed, he devoted his' time to writing a symphony, string quartets, and piano pieces.

Write about an Image

Using the different types of pronouns you learned about in this chapter, write five to ten sentences describing the performers in the photo. Then underline the pronoun(s) in each sentence and write the type of pronoun it is.

Example: <u>One</u> of the performers holds an orange trash can. Indefinite pronoun

> ### English Success Tip: It Is Not Necessary to Start a Sentence with *It*
>
> Sometimes *it* is used as a subject of a sentence without referring to a specific word. Grammarians call this the "dummy it." When *it* is the subject, the reader must stop to figure out what *it* refers to. When possible, use the real subject.
>   **Unnecessary it:** It is easy to download music.
>   **Real subject:** Downloading music is easy.
> *It* is often used in conversation to talk about the weather and time:
>   It is two o'clock.   It is raining outside.
> Use *it* as a subject only when there is no other way to express the sentence.

For support in meeting this chapter's objectives, log in to www.mywritinglab.com, go to the Study Plan tab, click on **Pronouns** and choose **Pronouns, Pronoun Reference and Point of View, Pronoun Antecedent Agreement, and Pronoun Case** from the list of subtopics. Read and view the videos and resources in the Review Materials section, and then complete the Recall, Apply, and Write exercises in the Activities section. You can check your scores and overall progress by using the Gradebook.

CHAPTER 25

Nouns and Noun Markers

Theme: *Travel and Tourism*

Learning Objectives

After working through this chapter, you will be able to:

LO 1 Identify nouns.

LO 2 Identify and use common, proper, compound, and collective nouns.

LO 3 Use singular and plural nouns.

LO 4 Choose appropriate noun markers.

LO 1 What Is a Noun?

Nouns are words used to name people, things, activities, and ideas. There are more nouns than other kinds of words in the English language. Along with verbs, nouns are the chief building blocks of a sentence.

Nouns in Context

In the following passage about museums, the nouns are highlighted.

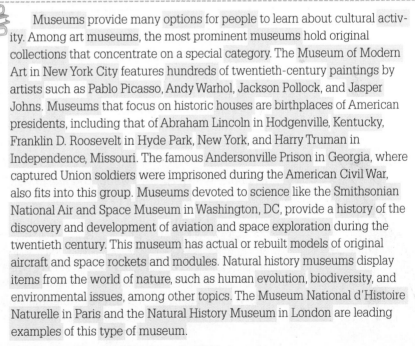

Museums provide many options for people to learn about cultural activity. Among art museums, the most prominent museums hold original collections that concentrate on a special category. The Museum of Modern Art in New York City features hundreds of twentieth-century paintings by artists such as Pablo Picasso, Andy Warhol, Jackson Pollock, and Jasper Johns. Museums that focus on historic houses are birthplaces of American presidents, including that of Abraham Lincoln in Hodgenville, Kentucky, Franklin D. Roosevelt in Hyde Park, New York, and Harry Truman in Independence, Missouri. The famous Andersonville Prison in Georgia, where captured Union soldiers were imprisoned during the American Civil War, also fits into this group. Museums devoted to science like the Smithsonian National Air and Space Museum in Washington, DC, provide a history of the discovery and development of aviation and space exploration during the twentieth century. This museum has actual or rebuilt models of original aircraft and space rockets and modules. Natural history museums display items from the world of nature, such as human evolution, biodiversity, and environmental issues, among other topics. The Museum National d'Histoire Naturelle in Paris and the Natural History Museum in London are leading examples of this type of museum.

(Adapted from *Travel and Tourism* by Paul S. Biederman)

LO 2 Types of Nouns

Nouns can be grouped to make them easy to understand and identify: common and proper nouns, compound nouns, and collective nouns.

Common and Proper Nouns

A **common noun** is a word that refers to a general person, place, thing, activity or idea. A common noun begins with a lowercase letter unless it is the first word in a sentence. A **proper noun** is a word that refers to a specific person, place, thing, activity or idea and begins with an uppercase letter no matter where it is placed in a sentence.

Common nouns	Proper nouns	Examples
pilot	Charles Lindbergh	Charles Lindbergh was the first pilot to make a nonstop flight alone across the Atlantic Ocean in May 1927.
hotelier	Cesar Ritz	Cesar Ritz was a famous Swiss hotelier.
city	Las Vegas	Gambling was legalized in the city of Las Vegas in 1931.
airplane	Cessna	Cessna is the world's largest manufacturer of private airplanes.

PRACTICE 25.1 Writing Common Nouns

List ten common nouns that are items that can be placed in a large suitcase.

_____

_____

PRACTICE 25.2 Using Proper Nouns in Sentences

Working in small groups of two or three, answer the following questions using proper nouns. On a separate sheet of paper, write your answers in complete sentences and underline each proper noun. In each sentence, use the name of the person who answered the question.

Example: Which country would you like to visit?

Alcee would like to visit Egypt.

1. What is the name of the city or town you live in now?

2. What is the name of a tourist site you have visited?

3. What countries are your relatives or your ancestors from?

4. What is the name of your favorite park, theater, or museum?

5. What is the name of a hotel or motel that you have heard about or stayed in?

Compound Nouns

A **compound noun** consists of more than one word: for example, two nouns (*tour package*); a preposition and noun (*underground*); an adjective and a noun (*monthly rates*); or an *-ing* verb and a noun (*swimming pool*).

Compound nouns have three forms.

Compound noun form	Examples
one word	keyboard, flashlight, bedroom, database
two words	police officer, seat belt, swimming pool, real estate
hyphenated	sister-in-law, editor-in-chief, passer-by

TIP	Consult a good dictionary to check the spelling of compound nouns.

PRACTICE   Writing Compound Nouns

25.3   List five compound nouns for each of the following words. Use a dictionary if needed.

Example: paper <u>paperback, paperwork, paper towel, paper clip, newspaper</u>

1. air _____

2. fire _____

3. rain _____

Grammar Reminder: For more information about subject-verb agreement with collective nouns, see Chapter 21.

Collective Nouns

Collective nouns refer to a group of people or things. They can describe the group as a whole or the individuals in the group. Collective nouns are singular if the members in the group are acting as a unit, but they are plural if the members are acting as individuals.

Here are some common collective nouns:

army	class	crowd	group	senate
audience	club	family	jury	society
band	committee	gang	public	team

LO 3 Singular and Plural Nouns

A **singular noun** refers to one person, place, thing, activity, or idea. A **plural noun** refers to more than one.

Regular Plural Nouns

Most singular nouns form their plurals by adding *-s* to the end of the noun.

> **Singular nouns:** railroad, customer, island
>
> **Plural nouns:** railroads, customers, islands

Some nouns form their plurals using different rules as explained in the following chart.

Forming Noun Plurals		
Noun	Add for Plural	Examples
Most nouns ending in -s, -ss, -sh, -ch, -x, or -z, including names that end in -s	-es	bus, buses Jones, Joneses church, churches kiss, kisses fox, foxes wish, wishes buzz, buzzes
Most nouns ending in a *vowel* + -o, including all names of people ending in -o	-s	Grasso, Grassos stereo, stereos patio, patios tattoo, tattoos radio, radios video, videos
Most nouns ending in a *consonant* + -o	-es	echo, echoes tomato, tomatoes hero, heroes veto, vetoes potato, potatoes volcano, volcanoes *Exceptions:* auto, autos piano, pianos Latino, Latinos solo, solos memo, memos soprano, sopranos
Most nouns ending in a *vowel* + -y, including names of people	-s	boy, boys key, keys day, days Riley, Rileys holiday, holidays turkey, turkeys
Most nouns ending in a *consonant* + -y	Change *y* to *i* and add -es	baby, babies country, countries berry, berries salary, salaries company, companies spy, spies *Exception:* With proper nouns, add -s the Kellys, the O'Gradys
Most nouns ending in -f, -fe, or -lf	Change the *f* to *v* and add -s or -es	elf, elves loaf, loaves half, halves self, selves knife, knives wife, wives *Exceptions:* belief, beliefs staff, staffs chief, chiefs
Compound nouns: one word two words Hyphenated nouns	 -s -s to last word Check the dictionary.	 keyboard, keyboards police officer, police officers sister-in-law, sisters-in-law grown-up, grown-ups

PRACTICE Forming Plural Nouns

25.4 Spell the plural form of each of the following nouns.

1. emergency <u>emergencies</u>
2. journey _____
3. Marotta _____
4. passer-by _____
5. stepmother _____

6. family _____
7. tomato _____
8. calf _____
9. veto _____
10. yourself _____

Irregular Plural Nouns

Irregular nouns do not form plurals by adding -s or -es. The following chart explains the rules and exceptions.

Forming Irregular Plural Nouns	
Irregular Plural Nouns	**Examples**
Nouns with different plural forms	child, children mouse, mice foot, feet ox, oxen man, men woman, women
Nouns that have the same singular and plural forms	deer, sheep, equipment *Names of fish:* cod, halibut, perch, salmon
Nouns that end in -s with no singular form	*Tools/instruments:* scissors, tweezers, pliers, tongs *Clothes:* pants, jeans, pajamas, shorts *Eyewear:* binoculars, glasses, goggles
Nouns that end in -s but are singular	economics, gymnastics, mathematics, measles, news, mumps
Plural nouns that do not end in -s	people, police, cattle
Nouns that are both singular and plural	headquarters, species, crossroads

TIP | The words *persons* and *people* are both used to refer to more than one individual; however, the preferred usage is *people*. *Persons* is preferred in legal contexts: Vehicles with fewer than three **persons** may not use the restricted highway lane.

PRACTICE   Changing Plural Nouns to Singular Nouns

25.5   Write the singular form for each of the plural nouns. If the form does not change, write NC for "no change."

1. economics _____NC_____
2. feet _____
3. children _____
4. pants _____
5. sheep _____
6. jeans _____
7. teeth _____
8. ladies _____

PRACTICE   Editing for Plural Noun Errors

25.6   Proofread the following paragraph for eight errors in plural nouns.

[1]Traveler who want to visit natural areas that conserve the environment and help the local people will enjoy going to the Sukau Rainforest in Malaysia. [2]The Sukau Rainforest Lodge is a twenty-room **ecolodge**. [3]It is located on the Kinabatangan River, which is Malaysia's second-longest river. [4]The nearby Kinabatangan Wildlife Sanctuary is famous for its wildlife, including elephants, monkies, and orangutans. [5]Visitor can observe wildlife from the comfort of riverboats or hike along jungle walkways. [6]The area is also known for the Gomantong Caves, home to an estimated two million bats. [7]Many other animal specie can be observed. [8]Hoofed mammals, which are active at night, include deers, cattles, and pig. [9]Birds are plentiful, with over 200 different type in the region.

(Adapted from *Travel and Tourism* by Paul S. Biederman)

ecolodge a special type of hotel, usually located in or near a protected area and managed in a way that conserves the environment

Mass Nouns

Mass nouns are nouns that have only singular forms. Usually, they are idea words or substances, such as things in liquid or mass forms that cannot be easily counted. Examples of mass nouns are listed below.

> **Whole groups or categories:** food, fruit, clothing, equipment, money, traffic, homework, mail, makeup, scenery, wildlife
>
> **Idea words:** advice, information, work, news, slang, vocabulary, evidence, fun, music
>
> **Fields of study:** chemistry, history, mathematics, psychology, marketing, anthropology
>
> **Languages:** English, French, Chinese, Spanish, Russian
>
> **Sports and activities:** driving, studying, swimming, soccer, chess, jogging, traveling
>
> **Solids and elements:** ice, bread, butter, glass, brass, meat, wood, plastic, cotton, hydrogen, oxygen
>
> **Natural phenomena:** fog, rain, lightning, sleet, snow, darkness, light, fire, gravity, cold
>
> **Medical conditions:** measles, mumps, AIDS, arthritis, flu, tuberculosis
>
> **Liquids:** juice, water, oil, blood, soup, gasoline, wine, coffee
>
> **Things made up of small pieces:** rice, corn, flour, hair, salt, sand, sugar, pepper, dust

Expressing Quantity with Mass Nouns To express quantity with a mass noun, add a quantity or container word or phrase in front of the mass noun.

> **Quantity words**: *a little* salt, *any* evidence, *less* work, *some* rice, *a great deal of* money
> **Possessive and demonstrative pronouns**: *his* music, *her* makeup, *this* clothing
> **Container words**: *gallon* of milk, *teaspoon* of sugar, *bottle* of water, *glass* of juice, *bowl* of soup, *tube* of toothpaste, *piece* of furniture

PRACTICE   Editing Singular and Plural Nouns

25.7   There are six mistakes in the use of plural nouns in this paragraph. Find and correct the errors.

Example: ¹In the United States, Coney Island was the birthplace of the ~~amusements~~ *amusement* park, the roller coaster, and the hot dog.

²Long before Disneyland, Six Flags, and Universal Studios, many American went to Coney Island and its amusement park. ³Coney Island is located on the south shore of Brooklyn, New York, facing the Atlantic Ocean. ⁴It started out as an upscale seaside resort after the Civil War in the mid-1800s with hotel, restaurants, and bathing facilities. ⁵In the 1920s, Coney Island became the nation's first mass tourism amusement park. ⁶Visitors could ride a choice of thrilling roller coasters, ferris wheels, and carousels, buy souvenir, and eat fast food. ⁷They could also go for a swim in the ocean or sit in the sands on the beach. ⁸During the summer, especially on weekend, a million visitor a day were not uncommon. ⁹Today, the crowds are not as massive. ¹⁰However, Coney Island still reflects the same mixing of Brooklyn's diverse population and languages as it did in the last century.

(Adapted from *Travel and Tourism* by Paul S. Biederman)

LO 4   Noun Markers

Noun markers are words that signal that a noun will follow. They sometimes tell if a noun is singular or plural.

> Many billions of dollars are spent every year on conventions and meetings, and cities compete vigorously for this business because of its economic impact.

This chart lists the types of noun markers with examples of their use in a sentence.

Noun Markers

Type	Markers
Articles	*a, an, the* Conventions and meetings are a significant part of the travel and tourism sector.
Demonstrative pronouns	*this, that, these, those* These conventions and meetings are held by many different groups such as professional and trade organizations.
Indefinite pronouns	*all, any, both, each, either, enough, every, few, fewer, less, little, many, more, most, much, neither, no, several, some* Some meetings are held for training employees. Government agencies stage meetings of all kinds.
Numbers	*one, two, three, four, etc.; first, second, third, etc.* Paris is one city that has become a popular host for international meetings.
Possessive nouns	*the teacher's, Javier's, a manager's* A planner's job is to arrange and carry out all the details related to a variety of meeting formats.
Possessive adjectives	*my, your, his, her, it, our, their, whose* A trade show gives suppliers of goods and services an opportunity to show their latest products.

Grammar Reminder:
For more information about these noun markers, see the adjectives section of Chapter 26.

Frequently Confused Noun Markers

Some noun markers have specific uses and are frequently confused.

A, An, The

a, an	• refers to a noun that is not specific • used when it is not important to know the specific noun or when the specific is not known	Marie takes a bus to work.
the	• refers to one specific noun • used if the noun is known or if the noun has been mentioned before; can also refer to one of a kind.	Marie takes the Route 6 bus that stops at Cheltenham and Ogontz Avenues.
no article	• with mass nouns that refer to a general term such as *life* or *water* • with nouns that are languages, sports, and academic subjects	~~An/The~~ Exercise can be tiring.

PRACTICE   Using *A, An,* or *The*

25.8   In the space provided, write *a, an,* or *the* before each noun. If no noun marker is needed, write an *X*.

Example: <u>X</u> People travel to experience other cultures and meet new people.

[1]Tourism can have a positive social and cultural impact on communities. [2]First of all, tourism has made _____ significant contribution to international understanding. [3]World tourism organizations recognize that tourism is a way to enhance respect for human rights without distinction as to race, sex, language, or religion. [4]In addition, tourism gives people _____ opportunity to see how others live. [5]Also, _____ tourists can interact socially with people in _____ host community. [6]A London pub or a New York café are good places for _____ social interaction. [7]Even a visit to another part of _____ United States would be socially and culturally stimulating. [8]For example, New Orleans has _____ very diverse social and cultural heritage. [9]Over the years, _____ Spanish, French, British, and Americans have lived in New Orleans. [10]The food, music, dance, and social norms are unique to the area.

(Adapted from *Introduction to Hospitality Management* by John R. Walker)

Many, Much/Few, Less, Little

Many and *few* are used with plural nouns.

> People like to travel for many reasons.
> Few people would refuse a chance to travel.

Much, less, and *little* are used with mass nouns.

> Some people do not have much time to travel.
> Soft adventure travelers like controlled trips with less risk.
> Hard adventure travelers have little fear of being exposed to risk.

This, That/These, Those

This and *these* refer to people or things that are near to the speaker. *That* and *those* refer to people or things that are far.
Use *this* and *that* before singular nouns.

> This research helps the travel industry.
> That desire to get away was important to most age groups.

Use *these* and *those* before plural nouns.

> These tourists want to relax and get rid of stress.
> Those tourists want to see and do new things.

PRACTICE Find Noun Markers

25.9 Circle the appropriate noun marker in the parentheses. If no noun marker is needed, circle the *X*.

Example: (The, [X]) Early humankind first imagined traveling to the moon, planets, and stars by viewing the night sky.

1. The first tourist trips into (X, the) space involved (a, the) flight that circled the earth.
2. (These, X) Two or three travelers and an experienced pilot were launched from (a, an) aircraft at nine miles above the earth.
3. They rocketed to an altitude of 60 miles, considered the end of the earth's atmosphere, and then (these, they) turned around.
4. (This, these) trip took about an hour.
5. Passengers saw a (few, little) spectacular views of earth as well as several minutes of weightlessness.
6. As technology improved, spaceships were able to fly higher and reach (the, X) orbiting altitude.
7. (Those, this) orbiting vehicles were small and uncomfortable and had (few, little) amenities.
8. In the first decade of 2000, orbital travel cost $500,000 for a two-day journey and $1 million for (a, X) five days.

(Adapted from *Travel and Tourism* by Paul S. Biederman)

> **TIP**
>
> A quick way to identify a noun is to test it by answering one of these questions:
>
> | | |
> |---|---|
> | Can the word follow *a, an,* or *the*? | **The** _____ is here.
 It is on **a** _____. |
> | Can you put a possessive pronoun in front of it? | **My** _____ is wonderful.
 Where are **their** _____? |
> | Can you put a quantity word in front of it? | **Three** _____ are in the box.
 Give me **some** _____. |

Writing Assignments

Review: Nouns

The following passage has errors in singular nouns, plural nouns, and noun markers. Find and correct them.

¹To understand the way people eat now, we have to look back about 500 years ago when plants, animals and microbes were transferred among the Americas, Europe, Asia, and Africa. ²The plants and animals survived deadly journies and successfully adapted to new climates. ³Seeds traveled in the cuffs or pleats of the clothing of persons. ⁴They also were caught in the fabric of cloth bundles and sacks.

⁵From Eurasia to the Western and Southern hemispheres went wheat, sugars, rices, and fruit such as banana, coconuts, apples, pears, apricot, peachs, plums, cherrys, and olives. ⁶Animals that provided meat and dairy were also transported. ⁷Yams, okra, and collard greens were among the much vegetables that made the crossing from Africa.

⁸Quinine, a medicinal plant from Peru, had enormous long-term importances because it could control the effects of malaria. ⁹Native Americans provided tobacco, which was thought to aid digestion. ¹⁰Most important gifts from New World were corn and white and sweet potatos.

¹¹These informations about the transfer of plants and animals was considered largest ever made on earth.

(Adapted from *The World* by Felipe Fernandez-Armesto)

Write about an Image

The large size of South America makes its climate varied. Each region has its own characteristic weather conditions.

Study the map of Latin America on the next page. Notice that the legend at the bottom is color coded to match the region on the map. The legend describes the region and its climate. Write a sentence describing the climate of each of the 7 regions (for a total of 7 sentences). Underline the common and proper nouns and noun markers in each sentence.

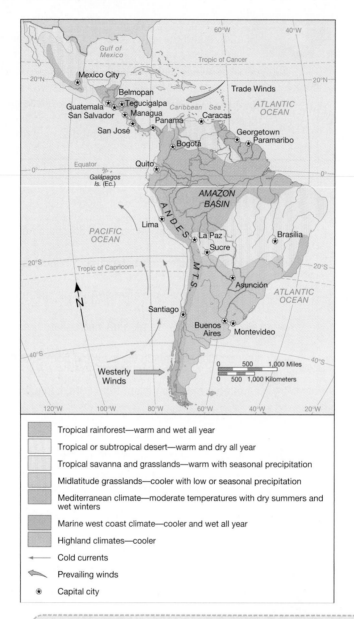

Tropical rainforest—warm and wet all year

Tropical or subtropical desert—warm and dry all year

Tropical savanna and grasslands—warm with seasonal precipitation

Midlatitude grasslands—cooler with low or seasonal precipitation

Mediterranean climate—moderate temperatures with dry summers and wet winters

Marine west coast climate—cooler and wet all year

Highland climates—cooler

⟵ Cold currents

↙ Prevailing winds

✳ Capital city

English Success Tip: Use a Dictionary to Check for Noun Forms

If you are looking for information about a specific noun, you can find it in a print or online dictionary. You can find some of these features of nouns:

- **Part of speech:** The dictionary gives a word's part of speech, usually abbreviated. The abbreviation for a noun is *N* (or *n*).
- **Singular and plural forms:** If the noun has an irregular plural form, it is listed right after the singular form.
- **Common or proper noun:** Proper nouns are capitalized.
- **Compound nouns:** The dictionary shows the correct form, a one-word, two-word, or a hyphenated compound noun.

For support in meeting this chapter's objectives, log in to www.mywritinglab.com, go to the Study Plan tab, click on **Nouns and Noun Markers** and choose **Nouns, Prepositions, and Articles** from the list of subtopics. Read and view the videos and resources in the Review Materials section, and then complete the Recall, Apply, and Write exercises in the Activities section. You can check your scores and overall progress by using the Gradebook.

CHAPTER 26

Adjectives and Adverbs

Theme: *Culinary Arts*

Learning Objectives

After working through this chapter, you will be able to:

LO 1 Identify adjectives and adverbs.

LO 2 Use adjectives correctly.

LO 3 Use adverbs correctly.

LO 4 Use the comparative forms of adjectives and adverbs.

LO 1 What Are Adjectives and Adverbs?

Adjectives and adverbs are modifiers. They make the words they modify more specific. However, adjectives and adverbs are used differently.

- Adjectives describe or limit nouns or pronouns:
  Food preparers should have a basic understanding of nutrition.
- Adverbs describe a verb, an adjective, or another adverb:
  The human body only survives a short time without water.
  Many dishes can be made more nutritious.
  Chefs are very often asked to modify dishes served to guests with health concerns.

Adjectives and Adverbs in Context

In the following passage about food and health, the adjectives and the adverbs are highlighted.

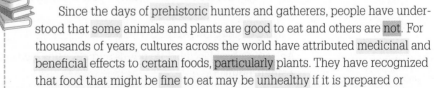

Since the days of prehistoric hunters and gatherers, people have understood that some animals and plants are good to eat and others are not. For thousands of years, cultures across the world have attributed medicinal and beneficial effects to certain foods, particularly plants. They have recognized that food that might be fine to eat may be unhealthy if it is prepared or stored improperly.

Not until the past few decades have people become increasingly concerned about the way foods affect their health and the specific foods that promote good health and longevity. These consumer concerns have had an impact on the food service industry. As a result, culinary students now study nutrition as part of their training. The relationship of the way people eat to the prevention of chronic weakening diseases such as obesity, diabetes, and heart disease will greatly influence what is served in restaurants and sold in stores.

(Adapted from *On Cooking* by Sarah R. Labensky and Alan M. Hause)

LO 2   Adjectives

Adjectives describe or limit nouns and pronouns. They specify which one, whose, how much, or how many, as explained in the following chart. Notice that these words can function as adjectives:

> possessive pronouns: my recipe, their restaurant
> possessive nouns: Ricardo's gazpacho, chef's kitchen
> nouns: vegetable garden, garden vegetables
> indefinite pronouns: several tomatoes, another salad

Adjectives and Examples	
Which one	Fresh vegetables have become popular choices in restaurants.
	This trend reflects the demands of consumers.
Whose	A chef's preference is to select his or her vegetables at the peak of their season.
	Everyone's diet should include vegetables.
How many/how much	Restaurants can purchase some vegetables already cleaned and cut, which saves both time and waste.
	Celery is packed in fifty-five pound cartons containing eighteen to forty-eight heads.
	Some vegetables are labeled 100 percent organic.
What kind	Recently, increasing numbers of people are adopting a vegetarian diet for its important health benefits.
	The demand for scrumptious, low-fat, fresh meals has increased, and many restaurants are finding creative ways to add vegetarian choices to their menus.
	Some Indian dishes can be traced to religious traditions.

Adjectives do not have singular or plural forms. Do not add an *-s* to an adjective.

> My professor gives ~~difficults~~ difficult assignments.
> I have a ~~five-years-old~~ five-year-old sister.

Placement of Adjectives

Adjectives are placed before nouns and after linking verbs. Several adjectives may modify a single noun.

> **TIP**   Some common linking verbs are *am, is, are, was, were, being, been, appear, become, remain, feel, seem,* and *look.*

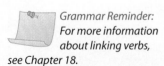
Grammar Reminder: For more information about linking verbs, see Chapter 18.

Before nouns	Herbs refer to the large group of sweet-smelling plants.
After linking verbs	Sweet basil is flavorful.
In pairs or a list	Sweet basil is an herb with green, tender leaves and a strong, warm, peppery flavor.

PRACTICE   Identifying Adjectives

26.1   Underline the adjectives in the following sentences. A sentence may have more than one adjective.

Example: The menu is the soul of <u>every</u> restaurant.

1. Most menus offer consumers enough selections to build an entire meal.
2. Food service operations may have separate menus for breakfast, lunch, and dinner.
3. If brand names are used, those brands must be served.
4. A typical North American meal consists of three courses.
5. The first course may be a hot or cold appetizer, soup, or salad.
6. The second course is the entrée or main dish, usually meat, poultry, fish or shellfish along with a vegetable and starch.
7. A sweet preparation or fruit and cheese is offered for dessert, the third course.
8. For a meal served in the European tradition, the salad would be presented as a palate cleanser after the main dish and before the dessert.

palate cleanser a food offered in the middle of a meal to remove lingering flavors so that the next course may be enjoyed

(Adapted from *On Cooking* by Sarah R. Labensky and Alan M. Hause)

Participles as Adjectives

Participles are verb forms that can act as adjectives. Present participles end in *-ing*. Past participles end in *-ed* or have an irregular form.

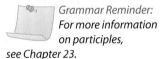

Grammar Reminder: For more information on participles, see Chapter 23.

Many food service operations use prepared condiments and flavorings. Old Bay seasoning is widely used in making boiled shrimp or crab.

Cooking oils are refined from various seeds, plants, and vegetables. To sauté foods properly, put a small amount of fat into the frying pan and pay attention to heating time.

Using Commas with Adjectives

Do use commas between coordinate adjectives. Coordinate adjectives equally modify the same noun; it does not matter which one comes first.

Original order: Thousands of years ago, spices were used for therapeutic, cosmetic, medicinal, and culinary purposes.

Switched order: Thousands of years ago, spices were used for cosmetic, culinary, medicinal, and therapeutic purposes.

Do not use a comma in these situations:

ø no comma between the last adjective and the noun	Dried herbs and spices should be stored in a cool, dry ø place.
ø no comma before or after the *and* between two adjectives	Herbs and spices are an inexpensive ø and ø tasty way to bring variety to food.
ø no comma between cumulative adjectives. The first adjective modifies the next and so on. The order of adjectives cannot be changed.	Hot spicy food became common in the fifth century.

> **TIP** To decide whether or not to use commas, use the following tests:
>
> **The *And* Test**: Place *and* between the adjectives. If the sentence still makes sense, then place a comma between the adjectives.
> **The Reversing Test**: Reverse the order of the adjectives. If the sentence makes sense, then place a comma between the adjectives.

PRACTICE Using Commas with Adjectives

26.2 Insert commas where they are needed between adjectives. Some sentences are correct.

Example: Aleppo pepper has a sharp, sweet, fruity flavor.

1. The spice anise is used in pastry fish shellfish and vegetable dishes.
2. Annatto seeds give a bright yellow-orange color to foods, and they are often used in cheeses and margarine.
3. Fresh capers are not used; the salty and sour flavor develops after they are soaked in strongly salted white vinegar.
4. Caraway, the world's oldest spice, is used for its fragrant spicy taste.
5. Mustard seeds are small hard spheres with a bitter flavor.
6. Black white and green peppercorns come from the same plant but are picked at different times.
7. Wasabi is a pale green root that is similar but unrelated to horseradish.
8. Sesame seeds are native to India; they are small flat ovals and have a nutty earthy taste when roasted or ground.

LO 3 Adverbs

Adverbs describe a verb, an adjective, or another adverb. They specify how, how often, when, where, and to what extent.

Adverbs and Examples	
Type of Information	Examples
How	Insects and rodents can quickly spoil food.
How often	An insect or rodent infestation should be dealt with immediately.

(continued)

When	Yesterday, we saw rat droppings in the kitchen.
Where	We looked for the rat everywhere but could not find it.
To what extent/how much	A rodent **infestation** is a very serious health risk.

infestation problem caused by a pest being present in large numbers

Many adverbs, such as *badly* and *quickly*, end in *-ly* and are easy to recognize. However, some adverbs do not end in *-ly*:

always fast quite less never not often seldom very well

Conjunctive Adverbs

Conjunctive adverbs are used as transitions between ideas to connect two independent clauses or within a sentence to show addition, time, contrast, effect, and summary. Examples are *however, therefore, consequently, moreover, otherwise, furthermore.*

Competitive cooking television shows, moreover, have caused enrollment in culinary schools to increase.

Placement of Adverbs

Some adverbs can be placed at the beginning, middle, or end of a sentence. Others need to be placed next to the word they modify.

Adverb use	Example
Describe a verb	Kitchen workers should learn to operate equipment properly.
Describe an adjective	Kitchens are filled with very dangerous objects.
Describe an adverb	Kitchen accidents are almost always caused by carelessness.

> **TIP**
>
> Some adverbs can change their meaning depending on where they are placed in a sentence. A few of them are *almost, ever, hardly, nearly, only,* and *quite.* Notice the difference in the meaning of *only* in the following sentences.
>
> Only my boss asked to taste the food.
>
> My boss only asked to taste the food.
>
> My boss asked to taste only the food.

Using Commas with Adverbs

Do use a comma after an adverb that introduces a sentence.

Tomorrow, I have to work a double shift.

Do use commas before and after conjunctive adverbs that interrupt a sentence.

The restaurant, however, will be closed for renovations next week.

> **PRACTICE** Identifying Adverbs
> **26.3**   Circle the adverbs.

Example: Wine making ⟦probably⟧ began 5,000 years ago in ancient Mesopotamia (today's Iraq).

1. Containers with traces of wine that once filled them have been found in tombs of Egyptian pharaohs.

2. Images and written records about grapes and wine suggest that the upper classes of Egypt enjoyed wine that was mostly sweet.

3. Wine was equally prized by the upper classes of ancient Greece.

4. When the Romans dominated Greece, wine became available to the lower classes because of its unusually low prices.

5. By the 1700s, France quickly became the greatest of the European wine-making nations.

6. Now, wine from many countries commands respect throughout the world.

7. Modern technologies have given wine makers control over almost every aspect of the process.

(Adapted from *On Cooking* by Sarah R. Labensky and Alan M. Hause)

Using Adjectives and Adverbs Correctly

Use an adverb, not an adjective, to modify a verb.

Food should be presented ~~proper~~ properly to diners.
The food should be arranged ~~neat~~ neatly.

Use correct irregular adjective and adverb forms.

Adjective	Adverb
good	*well*
The food tasted good. The restaurant served good food.	The food was prepared well.
Use *well* when referring to health: Eating chicken soup may help a person with a cold feel well.	
bad	*badly*
The meal tasted bad. The chef cooked a bad meal.	The chef cooked badly.
real	*really*
The chef used real sugar in the dessert, not an artificial sweetener.	The dessert was really sweet.

PRACTICE Using Adjectives and Adverbs Correctly
26.4 Circle the correct adjective or adverb.

Example: Fish and shellfish have become (increasingly, increasing) popular in recent years.

1. Good-quality fish and shellfish are now (easily, easy) available to almost every food-service operation.
2. Many fish and shellfish are (real, really) expensive and go bad (quick, quickly).
3. Fish can be hard to identify because many fish look (similarly, similar).
4. The FDA publishes a (regular, regularly) updated list of approved names for food fish.
5. Fish must be cooked (good, well) enough so that it is firm, not mushy and soft.
6. If the fish smells (bad, badly), throw it out.
7. Fish and shellfish inspections are performed (voluntary, voluntarily).
8. Grade A fish must look (good, well) with no physical marks or defects.

(Adapted from *On Cooking* by Sarah R. Labensky and Alan M. Hause)

LO 4 Comparatives and Superlatives

Adjectives and adverbs have forms for comparing two or more people or things. The **comparative form** compares two people or things. The **superlative form** compares three or more people or things.

Forming Adjective and Adverb Comparatives and Superlatives

syllable one or more letters used to make a single sound

Comparatives and superlatives are formed according to the number of **syllables** in the adjective or adverb.

Forming Comparative and Superlative Adjectives and Adverbs		
Adjective or Adverb Form	Comparative	Superlative
One syllable ending in a consonant	add -er	add -est
fast	faster	fastest
soon	sooner	soonest
One syllable ending in -e	add -r	add -st
large	larger	largest
late	later	latest
One syllable ending in a vowel and consonant	double the consonant and add -er	double the consonant and add -est
big	bigger	biggest
Two or more syllables	add *more* + word	add *most* + word
thoughtful	more thoughtful	most thoughtful
convenient	more convenient	most convenient

(*continued*)

Adjective or Adverb Form	Comparative	Superlative
Two syllables ending in -y	change the -y to an -i and add -er	change the -y to an -i and add -est
pretty	prettier	prettiest
Adverbs ending in -ly	use *more* + adverb	use *most* + adverb
carefully	more carefully	most carefully

Some adjectives can follow either rule:

Two-syllable adjective	Comparative	Superlative
clever	cleverer, more clever	cleverest, most clever
gentle	gentler, more gentle	gentlest, most gentle
friendly	friendlier, more friendly	friendliest, most friendly
quiet	quieter, more quiet	quietest, most quiet
simple	simpler, more simple	simplest, most simple

> **TIP** Be sure to use the correct word order for comparative and superlative forms.
>
> *–er* form: use *than* before the second item being compared
>
> At my house, chocolate ice cream is **more popular** than other flavors.
>
> *–est* form: use *the* because one thing is compared to the rest of the group.
>
> At my house, chocolate ice cream is **the most popular** flavor.

PRACTICE   Using Comparative and Superlative Adjectives and Adverbs

26.5   Correct any errors in the use of comparative or superlative adjectives and adverbs. Remember, the comparative compares two people or things, and the superlative compares three or more people or things. One sentence is correct.

duller
Example: A cold food product has a ~~more dull~~ flavor than a warm product.

1. Because they are served cold, some ice creams and custards have to be made more sweeter.

2. Frozen custard contains a highest percent of egg yolks and cream than standard ice cream.

3. Gelato is an Italian style ice cream with a more low milk fat content than American products.

4. Today, low-fat ice cream is richer, creamier, and more smooth than it used to be.

5. New stirring methods most thoroughly separate the tiny milk fat globules than the older method.

6. Frozen yogurt uses yogurt as a base, which makes it easiest to digest than ice cream.

7. Frozen yogurt is not more healthy than regular yogurt if it has large amounts of sugar and fat.

8. Gelato is more thicker than ice cream because it does not have much air in it from churning or stirring.

9. The top four more popular flavors of ice cream are vanilla, chocolate, butter pecan, and strawberry.

10. Recently, candy and ice cream companies have been partnering to produce more tasty ice creams.

Irregular Comparatives and Superlatives

Some adjectives and adverbs have irregular comparative and superlative forms.

Adjective or Adverb	Comparative	Superlative
bad, badly	worse	worst
good, well	better	best
much, many	more	most
little (amount)	less	least
far (distance)	farther	farthest

PRACTICE 26.6 Using Irregular Comparative and Superlative Forms

Choose the correct irregular comparative or superlative form.

Example: Is buying organic food really (better, best) for you?

1. Few studies have been conducted to prove that organic food is (more, the most) nutritious than non-organic food.

2. Higher prices for organic food are due to (more, the most) expensive farming and tighter government regulations.

3. Organic farms yield (less, the least) produce than non-organic farms do.

4. Organic food is (more, the most) expensive of all foods.

5. Some experts say that organic farming has (less, the least) impact on the environment than other types of farming.

6. Non-organic strawberries, apples, carrots, and grapes are foods that have the (more, most) pesticide and insecticide residues remaining on them.

7. Non-organic vegetables that have (less, the least) amount of pesticide and insecticide residues are asparagus, avocados, and cabbage.

8. Some people will travel (farther, the farthest) to buy organic food than to buy non-organic food.

9. It is (better, best) to buy organic or non-organic produce from local farmers than from supermarkets because it is fresher and the nutrients are at their peak.

10. Eating more fruit and vegetables and eliminating junk food is the (better, best) thing people can do for their health.

Writing Assignments

Review: Adjectives and Adverbs

Circle and correct the errors in adjectives and adverbs. Two sentences are correct.

Example: [1]America has become a service-oriented economy, and people are traveling and dining out oftener than ever before. *More often*

[2]The demand for hospitality managers has never been greatest than now. [3]However, the hospitality field is the worse choice for people looking for a regular five-day 40 hour workweek with weekends off. [4]Hospitality professionals get paid to work when other people are enjoying themselves. [5]Recently, companies have come to realize that to keep their managers, they cannot expect managers to work endless hours with least time off. [6]Much companies now limit the number of hours managers work.

[7]Not every person matches good with every hospitality position. [8]Some positions require high energy and excellent people skills. [9]Others call for people who can work quiet and pay attention to details. [10]If managers do not choose employees more better, they may hire the wrong people. [11]The positions will not be filled successful, and managers will be stuck with poor employees.

[12]After graduating from college, people may take any available management position that pays good. [13]Once they get used to making adequate money, they may find least satisfaction with the job. [14]The mismatch becomes obvious, and they may change jobs more soon than they would like. [15]People who work at a job that is not a good match will find it more hard to be effective managers. [16]College students should think about what is real important to them before taking a job in the hospitality field. [17]They need to figure out who they are and what they like to avoid making a worse choice.

(Adapted from *Introduction to Hospitality Management* by John R. Walker)

Write about an Image

Compare the nutritional information for the two snack chips on page 447. Write five to eight sentences about their differences using comparatives and superlatives.

Example: Cheddar and sour cream chips are **higher** in fat than tortilla chips.

Cheddar and Sour Cream Chips	
Serving Size: 1 Big Grab bag ● 1.5 oz ● 42.5g	
Amount Per Serving	
Calories 240	Calories from Fat 140
	% DV
Total Fat 15g	**23**%
Saturated Fat 4g	**20**%
Trans Fat 0g	
Cholesterol 0mg	**0**%
Sodium 350mg	**15**%
Total Carbohydrate 21g	**7**%
Dietary Fiber 2g	**8**%
Sugars <1g	
Protein 3g	**6**%
Vitamin A 0%	Vitamin C 15%
Calcium 2%	Iron 2%
Vitamin E 10%	Thiamine 6%
Niacin 10%	Vitamin B6 6%
Phosphorus 0%	Zinc 2%
Unofficial Pts: 6	**©DietFacts.com**

Percent of Calories from:
Fat-58.3%   Carb-35%   Protein-5%
(Total may not equate 100% due to rounding.)

Tortilla Chips	
Serving Size: 1 bag ● 1.125 oz ● 31.8g	
Amount Per Serving	
Calories 140	Calories from Fat 35
	% DV
Total Fat 4g	**6**%
Saturated Fat 1g	**5**%
Trans Fat 0g	
Cholesterol 0mg	**0**%
Sodium 240mg	**10**%
Total Carbohydrate 24g	**8**%
Dietary Fiber 2g	**8**%
Sugars 3g	
Protein 2g	**4**%
Vitamin A 0%	Vitamin C 2%
Calcium 2%	Iron 2%
Thiamine 2%	Riboflavin 2%
Niacin 6%	Vitamin B6 10%
Phosphorus 8%	
Unofficial Pts: 3	**©DietFacts.com**

Percent of Calories from:
Fat-25%   Carb-68.6%   Protein-5.7%
(Total may not equate 100% due to rounding.)

English Success Tip: Hopefully Very Awesome Advice to Share Together

Precise adjectives and adverbs enrich your sentences. However, overused or repetitious adjectives or adverbs are not effective.

Overused Adverbs

Avoid using adverbs that do not add meaning to the sentence. Examples are words like *very, totally, basically, hopefully, extremely, really, quite,* and *so.* Notice how the meaning of the next two sentences do not change when the overused adverbs are removed:

> The movie's ending was ~~very~~ surprising.
> The movie had a ~~really~~ sad ending.

Repetitious Words

Some word combinations say the same thing twice. Here's a brief list:

advance planning	cheap price	close proximity	commute back and forth
each and every	end result	free gift	regular routine

Check your papers for overused adverbs and repetitious words and find appropriate substitutes.

For support in meeting this chapter's objectives, log in to www.mywritinglab.com, go to the Study Plan tab, click on **Adjectives and Adverbs** and choose **Adjectives and Adverbs** from the list of subtopics. Read and view the videos and resources in the Review Materials section, and then complete the Recall, Apply, and Write exercises in the Activities section. You can check your scores and overall progress by using the Gradebook.

Using Correct Punctuation, Mechanics, and Spelling

Commas, Semicolons, and Colons

Theme: *Business and Marketing*

Learning Objectives

After working through this chapter, you will be able to:

LO 1 Identify commas, semicolons, and colons.

LO 2 Use commas to separate words in a series, introductory words and word groups, interrupter words and phrases, sentences, dates and addresses, and quotations.

LO 3 Use semicolons to connect two related sentences and to simplify a series.

LO 4 Use colons to signal a series or a long quotation, to separate titles and subtitles, and hours and minutes.

LO 1 What Are Commas, Semicolons, and Colons?

Commas, semicolons, and colons are three important punctuation marks used within sentences to separate words or groups of words. They help readers understand which words go together. Each mark looks different:

comma   ,   semicolon   ;   colon   :

Commas, Semicolons, and Colons in Context

Notice the use of commas, semicolons, and colons in the following passage about psychological pricing in marketing.

> Most consumers don't have all the time, ability, or information they need to figure out whether they are paying a good price for an item, which includes the following: researching the different brands or stores, comparing prices, and getting the best deals. Instead, they may rely on certain information that signals whether a price is high or low. For example, the fact that a product is sold in a respected and admired department store might signal that it is worth a higher price.
>
> As a result, many sellers consider the psychology of prices. For example, many consumers use price to judge quality. Consumers perceive higher-priced products as having higher quality. A $100 bottle of perfume may contain only $3 worth of scent, but some people are willing to pay the $100 because this price indicates something special.
>
> A retailer might show a higher manufacturer's suggested price next to the marked price, which would indicate that the product was originally priced much higher. Another approach is displaying a less expensive product next to a more expensive one; as a result, the shopper would think that the less expensive product was in the same class.
>
> (Adapted from *Marketing* by Gary Armstrong and Philip Kotler)

LO 2 Commas

Commas are used more frequently than other punctuation marks. This section explains seven ways to use commas.

In a Series

Use a comma after each word in a series and right before the *and* or *or*. A **series** is a list of three or more words, phrases, or clauses.

Series of words	In the 1960s, people did not know about personal computers, cell phones, iPods, or the Internet.
Series of phrases	Companies need to keep up with new technologies, update their products, and take advantage of new opportunities.
Series of clauses	Every new technology replaces an older technology, and as a result, CDs hurt phonograph records, digital photography hurt the film business, and mp3 players hurt the cassette tape player industry.

Do not use commas if each of the items in the series is connected with *and* or *or*.

Technology has released such wonders as antibiotics **and** robotic surgery **and** credit cards.

PRACTICE Using Commas with Items in a Series
27.1

Underline each series of three or more items and add commas to separate the items.

Example: Companies collect information about consumers, competitors, and developments in the marketplace.

trade show an event at which goods and services in a specific industry are shown and demonstrated

1. They use techniques such as observing consumers going to **trade shows** and monitoring consumer reviews on the Internet.
2. Companies monitor blogs and Internet sites to find out what people are saying about their products their performance and their reputation.
3. They also monitor their competitors' new strategies product launches or techniques.
4. Suppliers resellers and key customers can offer important information about other companies.
5. Competitors can learn about other companies by reading their annual reports visiting trade show exhibits and checking their web pages.
6. Spies from other companies could pose as company drivers internal security guards or executives.
7. For a fee, companies can subscribe to over 3,000 online databases and search services such as ProQuest LexisNexis and Dow Jones News Retrieval.
8. Most companies are now training employees to protect information from competitors to collect information and to avoid using illegal means to get secret company information.

(Adapted from *Marketing* by Gary Armstrong and Philip Kotler)

Introductory Words and Word Groups

Use a comma after introductory expressions, phrases, and clauses.

Introductory transitional words and phrases	First, all products go through several phases and complete their life cycles.
	As a result, newer, better products come along.
Introductory prepositional phrase	Through research and development, a company can create an original product.
Introductory verbal phrase *Exception:* when followed by a verb	Testing the new product, the company found that consumers would buy it.
	Finding a new product to develop can be expensive.

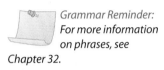

Grammar Reminder: For more information on phrases, see Chapter 32.

PRACTICE Using Commas with Introductory Words and Phrases

27.2 Underline the introductory words or phrases and place a comma after them. If the sentence is correct without a comma, write *C*.

Example: ¹In fact, studies indicate that up to 90 percent of all new consumer products fail.

²For example of the new food, beverage, and beauty products each year, at least 70 percent fail within that year. ³First the product may be poorly designed. ⁴Despite poor research results a high-level executive might push a favorite idea. ⁵Priced too high a product will not sell. ⁶On the other hand sometimes competitors fight back with a cheaper or better product.
⁷Behind each failed product are wasted money and hopes. ⁸Failing to bring value to customers Smokeless cigarettes never sold well.
⁹Therefore to create successful new products, companies must take a customer-based, systematic approach.

(Adapted from *Marketing* by Gary Armstrong and Philip Kotler)

Interrupter Words and Phrases

Use commas around interrupter words and phrases. An interrupter can be removed without changing the sentence's meaning.

Words or phrases that add information	People born between 1977 and 2000, called Millennials or Generation Y, are a diverse group.
	Millennials, who grew up with computers and the Internet, are consumers of all means of communication.
	Kim, an international student, uses her cell phone to stay in touch with friends and family throughout the day.
Transitions	Reaching the Millennials, therefore, requires creative marketing approaches.

PRACTICE Using Commas with Interrupters

27.3 Underline the interrupters and place commas to set them off from the rest of the sentence.

Example: In 1955, Ray Kroc, a 52-year-old salesman of milk-shake-mixing machines, discovered a number of seven similar restaurants owned by Richard and Maurice McDonald.

1. Kroc saw the McDonald brothers' fast-food concept as a perfect fit therefore for America's on-the-go lifestyles.

2. Kroc bought the small chain for $2.7 million, and of course the rest is history.

3. McDonald's quickly grew as a matter of fact to become the world's largest fast-feeder.

4. The Golden Arches are I believe one of the world's most familiar symbols.

5. Just as the marketplace provided opportunities for McDonald's however it has also presented challenges.

6. The company has struggled after all to address changing consumer lifestyles.

7. Fast-casual restaurants those offering imaginative meals in fashionable surroundings were attracting customers.

8. Americans were in addition looking for healthier eating options.

9. McDonald's has made major efforts with its plan to improve business Plan to Win.

10. Yes even McDonald's character Ronald McDonald is trimmer and fitter.

(Adapted from *Marketing* by Gary Armstrong and Philip Kotler)

Compound Sentences

Use a comma before the coordinating conjunction (*and, but, for, nor, so, yet*) that connects two independent clauses in a compound sentence.

Grammar Reminder: For more information about compound sentences, see Chapter 19.

In the past, most catalogs were printed, but today, more catalogs are online. Companies have not given up their printed catalogs, for they convince shoppers to use the online versions.

PRACTICE Using Commas in Compound Sentences

27.4 Edit the following passage by adding commas to the compound sentences.

Example: Direct marketing is a selling approach, and technology has helped to transform it.

mass-media advertising selling through television, radio, newspapers

direct marketing selling directly to the consumer by sending catalogs, email and by calling people

[1]Many companies still use **mass-media advertising** but they supplement with **direct marketing**. [2]Other companies use direct marketing as the only approach for it is convenient, easy, and private. [3]Direct marketers never close their doors and customers do not have to battle traffic. [4]Good catalogs and website give a great deal of information so shoppers do not have to depend on retail salesperson who may not know as much about a product. [5]Shoppers can learn about products and services on their own yet they can interact with sellers by phone on the seller's website if necessary.

Complex Sentences

Use a comma after an introductory dependent clause. In most cases, do not use a comma if the sentence ends with a dependent clause.

> If a company wants to compete in today's market, it should consider creating a website.

> A company should consider creating a website if it wants to compete in today's market.

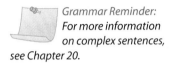
Grammar Reminder:
For more information
on complex sentences,
see Chapter 20.

Use a comma for nonessential dependent clauses. A dependent clause is nonessential when it can be left out without changing the meaning of the sentence.

> **Nonessential, no commas**: The brand website, which is the most basic type, is designed to inform people about the company's products without selling them.

> **Essential, no commas**: Marketers must design a site that will get consumers to visit it and come back.

PRACTICE **Using Commas in Complex Sentences**

27.5 Edit the passage by adding commas to complex sentences.

Example: ¹Many people prefer online shopping because it offers shoppers many advantages. No comma.

post to make information
available online

> ²People who do not like fighting traffic or looking for parking spaces enjoy shopping online. ³As long as they can connect to the Internet they can shop. ⁴Time is not a problem either because online stores never close. ⁵Also, when people want to find out more about a product they can do their own independent research. ⁶They can visit company websites for information although the company may not sell the product. ⁷To find out what others think customers can visit product websites that invite customers to review products. ⁸The reviews are **posted** whether they are good or bad. ⁹Although customer reviews are helpful shoppers may prefer to visit websites with reviews written by experts. ¹⁰People can also compare prices online so that they can find the most reasonable price for a product. ¹¹The cost to have the product sent does not have to be a concern since many companies offer free or discounted shipping. ¹²Another benefit of online shopping is product availability. ¹³A desired product can be found online whereas it may not be available locally. ¹⁴A greater variety of products and items that are hard to find can be found online anywhere in the world. ¹⁵Finally, shoppers do not have to worry about receiving an item with missing parts or mangled boxes.

Dates and Addresses

Use commas for dates and addresses according to these rules:

Commas for Dates	Examples
Between the date and the year	October 31, 2001
	The first iPod was released on October 23, 2001.
Between the day and the date	Tuesday, October 31, 2001
	The first iPod was released on Tuesday, October 23, 2001.

(Continued)

(Continued)

After the year	The first iPod was released on October 23, 2001, and the rest is history.
Note: no comma between the month and the day or the month and the year	The first iPod was released on October 31.
	The first iPod was released in October 2001.
Commas for Addresses	**Examples**
Between the street, city or town, and state	The college bookstore is located at 123 Main Street, Phoenix, Arizona.
After the state or country within a sentence	The college bookstore is located at 123 Main Street, Phoenix, Arizona, right next to the student center.
	The U.S. Toyota sales president travels to Toyota City, Japan, at least once a year.
Note: no comma before a zip code	His mailing address is 123 Main Street, Phoenix, AZ 85003.

PRACTICE **Using Commas with Dates and Addresses**

27.6 Add commas to the following passage.

Example: ¹Bill Gates was born on Friday, October 28, 1955.

²Gates grew up in Seattle Washington with his parents and two sisters. ³In 1973 Gates enrolled as a freshman at Harvard University in Cambridge Massachusetts. ⁴When he was a junior, Gates took a leave of absence from Harvard to work with his friend Paul Allen at a microcomputer company in Albuquerque New Mexico in November 1975. ⁵Gates and Allen developed a partnership called "Micro-Soft," and on November 26 1976 the trade name "Microsoft" was registered in New Mexico. ⁶The first retail version of Microsoft Windows was launched on November 20 1985 and the company struck a deal with IBM in August to develop a system called OS/2. ⁷Gates took a management and executive role in Microsoft from 1975 to 2006. ⁸He decided to dedicate more time to **philanthropy** on June 15 2006 and his last full-time day at Microsoft was Friday June 27 2008. ⁹The Microsoft Corporation is located at One Microsoft Way Redmond WA 98052.

philanthropy helping the poor, especially by giving money

Direct Quotations

Direct quotations can be introduced by a signal phrase or integrated in a sentence. A signal phrase identifies the person making the statement using words such as "she states" or "he writes."

Use commas to separate the signal phrase from the direct quotation according to the following rules:

Signal phrase at the beginning	He said, "The aim of marketing is to affect customers' buying behavior."
Signal phrase in the middle	"The aim of marketing," he said, "is to affect customers' buying behavior."
Signal phrase at the end	"The aim of marketing is to affect customers' buying behavior," he said.

Do not use a comma when the quotation is integrated with the sentence:

> Kolter emphasizes that "the aim of marketing is to affect customers' buying behavior."

PRACTICE Using Commas with Quotations

27.7 Insert commas within the following quotations.

rumble to make a continuous low sound

Example: Armstrong and Kolter said, "Harley-Davidson has **rumbled** its way to the top of the heavy-weight motorcycle market."

1. One sports T-shirt said "I'd rather push a Harley than drive a Honda."
2. "You take off the leather jacket and pants and the helmet, and you'll never know who you'll find" said one Harley fan.
3. "Independence, freedom, and power " stated a Harley-Davidson executive "were the universal Harley appeals."
4. One analyst remarked "It's much more than a machine. It is part of their own self-expression and lifestyle."
5. "We sell a dream here" points out a Harley-Davidson dealer.
6. According to Armstrong and Kolter "The average Harley customer is a 47-year-old male with an average household income of $82,000."
7. "Harley-Davidson's marketers spend a great deal of time" they said "thinking about customers and their buying behavior."

(Adapted from *Marketing* by Gary Armstrong and Philip Kotler)

LO 3 Semicolons

Use semicolons to connect two related sentences and simplify a series of items.

Connect two related sentences

> Money is a medium of exchange; we use it as a way of buying and selling things. Money keeps its value; therefore, it can be used for future purchases.

Simplify a series of items

> The most spendable forms of money are cash, paper money and metal coins; a check, an order instructing a bank to pay a payee; and a checking account, bank account funds owned by the depositor.

(Adapted from *Business Essentials* by Ronald J. Ebert and Ricky W. Griffin)

PRACTICE Using Semicolons

27.8 Add semicolons to the following sentences.

Example: There is a saying that money makes the world go round; however, the cultures of the world have different attitudes towards it.

1. In some countries, money is exchanged with respect Japan is a good example.
2. Money is rarely passed from hand to hand in Japan instead, people pick up money from little trays and dishes placed next to cash registers.
3. Also, it is not good form to talk about how much you make or have in the bank these are private matters.

4. This is also true in the United Kingdom it is often considered bad manners to talk about money.

5. In some places, people have a more relaxed attitude towards money the United States is one of them.

6. People in the United States freely discuss how much they make how much they paid for their houses and how much they have.

7. Notes and coins are exchanged with little formality in the United States people put bills on a counter or slap them into someone's hand.

8. In some countries, money helps set apart a country from its neighbors people often feel a sense of pride toward their national currencies.

9. In 2002, the euro replaced the currencies of twelve European nations officials worried that many Europeans would not want to give up their currencies.

10. However, people made the switch easily old currencies disappeared quickly.

(Adapted from *Business Essentials* by Ronald J. Ebert and Ricky W. Griffin)

LO 4 Colons

Use a colon in the following ways:

To introduce a list of items at the end of a complete sentence

Securities include the following: stocks, bonds, and mutual funds.

mutual funds amounts of money that are managed by an investment company

To introduce a quotation

Ebert and Griffin caution students about the securities markets: "**Mutual funds** trading is a risky industry featuring rapid buying and selling in the financial marketplace."

To introduce a second sentence that explains or adds details to the first

Sachi decided to take the company's offer: the company will pay for her college courses as long as she maintains a B average.

To separate titles and subtitles

The required textbook for our class is *Marketing: An Introduction*.

To separate hours and minutes

Our class begins at 10:30 a.m.

Do not use a colon after a verb:
Three ways financial professionals manage mutual funds are✗creating, buying, and selling.

PRACTICE Using Colons

27.9 Add colons to the following sentences.

Example: Many brand names have become identified with the product category: Kleenex, Levi's, Jell-O, Scotch Tape, and Ziploc.

1. The following brand names became generic aspirin, nylon, escalator, thermos, and shredded wheat.

2. According to Armstrong and Kolter, a brand name should have these qualities "(1)It should suggest something about the product's benefits and qualities.

extendable using the brand name in one category that people know well to market a new product in another category, for example Sun-Maid raisins and Sun-Maid raisin muffins

(2) It should be easy to pronounce, recognize, and remember. (3) The brand name should be distinctive. (4) It should be **extendable**. (5) The name should translate easily into foreign languages. (6) It should be capable of registration and legal protection."

3. A brand name should be extendable Amazon.com began as an online bookseller but chose a name that would allow expansion into other categories.

4. To learn about marketing to improve people's well-being, read the book *Social Marketing Improving the Quality of Life*.

5. The Super Bowl, which usually begins around 6 30 p.m. Eastern Standard Time, has a lot to offer advertisers because it is the most-watched television event of the year.

(Sentences 1–4 adapted from *Marketing* by Gary Armstrong and Philip Kotler)

Writing Assignments

Review: Commas, Semicolons, and Colons

Add commas, semicolons, and colons as needed to the following passage.

[1]When most people think of athletic footwear global brands such as Nike and Adidas come to mind. [2]However a small, new company called And1 quickly made a name for itself. [3]The company began as a graduate school research project for Jay Coen Gilbert Seth Berger and Tom Austin. [4]The idea for the name And1 came from a phrase that basketball broadcasters use.

[5]The company started out with "trash talk" tee shirts which became a huge success. [6]Trash talk is a form of **boasting** or insulting another player. [7]For example one slogan said "Call 911. I'm on fire." [8]Soon after And1 added shoes and shorts to its product line. [9]The clothing and shoes were designed to appeal to eleven- to seventeen-year-olds who were hard core "ballers" the street name for basketball players. [10]And1 became very popular among children teenagers and young adults. [11]The clothing is meant for those who love basketball but it is not meant for those who want to make a fashion statement.

[12]At the core of its business is a growing line of tapes that highlight the skills of **playground legends** showing their incredible moves. [13]One successful promotional activity was "mixtapes" created by talented streetball players these mixtapes show the players doing tricks with the basketball. [14]Also, And1 conducted a summer tour **showcasing** the talents and footwear of more than fifteen top streetball players.

[15]In 2009, Ebert and Griffin said "And1 is successful because it knows hires and promotes to its target market." [16]To help keep itself fresh And1 hires mostly younger staffers and pays close attention to their advice. [17]In addition And1 knows that most high school basketball players do not go on to play in college or professionally therefore And1 donates money to projects that emphasize and contribute to education.

(Adapted from *Business Essentials* by Ronald J. Ebert and Ricky W. Griffin and http://wep.wharton.upenn.edu/newsletter/spring07/allstar.html)

boasting talking proudly about one's abilities

playground legend a person who is well known for playing basketball at neighborhood basketball courts

showcasing displaying something to its advantage

Write about an Image

Study the photograph showing a young woman who has just bought her first car. Write ten sentences about the photograph applying the rules you learned in this chapter about commas, semicolons, and colons.

> ### English Success Tip: Punctuate to Separate, Not to Pause
>
> If you have been using the "place a comma when you pause" method, you may end up with unnecessary commas. In spoken English, pauses are important because they give listeners a chance to get the meaning. On the other hand, readers of written English do not need pauses because they can go back and reread a sentence or passage.
>
> As you have learned in this chapter, commas are used according to specific rules. With some practice, you can learn to use commas effectively.

For support in meeting this chapter's objectives, log in to www.mywritinglab.com, go to the Study Plan tab, click on **Commas, Semicolons, and Colons** and choose **Commas, Semicolons, Colons, Dashes, and Parentheses** from the list of subtopics. Read and view the videos and resources in the Review Materials section, and then complete the Recall, Apply, and Write exercises in the Activities section. You can check your scores and overall progress by using the Gradebook.

Other Marks of Punctuation

Theme: *Fashion*

Learning Objectives

After working through this chapter, you will be able to:

LO 1 Use the apostrophe to form contractions and show ownership.

LO 2 Use quotation marks to set off exactly quoted words, titles of short works, and parts of whole works.

LO 3 Use hyphens, dashes, and parentheses correctly.

LO 1 What Are Other Marks of Punctuation?

Apostrophes, quotation marks, hyphens, dashes, ellipses, and parentheses are punctuation marks. Each of these marks is used for specific reasons according to special rules.

> apostrophe '   quotation marks " " ' '   hyphen -
>
> dash —   parentheses ( )

Other Punctuation Marks in Context

In the following passage about the growing size of Americans and items made to fit them, the marks of punctuation covered in this chapter are highlighted.

> [1]As we Americans are getting bigger (the Centers for Disease Control and Prevention in Atlanta estimate that roughly a third of Americans are overweight, with 20 percent of us qualifying as obese), so, too, is our stuff. [2]Cars are getting larger, of course—the 2004 Ford Excursion fits eight average-size passengers (or roughly six obese ones). [3]And apparently so are the people driving them—the Excursion's driver's seat is 40 inches wide. [4]The same goes for our places of worship. Thomas McElheny, the CEO of Church Plaza, a manufacturer of "worship furniture" based in Florida, says that whereas 18 inches per worshipper used to be the allotment when fitting for pews, most churches now require 21 inches. [5]Church Plaza's pews have been made to support an almost miraculous 1,700 pounds per seat. [6]"The last thing you want is the tragedy of a chair collapsing in church," McElheny says. [7]But it's not only more sitting space we require. [8]For football enthusiasts, Russell Athletic now makes an XXXXXL (that's five X's) team jersey. [9]This fits a 62-inch-wide chest and an even larger belly, if the jersey's mesh-blend stretchiness is put to full use. [10]But high-end clothiers have also come to recognize the value of getting into plus sizes, which now account for about 5 percent to 10 percent of the male clothing market and, by some estimates, as much as 20 percent of the female market.
>
> (From "Supersize It" by James Verini, http://www.slate.com/id/2096457/)

LO 2 Apostrophes

An apostrophe is a mark of punctuation that is used to form contractions or to show ownership.

Apostrophes with Contractions

A **contraction** is a shortened form of two or more words. An apostrophe is used in place of the letters that are missing.

She's majoring in fashion design.   She's = She + is
It's a career with excellent employment options.   It's = It + is

Contractions formed from a pronoun and verb:

I + am = I'm	he + is = he's	you + are = you're	she + has = she's
they + have = they've	we + had = we'd	I + will = I'll	he + would = he'd

Contractions formed from a helping verb and *not*:

are + not = aren't	can + not = can't	could + not = couldn't	do + not = don't
does + not = doesn't	did + not = didn't	has + not = hasn't	have + not = haven't
is + not = isn't	was + not = wasn't	will + not = won't	would + not = wouldn't

! Contractions are not commonly used in academic writing.

PRACTICE   Adding Apostrophes to Contractions

28.1   Add apostrophes to contractions in the following sentences.

shouldn't
Example: Some people think furs shouldnt be used to make clothing items.

1. They dont like to see animals killed for their fur.
2. Organizations such as People for the Ethical Treatment of Animals (PETA) havent been happy with the way fur farmers treat animals.
3. As a result, the fur industry saw that it wasnt raising the animals in a good way.
4. Fur farmers realize they have to be sure that the animals wont experience a painful death.
5. Fur trappers cant trap animals that are **endangered species** because of government regulations.
6. An experienced animal trapper tries to trap the animals he wants, not the ones he doesnt want.

endangered species a type of animal or plant that might stop existing because there are only a few of this type alive

7. Research is being done to make certain that trappers arent using cruel methods to trap animals.

8. The use of fur in the fashion industry isnt going to stop because theres a market for it.

(Adapted from *Fashion, Apparel, Accessories, and Home Furnishings* by Jay Diamond and Ellen Diamond)

Apostrophes to Show Ownership

Apostrophes are used with nouns and indefinite pronouns to show ownership. Words that show ownership are called **possessives**.

Hernando's girlfriend designs and sews her own clothes.

She wants to design women's clothing and become famous.

Singular Nouns   To make singular nouns or indefinite pronouns possessive, add an apostrophe and an -s.

Singular nouns not ending in -s	Antoinette's jeans were expensive. A designer creates a product with the customer's needs in mind.
Singular nouns ending in -s *Note:* If the added –s makes the word hard to pronounce, it can be omitted.	College students are the business's best customers. Delores's clothing is fashionable. Or Delores' clothing is fashionable.
Family names ending in -s	Mr. Rodrigues's company is in Honduras.
Indefinite pronouns ending in -*body* **or** -*one* (*anybody, anyone, somebody, someone, everybody, everyone, nobody, no one*)	Everyone's shirt had long sleeves. Someone's hat was left in the classroom.
Singular compound nouns	My father-in-law's factory makes zippers.

Plural Nouns   Regular plural nouns usually end in -s. To make plural nouns possessive, add an apostrophe. Notice the possessive form of irregular plural nouns.

Plural nouns ending in -s	Magazine editors' preferences appear in their monthly fashion magazines. Designers' ideas come from many different sources.
Plural nouns not ending in -s	Children's clothing started to be produced early in the twentieth century. International trends and styles have influenced men's clothing.
Plural family names	The Rodrigueses' home is in San Antonio, Texas.
Plural compound nouns	My brothers-in-law's store sells clothing for large men.

Grammar Reminder: See Chapter 25 for more information about regular and irregular noun plurals.

Individual and Joint Ownership To show that two people own one thing, add an apostrophe and *-s* to the second name.

> Sheree and Vanessa's clothing store is called SherVan.

To show that two people each own something separately, add an apostrophe and *-s* to both names.

> Sheree's and Vanessa's stores were originally in different towns.

TIP

Your possessive form is correct if you can turn it into an "of" expression.

Hernando's girlfriend   girlfriend of Hernando
women's clothing   clothing of the women

PRACTICE Adding Apostrophes to Make Singular and Plural Possessives

28.2   Rewrite the phrases by putting the noun or indefinite pronoun that comes after the "of the" into the possessive form.

Example: the uniform of the player   the player's uniform
        the uniforms of the players   the players' uniforms

1. the shoes of the child   _____
2. the glasses of Chris   _____
3. the clothes of Lee and Wei, joint ownership _____
4. the hat of Mr. Gonzales   _____
5. the hat of the Gonzaleses   _____
6. the jacket of someone   _____
7. the stores of Santos and Alexis, individual ownership _____
8. the jackets of the men   _____
9. the employee of the brother-in-law   _____
10. the dresses of the sisters-in-law   _____

Apostrophes with Abbreviations and Numbers

Capital letters and abbreviations do not need apostrophes	The students received As and Bs on their projects. The college awarded 250 BAs last winter.
Use apostrophes for lowercase letters so they will not be mistaken for words	The word *choose* has two o's.
No apostrophes are needed for decades: 1990s, 2000s, 2010s	Tattoos were a popular fad of the 1990s.
No apostrophes are needed for numbers: 5s, 10s, 20s	Her cell phone number ends with two 5s.

Apostrophes with Time and Quantity Words

Words such as *minute, hour, day, week, month, year,* and *summer* express time. Words such as *dollar, pound,* and *mile* express quantity. Add an apostrophe and *-s* to show ownership.

Singular	Plural
He paid one month's rent for his studio.	He paid two months' rent for his studio.
She had one year's experience working as a buyer.	She had three years' experience working as a buyer.
It is hard to survive on one dollar's worth of food a day.	It is easier to survive on twenty-five dollars' worth of food a day.

PRACTICE   Adding Apostrophes to Show Ownership

28.3   Add apostrophes to words that show ownership in the following sentences.

Today's children's

Example: Todays childrens clothing is far different from the products that were available in the early twentieth century.

1. Boys and girls clothes in the early 1900s were not fashionable.
2. Many outfits children wore were cut down and remade from their parents old clothes.
3. Yesterdays children did not get to decide what they wanted to wear.
4. They had to wear a parents selection for them.
5. Their clothes were small versions of adults clothing styles.
6. Today, successful television programming has influenced this generations styles and fashions.
7. Peer groups also play a part in young consumers preferences.
8. When an adults style is popular, it is often copied for children.

(Adapted from *Fashion Apparel, Accessories, and Home Furnishings* by Jay Diamond and Ellen Diamond)

Avoid Problems with Apostrophes

Avoid confusing contractions with possessive pronouns.

Contraction		Possessive Pronoun	
it's (it is)	It's on sale.	its	The store has its sale on Saturday.
you're (you are)	You're going to buy a new pair of jeans.	your	Your new jeans cost $100.
they're (they are)	They're buying the latest fashions.	their	Their new outfits are fashionable.
who's (who is)	Who's the best dressed at school?	whose	Whose sweater is this?

Avoid confusing singular possessive nouns with plural nouns.

singular	singular possessive	plural	plural possessive
lady	lady's	ladies	ladies'
The lady shopped for a new pair of shoes.	The lady's shoe size was a 12.	Some ladies have large feet.	The store did not have any ladies' shoes in size 12.
employee	employee's	employees	employees'
The employee brought his lunch to work.	The employee's wife prepared his lunch.	Many employees prefer to buy their lunch at the company cafeteria.	The employees' cafeteria has a large selection of food.

> **TIP** | Do not use an apostrophe before an *-s* verb ending.
>
> starts
> The class ~~start's~~ in ten minutes.

PRACTICE Edit for Apostrophes

28.4   Add apostrophes where needed or correct incorrectly used apostrophes.

Handbags
Example: [1]~~Handbag's~~ are an extremely important part of the fashion business.

[2]Not long ago, handbag makers designed their handbags to go with clothing and shoe manufacturer's styles. [3]A designers' signature appeared on a label inside the bag. [4]During the 1970's, designer signatures started to appear on the bags themselve's.[5] The designer handbag popularity began when a famous LV logo was displayed on an expensive vinyl handbag collection, and a large number of customers' immediately bought them.

[6]In todays' environment, the designer bag market continue's to expand. [7]Prada, for example, one of the worlds upscale names, markets a collection of handbags that sells for over $1,000. [8]The publics' acceptance of these designer label handbags has become important in the retail market. [9]Many fashion retailers have set aside separate departments in their stores to feature individual designers names. [10]Still, comparatively inexpensive

handbags produced outside of the United States account for much of the industrys' sales. [11]Copies of designer bags can be found at flea markets and street vendor's stands around the world.

(Adapted from *Fashion Apparel, Accessories, and Home Furnishings* by Jay Diamond and Ellen Diamond)

Quotation Marks

Quotation marks are placed at the beginning and end of words, phrases, or sentences. There are two types, double and single, and each has a specific use.

DOUBLE QUOTATION MARKS: " "   SINGLE QUOTATION MARKS: ' '

Quotation Marks with Direct Quotations

A **direct quotation** reports the exact wording of a speaker or writer. Most quotations are introduced by a signal phrase, which is made up of the author's name and a verb that introduces the quotation and fits what the author is saying. Notice how quotation marks, capital letters, periods, and commas are used in the following examples.

Signal Phrase and Direct Quotation
Famous twentieth century French designer Coco Chanel said, "Fashion is made to become unfashionable."

Signal Phrase Interrupting a Direct Quotation
"Fashion," said Coco Chanel, "is made to become unfashionable."

Signal Phrase at the End of a Direct Quotation
"Fashion is made to become unfashionable," said Coco Chanel.

Complete Sentence Introducing a Direct Quotation
Coco Chanel explains her attitude toward fashion: "Fashion is made to become unfashionable."

Two Quoted Sentences with a Signal Phrase
"I don't design clothes," comments designer Ralph Lauren. "I design dreams "

Quotation Marks with a Question as the Direct Quotation
A. J. Esther once asked, "What do nudists wear on casual Fridays?"

Quotation Marks with a Direct Quotation in Your Own Sentence
Who said, "I base most of my fashion sense on what doesn't itch"?

> *Writing Reminder:*
> *For more information on using signal phrases with quotations in documented papers, see Chapter 16.*

PRACTICE Using Quotation Marks

28.5   Underline the signal phrase and punctuate the quotation. Remember to capitalize the first word of a quoted sentence.

Example: "Fashion is never in crisis because clothes are always necessary," <u>says Achille Maramotti</u>, founder of Max Mara.

1. clothes don't make a man   states Herbert Harold Vreeland, but clothes have got many a man a good job

2. Comedian Gilda Radner offers her humorous point of view about fashion   I base my fashion taste on what doesn't itch

3. I knew exactly what I wanted to do   explains designer Tommy Hilfiger   I wanted to build a brand of clothing around my own attitude and my own lifestyle

4. According to writer Henry David Thoreau   every generation laughs at the old fashions but follows religiously the new

5. I don't know who invented the high heel but all men owe him a lot   said Marilyn Monroe

6. Woolfgang Joop comments   I think that fashion is about surprise and fantasy It's not about rules

7. if men can run the world why can't they stop wearing neckties? asks journalist Linda Ellerbee how intelligent is it to start the day by tying a little noose around your neck?

Using Single Quotation Marks Use single quotation marks for a quotation that is inside another quotation.

chapeaus the French word for hats

According to Jay Diamond and Ellen Diamond, "French designers have always designed 'chapeaus' that brought excitement to fashion events."

(Adapted from *Fashion Apparel, Accessories, and Home Furnishings* by Jay Diamond and Ellen Diamond)

Quotation Marks or Italics with Titles

Use quotation marks for titles of short works and parts of whole works. Use *italics* for titles of whole or long works. The following chart gives examples.

Quotation Marks versus Italics for Titles	
Quotation Marks for Short Works and Parts of Whole Works	**Italics for Whole Works or Long Works**
Short Story or Chapter in a Book: "The Necklace"	**Book:** *The Complete Short Stories of Guy de Maupassant*
Short Poem: "The Men Who Wear My Clothes"	**Long Poem:** *The Odyssey*
One Show in a Television Series: "We Expect Fashion"	**Television Series as a Whole:** *Project Runway*
Song: "My Adidas"	**Record Album:** *Run DMC Greatest Hits*
Encyclopedia Article: "History of Fashion"	**Encyclopedia:** *Britannica Online Encyclopedia*
Website Article: "Vera Wang: Medieval Modern"	**Website:** *fashionwiredaily.com*
Magazine or Newspaper Article or Essay: "Street Style"	**Magazine or Newspaper:** *Essence Magazine*
Skit, Monologue, or Short Commercial: "Hurt You" (Geico Caveman commercial)	**Play or Movie:** *The Devil Wears Prada*

Writing Reminder: Titles must also be capitalized correctly. For information about how to capitalize titles, see Chapter 29.

PRACTICE   Using Quotation Marks or Italics with Titles
28.6   Add quotation marks or italics to the titles.

Aesop a Greek who lived from 620 to 560 BC and was known for his stories with lessons

Example: The lesson of **Aesop's** story "A Wolf in Sheep's Clothing" is that appearances can make you believe something that is not true.

1. Chapter 2 of the textbook in Inside Fashion Design is called What Does a Designer Do?

2. The short story Clothes, written by Chitra Banerjee Divakaruni, is about a woman from India who is caught between two worlds, India and the United States.

3. On the Job, an episode of a cable television program, The Fashion Show, had contestants work for a top designer.

4. Blue Suede Shoes is considered the first rock and roll song, written and first recorded by Carl Perkins in 1955.

5. Apparel News, a weekly newspaper that covers California manufacturers and fashion trends, had an article entitled Night and Day.

Avoid Problems with Quotation Marks

Follow these guidelines to avoid mistakes with quotation marks.

- Do not put quotation marks around the title of your own essay.

   "Peer Pressure and Fashion"   Peer Pressure and Fashion

- Do not put quotation marks around indirect quotations. An **indirect quotation** reports what someone else says.

   Direct quotation: Carmella told me, "My favorite store is having a sale."
   Indirect quotation: Carmella told me that her favorite store was having a sale.

- Add quotation marks to sentences that begin with a form of the verb *ask*.

   Incorrect: They asked do I want to pay cash or pay with a credit card?
   Correct: They asked, "Do I want to pay cash or pay with a credit card?"

PRACTICE   Avoiding Problems with Quotation Marks
28.7   Add or remove the quotation marks. Remember to use a capital letter for the first word of a quoted sentence.

Example: The title of my essay was "How to Create a Design Portfolio."

1. Davon asked me, why do you get dressed up to come to school?

2. Natasha told me that "her mother taught her how to sew."

3. She had to read a chapter called Retailing Strategies for Success.

4. Sara got the best grade in the class for her essay "Dressing for the Workplace."

5. The production manager asked, how much is each garment going to cost us to manufacture?

Hyphens, Dashes, and Parentheses

Hyphens

Hyphens are short horizontal lines used to divide a word or form a compound word. There is no space between the hyphen and the word or letters in front of it or after it. The following explains how to use hyphens.

- Use a hyphen to form certain compound words.

  Compound modifiers: Our Spanish-speaking employees help us communicate with businesses in South and Central America.
  Compound nouns: We had to talk to an attorney-at-law about licensing our T-shirts.

- Use a hyphen with spelled out numbers and fractions.

  One-tenth of all clothing sales occurred online in 2009.
  Ashley is twenty-two years old and has her own line of fashions.
  Her twenty-five-year-old cousin wants to open a clothing boutique.

- Use a hyphen to divide a word with at least two syllables at the end of a line. Place the hyphen on the same line, not the next line. Leave two letters at the end of the line and three letters at the beginning of the next line.

  While New York City still reigns as America's fashion capital, others in re-gional markets continue to make progress.

> **TIP** Check an up-to-date dictionary for the use of hyphens with compound nouns and the correct syllable breaks for words.

Dashes

Dashes look like two hyphens next to each other and are used to add nonessential information to a sentence. Word processing programs often change the two hyphens into one long dash. There is no space between the word in front of the dash and the word after the dash.

  Showroom models have the body proportions used in fashion drawings—broad shoulders, narrow hips, and long legs—so they can show samples effectively.

 Dashes are considered informal and are not usually used in academic writing. Use commas instead to set off nonessential information.

Parentheses

Parentheses are curved punctuation marks that appear in pairs, one at the beginning of the word, phrase, or sentence, and one at the end. The following chart explains how parentheses are used.

How to Use Parentheses

Uses for Parentheses	Examples
To clarify information	Most manufacturers *knock off* (copy identically, or slightly change) good selling clothing styles.
To include nonessential information	The design department will meet on Monday at 2:00 p.m. (Please save the date.)
To enclose numbers in a list	The three major departments of an apparel firm are (1) design, (2) production, and (3) sales.
To give an acronym	Many apparel manufacturers use computer-aided design (CAD).
To refer to a page, chapter, or graphic	The designer develops a line using all of his creative talents (Figure 7.1).

TIP | Numbered lists are more common in scientific, technology, and business writing but not in other types of academic writing. Instead, simply use commas.

PRACTICE   Using Hyphens, Dashes, and Parentheses

28.8   Add hyphens, dashes, and parentheses.

Example: The first man-made fiber was called rayon.

1. First developed by a French chemist in 1850, rayon was made from cellulose a plant fiber .
2. Rayon was first produced in the United States in 1910 at a fiber factory in Pennsyl vania.
3. Spandex is a synthetic fiber known as elastane in Europe and other parts of the world that has become a very popular fabric.
4. Spandex is made of at least eighty five percent polymer polyurethane, a toxic chemical.
5. There are twelve major groups of manufactured fibers Table 2.2 .
6. Four natural fibers used to make clothing are 1 cotton, 2 flax, 3 wool, and 4 silk.
7. About 10,000 years ago in central Asia, a man discovered that sheep in addition to food could provide a soft, warm covering.
8. Camel's hair, which comes from Mongolian and Tibetan camels, has a wool like texture that is used for coats and suits.
9. Flax is a gold colored plant whose stems are used for fiber to make linen.
10. Silk was discovered about 4,000 years ago and is produced by a process called sericulture the raising and keeping of silkworms to make silk .

(Some information adapted from *Fashion Apparel, Accessories, and Home Furnishings* by Jay Diamond and Ellen Diamond)

Writing Assignments

Review: Punctuation

Correct the errors in using apostrophes, quotation marks, hyphens, dashes, and parentheses.

"Leather."

Example: [1]Chapter 3 in our textbook is titled 'Leather.'

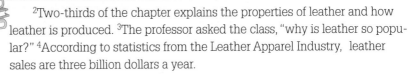

[2]Two-thirds of the chapter explains the properties of leather and how leather is produced. [3]The professor asked the class, "why is leather so popular?" [4]According to statistics from the Leather Apparel Industry, leather sales are three billion dollars a year.

[5]Leather is the general term for all hides (pelts of the large animals) or skins (pelts from smaller animals). [6]Leather's physical properties make the final products functional as well as fashionable. [7]When compared with fabrics, leather is far superior in terms of it's ability to resist tearing. [8]Ladies' and men's leather shoes absorb moisture, retain their shape, and adjust to outside temperatures.

[9]Hundreds of dyes are used to color leather, but the four most common dyes are 1 acid dyes, 2 metalized dyes, 3 direct dyes, and 4 basic dyes. [10]Authors Jay and Ellen Diamond said, "certain precautions must be taken when leather is made into products." [11]The Leather Apparel Association established guidelines for the leather industry to benefit manufacturer's and consumer's.

(Adapted from *Fashion Apparel, Accessories, and Home Furnishings* by Jay Diamond and Ellen Diamond)

Read the following paragraph about the history of jeans. Then, follow the instructions on page 472.

[1]Denim jeans have become a basic apparel item worn by almost all consumers. [2]Jeans were first made by Levi Strauss, a German tailor who emigrated to California in the mid-nineteenth century to mine for gold. [3]He was unsuccessful as a miner and began to manufacture sturdy work pants out of heavy canvas twill, imported from France, called *serge de Nimes*. [4]This was shortened to *denim*. [5]Denim was died with indigo dye made from plants imported from India. [6]This dye was duplicated chemically in the twentieth century. [7]The dye bleeds, and denim apparel gradually become softer blue after being washed many times. [8]Later, famous designers from Europe and the United States stepped in to establish the jean as status fashion.

(Adapted from *Inside Fashion Design* by Sharon Lee Tate)

Add signal phrases and quotation marks to the following sentences as directed.

Example: Add a signal phrase at the beginning of sentence 1 and quotation marks to the sentence.

According to Sharon Lee Tate, "Denim jeans have become a basic apparel item worn by almost all consumers."

1. Add quotation marks to sentence 2 and a signal phrase at the end of the sentence.

   _____

   _____

2. Add a signal phrase in the middle of sentence 7. Then add quotation marks where needed.

   _____

   _____

3. Add a complete sentence to introduce the author and quotation for sentence 3. Follow the introductory sentence with the direct quotation.

   _____

   _____

4. Add a signal phrase at the beginning of sentence 5 and quotation marks to the direct quotation.

   _____

   _____

✔ **English Success Tip: Avoid the Exclamation Point!!!!**

! The exclamation point is a punctuation mark that is used at the end of a word, phrase, or sentence to show excitement, shock, or surprise. It is also used after some commands.

Congratulations!   The concert was great!   Stop!   Somebody help me!

Exclamation points are rarely used in academic writing. Therefore, limit the use of exclamation points to informal writing situations.

For support in meeting this chapter's objectives, log in to www.mywritinglab.com, go to the Study Plan tab, click on **Other Punctuation** and choose **Quotation Marks, Apostrophes, and Semicolons, Colons, Dashes, and Parentheses** from the list of subtopics. Read and view the videos and resources in the Review Materials section, and then complete the Recall, Apply, and Write exercises in the Activities section. You can check your scores and overall progress by using the Gradebook.

CHAPTER

29

Spelling and Capitalization

Theme: *World Geography*

Learning Objectives

After working through this chapter, you will be able to:

LO 1 Apply spelling rules for words with *ei* and *ie*, prefixes, and suffixes.

LO 2 Capitalize first words of sentences, proper nouns, proper adjectives, and titles.

What Are Spelling and Capitalization?

Spelling is the forming of words with letters in the correct order. **Capitalization** is the practice of using capital letters at the beginning of certain words. Spelling and capitalization are essential to good writing. Each of these skills has specific rules.

Spelling and Capitalization in Context

In the following passage about how geography connects people, places, and regions of the world, capitalized nouns and words frequently misspelled are highlighted.

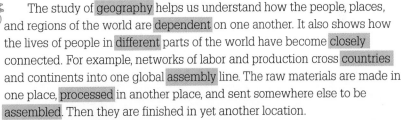

The study of geography helps us understand how the people, places, and regions of the world are dependent on one another. It also shows how the lives of people in different parts of the world have become closely connected. For example, networks of labor and production cross countries and continents into one global assembly line. The raw materials are made in one place, processed in another place, and sent somewhere else to be assembled. Then they are finished in yet another location.

A pair of Lee Cooper jeans, for instance, was assembled in many places. First, the cotton was grown and picked in Benin, a country in West Africa. The denim fabric was made and dyed in Milan, Italy. Then, the denim was colored with a synthetic dark blue dye from Germany. Next, the denim was stonewashed using pumice, a stone used to give the jeans a worn appearance. The pumice came from a volcano in Turkey. Then, the jeans were assembled. The thread to sew the jeans was from Lisnaskea, Northern Ireland. Teeth for the zippers were made in Japan, while the brass rivets were made out of copper from Namibia in southern Africa, and zinc from Australia. The sewing took place in Jebel, Tunisia. Finally, they were sold in a store in the United Kingdom.

(Adapted from *World Regions in Global Context* by Sallie A. Marston et al.)

LO 1   Spelling

Spelling correctly is an important part of good writing. An incorrectly spelled word may confuse readers or give them a bad impression of your writing. Although spell-checking programs are helpful, they cannot tell the difference in meaning between words such as *two*, *too*, or *to* and *hear* or *here*.

Spelling in English can be difficult. For one, words are not always spelled the way they sound. Also, many words were brought into English from other languages. The best way to improve your spelling is to learn the rules and when in doubt, look in a dictionary.

Consonants, Vowels, and Syllables

Spelling rules use specific terms: consonants, vowels, and syllables.

The letters of the English alphabet are divided into consonants and vowels.

> **Consonants**: *b, c, d, f, g, h, j, k, l, m, n. p, q, r, s, t, v, w, x, y, z*
> **Vowels**: *a, e, i, o, u,* and sometimes *y*

Syllables are single units of sound. A syllable always contains a vowel.

> syl-la-ble   con-so-nant   vow-el

Spelling Rules for *ei* and *ie*

A well-known memory aid for *ei* and *ie* is this: *i* before *e* except after *c* or when the *ei* is pronounced *ay*. However, there are some exceptions.

i before *e*	achieve, believe, field, friend, piece
except after *c*	ceiling, conceive, deceive, perceive, receipt
or when *ei* is pronounced *ay*	eight, beige, freight, rein, veil
	Exceptions: ancient, caffeine, conscience, foreign, forfeit, height, leisure, neither, protein, science, society

PRACTICE   Applying the *ei* and *ie* Rule

29.1   Insert *-ei* or *-ie* in the following words.

Example: rel_____*ie*_____ve

1. rec_____ve
2. n_____ghbor
3. pr_____st
4. ch_____f
5. y_____ld

6. h_____ght
7. n_____ce
8. gr_____f
9. hyg_____ne
10. sl_____gh

Spelling Rules for Prefixes

A **prefix** is a letter or group of letters added to the beginning of a word to change the meaning and make a new word.

> mis (meaning *wrong*) + spell = misspell

Some common prefixes are listed in the following table.

Prefix	Meaning	Example
ab-	from	absent
ad-	to	adhere
be-	by	between
con-, com-, co-	with	conjunction
de-	from	depart
dis-, di-	not	disagree
en-	within	enclose
ex-	out	exclude
in-, il-, ir-, im-	not	inadequate
pre-	before	pretest
pro-	forward	proceed
re-	again	replace
sub-	under	subway
un-	not	unfair

TIP Here is a tip to help you remember how to use *-in, -il, -ir,* and *-im.*

Use *-il* before words that begin with *-l*: illogical, illegible, illiterate
Use *-ir* before words that begin with *-r*: irrelevant, irresponsible, irrational
Use *-im* before words that begin with *-m* or *-p*: immoral, impatient, immature
Use *-in* before words that begin with any other letter: inadequate, inflammable

PRACTICE Adding Prefixes

29.2 Correct any words that are not spelled correctly. Write *C* if the word is correct.

Example: unecessary **unnecessary**

1. disappear
2. overeact
3. consider
4. ilegal
5. comunicate

6. ennvision
7. substitute
8. fullfill
9. unoticed
10. adress

Spelling Rules for Suffixes

A **suffix** is a letter or group of letters added to the end of a word to change the meaning and make a new word. The spelling of a word can change when a suffix is added.

Here are some common suffixes.

Suffix	Meaning	Example
-able	able to	capable
-ance	act, fact	acceptance
-ation	action, state, result	occupation
-ence	state or condition, action	dependence
-er	one who does, more	teacher
-ful	full of	peaceful
-ible	able, likely	possible
-ion	action or process	celebration
-ish	like	childish
-ism	state or quality	heroism
-ist	doer, believer	novelist
-ity	state, quality, condition	prosperity
-ize	make, cause to be, treat with	criticize
-less	without	fearless
-ly	like	friendly
-ment	action, process, or act	excitement
-ness	quality	kindness
-ous	full of	religious

TIP | The suffix *-ful* has only one *–l* at the end: wonder**ful**, play**ful**, thank**ful**.

English has special spelling rules for adding suffixes to words. Read and study the rules for adding suffixes to words ending in *-e*, words ending in a consonant and *-y*, doubling the final consonants.

Adding Suffixes to Words Ending In *-e*

- If the suffix begins with a consonant, keep the *–e* and add the suffix.

     care + ful = careful   announce + ment = announcement

- *Exceptions:* Drop the *-e* when it has a vowel in front of it.

     argue + ment = argument   true + ly = truly   nine + th = ninth

- If the suffix begins with a vowel, drop the *-e* and add the suffix.

     move + able = movable   admire + ation = admiration

- *Exceptions:* Keep the *-e* when the word has a soft *-ce* or *-ge* sound

     judge + ment = judgment   notice + able = noticeable

PRACTICE Adding Suffixes to Words Ending in -*e*

29.3 Apply the rules to add the suggested suffix to each word.

Example: place + ment ___placement___

1. care + less _____
2. use + age _____
3. continue + ous _____
4. announce + ment _____
5. value + able _____
6. battle + ing _____
7. nine + th _____
8. sue + ing _____
9. advise + able _____
10. manage + able _____

Adding Suffixes to Words Ending with a Consonant and –*y*

- If the word ends with a consonant + -*y*, change the -*y* to an -*i* and add the suffix.

    worry + ed = worried   eighty + eth = eightieth

- *Exceptions:* If the suffix begins with an -*i* or if it ends a proper name, keep the -*y*.

    cry + ing = crying   Stravinsky + -*s* = Stravinskys

- If the word ends with a vowel + -*y*, keep the -*y* and add the suffix.

    pay + ment = payment   delay + ing = delaying

- *Exceptions*: pay + ed = paid   say + ed = said

PRACTICE Adding Suffixes to Words Ending with a Consonant and -*y*

29.4 Apply the rules to add the suggested suffix to each word.

Example: terrify + ing ___**terrifying**___

1. beauty + ful _____
2. satisfy + ed _____
3. rely + able _____
4. joy + ful _____
5. happy + er _____
6. delay + ing _____
7. O'Reilly + s _____
8. fly + ing _____
9. messy + ier _____
10. day + s _____

Doubling the Final Consonants before Adding a Suffix

One Syllable Words

- If the word ending in a consonant + vowel + consonant has one syllable, double the final consonant.

    hop + ing = hopping   drip + ing = dripping

- *Exceptions:* Do not double the last consonant when the words end in *-w, -x, or -y.*

    sew + ing = sewing   fix + ing = fixing

- If the word ends with two or more consonants, do not double the final consonant.

    debt + or = debtor   wish + ed = wished

- If the word ends with two or more vowels and a consonant, do not double the final consonant.

    tear + ing = tearing   sweet + est = sweetest

Words with Two or More Syllables

Knowing which syllable is stressed (emphasized) when saying a word is helpful to understanding these rules.

- **First syllable stressed: hap**pen **en**ter

- **Second syllable stressed: be**gin com**mit** e**quip**

- If the first syllable is stressed, do not double the final consonant.

    happen + ed = happened   enter + ing = entering   accept + ed = accepted

- If a word has more than one syllable, and the last syllable is stressed, double the final consonant.

    begin + ing = beginning   commit + ed = committed   equip + ed = equipped

---

PRACTICE   Doubling Final Consonants before Adding Suffixes

29.5   Apply the rules to add the suggested suffix to each word.

EXAMPLE: travel + ing ___travelling___

1. occur + ed _____
2. benefit + ing _____
3. prefer + ed _____
4. excel + ed _____
5. thin + est _____
6. plan + ing _____
7. big + est _____
8. show + ing _____

Spelling Out Certain Words

Some words should be spelled out in academic writing.

numbers that begin sentences	**Fifty** percent of Southeast Asia's people live in cities.
	Sixteen hundred different languages are spoken in India.
numbers under 100	**ten**, not 10
	twenty-four, not 24
units of measurement	**inches**, not in.
	feet not ft.
	miles per hour, not mph
days, months, and holidays	**Monday**, not Mon.
	August 6, not Aug. 6
people's first names	**William**, not Wm.
courses in general	**English**, not Eng.
	biology, not bio.

PRACTICE   Spelling Out Words

29.6   Correct any numbers or abbreviations that should be spelled out.

Example: Native people of Amer. domesticated the wild tobacco plant more than 5,000 years ago. **America**

1. They grew 2 main types of tobacco.

2. One type was grown in the northeastern U.S. and Can.

3. Another type of tobacco was grown in Central and S. America.

4. Native people in these countries developed all of the ways to use tobacco, such as smoking, inhaling, and chewing before people from Eur. came to the Americas.

5. Sailors and merchants carried these customs to Spain and Portugal, and by the end of the seventeenth century, the tobacco trade was 1 of the important parts of the world economy.

6. In 1620, 40,000 lbs. of tobacco were exported from Virginia to England.

7. 1770 was the year that the oldest tobacco shop in the United States opened in Lancaster, PA.

8. During the American Revolution, Benj. Franklin got a loan from France by promising to repay France with tobacco if he did not have the money.

9. 46 million residents of the United States smoke cigarettes.

10. In China, the largest producer of tobacco, a large percentage of males between the ages of 15 and 69 smoke, according to 2008 statistics.

(Adapted from *World Regions in Global Context* by Sallie A. Marston et al.)

Avoiding Clipped Words

Avoid using clipped words in college writing. A clipped word is the shortened form of a word.

Commonly Used Clipped Words			
ad	advertisement	phone	telephone
burger	hamburger	photo	photograph
exam	examination	teen	teenager
fridge	refrigerator	typo	typographical error

LO 2 Capitalization

Capitalization is the practice of using capital letters at the beginning of certain words.

Capitalize First Words of Sentences

As a world region, Europe is located between the Americas, Africa, and the Middle East.

Marston, Knox, and Liverton state, "Overall, Europe accounts for almost two-fifths of world trade."

Capitalize Proper Nouns and Proper Adjectives

Proper nouns and proper adjectives are capitalized according to these rules.

Names of People	
First, middle, and last names and initials	George Herbert Bush
	Simone de Beauvoir
	Thomas A. Edison
	Shamu
Names with more than one part	Tom MacGregor
	Maureen O'Hara
	Oscar de la Hoya
	Rocco De Luca
Initials and abbreviations that come before or after names	Jonas Salk, M.D.
	Mr. Peter T. Roth
	Sr. Perez
	J. K. Rowling
	James Carter, Jr.
Titles before names	Senator Reed
Names of relationships when they replace proper names	Aunt Yolanda But: My aunt will visit next week.
	Please ask Father for the car keys. *But:* My father has the car keys.

> **TIP** Always capitalize the pronoun **I**.
>
> Capitalize *the* in front of a name when it is part of the formal name.

Other Proper Nouns and Adjectives

Names of groups: organizations, teams, government bodies, institutions	National Audubon Society New York Giants Central High School United Nations Pennsylvania State University
National and ethnic groups and their languages	Chinese Haitian Navaho African American Hispanic *Note:* In current practice, the terms *black* and *white* are not capitalized when referring to a group of people.
Specific places: cities, counties, states, countries, continents, islands, streets, regions, bodies of water	Rio de Janeiro Atlantic Ocean Broward County Main Street New Mexico Houston, Texas South America Lake Erie Korea the West
Historical events, periods, movements	World War II the Romantic Period the Space Age the Civil Rights Movement
Days of the week, months, holidays	Friday December Independence Day New Year's Day Ramadan
Religions, their followers, sacred writings, deities	the Bible the Koran (or Qur'an) the Torah

(Continued)

Other Proper Nouns and Adjectives (*Continued*)

	the Vedas
	Christianity, Christians
	Islam, Muslims
	Judaism, Jews
	Buddhism, Buddhists
	Jehovah
	God
	Allah
	Buddha
Planets, stars, constellations, heavenly bodies	Mars
	Sirius
	Andromeda
	the Milky Way
Businesses and brand names	Amazon.com
	Dell
	Taco Bell
	Kodak
	Levi's
	Colgate
	Kleenex
	Gatorade
Internet terminology	Internet
	World Wide Web
	RAM
	Wi-Fi
	But: website, web page

> **TIP** | Check an up-to-date dictionary if you are not sure about the capitalization of a word.

PRACTICE Capitalizing Proper Nouns and Adjectives

29.7 Capitalize proper nouns and proper adjectives.

Example: The most populated region of the world is east asia. **East Asia**

1. This region of consists of china, japan, mongolia, north and south korea, and taiwan.

2. Since the death of mao zedong, leader of the communist party of china, china has had an important affect on the world economy.

3. In 2001, china was admitted to the world trade organization.

4. Skilled chinese garment workers can be hired for $30 for a 60-hour week; as a result, retailers in europe and the united states pay less for the item than they would in toronto or hong kong.

5. The chinese automobile market is attractive to western manufacturers.

6. In 1985, volkswagen was the first to have a factory there.

7. A partnership was formed between general motors and shanghai automotive industry corporation.

8. Other foreign manufacturers operating in china include honda, toyota, nissan, and most recently bmw and mercedes.

9. More than 50,000 taiwanese firms have established operations in china.

10. The center of the south korean footwear industry, pusan, has lost business to china.

11. Originally based in japan, pioneer has moved its manufacture of dvd recorders to cities in china.

12. The philosophy of confucianism is the most widely recognized belief system in china.

13. Formalized religions include taoism, tibetan buddhism, and islam.

14. The official language of china is mandarin.

15. Other languages spoken on a regular basis are cantonese, xiang, minn, and hakka; fifty-three ethnic minorities have their own languages.

(Adapted from *World Regions in Global Context* by Sallie A. Marston et al.)

Capitalize Titles

Capitalize the first and last words of a title.

> *World Regions in Global Context*

Capitalize a word that comes after a colon or semicolon.

> *World Regions in Global Context: Peoples, Places, and Environments*

Do not capitalize these words unless they appear at the beginning or end of the title or after a colon or semicolon.

Articles: *a, an, the*

Prepositions fewer than five letters: *at, by, down, in, into, of, off, on, up, to* and so on

Conjunctions of fewer than five letters: *and, but, for, nor, or, so, yet*

Article title: "Scientists Capture Haiti Disaster with High-Tech Imaging System"

Book title: *The Discoverers: A History of Man's Search to Know His World and Himself*

For more information about using italics or quotation marks for titles, see Chapter 28.

> **PRACTICE**
> **29.8**
> **Capitalizing Titles**
>
> Add capital letters to the titles.

Example: *a dictionary of geography* **A Dictionary of Geography**

1. *around the world in 80 days*
2. "inspiring tomorrow's geographers"
3. *antarctica: the blue continent*
4. "a history and overview of earth day"
5. "seismologists use ultrasounds to assess quakes faster"
6. *journal of cultural geography*
7. "climbing volcanoes in mexico"
8. "tsunamis: how safe is the united states?"
9. *maps: finding our place in the world*
10. *the village by the sea*

Avoiding Capitalization Errors

The following words do not need to be capitalized:

names of seasons	Our class will take a field trip to Bear Mountain this **spring**.
subjects in general	Ricardo is taking a **geography** class this semester.
directions	To get to the mall, go **east** on Main Street.
titles not attached to names	Our geography **professor** is well known in the field.
	My **mother** is proud of my good grades in geography.

> **PRACTICE**
> **29.9**
> **Correcting Errors in Capitalization**
>
> Correct any capitalization errors.

Example: John Pennekamp Coral Reef State Park is located North of Key Largo, Florida. **north**

1. Last year, my Geography class took a two-day field trip there, which turned out to be better than I expected.
2. Our Professor planned the trip so that we could learn about the unique coral reef formations and mangrove swamps.
3. The last thing on Earth that I wanted to do was to spend two nights in the Florida Keys' heat and humidity.
4. I had never been to Key Largo before, but my Dad, who used to go on fishing trips there before he married my Mother, told me that I would enjoy it.
5. Before we went on the trip, we looked for information about the park on the internet.
6. We found several informative websites that described Pennekamp's History, Geography, and Activities.

7. I would have preferred an air-conditioned hotel room instead of in a tent on the campgrounds, but I made sure to bring my Off! brand Insect Repellent and plenty of Sunscreen.

8. We packed our Snorkels and Masks so that we could get a firsthand look at the diverse sea life and coral formations in the shallow waters near the park.

9. My friend's Aunt told us to watch out for the jellyfish called the Portuguese Man of War, but several students received painful stings while in the water.

10. Fortunately, we had brought some Meat Tenderizer, which helped to stop the stinging.

11. While driving North to get home, we talked about how awful Professor Tarpon's cooking was but also about what we learned about the geography of the area.

12. I wrote an article about Pennekamp Coral Reef State Park for the College newspaper.

Writing Assignments

Review: Spelling and Capitalization

Correct any spelling and capitalization errors in the following passage.

Example: [1]The continent of antarctica is located over the south pole.
                          Antarctica   South Pole

[2]During the six-month Winter, the Sun does not rise above the horizon, so the continent stays in twilight. [3]The temperature averages minus sixty deg., and by sept. each year, half of the surrounding Ocean is frozen. [4]The frozen area creates a large ice pack that has an area of 32 mil. mi. and a thickness of 6.6 ft.

[5]Glaciers and snowfields cover most of the continent; the largest glaciers, such as the lambert and the beardmore, are so large that they force huge amounts of ice into the seas. [6]The landscapes of antarctica are almost completely silent because nothing grows in the region, and the Sea is quiet because it is frozen for most of the year. [7]The most active and noisy residents are the millions of Seals and Penguins and the occasional giant blue whale coming to the surface offshore.

[8]Although few people live there, many are interested in antarctica for scientific research and for using its natural resources such as Iron Ore, Coal, Gas, and Oil that may lie beneath it.

[9]Between 1911 and 1912, britain's Capt. Rob. F. Scott and norwegian explorer Roald Amundsen raced to the south pole to claim it. [10]Amundsen arrived in Dec. 1911, and Scott arrived on Jan. 18, 1912, but Scott and his companions died when bad weather slowed them down and they ran out of food.

[11]In 1958, the antarctic treaty was created and signed by 45 countries. [12]The Treaty baned nuclear tests and the disposal of radioactive waste. [13]It also ensured that the continent can only be used for peacefull purposes, mainly for scientific research.

[14]There are no airports in the entire continent and only one hotel on king george island, so military personnel, scientists, and staff must be flown in on aircraft equiped with skis. [15]Cruises are the most popular tourist activity, but organized tours also offer mountain climbing, kayaking, sailling, camping, and even scuba diving. [16]Many ecologists have noticed that the number of petrels, birds that live a long time, has decreased. [17]They think the reasons could be the presence of humans or the increase of commercial fishing, some of which is illegal. [18]There is also growing concern that global warming is threatening the continent, especially the Antarctic peninsula, where temperatures are warming.

(Adapted from *World Regions in Global Context* by Sallie A. Marston et al.)

Write about an Image

Imagine that you are a geographer who has just discovered the island in the photograph on page 487. On a sheet of paper, write down the features of the island. Include details such as location, names of bodies of water, the island's physical appearance, weather, plants and trees, insects, birds, and wildlife. Give names to these items.

Write five to eight sentences. Check for spelling and capitalization errors. Describing your observations and thoughts the day you arrived on the island.

English Success Tip: Learn to Spell in Two Minutes (or Less)

If you have trouble with spelling, you can learn to spell a new word in a short time by using the **Look**, **Say**, **See**, **Write** method. This method involves following four simple steps:

Look: Look at the word to become familiar with the way it is spelled.

Say: Say the word out loud. Break the word into smaller parts or syllables. Check a dictionary for the syllables of the word if you do not know them. Say the word using rhythm or sing the word. Find a word that rhymes and say the two words together. You can even make up a song out of the word.

See: See the word spelled correctly in your mind. Close your eyes and create a mental image of the word. Picture the word in color or in a colorful setting.

Write: Write or type the word as you remember it. Play with the style and size of the letters of the word. Try writing the word in the air with your finger.

For support in meeting this chapter's objectives, log in to www.mywritinglab.com, go to the Study Plan tab, click on **Spelling and Capitalization** and choose **Spelling and Capitalization** from the list of subtopics. Read and view the videos and resources in the Review Materials section, and then complete the Recall, Apply, and Write exercises in the Activities section. You can check your scores and overall progress by using the Gradebook.

Improving Your Writing

Concise and Appropriate Words

Learning Objectives

After working through this chapter, you will be able to:

LO 1 Choose concise words to make writing precise, understandable, original, and accurate.

LO 2 Choose bias-free words when writing about gender, age, disability, ethnicity, and race.

LO 3 Use commonly confused words correctly.

What Are Concise and Appropriate Words?

Writers' word choices reveal a great deal about them and give readers a positive or negative impression. Concise and appropriate words are important features of good academic and workplace writing.

Words that are **concise** express what needs to be written without unnecessary words. Words that are **appropriate** are suitable for a particular situation or occasion. They are essential when writing about gender, age, disability, ethnicity, and race.

Concise and Appropriate Words in Context

The following two letters were written by **Medicare** employees. Medicare receives many false claims from health care providers every year. To reach these providers more effectively, they changed their original letter to make it concise and understandable.

Medicare U. S. government health insurance for people over 65

Medicare Fraud Letter: Wordy

Investigators at the contractor will review the facts in your case and decide the most appropriate course of action. The first step taken with most Medicare health care providers is to reeducate them about Medicare regulations and policies. If the practice continues, the contractor may conduct special audits of the providers' medical records. Often, the contractor recovers overpayments to health care providers this way. If there is sufficient evidence to show that the provider is consistently violating Medicare policies, the contractor will document the violations and ask the Office of the Inspector General to prosecute the case. This can lead to expulsion from the Medicare program, civil monetary penalties, and imprisonment. (111 words)

Medicare Fraud Letter: Concise

We will take two steps to look at this matter: We will find out if it was an error or fraud. We will let you know the result. (28 words)

LO 1 Choose Concise Words

Writing that is concise expresses what needs to be written without unnecessary words.

Avoid Wordy Expressions

Wordy expressions contain more words than are necessary. The following chart lists some wordy expressions and gives precise words to replace them.

Wordy	Precise
a great number of	many
as a result of, due to the fact that, for the reason that	because
at that time	then
at a rapid rate	fast
at the present time, in this day and age	now
despite the fact that, in spite of the fact that	although
for the purpose of	for, to
in the event that	if
in the near future	soon
last but not least	last

TIP

Some college writers add unnecessary words to make their paper longer to meet assignment requirements. Adding unnecessary words makes writing wordy and less effective.

PRACTICE Replacing Wordy Expressions

30.1   Replace wordy expressions with precise words, and rewrite each sentence.

Example: At this point in time, the committee needs to meet for the purpose of planning the community outreach projects.
Now, the committee needs to meet to plan the community outreach projects.

1. In this day and age, with so many people out of work, we need to hold a Thanksgiving food drive in the near future.

   _____

2. Due to the fact that the holidays are approaching at a rapid rate, we will place boxes for food donations at the local supermarkets.

   _____

3. We hope to collect enough food to fill the homeless shelter's pantry despite the fact that many people are struggling financially.

   _____

4. The company also plans to collect a great number of holiday gifts for the children in the domestic abuse shelter for the reason that they may not receive any presents.

_____

5. Last but not least, during the holidays, we plan to volunteer along with shelter officials to prepare and serve meals in the event that there are large crowds.

_____

Avoid Redundant Expressions

A **redundant expression** uses two or more words that mean the same thing. The chart below gives examples of redundant expressions and explains why they are redundant.

Redundant expression	Why is the expression redundant?
and also	_And_ and _also_ mean the same thing.
three in number	_Three_ is a number.
combine into one	_Combine_ means to join together to make a single thing or group.
consensus of opinion	_Consensus_ is a generally accepted opinion.
each and every	_Each_ means every person or thing in a group, and _every_ means all members of a group.
first and foremost	_First_ and _foremost_ mean the same thing.
month of June	_June_ is the name of a month.
new innovation	_Innovation_ means something new.
past experience	_Experience_ is something that happened in the past.
past history	_History_ consists of past events.
red in color	_Red_ is a color.
same identical	_Identical_ means exactly the same.
small in size	_Small_ is a size.
the reason why is because	_Reason, why_, and _because_ all mean the same thing.
true fact	A _fact_ is something that is true.
3 p.m. in the afternoon	The abbreviation _p.m._ means afternoon (or evening).
unexpected surprise	A _surprise_ is something unexpected.

PRACTICE   Replacing Redundant Words, Phrases, and Sentences

30.2   Revise this letter for redundant words and phrases. Some of the sentences can be eliminated.

Dear Ms. Mendoza:

[1]Thank you for your interest in joining the new recruits here at Dynatech.

[2]We welcome this opportunity to conduct a full and complete review of your

application and résumé.

[3]First and foremost, we will consider your unique skills and past experience to see how they match our present needs. [4]We will review our needs and determine the appropriateness of your skills and experience. [5]If and when there is a consensus of opinion that a suitable opening is available, we will contact you in the next few weeks to schedule an interview.

[6]On the other hand, if you don't hear from us, we will keep your résumé in our active file for at least six months. [7]It is Dynatech's policy to keep reésumés active for at least six months even if an applicant doesn't hear from us. [8]During that period of time, we will continue to consider you for each and every appropriate position that becomes available.

[9]Thank you again for your interest in joining the team here at Dynatech.

Sincerely,

Vanessa Blake

(From *Be Your Own Editor* by Beverly A. Vanzo)

Avoid Inflated Words

Some writers use long words to make their writing sound more intelligent and impressive. While a good vocabulary is an asset, writing that is more difficult to read and understand is less effective.

> **Inflated**: During the preceding year, the company accelerated operations.
> **Readable**: Last year, the company sped up operations.

The following chart lists some words that writers think are impressive, called **inflated words**, and words to replace them that make writing more readable.

Inflated and Readable Words	
Inflated words	**Readable words**
ascertain	find out
commence	begin
encounter	meet, meeting
equitable	fair
finalize	finish, complete
modification	change
methodology	method
necessitate	need
termination	end
utilize	use

PRACTICE   Using Readable Words

30.3   Replace the inflated words with readable words. Some sentences have more than one inflated word that needs to be replaced.

finished
Example: The architects have ~~finalized~~ the plans for the new building.

1. After meeting with the city planners, they ascertained that the building was too tall.
2. The construction could not commence until the plans were modified.
3. After an encounter between the two groups, they reached an equitable solution.
4. By changing their methodology, the architects found a way to create more space.
5. Their change in plans necessitated the builders to utilize the lot next to the site and build out instead of up.

Avoid Clichés

Choosing words and expressions that are original makes writing fresh and interesting. On the other hand, using clichés has the opposite effect; a **cliché** is an expression that has been overused and is unoriginal and boring.

Raoul was sweating like a pig while mowing the lawn on a hot summer day. Stephanie was upset when she saw that one of the new tires on her car was flat as a pancake.

The following are some examples of clichés:

all talk no action	arm and a leg	better late than never
between a rock and a hard place	blind as a bat	easier said than done
fifteen minutes of fame	hard as a rock	knock on wood
no pain no gain	raining cats and dogs	strong as an ox
stubborn as a mule	this day and age; this point in time	work like a dog

PRACTICE   Replacing Clichés

30.4   Replace the underlined clichés in the following sentences with more original words or expressions.

sick
Example: The patient was as sick as a dog when he arrived at the emergency room.

1. Getting him signed in at the front desk was like pulling teeth because he did not cooperate.
2. The nurse had to think outside the box to get the patient to answer questions, which seemed to go in one ear and out the other.
3. The staff was between a rock and a hard place with the patient who clearly needed help.
4. When the patient calmed down, the nurses decided to strike while the iron was hot and moved him into an examination room.

5. Although the patient was <u>a pain in the neck</u>, the medical team stayed with him and gave him the treatment he needed.

Avoid General Words

Specific words help the reader create a mental picture and make writing more accurate and interesting. In contrast, **general words** are less specific and can mean different things to different readers.

> **General:** job   **Specific:** senior accountant for Softbyte Press
> **General:** person   **Specific:** Sarah Jones, production manager
> **General:** One of our workers was injured by a piece of equipment recently.
>
> **Specific:** Alan Hill suffered a broken thumb while working on a lathe yesterday.
>
> (From *Technical Communication* by John Lannon)

Examples of general adjectives are *good, a lot, awful, awesome, bad, beautiful, big, cute, difficult, exciting, expensive, fantastic, fine, funny, glamorous, interesting, many, nice, pretty, several, some, ugly,* and *unusual.*

PRACTICE   Choosing Specific Words

30.5   Revise the following sentences changing vague words to specific ones.

Example: The office worker keyboarded the report.
The administrative assistant keyboarded the quarterly earnings report.

1. Spencer is a very lazy worker.

_____

2. The patient was not feeling too well.

_____

3. We need this information as soon as possible.

_____

4. The kitchen staff prepared the food.

_____

5. We had a good meeting.

_____

6. Bad weather in our area damaged the computer systems.

_____

7. At our auto shop, we can fix anything.

_____

LO 2   Choose Appropriate Words

Choosing appropriate words is essential when writing about gender, age, disability, ethnicity, race, and sexual orientation. If you have any biases, they may show up in your writing without your realizing it. A **bias** is a personal opinion that influences your judgment, usually in an unfair way. Bias in writing gives a negative image about a person or group and disrespects readers. Bias-free writing treats people fairly.

Bias-free Language for Gender

Gender-biased words and expressions give inaccurate ideas about men and women. Use *he or she* or the plural form *they* to refer to nouns when the gender is not known.

> **Biased:** A good lawyer will make sure that **his** clients are aware of their rights.
>
> **Unbiased:** A good lawyer will make sure that **his or her** clients are aware of their rights.

Replace words such as job titles and qualities that stereotype men and women. A **stereotype** is a fixed idea that people have about what someone or something is like, especially an idea that is wrong. For example, many people assume that nurses and teachers are females, while doctors and company presidents are males.

Words that stereotype men	Replacements
businessman, fireman, policeman, salesmen	*business person, fire fighter, police officer, sales associate*
Words that stereotype women	Replacements
female doctor, maid, waitress, housewife, working mother	*doctor, house cleaner, server, homemaker, worker*

Bias-free Language for Age

The use of negative stereotypes and language aimed at specific age groups is considered **ageism**. In the U.S. culture, ageism is directed toward older adults; aging is viewed in a negative way in language and in the media.

Avoid words like *senior citizen, old folks, seniors, golden agers, grandmotherly, elderly,* and *80-years-young.* Avoid reference to a person's age when it is not relevant.

> **Ageist:** Representative Brown, **an elderly politician**, has decided to run for another term in office.
>
> **Not ageist:** Representative Brown has decided to run for another term in office.
>
> **Ageist:** Maria Ramirez, **59**, has just joined our finance department.
>
> **Not ageist:** Maria Ramirez has just joined our finance department.

Bias-free Language for Disability

A **disability** is an illness, injury, or condition that makes it difficult for someone to do the things that other people do.

Avoid words like *handicapped* or *crippled*; instead, use *disabled*. In general, avoid referring to a person's disability. If the reference is necessary, use words that treat disabilities or illness in a neutral way.

> **Biased:** The AIDS **victim** received a promising new treatment.
>
> **Unbiased:** The AIDS **patient** received a promising new treatment.
>
> **Biased:** Ford Smith, **a blind employee**, had the highest number of sales this month.
>
> **Unbiased:** Ford Smith had the highest number of sales this month. (Do not mention disability unless necessary or relevant.)

Bias-free Language for Ethnic and Racial Groups

An **ethnic group** refers to people of the same race or nationality who share a distinctive culture. A **racial group** is a set of individuals who share physical characteristics or biological descent.

Avoid identifying people by their ethnic or racial group, but if a label is necessary, be sure to use an acceptable word for that label. Words that are insulting to any ethnic or racial group should be avoided.

> **TIP**
>
> Whether to use African American or black, Pacific Islander or Asian, or Hispanic American or Latino, for example, depends on many things such as group or individual preference.

Bias-free Language for Sexual Orientation

Sexual orientation is a person's emotional, romantic, and/or sexual attraction to the same, opposite, or both sexes. Identify people by what they do rather than by their sexual orientation.

PRACTICE   Using Bias-Free Language

30.6   Revise words, phrases, or sentences that use biased language.

Example: The committee wants to hire the right man for the job. Replace *man* with *person*.

1. Candidate Rocio Perez, married and the mother of a ten-year-old, will attend the debate.
2. Senior citizen Paul Ormand is still an active, successful sales representative.
3. I will have my girl make the appointment.
4. The president of the company, a woman, met with her sales staff.
5. An **epileptic**, Lisa has no trouble doing her job.
6. Our department has completed a man-sized job.
7. The male nurse won the patient's confidence.
8. The team consisted of two female astronauts, one male navigator, and three male technicians.
9. Rudolph Giuliani, Italian-American lawyer and politician, served as mayor of New York from 1994 to 2001.
10. Every teacher should prepare and submit her lesson plans by Friday.

epileptic someone who has epilepsy, a condition of the brain, which causes a person to become unconscious for short periods or to move in a violent and uncontrolled way

LO 3   Commonly Confused Words

Some words can be confused because they sound alike or look alike. Writers cannot depend on spell-checkers to find errors when words sound alike but have different spellings and meanings. Look over the list of commonly confused words to review those you are not familiar with.

Easily Confused Word Pairs and Examples

accept to receive, admit, or believe	**except** not including
The company **accepted** Gerry's application.	All of the candidates **except** Gerry were called in for interviews.
affect to have an influence on something	**effect** something that happens because of something else
The new manager has **affected** us in a positive way.	The new manager has had a positive **effect** on our department.
a lot a large number, very much	**alot** an incorrect spelling, making two words into one
A lot of employees bring their children to the company daycare center.	
already before the present time	**all ready** prepared for what one is about to do or experience
Our team had **already** done the research, so the report was easy to write.	Our team was **all ready** to write the report.
been the past participle of the verb *be*	**being** the *-ing* form of the verb *be* (present progressive)
Charlemane has **been** an administrative assistant for two years.	Charlemane was **being** helpful when she offered to work late to finish our paperwork.
break to damage something, to interrupt, to ignore, to stop; an opportunity, an interruption	**brake** a device that slows or stops the movement of a vehicle
Getting a job at the prestigious accounting firm was the **break** she had hoped for.	Juan quickly pressed down on the **brake** to stop the truck.
The copier **breaks** frequently.	
breath air taken in or let out of lungs	**breathe** to take air into the lungs and let it out again
Selma took a deep **breath** before giving her presentation.	Selma learned that she should **breathe** deeply when she is stressed.
complement to help make someone or something more complete	**compliment** a remark or action that expresses approval, admiration, or respect
Copies of letters of recommendation **complemented** Aiden's résumé.	The interviewer **complimented** Aiden on his résumé.
conscience the sense of right and wrong that enables one to decide between right and wrong acts or behavior	**conscious** aware of what is happening, something intentional
	The boss became **conscious** of the employee's poor work.
He had a guilty **conscience** after he lied about being too sick to go to work.	He made a **conscious** decision to fire the employee.

PRACTICE Choosing the Correct Word

30.7   Some of the boldfaced words in the following sentences are not correct. If the word is not correct, write the correct word above it. If the word is correct, write a *C* above it.

A lot
Example: ~~Alot~~ of frustrated consumers go online to complain about problems with products.

1. Consumers who write product reviews seem to **complement** products less and complain more.

2. For example, when a product **brakes**, the online consumer may not know where to look for help.

3. When they write to companies for help, they are **all ready** frustrated.

4. To add to the problem, these consumers are **effected** by poor online service.

5. Some companies are **conscious** of the problem and have **been** setting up consumer social networks where consumers' questions and comments are **excepted**.

6. Employees representing companies that sell the products are **already** with answers to consumers' questions.

7. Customers can **breath** a sigh of relief knowing that the company cares about them and is **being** helpful.

More Easily Confused Word Pairs and Examples

decent socially acceptable, appropriate

He always wears **decent** clothing to work.

descent a movement downward, ancestral background

The airplane's **descent** was not smooth due to the storm.

---

elicit to get a reaction, produce a response

The stockbroker tried to **elicit** a positive reaction to his financial plan for the client.

illicit illegal or not socially approved of

His **illicit** sales of company stock got him fired.

---

everyday commonplace, ordinary

Buying a cup of coffee on the way to work was an **everyday** routine for Marie.

every day occurring or done each day

Marie buys a cup of coffee **every day** on her way to work.

---

imply to suggest something without saying it directly

Though he did not state it directly, the manager **implied** that some people would be laid off.

infer to reach an opinion with available information or facts

We **inferred** from his announcement that our jobs were safe.

---

it's a contraction of *it is*

It's going to be a difficult work day because several employees are sick.

its possessive form of *it*

The company displayed **its** new logo at the entrance to the building.

---

knew the past tense of *know*, which means to be well informed about, to recognize

Jessie **knew** how to write a good memo.

new recently created, not previously used or owned

Jessie was promoted to a **new** position because of her writing skills.

---

know to be well informed about, to recognize

I **know** I need to take more business courses.

no not any, the opposite of yes

No stores are open right now.

---

lose not be able to find, to be defeated, to have less of

The store did not **lose** money this month.

loose not attached, not tight

Chris likes to wear **loose** clothing to work to be comfortable while sitting at a desk all day.

---

passed the past tense of *pass*, which means to go or move forward, to succeed

Vanessa **passed** her nursing certification exam. Alex **passed** me in the hallway without saying hello.

past the time before and until now

Vanessa spent the **past** two years studying to be a nurse.

PRACTICE Choosing the Correct Word

30.8   Some of the boldfaced words in the following sentences are not correct. If the word is not correct, write the correct word above it. If the word is correct, write a *C* above it.

illicit
Example: Employees who observe ~~elicit~~ or unethical behavior in their companies may
C
not **know** how to deal with it.

1. Talking to a supervisor about an action that the employee has observed **everyday** may not be an option.

2. The supervisor may **infer** that the employee is not loyal to the company even if the supervisor does not say it.

3. On the other hand, the supervisor may be upset that the employee **new** about the behavior and wants to take action.

4. When the employee has **no** options, he or she may report the individual to **illicit** help from the company ethics hot line or the news media.

5. Sometimes, **it's** the only way to bring a problem to management's attention.

6. As a result, the employee who made a **descent** decision to expose the problem may **loose** his or her job.

7. From **passed** experience, companies have set up formal ways to report problems such as rule breaking, criminal activity, and cover-ups.

More Easily Confused Word Pairs and Examples

piece a part or piece of something

The people attending the conference were asked to sign in on a **piece** of paper.

peace calm and quiet, a time where there is no war

Miranda enjoyed the **peace** and quiet in the office after the employees went home for the day.

principle a rule of behavior or a basic truth

We buy recycled paper for the copier as a matter of **principle**.

principal first in importance or a person in charge of a school

A good way to remember **principal** is the sentence, The principal is your pal.

The **principal** reason for the budget crisis is overspending.

quiet making little or no noise or without much activity

The noise of the construction work taking place outside of the building disturbed our normally **quiet** office.

quit to go away or to give up

James **quit** his job because he found a better position.

quite very or really

The workers were **quite** disturbed by the noise.

rise to move up from a lower to higher position or to increase

As we started the corporate race Saturday morning, the sun began to **rise**.

raise an increase in salary or to cause to rise, to increase in size, value, or amount

The corporate race **raised** $10,000 for charity.

(Continued)

More Easily Confused Word Pairs and Examples (*Continued*)

site a place where something is, was, or will be

The new **site** for the company is downtown next to the bank.

cite to mention something as proof or to repeat a passage from

In his proposal, James **cited** evidence from two specialists in the field.

sight the ability to see, range of vision, anything that is seen

Pat's **sight** got worse from working at the computer every day.

---

stationary not moving, still

The subway remained **stationary** while passengers got off.

stationery paper on which one writes

Stationery includes envelopes and will help people remember the *e*.

---

suppose to expect or believe, make a suggestion

The attorney **supposed** that the jury would not take long to reach a verdict.

supposed past and past participle of *suppose*, also to describe something believed to be true but not proven or required or permitted

Employees are not **supposed** to smoke in the rest rooms.

---

taught the past tense and past participle of *teach*, meaning to provide knowledge

The representative **taught** us how to operate the new equipment.

thought the past tense and past participle of *think*, meaning to formulate in the mind

We **thought** the new equipment would be easy to operate, but it was not.

---

their possessive form of the pronoun *they*

Their meetings are always scheduled for 4 p.m.

they're contraction meaning *they are*

They're meeting at 4 p.m. in the conference room.

there a location other than here

The conference room is located over **there**, next to the main entrance.

PRACTICE   Choosing the Correct Word

30.9   Some of the boldfaced words in the following sentences are not correct. If the word is not correct, write the correct word above it. If the word is correct, write a *C* above it.

Example: The teachers of Sun County are ~~quiet~~ *quite* upset.

1. They have not had a **raise** in three years, and **their** thinking of going on strike.

2. The **principle**, who had always supported them, **taught** that he should stay neutral.

3. He has to remain **quiet** and keep the **piece** between the teachers and the school board.

4. The teachers threatened to **raise** up and organize a strike at the **cite** of the main administrative center.

5. They listed **they're** grievances in a letter typed on a **piece** of school **stationary** and sent it to the local newspaper.

6. The teachers **suppose** that the school board would reconsider its decision.

7. The school board said it would give them more money if the city would **raise** taxes.

More Easily Confused Word Pairs and Examples

then at that time, next or after that

> Jamal made sure his schedule for Friday was clear, and **then** he made several appointments.

than used to join two items in comparison

> Jamal is busier on Thursday **than** he is on Friday.

threw past tense of throw, to send through the air

> She **threw** the old copy of the report in the trash.

though although, despite the fact that

> **Though** Clarisse spent several hours preparing her presentation, she was not happy with it.

through from one end or side to the other or having finished

> Tony looked **through** the files but could not find the document.

thru abbreviated slang for *through*; not appropriate in standard English

to in the direction of, for the purpose of

> Employees are not allowed wear jeans **to** work.

too in addition, very

> Chet took **too** many days off last month.

two the number which is the sum of one and one

> Hank had to give **two** speeches, one to the clients and the other to the company president.

use to put into service, to reduce

> Taylor always **uses** spell-check while he writes.

used past tense and past participle of *use*, previously owned; followed by *to* the expression *used to* means accustomed to

> Taylor **used** spell check after writing his memo.

we're the contracted form of *we are*

> **We're** meeting with the attorneys this morning.

where in, at, or in what place

> **Where** will the meeting take place?

were past tense of **be** for second person singular and first, second, and third person plural

> Jennifer and Amy **were** on maternity leave in January.

whether if, used to refer to one or more possibilities

> Keith did not know **whether** the boss had read his report.

weather the condition of the atmosphere such as temperature, rainfall, cloudiness, etc.

> The stormy **weather** caused many employees to be late.

who's contracted form of *who is*

> **Who's** writing the operating manual for the new equipment?

whose used to talk or ask about the person or thing something belongs to

> The writer **whose** email message is well written is the most effective.

write to record information

> Sometimes, employees **write** and print a message as a permanent, secure record.

right correct, morally good or acceptable, suitable

> Attention to email etiquette is the **right** approach in the business environment.

your possessive form of *you*

> We were impressed with **your** former boss's letter of recommendation.

you're contracted from of *you are*

> **You're** hired.

PRACTICE Choosing the Correct Word

30.10 Some of the boldfaced words in the following sentences are not correct. If the word is not correct, write the correct word above it. If the word is correct, write a *C* above it.

through
Example: Written communication can be enhanced ~~thru~~ visual elements, such as charts or pictures.

1. Sometimes, visuals can convey message points more effectively **then** words.

2. They can provide more information **too** while holding the reader's attention.

3. Busy readers **who's** time is limited often skip **threw** the written words and look at the visuals to get the central meaning of the message.

4. The designer must be careful that the **right** images are **use** because they can mean different things in different cultures.

5. Also, a poorly designed visual can confuse **you're** readers.

6. **Through** the use of powerful software, everyday business communicators can produce high quality images and video, and **were** using the software more often.

7. **Weather** an individual has high or low reading skills, he or she can understand visuals.

Writing Assignments

Review: Concise and Appropriate Words

The following is a letter from a school principal to parents. Revise the letter so that parents can easily understand it. Try to reduce the message to two sentences.

Dear Parent:

We have established a special phone communication system to provide additional opportunities for parent input. During this year we will give added emphasis to the goal of communication and utilize a variety of means to accomplish this goal. Your inputs, from the unique position as a parent, will help us to plan and implement an educational plan that meets the needs of your child. An open dialogue, feedback, and sharing of information between parents and teachers will enable us to work with your child in the most effective manner.

Dr. George B. Jones

Principal

(From "Writing in Your Job" by William Zinsser in *Strategies for Business and Technical Writing* by Kevin J. Harty)

Write about an Image

In the photograph, one employee is gossiping to another while the third tries to hear what they are saying. **Gossip** is conversation or reports about other people's private lives that might be unkind, disapproving, or not true.

In many instances gossiping would be considered unethical; for example, when you use it to unfairly hurt another person, when you know it's not true, when no one has the right to such personal information, or when you are breaking a promise of secrecy.

(From *Human Communication* by Joseph A. DeVito)

Write eight or more sentences that tell about an experience you had or heard about that involved gossip. As an alternative, you can write sentences about what you think is happening in the photograph. Make sure that your word choices are concise and appropriate.

English Success Tip: Word Choice and Cross-Cultural Communication

In this chapter, you have learned to choose words carefully when writing about gender, age, ethnicity, race, and disabilities. Communication problems can also occur between native English speakers and English learners. Word choice plays an important role in **cross-cultural communication** between people from different cultures with different native languages.

When writing for college or workplace audiences, be sensitive to the needs of the cross-cultural audience.

1. Use simple, clear language.
2. Use transitional words and expressions.
3. Avoid humor and references to popular culture.

(Adapted from *Business Communication Today* by Courtland L. Bovée and John V. Thill)

For support in meeting this chapter's objectives, log in to www.mywritinglab.com, go to the Study Plan tab, click on **Concise and Appropriate Words** and choose **Easily Confused Words** from the list of subtopics. Read and view the videos and resources in the Review Materials section, and then complete the Recall, Apply, and Write exercises in the Activities section. You can check your scores and overall progress by using the Gradebook.

CHAPTER 31

Consistency and Parallelism

Theme: *Nursing*

Learning Objectives

After working through this chapter, you will be able to:

LO 1 Maintain consistency in person.

LO 2 Maintain consistency in number.

LO 3 Maintain consistency in verb tense and voice.

LO 4 Maintain parallelism with words, phrases, and clauses.

What Are Consistency and Parallelism?

Consistency is the use of words, phrases, or clauses that match. **Parallelism** is the use of the same forms of words, phrases, or clauses when they appear in pairs, in groups, or in lists.

Consistency of person and number	Florence Nightingale was the founder of modern nursing, and she earned the title of "Lady with the Lamp" for her nightly rounds visiting wounded soldiers.
Consistency of verb tense	Mary Mahoney, who was the first African-American professional nurse, constantly worked to promote equal opportunities.
Parallelism	Clara Barton was an American teacher, nurse, and humanitarian, and during the United States Civil War, she established an agency to obtain and deliver supplies to wounded soldiers.

Consistency in Context

In the following passage about the importance of critical thinking for nurses, examples of consistency in person and number, verb tense, and parallel structure are highlighted.

¹Critical thinking is essential to safe, competent, skillful nursing practice. ²Every day, nurses have to make vital decisions that may determine the well being of their clients and even their survival. ³Often, nurses have to think and act in situations where there are neither clear answers nor standard procedures. ⁴In order to make decisions, nurses must use and learn a large amount of knowledge. ⁵They cannot function if they limit themselves to the information they learned in school or in books. ⁶Treatments, medications, and technology change constantly. ⁷Also, a client's condition may change from minute to minute. ⁸Therefore, nurses need to master critical thinking

skills to process and to evaluate information they previously learned and new information they have and will continue to learn.

(Adapted from *Fundamentals of Nursing* by Audrey Berman et al.)

LO 1 Consistency in Person

Pronouns and singular and plural forms should be used consistently in a sentence. A sentence that is consistent in person uses the same pronoun form throughout the sentence to refer to the same person. The three types of personal pronouns in their singular and plural forms are as follows:

Person	Singular	Plural
first	I, me	we, us
second	you	you
third	he, she, it; him, her, it	they, them

Not consistent	THIRD SECOND
	If a person wants to be a nurse, you need to fulfill the educational requirements and pass a licensing examination.
Consistent	THIRD THIRD
	If a person wants to be a nurse, he or she needs to fulfill the educational requirements and pass a licensing examination.

PRACTICE 31.1 Correcting Problems in Person

Correct the shifts in person in the following sentences.

Example: In the early days of nursing education, students trained in hospitals, and a
                                                                                    students
~~student~~ learned by working directly with patients.

1. Student nurses learned on the job, and one had to be supervised by an experienced nurse.
2. During that time, the nursing students did not study a standardized curriculum; instead, you had to meet the needs of the hospital.
3. Hospital administrators liked the idea of hospital training so that we could take advantage of free or inexpensive staffing for the hospital.
4. Unfortunately, because nurses had different sets of skills, you could not give proper care to all patients.
5. In 1901, Congress authorized the Army Nurse Corps to train nurses in life-saving techniques that one could use on the battlefields.
6. In 1905, Annie Walburton Goodrich changed nursing education in the United States; they established guidelines for proper nursing instruction.
7. Goodrich paved the way for women in nursing when one became the first dean of studies in Yale's Nursing School, established in 1923.

LO 2 Consistency in Number

A sentence that is consistent in number uses either the singular or plural form throughout the sentence.

Not consistent	SINGULAR A licensed practical nurse (LPN) usually provides basic direct PLURAL technical care to their clients.
Consistent	SINGULAR A licensed practical nurse usually provides basic direct technical care SINGULAR to his or her clients.

PRACTICE 31.2 Correcting Problems with Number

Correct any problems with consistency in number in the following sentences.

his or her

Example: A licensed practical nurse (LPN) must work under the supervision of ~~their~~ Registered Nurse (RN).

1. In most states, LPNs are not permitted to give certain drugs or perform blood transfusions to his patients.

2. Many LPN programs last nine to twelve months, and it provides both classroom and clinical experiences.

3. At the end of the program, the graduate takes the National Council Licensure Examination to obtain their license.

4. The registered nurse (RN) is responsible for assessing their client's condition, planning care, and evaluating the effect of the care provided.

5. A person can become an RN when they complete one of these programs: associate's degree in nursing, baccalaureate degree in nursing, or nursing diploma.

6. A popular degree program is the associate's degree in nursing because once the student completes them, the student can apply for an entry-level position with benefits.

Grammar Reminder:
For more practice with pronoun-antecedent agreement, see Chapter 24.

7. After completing any of these programs, a nurse must pass a national licensing examination, and they also may need to pass a state examination.

LO 3 Consistency in Verb Tense and Voice

A sentence that is consistent in verb tense uses the same verb tense throughout a sentence unless the time changes. A sentence that is consistent in voice uses either active or passive voice.

Present and Past

A sentence's verb tense is consistent when the verbs do not change unnecessarily from present to past or from past to present.

Not consistent	PRESENT	PAST
	Nurses work in hospitals, but today they also worked in clients' homes, community agencies, and clinics.	
Consistent	PRESENT	PRESENT
	Nurses work in hospitals, but today they also work in clients' homes, community agencies, and clinics.	

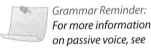

Grammar Reminder:
For more information on present and past tense, see Chapters 21 and 22.

Active Voice to Passive Voice

English verbs have two voices: active voice and passive voice. A sentence is consistent in voice when the verbs do not change unnecessarily from active to passive or passive to active.

The **active voice** is the form of the verb used when the subject performs the action.

The registered nurse (RN) assesses the client's health status.

The **passive voice** consists of a form of the verb *be* and the past participle. The passive voice focuses on the receiver of the action. The subject of the sentence, however, is not the performer.

The client's health status is assessed by the registered nurse (RN).

Not consistent	An experienced nurse uses past knowledge and skill to diagnose a patient, but guidelines are needed by novice nurses.
Consistent	An experienced nurse uses past knowledge and skill to diagnose a patient, but novice nurses need guidelines.

Grammar Reminder:
For more information on passive voice, see Chapter 23.

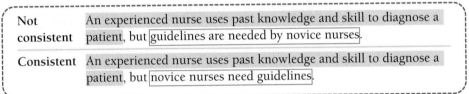

PRACTICE   Keeping Verb Tenses Consistent

31.3   Correct verb tenses that are not consistent in the following sentences.

Example: Home nursing care services is a growing sector of the health care system be-
                                     need
cause more people ~~needed~~ it.

1. Home health care workers go to people's homes, and a trusting relationship with the client and family must be established by the nurse.

_____

2. Nurses get to know the client and family well when they cared for the clients over a period of weeks or months in their homes.

_____

3. These nurses give hands-on care for all types of health conditions; they also did physical assessments, changed wound bandages, and supervise different therapies.

_____

4. Consultations are had by home health care workers with other health care providers so that they can improve their client's nursing care.

_____

5. A family can request a home health care worker from an agency or a client may be referred by a doctor, nurse, social worker, or therapist.

_____

6. Home health care cannot begin without an order from a doctor; the doctor also had to approve a treatment plan.

_____

LO 4 Consistency in Structure: Parallelism

Parallelism, also called parallel structure, is the use of the same forms of words, phrases, or clauses when they appear in pairs, in groups, or in lists.

Words, Phrases, or Clauses in Pairs

When words, phrases, or clauses appear in pairs, they should be in the same form.

Words	A health assessment differs with children and adults.
Phrases	With children, the nurse should proceed from the least uncomfortable to the most uncomfortable.
Dependent clauses	The nurse should explain when the examination will take place and what will happen during the exam.
Independent clauses	The examination room should be well lighted, and the equipment should be efficiently organized.

Not consistent	A nurse can wear *either* a disposable water-resistant gown *or* an apron that is made out of plastic during procedures when the uniform is likely to become soiled.
Consistent	A nurse can wear *either* a disposable water-resistant gown *or* a plastic apron during procedures when the uniform is likely to become soiled.

PRACTICE   Consistency through Parallel Words, Phrases, or Clauses in Pairs
31.4   Rewrite the following sentences so that the pairs of words, phrases, or clauses are parallel.

Example: A physical examination can be organized using either a head-to-toe approach or one that uses a body systems approach.

A physical examination can be organized using either a head-to-toe approach or a body systems approach.

1. Usually, the nurse records a general impression about the client's overall appearance and status of health.
   _____

2. The head-to-toe approach begins the examination at the head, and the toes are last.
   _____

3. The nurse assesses all body parts and comparing findings on each side of the body.
   _____

4. The nurse can either give a complete examination or focus on what the problem area is.
   _____

5. Nurses use a written format or a format that is on a computer that organizes the information from the examination.
   _____

6. The information gathered during the assessment must be complete, and accuracy is also important.
   _____

7. The nurse double-checks the information when the data from the nursing interview does not agree with physical examination data.

---

8. To collect data accurately, nurses need to be able to separate facts from interpreting to avoid making a mistake that could affect the client's safety.

Words or Phrases in a Series, List, or Outline

Each word or phrase that is in a series, list, or outline must be parallel.

Series of Items or Numbered List within a Sentence

A series of items	The nursing process consists of assessing, diagnosing, planning, implementing, and evaluating.
A numbered list of items within a sentence	The nursing process consists of (1) assessing, (2) diagnosing, (3) planning, (4) implementing, and (5) evaluating.

Not consistent	Assessing the patient includes collecting, organizing, validating, and an objective record of the information.
Consistent	Assessing the patient includes collecting, organizing, validating, and recording the information objectively

Bulleted or Outlined Items

Bulleted items	A nurse asks the patient for the following information about his or her health history:

- childhood illnesses
- childhood immunizations
- allergies
- accidents and injuries
- hospitalization for serious illnesses
- medications

Outlined items

I. Social Data
   A. Family relationships/friendships
   B. Ethnic affiliation
   C. Educational history
   D. Occupational history
   E. Economic status
   F. Home and neighborhood conditions

(Adapted from *Fundamentals of Nursing* by Audrey Berman et al.)

Compare the bulleted lists below. Items on the list that are consistent are highlighted.

Not Consistent	Consistent
Important Times for Medication Check	Important Times for Medication Check
• On admission	• On admission
• During shift reports	• During shift reports
• During transfers	• During transfers
• New medication orders	• During new medication orders
• When the patient is discharged	• Upon patient discharge

PRACTICE Consistency through Parallel Series, Bulleted Lists, and Outlines

31.5 Revise the sentences, lists, or outlines that have series, bulleted lists, or outlines that are not consistent.

Example: An infection can be transmitted through any of the following mechanisms: (1) direct transmission, (2) that which is indirect, and (3) airborne transmission.

An infection can be transmitted through any of the following mechanisms: (1) direct transmission, (2) indirect transmission, and (3) airborne transmission.

1. An infection can be directly transmitted from one person to another through touching, biting, or a kiss.

_____

2. Droplet spread is another form of transmission that occurs through a sneeze, coughing, singing, or someone talking.

_____

3. The droplet sprays from the infected person into healthy person's mucous membranes of the eye, nose, or the person's mouth when the individuals are within three feet of one another.

_____

4. Uninjured skin is the body's first line of defense against infections and protects it because of these characteristics:
   - Dryness as a deterrent
   - Resident bacteria
   - Acidity inhibits bacterial growth

5. I. Steps for hand cleaning with alcohol-based antiseptic hand rub
   A. Apply palm full of product into cupped hand.
   B. Next, you should rub palms against palms.
   C. **Interlace** fingers palm to palm.
   D. Rub palms to back of hands.
   E. Don't forget to rub each finger individually on all sides.
   F. It is important to continue until product is dry.

   A. _____

   B. _____

   C. _____

   D. _____

   E. _____

   F. _____

interlace cross one finger over and under another, as if woven together

grooming making yourself ready to be seen

6. The following practices can reduce a person's chance of infection: (1) cleansing and **grooming** the body, (2) eating a well balanced diet, (3) enough fluid, (4) getting adequate sleep, and (5) excessive stress.   The following practices can reduce a person's chance of infection: (1) cleansing and grooming the body, (2) eating a well-balanced diet, (3) drinking enough fluid, (4) getting adequate sleep, and (5) reducing stress.

(Adapted from *Fundamentals of Nursing* by Audrey Berman et al.)

Writing Assignments

Review: Consistency and Parallelism

Edit the following paragraph for the ten errors in consistency in person and number, verb tense, and parallelism.

¹Nurses and nursing students need to examine the values they hold about life, death, health, ~~and~~ values ~~about illness~~.² In their daily work, nurses deal with intimate and basic human events such as ~~babies being born~~, death, and suffering. ³They must decide the morality of their own actions when they face the many ethical issues of these sensitive areas. ⁴Because of the special nurse-client relationship, nurses are the ones who support and ~~speak~~ ~~speaking~~ for clients and families who face difficult choices. ⁵They also ~~had~~ to support the people who are living the results of choices that others make for and about them.

⁶Being involved in ethical problems and making difficult decisions are stressful for nurses. ⁷~~You~~ may be torn between obligations to the client, the family, and ~~the person who is the employer~~. ⁸What is in the client's best interest may be the opposite of what the nurses personally believe.

⁹They also need to identify clients' values as they affect and ~~are related~~ to a particular health problem. ¹⁰~~The nurse rarely, if ever, offers~~ an opinion when the client asks for it, but if they do, ~~great care is taken by them when giving their opinion~~. ¹¹Since each situation is different, nurses' choices for ~~his or her~~ own life may not apply to the client's circumstances.

¹²Although their input is important, in reality several people are usually involved in making an ethical decision. ¹³The client, family, spiritual support persons, and other members of the health care team work together in reaching ethical decisions. ¹⁴Therefore, collaboration, communication, and compromise are important skills for nurses.

(Adapted from *Fundamentals of Nursing* by Audrey Berman et al.)

Write about an Image

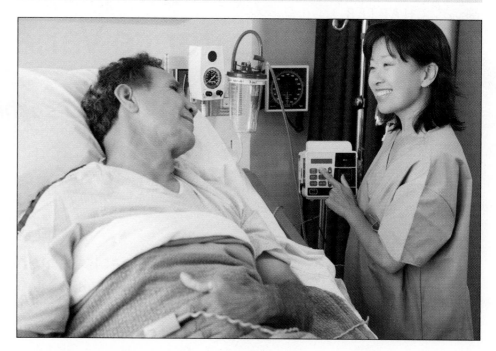

Write five to eight sentences about an experience you or someone you know had with a nurse or other health care worker. Check your sentences for consistency in person, number, verb tense, and parallelism. Reread several times to catch any errors.

English Success Tip: In Technical Writing, Every Word Carries the Message

Writing in the technical fields can take many different forms. For example, nurses must record information about their patients on charts, which are legal records of everything that happened during a patient's stay at a hospital. A chart that is not accurate can affect the patient's care.

Effective writing should follow these three guidelines.

1. **Organization:** Focus on the important ideas and concepts and present them in a logical pattern.
2. **Details:** Make sure the information is accurate, reliable, and precise; include necessary details only.
3. **Sentences:** Use words that are easy to understand and write sentences that make a point concisely.

For support in meeting this chapter's objectives, log in to www.mywritinglab.com, go to the Study Plan tab, click on **Consistency and Parallelism** and choose **Consistent Verb Tense and Active Voice, Parallelism, and Abbreviations and Numbers** from the list of subtopics. Read and view the videos and resources in the Review Materials section, and then complete the Recall, Apply, and Write exercises in the Activities section. You can check your scores and overall progress by using the Gradebook.

CHAPTER 32

Sentence Variety

Theme: *Teaching*

Learning Objectives

After working through this chapter, you will be able to:

LO 1 Add variety to your writing by using a mixture of simple, compound, and complex sentences.

LO 2 Add variety through the use of phrases.

LO 3 Add variety through the use of compound subjects and verbs, and adjectives and adverbs.

What Is Sentence Variety?

Sentence variety is the use of a mixture of sentence types and descriptive words and phrases in a piece of writing. Writing that lacks variety is not interesting to read.

Sentence Variety in Context

Compare the following two passages about teaching reading and writing. The first one illustrates writing that lacks variety. Most of the sentences are simple, and words and phrases are repeated.

[1]Education researchers and reading teachers had beliefs. [2]This was before the 1970s. [3]Their beliefs were about reading and writing. [4]Reading should be taught before writing. [5]They thought that students should learn some things first. [6]They thought that students should learn to form letters. [7]They also thought that students should learn to spell. [8]Then, in the 1970s, research showed something new about teaching reading and writing. [9]The research was the work of Read and Chomsky. [10]It showed that reading and writing develop at the same time.[11]Now the trend is different. [12]The trend is to encourage students to write as early as possible. [13]They do not have to know how to form letters. [14]They do not have to know how to spell in Standard English. [15]They are encouraged to get their ideas down in any way possible. [16]They should draw pictures. [17]They should scribble. [18]They should invent their own letters. [19]These are early forms of writing. [20]These early forms create a natural sequence. [21]The natural sequence is for learning to write.

This next paragraph is a revision of the first. One improvement is the use of a variety of simple, compound, and complex sentences. Also, combining words and using descriptive phrases got rid of the repeated ideas.

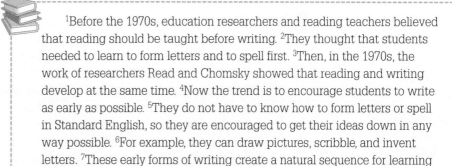

[1]Before the 1970s, education researchers and reading teachers believed that reading should be taught before writing. [2]They thought that students needed to learn to form letters and to spell first. [3]Then, in the 1970s, the work of researchers Read and Chomsky showed that reading and writing develop at the same time. [4]Now the trend is to encourage students to write as early as possible. [5]They do not have to know how to form letters or spell in Standard English, so they are encouraged to get their ideas down in any way possible. [6]For example, they can draw pictures, scribble, and invent letters. [7]These early forms of writing create a natural sequence for learning to write.

(Adapted from *Teaching Exceptional, Diverse, and At-Risk Students in the General Education Classroom* by Sharon Vaughn et al.)

LO 1 Achieving Variety by Mixing Sentence Types

Using a mixture of simple, compound, and complex sentences makes writing more interesting to read. When most sentences are short, the writing sounds elementary, indicating that the writer's thoughts are simple. When too many simple sentences are combined into one very long sentence, the relationship between the ideas is lost.

adaptation a change in the way a teacher presents a topic to make it understandable to learners with special needs

Too many short sentences and repeated ideas:

Tony took a course. The course was on making **adaptations**. The adaptations were for students. The students have special learning needs.

Revised:

Tony took a course on making adaptations for students with special learning needs.

Too many simple sentences combined:

Tony took a course, and it was on making adaptations, and the adaptations were for students, and the students have special learning needs. His classroom teaching was videotaped, and a graduate student served as a peer coach, and Tony wanted help with teaching social studies, and Tony watched the videotape, and he was not happy, and he saw his mistakes, so he decided to change his teaching style.

Here is the revised passage with sentence variety:

Grammar Reminder: For more information about and practice with sentence types, see these chapters: simple sentences, Chapter 18; compound sentences, Chapter 19; complex sentences, Chapter 20.

Tony took a course on making adaptations for students with special learning needs. Because he wanted help with teaching social studies, he asked a graduate student to serve as a peer coach. Tony's classroom teaching was videotaped. After watching the videotape, he saw his teaching mistakes, and he decided to change his teaching style.

(Adapted from *Teaching Exceptional, Diverse, and At-Risk Students in the General Education Classroom* by Sharon Vaughn et al.)

PRACTICE Varying Sentence Types

32.1 Add variety to the simple sentences in this paragraph by combining some of them. Include two compound and two complex sentences. When you are finished, label your sentences: *S* for simple; *CD* for compound; and *CX* for complex.

¹Faimon Roberts is a seventh- and eighth-grade science teacher. ²He teaches at Louisiana State University Laboratory School. ³Faimon's primary responsibility is teaching students to learn in science classes. ⁴He has taught for more than twenty years. ⁵In that time, he has learned. ⁶Students need to get ready to listen and read. ⁷Their minds are on a million different things. ⁸Pre-learning activities help them focus. ⁹Faimon has learned the importance of setting a purpose for learning. ¹⁰This helps some students. ¹¹These students get lost. ¹²They need help reading science textbooks. ¹³They need help hearing a lecture. ¹⁴Also, the teacher needs to show students the textbook organization.

_____

_____

_____

_____

_____

_____

(Adapted from *Teaching Exceptional, Diverse, and At-Risk Students in the General Education Classroom* by Sharon Vaughn et al.)

LO 2   Achieving Variety with Phrases

Using prepositional and participial phrases also adds variety to your sentences.

Prepositional Phrases

Prepositional phrases are descriptive word groups that act as adjectives or adverbs. They begin with a preposition and end with a noun or a pronoun. Some examples of prepositional phrases are *during the lesson, in small groups, about a student.*

You can use prepositional phrases to add variety in two ways:

1. Place a prepositional phrase at the beginning of or within a sentence.

   Within the sentence:

   Children continue to develop language skills through the school-age years.

   At the beginning:

   Through the school-age years, children continue to develop language skills.

TIP   When one or more prepositional phrases are placed at the beginning of a sentence, follow them with a comma.

2. Combine several shorter sentences with prepositional phrases into one longer sentence.

Short sentences:

Opportunities to teach language can occur. They can occur in the classroom. They can occur on the playground.

Combined:

Opportunities to teach language can occur in the classroom and on the playground.

Grammar Reminder: For more information on prepositional phrases, see Chapter 18.

PRACTICE 32.2 Varying Sentences with Prepositional Phrases

Part A

Rewrite the sentence so that the prepositional phrase is at the beginning.

Example: Young children learn to use language through interaction with people.
Through interaction with people, young children learn to use language.

1. Children between the ages of one and a half to two can recognize some printed symbols, such as brand names.

2. Children begin to understand how language works from ages two to six.

3. Children can separate words into syllables at this age.

4. They can correct their own speech to help the listener understand in response to a listener's request.

Part B

Rewrite the sentence by combining sentences with short prepositional phrases into one longer sentence.

Example: General education teachers play a role. They play a role of observer and listener. They listen for students with communication problems.

General education teachers play a role of observer and listener for students with communication problems.

1. Classroom teachers get to observe students. They observe students in the classroom. They also observe them on the playground.

2. Students have opportunities. These are students with communication disorders. They have opportunities for language development. The opportunities are in the classroom.

speech and language pathologist a specialist who evaluates and treats communication disorders

3. Some students get help. They get help from a **speech and language pathologist**. They get help for thirty minutes several times a week.

_____

4. Teachers should create a safe environment. The environment is for student communication. The environment should be without pressures and tensions.

_____

Appositive Phrases

An **appositive phrase** consists of a noun and its modifiers. It describes, defines, or re-names another noun or pronoun. An appositive phrase most often appears after the word it describes. To add variety, combine two sentences that have nouns or pronouns that refer to the same thing by turning one sentence into an appositive phrase.

> **Two sentences:**
>
> Mathematics instruction has become a growing national concern. Mathematics instruction is a central topic in education.
>
> **One sentence with an appositive:**
>
> Mathematics instruction, a central topic in education, has become a growing national concern.

> **TIP** | Use commas before and after appositive phrases that are not essential to the meaning of the sentence.

PRACTICE Changing Sentences to Appositive Phrases
32.3   Combine the following pairs of sentences by changing one of the sentences to an appositive phrase. Remember to place the appositive phrase next to the word it describes, defines, or names. Underline the appositive phrase in the revised sentence.

Example: One reason students display poor math performance can easily be corrected. The reason is inappropriate or inadequate instruction.

One reason students display poor math performance, inappropriate or inadequate instruction, can easily be corrected.

1. Dennis Chun is a fifth grade teacher. Dennis Chun checks his students' math work frequently and provides immediate feedback.

_____

2. Mr. Chun asked students to complete a worksheet using skills from a new lesson. The lesson was dollar signs and decimal points in subtraction problems.

_____

3. He moved quickly from student to student using an effective method. A method was immediate feedback and positive support.

_____

4. Mr. Chun stopped to help Cyndi. She was one of the students having trouble with the first problem.

_____

5. This teacher's methods have helped his students gain a positive attitude toward the subject. The methods are his effective instruction and his interest in math.

_____

Participial Phrases

A participial phrase is a group of words that begins with a participle and contains other words related to it. A participial phrase is used as an adjective to describe a noun or pronoun and is placed next to the word it modifies. A present participle is a verb form that ends in -ing, such as _studying_, _teaching_, and _learning_; a past participle is a verb form that ends in -ed/en, such as _studied_, _given_, and _learned_.

To add variety, combine two sentences that have the same subject into one by changing one sentence to a participial phrase.

Move this sentence to the previous paragraph. Drop the subject of the sentence you want to change to a participial phrase. Place the participial phrase next to the word it modifies.

Phrases with Present Participles When two sentences have the same subject and when the verbs express actions that are happening at the same time, you can change one sentence into a present participial phrase.

Two sentences:

Teachers encourage their students to read. Teachers supply their classroom with interesting reading materials.

One sentence with a present participial phrase:

Encouraging their students to read, teachers supply their classrooms with interesting reading materials.

Supplying their classroom with interesting reading materials, teachers encourage their students to read.

PRACTICE Combining Sentences: Using Present Participial Phrases

32.4 Combine the following pairs of sentences by changing one of the sentences to a present participial phrase. Remember to place the phrase next to the word it describes. Underline the phrase.

Example: Ms. Graziose models reading. She reads out loud to students and reads silently when they do.

Modeling reading, Ms. Graziose reads out loud to students and reads silently when they do.

_____

1. The teacher talks about books she has read. This shows that she enjoys reading.

2. Community leaders, parents, and grandparents frequently visit the class. They read to students and listen to students read.

3. Children hear stories over and over again. They become familiar with the book.

4. Children begin by saying some of the words and phrases. Eventually, they can read most of the book along with the person reading to them.

5. Students read stories they have written themselves. They are motivated to read their story over and over again.

Phrases with Past Participles When two sentences have the same subject, you can combine them by changing one sentence into a past participial phrase.

Two sentences:

The teacher was annoyed that students were writing on the desks. The teacher discussed the problem with the class.

One sentence with a past participial phrase:

Annoyed that students were writing on the desks, the teacher discussed the problem with the class.

PRACTICE   Combining Sentences: Using Past Participial Phrases

32.5   Combine the following pairs of sentences by changing one of the sentences to a participial phrase that begins with a past participle. Remember to place it next to the word it describes. Underline the phrase.

Example: The students were influenced by the discussion about destroying school property. They came up with a solution.

Influenced by the class discussion about destroying school property, the students came up with a solution.

1. The students were determined to keep writing on the desks. However, they figured out a safe way to do it.

2. The students placed masking tape around the edges. The students protected the desks.

3. They were called reference borders. They could be used to record ideas or misspelled words.

_____

4. The students were concerned that the reference borders would be used for cheating. The students set up class rules.

_____

5. The students were asked about the activity. They said they liked solving a real-life problem together.

_____

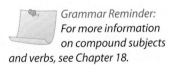

Grammar Reminder:
For more information
about participles as
adjectives, see Chapter 26 and for
past participles, see Chapter 23.

(Adapted from _Teaching Exceptional, Diverse, and At-Risk Students in the General Education Classroom_ by Sharon Vaughn et al.)

LO 3 Achieving Variety with Words

Short sentences can be combined to create sentence variety by using compound subjects and verbs and adjectives and adverbs.

Compound Subjects and Verbs

Combining short sentences by using compound subjects and verbs can make them more interesting and varied.

A **compound subject** is made up of two or more subjects that share the same verb. The two subjects can be joined with _and, or, either … or, neither … nor,_ or _not only … but also._

Two short sentences that share the same verb:

Juanita worked on the math problem. Marcel worked on the math problem.

Two sentences combined with a compound subject:

Juanita and Marcel worked on the math problem.

A **compound verb** is made up of two or more verbs that have the same subject. The verbs are joined by coordinating conjunctions such as _and, but,_ or _or._

Two short sentences with the same subject:

The teacher made the rules for the class. The teacher explained them to the students.

Two short sentences combined with a compound verb:

The teacher made the rules for the class and explained them to the students.

Grammar Reminder:
For more information
on compound subjects
and verbs, see Chapter 18.

PRACTICE Joining Ideas with Compound Subjects or Compound Verbs

32.6 Combine the two short sentences into one by using a compound subject or compound verb.

Example: Students become fearful after punishment. Students may resent the teacher.

Students become fearful after punishment and may resent the teacher.

_____

1. Laura uses class meetings to solve crises. Laura deals with immediate problems.

_____

2. Laura has regularly scheduled class meetings. Joan has regularly scheduled class meetings.

_____

3. Teachers place written recognitions of classmates in the recognition box. Students place written recognitions of classmates in the recognition box.

_____

4. Joan brings the recognition box to the class meeting. Joan passes it around to each student.

_____

5. Each student selects a slip from the recognition box. Each student takes a turn reading one recognition.

_____

Adjectives and Adverbs

Another way to achieve variety is to combine short sentences by using adjectives and adverbs that describe the same word.

An **adjective** describes a noun (a person, place, thing, idea, or activity). Combine short sentences that describe the same noun by creating a series of adjectives:

> **Short sentences**: Teachers should listen to students in a calm manner. Teachers should listen to students in a thoughtful manner.

> **Combined**: Teachers should listen to students in a calm, thoughtful manner.

An **adverb** describes verbs, adjectives, or other adverbs. Combine short sentences that use adverbs to describe the same verb:

> **Short sentences**: Joan teaches her lessons skillfully. She also teaches them effectively.

> **Combined**: Joan teachers her lessons skillfully and effectively.

For variety, try starting a sentence with an adverb:

> Generally, praising students helps to raise their self-esteem.

Grammar Reminder: For more information about adjectives and adverbs, see Chapter 26.

PRACTICE 32.7 Joining Ideas with Descriptive Words

Combine the two short sentences by using adjectives or adverbs.

Example: The best way to learn language is through a meaningful activity. The quickest way to learn language is through a meaningful activity.

The best, quickest way to learn language is through a purposeful activity.

Barrier game: A game where each student works behind a piece of wood or cardboard that prevents another student from seeing what he or she is doing.

1. Speech and language teachers use barrier games with an entire class or with pairs of students. They use **barrier games** frequently.

_____

2. Students work in pairs with blocks for building or paper and colors for making a picture. They usually work in pairs.

_____

3. Each student works behind a barrier. The barrier is made of wood or heavy cardboard.

_____

4. The lead student builds a structure or picture. The structure or picture is simple.

_____

5. The lead student gives the second student the instructions to make his or her design. The lead student gives the instructions slowly and carefully.

_____

6. The barrier is removed, and the two students compare their projects. The barrier is removed last.

_____

Writing Assignments

Review: Sentence Variety Strategies

The following passage lacks sentence variety. Revise the groups of sentences using the suggested strategies.

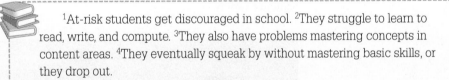

[1]At-risk students get discouraged in school. [2]They struggle to learn to read, write, and compute. [3]They also have problems mastering concepts in content areas. [4]They eventually squeak by without mastering basic skills, or they drop out.

1. Combine sentences 2 and 3 into a compound sentence.

_____

_____

2. Begin sentence 4 with a modifier.

_____

_____

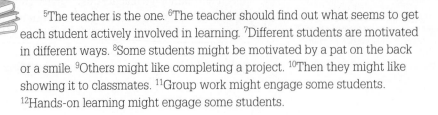

⁵The teacher is the one. ⁶The teacher should find out what seems to get each student actively involved in learning. ⁷Different students are motivated in different ways. ⁸Some students might be motivated by a pat on the back or a smile. ⁹Others might like completing a project. ¹⁰Then they might like showing it to classmates. ¹¹Group work might engage some students. ¹²Hands-on learning might engage some students.

3. Combine sentences 5 and 6 into a complex sentence.

_____

4. Begin sentence 8 with "a pat on the back or a smile."

_____

5. Combine sentences 9 and 10 into a compound sentence. Use a transition expression as a connector.

_____

6. Combine sentences 11 and 12 by using a compound subject.

_____

(Adapted from *Teaching Exceptional, Diverse, and At-Risk Students in the General Education Classroom* by Sharon Vaughn et al.)

Write about an Image

Choose a teacher who was effective *or* ineffective, and write five to eight sentences providing specific examples to support the word "effective" or "ineffective." Alternatively, write five to eight sentences about the classroom in the photograph. Then analyze your sentence variety by following the instructions in the *English Success Tip: How to Check Your Writing for Sentence Variety* (page 525). If necessary, edit your sentences to achieve sentence variety.

English Success Tip: How to Check Your Writing for Sentence Variety

Varying sentence length and patterns can make your writing enjoyable to read. Here is a method you can use to check your own writing for sentence variety. Begin by choosing one of your paragraphs that is a minimum of one hundred words. Number each sentence.

Using the chart below, fill in the information about your paragraph.

1. Count the words in each sentence.
2. Write down the type of sentence: simple, compound, or complex.
3. Write the first four words of each sentence.
4. Using the information you wrote down in the chart, analyze your writing by looking for variety in sentence types, length, beginnings, and phrases.

Sentence number	Number of words in each sentence	Type of sentence: simple, compound, complex	First four words of each sentence
1.			
2.			
3.			
4.			
5.			
6.			
7.			
8.			

If you have discovered that your writing needs more variety, refer to the ideas in this chapter whenever you revise a paper.

For support in meeting this chapter's objectives, log in to www.mywritinglab.com, go to the Study Plan tab, click on **Sentence Variety** and choose **Varying Sentence Structure** from the list of subtopics. Read and view the videos and resources in the Review Materials section, and then complete the Recall, Apply, and Write exercises in the Activities section. You can check your scores and overall progress by using the Gradebook.

Reading

CHAPTER 33

Active Reading

Learning Objectives

After working through this chapter, you will be able to:

LO 1 Describe the stages of the active reading process.

LO 2 Use prereading strategies to prepare for reading.

LO 3 Use reading strategies to improve your comprehension.

LO 4 Reflect upon and interpret what you have read.

As a college student, you will be doing quite a bit of reading. The types of reading materials for college assignments will vary. These include textbooks, academic journals, and magazine and newspaper articles. In English courses like the one you are taking now, you may also read essays and fiction.

Textbooks, academic journals, and magazine and newspaper articles have different features. When you know how a reading is organized, you can decide on the best reading strategy to use. The chart below describes the features each type of reading:

Features of College Reading Materials	
Type of Reading	Features
Textbooks	■ Units, chapters, and sections ■ Headings and subheadings ■ Chapter summaries
Journal Articles	Follow a standard format: ■ Short summary ■ Introduction to the subject of the article ■ Review of research that has already been done on the subject ■ Methods of research ■ Discussion of the results
Magazine and Newspaper Articles	■ A lead gets the reader interested and is followed by the main point of the article ■ Body paragraphs are short so that the reader can get the information quickly ■ Writer often concludes with a final thought on the subject

LO 1 What Is Active Reading?

When your professors assign reading materials, they expect you to learn, think about, and respond to those materials. Learning how to be an active reader will help you get the most out of your reading assignments.

Active reading is the use of a variety of strategies before, during, and after you read to help you understand, learn, and study what you have read. Active reading takes time and effort, but you will get more from your reading than if you simply read and highlight.

The active reading process has three stages: (1) getting ready to read, (2) understanding the reading, and (3) remembering and thinking about the reading.

LO 2 Stage 1. Getting Ready to Read

In this stage, you prepare to read by looking over the material to find out what it is about, what you already know about the topic, what your purpose for reading is, and how difficult the reading is. Here is a checklist of things to think about as you prepare to read:

- -

GETTING READY TO READ CHECKLIST

What is the reading about? The reading material offers clues about its content.

☐ Look at the title for the subject of the reading or an idea about how the author feels about it.

☐ Look through the reading itself.

- **In textbook chapters:** chapter objectives, introduction, headings, subheadings, visuals, chapter summary, chapter study questions
- **In magazine and newspaper articles:** background and main idea after the lead, the writer's final thought at the end
- **In academic journal articles:** the summary and results of the research

What do you already know about the subject? Having some knowledge about the subject makes reading easier.

☐ Think about the topic and what background knowledge you have.

☐ Do a brief online search to learn more.

What is your purpose for reading? Having a purpose helps you focus on getting the information you need.

☐ to learn information for a test
☐ to write a summary
☐ to make an outline
☐ to be prepared to discuss the main ideas
☐ to write an essay about some aspect of the reading
☐ other

How difficult is the reading? A more difficult reading will require more time and energy.

☐ new vocabulary words
☐ new ideas
☐ difficult reading level
☐ explanations that are hard to understand

- -

Getting Ready to Read Graphic Organizer

Instead of just thinking about the questions in this stage of the reading process, become an active reader by filling in key elements of any reading assignment in the graphic organizer shown on page 530. A completed organizer for the reading at the end of this section titled "Beauty May Be Only Skin Deep, but Its Effects Go on Forever: Stereotypes in Everyday Life" is shown on page 533.

Getting Ready to Read Graphic Organizer

Title and Author of Reading:

Type of Reading:

Topic of Reading from its Clues:

Your Knowledge of This Topic:

Purpose for Reading:

Unfamiliar Words or Concepts:

Word/Concept	Definition

LO 3 Stage 2. Understanding the Reading

An important part of the active reading process occurs while you are reading. Instead of silently reading and highlighting, take control of your reading by using strategies that help you understand and learn the materials. Three of these strategies are annotating, RAP, and Click and Clunk.

Annotating

Annotating is the process of writing comments and notes directly on the reading materials. Annotating keeps you involved in your reading. Also, writing notes and comments are helpful for paragraph summaries, questions about the material, important vocabulary words and definitions, and your thoughts or opinions. When you annotate, your notes will stand out so that you can find important information later.

Before annotating, read the section or passage to get a sense of what it is about. You can write notes and comments, use symbols, or draw concept maps. If you prefer to use symbols, it is a good idea to make a set of symbols that you plan to use every time you annotate. For example, you can use circles for words you need to look up or learn or put boxes around important ideas. Another way to annotate is to draw concept maps in the margins.

Turn to page 533 to see an annotated version of the textbook excerpt "Beauty May Be Only Skin Deep, but Its Effects Go on Forever: Stereotypes in Everyday Life."

Writing Reminder. For more information on concept maps, see Chapter 2.

RAP

RAP is an active reading strategy to use while you are reading to check your understanding. This is especially helpful when the material is difficult or when your mind starts to wander. RAP can be done silently or out loud. It consists of three parts: Read, Ask, and Paraphrase.

- Read a paragraph or section.
- Ask yourself what the main ideas are.
- Put the main ideas in your own words.

Click and Clunk

Click and Clunk is another strategy for checking reading comprehension or figuring out words you do not know. Say "click" to yourself when you understand and "clunk" when you come across something that is confusing. Clunks are things that you should pay more attention to.

Responding to Clunks	
When you don't understand part of the reading	■ Reread the passage. ■ Reread a few sentences after it for further explanation.
When you don't understand a word	■ Reread the sentence for clues. ■ Reread the sentences before and after. ■ Look for smaller words within the word. ■ Look it up in a dictionary.

LO 4 Stage 3. Remembering and Thinking about the Reading

The active reading process does not end when you have read the very last word of the material.

Remembering the Reading

To remember what you have read, use your annotations and notes to make a concept map, an outline, or a graphic organizer. The reading organizer on page 532 can be used for textbooks. Rows can be added as needed.

Reading Graphic Organizer

Change Titles, Headings, and Topic Sentences into Questions	Write the Answers to the Questions by Putting the Information in Your Words

Reacting to and Thinking about the Reading

Writing about the reading in a journal gives you an opportunity to reflect on the reading in a personal way, to express your thoughts and opinions. Here are some focused questions you can answer in a reading journal:

- Did the reading change your thinking?
- Can you connect the reading to something else you have read or know about?
- What was interesting in the reading?
- Do you agree or disagree with the author?
- Did you gain any new insights?

Tori's Getting Ready to Read Graphic Organizer: Sociology Text

Title of Reading: "Beauty May Be Only Skin Deep, but Its Effects Go on Forever: Stereotypes in Everyday Life"—from Essentials of Sociology by Henslin

Type of Reading: Textbook

Topic of Reading from Its Clues:

Chart: How Self-Fulfilling Stereotypes Work
"Stereotypes" is in bold and defined
Title gives the idea that the excerpt will be about how beauty affects our everyday life

Your Knowledge of This Topic:

I have heard the expression "beauty is only skin deep." According to the dictionary, the quote means that physical beauty is superficial and not as important as intellectual, emotional, and spiritual qualities--but I think our culture and the media focus on how important physical beauty is. Women have a lot of pressure to look beautiful to the point where they want to get plastic surgery and go on extreme diets.

Purpose for Reading: Assigned in English class. I have to write a summary of it.

Unfamiliar Words or Concepts:

Word/Concept	Definition
self-fulfilling stereotype	the idea that a person will behave the way others think he or she will behave
ingenious	very clever and skillful
homely	not good-looking
reserved	tending to keep your feelings or thoughts private and hidden
permeate	to spread through something, to be present in every part of it
revenues	income

An Illustration of Active Reading

Tori was assigned to read a section of her textbook, *Essentials of Sociology* by James M. Henslin. Here is how she approached this assignment.

Tori first scanned the selection on page 534 to preview it. She used the Getting Ready to Read Graphic Organizer on page 530 to prepare for reading.

As she read the selection carefully, Tori annotated it.

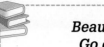

Beauty May Be Only Skin Deep, but Its Effects Go on Forever: Stereotypes in Everyday Life

Purpose of experiment— are stereotypes self-fulfilling?

Description of experiment

?? Look up

1   Mark Snyder, a psychologist, wondered whether stereotypes—our assumptions of what people are like—might be self-fulfilling. He came up with an <u>ingenious</u> way to test this idea. He (1993) gave college men a Polaroid snapshot of a woman (supposedly taken just moments before) and told them that he would introduce them to her after they talked with her on the telephone. Actually, the photographs—showing either a pretty or a homely woman—had been prepared before the experiment began. The photo was not of the woman the men would talk to.

Men reacted more positively to photo of pretty woman

2   <u>Stereotypes came into play immediately.</u> As Synder gave each man the photograph, he asked him what he thought the woman would be like. The men who saw the photograph of the attractive woman said that they expected to meet a poised, humorous, outgoing woman. The men who had been given a photo of the unattractive woman described her as awkward, serious, and unsociable.

Main idea

3   <u>The men's stereotypes influenced the way they spoke on the telephone to the women,</u> <u>who did not know about the photographs.</u> The men who had seen the photograph of a pretty woman were warm, friendly, and humorous. This, in turn, affected the women they spoke to, for they responded in a warm, friendly, outgoing manner. And the men who had seen the photograph of the homely woman? On the phone, they were cold, reserved, and humorless, and the women they spoke to became cool, reserved, and humorless. Keep in mind that the women did not know that their looks had been evaluated—and that the photographs were not even of them. In short, stereotypes tend to produce behaviors that match the stereotype. This principle is illustrated in this figure:

Summary of how stereotypes shape our attitudes

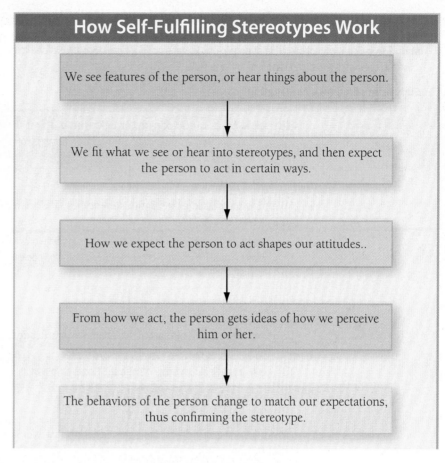

How Self-Fulfilling Stereotypes Work

We see features of the person, or hear things about the person.

↓

We fit what we see or hear into stereotypes, and then expect the person to act in certain ways.

↓

How we expect the person to act shapes our attitudes..

↓

From how we act, the person gets ideas of how we perceive him or her.

↓

The behaviors of the person change to match our expectations, thus confirming the stereotype.

Effects of being attractive

4   Although beauty might be only skin deep, its consequences permeate our lives (Katz 2005). Beauty bestows an [1]advantage in everyday interaction, but it also has other effects. For one, if you are physically attractive, you are [2]likely to make more money. Researchers in both Holland and the United States found that advertising firms with better looking executives have [3]higher revenues (Bosman et al. 1997; Pfann et al. 2000). The reason? The researchers suggest that people are more willing to associate with individuals whom they perceive as good-looking.

Men	Women
• Shown photos of women	• Did not see photos of men and didn't know about photos
• Were warm and friendly to pretty woman, cold to homely woman	• Responded the same way that men talked to them

After annotating the selection, Tori made a reading map of it. To map the supporting evidence and explanation, she used the chart from the reading and added the information about the experiment to it.

Tori's Reading Map

Main Idea: Our assumptions of what people are like are self-fulfilling; stereotypes tend to produce behaviors that match the stereotype.

Supporting Evidence/Explanation

> We see features of the person, or hear things about the person.
> College men were shown photo of pretty or homely woman.

> We fit what we see or hear into stereotypes, and then expect the person to act in certain ways.
> The men described how they thought the woman would act: positive traits for pretty woman, negative traits for homely woman.

> How we expect the person to act shapes our attitudes.
> On the phone, the men were warm and friendly to the pretty woman and cold and reserved to the homely woman.

> From how we act, the person gets ideas of how we perceive him or her.
> The women got an idea of what the men thought of them from the way the men talked to them.

> The behaviors of the person change to match our expectations, thus confirming the stereotype.
> The way the men spoke to the women affected the way they spoke to the men.

Conclusion

> Researchers suggest that people are more willing to spend time with individuals that they think are good looking.

For support in meeting this chapter's objectives, log in to www.mywritinglab.com, go to the Study Plan tab, click on **The Reading Process** and choose **Critical Thinking: Responding to Text and Visuals** from the list of subtopics. Read and view the videos and resources in the Review Materials section, and then complete the Recall, Apply, and Write exercises in the Activities section. You can check your scores and overall progress by using the Gradebook.

ILLUSTRATION
Theme: *Communication*

<table>
<tr><td>Culture Shock:</td><td>Joseph A Devito, excerpt from The Interpersonal Communication Book</td></tr>
<tr><td></td><td>Michael A. Lev, "Letter from Tokyo"</td></tr>
</table>

NARRATION
Theme: *Sociology*

<table>
<tr><td>The Power of Peer Pressure:</td><td>James M. Henslin, excerpt from Essentials of Sociology</td></tr>
<tr><td></td><td>Julia Alvarez, "Names/Nombres"</td></tr>
</table>

DESCRIPTION
Theme: *History*

<table>
<tr><td>The Face of the Holocaust:</td><td>Robert A. Devine et al., excerpt from America Past and Present</td></tr>
<tr><td></td><td>Elie Wiesel, excerpt from Night</td></tr>
</table>

PROCESS
Theme: *Hospitality*

<table>
<tr><td>Guest Service:</td><td>John R. Walker, excerpt from Introduction to Hospitality Management</td></tr>
<tr><td></td><td>Jane Engle, "Server Tips: How to Get More Out of Customers"</td></tr>
</table>

COMPARISON AND CONTRAST
Theme: *Video Game Design*

<table>
<tr><td>Male and Female Players and Characters in Video Games:</td><td>Ernest Adams and Andrew Rollings, excerpt from Game Design and Development</td></tr>
<tr><td></td><td>Sheri Graner Ray, "But What if the Player Is Female?"</td></tr>
</table>

CLASSIFICATION
Theme: *Health and Wellness*

<table>
<tr><td>Mind-Body Therapies:</td><td>Barbara Kozier and Glenora Erb, excerpt from Fundamentals of Nursing</td></tr>
<tr><td></td><td>Shirley Archer, "Meditation: Just the Basics: An Introduction to the Styles and Benefits of Regular Practice"</td></tr>
</table>

CAUSE AND EFFECT
Theme: *Psychology*

<table>
<tr><td>Aggression:</td><td>Richard J. Gerrig and Philip G. Zimbardo, excerpt from Psychology and Life</td></tr>
<tr><td></td><td>Dave Barry, "All the Rage"</td></tr>
</table>

DEFINITION
Theme: *Anthropology*

<table>
<tr><td>Race:</td><td>Carol R. Ember, Melvin Ember, and Peter N. Peregrine, excerpt from Anthropology</td></tr>
<tr><td></td><td>Charisse Jones, "Light Skin versus Dark"</td></tr>
</table>

ARGUMENT
Theme: *Education*

Managing Student Behavior: Sharon Vaughan, Candace S. Bos, and Jeanne Shay Schumm, excerpt from *Teaching Exceptional, Diverse, and At-Risk Students in the General Education Classroom*

Alan Bloom and S. Campbell, "Making Cell Phones in the Class a Community Builder (Pro and Con)"

| ILLUSTRATION | Theme: *Communication* |

Culture Shock

When you go to a new place, a country, city, or even a college, you may find that the culture is different from your own. These differences may make it difficult for you to adjust at first. Read the following textbook excerpt and compare your reactions to a new culture with those described by the author.

Getting Ready to Read: Use the graphic organizer on page 530 to preview the reading.

Excerpt from *The Interpersonal Communication Book*
Joseph A. DeVito

1   **Culture shock** is the psychological reaction you experience when you're in a culture very different from your own. Culture shock is normal; most people experience it when entering a new and different culture. Nevertheless, it can be unpleasant and frustrating. When you lack knowledge of the rules and customs of the new society, you cannot communicate effectively. In your culture shock you may not know basic things:

- how to ask someone for a favor or pay someone a compliment
- how to extend or accept an invitation for dinner
- how early or how late to arrive for an appointment
- how long you should stay when visiting someone
- how to distinguish seriousness from playfulness and politeness from indifference
- how to dress for an informal, formal, or business function
- how to order a meal in a restaurant or how to summon a waiter

2   Anthropologist Kalervo Oberg, who first used the term *culture shock*, notes that it occurs in stages. These stages are useful for examining many encounters with the new and the different. Going away to college, moving in together, or joining the military, for example, can result in culture shock. Let's use the example of moving away from home into your own apartment to illustrate Kalervo's four stages:

Stage One: The Honeymoon. At first you experience fascination, even enchantment with the new culture and its people. You finally have your own apartment. You're your own boss. Finally, on your own! When in groups of people who are culturally different, this stage is characterized by cordiality and friendship in these early and superficial relationships. Many tourists remain at this stage, because their stay in any one foreign country is so brief.

Stage Two: The Crisis. Here, the differences between your own culture and the new setting create problems. No longer do you find dinner ready for you unless you cook it yourself. Your clothes are not washed or ironed unless you do them yourself. Feelings of frustration and inadequacy come to the fore. This is the stage at which you experience the actual shock of the new culture. One study of foreign students coming from more than 100 countries and studying in 11 different countries found that 25% of the students experienced depression.

Stage Three: The Recovery. During this period you gain the skills necessary to function effectively. You learn how to shop, cook, and plan a meal. You find a local laundry and figure you'll learn how to iron later. You learn the language and ways of the new culture. Your feelings of inadequacy subside.

Stage Four: The Adjustment. At this final stage, you adjust to and come to enjoy the new culture and the new experiences. You may still experience periodic difficulties and strains, but on the whole, the experience is pleasant. Actually, you're now a pretty decent cook. You're even coming to enjoy it. You're making a good salary, so why learn to iron?

People may also experience culture shock when they return to their original culture after living in a foreign culture, a kind of reverse culture shock. Consider, for example, Peace Corps volunteers who work in rural and economically deprived areas. On returning to Las Vegas or Beverly Hills, they too may experience culture shock. A sailor who serves long periods aboard ship and then returns to an isolated farming community may experience culture shock. In these cases, however, the recovery period is shorter and the sense of inadequacy and frustration is less.

Understanding the Reading

1. What is culture shock?

_____

2. List three basic things a person experiencing culture shock may not know.

_____

3. List the four stages of culture shock.

_____

Map the Reading.   Create a graphic organizer that maps the main idea and the stages of culture shock.

Vocabulary in Context.   Write a definition for each of these words as they are used in the reading. Look for words or phrases that help you figure out the meaning. Then check your answer with the dictionary definition.

Word	Para.	Definition
enchantment	2	_____
cordiality	2	_____
superficial	2	_____
frustration	2	_____
inadequacy	2, 3	_____
periodic	2	_____
subside	2	_____

Thinking and Writing about the Reading

1. **Quick Write:** In the reading, DeVito says, "Going away to college, moving in together, or joining the military, for example, can result in culture shock." Write about a time when you or someone you know experienced culture shock.

2. **Quick Write Jump Off:** Expand on the quick write assignment by writing a paper giving examples of culture shock that you have experienced yourself or have observed.

3. **Summary:** Using your reading map, write a summary of the textbook excerpt.

4. Imagine that you have a neighbor who has just moved to your area from another country. That person does not speak English well and does not know the area. You have decided to help the individual adjust to the new culture. Which rules and/or customs do you think are most important for the person to know? Write a guide giving examples of those most important rules and/or customs.

This newspaper article, written by journalist Michael A. Lev when he served as a foreign correspondent in Tokyo, gives readers a view of Japanese culture from an American's perspective. As you read, also consider what the Japanese must have thought about his actions.

Getting Ready to Read: Use the graphic organizer on page 530 to preview the reading.

Letter from Tokyo
Michael A. Lev

1   Tokyo—The day of the naked cheeseburger could have turned ugly. The ex-New Yorker in me wanted to scream and yell. But the journalist in me recognized a chance to gain insight into Japanese society, or at least to have a classic native experience—like being in Manhattan and getting accosted by an arrogant panhandler.

2   It was lunch time, and my Japanese interpreter, Naoko Nihiwaki, and I were at a Tokyo hamburger restaurant called One's. Naoko ordered the One's burger, and I picked the cheeseburger.

3   When our food came, Naoko's hamburger looked fabulous—a thick juicy patty heaped with fresh lettuce and tomato. My cheeseburger was naked. It looked sad. In halting Japanese, I called over the proprietor.

4   "Excuse me," I said. "My cheeseburger doesn't have lettuce or tomato. Can I have some please?"

5   She gave me a quizzical look.

6   "No."

7   No? My pulse immediately quickened beyond my Japanese fluency level, and Naoko was forced to begin interpreting. "Just bring some lettuce and tomato. I'll pay for it."

8   "Sorry. The cheeseburger doesn't come with lettuce and tomato."

9   I didn't back down, so she got tough. "Cheeseburgers don't get lettuce and tomato; that's not how they come," she said, adding, "Even for a child, we wouldn't do anything different."

10   Her final offer: "If you don't want the cheeseburger, I'll take it back and make you a One's burger."

11   "That's absurd. Just cut me some tomato slices and bring them on a napkin."

12   The woman got so excited that even Naoko had trouble deciphering her. The tomato and lettuce aren't the right size for the cheeseburger, she argued. They won't mesh properly with the cheese.

13   She grabbed my cheeseburger from me. She returned later with a freshly cooked One's burger and a dirty look.

14   I label this run-in with Japanese inflexibility the "kir effect" because of what happened to Masao Miyamoto, an author and social critic I know.

15   Miyamoto went to a hotel bar, saw an open bottle of white wine on display and ordered a glass. Sorry, he was told, white wine isn't on the menu. It's used to make kir, a wine cocktail with **cassis**. Thinking quickly, Miyamoto ordered a kir—hold the cassis.

cassis   a sweet, alcoholic drink made from cassis berries

16   Long negotiations ensued with the waiter, with the maitre d', with the assistant manager. Finally, he got his drink, but he was told to please never come back.

17   These moments of exasperation reflect a culture in which order reigns. It is a cliché, but it's true: Japan is a group-oriented society. If everyone did their own thing, this tiny overpopulated archipelago would descend into chaos, the thinking goes.

18   In some ways, it's a great system. Riding a bicycle in Tokyo is a pleasure, even on crowded sidewalks. The rule is, ring your bicycle bell once and pedestrians ahead will step to the side. Works every time.

19   Just don't question the rules. While buying an expensive cellular telephone, the salesman asked for my Japanese residency card. I had my temporary card with permanent ID number but had not yet received the credit-card size permanent card with photograph.

20   "Sorry," he said. "Come back when you have it."

21   "But it's the correct ID number," I explained. "I just have it on a sheet of paper instead of on a credit card."

22   He continued to pack up the paperwork. I insisted that he call headquarters. I needed the phone, didn't he need the sale? He returned sucking his teeth and shrugging. "It would be a little difficult," he said, using the Japanese phrase for "impossible."

23   If I were Japanese, I would have been expected to apologize and leave the store for causing trouble. Instead, Naoko, who has lived in America and understands our strange ways, went to work. There were belabored discussions by telephone with several parties and then a visit to the local telephone company office. Proposals. Counteroffers. Liberal use of the phrase "a little difficult." But I finally got my phone.

24   Miyamoto sees the issue in harsh terms: Japanese society does not teach or tolerate independent thinking. All decisions are reached by consensus. Everything is done **by the book**.

by the book according to standard procedures

25   I was stopped for speeding not long ago. Instead of producing a Japanese or an American driver's license, I showed my international driver's license. The cop had never seen one before. I knew he was impressed with how official it looked, but he was confounded by the identification numbers. They didn't correspond with the number of blank spaces on his speeding-ticket form.

26   Would he risk filling out a messy ticket with numbers that didn't fit in the boxes?

27   No way. He let me go.

Understanding the Reading

1. What is the main idea of the reading?

_____

2. The author gives four examples to support his main idea. Using a phrase for each, list them.

_____

3. How do you think the Japanese people involved in the examples viewed the author?

_____

Map the Reading.   Create a graphic organizer that maps the main idea, the examples and conclusion.

Vocabulary in Context.   Write a definition for each of these words as they are used in the reading. Look for words or phrases that help you figure out the meaning. Then check your answer with the dictionary definition.

Word	Para.	Definition
panhandler	1	_____
accosted	1	_____
deciphering	12	_____
archipelago	17	_____
belabored	23	_____

Thinking and Writing about the Reading

1. **Quick Write:** Write about a frustrating experience that you or someone you know had with an employee in a restaurant or a store.

2. **Quick Write Jump Off:** Expand on the quick write assignment by writing an illustration paper about frustrating experiences with employees.

3. **Summary:** Using your reading map, write a summary of the essay.

4. The author ran into trouble when he tried to suggest solutions that were not according to standard procedures. Write an illustration paper providing examples of rules or regulations (either in the United States or a culture you are familiar with) that must be followed by the book.

Connecting the Illustration Readings

1. What connections can you make between the textbook passage "Culture Shock" and the newspaper article "Letter from Tokyo"?

   _____

   _____

2. In the reading "Culture Shock," you learned about the four stages of culture shock: Stage 1: The Honeymoon; Stage 2: The Crisis; Stage 3: The Recovery; Stage 4: The Adjustment. Which stage has Michael A. Lev reached? What evidence can you find in his essay to support your opinion?

   _____

   _____

NARRATION   Theme: *Sociology*

The Power of Peer Pressure: The Asch Experiment

The pressure to conform is motivated by the human need to be liked, to be correct, or to fit a social role. Changing your thinking or behavior to fit into a group can have positive or negative effects. As you read this textbook excerpt, think about how you would have reacted as a student in Dr. Asch's experiment.

Getting Ready to Read: Use the graphic organizer on page 530 to preview the reading.

Excerpt from *Essentials of Sociology*
James M. Henslin

1   How influential are groups in our lives? To answer this, let's look first at *conformity* in the sense of going along with our peers. Our peers have no authority over us, only the influence we allow.

2   Imagine that you are taking a course in social psychology with Dr. Solomon Asch and you have agreed to participate in an experiment. As you enter his laboratory, you see seven chairs, five of them already filled by other students. You are given the sixth. Soon the seventh person arrives. Dr. Asch stands at the front of the

3   room next to a covered easel. He explains that he will first show a large card with a vertical line on it, then another card with three vertical lines. Each of you is to tell him which of the three lines matches the line on the first card.

3   Dr. Asch then uncovers the first card with the single line and the comparison card with three lines. The correct answer is easy, for two of the lines are obviously wrong, and one is exactly right. Each person, in order, states his or her answer aloud. You all answer correctly. The second trial is just as easy, and you begin to wonder why you are there.

4   Then on the third trial, something unexpected happens. Just as before, it is easy to tell which lines match. The first student, however, gives the wrong answer. The second gives the same incorrect answer. So do the third and the fourth. By now, you are wondering what is wrong. How will the person next to you answer? You can hardly believe it when he, too, gives the same wrong answer. Then it is your turn, and you give what you know is the right answer. The seventh person also gives the same wrong answer.

5   On the next trial, the same thing happens. You know that the choice of the other six is wrong. They are giving what to you are obviously wrong answers. You don't know what to think. Why aren't they seeing things the same way you are? Sometimes they do, but in twelve trials they don't. Something is wrong, and you are no longer sure what to do.

6   When the eighteenth trial is finished, you heave a sigh of relief. The experiment is finally over, and you are ready to bolt for the door. Dr. Asch walks over to you with a big smile on his face and thanks you for participating in the experiment. He explains that you were the only real subject of the experiment! "The other six were stooges. I paid them to give those answers," he says. Now you feel real relief. Your eyes weren't playing tricks on you after all.

7   What were the results? Asch tested fifty people. One third (33 percent) gave in to the group half the time, giving what they knew to be wrong answers. Another two out of five (40 percent) gave wrong answers but not as often. One out of four (25 percent) stuck to their guns and always gave the right answer. I don't know how I would do on this test (if I knew nothing about it in advance), but I like to think that I would be part of the 25 percent. You probably feel the same way about yourself. But why should we feel that we wouldn't be like *most* people?

8   The results are disturbing, and more researchers have replicated Asch's experiment than any other study. In our land of individualism, the group is so powerful that most people are willing to say things that they know are not true. And this was a group of strangers! How much more conformity can we expect when our group consists of friends, people we value highly and depend on for getting along in life?

Understanding the Reading

1. What is the main idea of the textbook excerpt?

_____

2. Summarize the Asch experiment.

_____

3. What were the results of the Asch experiment and why were they disturbing?

_____

Map the Reading.   Create a graphic organizer that maps the main idea, the events of the experiment and conclusion.

Vocabulary in Context.   Write a definition for each of these words as they are used in the reading. Look for words or phrases that help you figure out the meaning. Then check your answer with the dictionary definition.

Word	Para.	Definition
conformity	1	_____
heave a sigh of relief	6	_____
bolt for	6	_____
stooges	6	_____
stuck to their guns	7	_____

Thinking and Writing about the Reading

1. **Quick Write:** Conformity is defined as behavior that follows the usual standards expected by a group or society. Write about a time when you or someone you know conformed to the standards of a group or society. The situation could have been positive or negative.

2. **Quick Write Jump Off:** Develop your quick write story into a narrative paper. Your main idea sentence should make a point about the meaning or importance of the experience or event.

3. **Summary:** Using your reading map, write a summary of the textbook excerpt.

4. Nonconformity is the refusal to follow those standards. Write a narrative paper about an incident in which you or someone else did not conform to the standards of a family, group, or society. You can use a personal experience or retell a story you read about or saw on television or in a movie.

Has anyone ever mispronounced your name? Imagine the frustration many immigrants experience when English speakers have difficulty with their names. To avoid this, some people translate their names to English equivalents or replace them with American names. While reading this personal essay, notice how names play an important role in the author's struggle for identity in a new culture.

Getting Ready to Read: Use the graphic organizer on page 530 to preview the reading.

Names/Nombres
Julia Alvarez

1   When we arrived in New York City, our names changed almost immediately. At immigration, the officer asked my father, *Mister Elbures*, if we had anything to declare. My father shook his head, "No," and we were waved through. I was too afraid we wouldn't be let in if I corrected the man's pronunciation, but I said our

name to myself, opening my mouth wide for the organ blast of the *a*, trilling my tongue for the drum-roll of the *r*. *All-vah-rrr-es!* How could anyone get *Elbures* out of that orchestra of sound?

super superintendent; the person who manages an apartment building

2   When we moved into our new apartment building, the **super** called my father *Mister Alberase*, and the neighbors who became mother's friends pronounced her name *Jew-lee-ah* instead of *Hoo-lee-ah*. I, her namesake, was known as *Hoo-lee-tah* at home. But at school, I was *Judy* or *Judith*, and once an English teacher mistook me for *Juliet*.

3   It took awhile to get used to my new names. I wondered if I shouldn't correct my teachers and new friends. But my mother argued that it didn't matter. "You know what your friend Shakespeare said, *'A rose by any other name would smell as sweet.'*" My father had gotten into the habit of calling any famous author "my friend" because I had begun to write poems and stories in English class.

4   By the time I was in high school, I was a popular kid, and it showed in my name. Friends called me *Jules* or *Hey Jude*, and once a group of troublemaking friends my mother forbade me to hang out with called me *Alcatraz*. I was *Hoo-lee-tah* only to Mami and Papi and uncles and aunts who came over to eat *sancocho* on Sunday afternoons—old world folk whom I would just as soon go back to where they came from and leave me to pursue whatever mischief I wanted to in America. JUDY ALCATRAZ: the name on the Wanted Poster would read. Who would ever trace her to me?

5   My older sister had the hardest time getting an American name for herself because *Mauricia* did not translate into English. Ironically, although she had the most foreign-sounding name, she and I were the Americans in the family. We had been born in New York City when our parents had first tried immigration and then gone back "home," too homesick to stay. My mother often told the story of how she had almost changed my sister's name in the hospital.

6   After the delivery, Mami and some other new mothers were cooing over their new baby sons and daughters and exchanging names and weights and delivery stories. My mother was embarrassed among the Sallys and Hanes and Georges and Johns to reveal the rich, noisy name of *Mauricia*, so when her turn came to brag, she gave her baby's name as *Maureen*.

7   "Why'd ya give her an Irish name with so many pretty Spanish names to choose from?" one woman asked.

8   My mother blushed and admitted her baby's real name to the group. Her mother-in-law had recently died, she apologized, and her husband had insisted that the first daughter be named after his mother, *Mauran*. My mother thought it

the ugliest name she had ever heard, and she talked my father into what she believed was an improvement, a combination of *Mauran* and her own mother's name, *Felicia*.

9   "Her name is *Mau-ree-shee-ah*," my mother said to the group of women.

10   "Why that's a beautiful name," the new mothers cried. *"Moor-ee-sha, Moor-ee-sha,"* they cooed into the pink blanket. Moor-ee-sha it was when we returned to the States eleven years later. Sometimes, American tongues found even that mispronunciation too tough to say and called her *Maria* or *Marsha* or *Maudy* from her nickname *Maury*. I pitied her. What an awful name to have to transport across borders!

11   My little sister, Ana, had the easiest time of all. She was plain *Anne*—that is, only her name was plain, for she turned out to be the pale, blond "American beauty" in the family. The only Hispanic thing about her was the affectionate nicknames her boyfriends sometimes gave her. *Anita*, or as one goofy guy used to sing to her to the tune of the banana advertisement, *Anita Banana*.

12   Later, during her college years in the late '60s, there was a push to pronounce Third World names correctly. I remember calling her long distance at her group house and a roommate answering.

13   "Can I speak to Ana?" I asked, pronouncing her name the American way.

14   "Ana?" The man's voice hesitated. "Oh! You must mean *Ah-nah*!"

15   Our first few years in the States, though, ethnicity was not yet "in." Those were the blond, blue-eyed, bobby sock years of junior high school before the '60s ushered in peasant blouses, hoop earrings, **serapes**. My initial desire to be known by my correct Dominican name faded. I just wanted to be Judy and merge with the Sallys and Janes in my class. But inevitably, my accent and coloring gave me away. "So where are you from, Judy?"

16   "New York," I told my classmates. After all, I had been born blocks away at Columbia Presbyterian Hospital.

17   "I mean, *originally*."

18   "From the Caribbean," I answered vaguely, for if I specified, no one was quite sure on what continent our island was located.

19   "Really? I've been to Bermuda. We went last April for spring vacation. I got the worst sunburn! So, are you from Portoriko?"

20   "No," I sighed. "From the Dominican Republic."

21   "Where's that?"

22   "South of Bermuda."

serapes colorful shawls

23   They were just being curious, I knew, but I burned with shame whenever they singled me out as a "foreigner," a rare, exotic friend.

24   "Say your name in Spanish, oh please say it!" I had made mouths drop one day by rattling off my full name, which according to Dominican custom, included my middle names, Mother's and Father's surnames for four generations back.

25   "Julia Altagracia Maria Teresa Alvarez Tavares Perello Espaillat Julia Pérez Rochet González," I pronounced it slowly, a name as chaotic with sounds as a Middle Eastern bazaar or market day in a South American village.

26   My Dominican heritage was never more apparent than when my extended family attended school occasions. For my graduation, they all came, the whole lot of aunts and uncles and the many little cousins who snuck in without tickets. They sat in the first row in order to better understand the Americans' fast-spoken English. But how could they listen when they were constantly speaking among themselves in florid-sounding phrases, **rococo** consonants, rich, rhyming vowels?

rococo fancy, ornate style of art of the early eighteenth century

27   Introducing them to my friends was a further trial to me. These relatives had such complicated names and there were so many of them, and their relationships to myself were so convoluted. There was my Tia Josefina, who was not really my aunt but a much older cousin. And her daughter: Aida Margarita, who was adopted, una hija de crianza. My uncle of affection, Tio Jose, brought my *madrina* Tia Amelia and her *comadre* Tia Pilar. My friends rarely had more than a "Mom and Dad" to introduce.

28   After the commencement ceremony my family waited outside in the parking lot while my friends and I signed yearbooks with nicknames which recalled our high school good times: "Beans" and "Pepperoni" and "Alcatraz." We hugged and cried and promised to keep in touch.

29   Our goodbyes went on too long. I heard my father's voice calling out across the parking lot. *"Hoo-lee-tah! Vamonos!"*

30   Back home, my *tios* and *tias* and *primas*, Mami and Papi, and *mis hermanas* had a party for me with *sancocho* and a store-bought *pudin*, inscribed with Happy Graduation, Julie. There were many gifts—that was a plus to a large family! I got several wallets and a suitcase with my initials and a graduation charm from my godmother and money from my uncles. The biggest gift was a portable type-writer from my parents for writing my stories and poems.

31   Someday, the family predicted, my name would be well-known throughout the United States. I laughed to myself, wondering which one I would go by.

Understanding the Reading

1. What is the main idea of the narrative essay?

_____

2. How does the title of the narrative "Names/Nombres" suggest the writer's conflict?

_____

3. Why does the writer spell out different pronunciations of names?

_____

Map the Reading.   Create a graphic organizer that maps the events in the narrative in chronological order. Notice that some details take place when the Alvarezes first tried immigration.

Vocabulary in Context.   Write a definition for each of these words as they are used in the reading. Look for words or phrases that help you figure out the meaning. Then check your answer with the dictionary definition.

Word	Para.	Definition
declare	4	_____
trilling	4	_____
sancocho	9	_____
florid	12	_____
pudin	16	_____

Thinking and Writing about the Reading

1. **Quick Write:** Being accepted into a group is important to children, especially in school. Write about a time when you or someone else was not accepted into a group at school.

2. **Quick Write Jump Off:** Develop your quick write into a narrative paper. Your main idea sentence should make a point about the meaning or importance of the experience or event. Include the setting, characters, conflict, events, and resolution.

3. **Summary:** Using your reading map, write a summary of the narrative essay.

4. "Names/Nombres" reminds us of how names can affect our self-image and identity. Write a narrative paper about a positive or negative experience with your name or the name of someone you know.

Connecting the Narrative Readings

1. What are the similarities between "The Power of Peer Pressure: The Asch Experiment" and the essay "Names/Nombres"?

_____

2. What do both readings conclude about the people's need to conform?

_____

DESCRIPTION	Theme: *History*

The Face of the Holocaust

When the U.S. generals and soldiers opened the doors of the Nazi concentration camps to free the people imprisoned, they were not prepared for what they found. Even those who had experience in fighting and had seen death and destruction were sickened by the unspeakable conditions. As you read this textbook excerpt, imaging what it must have been like for the liberators and the prisoners.

Getting Ready to Read: Use the graphic organizer on page 530 to preview the reading.

Excerpt from *America Past and Present*
Robert A. Divine et al.

1   The liberation of the Nazi death camps near the end of World War II was not considered an important goal to be achieved; nor was it a planned operation. Since 1942, the U.S. government had known that the Nazis were murdering Jews in groups, but officials of the Roosevelt administration were divided on what to do about it. Some argued for air raids on the death camps, even if such raids were likely to kill large numbers of the Jewish inmates. Others strongly stated that the air raids alone would not stop the killing, that they would divert resources from the broader attack against Germany, and that military victory was the surest path to the liberation of the camps. In part because no one in the United States comprehended the full extent of the evil of Hitler's "final solution," Roosevelt sided with the latter group, and no special action was taken against the death camps. As a result, it was by chance that Allied forces first stumbled upon the camps, and the GIs who threw open the gates to that living hell were totally unprepared for what they found.

2   *Inside the Vicious Heart*, Robert Abzug's study of the liberation of the concentration camps, discusses the phenomenon of the inability to see the obvious because the truth is so horrible. He calls it "double vision." Faced with a revelation so terrible, witnesses could not fully comprehend the evidence of the systematic murder of more than six million men, women, and children. But as the Allied armies advanced into Germany, the shocking evidence increased. On April 4, 1945, the Fourth Armored Division of the Third Army unexpectedly discovered Ohrdruf, a relatively small concentration camp. Ohrdruf's liberation had a tremendous impact on American forces. It was the first camp discovered in its original state with its shocking display of the dead and dying. Inside the compound, corpses were piled in heaps in the barracks. An infantryman recalled, "I guess the most vivid recollection of the whole camp is the pyre that was located on the edge of the camp. It was a big pit, where they stacked bodies—stacked bodies and wood and burned them."

3   On April 12, generals Eisenhower, Bradley, and Patton toured Ohrdruf. The generals, professional soldiers familiar with the damage and destruction of battle, had never seen anything like it. Years later, Bradley recalled, "The smell of death overwhelmed us even before we passed through the stockade. More than 3200 naked, extremely thin bodies had been flung into shallow graves. Others lay in the street where they had fallen.

4   Eisenhower ordered every available armed forces unit in the area to visit Ohrdruf. "We are told that the American soldier does not know what he is fighting for," said

Eisenhower. "Now at least he will know what he is fighting against." He urged government officials and journalists to visit the camps and tell the world. In an official message Eisenhower summed it up:

> We are constantly finding German camps in which they have placed political prisoners where unspeakable conditions exist. From my own personal observation, I can state unequivocally that all written statements up to now do not paint the full horrors.

5   On April 11, the Timberwolf Division of the Third Army uncovered Nordhausen. They found three thousand dead and only seven hundred survivors. The scene sickened battle-hardened veterans:

> The odors, well there is no way to describe the odors . . . . Many of the boys I am talking about now—these were tough soldiers, there were combat men who had been all the way through the invasion—were ill and vomiting, throwing up, just at the sight of this.

6   For some, the liberation of Nordhausen changed the meaning of the war.

> I must also say that my fellow GIs, most thought that any stories they had read in the paper…were either not true or at least exaggerated. And it did not sink in, what this was all about, until we got into Nordhausen.

7   If the experience at Norhausen gave many GIs a new sense of mission in battle, it also forced them to distance themselves from the realities of the camps. Only by closing off their emotions could they go about the shockingly horrible task of sorting out the living from the dead and taking care of survivors. Margaret Bourke-White, whose *Life* magazine photographs brought the horrors of the death camps to millions on the home front, recalled working "with a veil over my mind."

People often ask me how it is possible to photograph such atrocities. In photographing the murder camps, the protective veil was so tightly drawn that I hardly knew what I had taken until I saw prints of my own photographs.

8   By the end of 1945, most of the liberators had come home and returned to non-military life. Once home, their experiences produced no common moral responses. No particular pattern developed in their occupational, political, and religious behavior, beyond a fear of the rise of postwar totalitarianism shared by most Americans. Few spoke publicly about their role in the liberation of the camps; most found that after a short period of grim fascination, their friends and families preferred to forget. Some had nightmares, but few reported being tormented by memories. For the liberators, the ordeal was over. For the survivors of the Holocaust, liberation was but the first step in the difficult, painful process of rebuilding broken bodies and destroyed lives.

Understanding the Reading

1. What is the main idea of the reading?

_____

2. The U.S. government knew that the Nazis were murdering large numbers of Jews, but the officials of President Roosevelt's administration had different opinions about what to do about it. What were the opinions?

_____

3. Describe what the troops found at Ohrdruf and Nordhausen.

_____

Vocabulary in Context.   Write a definition for each of these words as they are used in the reading. Look for words or phrases that help you figure out the meaning. Then check your answer with the dictionary definition.

Word	Para.	Definition
air raids	1	_____
revelation	2	_____
infantryman	2	_____
pyre	2	_____
stockade	3	_____
atrocities	7	_____
veil	7	_____
totalitarianism	8	_____

Thinking and Writing about the Reading

1. **Quick Write:** For a brief moment, remember something terrible that you have witnessed. Write about why it is difficult to think about.

2. **Quick Write Jump Off:** Turn your quick write into a description of that terrible scene that you wrote about.

3. **Summary:** Using your reading map, write a summary of the textbook excerpt.

4. Write a paper describing a war scene from any period in the history of the world. You may choose a photograph or write from personal experience. For example,

you can describe a scene during or after the September 11, 2001, terrorist attacks. To find war photographs, look in history textbooks or search online.

Elie Wiesel was fifteen years old when he and his family were deported by the Nazis from Romania to the Auschwitz concentration camp in Poland. After the American army freed the camps, Wiesel was hospitalized. While there, he wrote the outline for the book *Night*, describing his experiences during the Holocaust. However, he was not ready to publicize his experiences and waited ten years to write the book. Wiesel has continued writing novels and has won many awards for his humanitarian work. As you read this excerpt, imagine what it must have been like for a teen-aged boy to arrive at a concentration camp.

Getting Ready to Read: Use the graphic organizer on page 530 to preview the reading.

Excerpt from *Night*
Elie Wiesel

1   Never shall I forget that night, the first night in camp, that turned my life into one long night, seven times sealed.

2   Never shall I forget that smoke.

3   Never shall I forget the little faces of the children, whose bodies I saw transformed into smoke under a silent sky.

4   Never shall I forget those flames that consumed my faith forever.

5   Never shall I forget that nocturnal silence which deprived me for all eternity of the desire to live.

6   Never shall I forget those moments that murdered my God and my soul and turned my dreams to ashes.

7   Never shall I forget those things, even were I condemned to live as long as God Himself.

8   Never.

9   The Barrack we had been assigned to was very long. In the roof some blueish skylights. This is what the antechamber of Hell must look like. So many crazed men, so much shouting, so much brutality!

10   Dozens of inmates were there to receive us, sticks in hands, striking anywhere, anyone, without reason. The orders came:

11   "Strip! Hurry up! *Raus*! hold on only to your belt and shoes . . . ."

12   Our clothes were to be thrown on the floor at the back of the barrack. There was a pile there already. New suits, old ones, torn overcoats, rags. For us it meant true equality: nakedness. We trembled in the cold.

13   A few **SS** officers wandered through the room, looking for strong men. If vigor was that appreciated, perhaps one should try to appear sturdy? My father thought the opposite. Better not to draw attention. (We later

Copyright © 2011 Pearson Education, Inc.

SS a major organization under Adolph Hitler and the Nazi Party; responsible for the majority of war crimes

found out that he had been right. Those who were selected that day were incorporated into the Sonder-Kommando, the Kommando working in the crematoria. Bela Katz—son of an important merchant of my town—had arrived in **Birkenau** with the first transport, one week ahead of us. When he found out we were there, he succeeded in slipping us a note, having been chosen because of his strength, he had been forced his own father's body into the furnace.)

Birkenau the extermination camp in the Auschwitz complex; site of the crematories

14   The blows continued to rain on us:

15   "To the barber!"

16   Belt and shoes in hand, I let myself be dragged along to the barbers. Their clippers tore out shaved every hair on our bodies. My head was buzzing; the same thought over and over: not to be separated from my father.

17   Freed from the barbers clut dies, we began to wander about the crowd, finding friends, acquaintances. Every encounter filled us with joy—yes, joy: "Thank God! You are still alive!"

18   Some were crying. They used whatever strength they had left to cry. Why had they let themselves be brought here? Why didn't they die in their beds? Their words were interspersed with sobs.

19   Suddenly, someone threw his arms round me in a hug: Yechiel, the Sighetel rebbers brother. He was weeping bitterly. I thought he was crying with joy at still being alive.

20   "Don't cry, Yechiel," I said. "Don't waste your tears . . . ."

21   "Not cry? We're on the threshold of death . . . . Soon we shall be inside . . . . Do you understand? Inside. How could I not cry?"

22   I watched darkness fade through the blueish skylights in the roof. I no longer was afraid. I was overcome by fatigue.

23   The absent no longer entered our thoughts. One spoke of them—who knows what happened to them?— but their fate was not on our minds. We were incapable of thinking. Our senses were numbed, everything was fading into a fog. We no longer clung to anything. The instincts of self-preservation, of self-defense, of pride, had all deserted us. In one terrifying moment of lucidity, I thought of us as damned souls wandering through the void, souls condemned to wander through space until the end of time, seeking redemption, seeking oblivion, without hope of finding it.

Understanding the Reading

1. What is the author describing in this excerpt?

2. What is the dominant impression of the excerpt?

3. In paragraph 18, the author writes, "It was no longer possible to grasp anything." What does he mean?

Map the Reading.   Create a graphic organizer that maps Wiesel's descriptive excerpt.

Vocabulary in Context.   Write a definition for each of these words as they are used in the reading. Look for words or phrases that help you figure out the meaning. Then check your answer with the dictionary definition.

Word	Para.	Definition
nocturnal	3	
antechamber	4	
barracks	4	
truncheons	5	
crematories	8	
blunted	18	
lucidity	18	
oblivion	18	

Thinking and Writing about the Reading

1. **Quick Write**: What does it mean to feel hopeless? Write about a time when you or someone you know felt hopeless.

2. **Quick Write Jump Off**: Develop your quick write into a descriptive paper about a situation of hopelessness. Consider what caused the feeling of hopelessness and how the individual(s) responded to it.

3. **Summary.** Using your reading map, write a summary describing Wiesel's excerpt.

4. The first three paragraphs of the excerpt begin with the words "Never shall I forget … ." These paragraphs describe the narrator's reactions to his experience during his first night at the concentration camp. His words also carry a message about the Holocaust to all of humanity. Write a paper explaining the two ways of interpreting "Never shall I forget."

Connecting the Description Readings

1. "The Face of the Holocaust" and the excerpt from *Night* present two different views of the Holocaust. Explain the differences.

2. The Holocaust is one of many examples throughout history of intolerance—of people's refusal to accept ideas, beliefs, or people who are different. Describe a situation of intolerance that happened in the recent past or that is occurring now.

Guest Service

Walt Disney theme parks are popular travel destinations around the world: California, Florida, Hong Kong, Tokyo, and Paris. The success of Disney's theme park business is a result of its commitment to exceptional customer service. As you read this textbook excerpt, note how Disney expects employees to serve and care for guests during their visit to the parks.

Getting Ready to Read: Use the graphic organizer on page 530 to preview the reading.

Excerpt from *Introduction to Hospitality Management*
John R. Walker

To all who come to this happy place: Welcome! Disneyland is your land; here, age relives fond memories of the past, and here youth may savor the challenge and promise of the future.

Disneyland is dedicated to the hard facts that have created America, with the hope that it will be a source of joy and inspiration to all the world.

—Disneyland Dedication Plaque, July 17, 1955

1   When Walt Disney conceived the idea to build Disneyland, he established a simple philosophical approach to his theme park business, based on the tenets of quality, service, and show. Walt Disney was committed to service. Disney's mission statement is simple: "We create Happiness." To reinforce the service concept, Disney has guests, not customers, and cast members, not employees. Disney's ability to create a special brand of magic requires the talents of thousands of people fulfilling many different roles. However, the heart of it is the frontline cast members. Through the processes of hiring and training, cast members learn how Disney expects them to serve and care for guests during their visit to the park or resort.

2   Disney uses a 45-minute team approach to interviewing called *peer interviews*. In one interview there may be four candidates and one interviewer. The candidates may include a housewife returning to the work force, a teacher looking for summer work, a retiree looking for a little extra income, or a teenager looking for a first job. All four candidates are interviewed in the same session. The interviewer looks for how they individually answer questions and how well they interact with each other—a good indicator of their future onstage treatment of guests. The most successful technique used during the 45 minutes is to *smile*. The interviewer smiles at the people being interviewed to see if they *return the smiles*. If they don't, it doesn't matter how well they interview. They won't get the job.

3   On the first day at work, every new Disney cast member participates in a one-day orientation program at the Disney University, "Welcome to Show Business." The main goal of this experience is to learn the Disney approach to helpful, caring, and friendly guest service. The cast member training follows the Disney service model.

Smile. This is the universal language of hospitality and service. Guests recognize and appreciate the cast members' warmth and sincerity.

Make eye contact and use body language. This means stance, approach, and gestures. For instance, cast members are trained to use *open* gestures for directions, not pointed fingers, because open palms are friendlier and less directive.

Respect and welcome all guests. This means being friendly, helpful, and going out of the way to exceed guests' expectations.

Value the magic. When stage cast members are on stage, they are totally focused on creating the magic of Disneyland. They don't talk about personal problems or world affairs, and they don't mention that you can find Mickey in more than one place.

Initiate guest contact. Cast members are reminded to actively initiate guest contact. Disney calls this being aggressively friendly. It is not enough to be responsive when approached. Cast members are encouraged to take the first step with guests. They have lots of little tricks for doing this, such as noticing a guest's name on a hat and then using the name in conversation or kneeling to ask a child a question.

Use creative service solutions. For example, one Disneyland Hotel cast member recently became aware of a little boy who had come from the Midwest with his parents to enjoy the park and then left early because he was ill. The cast member approached the supervisor with an idea to send the child chicken soup, a character plush toy, and a get-well card from Mickey. The supervisor loved the idea, and all cast members are now allowed to set up these arrangements in similar situations without a supervisor's approval.

End with a "thank you." The phrases cast members use are important in creating a service environment. They do not have a book of accepted phrases; rather, through training and coaching, cast members are encouraged to use their own personality and style to welcome and approach guests, answer questions, anticipate their needs, thank them, and express with sincerity their desire to make the guest's experience exceptional.

4   How does this training translate into action? When a guest stops a street sweeper to ask where to pick up a parade schedule and the sweeper not only answers the question but recites the parade times from memory, suggests the best viewing spots on the parade route, offers advice on where to get a quick meal before parade time, *and* ends the interaction with a pleasant smile and warm send-off, people can't help but be impressed. It also makes the sweepers feel their jobs are interesting and important, which they are.

5   Once the initial cast member training is completed, these concepts must be applied and are continually reinforced by leaders who possess strong coaching skills.

Understanding the Reading

1. What is the main idea of the reading?

_____

_____

2. Explain two of the approaches of the Disney service model that cast members learn when they go through the training process.

_____

_____

3. Give an example of how the training translates into action.

_____

_____

Map the Reading.   Create a graphic organizer that maps the textbook excerpt.

Vocabulary in Context.   Write a definition for each of these words as they are used in the reading. Look for words or phrases that help you figure out the meaning. Then check your answer with the dictionary definition.

Word	Para.	Definition
tenets	1	_____
stance	3	_____
responsive	3	_____

Thinking and Writing about the Reading

1. **Quick Write:** Write about the training process you experienced for a job or volunteer service, or the process you used to train someone.
2. **Quick Write Jump Off:** Develop your quick write into an instructional or informational process paper.
3. **Summary:** Using your reading map, write a summary of the textbook excerpt.
4. In your daily life, you have had contact with many types of service providers as a consumer, an employee, or a student. Choose a service provider whose customer service needs improvement. Write a process paper about the steps management should take to improve its customer service.

Service is important to a restaurant's success and failure from the time customers enter a restaurant to the time they leave. This newspaper article reports the results of researcher Michael Lynn's study "Mega Tips: Scientifically Tested Techniques to Increase Your Tips." As you read, think about your own experiences with restaurant servers and the techniques they used that influenced the amount you left for a tip.

Getting Ready to Read: Use the graphic organizer on page 530 to preview the reading.

Server Tips: How to Get More Out of Customers
Jane Engle

1   Your waitress tells jokes, touches you on the shoulder and draws pictures on the check. Does she have a thing for you? Think again. She may be angling for a bigger tip, using a list of 14 suggestions from a researcher's new booklet.

2   "Mega Tips: Scientifically Tested Techniques to Increase Your Tips," by Michael Lynn, an associate professor at the Cornell University School of Hotel Administration in Ithaca, N.Y., is based on more than 25 years of studies by Lynn and others.

3   Among other tactics Lynn suggests to servers is to recommend higher-priced entrees, wear unusual clothing, introduce themselves, call customers by name and even offer sunny weather forecasts.

4   You may be wondering where service fits in. It doesn't. Which is the most surprising conclusion in Lynn's work. If you thought you were, at most, mildly confused about how much to leave servers, read on. It turns out that we don't know our own minds, much less the mores of tipping.

5   People typically say they tip to reward good service, Lynn said, which seems logical, "but it's obviously not true."

6   In his studies, he asked diners to rate their server's performance based on attentiveness, knowledge, promptness and other measures. Then he tallied the tips. The two numbers had little correlation. Service quality accounted for only 4 percent of the differences in diners' tips, he found.

7   What does boost tips, he said, are higher meal tabs and servers' actions that help them connect with their patrons.

8   Research shows the bill's total accounts for about 70 percent of the differences in tips—hardly a shock, given that most people tip on a percentage of the check; the usual recommendation is 15 to 20 percent. That's one reason savvy servers prompt diners to choose pricier entrees and extras such as appetizers, after-dinner drinks and desserts.

9   Such suggestive selling works well during slow times. During busy times, the best strategy is "get 'em their entrees, get 'em out," said Lynn, who worked his way through college as a bartender, busboy and waiter. Better to have a table of four wolfing down $20 rib-eye steaks than dawdling over $2 coffees and $5 slices of cake. No wonder some diners feel they're being rushed out the door on Saturday nights. They are.

10   But it's the customer-server rapport that's really revealing. What we're buying with restaurant tips is not service, Lynn contended, but social approval from our server and tablemates. The motive: "I don't want them to think I'm a cheapskate and a bad guy." If we feel a personal connection with a server, we care more about what she or he thinks of us. We're willing to pay more for that approval, so we tip more, Lynn said.

11   Many of Lynn's tactics will sound familiar to frequent diners. His advice to servers:

- Wear something unusual. "This will help customers perceive you as an individual rather than a faceless member of the staff." In one study, waitresses who wore flowers in their hair earned 17 percent more in tips than those who didn't.

- Introduce yourself by name. This can "make you seem friendly and polite and make the customer feel more empathy for you." In a study at a Charlie Brown's restaurant in Southern California, taking this step increased average tips from $3.49 to $5.44.

- Squat next to the table. This makes you more equal to the customer, brings your face closer and improves eye contact. In one study, this action earned about $1 more per table in tips.

- Touch your customers, preferably on the shoulder (which feels less private than other zones) for a second or two. Effect on tips: As much as 17 percent was left, up from 12 percent. Diners may flinch at this idea, but that's because "people don't know what they like," Lynn said. They may not even notice they're being touched, but no matter, they'll still tip more.

- Repeat customers' orders, word for word. This increases others' "liking for and interpersonal closeness to the imitator." In a Netherlands study, it also doubled tips.

- Call customers by name. It's flattering—and profitable, earning 10 percent more in tips at several Kansas restaurants studied.

- Draw on the check. A "smiley face" personalizes the transaction and improves customers' mood. In a study at a Philadelphia restaurant, this increased waitresses' tips by nearly 18 percent but, oddly, had no significant effect on waiters' tips.

- Smile. At a Seattle cocktail lounge, a waitress earned 140 percent more in tips when she sported a "large, open-mouthed smile."

- Write "thank you" on checks. This may make diners "feel obligated to earn that gratitude by leaving larger tips." In one study, the average tip went up from 16 to 18 percent on a "thank you."

- Give customers candy. "People generally feel obligated to reciprocate when they receive gifts from others." Effect on tips in one study: 23 percent instead of 19 percent.

12   My favorite suggestion is to write a favorable weather forecast on the check.

13   "Sunny weather puts people in a good mood, and people in a good mood leave bigger tips than those in a bad mood," Lynn's booklet says. The payoff in one study: 19 percent more in tips.

14   Manipulative?

15   "Of course," Lynn said.

16   He acknowledged that there are insincere servers "who hate a customer's guts, and yet they smile, write 'thank you' on the check and 'come again.'" But more common, he said, are servers who like their customers and want to please them but aren't sure how. That's where his pointers come in.

17   Diners who don't care to become best friends with their server or who cringe at being touched by a stranger may find Lynn's work dispiriting be-cause it looks as though "Hi, I'm Mike, I'll be your waiter" isn't going away soon—at least not at the middle-brow eateries that Lynn's studies focus on.

18   Lynn, by the way, takes his own advice. He tips 15 to 20 percent or even 40 percent if he's at a regular lunch spot, he said.

19   "It really depends," he added, "on how much I like the server."

Understanding the Reading

1. What is the main idea of the article?

_____

_____

2. List four of the tactics Lynn suggests to get bigger tips.

_____

_____

3. What does research show that customers are buying with their tips?

_____

_____

Map the Reading.   Create a graphic organizer that maps the article.

Vocabulary in Context. Write a definition for each of these words as they are used in the reading. Look for words or phrases that help you figure out the meaning. Then check your answer with the dictionary definition.

Word	Para.	Definition
tally	6	_____
correlation	6	_____
rapport	10	_____
empathy	11	_____
reciprocate	11	_____
manipulative	14	_____
dispiriting	17	_____

Thinking and Writing about the Reading

1. **Quick Write:** Your college provides many services to students such as advisement, registration, campus safety, department chairs, and administrative assistants. Write about a problem you or someone you know experienced with service at your college.

2. **Quick Write Jump Off:** Develop your quick write into a paper about the steps you took to correct the problem or the steps the service person took to resolve it.

3. **Summary.** Using your reading map, write a summary of the article.

4. Imagine that you have been asked to train someone to do a job that you are doing now or that you once did. Write a paper that explains the steps you follow to perform your job. If you have never been employed, explain the steps that you follow to perform a job at home. Include tips that will help the individual do an exceptional job.

Connecting the Process Readings

1. In their passage "Service," textbook authors Gregoire and Spears write, "Service can be thought of as an American way of life, and in America each individual holds power." Explain how each of the readings supports this statement.

2. Each reading offers advice for dealing with customers. Is any of the advice in the readings useful to you now or in future employment?

COMPARISON AND CONTRAST   Theme: *Video Game Design*

Male and Female Players and Characters in Video Games

Video game designers want players to be able to identify with and believe in the characters they create. To create appealing characters, designers need to consider the differences in the way males and females view them. As you read this excerpt adapted from a textbook, think about how female characters are portrayed in video games.

Getting Ready to Read: Use the graphic organizer on page 530 to preview the reading.

Excerpt from *Game Design and Development: Fundamentals of Game Design*
Ernest Adams and Andrew Rollings

The Goals of Character Design

1   Character design is an important part of telling stories and getting an emotional reaction in both stories and games. Players need well-designed characters to identify with and care about—heroes to cheer and villains to boo. The character we play and those we interact with help make the game world believable to us. The best games also include complex characters designed to get the player interested or make the player think. If characters aren't interesting or appealing, the game will be less enjoyable.

2   Avatar characters have an extra responsibility: The player must want to step into their shoes, to identify with them, and to play as them. We use the term *avatar* to refer to a character in a game who serves as the main character that the player controls.

3   The goal of character design is to create characters that people *find appealing* (even if the character is a villain), that people can *believe in*, and that the player can *identify with* (especially in the case of avatar characters). If possible, the character should do these things well enough and be different enough that players will remember them.

Male and Female Character Design

4   Early in the history of video games, some designers worried that male players, who used to make up the majority game players, would not want to play female avatars. They thought that men might find identifying with a female character somewhat threatening. Lara Croft, the main character of the popular Eldos' *Tomb Raider* video game series, demonstrated that this is not a problem as long as the character is acting in a role that men are comfortable with. Lara takes part in traditionally masculine activities, so men are happy to enter the game as Lara. They might be less comfortable with an avatar who took part in more traditionally feminine activities.

5   Women, of course, are expected to identify with male heroes most of the time. This was true even before computer games were invented. Until recently, few books, movies, TV shows, or video games about adventurous activities featured female heroes. Even today, there are not many female heroes. Women get tired of playing male heroes, and they appreciate the chance to play as female characters. At the same time, however, women aren't that interested in playing hypersexualized, imaginary characters.

6   Hypersexualization is the practice of making the sexual features of men and women bigger in order to make them more sexually appealing, at least to teenagers. Male characters get extra-broad chests and shoulders, huge muscles, large jaws, and oversized hands and feet. Female characters get very large breasts, extremely narrow waists, and wide hips. They wear clothing that is too small so that their physical attributes show as much as possible. Also, they are shown in positions that make people think about sex. Both males and females are unusually tall, with extra long legs and with heads that seem smaller than their bodies. The women wear

Lara Croft

Blood Rayne

Heather

high heels that make them seem even taller. Such female characters are so extreme that women players do not identify with them. Rayne from the *Blood Rayne* series is an example of a hypersexualized avatar. Rayne is a half-human, half vampire video game character. On the other hand, Heather, the teenage avatar from *Silent Hill 3*, is an avatar that women players can identify with; she looks like a real woman, not a woman in a lingerie advertisement.

7   In general, male players don't actually identify with their avatars as much as female players do. Men treat an avatar as more of a puppet than a person, something they control. Men are more willing to take the avatar provided by the game and happily use it. In contrast, women tend to see an avatar as a part of their own personalities and as a way to express themselves. One of the best things a game designer can do to make the game more attractive to female players is to let them to customize the avatar—to choose his or her clothes, accessories, and weapons (if any).

8   When possible, it's better to give the player a choice of male or female avatars, but it can be difficult to write a story that works with either males or females. Writers would have to develop the story more, which would be more expensive.

Understanding the Reading

1. What is the main idea of the reading?

_____

_____

2. List the differences between how men and women feel about avatars (main characters).

_____

_____

3. What does "hypersexualization" mean? Give an example for a male and a female character.

_____

_____

Map the Reading.   Create a graphic organizer that maps the textbook passage.

Vocabulary in Context. Write a definition for each of these words as they are used in the reading. Look for words or phrases that help you figure out the meaning. Then check your answer with the dictionary definition.

Word	Para.	Definition
villains	1	
appealing	1, 3	
identifying with	4	
attribute	6	
customize	7	

Thinking and Writing about the Reading

1. **Quick Write:** Do you enjoy playing video games (including Wii)? Why or why not?
2. **Quick Write Jump Off:** Write a paper explaining why you do or do not like to play video games.
3. **Summary.** Using your reading map, write a summary of the article.
4. Male and female roles are clearly defined in the United States. From birth children are given toys that strengthen these roles. Boys' games and toys are designed to encourage aggression, competition, and controlled violence, while girls' games and toys are designed to encourage taking care of others, being friendly, and being willing to give in to the wishes of others. Think about the games you play (or used to play as a child). Interview someone to find out about the games he or she plays (or played as a child). Write a paper about the differences between games played by boys and girls.

To date, game developers have focused more on males rather than females. The number of women who enjoy playing video games has increased significantly, but few games that appeal to them are available. Strong female lead characters with their exaggerated curves and skimpy outfits tend to insult rather than please women gamers. As you read this excerpt from a book, note the differences between what males and females look for in video games.

Getting Ready to Read: Use the graphic organizer on page 530 to preview the reading.

But What If the Player Is Female?
Sheri Graner Ray

1 Girls that play Barbie games do grow up. With no titles for them to graduate to, they simply spend their money elsewhere. It doesn't have to be this way.

2 By looking at the differences in male and female entertainment criteria, and applying this information to the titles the industry is developing, it is possible to remove the barriers that prevent the female market from

Doom a first-person shooter game with graphic and interactive violence and evil, cruel imagery

accessing those titles. And it is possible to do this without putting **Doom** into a pink box or making games about fuzzy kittens.

3   It can be done by looking at some of the basic foundations of game design and recognizing that males and females may deal with game basics in very different ways. From the first contact with a title, their differences in approach can be seen.

4   The avatar is the first thing a player comes in contact with, usually on the package cover. How the players experience the game through their avatars can be greatly enhanced with an understanding of the importance of avatar presentation and representation. When the female avatar is **hypersexualized**, it is highly likely the female player won't even consider the title. This "eye candy" may be pleasing for male players, but they are a barrier for female players.

hypersexualized making the sexual features of men and women bigger in order to make them more sexually appealing

5   Also, providing avatars that are gender stereotyped in their roles in the game, or are limited in what they can do, serves to push away the female audience. Likewise, if designers know that sexually-oriented humor that contains "put-downs" of females will cause female players to walk away, they can avoid unintentionally adding content that will drive away a sizeable portion of their sales audience.

6   Differences in learning styles can affect whether or not a player actually plays the game when they first come in contact with the tutorial and, if it is a demo, whether the player actually buys it. Females want a modeling style of learning, whereas males prefer a more explorative method. If designers keep this in mind, they can work to develop tutorial styles that will best benefit both genders and make game tutorials seamless and natural for all players; the player is encouraged to enter the game, and their level of enjoyment is increased (Gottfried 86).

7   Even the basic concept of the game can be a barrier for some players. The concept of conflict usually serves as the basic idea for any game title. If it is apparent from the game description that the resolution of the conflict is only going to be handled in the traditionally male manner—that is, a fight— then this will turn away those players that would normally choose other types of solutions, such as negotiation or compromise. With the knowledge of how each gender handles conflict, designers can build resolutions into their games that complement both styles and appeal to both audiences.

8   The stimuli designers use to capture their audience and keep their attention can have an effect on which markets find the title attracting

interest as well. Males are physically stimulated by visual input. Females may enjoy visual stimulus, however, the do not have a physical response to it. Their response comes from things they can feel or touch. So games that rely on fast movement and visual special effects may not capture the female market as well as they do the male market. By understanding the difference, designers can balance the stimuli they are using for their game and attract and keep a greater percentage of their players.

9   When the players have actually entered the game, how they are rewarded for their successes can either reinforce a positive game experience, or it can make the players less motivated. While males prefer punishment for error in a game, females prefer forgiveness. Punishment for errors is the classic method by which games are resolved. The player is given a limited number of "lives" and has only so many "chances" to succeed. If they do not succeed, then they are usually returned to the beginning of the level, and all progress on that level is lost.

10   Forgiveness for error means the loss is not permanent. Instead, it is a temporary loss, or progress toward the final goal is slowed; but it can be re-gained quickly, normal gameplay resumed, progress can be continued. There is no "dying" and starting over.

11   Often for females, the reward of "winning" or achieving a high level is simply not enough reason to play a game. They want to find a solution that is beneficial and socially significant. They want to accomplish something, rather than "win." By understanding this, designers can adapt their reward system and their victory conditions to work better with different player expectations.

Reference

Gottfried, Allen W., and Catherine Caldwell Brown. *Play Interactions, The Contribution of Play Materials and Parental Involvement to Children's Development.* Lexington Books: Mississippi, 1986.

Understanding the Reading

1. What is the main idea of the reading?

_____

_____

2. List the different ways males and females approach video games.

_____

_____

_____

3. What are three things that game designers should consider to attract women to play?

_____

_____

Map the Reading.   Create a graphic organizer that maps the article.

Vocabulary in Context.   Write a definition for each of these words as they are used in the reading. Look for words or phrases that help you figure out the meaning. Then check your answer with the dictionary definition.

Word	Para.	Definition
barriers	2	_____
accessing	2	_____
gender stereotyped	5	_____
explorative method	6	_____
modeling style of learning	6	_____
seamless	6	_____
complement	7	_____
stimuli	8	_____

Thinking and Writing about the Reading

1. **Quick Write:** Video games and other forms of media, such as television, movies, and the Internet, present images of males and females that have a strong influence on us—how we should look and act, what we should buy, and often what we should think. Write about how the media has influenced people's actions, appearance, purchases, or thoughts.

2. **Quick Write Jump Off:** Write a paper about specific changes you made in yourself or your life because of the influence of the media.

3. **Summary:** Using your reading map, write a summary of the article.

4. Write a paper in which you compare your image of yourself to a media image of your gender (such as television shows, fashion magazines, movies, Internet, etc.).

Connecting the Comparison and Contrast Readings

1. "Male and Female Players and Characters in Video Games" and "But What If the Player Is Female?" explain that males and females experience a video game differently. What are those differences?

2. Both articles point out that many females are not interested in playing hypersexualized female characters. Look at the photographs of video game heroine avatars Lara Croft and Rayne on page 564. Why might some females object to these characters? Why do they appeal to males?

Mind-Body Therapies

For centuries, people have believed that the mind and the body should be treated as a whole. Today there is new interest in these traditions as alternative healing practices. As you read this textbook excerpt, note the mind-body therapies you have heard about.

Getting Ready to Read: Use the graphic organizer on page 530 to preview the reading.

Excerpt from *Fundamentals of Nursing*
Barbara Kozier and Glenora Erb

1   Mind-body therapies are considered alternative medical practices. Some of these have been practiced all over the world. Many have been handed down over thousands of years and are based on medical systems of ancient people.

2   In mind-body therapies, individuals focus on realigning or creating balance in mental processes to bring about healing. These therapies include yoga, meditation, hypnotherapy, guided imagery, and, qigong, t'ai chi.

Yoga

3   Yoga has been practiced for thousands of years in India, where it is a way of life that includes models of right and wrong behavior and mental and physical exercises aimed at producing spiritual enlightenment. It is a method for life that can complement and enhance any system of religion, or it can be practiced completely apart from religion. The Western approach to yoga tends to be more fitness oriented with the goal of managing stress, learning to relax, and increasing vitality and well-being. A typical yoga session lasts twenty minutes to an hour. Some people spend thirty minutes doing the poses and another thirty minutes doing breathing practices and mediations. Others spend the majority of the time doing poses and end with a short meditation or relaxation procedure. Even for those who are inactive and out of shape, sick, or weak, sets of easy exercises can help to loosen the joints and stimulate circulation. If practiced regularly, these simple exercises alone make a great difference in people's health and well-being.

Meditation

4   Meditation is a general term for a wide range of practices that involve relaxing the body and easing the mind. Meditation is a process that people can use to calm themselves, cope with stress, and, for those with spiritual inclinations, feel as one with God or the universe. Meditation can be practiced individually or in groups and is easy to learn. It requires no change in belief system and is compatible with most religious practice.

5   If practiced regularly, such as twenty minutes twice a day, meditation produces widespread positive effects on physical and psychologic functioning. The **autonomic nervous system** responds with a decrease in heart rate, lower blood pressure, decreased breathing rate and oxygen use, and a lower arousal threshold. People who meditate say that they have clearer minds and sharper

autonomic nervous system
part of the nervous system that regulates key functions of the body including the activity of the heart muscle, the muscles of the intestinal tract, and the glands

thoughts. Meditation's lasting effects—improved stress-coping abilities—are a protection against daily stress and anxiety. All other self-healing methods are improved with the practice of meditation.

Hypnotherapy

6   Hypnotherapy is the use of hypnosis in a wide variety of medical and psychologic disorders. Hypnosis is a trance state in which the mind is aware but not in its in its usual waking condition. An individual's concentration is focused and distraction is minimized. People in trances are aware of what is going on around them but choose not to focus on it and can return to normal awareness whenever they choose. Hypnosis is not a surrender of control; it is only an advanced form of relaxation. Hypnotherapy can be used to help people gain self-control, improve self-esteem, and become more independent. In some medical facilities, hypnosis is routinely used with a variety of conditions, usually with other forms of medical, surgical, psychiatric, or psychologic treatment. It can be used with nonmedical clients as well, in working through problems with anxiety and in changing bad habits. Depending on the complexity and seriousness of the complaint, treatment typically runs from two to ten sessions.

Qigong and T'ai Chi

7   A number of therapies focus on movement, body awareness, and breathing and their purpose is to maintain health as well as to correct specific problems. Qigong (pronounced *chee goong*) is a Chinese discipline consisting of breathing and mental exercises combined with body movements. T'ai chi (pronounced *teye chee*) arose out of qigong and is a discipline that combines physical fitness, meditation, and self-defense. Both disciplines consist of soft, slow, continuous movements. The softness of movements develops energy without nervousness. The slowness of the movements and the control required to perform them quiet the mind and develop one's powers of awareness and concentration. The movements themselves help develop strength and endurance.

8   Almost everyone can participate in movement-oriented therapies. They can be learned by the young and old, by people physically challenged or physically fit, and by those in good health and those recovering from long-term injury or illness. In China, eighty, ninety, and one hundred year old people get up every morning before dawn and go out to the parks to practice qigong or t'ai chi, even in the middle of winter. These Eastern practices can be done alone, in pairs or in large groups.

Understanding the Reading

1. What is the main idea of the reading?

_____

_____

2. Describe two types of mind-body therapies.

_____

_____

_____

3. Which two mind-body therapies would be helpful for people who prefer a more physical approach? Why:

_____

Map the Reading. Create a graphic organizer that maps the excerpt.

Vocabulary in Context. Write a definition for each of these words as they are used in the reading. Look for words or phrases that help you figure out the meaning. Then check your answer with the dictionary definition.

Word	Para.	Definition
alternative medical practices	1	_____
realigning	2	_____
spiritual enlightenment	3	_____
inclinations	4	_____
psychologic	5	_____
arousal threshold	5	_____

Thinking and Writing about the Reading

1. **Quick Write**: Write about a technique that you have used to calm your mind and/or body.
2. **Quick Write Jump Off**: Write a paper classifying the techniques you or people you know use to calm the mind and body.
3. **Summary**: Using your reading map, write a summary of the excerpt.
4. The mind-body connection refers to the way your body responds to the way you feel, think, and act. When you are upset, anxious, or stressed, your body sends you messages that something is not right. Write a classification paper about the ways a person's body may react physically to poor emotional health, such as headache, cold, or upset stomach.

Dr. Amen is an assistant clinical professor of psychiatry and human behavior at the University of California, Irvine School of Medicine. He teaches medical students and psychiatric residents about using brain imaging. Dr. Amen believes that people can change their brains with the appropriate treatments and skills for their brain type. As you read this excerpt from a website, note how your beliefs affect your thoughts.

Kill the Ants That Invade Your Brain
Daniel G. Amen, M.D.

1   The brain is a three-pound supercomputer. It is the command and control center running your life. It is involved in absolutely everything you do. Your brain determines how you think, how you feel, how you act, and how well you get along with other people. Your brain even determines the kind of person you are.

It determines how thoughtful you are; how polite or how rude you are. It determines how well you think on your feet, and it is involved with how well you do at work and with your family. Your brain also influences your emotional well-being and how well you do with the opposite sex.

2   Your brain is more complicated than any computer we can imagine. Did you know that you have one hundred billion nerve cells in your brain, and every nerve cell has many connections to other nerve cells? In fact, your brain has more connections in it than there are stars in the universe! Optimizing your brain's function is essential to being the best you can be, whether at work, in leisure, or in your relationships.

3   The thoughts that go through your mind, moment by moment, have a significant impact on how your brain works. Research by Mark George, MD, and colleagues at the National Institutes of Health demonstrated that happy, hopeful thoughts had an overall calming effect on the brain, while negative thoughts inflamed brain areas often involved with depression and anxiety. Your thoughts matter.

4   I often teach my patients how to metaphorically kill the ANTs that invade their minds. ANTs stand for Automatic Negative Thoughts. The ANTs are automatic. They just happen. But they can ruin your whole day, maybe even your life. For example, I once treated a college student who was ready to drop out of school. He thought he was stupid because didn't do well on tests. When his IQ (intelligence level) was tested, however, we discovered that he had an IQ of 135 (in the superior range). He just wasn't a good test taker. I have identified nine different kinds of ANT species, or ways your thoughts can distort incoming information to make you feel bad. Here are four ANT species:

Mind reading—predicting you know that another person is thinking something negative about you without them telling you. I often tell my patients that, "A negative look from someone else may mean nothing more than he or she is constipated. You don't know. You can't read minds. I have 25 years of training in human behavior and I still can't read anyone's mind."

Fortune telling—predicting a bad outcome to a situation before it has occurred. Your mind makes happen what it sees. Unconsciously, predicting failure will often cause failure. For example, if you say, "I know I will fail the test," then you will likely not study hard enough and fail the test.

Always or never thinking—this is where you think in words like always, never, every time, or everyone. These thoughts are overgeneralizations which can alter behavior. For example, I have a friend who asked out an attractive woman. She turned him down. He told himself that no one will ever go out with him again. This ANT prevented him from asking out anyone else for over nine months.

Guilt beatings—being overrun by thoughts of "I should have done . . . I'm bad because . . . I must do better at . . . I have to." Guilt is powerful at making us feel bad. It is a lousy motivator of behavior.

5   You do not have to believe every thought that goes through your head. It's important to think about your thoughts to see if they help you or they hurt you. Unfortunately, if you never challenge your thoughts you just "believe them" as if they were true. ANTs can take over and infest your brain. Develop an internal anteater to hunt down and devour the negative thoughts that are ruining your life.

6   Once you learn about your thoughts, you can chose to think good thoughts and feel good or you can choose to think bad thoughts and feel lousy. You can train your thoughts to be positive and hopeful or you can just allow them to be negative and upset you. That's right, it's up to you! You can learn how to change your thoughts and optimize your brain. One way to learn how to change your thoughts is to notice them when they are negative and talk back to them. If you can correct negative thoughts, you take away their power over you. When you think a negative thought without challenging it, your mind believes it and your brain reacts to it.

Understanding the Reading

1. What is the main idea of the reading?

_____

_____

2. What are Automatic Negative Thoughts (ANTs)?

_____

_____

3. Describe two of the Automatic Negative Thought species.

_____

_____

Map the Reading.   Create a graphic organizer that maps the excerpt.

Vocabulary in Context. Write a definition for each of these words as they are used in the reading. Look for words or phrases that help you figure out the meaning. Then check your answer with the dictionary definition.

Word	Para.	Definition
optimizing	2	_____
inflame	3	_____
metaphorically	4	_____
overgeneralizations	4	_____

Thinking and Writing about the Reading

1. **Quick Write:** Write about an Automatic Negative Thought you have had.
2. **Quick Write Jump Off:** Using Amen's types of Automatic Negative Thoughts, write a classification paper describing each one with details that apply to you or people you know.
3. **Summary:** Using your reading map, write a summary of the excerpt.
4. Write a classification paper about the ways people can overcome their negative thoughts.

Connecting the Classification Readings

1. Discuss which mind-body therapies would be most helpful in getting rid of negative thoughts.
2. How do mind-body therapies and "killing ANTs" bring about healing?

CAUSE AND EFFECT   Theme: *Psychology*

Aggression

Aggression is defined as behaviors that cause psychological or physical harm to another individual. This textbook excerpt includes responses of the authors' students when asked why they became aggressive in a particular situation. As you read, think about your behavior when you are angry or frustrated.

Excerpt from *Psychology and Life*
Richard J. Gerrig and Philip G. Zimbardo

1   Why are some individuals more aggressive than others? Take a moment to think back to the last time you engaged in aggressive behavior. It may not have been physical aggression: You may just have been verbally abusive toward some other individual, with the intent of causing psychological distress. How would you explain why that particular situation gave rise to aggression? Did you have a long history of conflict with the individual or was it just a one-time interaction? Did you act aggressively because of something very specific or were you just feeling frustrated at that moment? When we asked our own students to think about their aggressive acts, they have given us a variety of answers, as you will see in what follows.

Frustration-Aggression Hypothesis

2   I'd been having a really bad day. I needed to register late for a course. I couldn't find anyone to help me. When I was told for the thousandth time, "You've got to go to a different office," I got so angry I practically kicked a hole in the door.

3   This anecdote provides an instance of a general relationship captured by the frustration-aggression hypothesis. According to this hypothesis, frustration occurs in situations in which people are prevented or blocked from attaining their goals; a rise in *frustration* then leads to a greater probability of aggression. We can predict a certain level of aggression based on the frustration each individual experiences in an economy with rising unemployment. However, as people realize that expression of aggression may hurt their opportunity for employment, they do not act on that feeling of frustration.

Direct Provocation and Escalation

4   I was sitting in the library trying to get some work done. These two women were having a really loud conversation that was bothering a lot of people. I asked them to quiet down, and they pretty much ignored me. I asked again about five minutes later, and they only started talking louder. Finally, I told them they were both stupid, ugly jerks and that if they didn't shut up, I was going to pick them up and throw them out of the library. That worked.

5   *Direct provocation* will also give rise to aggression. That is, when someone behaves in a way that makes you angry or upset—and you think that the behavior is intentional—you are more likely to respond with some form of physical or verbal aggression. The intentionality of the act matters because you are less likely to interpret an unintentional act in a negative way.

6   A second characteristic of this anecdote, beyond provocation, is *escalation*. The failure of the initial attempts to change the situation led to feelings of frustration that also will increase the likelihood of more intense aggression.

Temperature and Aggression

7   It was a hot summer day, and the air conditioning in my car was broken. This guy cut me off. I chased after him and tried to run him off the road.

8   There is a strong relationship between how cold or hot it is and how likely it is that people will commit assaults. The relationship between temperature and assault is actually strongest in the late evening and early morning hours (that is, 9 p.m. to 3 a.m.).

9   In warmer weather, people are more likely to be outdoors and, therefore, are also more likely to be "available" as assault victims. Also, in the 9 p.m. to 3 a.m. house, people typically have fewer responsibilities. Furthermore, by late evening house, people may have been drinking alcohol or using other substances that lower their inhibition for aggression.

10   Certain situations are more likely to cause aggressive behavior. However, people make choices with respect to their display of aggression depending on their cultural values and norms.

Understanding the Reading

1. What is the main idea of the reading?

_____

_____

2. Explain the frustration-aggression hypothesis.

_____

_____

3. What causes people to control their display of aggression?

_____

_____

Map the Reading.   Create a graphic organizer that maps the reading.

Vocabulary in Context.   Write a definition for each of these words as they are used in the reading. Look for words or phrases that help you figure out the meaning. Then check your answer with the dictionary definition.

Word	Para.	Definition
anecdote	3	_____
hypothesis	3	_____
provocation	5	_____
escalation	6	_____
inhibition	10	_____

Thinking and Writing about the Reading

1. **Quick Write:** Write about a time when you behaved in an aggressive manner or when you saw someone behave agressively.
2. **Quick Write Jump Off:** Write a paper about the cause(s) and effect(s) of an instance of aggressive behavior.
3. **Summary:** Using your reading map, write a summary of the article.
4. Write a paper about the effects of violence in the news, movies, television, or video games.

Dave Barry is a Pulitzer Prize–winning writer and humor columnist. In this article, Barry takes a humorous view of instances in daily life that make him angry. As you read, consider whether or not there is some truth to his complaints.

Getting Ready to Read: Use the graphic organizer on page 530 to preview the reading.

All the Rage
Dave Barry

1   If you do much driving on our nation's highways, you've probably noticed that, more and more often, bullets are coming through your windshield. This is a common sign of Road Rage, which the opinion-makers in the news media have decided is a serious problem, ranking just behind global warming and ahead of Asia.

2   How widespread is Road Rage? To answer that question, researchers for the National Institute of Traffic Safety recently did a study in which they drove on the interstate highway system in a specially equipped observation van. By the third day, they were deliberately running motorists off the road.

3   "These people are MORONS!" their official report stated.

4   That is the main cause of Road Rage: the realization that many of your fellow motorists have the brain of a cashew. The most common example, of course, is the motorists who feel a need to drive in the left-hand, or "passing," lane, even though they are going slower than everybody else.

5   Nobody knows why these motorists do this. Maybe they belong to some kind of religious cult that believes the right lane is sacred and must never come in direct contact with tires. Maybe one time, years ago, these motorists happened to be driving in the left lane when their favorite song came on the radio, so they've driven there ever since, in hopes that the radio will play that song again.

6   But whatever makes these people drives this way, there's nothing you can do about it. You can honk at them, but it will have no effect. People have been honking at them for years: It's a normal part of their environment. They've decided that, for some mysterious reason, wherever they drive, there is honking. They choose not to ponder this mystery any further, lest they overburden their cashews.

7   I am familiar with the problem because I live and drive in Miami, Fla., which proudly bills itself as The Inappropriate-Lane-Driving Capital of the World, and where the left lane is thought of not so much as a thoroughfare as a public recreational area, where motorists feel free to stop, hold family reunions, barbecue pigs, play volleyball, etc. Compounding this problem is another common type of Miami motorist, the aggressive young male whose car has a sound system so powerful that the driver must go faster than the speed of sound at all times, because otherwise the nuclear bass notes emanating from his rear speakers will catch up to him and cause his head to explode.

8   So the tiny minority of us Miami drivers who actually qualify as normal find ourselves constantly being trapped behind people drifting along on the

interstate at the speed of diseased livestock, while at the same time we are being tailgated and occasionally bumped from behind by testosterone-deranged youths who got their driver training from watching the space-fighter battle scenes in Star Wars. And of course nobody EVER signals or yields, and people are CONSTANTLY cutting us off, and AFTER A WHILE WE START TO FEEL SOME RAGE, OK? YOU GOT A PROBLEM WITH THAT, MISTER NEWS MEDIA OPINION-MAKER?

9   In addition to Road Rage, I frequently experience Parking Lot Rage, which occurs when I pull into a crowded supermarket parking lot, and I see people get into their car, clearly ready to leave, so I stop my car and wait for them to vacate the spot, and . . . Nothing happens. They just stay there! WHAT THE HELL ARE THEY DOING IN THERE?? COOKING DINNER???

10   When I finally get into the supermarket, I often experience Shopping Cart Rage. This is caused by people—and you just KNOW these are the same people who drive in the left-hand lane—who routinely manage, by careful placement, to block the entire aisle with a single shopping cart. If we really want to keep illegal immigrants from entering the United States, we should employ Miami residents armed with shopping carts; we'd only need about two dozen to block the entire Mexican border.

11   What makes the supermarket congestion even worse is that shoppers are taking longer and longer to decide what to buy, because every product in America now comes in an insane number of styles and sizes. For example, I recently went to the supermarket to get orange juice. For just one brand of orange juice, Tropicana, I had to decide between Original, Homestyle, Pulp Plus, Double Vitamin C, Grovestand, Calcium or Old Fashioned; I also had to decide whether I wanted the 16-ounce, 32-ounce, 64-ounce, 96-ounce or six-pack size. This is WAY too many choices. It caused me to experience Way Too Many Product Choices Rage. I would have called Tropicana and complained, but I probably would have wound up experiencing Automated Phone Answering System Rage (" . . . For questions about Pulp Plus in the 32-ounce size, press 23. For questions about the Pulp Plus in the 64-ounce size, press 24. For questions about . . .").

12   My point is that there are many causes of rage in our modern world, and if we're going to avoid unnecessary violence, we all need to "keep our cool." So let's try to be more considerate, OK? Otherwise I will kill you.

Understanding the Reading

1. What is the main idea of the reading?

_____

_____

2. List the types of rage Barry classifies.

_____

_____

3. Give two examples Barry gives for road rage.

_____

_____

Map the Reading.   Create a graphic organizer that maps the reading.

Vocabulary in Context.   Write a definition for each of these words as they are used in the reading. Look for words or phrases that help you figure out the meaning. Then check your answer with the dictionary definition.

Word	Para.	Definition
ranking	1	_____
religious cult	5	_____
thoroughfare	6	_____
emanating from	6	_____
livestock	7	_____
tailgate	7	_____

Thinking and Writing about the Reading

1. **Quick Write:** Most of us have experienced one of the types of rage Barry writes about. Write about the reasons for your anger on the road, in the supermarket, or in a parking lot.
2. **Quick Write Jump Off:** Write a paper about the reasons you or others become angry on the nation's roads, supermarkets, or parking lots.
3. **Summary:** Using your reading map, write a summary of the article.
4. Write a paper about the causes and/or effects for people's impatience in our modern world.

Connecting the Cause and Effect Readings

1. Explain how the reasons for Dave Barry's rage fit the frustration-aggression hypothesis.
2. What is the difference between rage and aggression?

DEFINITION   Theme: *Anthropology*

Race

Races are invented by cultures, not biology. Ideas about race are learned through exposure to the beliefs of family, peers, culture, and social groups. In different societies around the world, race has been used to separate people and to treat them unequally. As you read this excerpt adapted from a textbook, notice how anthropologists view race and how their view differs from that of society.

Getting Ready to Read: Use the graphic organizer on page 530 to preview the reading.

Excerpt from *Anthropology*

Carol R. Ember, Melvin Ember, and Peter N. Peregrine

anthropologist someone who scientifically studies humans, their customs, beliefs and relationships

biologist a scientist who studies life science

1   In some societies, such as the United States, the idea that humans are divided into "races" is accepted as truth. People are asked for their "race" on the census. Most Americans probably believe that "races" are real, meaningful categories based on differences in skin color and other physical characteristics. However, this is not necessarily the case. You may have noticed that we put "races" in quotes. We have done so on purpose because most **anthropologists** believe that "race" is a meaningless idea when applied to humans. To understand why we say that, we first need to consider what the concept of race means in biology.

2   Biologists classify all forms of life into groups. Just as with animals, plants, and insects, biologists classify humans. They found that people living in different geographical locations in the world had different physical characteristics, such as skin color, hair texture, and facial features. **Biologists** classified these groups into *varieties*, or **races**. If people understood that the term *race* was just a system that biologists use to describe differences within a species from one population to the next, the concept of race would probably not be controversial. But, as applied to humans, racial groupings have often been thought to imply that some "races" are inferior to others.

3   Many anthropologists and others believe that the concept of race interferes with the search to explain how physical differences developed in humans. They have two reasons for this belief. One is the misuse and misunderstanding of the term *race*. The other is that race has been connected to racist thinking. In any case, classifying people by race is not scientifically useful in that search. Populations cannot be grouped according to certain characteristics because these characteristics vary from region to region.

4   How can groups be clearly divided into "races" if most people from one region show small differences from those in a neighboring region? Skin color is a good example. Groups of people who originally came from places close to the equator where the sun is strongest tend to have darker skin. Darker skin appears to protect the body from damaging ultraviolet radiation. For example, in the area around Egypt, there is a change of skin color as you move from north to south in the Nile Valley. Populations originating in places farther north developed lighter skin colors because the sunlight was not as strong.

5   Some of our physical differences make us think that it is possible to divide humans into races. However, when these physical characteristics are studied in detail, that cannot be concluded at all. It is an illusion that there are races. The diversity of human beings is so great and so complicated that it is impossible to classify the 5.8 billions of individuals into separate "races." Human populations do vary biologically in some ways, but it is important to understand that few of these ways are connected with each other. All humans are nearly alike genetically under the skin.

Understanding the Reading

1. What is the main idea of the excerpt?

_____

_____

_____

2. According to the authors of the reading, how do biologists define race?

_____

_____

_____

3. Why is the term *race* controversial?

_____

_____

_____

Map the Reading. Create a graphic organizer that maps the excerpt.

Vocabulary in Context. Write a definition for each of these words as they are used in the reading. Look for words or phrases that help you figure out the meaning. Then check your answer with the dictionary definition.

Word	Para.	Definition
census	1	_____
Species	2	_____
racist	3	_____
ultraviolet radiation	4	_____
originating	4	_____
illusion	5	_____
diversity	5	_____

Thinking and Writing about the Reading

1. **Quick Write:** We are not born with any beliefs about racial differences. What we think about race is learned. What messages have you received about race throughout your life? Write about what these messages are and where they came from.
2. **Quick Write Jump Off:** Write a paper about how the media, school, peers, family, and your experiences have influenced the way you think about race.
3. **Summary.** Using your reading map, write a summary of the excerpt.
4. The authors of the excerpt present the anthropologists' view that people can't be separated into races because human diversity is so great and so complicated. However, throughout history, people have used race as a basis for discrimination. Write a paper defining discrimination.

Colorism is a form or discrimination within racial groups in which there is skin tone variation. Members of the same race with lighter skin are treated more favorably than those with darker skin. As you read Clarisse Jones' magazine article "Light Skin versus Dark," think about how colorism influences the culture in the United States and other parts of the world.

Getting Ready to Read: Use the graphic organizer on page 530 to preview the reading.

Light Skin Versus Dark
Charisse Jones

1   I'll never forget the day I was supposed to meet him. We had only spoken on the phone. But we got along so well, we couldn't wait to meet face-to-face. I took the bus from my high school to his for our blind date. While I nervously waited for him outside the school, one of his buddies came along, looked me over, and remarked that I was going to be a problem, because his friend didn't like dating anybody darker than himself.

2   When my mystery man—who was not especially good-looking—finally saw me, he took one look, uttered a hurried hello, then disappeared with his smirking friends. I had apparently been pronounced ugly on arrival and dismissed.

3   That happened nearly fifteen years ago. I'm thirty now, and the hurt and humiliation have long since faded. But the memory still lingers, reinforced in later years by other situations in which my skin color was judged by other African Americans—for example, at a cocktail party or a nightclub where light-skinned black women got all the attention.

4   A racist encounter hurts badly. But it does not equal the pain of "colorism"—being rejected by your own people because your skin is colored cocoa and not cream, ebony and not olive. On our scale of beauty, it is often the high yellows—in the lexicon of black America, those with light skin—whose looks reap the most attention. Traditionally, if someone was described that way, there was no need to say that person was good-looking. It was a given that light was lovely. It was those of us with plain brown eyes and darker skin hues who had to prove ourselves.

5   I was twelve, and in my first year of junior high school in San Francisco, when I discovered dark brown was not supposed to be beautiful. At that age, boys suddenly became important, and so did your looks. But by that time—the late 1970s—black kids no longer believed in that sixties mantra, "Black is beautiful." Light skin, green eyes, and long, wavy hair were once again synonymous with beauty.

6   Colorism—and its subtext of self-hatred—began during slavery on plantations where white masters often favored the lighter-skinned blacks, many of whom were their own children. But though it began with whites, black people have kept colorism alive. In the past, many black sororities, fraternities, and other social organizations have been notorious for accepting only light-skinned members. Yes, some blacks have criticized their lighter-skinned peers. But most often

in our history, a light complexion had been a passport to special treatment by both whites *and* blacks.

7   Some social circles are still defined by hue. Some African Americans, dark and light, prefer light-skinned mates so they can have a "pretty baby." And skin-lightening creams still sell, though they are now advertised as good for making blemishes fade rather than for lightening whole complexions.

8   In my family, color was never discussed, even though our spectrum was broad—my brother was very light; my sister and I, much darker. But in junior high, I learned in a matter of weeks what had apparently been **drummed into the heads** of my black peers for most of their lives.

drummed into the heads to teach something to someone by repeating it a lot

9   Realizing how crazy it all was, I became defiant, challenging friends when they made silly remarks. Still, there was no escaping the distinctions of color.

10   In my life, I have received a litany of twisted compliments from fellow blacks. "You're the prettiest dark-skinned girl I have ever seen" is one; "You're pretty for a dark girl" is another.

11   A light-complexioned girlfriend once remarked to me that dark-skinned people often don't take the time to groom themselves. As a journalist, I once interviewed a prominent black lawmaker who was light-skinned. He drew me into the shade of a tree while we talked because, he said, "I'm sure you don't want to get any darker."

12   Though some black people—like film-maker Spike Lee in his movie *School Daze*—have tried to provoke debate about colorism, it remains a painful topic many blacks would rather not confront. Yet there has been progress. In this age of **Afrocentrism**, many blacks revel in the nuances of the African American rainbow. Natural hairstyles and dreadlocks are in, and Theresa Randle, star of the hit film *Bad Boys*, is only one of several darker-skinned actresses noted for their beauty.

Afrocentrism emphasizing the importance of African people in culture, philosophy, and history

13   That gives me hope. People have told me that color biases among blacks run too deep ever to be eradicated. But I tell them that is the kind of attitude that allows colorism to persist. Meanwhile, I do what I can. When I notice that a friend dates only light-skinned women, I comment on it. If I hear that a movie follows the tired old scenario in which a light-skinned beauty is the love interest while a darker-skinned woman is the comic foil, the butt of "ugly" jokes, I don't go see it. Others can do the same.

Understanding the Reading

1. What is the main idea of the article?

_____

_____

_____

2. How does Charisse Jones define "colorism"?

_____

_____

3. What is the history of "colorism"?

_____

_____

_____

Map the Reading.   Create a graphic organizer that maps the essay.

Vocabulary in Context.   Write a definition for each of these words as they are used in the reading. Look for words or phrases that help you figure out the meaning. Then check your answer with the dictionary definition.

Word	Para.	Definition
mantra	5	_____
synonymous	5	_____
subtext	6	_____
hue	7	_____
spectrum	8	_____
defiant	9	_____
provoke	12	_____
revel	12	_____
nuance	12	_____
bias	13	_____

Thinking and Writing about the Reading

1. **Quick Write:** Write about your experience with one or both of these:
   - not wanting to have someone as a friend because of his or her appearance, beliefs, residence, etc.
   - your being rejected or left out for similar reasons
2. **Quick Write Jump Off:** Discrimination is defined as the treatment of a person or particular group of people differently, especially in a worse way from the way you treat other people because of religion, sex, sexual orientation, color, disability, etc. Using this definition as a starting point, write a paper giving examples that support the definition. Include your quick write as one of the examples.
3. **Summary:** Using your reading map, write a summary of the excerpt.
4. People's positive and negative traits are often described in language through the use of labels. A label is a term used to describe a person based on one characteristic. Labels can be positive or negative. We label people according to the way they walk, talk, or dress, their beliefs, the crowd they associate with, their physical characteristics, economic status, and so on. How many labels do you use in one day without realizing it? Choose several label words that you use and write a paper explaining how those labels describe the individuals or groups of people.

1. What is the difference between the view of skin color in "Race" and in "Light Skin versus Dark"?
2. Is classifying people according to race a good or a bad idea? Why?

ARGUMENT   Theme: *Education*

Managing Student Behavior

Teachers need many skills to manage the tasks and situations that occur in the classroom every day. One of the primary concerns of new teachers is managing student conduct. Key to success in this area is establishing rules and consequences. In this excerpt adapted from a textbook, note the arguments for and against punishment.

Getting Ready to Read: Use the graphic organizer on page 530 to preview the reading.

Excerpt from *Teaching Exceptional, Diverse, and At-Risk Students in the General Education Classroom*
Sharon Vaughan, Candace S. Bos, and Jeanne Shay Schumm

1   Teachers must have effective ways to manage student behavior. They must set up clear, specific guidelines and consequences when students do not follow those guidelines. *Guidelines* in the classroom consist of procedures and rules. *Procedures* are ways of doing things in the classroom at specified times. They allow the classroom to run effectively. Students need to learn these procedures and use them every day so that the classroom will run smoothly.

Rules

2   **Rules** show students which classroom behaviors are acceptable and unacceptable. Teachers should not try to have a rule for every possible misbehavior. Instead they should develop a few general rules that help students figure out whether a behavior is or is not acceptable. These rules should be based on the teacher's standards for what is considered a behavior problem. Some teachers involve students in determining class rules and consequences. *Consequences* are the effects of acceptable or unacceptable behavior.

Punishment

3   **Punishment** is the opposite of reward. The purpose of punishment is to get the student to decrease or stop an undesirable behavior. Although punishment often reduces the undesired behavior, it does not guarantee that the desired behavior will occur. Thus, instead of teaching students to do what the teacher wants them to do, punishment simply teaches them to avoid doing what the teacher does not want them to do.

4   Following are some of the many significant arguments against the use of punishment:

- Punishment is often ineffective in the long run.
- Punishment often causes undesirable emotional side effects such as fear, aggression, and resentment.

- Punishment provides little information about what to do, teaching the individual only what *not* to do.
- The person who gives the punishment is often seen as harsh or negative.
- Punishment may not change a behavior, so the punishment has to be repeated.
- Fear of punishment often leads to escape behavior such as running out of the room or not completing a task.

5   Unfortunately, even though there are many arguments against the use of punishment, parents and teachers frequently use it. Why is punishment so frequently used? There are several reasons:

- because teachers may be unfamiliar with the effects of punishment.
- because teachers are not able to use a more positive approach effectively.
- because the student may quickly change the undesirable behavior, the person who does the punishing is highly rewarded.

6   Punishment should be used as a last resort and when behaviors are harmful to a student or others. If trying to change a student's behavior in a positive way has failed, the teacher should follow these guidelines for effective punishment:

- Tell the student ahead of time what the punishment will be for the undesirable behavior.
- Deliver the punishment right after the undesirable behavior.
- Apply the punishment every time the behavior occurs.
- If the behavior does not change, the punishment is ineffective and should be changed.
- Point out and reward the appropriate behaviors of the student.

Understanding the Reading

1. What is the main idea of the excerpt?

_____

_____

2. List three reasons against the use of punishment.

_____

_____

3. List the reasons teachers and parents use punishment.

_____

_____

Map the Reading.   Create a graphic organizer that maps the excerpt.

Vocabulary in Context.   Write a definition for each of these words as they are used in the reading. Look for words or phrases that help you figure out the meaning. Then check your answer with the dictionary definition.

Word	Para.	Definition
consequences	1	_____
standards	2	_____
resentment	4	_____
last resort	6	_____

Thinking and Writing about the Reading

1. **Quick Write:** Classroom management can be challenging for teachers. Write about a time when a teacher had a difficult time managing one or more students in a class.
2. **Quick Write Jump Off:** Using the situation that you wrote about in your quick write, write a paper arguing that the way the teacher handled the situation was either right or wrong.
3. **Summary:** Using your reading map, write a summary of the article.
4. Write a paper arguing for or against teacher punishment when behaviors are harmful to a student or others.

The use of electronic devices in college classrooms has brought about debate among college professors who have mixed opinions. Some feel that the lure of these devices can distract students from learning. In this article, two professors give their views on cell phone use in the classroom. As you read, think about which policy makes the most sense to you.

Getting Ready to Read: Use the graphic organizer on page 530 to preview the reading.

Making Cell Phones in the Class a Community Builder
Alan Bloom and S. Campbell

Cell Phones Do Not Distract in Class (Pro)

1   The first time a student's cell phone rang in my class, I was angry and frustrated. With their musical ringers, cell phones that go *off* in class are rude and distracting. But how to respond? I've never been very good at playing the heavy. Was there any way I could take this annoying occurrence and twist it so that it would contribute to a more positive classroom environment?

2   I've devised a "cell phone protocol" that has enabled me to make peace with the problem. As it appears in the syllabus, the protocol reads: **"Please turn off your cell phone ringer while in class. Mind you, violation of this protocol will demand punishment—though one that clearly does not infringe on your eighth amendment rights."** I then ask someone to identify the eighth amendment, and as a history professor, I'm happy to report that someone can always explain the constitutional limits on cruel and unusual punishment. I advise students to turn off their ringers in class, and I note that if someone's phone rings, he

or she will have to provide the class with food. It doesn't have to be an extravagant meal (remember the eighth amendment!), but there must be enough for everyone. In the beginning, I offered the possibility of a subsidy to economically unable students. However, I abandoned it once I realized that if student s could afford a cell-phone package, they could provide treats to about 30 classmates.

3   The community-building process develops in earnest when a phone actually rings in class. During an episode that otherwise involves an unpleasant exchange, there is now occasion for celebration, as students cheer at the possibility of their upcoming snack. The cell phone protocol, much like a kangaroo court in baseball, which exacts minor fines for small indiscretions, helps to build an esprit de corps and I push this outcome even further. When it is difficult to figure out whether the cell phone rang or was in vibration mode, I encourage the students to vote as to whether or not a violation has occurred.

4   So what are the drawbacks of this policy? There are few. The biggest is that even with my policy, cell phones still ring in class and they are just as rude and distracting. I see no way around this problem. In my class, students are distracted, but we grow closer as a result of it. The other potential problem is that an instructor might not want food in the classroom, fair enough, just have the punishment be something like telling a joke or sharing a poem.

5   The policy has also produced some wonderful surprises that make me proud of my students. Once a student decided to skip the standard fare of candy and brought in dried fruit. Although most of her peers (and her teacher) were disappointed with the healthy alternative, this student took the opportunity to encourage people to eat a more healthy diet. And at the end of this past semester, one of my quietest students informed the class that she was disappointed in a classmate who still hadn't brought in food for his transgression. The chastened student, who apparently had extra money on his meal card, brought in a buffet for his dumbfounded classmates.

6   Ultimately, though, the greatest advantage of the cell phone protocol occurs when someone's phone rings in class and the other students start hooting joyously. It doesn't make the phone ringing less distracting; but on the other hand, how often do you hear students cheering in the classroom?

—Alan Bloom

Cell Phones Do Distract in Class (Con)

7   In case you have ever had any doubts, research (reference below) now exists that proves that both students and teachers find cell phones ringing

in class distracting. The results also document strong support from students and faculty for policies against ringing cell phones. Although there was strong support against cell phones going off in class, the strength of that support was affected by age. The younger cohort in the study was more tolerant of cell phones than the older cohort.

8   The problem, of course, is that it is virtually impossible to prevent cell phones from ringing in class. They do ring, despite strongly worded statements in the syllabus, regular announcements in class, and threats of various sorts. Well, they don't actually ring, they beep out jingles, tunes, and other electronic sounds without pause until they are turned off or answered.

9   Ringing phones are distracting, and faculty, probably because we didn't grow up using cell phones, seem particularly annoyed when they do go off in class. If you want to generate discussion in the faculty mailroom, ask several folks standing there what they do about the problem. For many, there's something of a power issue involved here. Despite policies against cell phones in the syllabus, or announcements by the teacher that they must be turned off, right in the middle of an important point, one goes off. Everyone hears the phone and watches as someone (who is usually quite embarrassed) retrieves and silences it.

10   So what should a faculty member do when the inevitable occurs? Take the phone away? Accost the offender? Wail and carry on about how students show no respect? The problem with these loud and powerful responses is that most of the time they don't prevent the problem from recurring.

make a mountain out of a molehill make something seem much more important than it really is

11   It seems wiser not to **make a mountain out of a molehill.** That doesn't mean molehills have to be tolerated. Their offensiveness should indeed be pointed out. But when the distraction occurs, perhaps there is silence and then an attempt to regroup. "Now, where were we?" "What's the last thing you wrote in your notes?" "Do you understand what I was trying to explain?" The disruption becomes an opportunity to review and connect with what students are (or are not) understanding. This prevents the disruption from doing even more harm when it not only distracts but results in an unpleasant exchange that threatens the climate for learning.

—S. Campbell

Understanding the Reading

1. There are two articles in this reading. What is the main idea of each of the articles?

_____

_____

2. Explain how the professor of the first article deals with cell phone use in his class and how the students react to the policy.

_____

_____

3. Explain how the professor of the second article deals with cell phone use in his class.

_____

_____

Map the Reading.   Create a graphic organizer that maps the reading.

Vocabulary in Context.   Write a definition for each of these words as they are used in the reading. Look for words or phrases that help you figure out the meaning. Then check your answer with the dictionary definition.

Word	Para.	Definition
protocol	2	_____
subsidy	2	_____
indiscretion	3	_____
esprit de corps	3	_____
transgression	5	_____
chastened	5	_____
dumbfounded	5	_____
cohort	7	_____

Thinking and Writing about the Reading

1. **Quick Write:** Do any of your teachers have policies about the use of cell phones or other electronic devices in class? Write about those policies and explain whether or not they have been effective.
2. **Quick Write Jump Off:** Write a paper arguing for or against cell phone penalties.
3. **Summary:** Using your reading map, write a summary of the articles.
4. Text messaging or surfing the web during class has become commonplace and presents a different type of distraction. Argue for or against students being permitted to text message or surf the web during class.

Connecting the Argument Readings

1. "Managing Student Behavior" and "Making Cell Phones in the Class a Community Builder" address classroom management. The first article was written for the kindergarten through twelfth grade teacher, while the second article was written for the college teacher. Which information presented in the first article can be helpful to college teachers?
2. In "Managing Student Behavior," authors Vaughan, Bos, and Schumm point out, "Some teachers involve students in determining class rules and consequences." Do you think that cell phone interruptions and texting would stop if students had a voice in determining class rules and consequences of cell phone use in class?

Credits

Photo Credits

p. 1: © Jose Luis Pelaez Inc/Getty Images; p. 78: © Michael Newman/PhotoEdit; p. 79: © PNC/Getty Images; p. 97: © Mark Wilson/Boston Globe/Landov; p. 102: © Stephen Marks/Getty Images; p. 121: © Nikada/iStockphoto; p. 125: © Larry Lilac/Alamy; p. 142: © YinYang/iStockphoto; p. 145: © Francis G. Mayer/Corbis; p. 146 (top): © Dallas Museum of Art, gift of J.E.R. Chilton; p. 146 (bottom): © Christian Science Monitor/Getty Images; p. 152: © Steven Day/AP Images; p. 163 (both): © Blend Images/Alamy; p. 170: © Alistair Scott/Shutterstock; p. 174: © Enigma/Alamy; p. 194 (left): © Megan Duncanson, DBA MADART, Inc.; p. 194 (right): © Harvard Art Museum/Art Resource, NY; p. 201: © Image Source/Getty Images; p. 223: © Daniel Laflor/iStockphoto; p. 239: © Illustration Works/Alamy; p. 245: © Douglas Pulsipher/Alamy; p. 259 (top): © Andresr/Shutterstock; p. 259 (bottom left): © Tad Denson/Shutterstock; p. 259 (bottom right): Yuri Arcurs/Shutterstock; p. 264: © Photodisc/Getty Images; p. 283: Animal Care & Control of New York City; p. 285: © Tracy Tucker/iStockphoto;

p. 288: © AFP/Getty Images; p. 291: © Tetra Images/Getty Images; p. 335: © Rachel Watson/Getty Images; p. 340: © Jacob Wackerhausen/iStockphoto; p. 351: © Ilene MacDonald/Alamy; p. 352: © Jason Stitt/Shutterstock; p. 356: © Mike Kemp/Getty Images; p. 365: © Simone van den Berg/Shutterstock; p. 370: © James Steidl/Shutterstock; p. 375: © Livia Corona/Getty Images; p. 387: © Valentyn Volkov/Shutterstock; p. 395: © Mandy Godbehear/Shutterstock; p. 409 (top): © Roger Jegg/Shutterstock; p. 409 (bottom): © Corbis Super RF/Alamy; 424: © Fernando Alvarado/EPA/Corbis; p. 449: © Tina Chang/Corbis; p. 459: © Mandy Godbehear/Shutterstock; p. 487: © Maugli/Shutterstock; p. 489: © dbimages/Alamy; p. 504: © Somos Images/Alamy; p. 513: © Catherine Yeulet/iStockphoto; p. 524: © Bonnie Jacobs/iStockphoto; p. 527: © 2A Images/Getty Images; p. 551: © Roger-Viollet/The Image Works; p. 564 (top): © Paramount/courtesy Everett Collection; p. 564 (bottom): © Majesco Entertainment Company; p. 565: © TriStar Pictures/courtesy Everett Collection.

Text Credits

Schmalleger, Frank J., *Criminal Justice Today: And Introductory Text for the 21st Centure*, 10/e, Copyright © 2009. Reprinted by permission of Pearson Education, Inc., Upper Saddle River, NJ.

Chapter 1

Ember, Carol R., Ember, Melvin, and Peregrine, Peter N., Adapted from *Anthropology*. Copyright © Reprinted by permission of Pearson Education.

Chapter 2

Donatelle, Rebecca J., Adapted from *Access to Health*. Copyright © Reprinted by permission of Pearson Education. Jerome, Kyra, "Lunge Fitness," Copyright © 2010 Reprinted by permission of the author.

Chapter 3

Carter, Carol, et al., Adapted from *Keys to success*, 6/e, Copyright © Reprinted by permission of Pearson Education.

DeVito, *Human Communication*, pp. 17, 203, 268, 308, Copyright © 2006 by Pearson Education, Inc. Reproduced by permission of Pearson Education.

Ebert, Ronald J., Griffin, Ricky W., and Van Sykle, Barbara, Business Essentials, 6/e, Copyright © 2007. Reprinted by permission of Pearson Education, Inc., Upper Saddle River, NJ.

Henslin, *Essentials of Sociology: Down to Earth Approach*, *Text Excerpts* from pp. 98–99, 115, 119, 147, 351, 359–360, 390, and 1331–1334, Copyright © 2007 Pearson Education, Inc. Reproduced by permission of Pearson Education, Inc.

Yudkin, Jeremy, *Understanding Music*, (reprint) 5/e, Copyright © 2008. Printed and electronically reproduced by permission of Pearson Education, Inc., Upper Saddle River, NJ.

Chapter 11

Armstrong, Gary, and Kotler, Phillip, *Marketing: An Introduction*, 9/e, Copyright © 2009. Printed and electronically reproduced by permission of Pearson Education, Upper Saddle River, NJ.

Santiago, Gerardo, "My Real World Roommates," Copyright © 2010. Reprinted by permission of the author.

Welch, *Family Life Now: Conversations about Marriages, Families and Relationships*, *Text* excerpts from pp. 7, 252, 506, and 523, Copyright © 2007 Pearson Education, Inc. Reproduced by permission of Pearson Education, Inc.

Chapter 12

Bonta, Royce, "Clean Living," Copyright © 2010. Reprinted by permission of the author.

Donatella, Rebecca J., Adapted from *Access to Health*, Copyright © Reprinted by permission of Pearson Education.

Macionis, *Society: The Basics*, text excerpts from pp. 300, 328, and 470, © 2007 Pearson Education, Inc. Reproduced by permission of Pearson Education, Inc.

Wood, Wood, *World of Psychology*, *Text Excerpts* from pp. 116–117, 230, 330–331, 371, and 597, Copyright © 2008 Pearson Education, Inc. Reproduced by permission of Pearson Education, Inc.

Chapter 13

Henslin, *Essentials of Sociology: Down to Earth Approach*, *Text Excerpts* from pp. 98–99, 115, 119, 147, 351, 359–360, 390, and 1331–1334, Copyright © 2007 Pearson Education, Inc. Reproduced by permission of Pearson Education, Inc.

Jones, Howard, "Slam Dancing," Copyright © 2010. Reprinted by permission of the author.

Labensky, Sarah R., and Hause, Alan M., *On Cooking*, Copyright © Reprinted by permission of Pearson Education.

Welch, *Family Life Now: Conversations about Marriages, Families and Relationships*, Text excerpts from pp. 7, 252, 506, and 523, Copyright © 2007 Pearson Education, Inc. Reproduced by permission of Pearson Education, Inc.

Chapter 14

Byrd, Roxanne, "The Duck Problem," Copyright © 2010 Reprinted by permission of the author.

Welch, *Family Life Now: Conversations about Marriages, Families and Relationships*, *Text* excerpts from pages 7, 252, 506, and 523, Copyright © 2007. Pearson Education, Inc. Reproduced by permission of Pearson Education, Inc.

Chapter 15

Henslin, *Essentials of Sociology: Down to Earth Approach*, *Text Excerpts* from pp. 98–99, 115, 119, 147, 351, 359–360, 390, and 1331–1334, Copyright © 2007 Pearson Education, Inc. Reproduced by permission of Pearson Education, Inc.

Wood, Wood, *World of Psychology*, *Text Excerpts* from pp. 116–117, 230, 330–331, 371, and 597, Copyright © 2008 Pearson Education, Inc. Reproduced by permission of Pearson, Education, Inc.

Chapter 16

Adams, *Fundamentals of Game Design*, *Text Excerpts* from pp. 148–160, Copyright © 2010 Pearson Education, Inc. Reproduced by permission of Pearson Education, Inc.

Armstrong, Gary, and Kotler, Phillip, *Marketing: An Introduction*, 9/e, Copyright © 2009. Printed and electronically reproduced by permission of Pearson Education, Upper Saddle River, NJ.

Barkley, Elizabeth F., Adapted from *Crossroads*, Copyright © Reprinted by permission of Pearson Education.

DeVito, *The Interpersonal Communication Book*, pp. 48, 51–52, 141, 142, 179, 181–183, 201–211, 281–282, Copyright © 2007. Reproduced by permission of Pearson Education, Inc.

Donatella, Rebecca J., Adapted from *Access to Health*, Copyright © Reprinted by permission of Pearson Education.

Ebert, Ronald J., Griffin, Ricky W., and Van Sykle, Barbara, "Business Essentials," 6/e, Copyright © 2007. Reprinted by permission of Pearson Education, Inc., Upper Saddle River, NJ.

Labensky, Sarah R., and Hause, Alan M., Adapted from *On Cooking*, Copyright © Reprinted by permission of Pearson Education.

Chapter 17

Byrd, Roxanne, "Muscovy Ducks: A Campus Dilemma," Copyright © 2010. Reprinted by permission of the author.

Chapter 18

Ebert, Ronald J., Griffin, Ricky W., and Van Sykle, Barbara, *Business Essentials*, 6/e, Copyright © 2007. Reprinted by permission of Pearson Education, Inc., Upper Saddle River, NJ.

Wood, Wood, *World of Psychology*, *Text Excerpts* from pp. 116–117, 230, 330–331, 371, and 597, Copyright © 2008

Pearson Education, Inc. Reproduced by permission of Pearson, Education, Inc.

Chapter 19

DeVito, *Human Communication,* pp. 17, 203, 268, 308, Copyright © 2006 by Pearson Education, Inc. Reproduced by permission of Pearson Education.

DeVito, *The Interpersonal Communication Book,* pp. 48, 51–52, 141, 142, 179, 181–183, 201–211, 281–282, Copyright © 2007. Reproduced by permission of Pearson Education, Inc.

Chapter 21

Henslin, *Essentials of Sociology: Down to Earth Approach, Text Excerpts* from pp. 98–99, 115, 119, 147, 351, 359–360, 390, and 1331–1334, Copyright © 2007 Pearson Education, Inc. Reproduced by permission of Pearson Education, Inc.

Yudkin, Jeremy, *Understanding Music,* (reprint) 5/e, Copyright © 2008. Printed and Electronically reproduced by permission of Pearson Education, Inc., Upper Saddle River, NJ.

Chapter 22

Sayre, Henry M., *Humanities: The Culture, Continuity, and Change,* Book 6, 1/e, Copyright © 2008, Reprinted by permission of Pearson Edition, Inc., Upper Saddle River, NJ.

Chapter 25

Biederman, Paul, S., *Travel and Tourism: An Industry Primer,* 1/e, Copyright © 2008. Printed and electronically reproduced by permission of Pearson Education, Upper Saddle River, NJ.

Fernandez-Armesto, Felipe, Adapted from *The World,* Copyright © Reprinted by permission of Pearson Education.

Walker, John, *Introduction to Hospitality Management,* 1/e, Copyright © 2004. Printed and electronically reproduced by permission of Pearson Education, Inc., Upper Saddle River, NJ.

Chapter 26

Walker, John, *Introduction to Hospitality Management,* 1/e, Copyright © 2004. Printed and electronically reproduced by permission of Pearson Education, Inc., Upper Saddle River, NJ.

Chapter 27

Armstrong, Gary, and Kotler, Phillip, *Marketing: An Introduction,* 9/e, Copyright © 2009. Printed and electronically reproduced by permission of Pearson Education, Upper Saddle River, NJ.

Chapter 28

Diamond, Jay, and Diamond, Ellen, *Fashion Apparel and Accessories and Home Furnishings,* 1/e, Copyright © 2007. Printed and electronically reproduced by permission of Pearson Education, Inc., Upper Saddle River, NJ.

Tate, Sharon L., Adapted from *Inside Fashion Design,* Copyright © Reprinted by permission of Pearson Education.

Verini, James, "Supersize It: Our Waistlines Aren't All That's Expanding Our Stuff Is, Too," Slate, March 4, 2000. Copyright © 2000 Reprinted by permission.

Verini, James "Supersize It: Our Waistlines Aren't All That's Expanding Our Stuff Is, Too" Slate March 4, 2000. Copyright © 2000. Reprinted by permission.

Chapter 29

Martson, Sallie, Knox, Paul L., and Liverman, Diana, M., *World Religions in Global Context: People, Places and Environments,* 3/e, Copyright © 2008. Printed and Electronically reproduced by permission of Pearson Education, Upper Saddle River, NJ.

Chapter 30

Bovee, Courtland L., and Thill, John V., Adapted from *Communication Today,* Copyright © Reprinted by permission of Pearson Education.

DeVito, *Human Communication,* pp, 17, 203, 268, 308, Copyright © 2006 by Pearson Education, Inc. Reproduced by permission of Pearson Education.

Lannon, John, Excerpt from "Technical Communication," Copyright © Reprinted by permission of Pearson Education.

Vanzo, Beverly A., Excerpt from "Be Your Own Editor," Copyright © Reprinted by permission of Pearson Education.

Zinsser, William K., Excerpt from *On Writing Well,* Copyright © 1976, 1980, 1985, 1988, 1990, 1994, 1998, 2001, 2006 by William K. Zinsser. Reprinted by permission of the author.

Chapter 31

Berman, Audrey, J., Snyder, Shirlee, Kozier, Barbara J., and Erb, Glenora, "Kozier and Erb's Fundamentals of Nursing," 8/e, Copyright © 2008. Printed and electronically reproduced by permission of Pearson Education, Upper Saddle River, NJ.

Chapter 32

Vaughn, Sharron, et al., *Teaching Exceptional, Diverse, and At-Risk Student in the General Classroom,* pp. 75, 76, 79, 80,

85, 184, 313, 328, 355, 463, 467, Copyright © 2003. Reproduced by permission of Pearson Education, Inc.

Chapter 33

Adams, "Fundamentals of Game Design," Text Excerpts from pp. 148–160, Copyright © 2010 Pearson Education, Inc. Reproduced by permission of Pearson Education, Inc.

Alvarez, Julia, First published in *NUESTRO*, Copyright © 1985. By permission of Susan Bergholz Literary Services, New York, NY, and Lamy, NM. All rights reserved.

Amen, Daniel, Reprinted by permission of Dr. Daniel Amen.

Barry, Dave, "Road Warrior," *Miami Herald*, February 8, 1998. Copyright © 1998 by Dave Barry. Reproduced with permission.

Berman, Audrey, J., Snyder, Shirlee, Kozier, Barbara J., and Erb, Glenora, *Kozier and Erb's Fundamentals of Nursing*, 8/e, Copyright © 2008. Printed and electronically reproduced by permission of Pearson Education, Upper Saddle River, NJ.

Bloom, Alan, *Making Cell Phones in the Classroom a Community Builder, The Teaching Professor*, March, 2007. Copyright © 2007. Reprinted by permission of Magna Publications, Inc.

Campbell, Scott, "Cell Phones Do Not Distract in Class," from "Perceptions of Mobile Phones in College Classrooms: Ringing, Cheating, and Classroom Policies," *Communication Education*, 55.3 (2006) 280–294, Copyright © 2006 National Communication Association, reprinted by permission of Taylor & Francis Ltd., http://www.tandf.co.uk/journals on behalf of The National Communication Association.

DeVito, *The Interpersonal Communication Book*, pp. 48, 51–52, 141, 142, 179, 181–183, 201–211, 281–282, Copyright © 2007. Reproduced by permission of Pearson Education, Inc.

Divine, Robert A., Breen, T.H.H., Fredrickson, George M., Williams, R. Hal, Gross, Ariella J., and Brands, H.W., *America Past and Present*, Vol. 2, 9/e, Copyright © 2011,

pp. 802–803. Reprinted by permission of Pearson Education, Upper Saddle River, NJ.

Ember, Carol R., Ember, Melvin, and Peregrine, Peter N., *Anthropology*, Copyright © Reprinted by permission of Pearson Education.

Chapter 6

Gerrig, Zimbardo, *Psychology & Life: Discovering Psychology Ed.* pp. 571–575, (c) 2009 Pearson Education, Inc. Reproduced by permission of Pearson Education, Inc.

Graner-Ray, *Gender Inclusive Game Design*, 1/e, Copyright © 2004 Delmar Learning, a part of Cengage Learning, Inc. Reproduced by permission. www.cengage.com/permissions.

Jones, Charisee, "Light Skin vs. Dark Skin," *Glamour*, September, 1995. Copyright © 1995 Reprinted by permission of the author.

Lev, Michael A., "Lunch Served in 5 Easy Pieces," *Chicago Tribune* (News Section), March 31, 1998, page 7, Copyright © 1998 Chicago Tribune. Reproduced by permission. All rights reserved.

Vaughn, Sharron, et al., *Teaching Exceptional, Diverse, and At-Risk Student in the General Classroom*, 2/e, pp. 75, 76, 79, 80, 85, 184, 313, 328, 355, 463, 467, Copyright © 2000 by Pearson Education, Inc. Reproduced by permission of Pearson Education, Inc.

Walker, John, *Introduction to Hospitality Management*, 1/e, Copyright © 2004. Printed and electronically reproduced by permission of Pearson Education, Inc., Upper Saddle River, NJ.

Wiesel, Elie, Excerpt from *Night*, Copyright © 1972, 1985 by Elie Wiesel. English translation Copyright © 2006 by Marion Wiesel (Hill and Wang, 2006). Originally published as *La Nuit* by Les Editions de Minuit. Copyright © 1958 by Les Editions de Minuit. Used by permission of Georges Borchardt, Inc., for Les Editions de Minuit.

Wiesel, Marion, trans., Excerpt from *Night*, Translation Copyright © 2006 by Marion Wiesel. Reprinted by permission of Hill and Wang, a division of Farrar, Straus & Giroux, LLC.

Index